Bronze Head found in the River Alde, believed to represent the Emperor Claudius and to have been looted from Colchester.

Reports of the Research Committee
of the
Society of Antiquaries of London

No. XX
Published in conjunction with the Corporation of the Borough of Colchester

Roman Colchester

By

M. R. Hull, M.A., F.S.A.

with sections by M. A. Cotton, O.B.E., F.S.A., D. B. Harden, M.A., PH.D., F.S.A.,
J. W. Jackson, D.SC., F.S.A., and K. M. Richardson, M.A., F.S.A.
and an Introduction by
I. A. Richmond, C.B.E., F.B.A., V.-P.S.A.

50113

Oxford
Printed at the University Press by Charles Batey for
The Society of Antiquaries
Burlington House, London
and
The Corporation of the Borough of Colchester
1958

PRINTED IN GREAT BRITAIN

ACKNOWLEDGEMENTS

THE gratitude of all interested in Roman Britain, and especially of those resident in Colchester, is due to a multitude of people without whose direct or indirect collaboration this work could never have been completed. We owe much to the pioneer antiquaries, the early archaeologists, the private collectors, and the historians. Among official bodies the Town Council of the Borough of Colchester must take first place: few councils can have taken so consistent an interest in the antiquities of their town, and ever since the Council set aside a room in the Town Hall (in 1846) as the beginning of a Museum its attitude towards the archaeology of Colchester has been exemplary.

The Essex Archaeological Society has a long record of work of first-class importance, and for some time there was the Morant Club, which carried out a number of useful excavations. Outside bodies, too, have taken a great interest in the town, above all the Society of Antiquaries of London.

So we thank, of the older writers, Philip Morant (the County Historian), T. Cromwell, T. Wright, H. Jenkins, and E. L. Cutts. Of modern writers we are most deeply indebted to Sir Mortimer Wheeler and Professor C. F. C. Hawkes, both of whom have also excavated extensively in Colchester.

Of the Town Council we have to thank past Chairmen of the Museum Committee, but most notably Sir W. Gurney Benham, Alderman A. M. Jarmin, Alderman Henry Laver, and the present Chairman, Alderman L. E. Dansie; of the officers, the former Engineers W. Goodyear and H. Collins, and the present Mr. J. S. Orchard and his Deputy, F. N. A. Richardson.

Among private residents the following demand special mention: William Wire, postman and jeweller, for whose monumental manuscripts and drawings no praise is adequate; the collectors, J. Taylor, J. H. Pollexfen, and G. Joslin; Josiah Parish, artist, and more recently, besides H. Laver, the brothers H. E. and Philip Laver, the latter of whom devoted his life enthusiastically to Roman Colchester, making a contribution equal to, if not surpassing, that of Wire. Although he wrote but little, his contribution to knowledge and to the Museum was incalculable. We must also mention Mr. A. E. Mason, and record the indefatigable excavations of Mr. A. F. Hall, carried out over more than twenty-five years.

Perhaps I may be excused for referring also to the work of the Borough Museum, which reached a modern standard with the appointment of Mr. A. G. Wright as Curator in 1900. The work of the department has been invaluable and has reached out far beyond the four walls of the building. Here is the proper place to record our high appreciation of the work of the late E. J. Rudsdale, once a member of the staff. He took Wire for his model and followed him faithfully, as the frequency of his name in this book will show.

Finally, there is a multitude of men and women who have from time to time made themselves useful or acted as benefactors to Colchester archaeology. Here I would mention the representatives of H.M. Ministry of Works, the British Museum, and H.M. Ordnance Survey; also the students and others who have assisted with excavations and the preparation of their results. Their name is legion. Colchester is grateful to them all.

A final word of gratitude is due to the Museum staff, especially Mr. H. W. Poulter, whose photography, surveying, and levelling have been invaluable.

CONTENTS

LIST OF FIGURES IN THE TEXT

LIST OF PLATES

REFERENCES AND ABBREVIATIONS

A few titles of general application to Roman Colchester are included, although not mentioned in the text.

Accessions Books. The Accessions Registers of Colchester Museum.

Aislingen, see Knorr.

Aldhelm, Abbot of Malmesbury, *De Laudibus Virginitatis, c.* A.D. 670.

Ant. Journ. The Antiquaries Journal.

The Antiquary (1880–1915).

Antiquity, A Quarterly Review of Archaeology.

Anzeiger der Akad. der Wissenschaft zu Wien: philos.-hist. Klasse 1927.

Arch. Archaeologia, published by the Soc. of Antiquaries of London.

Arch. Ael. Archaeologia Aeliana, Journal of the Soc. of Antiquaries of Newcastle upon Tyne.

Arch. J. The Archaeological Journal, published by the Royal Archaeological Institute.

Archaeological News Letter.

Archaeology in England and Wales, 1914–31, by T. D. Kendrick and C. F. C. Hawkes (1933).

Arentsburg, Een Romeinsch Militair Vlootstation bij Voorburg, by Dr. J. H. Holwerda (1923).

Archives de la Commission des Monuments historiques.

Atkinson, D. 'A Hoard of Samian Ware from Pompeii' (*J.R.S.* iv, 27).

—— *Report on the Excavations at Wroxeter* (*the Roman City of Viroconium*) *1923–1927* (Birmingham Arch. Soc., 1942).

—— *The Romano-British Site in Lowbury Hill* (1916).

—— 'Caistor Excavations 1929' (*Norfolk Archaeology,* xxiv, 1929–31).

Augst, see Laur-Belart.

Avery, Sir G. 'The Site of Camulodunum' (*The Athenaeum,* Jan. 28, 1860).

Baldock. 'Roman and Pre-Roman Antiquities in Letchworth Museum', by W. P. Westell (*East Herts. Arch. Soc. Trans.* vii, 258).

Balmuildy. The Roman Fort at Balmuildy, by S. N. Miller (1922).

Beaumont, G. F. 'The Site of Camulodunum', *East Anglian Notes and Queries,* July 1894.

Bingen Mus. Cat. G. Behrens, *Katalog, Städtische Altertumssammlung,* Bingen (1920).

Benham, Sir Gurney. 'On Coel and Helena' (*Arch. Journ.* lxiv, 203 ff.; and *J.B.A.,* Dec. 1919, 229 ff.).

—— *Guide to Colchester.* (Many editions.)

B. J. Bonner Jahrbücher, published by the Verein von Altertumsfreunden im Rheinlande.

B.M. Catalogue. Catalogue of the Roman Pottery in the Dept. of Antiquities, British Museum, by H. B. Walters (1908).

Bonnin. Th. *Antiquités gallo-romaines des Éburoviques* (1860).

Book of Assemblies, Minute Books of the Colchester Town Council.

Brayley, E. W., and Britton, J. *The Beauties of Britain* (1810).

Brecon, see Wheeler.

B.R.G.K. Berichte der Römisch-Germanische Kommission.

Buckler, G. *Colchester Castle, a Roman Building,* pt. 1, 1876; pt. 2, 1877; pt. 3, 1879; pt. 4, 1882.

The Builder.

Bull. Ant. France. Bulletin de la Société des Antiquaires de France.

Bull. Mon. Bulletin Monumental.

Bury, J. B. *History of the Roman Empire* (1893).

Bushe-Fox, see *Richborough, Swarling,* and *Wroxeter.*

Caistor, see Atkinson.

Cam., see Camulodunum.

Camden, William. *Britannia* (1586).

—— *Britannia,* trans. with additions and improvements, by Edmund Gibson, 4th ed. (1772).

—— *Britannia,* trans. by Richard Gough, 1st ed. (1789).

Camulodunum. Camulodunum, First Report on the excavations at Colchester, 1930–39, by C. F. C. Hawkes and M. R. Hull. Report XIV of the Research Committee of the Soc. of Antiquaries of London (1947).

C. & W. Transactions of the Cumberland and Westmorland Archaeological Society.

Carter, Matthew. *A true relation of that honourable though unfortunate expedition of Kent, Essex, and Colchester in 1648* n.d.

Chapman & André, *A map of the County of Essex from an actual Survey taken in 1772, 1773, and 1774,* by John Chapman and Peter André (1777).

C.M.R. Colchester Museum Reports.

Christy, Miller. Articles in *Trans. Essex Arch. Soc.,* especially on Roman roads.

C.I.L. Corpus Inscriptionum Latinarum.

Clarke, J., 'Notes on Objects in the Mayer Collection relating to Essex' (*Trans. Hist. Soc. of Lancashire and Cheshire*, N.S. xiii, 1873).

Codrington, T. *Roman Roads in Britain.* (1903 onwards.)

Colchester Chronicle. MS. in the Colchester Oath Book.

Cohen, H. *Monnaies frappées sous l'Empire romain*, 2nd ed. (1880).

Coll. Ant. Collectanea Antiqua, by C. Roach Smith (1843 and later).

Collingwood, R. G. *The Archaeology of Roman Britain* (1930).

—— and Myres, J. N. L. *Roman Britain and the Early English Settlements* (1936).

Cottonian MSS., in British Museum.

Court Rolls. The Court Rolls of the Borough of Colchester (1310 to 1379), 3 vols. 1921, 1938, 1941).

Cromwell, T. *History of Colchester* (1825).

Crambeck. The Roman Pottery at Crambeck, Castle Howard, by P. Corder (1928).

Cumont, F. *Textes et monuments figurés relatifs aux mystères de Mithra*, ii (1896).

Cutts, Rev. E. L. *Colchester* (Historic Towns Series, 1885).

Y Cymmrodor. Published by the Hon. Society of Cymmrodorion.

D. Déch. Déchelette, J. *Les Vases céramiques ornés de la Gaule romaine* (1904).

Delglatigny, L. *Documents et notes archéologiques* (1925–7).

Dio Cassius, *History of Rome*, and its later part abridged by Xiphelinus.

Drag. Dragendorff. 'Terra Sigillata' (*Bonner Jahrbücher*, xcvi, xcvii, 1895, 1896).

Dugdale, Sir William, *Monasticon Anglicanum* (1655).

Duncan, Dr. P. M. 'A Survey of the Walls of Colchester' (*Trans. Essex Arch. Soc.*, o.s. i, 1 ff. 1858).

—— 'The Excavation of the cloaca in Holly Trees Meadow', ibid., o.s. v, 210 ff. (1873).

Essex County Standard, newspaper.

E.R. Essex Review.

Essex Weekly News, newspaper.

Ephemeris Epigraphica. C.I.L. Supplementum (1872–1913).

Evans, Sir J. *Ancient British Coins* (1864).

Firmicus, Julius de. *De Errore profanorum Religionum.*

Fontenoy, H. de. *Autun et ses Monuments* (1889).

Forrer, R. *Die römischen Terrasigillata-Töpfereien von Heiligenberg-Dinsheim und Ittenweiler im Elsass* (1911).

Furneaux, H. *Annals of Tacitus* (1891).

Fremersdorf, F. *Neue Beiträge zur Topographie des römischen Köln: Röm.-Germ. Komm. Forschungen*, xviii (1950).

Gaer, see *Brecon*.

Gellygaer. Ward J. *The Roman Fort of Gellygaer* (1902).

Gent.'s Mag. The Gentleman's Magazine.

Germania. Germania, published by the Römische-Germanische Kommission.

Gibbon, E. *The Decline and Fall of the Roman Empire.*

Gibson, E., *see* Camden.

Goodchild, R. G. 'The Origins of the Romano-British Forum' (*Antiquity*, no. 78, 1946).

Gough, R. *Tours*, MS. Bodleian, Top. Gen. e. 18, fol. 215, *and see* Camden.

Gould, J. Chalkley. *The Site of Camulodunum* (Chesterford) (1895).

Haltern, see Loeschcke.

Hardy, E. G. *Monumentum Ancyranum* (1923).

Hartshorne, the Rev. C. H. *On Colchester Castle* (1864).

Haverfield, F. *Ancient Town Planning*, 1913.

—— 'Quarterly Notes on Roman Britain' (*Antiquary*, xxxi, 1895, pp. 37 ff.)

Hawkes and Dunning. 'The Belgae of Gaul and Britain' (*Arch. Journ.* lxxxvii (1930), 140 ff.).

Heddernheim. Mitteilungen über Römische Funde in Heddernheim.

Henderson, B. W. *The Life and Principate of the Emperor Nero.*

Henkel, F. *Die römische Fingeringe der Rheinlande* (1913).

Hermet, F. *La Graufesenque* (1934).

Hettner, F. *Drei Tempelbezirke in Treverelande* (1901).

Hinks, R. P. *Catalogue of the Greek, Etruscan and Roman Paintings in the British Museum* (1933).

Hoare, Sir R. C. *Letter on the True Site of the Ancient Colony of Camulodunum* (1827). (Privately printed, 25 copies only, by Rutter of Shaftesbury.)

Hofheim. Das früh-römische Lager bei Hofheim in Taunus, by E. Ritterling (1913).

Horsley, J. *Britannia Romana* (1732).

Holt. Holt, Denbighshire. The Works Depot of the 20th Legion at Castle Lyons, by W. F. Grimes (*Y Cymmrodor*, xl, 1930).

Hull, M. R. *Short Guide to Roman Colchester* (1947).

Huntingdon, Henry of. *History of England.*

Illustrated London News.

J.B.A. Journal of the British Archaeological Association.

Jenkins, Rev. H. 'Observations on the Site of Camulodunum' (*Arch.* xxix (1842), 243–256).

—— *Colchester Castle once the Temple of Claudius* (1861, revised ed., 1869).

—— *An Appendix to the lecture on Colchester Castle, together with a Reply to the animadversions of the Rev. E. L. Cutts* (1853).

Jewry Wall, Excavations at the Jewry Wall Site, Leicester, by K. M. Kenyon. (Report XV of the Research Committee of the Soc. of Antiquaries of London, 1948.)

J.R.S. Journal of Roman Studies.

Kendrick, T. D., and Hawkes, C. F. C. *Archaeology in England and Wales 1914–1931* (1933).

K., Knorr, R. *Töpfer und Fabrikanten des Terra Sigillata des ersten Jahrhunderts* (1919).

—— *Die Terra Sigillata Gefäße von Aislingen* (1912).

—— *Die verzierten Terra Sigillata Gefäße von Rottenburg-Sumelocenna* (1910).

—— *Die verzierten Terra Sigillata Gefäße von Rottweil* (1907).

—— *Die verzierten Terra Sigillata Gefäße von Cannstadt* (1905).

—— and Sprater, F. *Die westpfälzischen Sigillata Töpfereien von Blickweiler und Eschweiler Hof* (1927).

Terra Sigillata-Gefäße des ersten Jahrhunderts mit Töpfernamen (1952).

Koenen, K. *Gefäßkunde* (1895).

Lanciani, C. *Ruins and Excavations of Ancient Rome* (1897).

Laur-Belart, R. *Führer durch Augusta Raurica* (1948).

Laver, H. Many articles in *Trans. Essex Arch. Soc.*; manuscripts in Museum.

Laver, P. G. Diary (two manuscript books kept as diaries at irregular intervals from 1922 onwards); many published articles and manuscripts.

Lodge, Rev. Barton. 'A Roman Sepulchral Monument found at Colchester' (*T.E.A.S.* v, 1870).

Loeschcke, S. *Lampen aus Vindonissa* (1919).

—— *Keramische Funde in Haltern* (1909).

—— *Das Tempelbezirk bei Trier*, Bände i u. ii.

London in Roman times (London Museum Cat. III, 1930).

Lowbury Hill, see Atkinson, D.

Lucas, A. *Ancient Egyptian Materials and Industries*, 3rd ed. (1948).

M. and S. Mattingly, H., and Sydenham, E. A. (later associated with others), *The Roman Imperial Coinage* (1923 and later).

Macdonald, Sir George. *Archaeology in England and Wales*, 1914–28. (*British Academy Supplemental Papers* VI, 1931.)

Mansi, G. D. *Sacr. Concil. Coll.* (Paris, 1901–13).

May, Thomas. *Catalogue of the Roman Pottery in the Colchester and Essex Museum* (Cambridge, 1930).

—— *The Pottery found at Silchester* (1916).

—— *Catalogue of the Roman Pottery in York Museum* (1903–11).

Mon. Hist. Brit. Monumenta Historica Britannica, ed. H. Petrie and J. Sharpe (Record Commission, 1848).

Monmouth, Geoffrey of. *Historia Rerum Britanniae.*

Morant, Rev. Philip. *History and Antiquities of Colchester* (1748).

—— *History and Antiquities of Essex* (1768).

Morning Chronicle, newspaper.

Mus. Disneianum. *Museum Disneianum, being a collection of . . . ancient fictile vases in the possession of John Disney* (1849).

Napper, H. F. 'The Site of Camulodunum' (*East Anglian Notes and Queries* (1894), 308.)

Newstead. Newstead: A Roman Frontier Post and its People, by J. Curle (1911).

Niederbieber. See Oelmann, F.

Notitia Dignitatum Imperii Romani.

Num. Chron. Numismatic Chronicle.

Oath Book, The Colchester. The Red Parchment Book of the Borough of Colchester.

O.R.L. Der Obergermanisch-Rhaetische Limes des Römerreiches.

Oelmann, F. *Die Keramik des Kastells Niederbieber: Materialen zur römisch-germanischen Keramik*, i, 1914.

Ospringe. Report on the Excavation of the Roman Cemetery at Ospringe, Kent, by W. Whiting, W. Hawley, and T. May (Report VIII of the Research Committee of the Soc. of Antiquaries of London, 1931).

Oswald, Felix. *Index of Potters' Stamps on Terra Sigillata* (1931).

—— *Terra Sigillata of Margidunum* (1948).

—— *Index of Figure Types on Terra Sigillata* (1936–7).

O. & P. Oswald and Pryce, *Introduction to the Study of Terra Sigillata* (1920).

Oxoniensia. Published by the Oxford Archit. and Hist. Soc.

Pachtère, F. de. *Paris à l'époque Gallo-Romaine* (1916).

Pelet, A. *Fouilles de la Porte d'Auguste à Nîmes*, 1849.

Phelps, W. *The History and Antiquities of Somerset-shire* (1836–9).

Phil. Trans. Philosophical Transactions of the Royal Society.

Plinius Secundus, C. *Historia Naturalium.*

Poltross Burn. 'The Milecastle on the Wall of Hadrian at the Poltross Burn', by J. P. Gibson and F. G. Simpson (*C. & W.* N.S. xi, 1911).

Promis, C. *Storia dell' antico Torino* (1869).

P.S.A.L. Proceedings of the Society of Antiquaries of London.

Ptolemaeus. *Geographia*, ed. Nobbe (1881).

R.C.H.M. The Royal Commission on Historical Monuments, *Inventory of the Historical Monuments of North-East Essex*, iii (1922).

Rahtz, P. 'The Roman Temple at Pagan's Hill' (*Somerset Arch. & N.H. Soc.* xcvi, 1951).

Reaney, P. H. *The Place Names of Essex* (1935).

Reid, J. S. *The Municipalities of the Roman Empire* (1913).

Richborough. First, Second, Third, and Fourth Report on the Excavation of the Roman Fort at Richborough, Kent, by J. P. Bushe-Fox. (Reports VI, VII, X, and XVI of the Research Committee of the Soc. of Antiquaries of London, 1926, 1928, 1932, 1949.)

Richmond, I. A. 'The Praetorian Camp at Rome' (*Papers of the British School at Rome*, x, 1927).

—— 'The Four Coloniae of Roman Britain', *Arch. Journ.* ciii, 1947.

—— *Roman Britain* (Britain in Pictures (1947)).

Ritt. Ritterling, see *Hofheim*.

Roach Smith, *see Coll. Ant.*

Romanelli, D. *Voyagia Pompeii* (1829).

Round, J. H. *The History and Antiquities of Colchester Castle* (1882).

—— 'On St. Helena', *English Historical Review*, Jan. 1922.

Rouse, J. *Views of Hastings Castle* (1825).

Rhys, J. *Celtic Britain* (1884).

Rye, W. *Dr. J. H. Round and his Recent Attack on Mr. Walter Rye* (1922).

Salmon, N. *History of Essex* (unfinished) (1740–2).

Scarth, Rev. H. M. 'On Roman Remains discovered at Camerton' (*Proc. Somerset Arch. & N.H. Soc.* xii, 1861–2).

Schultze, R. 'Die Römischen Stadttöre, in *B.J.* cxviii, 280 ff.

Segontium, see Wheeler.

Silch. Silchester, *see* May.

Simonett, C., *Tessiner Gräberfelder* (1941).

Skinner, Rev. J. *Proc. Somerset Arch. and Nat. Hist. Soc.* xi, 174 (1861–2). See also Phelp's *History of Somerset.*

Stanfield, J. A. 'Unusual Forms of Terra Sigillata' (*Arch Journ.* lxxxvi, 1929).

Stevenson, S. M. *Dictionary of Roman Coins* (1889).

Studies presented to D. M. Robinson, ed. G. E. Mylonas, vol. i (1951).

Stukeley, William. *Letters, Diaries* (Surtees Soc. 73, 76, 80, 1882, 1883, 1889).

Suetonius, C. Tranquillus. *Lives of the Caesars, Caligula and Claudius.*

Sumner, H. *A descriptive account of the Roman Pottery at Ashley Rails* (1919).

Swanpool. 'A Romano-British pottery Kiln at Swanpool, nr. Lincoln, by G. Webster and N. Booth (*Ant. Journ.* xxvii, 1947).

Swarling. Excavation of the Late Celtic Urnfield at Swarling, Kent, by J. P. Bushe-Fox. (Report V of the Research Committee of the Soc. of Antiquaries of London, 1925).

Tacitus, Cornelius. *Annales; Historiae; Agricola.*

T.E.A.S. Transactions of the Essex Archaeological Society.

Toutain, J. *Les cultes päiens dans l'empire romain*, n.d.

Unverzagt, F. *Die Keramik des Kastells Alzei* (1916).

Vet. Mon. Vetusta Monumenta, published by the Society of Antiquaries (1747–1893).

Webb, P. H. 'The Coinage of Allectus' (*Num. Chron.*, 4th ser. vi).

—— 'The reign and coinage of Carausius' (*Num. Chron.*, 4th ser. vii, 1908).

—— *Roman Imperial Coinage*, vol. v.

Wheeler, R. E. M. (now Sir Mortimer). 'An Insula of Roman Colchester', Morant Club (1921) and *T.E.A.S.* xvi, 7 ff.

—— 'A Further Note on the Vaults under Colchester Castle' (*J.R.S.*, x, 87).

—— 'The Balkerne Gate, Colchester' (*T.E.A.S.* xv, 172 ff.).

—— *The Roman Fort near Brecon* (Cymmrodorion Soc. Publications, 1926).

—— *Segontium and the Roman occupation of Wales* (Cymmrodorion Soc. Publications, 1924).

Wheeler, R. E. M. *London in Roman times* (London Mus. Cat. III, 1930).

—— and T. V. Wheeler, *Verulamium; A Belgic and Two Roman Cities* (Report XI of the Research Committee of the Soc. of Antiquaries of London, 1936).

—— and Laver, P. G., 'Roman Colchester' (*J.R.S.*, ix, 1919).

Wright, T. *History and Topography of Essex* (1836).

Wroxeter. Excavations on the Site of the Roman Town at Wroxeter, Shropshire in 1912, 1913, 1914, by J. P. Bushe-Fox (Reports I, II, IV of the Research Committee of the Soc. of Antiquaries of London, 1913, 1914, 1916.) *See also* Atkinson.

York, see May.

Zugmantel. O.R.L. No. 8.

INTRODUCTION

By I. A. RICHMOND, C.B.E., F.B.A. V.-P.S.A.

THE decision to create the Roman chartered town at Colchester, named *Camulodunum*, *Colonia Victricensis*, or *Colonia*,[1] was made in A.D. 49 by the governor of Britain, Ostorius Scapula, as part of a double programme. The war against the Silures and Caractacus, about to reach its decisive phase, demanded from East Anglia the transfer of a legion to the western front; but the eastern tribes upon whom the hold was thus relaxed, the conquered Trinovantes of Essex and the allied Catuvellauni of Hertfordshire and Iceni of Norfolk, required a reliably loyal urban community to steady them or even to curb them, and above all to guide them into the way of Romanized provincial society. All this is indicated by Tacitus,[2] who describes the prime military considerations and summarizes the purpose of the projected *colonia* as 'subsidium adversus rebellis et imbuendis sociis ad officia legum'.

   The site chosen for the new town appears to have been close to the disused legionary fortress, from which the troops had now been transferred to Western Britain. This is indicated by the two tomb-stones of serving soldiers, the centurion of the Twentieth Legion, Favonius Facilis,[3] and the Thracian auxiliary trooper Longinus,[4] both of which were standing unweathered by the side of an early westward road when they were defaced and thrown down in the revolt of A.D. 61. But the precise site and size of the fortress are unknown, and the difficulty of the question is not lessened by the consideration that in the initial stage of the conquest not only a fortress but temporary camps, labour camps, and large supply compounds will surely have taken up much space over a very wide area. The Fingringhoe gravel pits, down river from Colchester, have yielded military finds[5] suggestive of this type of occupation, and emphasizing that the entire area of the captured *oppidum* of Cunobelinus, on the tongue between the rivers Colne and Roman, was at the disposal of the military to use freely, regardless of any considerations but their own convenience. The Column of Trajan depicts precisely this kind of action in progress in the captured capital of Decebalus at Sarmizegethusa.[6]

   It was, then, the existence of a specifically reserved military site, as later at Lincoln[7] or Gloucester,[8] which dictated the choice of ground for the new *colonia*. But the ancient native history of the place must also enter into consideration. The new town was to serve as the religious centre of the province, where loyalty was to be expressed in the cult of the Emperor who had founded it. The cult and its ceremonies, in their new and splendid setting, itself surrounded by the buildings and atmosphere of a Roman urban community, were nevertheless associated with a site significant in British tradition. Camulodunum was the one native centre

---

[1] 'Colonia Victricensis quae est in Britannia Camaloduni', *C.I.L.* xiv, 3955 = *I.L.S.* 2740, *Colonia*, *It. Ant.* 474, 4. It will be observed that the spelling *Camalodunum* is not without ancient authority and recurs, even if the manuscript tradition might be doubted, in Pliny, *N.H.* ii, 187. For the form Camulodunum, which is certainly correct, see Tac. *Ann.* xiv, 31, 32, *It. Ant.* 480, 4, and *Tab. Peut.* reproduced *Archaeologia*, xciii, pl. I: also the coin of Cunobelinus, *Archaeologia*, xc, pl. III, 22.

[2] Tac. *Ann.* xii, 32: 'Silurum gens non . . . mutabatur, quin bellum exerceret castrisque legionum premenda foret. Id quo promptius veniret, coloniam Camulodunum, valida veteranorum manu deducitur in agros captivos subsidium adversus rebellis et imbuendis sociis ad officia legum.'

[3] *C.I.L.* vii, 90: see p. 251 and plate II, A, below.

[4] *J.R.S.* xviii, 212–13, pl. XXIII: see p. 251 and plate II B, below.

[5] p. 1, below.

[6] Cichorius, *Die Reliefs der Traianssäule*, scenes cxxiv–cxxv.

[7] *Arch. Journ.* ciii, 65.

[8] *J.R.S.* xxxii, 41, fig. 5, also, p. 51.

which had ever served anything like a hegemony of Britain:[1] for had not Cunobelinus been thought of as *Rex Britannorum*? And while under the new dispensation some tribal representatives might feel a sense of glory departed, others would rejoice that a cruel and relentless aggressor had been annihilated by the very power in whose society they were already playing a valued part. Even within the tribal structure of the locality aristocratic partisanship and family jealousy had created[2] among the Trinovantes a pro-Roman party, from which were no doubt drawn many of the *incolae*, or native in-dwellers, who were incorporated[3] in the new Roman community. The choice was thus not without its effect upon native political feeling.

Time was so soon to show that Ostorius had miscalculated the reserves of loyalty available, but little is known archaeologically or otherwise of the new *colonia*, which eleven years later, in A.D. 61, perished in flames[4] during Boudicca's savage revolt. The heavily burnt layers left below the later Roman town by those very fires make it plain, however, that the *colonia* occupied the site upon which it was in due course rebuilt. In the western half of this area, on the summit of the ridge, five clear instances[5] (in insulae 10, 11, 17, 19, and 28) are recorded of burnt buildings or deposits securely linked with the destruction of A.D. 61: and it will be observed that two of them (in insulae 19 and 28), involving large stocks[6] of imported pottery and glass, are related to commerce. Similar deposits have been claimed[7] to exist at the east end of the site, in insula 38, and there is no doubt of their existence below the north–south street[8] dividing insulae 7 and 15 from insulae 8 and 16. Traces of an early burnt layer[9] were also noted below the extensive remains of private houses in insula 6. It would thus appear that the original *colonia* covered about as much ground from east to west as its successor and extended, in the west at least, no less far from north to south. Defences did not exist, as is specifically stated[10] by Tacitus.

This significant distribution of early remains forms the setting for the very large temple platform carrying the Norman castle; and its inclusion within the area of the Boudiccan destruction strongly supports the view[11] that it was in fact the temple of Divus Claudius. Its impressive vaulted substructure, deliberately earth-filled during construction and forgotten until its recognition a generation ago, is here published in detail[12] for the first time. Its importance as the religious centre of the provincial council explains both the great size of the temple and the provision of a large precinct surrounding it. The total removal of the Boudiccan layers of burning must be explained by thorough ritual cleansing.[13] The surrounding buildings in fact do not exhibit the same fresh construction as does the temple platform. The southern monumental arcade and drain incorporate re-used materials, including decorative details in alabaster, in the aggregate of their core,[14] while the northern group[15] seems to be later than a street contemporary with the post-Boudiccan grid. Thus, while the temple

[1] Suetonius, *Gaius*, 44, 2.

[2] Ibid. for the party of Adminius; cf. the comment by J. Toynbee, *Trans. Essex Arch. Soc.*, N.S. xxv, 10 on the bust of Gaius from site 91 or 92 (pl. XLII).

[3] Tac. *Ann*. xiv, 32: 'impedientibus qui occulti rebellionis conscii consilia turbabant' implies in-dwellers hindering the counsels of the colonists.

[4] Ibid.

[5] See pp. 98 (insula 10), 104 (insula 11), 148–9 (insula 17), 153–8 (insula 19), 198–202 (insula 28).

[6] pp. 153–8, 198–202.

[7] p. 214.

[8] p. 74.

[9] p. 81: the date, however, does not appear to have been precisely defined.

[10] Tac. *Ann*. xiv, 31: 'coloniam nullis munimentis saeptam'.

[11] Wheeler and Laver, *J.R.S.* ix, 146–8.

[12] pp. 162–91.

[13] Tac. *Hist*. iv, 53: 'haruspices monuere ut reliquiae prioris delubri in paludes aveherentur', of the Roman Capitol.

[14] p. 175.

[15] p. 180.

platform, indestructible and made of completely fresh materials, may be regarded as Claudian, the evidence provided by excavation would suggest that the subsidiary buildings may well be later than A.D. 61. As for the temple itself, its very large size, 80 × 105 ft., far outstrips the normal temples of *coloniae*, though it is not as large as the provincial temple of Gallia Narbonensis at Narbonne,[1] which measures some 118 by 158 ft. Some of its stone-work comprised building-blocks of alabaster, already noted as built damaged into a later drain, and there were fragments of thick white plaster mouldings, all of which hint at an appropriate richness of furnishings. Its position deserves comment. The temple did not dominate the town, but lay aside from its main centre and high point. This may well have been due to deliberate policy; for it will be recalled that at Lyons (Lugdunum), the cult-centre of the Three Gallic provinces was situated[2] at the confluence of the Rhône and the Saone, while the *colonia* occupied the summit of Fourvière. It is thus unlikely that the provincial cult was combined with the town-centre of the *colonia*, which will have occupied the heart of the urban area, rather than its fringe. In that heart may well also have lain the *curia* and perhaps the theatre, the two buildings of which Tacitus and Dio Cassius make incidental mention[3] in relating the portents which were the prelude to disaster. An eloquent relic of the disaster and of the looting which followed is the bronze head[4] of Claudius found in the river Alde at Rendham in 1907. Its scale, which is only life-size, precludes any notion that it was the cult-statue from the temple of Claudius itself, and the point is corroborated by its distinct inferiority[5] as a portrait. But it may well have adorned another public building, for example, the theatre[6] or the *curia*, and it remains one of the most dramatic witnesses of the temporary but total overthrow of Roman influence and power.

The second *colonia*, built after the Boudiccan destruction, was once again unprovided with walls, a fact which underlines the complete and merciless suppression which followed the revolt. But the known Roman street-grid undoubtedly belongs to this town, whether or not it reflects the intentions of the original builders or actually follows their less substantially marked lines. Proof of date is not lacking. Not only does at least one street[7] overlie the Boudiccan destruction layer, but an important east-to-west street[8] embodied in its primary metalling an *as* of Nero, a coin which cannot have got there until after A.D. 64, the year to which the first Neronian copper issues belong. The new streets were not everywhere laid out very precisely. Discrepancies on the through lines occur at the north-east corners of insulae 10 and 18, on the north side of insula 38, and on the east side of insulae 7 and 15, the last obliquity forming a contrast with the normal division between insulae 23 and 24. Again, it is certain that the main east-to-west street, between Balkerne Gate and East Gate, is not straight, but dog-legged. The reason for this divergence is provided by the new front of the precinct of the Temple of Claudius. As now reconstructed, the Temple occupied[9] a great court, shown in 1950 to have been somewhat irregularly planned at the back, where it was built up on the northward slope. It will be observed that the court is not planned with the Temple on its axis,

[1] *Gallia*, xiv, 10, fig. 8.

[2] P. Wuilleumier, *Fouilles de Fourvière à Lyon*, plan A.

[3] Tac. *Ann.* xiv, 32: 'fremitus in curia eorum auditos; consonuisse ululatibus theatrum'. Cass. Dio. lxii, 1, 2, from another source, but perhaps the same as used by Tacitus.

[4] Macdonald, *J.R.S.* xvi, 3–7.

[5] Here the Frontispiece: for the size see *J.R.S.* xvi, 6, note 2: for the work as a portrait, J. Toynbee, *Trans. Essex Arch. Soc.*, N.S., xxv, 11.

[6] Cf. the seated statue of Augustus from the theatre at Arles, S. Reinach, *Répertoire de la statuaire*, iii, 275, 7.

[7] p. 74.

[8] pp. 66–67, fig. 27.

[9] p. 161, fig. 81.

whether because another monument shared the place of honour or simply because the court was planned later, and irregularly throughout. The over-all dimensions of the entire block of buildings are not precisely established, but are not less than 536 by 426 ft.[1] In front of the main flight of steps lay a large altar, flanked by two oblong pedestals and bordered on three sides by a drain. This is reminiscent of the altar of Rome and Augustus at Lugdunum,[2] which stood between statues of Victory. The main street front was occupied by a great ornamental screen-wall,[3] associated with a monumental central entrance with attached angle-columns and itself consisting of panel-walls linking large ashlar-faced piers projecting north and south. The piers seem to have carried arcades, and to have been associated with free-standing columns on its inner front, but treated as squared piers externally, the whole elaborate structure being carried upon a platform of masonry, 15 ft. wide. The walling itself was marble-faced and no less than eight foreign varieties[3] of facing-slabs have been recognized as well as a Greek porphyry and much British Purbeck marble. The fact that this elaborate front projected southwards across the line of the main east-to-west street has already been noted, and it seems likely that the Temple precinct could be entered from both ends, no doubt by pedestrians only. These entrances would close a vista down the main street to east and west.

There is little to hint even at the whereabouts of the principal buildings of the *colonia*, as opposed to those of the province: nor is there much clue to their size or nature. Speed's record in 1610, of a curving series of houses[4] in insula 3, and the very solid curved foundation observed in insula 13 might hint at amphitheatre and theatre respectively; and it is useful to recall how at Aosta[5] the theatre is fitted to the plan by the addition of features which square it. Again, it is clear that the site of a public building, with foundations so solid as to require explosives to remove them, was occupied in 1910 by the Technical College,[6] but the nature of the structure is wholly unknown. The remains recorded in insula 30, opposite the Temple of Claudius, are hardly so certainly indicative of public building as to permit a sure conclusion.

It is indeed particularly unlucky that the single building which has been thoroughly excavated, the so-called *mithraeum* in insula 15, should have yielded neither structures nor associated evidence which conclusively proclaim its purpose. The case for a *mithraeum* advanced by Mr. Hull (pp. 112–13) is hard to accept in the total absence of Mithraic cult-objects, while the slots explained as bench-foundations do not in fact follow the expected lines, as a comparison with Carrawburgh[7] will show. Another demonstrable weakness is the lack of wall decorations and the rough nature of the floor. Indeed the character of the work aligns it with the underground chamber at Burham, Kent, now generally accepted[8] as a cellar, the grooves in the floor being explicable as for bins or racks. At present the most significant archaeological contribution of the excavation is the rubbish tipped into the building in the middle of the fourth century, including a most valuable series of coarse pottery, fully illustrated by Mr. Hull below (figs. 60–71). The building may thus after all belong to the

[1] p. 162.
[2] Strabo, *Geogr.* iv, 3, 2 mentions the βωμὸς ἀξιόλογος, while in *B.M.C.* i, pl. 21, 1, 2, 4, 5 are figured the altar and statues of Victory.   [3] pp. 188–9, report by Mrs. J. E. Morey.
[4] p. 80.
[5] P. Barocelli, *Notizie degli scavi*, 1941, 18, fig. 1.

[6] p. 96.
[7] The difference is that at no time were the ends of the benches connected across the nave by any structure, while they were not left open at one end, as is the western alleged bench-foundation at Colchester.
[8] R. F. Jessup, *Arch. Cantiana*, lxx (1956), 168–71.

domestic series, still best illustrated (fig. 36, p. 82) by the houses excavated in insula 6 in 1920. On a frontage 265 ft. long were found two courtyard houses, and one strip house, and, while their plans were by no means fully recoverable, it was clear that they shared a common street-front along which they were tightly packed and aligned. Some traces of the regulated allot-ment of land within the *colonia* is revealed here, based, as at Orange,[1] upon street-frontages. The phenomenon[2] is one of urban life and its stricter control, in sharp contrast with the sprawling distribution of houses in some of the cantonal capitals. The same tight planning in relation to the street front, with a curved wall to respect a small independent building, occurs in insula 9, close to the west wall of the *colonia* (fig. 39, p. 94). As to the general level of civilization, in domestic or public building, the impressive testimony is still provided by its mosaic pavements, largely the fruit of chance discovery and largely no doubt domestic. Their distribution is thickest in the western two-thirds of the town, showing that here lay the concentration of wealth and urbanization.

Next come the defensive walls, thoroughly pillaged in post-Roman days for their tile and septaria facing, and often reduced to a mass of intractable core, a stubborn relic of Roman structural ability. These walls are now dated as certainly not earlier than A.D. 150, and would take their place naturally enough, in view of the prestige of the town, as one of the first in the series of new town-walls erected in Britain about the end of the second century.[3] Their characteristics differentiate them sharply from defensive works of the later third century. They are devoid of external bastions and their principal gateways are furnished with double or single carriage-ways, flanked by a pair of foot-ways. The tile lacing-courses, sometimes considered as of late date, are matched by the similar lacing-courses used in the Augustan town walls[4] of Alba Pompeia and Turin. In their own right the Colchester gateways are of the greatest interest. The small north-east gateway, with single tower-crowned entry recessed between curved in-turns of the town wall, is of special interest in view of its close resemblance to the north and south gates of Silchester, and the fallen remains of an upper story allow of attempts at reconstruction, too rarely aided in Britain by actual masonry. It is not quite cer-tain whether the north gate had one portal or two, but it is most likely, as Mr. Hull suggests (p. 34), to have conformed to the same pattern. According to local tradition, the east gate had a single carriage-way and two footways, like the gates of Roman Lincoln.[5] In that case, it was eclipsed in splendour by the West or Balkerne Gate. The austere reconstruction here offered (fig. 4) perhaps hardly does justice to the monumentality of the structure; for it omits the strip pilasters which were always a feature of the façade, even after reconstruction. These imply, as at the gates of the Castra Praetoria[6] or at the gates[7] of Spello, a flat architectural framework, whose effect would be to enrich and enliven the façade. But this type of decora-tive façade, however simple, carries with it the necessity to counterbalance the width and height of the main portals by at least two upper stories, if not three, and these themselves can hardly have been devoid of architectural framing. Thus, the very decoration of the gate proves that it formed a positively theatrical stage-setting for the principal entry to the town.

---

[1] *J.R.S.* xxxii, 70, where the *merides* are identified with frontages of ribbon development outside the walls.

[2] F. Haverfield, *Ancient Town-planning*, 131.

[3] P. Corder, *Arch. Journ.* cxii, 23–24.

[4] Rivoira, *Roman Architecture*, p. 47, fig. 52 (Alba Pompeia), p. 49, fig. 54 and p. 50, fig. 55 (Turin).

[5] *Arch. Journ.* ciii, 31, pl. v, *a*.

[6] *P.B.S.R.* x, p. 22, pl. vi.

[7] *P.B.S.R.* xiii, p. 57, fig. 8; p. 60, fig. 11.

Richer are the vanished Porta Aurea at Ravenna, or the extant Porta dei Borsari at Verona, both examples[1] of first-century planning which are here echoed in the same way as the Augustan designs of Nîmes or Autun are reflected[2] in the late second-century monumental gateways of Verulamium.

These imposing defences and monumental gateways attest the pride and prosperity of the late second-century *colonia*, as well as a new need to protect it, whatever the precise cause. The wealth of the place is reinforced by a consideration of external structures. The rich tombs with Purbeck marble inscriptions, of which two examples[3] survive, one commemorating an *eques Romanus*, attest wealthy citizens among whom might well rank the retired centurion[4] of the Twentieth Legion, whose promotions are so proudly proclaimed: so do the sculptures, such as the fragmentary veiled head[5] from the Royal Grammar School, the famous Sphinx[6] from the Oxford Road, or the togate figure[7] from Manor Road. But no less impressive are the suburban temple sites, now published in detail for the first time. The most remarkable is undoubtedly Gosbecks, where a native shrine surrounded by a ditched enclosure was superseded in Roman times by a double portico, presumably comprising external and internal covered walks surrounding the temple precinct, as at Verulamium.[8] The temple is of native Romano-Celtic type, again as at Verulamium. But while the Verulamium temple occupies the centre of its enclosure, the Gosbecks temple lies in the south-east corner. Most of this detail is provided by air-photography, which excavation has so far been insufficient to corroborate. The ditch of the native shrine, however, appears to have been open until Antonine times at least (p. 264), and this confirms the general impression conveyed by the finds, of a late development of the site. The temple precinct lay at the west end of a much larger pair of enclosures (fig. 113, p. 260), whose purpose remains obscure, while to the south lay a large theatre 270 ft. in diameter (fig. 115, p. 268). Although the basis of comparison is slender, in the sense that excavation had yet to reveal the details of this spectacular site, it is none the less clear that comparisons with such Gallic establishments[9] as Sanxay, Drevant, or Vieux are justified. As to the god or gods there worshipped, Mercury, the god of trade and wealth, was certainly one of them, is shown by the discovery on the site of the elegant bronze statue thought to have formed part of a larger composition.

Gosbecks lies some two miles south-west of Colchester: the other sites lie closer, and their foundation is later. The best known is at Sheepen (fig. 106, p. 225), where another large walled precinct, 460 by 395 ft. over-all, enclosed a fine Romano-Celtic temple, approximately 64 ft. square (fig. 107, p. 226), whose erection is associated with coins of Domitian, and may date from about the turn of the century. A second similar but smaller temple (41 × 36 ft.) lay outside the walled precinct to the north-west (fig. 106, p. 225). The date of its erection is less precisely substantiated than that of the larger work, but it is not earlier than the third century and may well fall within its second half.

The temple discovered at the Royal Grammar School playing-field (fig. 110, p. 237) plainly

---

[1] Kähler, *Römische Mitteilungen*, 1, 175 Abb. 1, 179 Abb. 4 (Ravenna), dated to A.D. 43 (*C.I.L.* xi, 1, 7, no. 5): Schultze, *Bonner Jahrbücher*, 118, Taf. 23 (Verona).

[2] *Bonner Jahrbücher*, 118, Taf. 20, 21 (Autun).

[3] *E.E.* ix, 1007 (eques Romanus), 1008: a third is *E.E.* vii, 845.

[4] *C.I.L.* vii, 91, see p. 254 below.

[5] p. 254 now published by J. Toynbee, *Trans. Essex Arch.*

Soc., N.S. xxv, 13, pl. v, 2.

[6] Plate xxxviii, B, below: also *J.R.S.* ii, 148, fig. 16.

[7] p. 253.

[8] Wheeler, *Verulamium*, pl. xxxviii.

[9] Sanxay, J. Formigé, *Gallia* iii, 43–120; Drevant, *Bulletin monumental*, xxxii, 97; Vieux, *Mémoires de la Société des Antiquaires de Normandie*, xxi, 458–85.

had a more complicated history, and the remains were apparently so much robbed that the plan was not recovered accurately. The temple itself was identified as a rectangular stone building 21×30 ft. over-all, occupying the middle of a polygonal enclosure bounded by a narrow ditch which probably contained a palisade. The question whether the stone temple and palisade are contemporary is raised by the fact that the ditch was in due course rendered obsolete by a new stone-walled enclosure, planned as an irregular pentagon, which, however, respected the curving north-west side of the earlier boundary. Within the new enclosure, and obliterating the south end of the old boundary, lay a rectangular building $61 \times 28\frac{1}{2}$ ft. over-all. In and near a large pit, which once again was found to respect the early boundary, came to light two bronze dedications[1] to Silvanus, one adding his native name Callirios. A small but spirited votive stag[2] in bronze came from the large pit. There is a high proportion of Trajanic coins from the site, but their connexion with actual structures is not established.

Other religious structures and sites are less circumstantially authenticated. It seems highly likely that the grounds of St. Mary's Hospital (once the Union) contained another temple of Romano-Celtic type. Isolated finds, which may be strays, do not necessarily prove the site of a temple. But the dedication[3] to Matres Suleviae by a *peregrinus* from the Cantii is worth noting for its introduction of a foreign cult, not unknown elsewhere in Britain. No less interesting is the well-known bronze tablet[4] from St. John's Abbey, dedicated by a Caledonian of noble lineage to Mars Medocius Campensium and to the Victory of the Emperor Severus Alexander. This must belong to the years 222–35, and its expression of loyalty must be one of the consequences of a Caledonian treaty, the dedicator being a friendly chief. It may well be significant that *Brittones gentiles*, from beyond the provinces, were at this time quartered in Germany[5] and that Colchester was a principal port for the Rhineland, as Harwich is today.

The tale of external structures is not exhausted by tombs and temples. The town may indeed have been surrounded by a population of squatters, very much as was Clermont Ferrand in the days of Sidonius Apollinaris.[6] But there were also more substantial dwellings. A small suburb with substantial houses (pp. 243–4) was situated outside the Balkerne Gate, and another just outside the south-west angle (p. 244). Buildings of importance (p. 242), but uncertain nature, lay below the Water-works, outside the north-west corner of the town. A group of houses of some pretension lay just north of the crossing of the Colne, where no doubt a Roman bridge existed, though attempts to recognize its structure are in themselves unconvincing (pp. 241–2).

Such manufactures as went on inside the town are unknown. But in the suburbs were situated industries which depended upon the extraction of raw materials from the soil and demanded space for their work as well. At Colchester these were principally potteries.

Late in the second century makers of Samian ware arrived in Camulodunum to establish the only sizeable centre of such manufactures known in Britain. At least fourteen individual potters are known, and among them Acceptus (p. 249) was making colour-coated beakers marked with a common stamp. At least twenty-five kilns are known. Their distribution is

---

[1] p. 239, with references there quoted: also plate xxxvii, A and B.

[2] See plate xxxvii C; the animal might well come from a tripod. cf. M. V. Taylor, *Ant. Journ.*, xxiv, 22–26.

[3] p. 240; also *E.E.* vii, 844.

[4] p. 240; also *E.E.* ix, 1005.

[5] Rowell, *Yale Classical Studies*, vi, 88 ff.

[6] C. E. Stevens, *Sidonius Apollinaris* 144–7.

wide and would ring the urban area, were examples also to be discovered on the east. But the principal concentrations yet recognized lie to west and north-west, beyond St. Mary's Hospital and close to Kingswode Hoe. The potters' fields lie close to those associated with coarse wares, which also abound. Tileries, of which very large numbers must have existed, in view of the abundant use of tiles for building and roofing, have been noted in the area of the Sheepen by-pass, well to the north-west of the town.

THE APPROACHES TO ROMAN COLCHESTER

(a) THE SEA APPROACHES

So far as our records extend, Colchester has always been a Port Authority, and there is ample evidence from imports that it was a flourishing port in ancient times. The area allocated to its jurisdiction is a large part of the northern quarter of the Thames estuary, extending from West Ness at St. Osyth to Mersea Stone and thus including many creeks and mudflats, and, of course, the famous oyster fishery.

When Cunobelin established his capital at Camulodunum he probably did so for maritime facilities. These he could very well have obtained elsewhere in a region like this, most notably perhaps at Maldon, where there is a broad and deep water approach. But Camulodunum was already a royal seat of some long standing, and it is possible that some or many of the defences which shut it off as a huge promontory fortress were already in existence. Hence the choice of the site on the narrow, shallow, and muddy Colne.[1]

The approach from the sea is, to the eye, wide and easy. But many parallel sandbanks traverse the Thames estuary from NE. to SW., among which the currents are treacherous. The mouth of the Colne–Blackwater estuary is closed by such a bank, the Buxey Sands, which only leaves three useful channels. One is by the coast on the north, the second a narrow channel, called the Raysand, which comes up from the south, passing the Saxon Shore fort at Bradwell-on-Sea. The third is a very narrow channel called the Spitway, which passes through the middle of the sandbank. Marked as it now is, it is easy to find in good weather; without marks it would be hard to recognize at all times. Of course, these banks change, and they may have been very different 2,000 years ago.

To one sailing up the Colne there is no high ground on the left close to the water until the marshes are ended abruptly by the flat-topped bluff of Fingringhoe Wick. There were Roman villas on both banks right up to Colchester.[1] On Fingringhoe Wick, gravel-workings on a most extensive scale have removed at least two villas of unproven date and an area surrounded by a ditch of medium size. From this has come a great quantity of small finds of Claudian date and of a military nature, including a bronze camp-kettle. The absence of building-remains shows that the troops were in tents or huts. The area, according to the workmen, was full of small rubbish-pits, in which oyster-shells, food-bones, and most of the pottery, coins, and brooches, &c., were found. The pits appeared to be in regular rows. The remains are nearly all in private hands and cannot be reported here.

In the absence of roads pointing to this site, and in view of its position, it seems almost certain that it was a base for the fleet during, or even after, the invasion.

We have no indication whatever of the location of the Roman harbour. It may well have been that, while British boats (whatever their nature) could reach a point well upstream and near the native site, the Roman merchant ships had to tie up lower down. The place may have been the present Hythe, and it will be noted that the line of the Roman road at Gurney Benham House, if prolonged, continues by an almost straight line of modern streets (Magdalen and Barrack Streets) to the Hythe. Trenches cut across Barrack Street opposite Paxman's works, however, showed no sign of ancient road-metalling.

But the Hythe was known as 'New Hythe' from 1276 to the seventeenth century, in contradistinction, we are told, to the 'Old Hethe' which was supposedly the earlier harbour. But the latter place is, now at least, not on the river and has always been spelt 'Hethe', which locally means 'Heath'. In fact the only evidence for a medieval Old Hythe is the name New Hythe.[2] Roman coins and pottery are found in the river at the Hythe, but not in sufficient numbers to prove the position of a landing-place.

(b) THE LAND APPROACHES

The approaches to Roman Colchester by land consisted of an unknown number of Roman roads, but, while much has been written on the Itineraries and much on the roads themselves, practically no work has

---

[1] *Cam.*, pp. 2, 3.

[2] Morant says, *Colch.*, 1748, ii, 23; *Essex*, 1768, i, 127: 'At what time this (older) harbour came to be neglected and another one made, I never could find.' There is really no evidence for another harbour at all.

been done with the spade. The chief writers are Codrington,[1] H. Laver,[2] and Miller Christy,[3] the latter giving a large bibliography.

Several writers have emphasized the lack of good road-metal in Essex. This is true of the clay lands, but in the gravel areas the flinty glacial gravel makes a first-class road material and is available in unlimited quantities. To what extent the Colonia used this to embank its roads generally, and in the clay areas particularly, we do not know, for little remains in Essex in the way of embanked roads. This may be because they have been robbed for gravel, which would be all the more precious in the clay areas.[4]

The sources of information regarding the roads which may have existed are very inadequate. In the first place one may assume that there was a direct road between Londinium and Colonia. One sees that there now is such a thing and assumes it was always so. One looks for a road from Colchester towards St. Albans and finds an undoubted one in Stane Street, which is straight as far as Bishop Stortford. But when one applies this method to find roads from Colchester to Norwich, Cambridge, or Great Chesterford there is no easy answer. The two Antonine Itineraries which mention Colchester (one as Colonia, the other as Camulodunum) agree in placing it about 50 miles from London, which it is, so the road must have been nearly straight. But beyond Colchester both these routes are quite lost, for we have no clues as to where the places named lie, except that Stratford St. Mary could well be *Ad Ansam*. The mass of writings of authors of varying period and erudition is composed of superficial observations, guesses, and theories which are confusing and without substantiation. Hitherto, air-photographs have failed to fill the gap.

The frontispiece of the *Camulodunum* Report shows what was known of the roads and earthworks around Colchester in 1947. There is little if anything to add to this plan as yet, but the details regarding many entries upon it are here published for the first time. The defensive earthworks are left for a later report, except in the case of minor works, such as camps and enclosures. However confident we may feel about straight lines (such as Stane Street) converging upon Colchester, they seem (as indeed they do elsewhere) to disappear as they approach the town. At various times there have been attempts to explain one or other of the linear earthworks as a road. We may mention the survey of the Rev. T. Lufkin and Payler Smith in 1722,[5] and the

excursus by H. Jenkins in *Arch.* xxix, 251 (and pl. xxx). So determined was Jenkins to make the Lexden Rampart a road that he would carry it on a bridge over the road from London! The Lavers did not consider this rampart to be a road, but did sometimes regard as a road an earthwork which they identified as running from the south end of Bluebottle Grove to near Heath Cottage, and so by Olivers Thicks to Layer de La Haye vicarage. This, however, is a rampart, and P. G. Laver only termed it a road from Bluebottle Grove to Heath Cottage.[6] We have no reason to regard it as a road, though in fact we know little of its nature.

One of the engravings made by Benazach for Stukeley shows the Roman road to 'Ad Sturiam' (the river Stour) running east of north from the East Gate. No doubt the line of Land Lane is intended—it is labelled 'Stratford Street', a term otherwise unknown. There is no reason to suppose Land Lane was a Roman road, and no evidence for any continuation of it.

1. ROADS FROM THE WEST

I. *From St. Albans and Braughing.* We can feel satisfied that Stane Street is a prehistoric track, which was romanized, and the remains of it are very straight in Essex. It enters Camulodunum passing through Gryme's Dyke just south of King Coel's Kitchen.

II. *From London.* It has been universally accepted that the modern road represents this, and it joins Stane Street at Marks Tey. With arguments regarding its nature or course we are not here concerned, but repeated observations of trenches cut in it have failed to show an earlier road-surface beneath it.[7]

IIA. It has been observed that between Kelvedon and Marks Tey a minor modern road branches off to the right, and after a short leg of some 100 yards sets a perfectly straight course for 2 miles through Easthorpe, bearing a little north of east, and running almost exactly parallel to Stane Street at an interval of 2,400 yards.[8] This has been referred to as an alternative route from London to Colchester, and, although east of the straight portion there is little whereby to trace its course, a case could be made out for its connexion with a bank in Gol Grove. More important perhaps is the fact that it points directly to the complex occupation-site on Gosbecks Farm (p. 259). No work has been done on this line, and it does not show on air-photographs. It would be interesting to know whether the straight portion really had a continuation, or whether

[1] T. Codrington, *Roman Roads in Britain*, 214–20.

[2] *T.E.A.S.* n.s. iii (1889), 123 ff.

[3] Ibid. xv, 190 ff.

[4] Christy, loc. cit. 195; Horsley, *Britannia Romana* (1732), 331.

[5] Used by Morant in a note at the end of Lexden Parish.

[6] There is a manuscript plan by P. G. Laver in the Museum showing linear earthworks in blue and what he considered to be Roman roads in red.

[7] With one possible exception near Kelvedon.

[8] Measured from the map. For first notice of it see Miller Christy in *T.E.A.S.* xvi, 127; xvii, 97 ff.

it is to be compared with the roads which, pointing NE., stop equally suddenly at Dunmow and Gosfield.

We now come to the much-debated question of the course which was long held to be that of the London Road.[1] Jenkins was the first to show (on his plan) a line from the Balkerne Gate to the south end of Bluebottle Grove. Thence the bank of a large rampart leads on to the east end of Dugard Avenue, on the Straight Road. From this point, where Jenkins speaks of a 'Roman milliary or beacon' (a mound, of which no trace could be found in 1936), he wanders away to the SW. H. Laver, followed by P. G. Laver, examined the line more thoroughly: from the Balkerne Gate the road crossed Lexden Road diagonally just beyond the Hospital, 'on its way to the south end (of Bluebottle Grove). . . . In cutting the drain in Rawstorn Road (SW. of **110**) in 1884 the workmen cut through considerable remains, and also in the road at the back of Mr. Brightwell's playground (**36**) (in Manor Road), but here only about 9-inches thick of the foundation remained.' . . . 'In the playground of the Grammar School (between **112** and **113**) is a considerable depth of stones, and it was also cut through opposite the fourth house on the left in Beverley Road, and close to this spot Mr. G. Joslin discovered his well-known tombstone (**15**). In West Lodge Road in the same line, in 1884 the workmen came onto it in laying the waterpipes, and these are placed on its even surface.[2] No remains have been seen by me between the end of the Avenue and the earthwork at the back of Lexden Park (i.e. Bluebottle Grove) . . . but, . . . before the stones were removed, and the land had not so long been in cultivation, the course might easily be traced by the altered appearance of the crops directly across the fields, from the end of the Avenue[3] to the south end of the Bluebottle Grove.'

From this point the rampart continues the line westwards to the east end of Dugard Avenue (formerly Peartree Lane) 'it then makes a bend towards the NW. going directly across two fields to a spot in Gryme's Dyke, where the ditch has never been excavated. . . . Across these two fields the plough has almost obliterated it, but it may be readily traced (as a crop mark) in a dry spring. I have also made some sections and find, under about 15 in. of soil, that there still exists about a foot in thickness of stones, nearly 14 yards wide, under which the topsoil has been removed. These stones seem to have been mixed with chalk or lime and rammed down very thoroughly, many, in fact most of them being broken in the operation. The labourer I employed (said) . . . "it was very odd, he

had found a road, covered up, harder than the turnpike".'

From the opening through Gryme's Dyke H. Laver took his road thus: 'a line to the present bridge at Stanway . . . will take us near a raised hedge . . . across two fields to a modern road, where the crossing is distinct, and, still following the raised bank, which has on it a private road to Blackpits Farm, the house standing also on it, we follow the hedge to the road by a cottage near Stanway Villa, and find traces across this road and down the next hedge, the bank of which is unusually hard. After this the traces are very indistinct to Stanway Church, but in 1884, the spring being very favourable from its dryness, it was very easy to trace the course by the appearance of the growing crops. This latter part is still a right of way, a footpath following its course pretty closely.'[4]

P. G. Laver improves upon this line (manuscript map in Museum) leaving the main London Road east of Copford Lodge, and carrying on that same straight line to the field-boundary south of the church, continuing thence eastwards to pick up the crop mark and so to Black Pits Farm.

Neither of these theories has been tested on this portion west of Gryme's Dyke.

Within the dyke we have first to record P. G. Laver's notes:

'A pit was sunk at the entrance of Pope's Lane on Balkerne Hill . . . and revealed part of the Roman road as it emerged from the Balkerne Gate. The remains were fragmentary, owing to earlier trenching, which had, *inter alia*, destroyed the margins of the road so that their nature remains uncertain.' The following notes were taken: 'the present road metal is 8 in. thick (but in the sketch it is shown as 1–2 ft. thick, and in another MS. account it is shown as one foot 2 in.) below this was 4 in. of dark soil; under this was the Roman metalling of hard, rammed, bright red gravel, showing the camber on top, and from 12 to 18 in. thick. This lay on a foundation of grey clay 6 ins. thick, and then the natural sand.' The exact position of the pit is not shown. (Diary, 2/8/1922.)

In 1923 the road was cut again in Crowhurst Road (E. of **110**), during the laying of a waterpipe, at a depth of 3 ft. 6 in. It crossed the street at an angle, the north edge being 69 ft. north of the NE. corner of Papillon Road—'exactly on the line'. The sketch shows the road surface about 12 in. thick, extending over a width of 23 ft. from just opposite the north of the door of no. 41 to just north of the door of no. 43. It is lying on a bank of gravel, both sides sloping away steeply

---

[1] Cf. pl. XLIII.
[2] We cannot place this site. It can hardly be 'in the same line', see map.

[3] Read 'West Lodge Road' here for greater clarity.
[4] *T.E.A.S.* n.s. iii, 126–7, also 80, and vi, 19, where he says the crop mark is 60–70 yards left of the hedge.

(as if to a ditch), and here, on each side, black soil is indicated. A note observes that subsoil was showing in the bottom of the trench in places. (Diary, 18/12/1923.)

The line thus confirmed runs under the west end of Manor Road, where the lower half of a civil tombstone was found (36),[1] and runs under the main building of the Grammar School. But a manuscript by P. G. Laver, summarizing his notes, records the discovery between the north side of Beverley Lodge (now Gurney Benham House) and the boundary wall of 'a layer of hard stone which prevents plants from flourishing. It is about two feet below the surface' (N. of 113).

When Gurney Benham House (fig. 1) came into the hands of the Grammar School Mr. A. F. Hall decided to test this line, and so began a series of exploratory trenches which have proved most fruitful of results— and of problems. Examining the garden for the Laver Road he found a road indeed, but not running from NE. to SW., but almost due E.–W., with another smaller road coming in from the NW. Nothing fitted in with the 'Laver line'.

Nevertheless, long afterwards, some evidence was found, as shown on fig. 1 and on p. 7, that the road from the Balkerne Gate did actually follow the suggested line, joining the E.–W. road near the SE. corner of Gurney Benham House. This line we now accept.

Meanwhile, it was felt, doubt had been cast on the 'Laver line' as a whole, so it was examined further. The following details had been recorded: 'A trench for a water main slightly to the east of the centre line of Beverley Road, opposite Gilberd House (150) revealed a layer of largish gravel 8 in. below the present road surface, curved slightly in outline and 23 ft. wide. At one, and possibly two, points [was] a bed of buff clay under the clay being one foot deep at its thickest part [sic]. This is directly in line from the top of West Lodge Road to the Balkerne Gate.' (Diary, 17/4/1923.)

But a manuscript review of the line states: 'In Beverley Road the section showed that the road had been practically destroyed, but the boundary ditches were well shown and gave the width as about 27 ft.'

'At the top of West Lodge Road a foundation layer of buff clay 8 in. to one foot deep was found under the gravel of which the road was composed, the width here being 27 ft. as before.' (Diary, 19/3/1923.) (A sketch plan gives approximate position.)

Farther on, in Queen's Road: 'A trench cut at right angles to the South kerb of Queen's Road, just east of the boundary between Dacca House (which is on the corner of Victoria Road) and the house next to the east, revealed part of an old bank which formerly

bounded the fields on the south of the present road.' The bank sinks deeply to the north, and Laver thought this possibly showed remains of the ditch on the south side of the Roman road. (Diary, 17/4/1923.)

Now this line pointed to the Grammar School playing-field (1266a) (pl. XLIII), so Mr. Hall cut trenches over long stretches across the line. Here the subsoil was solid gravel. The field is quite flat. The gravel when exposed showed no trace of remains of a road-bank nor of marginal ditches;[2] though a ditch was found (179), possibly that of a minor rampart almost on the line of the one remaining at the south end of Bluebottle Grove.

In 1936 the writer undertook to examine the bank of the latter rampart, which runs west from the south end of Bluebottle Grove. The bank proved to be a massive linear rampart, faced with turf on the north, where lay a great ditch. This was no Roman road, but nevertheless it was felt that possibly metalling might have been laid upon it, which would have disappeared in subsequent ploughing. There was the more reason to suspect this because there was a second ditch on the south side of the rampart, about 12 ft. wide and 4 ft. deep. This seems to run all the way from Bluebottle Grove. As it approaches the (now single) ditch of the 'Triple Rampart' which runs N.–S. across our line, it tapers, turning slightly north, and runs into the larger ditch.

It was soon ascertained that no road-metal lay on the rampart, and if there ever had been a road built thereon the only way in which to prove it would be to find whether a causeway was built for it over the N.–S. ditch of the Triple Rampart. Accordingly, after this ditch had been proved on each side, a diagonal trench was dug in its filling approximately at right angles to the continuation of our line towards the passage through Gryme's Dyke. There was no doubt that the ditch had had a partial filling, which was capped with 9 in. of gravel metalling, with grey mud on top. When this causeway (if such it was) was made, the ditch had already silted up to a depth of 18 in. Upon this was dirty gravel, 4 in. thick, and then 6 in. of whitish material from the turf face of the N.–S. rampart. Then came 2 ft. of dirty red gravel, then a firm bed of rammed clayey loam.

The southern part of all this had been removed by an old gravel-pit, but what one may judge to be about half of the causeway remained. It seemed adequate, assuming that the road had dipped considerably into the ditch, to prove a deliberately made crossing at this point for a road. On the other hand, in plan, the behaviour of the south ditch hardly conforms to this theory,

---

[1] In his Diary, 21/7/1922, Mr. P. G. Laver says this stone was found during the sinking of a cesspool at no. 5 Hospital Lane, and a road-surface paved with cobbles was found in the yard. The Rev. H. Jenkins bought the stone for £10.

[2] These trenches were across the Laver line: the line we show, if projected, would fall farther east and miss Bluebottle Grove, but any road on it should have been found in the work done on field 1266.

and one must keep in mind that the whole may really be concerned with the finishing off of the end of the E.–W. rampart where it joined an earlier N.–S. rampart.

100 ft. south of it, and so the 'Laver line', as a Roman road, finally falls out of the running. For Mr. Hall was quite unable to find anything more than the ditch,

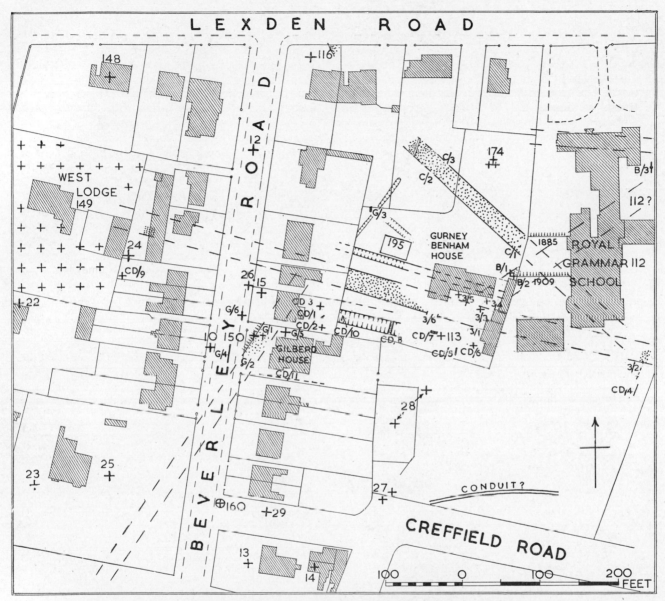

FIG. 1. Discoveries at and around Gurney Benham House (pp. 4–9).
(For 1885 on this plan read 1852.)

Feeling the matter was still uncertain, Mr. Hall now tested the next field (to the NW.), no. 1302, where H. Laver said he had excavated the road.

The 'Laver line' across this field and the next is very clear on air-photographs, and sometimes on the ground, as a dark line, indicating a ditch. Since Mr. Hall's work it has been established that the ditch in question does not aim at the opening in Gryme's Dyke, but at a point

the filling of which was exceptionally hard on top. It was 20 ft. wide and 5 ft. deep (from the present surface).

On the strength of these observations we advised the Ordnance Survey to omit the 'Roman Road' marked on the 'Laver line', except between the Balkerne Gate and Gurney Benham House. But we remain curious about the validity of the observations in

Beverley and West Lodge Roads, which we have been unable to check.

Before we pass on to describe Mr. Hall's other work on the roads, there are some other records left by P. G. Laver to be mentioned.

After describing the 'Laver line' he says: 'At some time the above line was altered, and it took the course shown on the plan[1]—that is it still ran diagonally to the south west, but at the back of the houses on the north side of Lexden Road, crossing the present road where it bends by St. Mary's Lodge' (now Vint Crescent, south of **101**). Of this line we know nothing at all, nor on what evidence the statement was made.

And here is the best place to mention two other lines shown on the same plan. One begins from the south corner of the former Lexden Heath and follows a line of rampart as far as Pretty Gate Farm (shown on pl. I, *Camulodunum*), where it is discontinued, pointing to the south end of Bluebottle Grove. The other has a detached portion (which might belong to the first) following the line of a fence in Gol Grove, and continuing NE. as a fence and a narrow line of trees to Warren Lane (about 150 yards north of Heckford Bridge). After a long gap the line is resumed at Well House (some 500 yards SW. of Brickwall Farm), whence it follows the road to that farm and thence a straight field boundary to Lexden Straight Road where it breaks off again. The only subsequent indication is a broken line through the orchard NW. of Oak Cottage and diagonally across the 'Roman Way' at Pretty Gate Farm. Here the line nearly converges on the previous one.

Unfortunately, once more we have no knowledge of P. G. Laver's reasons for showing these lines, and in the absence of confirmation, we feel that they are no more than theories.

2. ROADS AT GURNEY BENHAM HOUSE

We are indebted to Mr. A. F. Hall for the following account of the activities of the staff and boys of Colchester Royal Grammar School in exploring this area,[2] for, although initiated in collaboration with the Museum, the work is really that of Mr. Hall and his colleagues.

The Main Road to London (pl. XLII and fig. 2, iii)

Many trenches were cut in examining the well-built road which was found here (**195**) to be running on a course a little north of west. The section reproduced (fig. 2)[3] is typical. The road is quite elaborately built, and very wide (over 70 ft.) owing to its triple construction. On the north side is a light roadway nearly 20 ft. wide made of a concrete of pebbles and lime on clean loam. On the south lies another track of about the same width made of sand laid on loam. Presumably the north track is for foot passengers and the south for horses. Between these is the main bank of the road, for wheeled traffic. It is 27 ft. wide, but is flanked by disturbed areas, which, when critically examined, proved to contain traces of upright, boarded revetting with oblique supports. These certainly served to retain the edges of the bank, and there was no indication that they had served, either simultaneously, or alternatively, as wooden drains of the type found so often by the early streets in Köln.[4] In fact they showed that horizontal planks had been held up by vertical posts as a revetment, and the posts had been propped by slanting supports. The subsoil here is gravel, and to make the road the topsoil had been removed and a spread of loam (possibly mixed with lime) had been substituted to act as a bed for all three tracks. The main body of the central road was a bank of red sandy gravel, upon which lay a series of layers of lime and pebbles, which formed a succession of very hard road surfaces.

On the north there was a large ditch, the filling of which was partly covered by the footway and a small ditch. On the south there was a larger ditch with one uniform featureless filling.[5] The northern ditch was about 6 ft. wide and 3 ft. deep at the level of the base of the road-structure.

As to the course of this road, the portion explored has been very closely and accurately plotted, using the north edge and the revetted edges of the central track, all of which are parallel. The walled cemetery has the same alignment.[6] The line projected westwards passes just north of the site of the Longinus tombstone (**24**) (pl. I, B), and there the work of lowering the level of the ground exposed the road, part of which could be seen quite clearly. The stone was lying on its face, the head to the north at a depth of 3 ft. 6 in., which corresponds roughly to the Roman ground-level. At the time we had no knowledge of the three-track road. The observed position of the south edge of our piece of road, measured from the east and south walls of the site, gives a line about 7 ft. south of the line in Gurney Benham House (when projected), and even allowing for inaccuracy in judging the edges, this seems to indicate a slight swing to the south. The section was

---

[1] Presumably the tracing of the 6-in. map mentioned on p. 2, n. 6, is meant, where it duly appears.

[2] And many other similar works which he has carried out under the same or similar circumstances.

[3] *J.B.A.* 3 s. vii, 53.

[4] Fremersdorf, *Topographie*, i, *passim*.

[5] The 'Camp Ditch', see p. 273.

[6] See *Arch. J.* (1944), ci, 68.

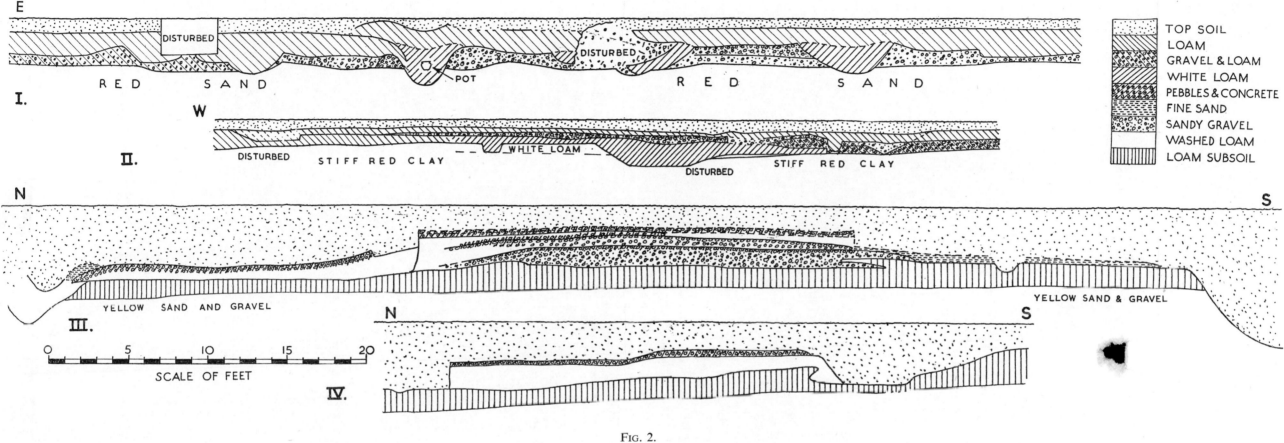

E

DISTURBED

RED   SAND   POT   DISTURBED   RED   SAND

I.

W

II.   DISTURBED   STIFF RED CLAY   — WHITE LOAM —   DISTURBED   STIFF RED CLAY

TOP SOIL
LOAM
GRAVEL & LOAM
WHITE LOAM
PEBBLES & CONCRETE
FINE SAND
SANDY GRAVEL
WASHED LOAM
LOAM SUBSOIL

N   S

YELLOW SAND AND GRAVEL   YELLOW SAND & GRAVEL

III.

0   5   10   15   20

SCALE OF FEET

N   S

IV.

FIG. 2.

I. Section of road at Rayner's Farm.   II. Section of road at Iron Latch Lane.

III. Section of three-track road at Gurney Benham House.   IV. Section of road to NW at Gurney Benham House.

taken from the exposed face, without digging, so that the appreciation of the quality of the various layers may be defective. There was loam at the bottom, with 6 in. of clay upon it. The two together should correspond to the loam under the road in fig. 2, iii. Upon this lay a bed of red gravel 2 to 6 in. thick and narrower than the metalling above it. South of this, at the same level, lay a layer of 3 in. of light clayey material, with a black line between it and the loam below. This corresponds to the sandy southern track of Mr. Hall's main section. The central track was built up of a bank of yellow gravel about 6 in. thick, with a hard gravel surface about 3 in. thick upon it. Bearing in mind that we did no dissection with the trowel, the resemblance to, and correspondence with, the former section is sufficiently convincing. Traces of revetting were not observed, nor of the slot in the south track, but we had no reason to search for either.

The further course of this road is not known. It may have connected directly, in an almost straight line, with the portion of metalling which was exposed in the garden of 'Ethelstowe'[1] in St. Clare Drive (**167**), some 50 yards south of Lexden Road. This would bring it partly under the latter over some of the distance. Its continuation would strike the spot where the Lexden Dyke has been destroyed.

The other possibility, that it turned slightly south and ran on the line of the road observed by P. G. Laver in Fitzwalter Road (**162**), is not so attractive, but points to a passable place through the ramparts; moreover it is pointing pretty well to the passage at King Coel's Kitchen.

Eastward of Gurney Benham House there has been little opportunity to examine the course. Mr. Hall has probed at 3/2 (fig. 1) immediately SE. of the Grammar School, close to the east boundary, and has located the metalling of the main bank there, and the south sand-track. He believes that the line is bending northwards a little, which he thinks may be bound up with the presence of the so-called 'Camp-ditch'. It should be noted that it is just about here (3/2) that the NW. road will make a junction with the three-track road.[2]

Junction of the road from the Balkerne Gate with the Three-track Road (fig. 1)

We have already stated and accepted the evidence for the existence of a road from the Balkerne Gate to a point approximately under the Grammar School. The question arises as to where exactly this road joined the three-track road. As Mr. Hall points out, H. Laver said in 1885 that the road was encountered in the school grounds. This must refer to discoveries during the terracing done in 1852. The existing line of the terrace can be seen on the west of the school and the 1852 line lay north of it. It is clear, therefore, that Laver did not see either the NW. road or the three-track road. The line from the Balkerne Gate would strike approximately under Gurney Benham House. In an attempt to check this, Mr. Hall made the following investigations.

A trial pit sunk at B/2 revealed extremely strong concreted road-metalling, bedded on the natural gravel. At B/1, in 1934, a trench for piping had cut through the festooned filling of a ditch apparently very obliquely, so that this ditch should be running NE. If so, it may very reasonably be regarded as the ditch of the road from the Balkerne Gate.

At B/3, east of the school, the Headmaster, Mr. J. F. Elam, cut a N.–S. trench in his lawn, and found a steeply sided ditch crossing it very obliquely and corresponding in character with that at B/1. It contained 'fairly numerous sherds, broken tile, and bones. Attempts by auger to pick up the line of this ditch further east have so far proved inconclusive, but further work is intended.'

These observations confirmed the possibility already suggested, and Mr. Hall sank three small trial-pits in search of the junction. He first exposed the surface of the centre of the three-track road north of 3/1, and at 3/1 he exposed the south edge of the central metalling. Twenty-seven feet north of this, where the northern edge should lie at 3/3, no edge could be found. At 3/4 again a road surface was found, and only 2 in. lower than the centre of the road (whereas the level of the northern side-track should be 2 ft. lower). Two more pits sunk at 3/5 showed road-metalling at the same high level.

There is thus revealed a certain amount of evidence to confirm the theory that the road from the Balkerne Gate joined the three-track road under the south face of Gurney Benham House, and did not go farther. The line laid down on the O.S. 25-in. map, edn. 1939, from the Balkerne Gate is too far to the west as it passes the corner of Manor Road, and if it be swung in to pass close by the site of the civilian tombstone (**36** on plan) it will hit our suggested point of junction, and the change of line does not invalidate previous observations.

3. GILBERD HOUSE (fig. 1)

Gilberd House, part of the Royal Grammar School, is now the sixth building on the east side of Beverley Road, south from Lexden Road. Joslin's house, at the

---

[1] The residence of P. G. Laver.
[2] Mr. Hall sees this part of the road east of Gurney Benham House as lighter-built (earlier?) than that westward, which could have been strengthened to carry traffic to the Balkerne Gate.

time of the discovery of the Centurion's tombstone, was the fourth. It works out well for the stone to have stood exactly as the Longinus stone, on the south side of the three-track road (or its predecessor). However, the position is such that it has been possible to argue that this Centurion's stone was evidence for the continuation of the road from the Balkerne Gate beyond Gurney Benham House. The other arguments to the same effect we have related. In his Diary (19/4/23) P. G. Laver records and sketches a cambered road-section which he saw revealed in a trench in the roadway (just east of the centre line) of Beverley Road exactly opposite the front of Gilberd House (G 4). He indicates the width as 23 ft., but claims it to be the road from the Balkerne Gate. Were it so, since it would cross the street at an angle of 53°, the actual width would only be 18 ft. He shows the metalling only 8 in. below the surface of the street, laid on thick clay of yellowish colour, which lies on sand. The general impression, however, is that the road ran E.–W. Mr. Hall accordingly began to explore the front garden of Gilberd House, expecting to establish its course.

The level of the ground here is higher than that in Beverley Road and there is nearly 3 ft. of topsoil. Trenching at once revealed that things were not as had been supposed. The site was much disturbed, in the first place, probably, by Joslin in excavating for graves, and later by masses of modern pipes and drains. In effect, evidence was gathered for a ditch crossing the site obliquely, accompanied on the east by a road. The west side of this ditch could not be found owing to disturbance of the ground. In the filling of it were found the remains of three human skeletons (**150**). Above the lowest two of these lay the skeleton of a dog, and an early bowl (form *Cam.* 221)[1] in polished black native ware was between the feet of one body. There was a vertical strip about 1 in. wide missing from the side of this bowl, which can hardly, therefore, be regarded as an undisturbed burial-pot (C.M. 129 and 130.47).

East of the ditch there were scattered and patchy evidences of a road-surface which was a curious, apparently artificial, layer of 'mortary' material lying directly on the natural gravel. A very dubious east edge for the road would make it 26 ft. wide. The damage to the road-surface may belong to graves, robbed by Joslin. One was cut into the road-material, which here

was 12 to 18 in. thick. Near it, but outside it, lay pieces of a human skull laid one inside another, perhaps left so by Joslin.

No more could be learnt in the very restricted space available, but a possible line of ditch and road was established, and this lies, as Mr. Hall points out, on the same line as the road which crosses Gosbecks Farm from the south. Nothing, however, was found to confirm or explain Laver's note, and the road found was not a continuation of that coming from the Balkerne Gate. Further work is desirable under better conditions, e.g. in gardens on Queen's Road.

4. THE ROAD POINTING NORTH-WEST

The discovery of this road was quite unexpected. The section, shown in fig. 2, iv, was taken at C/2, but the line was first picked up at C/1 where the section is not quite so definite. The course is plotted by the south margin. At C/2 the south edge was very clear, and vertical as if originally revetted and with a small bank of loam laid against it. There is little doubt that the north edge was also revetted, and this could be photographed at C/3. No revetting could be distinguished at C/1, but there was a posthole analogous to those associated with the revetting of the three-track road.

No ditch could be identified on the north side, but in its place was apparently artificial material which, at C/3, extended many feet northwards. Trenches cut north of C/1 for air-raid shelters showed a great depth of dark, made earth, in which were several cremation burials at varying depths (**174**).

In the C/1 section the road was pierced by an almost vertically sided pit or trench, and probing suggested that this occurs again several yards westwards. This can hardly be a draught ditch, for it does not occur at C/2.

This road has a surface of pebble concrete 22 ft. 6 in. wide. Its course, beyond our figure, is unknown.[2] We think it is premature to refer to it as the 'Cambridge Road', and prefer to reserve judgement, having regard to the possibility that some of these roads which are seen here and there may well prove to be part of the streets of a large early military encampment.[3]

Another exposure of roadway has to be recorded. This (**135,** and fig. 3) was found when building the NE.

---

[1] *C.M.R.* 1947, 28 and pl. IX, 6.

[2] Mr. Hall adds the following note: 'In the published account, in *J.B.A.* 3 s. vii, the plan shows this road bending north soon after leaving our site. This was because it was reported that a road ran SE. to NW. through allotments north of the Lexden Road (the large field 1085 behind St. Mary's Terrace). I later had an opportunity to dig on the alleged road, but found only mortary stuff, seemingly artificial; and so far as

a course could be guessed it would pass far north of our line. At the north edge of this alleged road was a small excavation (? ditch or grave) and at its edge a broken grey urn-base, with burnt bones' (**99** on plan). No road continued on this line across our area G (of 1934) on the top of the hill opposite.

[3] Since this was written this road has been uncovered again between C/1 and C/2 and a good photograph of the metalling obtained (22/5/53).

wing of the Hospital. The section was taken by Mr. F. Godfrey, Clerk of the Works. It shows that the surface was 3 ft. below the surface of Hospital Road. The Roman road itself was 18 ft. wide, with a small

it points exactly to the point of junction of the road last described with a projection of the line of the road from Gosbecks. What this may mean it is not possible to guess at the moment.

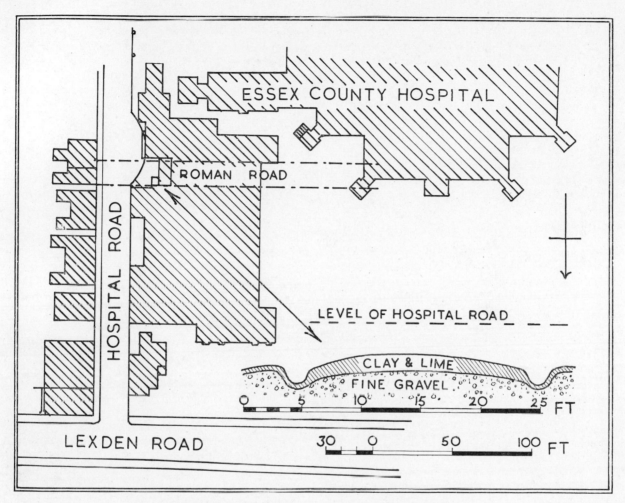

FIG. 3. Plan and section Roman road under the Hospital [135], p. 9.

ditch, 3 ft. wide, on each side. The subsoil is described as fine ballast, that is, small gravel, and the material of the road is described as 'clay and lime'. The thickness is not stated. The words 'clay and lime' are curious, and are directly related to a recent observation by Mr. Hall that he thought that the first (lowest) layer, or bed, of the three-track road was made of clay and lime. Note also the occurrence of clay and lime (or chalk) on the Gosbecks site (not necessarily, so far as we know, in connexion with roads).

This road under the Hospital is very clearly plotted, for course, by Mr. Godfrey, and it is remarkable that

5. THE ROADS TO THE SOUTH

IV. *Colchester to Maldon.* Many remains have been found at Heybridge and Maldon of both Iron Age and Roman date, including part of an Arretine platter of good period. There is no doubt that Heybridge[1] was a place of some importance even before the Conquest, but no road thence to Colchester had been suggested prior to the discovery, by air-photography, of the road passing the Gosbecks Farm site.[2] The line of it can be clearly seen as two parallel white lines, apparently about 35 ft. apart, centre to centre, in the southern

[1] Heybridge, *C.M.R.* 1913, 10, 11, pl. II; *Cam.* 19.　　　　[2] *Cam.* 18.

part and about 28 ft. in the northern part. It is visible from a point 300 yards NW. of Rayners Farm to a point 450 yards south of the Gosbecks temple. It passes under the junction of Olivers Lane with Gosbecks Road, and is not perfectly straight.[1] Projected northwards the line comes very near North Bridge, southwards a slight bend would suffice to bring it to the ford on Roman River, and most of the way from there to Garlands a more or less straight line can be followed, of roads and footpaths.

In 1936 a trench was cut across the line, against the north side of the south hedge of field 440, just east of Rayner's Farm. The section (fig. 2, i) was difficult to understand. The gravel subsoil had been cut about a good deal, and it was almost impossible to decide what had been moved and what not. However, the two pale lines on the photographs are two ditches, with rounded bottoms, lying at 30 and 55 ft. from our eastern zero point. The somewhat similar feature at 20 ft. seems accidental, for there are not three lines on the photographs. The three features are all distinguished by their remarkably white filling, in the midst of which lay, in the eastern one, a broken, but complete, beaker (as *Cam.*, pl. LVI, 108 BA), which belongs to the second half of the first century. The ware is Roman grey, and the date probably Flavian.

Between these two ditches, as might be expected, the gravel rises higher than elsewhere, except for one place west of the west ditch. Taking the top of this as the Roman level, the east ditch is about 3 ft. wide and 2 ft. 3 in. deep; the west ditch is doubtfully 6 ft. wide and 2 ft. deep. The disturbance in the middle is difficult to explain, for if continuous it should show on the photographs, while it can hardly be fortuitous, because, though it is certainly partly disturbed, its western half is not, and definitely contains the same white (turf?) material as found in the lateral ditches. The nature of this resembles that of the turf found in ramparts here, and also in the mound of the Gosbecks theatre. There is, however, no lamination in these ditches (nor in the theatre mound), and one wonders whether the material is actually turf or bleached surface soil, rain-washed from the road. This same stuff fills the lower part of the central excavation, but whether this could have been a 'draught-ditch' (compare *Cam.* 97, sections 52–56) or not we cannot say. It was certainly open at the same time as the side-ditches.

It could have been filled in and a new one made in some extensive rehabilitation of the road. The width of the road indicated is rather over 30 ft. in our diagram, but the uncertainty in which we are left by the features which resemble five ditches, and the difficulty in deciding which gravel is undisturbed and which may have been road-metal, makes definite conclusions impossible. One thing is certain, the 'tramline' exists in the ground and it is Roman. It was certainly a road.

The remains of the gravel bank are visible to the eye in field 1788 (SE. of temple and theatre) after deep ploughing, when they are turned to the surface and show as a yellowish (but broken) band.

Presumably by this road was carted the Kentish ragstone used for the theatre and other buildings at Gosbecks.[2] While the modern field-system disregards it completely, its relationship to the older one remains to be explored, and the air-photographs so far available are not adequate for this purpose.

V. *The road to Mersea.* On Mersea Island, 7 miles from Colchester, Roman remains have frequently been found. They include an opulent villa under the church, and the remarkable 'wheel-foundation' (probable tomb) east of it, at West Mersea, and on Barrow Farm a large Roman burial mound.[3]

It has long been assumed that there would be a road thither from Colchester. A course was laid out for it by H. Laver[4] beginning at St. Botolph's Gate[5] and running, with its ditch outside and its bank inside the Abbey Wall, along the Mersea Road as far as the fork at Plum Hall, thence following an intermittent line of ditch, bank, or footpath to Monk Wick Farm and beyond, to join the rampart in Berechurch Park.[6] Miller Christy thought the road might emerge by Scheregate or the Balkerne Gate (he surely means Head Gate) and pick up the modern road running south from Maypole Farm.

But all this is theory. The only positive evidence is that Mr. Rudsdale twice observed ancient road-metalling under the west side of St. Botolph's Street, opposite the Marlborough Head (**62**) and 50 yards farther south (**61**), apparently pointing to the gateway.

When part of the bank on the Mersea Road opposite Hyderabad Barracks was cut back and down to the level of the footpath, remains of cinerary urns were found (**146A**),[7] but no road-metalling. The bank

---

[1] It crosses fields 402 and 414 (O.S. 25-in., 1920, now, revision of 1939, all one field 1788) more or less clearly as far as field 1313 NW. of Rayner's Farm. This area is now built over.

[2] Without prejudice to its possible earlier existence contemporary with wooden buildings.

[3] Morant, ii, 424 ff.; Salmon, *History of Essex*, 434–5; *Arch.* xvi, 149; Gough's *Tours*, MS. in Bodleian, Top. Gen. e. 18, fol. 215; *T.E.A.S.* n.s. vi, 173; x, 325; *P.S.A.L.* xvi, 424; *T.E.A.S.* xvii, 128; *J.R.S.* xii, 260; *Ant. Journ.* iv, 267.

[4] *T.E.A.S.* n.s. iii, 79, 131 f.; ix, 327, followed by *R.C.H.M.*, pp. xxviii and 21. See also J. H. Round in *T.E.A.S.* xvi, 273.

[5] But on Major Bale's original drawing for the plan it begins, as a pencilled line, from the centre of the south front of the Castle!

[6] A section of this bank cut by Mr. Hall showed no road-metal.

[7] *C.M.R.* 1944, 37.

is not that of a road. In the present roadway, at the same spot, was a lead coffin (107), just below the surface, which has almost certainly been reduced to ease the gradient.

The area between Plum Hall and Monk Wick Farm is now covered by houses and the cemetery. A careful watch was kept on the work for signs of a road. None was found. A row of burials (197), native and Roman, just outside the west wall of the former cemetery might argue for a road passing by, but none has been seen, and we are far from Laver's line, and neither housing operations near, nor grave-digging, have found any traces of a road.

6. THE ROADS TO THE EAST

Though one might assume that a road emerged from the East Gate and crossed the river Colne (here tidal), immediately opposite, where there has been a bridge for centuries, with a ford beside it, no sign of Roman metalling has been seen under the present street. The gradient of the hill has also been reduced at the gate itself. But P. G. Laver has recorded that in May 1928 a trench cut along the entry to Crowther's factory cut through a road (198), lying just north of the present street. His sketch shows it as about 25 ft. wide, lying 3 ft. below the surface, metalled with gravel, including large stones, cambered, and about 12 in. thick at the middle. This lay on a bed of yellow brick-earth 35 ft. wide and 2 ft. thick, the whole standing up above the general black garden soil which alone appeared on each side of it. (Diary, 19/5/28.)

East of the river the roads are all guess-work.

VI. *Colchester to Beaumont Quay on Hamford Water.* Miller Christy[1] has tried to establish this line. If it existed it must have been simply to convey septaria stone from the coast.

VII. (?) *Colchester to Harwich or Dovercourt.* There are Roman sites in this direction, and H. Laver has suggested that the road out to Elmstead served Harwich and Dovercourt.[2]

VIII. *Colchester to Ipswich, or East Suffolk.* There is a general consensus[2] that the modern road from East Bridge to Stratford St. Mary (6 miles) follows, for the most part of its course, the line of a Roman road. This is probably correct, but we cannot discuss it here.

7. THE ROADS TO THE NORTH

IX. *Colchester to the north by Nayland.* Whether there was a Roman Rye Gate is unknown, though there is now a ford opposite its possible site. There are, however, no records of road-metalling found north or south of it. The NE. postern gate was not in use for much of the Roman period, but gravelling resembling road-metal was seen in May 1930, 30 yards east of the park boundary and 60 yards north of the gate. Its surface was much broken by pits containing human bones, which have been ascribed (we think without reason) to the siege of 1648.[3] P. G. Laver noted road-metal, which he took to indicate a ford, in the banks of the Colne at a point almost in line (159).[4] All this may indicate a road running north,[5] but we cannot accept it as a major road, for which we must look to the west.

The former arguments against the line of North Station Road[6] fail since the discovery that there was indeed a Roman North Gate, and Miller Christy is amply vindicated for his words—'I cannot help thinking that it [the Roman road] did in fact follow the present North Street and emerge from the North Gate, if not exactly on the line of the present street.' This seems now so probable, when one recalls the evidence for the abutment of a bridge on the line, that the lack of a road to the Rye Gate becomes noticeable and an argument that there was perhaps no gate of importance there. Yet the Roman cemetery seems to lie east of the line of the modern road, and it is perhaps too soon to decide that no road could have slanted across from Rye Gate towards North Station. When the By-pass Road was built careful watch was kept for evidence, but no trace of a road was seen anywhere at all.

At North Station the Roman road is supposed to have forked. P. G. Laver held that he had evidence for a Roman road following the West Bergholt Road out towards Bures, but lying behind the houses along the north side of the street.[7] However this may be, the main line is said to have held on to Mile End, which was at one time the end of the cultivated ground, and here it forked again as it entered upon Horkesley and Boxted Heaths. The western arm according to Jenkins was visible—'its agger or ridgeway more than three miles in length, formed a conspicuous object before the heath was enclosed. The modern road, called Horkesley Causeway, was made by levelling the

---

[1] *T.E.A.S.* xv, 203 and note 2. Roman remains have since turned up in Tendring Hundred, and actually near Kirby Quay and Elmstead.

[2] Ibid. n.s. iii, 130. One should also note the other modern road with straight sections, which passes through Trap Street and Fox Street.

[3] *C.M.R.* 1931, 7.

[4] Diary, 30/1/34.

[5] P. G. Laver claimed to have traced this road as far as an elm-tree which stood on the By-pass Road, between the houses 'Sunningdale' and 'Rascor', but this is purely theoretical. (Diary, 30/1/34.)

[6] *T.E.A.S.* n.s. iii, 129 f.

[7] He shows it (on a MS. map) as a straight line from a point in the modern road opposite Braiswick Lodge to the bend of the road north of the Railway Station.

materials of the Roman agger, and runs in a straight line through the parish of Great Horkesley to Nayland'.[1] There is nothing like this to be seen now, but Roman coins have been found along this line. There is no indication on the map of any road beyond Nayland or Bures.

An eastern fork crossed Boxted Heath, but both Christy and Laver disregard it, dismissing it as modern. But it is there as an open road across the heath on Chapman and Andre's map of 1777. Like the others, it has no visible continuation.

X. *The roads to the north-west.* It is to be assumed that one of the roads already discussed must have led to Venta Icenorum. The lack of a road to Cambridge has often been noticed, but perhaps it is the lack of a road to Great Chesterford which is the more surprising. To the present day, communications between Colchester and these two places are very poor. That there must have been a fairly direct route to Chesterford in Roman times may be regarded as certain, but a separate one to Cambridge would be unnecessary.

Apart from the modern roads on these two general lines, none of which look convincing,[2] there are two new indications of roads leading out in this direction.[3] Both fan out from King Coel's Kitchen, and appear on air-photographs as 'tramways', but are only visible for a very short distance. The more northerly bears about 313 degrees and is not visible beyond the railway, which it strikes at the bridge on Iron Latch Lane. In 1936 a section (fig. 2, ii) was cut 160 yards SE. of the bridge, at right angles to this line. The subsoil is red gravel, with reddish or brownish clayey loam on top. The band which appears on the air-photograph is associated with two layers of a very different nature. White loam takes the place of the red or brown loam over a width of 25 ft., and upon it lies a band of gravel, up to 6 in. thick, extending about 5 ft. farther than the white loam at each side. The loam was very white at the west side, where there may have been a small ditch, the filling the same as the brown loam, but not so compact. This is clearly a Roman road, but never truly ditched and perhaps never banked. The 35-ft. width of the gravel may be partly due to ploughing-down.

While this was being written the line of this road was cut under the modern road to Halstead. Here it had been slightly sunk below the general level, and the terrain had been wet, for the road consisted of a very thin layer of gravel laid upon faggots or fascines. Upon it lay some 9 in. of dark mud.

The second 'tramway' is much less distinct, and seems to run on a bearing of 280 degrees. It has not been examined.

A third 'tramway' appears on the air-photograph, bearing about 310 degrees, and ending on the edge of the gravel-pit in Dugard Avenue. It is not noticeable in the side of the pit. Both these last are recorded on the frontispiece-map of *Camulodunum*.

8. OTHER RECORDS RELATING TO ROADS

The following comments and notes in P. G. Laver's Diary are especially valuable.

162. 'When laying a water main along the west side of Fitzwalter Road a cambered road of gravel was revealed opposite Mr. D. W. Clarke's House. It lay 2 ft. 6 in. below the surface and was 18 ft. wide. The centre line (of the part exposed) was 15 ft. S. of the boundary wall between Messrs. Lazell and Clarke. The subsoil was gravel.' . . . 'I had traced (this road) as passing through the garden of H. Lazell and through the middle of the plantation in the Park, where, slightly changing its direction, it went through the Bluebell Grove bank . . . just to the south of (Lexden Park) house.' (20/8/1923.)

163 (not on map). 'When cutting a trench for a gas main on the west side of Lexden Straight Road, a road surface was cut through 33 ft. N. of the gate, . . . yards north from the corner of Cross Road.' This entry is confused, for there is no 'Cross Road', and even the distance from the gate is uncertain, for this is shown as 54 ft. on the sketch-plan. The road material was 18 in. thick and 18 ft. wide, resting on gravel. A sketch section shows 1 ft. of topsoil above a cambered road with a small, rounded ditch, 10 ft. wide and 3 ft. 6 in. deep (from the top of the road-metal), on the south side. (9/10/1923.)

The 'Cross Road', which is shown with a farmhouse in the north angle and was on the east side of the Straight Road, can only have been Heath Road, but this helps little, for the position of the gate (on the west side of the Straight Road) cannot now be recovered.

'This road apparently a continuation of the long plantation and walk from the back of Lexden Manor House to the west of the Straight Road; some evidence of a ditch both sides of the road, but most marked on the south.' (Ibid.)

164 (not on map). Some evidence of a bank in the field south of the wood which lies west of Iron Latch

---

[1] *J.B.A.* xix, 1863, 282; Miller Christy, loc. cit. 213.

[2] P. G. Laver (manuscript map in Museum) held as Roman the modern road from Cambridge, from Gallows Green to Eight Ash Green, and again from the third milestone to the slight angle just short of Gryme's Dyke, and again, after a short

interval, to just north of Cromwell Lodge, whence he takes it by a broken line to join the modern road just east of its junction with the By-pass Road. There is nothing convincing about this line.

[3] Both shown on the frontispiece-plan of the *Camulodunum* Report.

Lane led P. G. Laver to look for traces of a road, and in the hedge-bank, at the sharp curve in the west boundary of the field, he found exposed at the corner of the ('Lucy Miles') lane the metalling of a road, 16 in. below the surface, a cambered bank of gravel 10 in. thick and 27 ft. wide. He examined the fields towards Stanway Church without success. (21/10/23.)

165 (not on map). When a drain was being put in for the laundry, London Road, Stanway,[1] a good section of the ditch on the north side of the Roman road was revealed. P. G. Laver says he cannot remember any evidence of a (modern) ditch here in his time. His sketch shows a ditch 12 ft. wide, almost V-shaped, the centre approximately under the garden wall and the bottom 5 ft. below the level of the present footpath. The ditch is cut in gravel, the depth of which from the surface is not noted. (6/12/23.)

166. The sewer-trench cut along Fitzwalter Road, north of the tumulus, revealed a Roman road crossing the present road obliquely. The marginal sketch shows its apparent line as passing north of the inner angle of St. Clare and Fitzwalter Roads and just touching the east tip of a crescentic group of firs east of the tumulus. (9/12/23.)

P. G. Laver built and resided in the house called 'Ethelstowe' in St. Clare Drive. In the garden of this house, only a short distance south of Lexden Road, part of a Roman road was exposed (**167**), and Laver said he had also seen the ditch of it in the cutting for St. Clare Road itself, a little more to the east (**158**). Unfortunately, no plan or section of either exposure has survived.

All of this information remains very vague. As regards no. **162**, Laver gives no reasons for his assumed course, but it is noticeable that a line joining the road in Gurney Benham House to the opening at King Coel's Kitchen passes through the points he mentions. This provides an alternative line for this road, and a better one, since it passes through the gap in the Lexden Dyke which was explored in 1932.

No. **163** will be of no use until the road is found again. No. **164** is near, but not on, the line of the less distinct tramway pointing to King Coel's Kitchen. Its exact position is not known, however, and it may belong to this road.

No. **165** is merely a pointer. No. **166**, however, calls for comment, for, while **162** passes clear of the possible military fort, this line, if correctly apprehended, seems to pass through the middle of it. It also passes through a gap in the Lexden Dyke, south of that already mentioned. At one time Mr. A. F. Hall and the writer attempted to reconstruct possible lines of centuriation based on the theory that these roads were parallel and evenly spaced. Vertical roads to them could not be found, nor did the interval (about 125 yards) seem to fit with any Roman measurement, so the attempt was abandoned.

[1] Mr. W. Sadler informs me this laundry was a small place about opposite the Lexden Union.

II

THE TOWN WALLS

So well have the walls been preserved that even up to the eighteenth century they almost confined the town to its original shape, the only notable extension being weavers' houses to the south and the street to the Hythe. This is very clear on Speed's map of 1610 and on Stukeley's print. The outline of the Roman town can still easily be made out on the 6-in. map.[1]

Many Roman towns were abandoned and now lie under the plough, but their walls are usually well preserved (e.g. Silchester and Caistor-by-Norwich); others, like Caerwent, are now represented only by a village, but equally retain the outline of their defences. It is where there has been continuous occupation on a large scale (e.g. London, York) that the walls have been swept away or buried so as to require care to trace their former course. Colchester belongs to the first class, even though now built over. If it ever was completely abandoned it was not so for any lengthy period, but for a very long time it must have been a village.[2] In this time we may picture the stout old walls standing, whether cared for or not, and the ruined buildings within gradually disintegrating and swallowed up by vegetation. The small population lived in the poorest circumstances on the lines of Head Street and North Hill, and on High Street, where some divisions of property remain the same today as in Roman times (p. 159). These were the only Roman streets to survive. Of luxuries we find no trace, and only the sparsest trace of essentials such as pottery. The dissolution of the ruins was assisted from time to time by those who grubbed and burrowed into them for building material. Thus these two streets alone lie on the old street lines. Meanwhile the rest of the town became overgrown and largely grass fields or gardens. Finally, in the later Saxon period, when the population began to increase, new streets were laid out, on courses parallel to the two surviving streets, or to the town walls (which is nearly the same thing), but bearing no other relation to the Roman plan, for they run over Roman ruins; indeed, Trinity Church, the tower of which is late Saxon, stands across a Roman street.

What we do not know is when the Roman population left, or alternatively, how long it took to fade away.

The following description of the town walls begins at the Balkerne Gate and moves in a clockwise direction round the town. But a few preliminary remarks are desirable. The first extensive survey of the walls was made by Dr. P. M. Duncan in *Trans. Essex Arch. Soc.* o.s. i, 26 ff., hereafter referred to as 'Duncan'. A later article on them by P. G. Laver is in *J.B.A.*, n.s. xxvi, 22 ff. They enclose a rectangle of about 1,000 by 510 yards, with rounded angles. Morant[3] says a survey was made in 1746, when they were found to measure 9,280 ft.

---

[1] *Note:* The plan is irregular, for no obvious reason. The main axis (taken as a line from the west to east gates) bears 3° north of east. But the north wall bears only 85°, and the main part of the south wall 88°. The west wall bears not quite 1° east, and the east wall just over 356°. As a result, near the west end the town is 1,640 ft. across, near the middle, 1,750 ft., and near the east end 1,690 ft.

[2] This is only a slight modification of J. H. Round's view in *T.E.A.S.* xiv, 199.

[3] *History of Colchester* (1st edition, 1748), pp. 5–6; hereafter referred to as 'Morant'. Later references will be noted as necessary.

in circumference and to enclose a space of 108 acres, 2 roods, and 5 perches. Cromwell gives the circumference as 3,077 yards and the area enclosed as 118 acres, 1 rood, and 22 perches.[1]

The date of their erection has been much discussed, and the evidence available is brought together in this volume for the first time; a summary of the conclusions will be found on p. 62. It seems best now to suppose that they, with the earth rampart behind them, were not completed before the middle of the second century. Tacitus is quite clear that they did not exist in A.D. 60. They are not mentioned in history until A.D. 921, when the Saxon Chronicle tells us that the Danes were besieged in Colchester by the Saxons, who stormed the town and slew them all. In the same year Edward the Elder placed a strong garrison in Colchester and had the walls repaired.[2] The late P. G. Laver,[3] followed by others, thought traces of this work had been found in the east wall (see p. 42), but we think this not warranted. Perhaps something of it may yet be found to remain in the Balkerne Gate.

Later the Court Rolls of the town show that the bailiffs and commonalty kept a jealous, though unfortunately not unblinking, eye on the walls, summoning those who damaged the structure or built against it, or dug pits too near the foundations.[4]

Soon after this the wall was in so bad a state that the town had to repair it. We quote Morant (p. 6):[5] 'But more care seems to have been taken to repair and keep it [the wall] up in the time of King Richard II than in any other reign. For notice is taken in the Oath Book (5 Ric. II, 1381) that the Bailiffs and Commonalty were daily repairing the stone walls of the town where they most wanted. And that the king, in the 6th, 12th, and 17th of his reign (1382, 1388, 1393) did of his special grace and favour, exempt the Burgesses of Colchester from the charge of sending representatives to Parliament for three years, on the 6th and 17th and for five years on the 12th, upon account of the great expenses they were at in repairing their wall with lime and stone, for the safety of the town against all invaders. The same king, in the 16th of his reign (1392), granted his royal license to Ralph Agar, Stephen Baron, and Henry Bosse, impowering them to grant and assign . . . [property] . . . to the Bailiffs and the

[1] Cromwell, *History of Colchester*, 170.

[2] *Mon. Hist. Brit.* 380, 381; Duncan, 30.

[3] *J.B.A.*, n.s. xxvi, 31.

[4] *Court Rolls*, i, 5/6/1312, 'tallage assessed throughout the whole community for the repair of the walls and gates of the Borough of Colchester'.

26/6/1346. John de Larsele pleads not guilty to a charge by the bailiff of breaking down part of the stone wall of Colchester, viz. at Southsherd. Inquiry ordered. John atte Hyde, the same.

16/4/1352. Two maidservants of Geoffrey Chapman have broken the stone wall of the town and carried off the stones to the said Geoffrey's house. . . . Hugh, servant of John Pegon, and Robert de Kedyngton have done the same. . . . The servant of Wm. Mace is accustomed to do the same opposite the field of Colchester Castle.

31/10/1345. The bailiffs and commonalty leased . . . an empty place under the stone wall of Colchester, within the North Gate . . . .

Ibid. ii, 28/4/1354. John Pegon carried off stones of the town wall at Southsherd and exposed them for his own use. In mercy.

27/4/1360. Thos. Lamb for collecting at various times stones of the town wall and carrying them off to Peter Wisbeche's house. Adam Wistone for the same offence.

Ibid. iii, 17/1/1373. John Bolex, for digging sand under the stone wall of the town in North Strat. In mercy. And ibid. 53, Robert Champeneys, for doing the same.

Ibid., p. 190, 2/5/1379. Richard Packe, for collecting four cart-loads of stones which fell from the town wall, and hiding them at Northsherde, with the help of Thos. Matc.

Various names described as 'supra murum' probably indicate that certain families were already dwelling on top of the town wall.

Ibid., 2/10/1374. Robert Champeneys for digging sand under the stone wall of the town.

Ibid. iv, 101, 7/6/1382. The bailiffs and commonalty of the town are causing the stone walls of the town to be repaired day by day, as was very much wanted, and because John Hampton and Margaret his wife . . . hold a . . . house . . . joined to the stone wall at the East Gate, which obstructs the said repairing, it seems good to the bailiffs . . . that the house should be removed and rebuilt on a more suitable spot. (They granted another site and house, charging all expenses to the town, on account of the poverty of said John and Margaret, at a yearly rent of one halfpenny.)

[5] And see Cromwell, p. 171.

Commonalty and their successors, as a help towards mending and repairing the walls of the town.'

We shall see below (pp. 45–58) how evidence is coming to light to show what was done at this time.

'The like exemption . . . was granted . . . by king Henry IV in 1403 for six years, and by Henry V in 1421.'

The lands above mentioned, including those of the Hospital of the Holy Cross, had their revenues returned to them under Henry VII.

The walls naturally suffered much in the siege of 1648. '. . . One afternoon the besiegers . . . fired 140 great shot against the town wall, but did it very little hurt; only beat off the tops of two old towers upon it, and killed three men.'[1] On 1 September 1648, after the surrender, Fairfax wrote to the Mayor ordering tools 'for the demolishing of the workes and part of the walls about the town of Colchester'. But probably the only part really demolished was the SW. angle where the 'Royal Battery' was mounted.

From that time the walls were obsolete as a military protection, and it is regrettable that so many buildings were built upon or against them, with much resultant damage, in many places completely concealing them. On the other hand, there is no doubt that this circumstance has in some cases proved a protection to them.

During this period, when the walls were of neither military nor archaeological interest, several persons damaged them by cutting passages through them, and in other ways.

1. THE BALKERNE GATE
(PL. II, FIG. 4)

This is the main west gate of the town, facing London. By the time the earliest English records of Colchester begin (*c.* 1280) it had been put out of use and the London Road diverted to Head Gate. There is as yet no satisfactory evidence as to when this rather remarkable event took place. The change was complete and final, for the main street within the gate was built across, and the purpose of the gate itself was forgotten. Early references to it include the delightful name of Colkynges Castle, but the usual name was 'the Balkerne' or the 'Balcon' (without the word 'Gate'). In Morant's time, and back to the siege, it was regarded as a fort.[2] The meaning of the name is unknown. The philologists suggest that it refers either to the balks of the Saxon field system outside or to its wooden construction. The latter is puzzling, for it was not of wood, and the former is unconvincing.[3] The writer is no philologist, but suggests that since the gate was most notably blocked up there may be some connexion between Balkon, Balkerne, and blocked.[4]

Morant gives the 'Balkon' or 'chief bastion' but scant mention, and does not know that it was a gate. He is followed by Cromwell,[5] who implies that he thought it post-Roman, and says that the south guardroom was then (1825) used as a pigsty. Roach Smith followed (or inspired?) by Wire, and the Rev. C. H. Hartshorne recognized it as a gateway,[6] as did Duncan,[7] but neither understood its full extent. The four passage-ways were first recognized

---

[1] Matthew Carter, *A True Relation etc.*, 203.
[2] Ibid., 'the town being in all places very weak: neither had it any more than one flanker about it, and that very bad too, which was called the Old Fort or Balkon', 142.
[3] Reaney, 370.
[4] See *O.E.D.* Balk = Bar.
[5] Cromwell, 176–7.
[6] In *J.B.A.* ii. 31.
[7] Loc. cit. 48; *T.E.A.S.* i. 48.

by Mr. John Ward, who had a plan made by Mr. A. G. Wright.[1] Excavations were begun by the Morant Club in 1913 under the direction of Mr. H. Laver and Mr. E. N. Mason. The two northern piers were discovered and evidence of rebuilding found, but the sudden death of Mr. Mason put an end to the work.[2]

Excavations were resumed in 1917 under Major R. E. M. Wheeler (now Sir Mortimer), whose report was published in *T.E.A.S.* xv, 180. A later summary with some additional observations was published in the R.C.H.M., *Essex*, iii, 21 ff.[3] From these reports the following account is taken.

This is certainly the main west gate, and, facing London, and lacking any rival, it is probably the main gate of the town. It is the largest monument of its kind in Britain, unmatched in size and preservation, though sadly hemmed in by buildings, reservoir, iron railings, and even with a public house (the King's Head)[4] standing upon it, so that it provides a disappointing spectacle compared with what it could easily be.

The over-all dimensions are 107 ft. north to south and 39 ft. back to front, of which 30 ft. project forward from the face of the town wall. The walling is preserved to a height of 15 ft. and includes two complete archways (see plan, fig. 4).

First period. With the exception of the central pier, which seems to have been completely rebuilt, the dimensions of the original gate are now known.[5] There were two carriage-ways each 17 ft. wide, and two footways each 6 ft. wide. These four entrances were flanked by massive towers (fig. 4) each containing a large, almost quadrant-shaped guardroom, entered from the east by a passage 12 ft. long and 6 ft. wide, partly vaulted (pl. II, C). The vaults of the south guardroom and south footway are still standing. The latter passage is 32 ft. long (pl. II, B).

The character of the structure is exactly similar to that of the town wall, and Wheeler[6] is of the opinion that there is nothing to support the suggestion that the gate is a subsequent addition to the town wall. The foundations are of septaria and occasional flint, in loose, sandy mortar. The core of the walls is of the same material, but the mortar is of better quality and contains powdered tile. The normal facing is the same as that of the town wall, but is vastly inferior in the north face of the south wall of the south carriage-way.[7] This is most striking and suggests a late refacing. Only in the piers of the main front is there any difference. Here well-dressed tufa blocks are used. The tiles used measure 17 by 11 by 1½ in.[8] There are four quadruple tile courses between the Roman ground-level and the

spring of the vault over the footway. The north guardroom stands 15 ft. high, but is covered by the 'King's Head' (pl. III, A). The south (pl. II, C) is excavated to about Roman ground-level[9] and stands about 12 ft. high. The walls at the NE. corner bond perfectly into the east side (i.e. the massif on the line of the town wall). In the southern circuit the face is well preserved except for a hole filled with modern repairing, but the four courses of stone are not so regular as they might be; compare the excellent work of the north wall with that of the SW. circuit where it joins at the NW. corner. Here the courses do not register perfectly, and for a corner like this, with a pilaster on both outside faces, to be executed without tile is most remarkable.[10] The same imperfect bonding is noticeable at the joint of the north tower with the town wall. In fact it might be argued that the rounded walls of the guardrooms seem to have been added to a pre-existing gate and town walls, but Wheeler is against this view.

The carriage-ways are divided centrally by a pier which has been wholly or partly rebuilt. Of this pier only three courses of masonry remain above the rubble foundations. Twenty-four feet back from the outer face both masonry and foundations are broken off, so that the length of the pier is not known. The rubble foundations are clearly part of the original pier, but

---

[1] *Essex County Standard*, 23 April 1910.

[2] Mr. Mason's original notebook on the excavations is in the Musem.

[3] And, of course, *J.R.S.* ix. 141.

[4] Colloquially known as 'The Hole in the Wall'.

[5] They were obtained by Wheeler in 1917 by tunnelling under the 'King's Head'. The tunnel can still be inspected.

[6] *T.E.A.S.* xv, 180.

[7] This has not been remarked formerly.

[8] Wheeler has $8 \times 11 \times 1\frac{1}{2}$, clearly a misprint for 18, &c. Perhaps 17 is more accurate.

[9] When it was cleared a small oven was found in the Roman strata of the floor (Wheeler, note, p. 181). Ovens have been found in guard-chambers on Hadrian's Wall and elsewhere.

[10] It suggests that the masonry was covered by some form of facing.

BALKERNE GATE, COLCHESTER, RECONSTRUCTION.

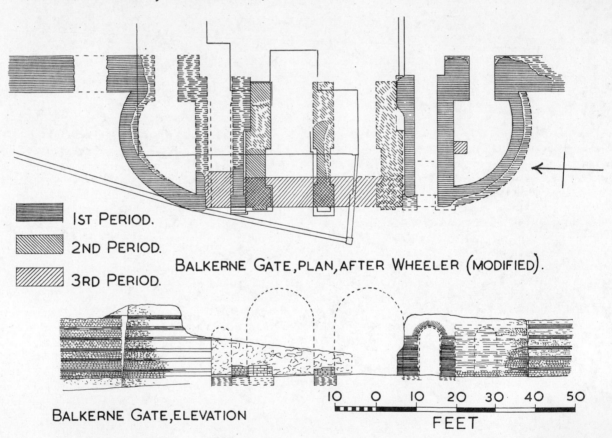

1ST PERIOD.

2ND PERIOD.

3RD PERIOD.

BALKERNE GATE, PLAN, AFTER WHEELER (MODIFIED).

BALKERNE GATE, ELEVATION

10   0   10   20   30   40   50

FEET

Fig. 4. The Balkerne Gate, Colchester, reconstruction, plan, and elevation of existing remains. Reconstruction by I. A. Richmond and M. Sisson; plan and elevation after *R.C.H.M.*

the ashlar is of period II. Some is of tufa, probably from the period I work, some is of an earthy limestone from the London clay, a stone rarely used in the earlier work. The hard pink mortar of the earlier period is replaced by a yellowish sandy mortar of poor quality.

The northern pier of the north carriage-way was found badly broken, but was doubtless symmetrical with the existing south pier. Its outer face was stepped down to bring it to the ground-level, already falling away to the north.

Most of the interior of the north tower is inaccessible. Mr. Mason sank a small shaft into it in 1913 and temporarily revealed part of the inner face of the walls.

The datable material found in the excavations was small. Sigillata of f. 29 dated A.D. 70–90 from the north junction with the town wall, and, from the foundation-sand and road-metal of the north footway, ff. 15/17 and 24/25. Then, low down in the road-metal by the foundations of the central pier, ff. 29 and 'transitional' 37.[1]

The second period. The north carriage-way was reduced by masonry added to its north side, and the central pier was apparently completely rebuilt in tufa, probably on the foundations of its predecessor. The yellow mortar of the rebuild is distinct. For this to happen the gate must have been in ruins, and the septaria used in the foundations of the reducing masonry is burnt, perhaps in the destruction of the previous building. The masonry had been robbed to below floor-level, and the foundation trench contained pottery assigned to the third and fourth centuries.

There is no doubt that what was thus observed in the northern part of the gate applied equally to the south, and that the south carriage-way was similarly reduced, but this remains undisturbed under a modern roadway.

The third period follows another destruction even more complete, for a rough wall, from 8 to 9½ ft. thick, has been found to run across the northern portal, and no doubt it continued across all the portals; it certainly extends partly over the south carriage-way. The rest is not accessible. It is without foundations, and consists of lumps of masonry (not separate stones or tiles) laid in the most unskilled manner in soft sandy mortar.

The date of this remarkable blocking-wall is most intriguing. It is clearly a desperate defence-measure taken when the gate was in complete ruin. It is therefore hardly likely to belong to the Roman period (quite apart from its uncivilized nature). It may well have been put up as a hasty defence by the Saxons during the raids and invasions which mark the end of the Roman occupation, or it may represent the work of the Danes or Saxons, or more precisely of Edward the Elder. It cannot be later than the Norman Conquest, and must be connected, even though remotely, with the closing of the gate and the building-over of the street within.

A cruder piece of masonry than this wall would be hard to find, and the mortar is so bad that the whole is now crumbling, nor could it be reset or pointed in order to save it.

The date of the first period has been the subject of varied opinions based upon very inadequate evidence. Such evidence as is now available falls under four headings:

1. The finds mentioned above; none of the potsherds found in the earliest strata need be later than A.D. 100, and several are undoubtedly Flavian. On the other hand, the relation of these strata to the structure is not recorded from the 1913 excavations, and the problem could not be reopened in 1917.

2. The plan is most remarkable. It is without known parallel; in Britain only one other site has produced gates with four portals, namely St. Albans, which are of more normal type and are not earlier than *c.* A.D. 180–90.

Amongst quadruple gates the Balkerne is exceptional in the peculiar plan of its towers and the extraordinary width of the carriage-ways, which are over 17 ft. wide, as compared with 11–13 ft. in the others (and 9–10 ft. at St. Albans). Most gates which project thus from the town wall have a so-called 'courtyard' built on to the inside, but the Porte-St-André at Autun lacks such a court, and the writer notes that, were there one here at Colchester, a wall should run on eastwards from the NE. corner of the south footway. But inspection of this corner shows it to be a finished corner of tile, with no continuation, so that a rear-court is improbable.

[1] For more detail see *T.E.A.S.* xv, 182.

3. The method of construction cannot be held to preclude an early period for the gate, and exhibits certain features which seem to militate against a late date.[1]

4. The evidence of history is not great, but what there is would make us place the building of the gate with that of the town walls,[2] and these, we are assured, had not been built in A.D. 61. But this simply means that the gate must be post-Boudiccan. Reason will be shown later (p. 62) for ascribing the town walls to *c.* A.D. 150.

The peculiar shape of the guardrooms and mode of junction with the town walls have, for years, discouraged all attempts at a restoration of this gate. Recently, however, Professor I. A. Richmond and Mr. Marshall Sisson have worked out a reconstruction upon which they are both agreed. A model has been built to their plans, and calls for a little explanation.

The two major problems outstanding, after one has grasped the simple implications of a four-portalled gateway 107 ft. wide, were the quadrant-shaped guardrooms and the large offset formed by the end of the town wall on each inner side of the gate. Structurally, guardrooms on this plan cannot have risen above the middle portion of the gate as individual towers. It was therefore decided that the whole gate must have been of one and the same height over all; almost an oblong building with rounded ends. Though devoid of architectural merit, this solves the problem of the towers. The offset shown by the town wall is not quite 7 ft., just enough to leave the thickness of the parapet wall stopping against the outside of the guardroom wall. The great width of the carriage-ways demands lofty arches which can hardly be put at less than 25½ ft. above the roadway, on which assumption the floor over the entrances must have been at least 27 ft. above the road.

If not absolutely necessary it would be at least natural to provide direct access from the rampart walk to the space over the gate, for otherwise the gate completely blocks the rampart walk. The peculiar projections formed by the town wall on each side are used in the reconstruction to provide space for a staircase, the first flight of which takes the walk up to the room over the gate, and a further flight connects to the roof. The latter we make a flat fighting-platform. Another story, roofed, might have been possible, but the plan is against a hip-roof.

Thus regarded the reconstruction is simple. No doubt it will not satisfy all, but it is something to be able to advance a plausible design.

As to the details of the façade, one can scarcely hope, in the circumstances, to make more

---

[1] Certain authorities on the Continent claim that the use of tile bonding courses can be proved to belong to the late Empire. This view cannot be sustained. Bonding was very necessary from the first, with the very bad septaria stone which had to be used here.

[2] In the Report of the Royal Commission on Historic Monuments there is a further comment on the Balkerne Gate. It is there associated with the 'Portes Monumentales' which were often constructed to mark the completion of a road undertaking, and the Arch of Augustus at Rimini and Trajan's Arch at Benevento were of this kind. Hence it is conjectured that the Balkerne Gate may have been erected to celebrate the completion of the romanization of the triangle of roads, London, Colchester, St. Albans, which must have been one of the earliest Roman works in the country. This raises a point for discussion, for it has been thought possible that the gate once stood alone, and the town wall was added later according to a preconceived plan. The point is made that, without the guardrooms, the building forms an independent rectangular block, and the guardrooms show signs of being later additions. It has been suggested that the central portion may have stood alone as a triumphal arch. The reply is that there never was a triumphal arch of this size, and the piers at the NE. and SE. angles, which form the respective halves of the entrances to the guardrooms, are integral with the building. It may be argued that there is some poor jointing and matching of courses on the inside of the outer angles of the guardrooms, but the outside looks good. There is some bad jointing at the north junction with the town wall, but the similarity of the work is complete, and it seems that, despite these few apparent discrepancies, we must regard the whole as of one build with the town walls.

than a guess. If it was ornate, nothing has survived of it. In the local dearth of building-material anything good would be most thoroughly robbed. But the same dearth might well be the cause of a very austere design, and this we have cautiously adopted, avoiding even pilasters, and offsets in the outer corners of the openings, despite the suggestion of them on the plan. We feel that we cannot hope to be nearly right in every detail, but that the general design cannot have been far different from ours.

On one important detail we are entirely without guidance. How the end of the rampart was treated we do not know, nor how access to it and the walk upon it was arranged. (But on this see Tower 1, below, p. 24).

Proceeding northwards from the Balkerne Gate the town wall is at first at its best, though there is a breach in it against the gate, made many years ago by a member of the Town Council, who was rebuked by his colleagues for his action. The following description of the wall is now given once and for all, and only aberrations from it will be noted in future. For 70 ft. north of the gate the facing is preserved as it rarely is elsewhere (pl. III, A).

The Roman town wall of Colchester is, so far as has been observed, of one uniform build, the variations being in points of detail insufficient to suggest work of different periods. The materials are tiles made locally, and septaria stone, squared as well as may be into rect-angular blocks of varying length. But the core between the faces is a concrete of yellowish mortar and roughly coursed, irregular pieces of septaria. The distance from face to face is usually 8 ft. 8 in., but the foundation is much wider, being 10–11 ft. Normally it is about 2–3 ft. deep, made of several courses of large blocks of septaria laid in mortar in an ample trench which was filled up with clay. Upon this the base of the wall was laid 9 ft. 6 in. wide, the face on each side consisting of one course of septaria capped by one of tile. This is clearly intended for ten Roman feet. Inside, the foundation projects about 18 in., outside, about 6, but not much is known of this. Upon the 9 ft. 6 in. base the upgoing wall was built with a 2–3-in. offset on the outside and a variable one of a few inches on the inside. The first courses were three of septaria. After this come four courses of tiles, and then four of stone and four of tile, alternately to the top. The joints are thick owing to the poor stone, and were plastered level with the stones and then marked off with the point of the trowel. This marking remains wherever the surface has been protected from frost. The pointing is done thus even where covered by the earth-bank. Few things have been found in the wall itself—a small red paving brick, and a denarius of Agrippina, which do not help to date it. In no case whatever has any demonstrably reused material been found in it, that is, no portions of architecture, inscriptions, or tombstones.[1]

The wall descends Balkerne Hill, the steepest slope of its course, not with majestic horizontal courses as in parts of Hadrian's Wall, but parallel to the surface. The present roadway lies over the line of the ditch, and so was always sunk, but has been both widened and further reduced so that the remains of the wall now stand on the top of a bank of soft sand with the founda-tions fully exposed. The soft subsoil here has repeatedly caused trouble even in modern times, but the wall itself has not moved recently, and, indeed, seems stable for the time being. But in time past it has received much damage, not all of which was due to the cannon of 1648. The first 70 ft. are very perfect, showing four of the quadruple lacing courses of tiles, with most of the

[1] A piece of grey marble sheathing found *in* the wall on Balkerne Hill in 1941 (C.M. 134.52) could be from a pre-Boudiccan building.

stone coursing in fair condition. The total height here, without the foundations (which are also visible), is still 13 ft. This is probably the best remaining piece. At its north end is a modern buttress of stone, which resembles a square projecting tower, and which must mislead many, for despite its ancient appearance it has been inserted to support the broken end of the wall, a very large mass of which is displaced and solely supported by the buttress.

There follows a gap of 185 ft., in which the great difference in the levels within and without the wall is very apparent and striking.

164. Exactly at the broken end of the wall where it resumes there is an internal tower (described below, p. 22). This, with the next 175 ft. of the wall, is inclined outwards to the west, and the wall is badly cracked and settled in places. There is then another gap of 125 ft. There may prove to be another tower where the wall resumes again, and shortly beyond this a private doorway has been made through the wall, but without cutting it, for the foundations are so high above the street outside that the door passes beneath them. Steps made on the inside, down to the door, revealed the inner facing of the wall in excellent condition, but after many years' exposure the face collapsed. It has been reset, but this is not the same thing, and this is the fate of any masonry long buried which is opened and left exposed to the frost in Colchester.

From here to the widely rounded NW. corner the wall is well preserved. Though much covered by the apron of the protective work the tile courses show through here and there, and the ground-level is gradually recovered until it is back to normal at the corner.

The following regarding the two gaps in the wall on Balkerne Hill is unpublished: From a manuscript note by H. Laver we learn that his father, Wm. Laver, told him that when he first came to live in Colchester the Roman town wall overhung the road near the top of Balkerne Hill in a very dangerous manner, and during the first ten years of the last century (i.e. 1800–10) this portion fell out into the road. 'To get this mass of masonry out of the road was a great task to the authorities for . . . the hardness of the mortar nearly defied the picks of the workmen. After some time there was an application made to the General in command of the troops in Colchester for assistance, and he gave permission for some of the engineers to break it up with gunpowder.' Some of the fragments were blown over the adjacent houses. Even after that the task was long in completion.

From an entry in Mr. Carr's Diary (in the Wire MSS.) we learn that the actual date of the above collapse was Saturday, 7 March 1795.

There is a reference in Wire to part of the wall falling out into Balkerne Lane and blocking the street a few years before 1858. This gives us the date of the second collapse lower down the hill.

2. SECTION I AND TOWER 1

(PLS. III, A, B; IV, A, FIG. 5; **164** on map)

In 1938, by permission of the County Council, a trench was cut inwards from the broken end of the Roman town wall across the line of the rampart.[1] In the first few minutes the wall was found to be faced, and it was soon clear that we had stumbled upon another of the few known interior towers of the walls of Colchester. This face, the south end of the tower, is 5 ft. 9 in. wide and well built, with the same courses as the wall itself, into which it is bonded. The angles are carefully executed in tile.

Subsequent work on the preservation of the wall necessitated the removal of much of the earth from the back of it, to relieve the pressure which it was feared might in time force it out into the street (as had happened twice before). This work revealed that the tower was $17\frac{1}{2}$ ft. long.

The construction is quite solid, the facing the same as that of the town wall, and the core similarly made of stones and mortar uncertainly coursed. There is a very slight offset of about 1 in. near the bottom, which should correspond to the ground-level at the time of erection. Above this the tower is perfectly preserved to a height of over 7 ft. The portion below the offset may well be regarded as foundation, though 15 in. of it is well faced with brick at the angles and three courses of septaria elsewhere. This part was largely plastered over so that the joints and sizes of the stones could not be seen. Lower down, the remaining 9 in. were almost completely covered, but the broken end of the wall showed that here the stones were rough and undressed. The total depth of the foundation from the offset was 4 ft. A tile near the base shows a deeply cut conto-mark.[2]

The foundation stood directly on soft yellow sand, which partly accounts for the instability along this part of the wall. The sand had been excavated to a depth of at least 2 ft. for the foundation trench. In it are two very black lines, the lower one of a peaty nature, about 1 in. thick, the upper like charcoal or carbonized vegetable matter, with another similar on top, the whole crowned by a layer of mortar 3 ft. wide and 4 in. thick, with another dark layer above. The mortar and the bulk of the sand was bounded on the east by a small gully 14 in. wide and 9 in. deep. East of

---

[1] *C.M.R.* 1944, 20–21.   [2] The brickmaker's tally of the number made.

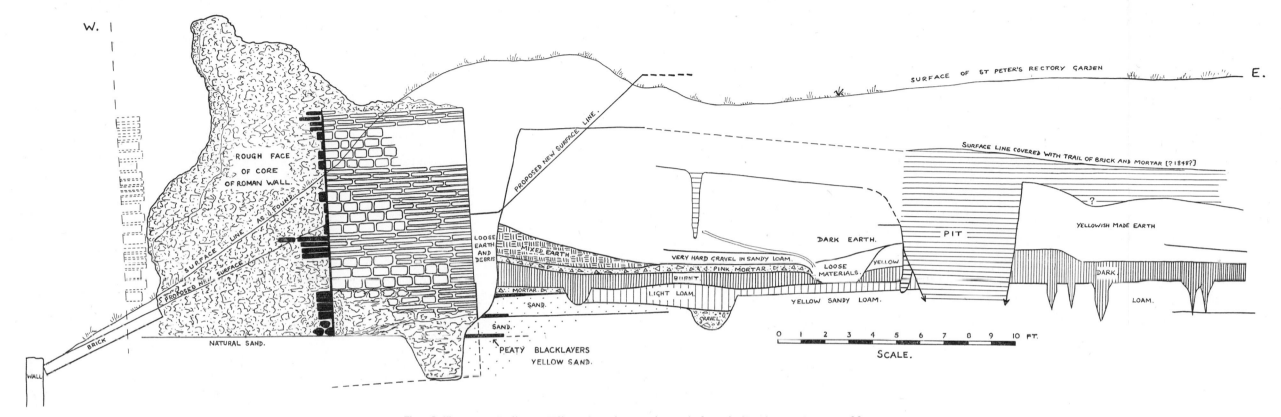

W.

E.

SURFACE OF ST PETER'S RECTORY GARDEN

SURFACE LINE COVERED WITH TRAIL OF BRICK AND MORTAR [?1848?]

ROUGH FACE
OF CORE
OF ROMAN WALL

PROPOSED NEW SURFACE LINE.

YELLOWISH MADE EARTH

?

DARK EARTH.

PIT

LOOSE
EARTH
AND
DEBRIS

MIXED EARTH

VERY HARD GRAVEL IN SANDY LOAM.

LOOSE
MATERIALS.

YELLOW

DARK

BURNT

PINK MORTAR

LIGHT LOAM.

MORTAR

YELLOW SANDY LOAM.

LOAM.

SAND.

GRAVEL

BRICK

SAND.

NATURAL SAND.

SAND.

PEATY BLACKLAYERS
YELLOW SAND.

WALL

0 1 2 3 4 5 6 7 8 9 10 FT.

SCALE.

FIG. 5. Tower on Balkerne Hill and section cut inwards from it (Section I). [164], p. 22.

this there was another rather larger gully, but at a lower level, marking the eastern limit of the sand. It was 1 ft. 9 in. wide and nearly a foot deep. Its filling was loose, washed gravel and its eastern lip was cut in a yellow sandy loam which appeared to be undisturbed. Above it the ground had been made up to the level of the top of the mortar layer by a spread of light-coloured loam.

The next layer was most striking, consisting of dark earth mixed with broken brick and mortar, the whole

bowl of Rhenish marbled ware f. 312. *Grey ware*: some 26 fragments of little character, but including f. 246, and a sub-Belgic rim like *Cam.* 218c, and one rim each of ff. 268 and 278 which may be of any date. There were also two large lumps of painted plaster, well back, and clear of the pink mortar.

The latest feature of this series is the appearance of T.S. f. 18/31, which we would not expect to see before A.D. 100. The question of whether the wall was cut through this layer cannot be settled at this point

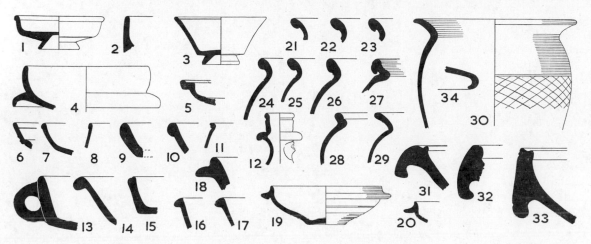

FIG. 5, A. Pottery from Section I (pp. 23–24). Scale ¼.

compacted into an extremely hard mass, which had a very red and burnt appearance. The thickness varied, being greatest against the wall. It is broken by another gully, beyond which the layer is resumed and continues unbroken through the section. This latter portion is lying on a thick bed of hard loam, in which particles of charcoal show that it is not undisturbed.

The next layer above was even more conspicuous and remarkable. It consisted entirely of comminuted pink mortar with fragments of tile and septaria, and was quite loose, and presumably came from some adjacent building.

The pottery from these two layers comprised: *Sigillata*: 21 fragments including forms 15/17(2), 18(2) (fig. 5, A, 6–7) 27(2), one fragment which looks Arretine in paste, 18/31(3), base of late first century f. 37, fragment f. Curle 11 or similar, and four fragments of good ware doubtfully second century. *Buff ware*: 24 fragments, chiefly of early flagons, some almost pipeclay, two were certainly *Cam.* f. 154, and so probably was a third; there was also a handle of f. 187, and a fragment of f. 186c, and a rim of a mortarium stamped SEXA (S reversed). This is a common name in Colchester and seems to belong to the late first century. The rim-form is *Cam.* 195B. There was also a fragment of a

because the whole has tilted, leaving a gap. It becomes very desirable to see the berm for evidence as to what layers may extend both sides of the wall. We are inclined to believe that the wall is cut through this layer.

The pink mortar fades away into the gully 14 ft. from the face of the tower. A bank of mixed earth was thrown up on top of it against the tower, perhaps to turn back storm-water from the wall.

Next a path or floor of very hard gravel in sandy loam, 7 or 8 in. thick and at least 6 ft. wide, was laid over the pink mortar. This also fades into the gully, the filling of which was divided by an old surface line from the material above. The upper filling contained sherds of colour-coated ware not earlier than the middle of the second century, giving a terminus for the underlying layers.

The material above was very difficult to observe owing to the unavoidable timbering and the presence of an enormous tree-stump with all its roots, and did not resemble that of the rampart as we had seen it elsewhere in Colchester. Above the hard gravel some grey earth with an old surface layer above it suggested a further banking against the tower, again so placed as to throw storm-water back to the gully. Later the gully silted up and became obsolete. At the east end of the section there was much broken tile and stone, lying on a hard dark layer containing oyster-shells. The pit in the centre prevented a certain corre-lation of these levels with those to the west.

The main mass of yellowish earth, containing much mortar and rubbish, and not resembling the usual rampart material, was over all the layers mentioned and was 3–4 ft. thick. Its top was difficult to follow and could not be seen behind the tree-stump. A large pit cut through it was filled with black earth. The appearance of a post-hole in its west side may be only due to a collapse of the side.

The last surface layer discernible was nearly 6 ft. 6 in. above the offset of the tower. It was covered with a litter of tile and mortar, and, as all finds at this level were recent, it seems reasonable to assume that it corresponds to the slighting of the town wall ordered by Fairfax in 1648.

If this is so, the main bank below, consisting of yellowish, made earth, is either the rampart bank or something of later date. It was by no means homo-geneous, the lower part being darker than the upper, and containing much broken tile and stone in places. The upper part was more yellow, and contained a nearly complete T.S. cup f. 33 (not stamped) (fig. 5, A, 3) and fragments of ff. 31, 33, 38, 45, and 79 (fig. 5, A, 1, 2, 4). Buff fragments resembled those from the kilns of c. A.D. 190 (fig. 5, A, 31), colour-coated wares included one Castor rim of f. 391 (fig. 5, A, 11); and four local fragments, one barbotined. The grey wares included the usual f. 278 (fig. 5, A, 30) and 268 (fig. 5, A, 24–25), and rims of platters, ff. 38, 39 (fig. 5, A, 13, 14). There was also an iron ring, part of a 'Celtic key', and half a whetstone. Another lot, from a grey band with stones near the wall in this upper part was exactly similar, but adds T.S. f. 79 and coarse form 259. The pottery is, therefore, all Antonine, and late, but we do not know how late the Antonine wares lasted.

The pottery from the black pit (fig. 5, A, 5, 8–10, 15–18, 21–23, 26–29, 32–34) includes these late Antonine wares but has in addition T.S. f. Lud. Tg. and among the colour-coated wares, fine metallic Rhenish ware, and the rim of a bead-rimmed bowl of Castor ware (fig. 5, A, 10), also a fine red flagon neck, f. 360 (fig. 5, A, 12); the grey wares include f. 305 (fig. 5, A, 18), and two rims with inside hollow for lid (ibid. 27, 28), but not so markedly as in the 'Derby-shire' ware. There were also tesserae, window glass, and half a whetstone. The whole seems third or fourth century, but it has to be admitted that there was, among this lot, a piece of recent brown-glazed ware.

The debris lying upon the bank, if bank it was, in-cluded flue tiles and red tesserae, fragments of bronze sheet, iron nails, and fragments of medieval and salt-glazed ware. The Roman pottery included many late mortarium rims of ff. 498, 500, 501, 502, 505; colour-coated ff. 308 and 391 (local) and chips of Castor ware; and 314; grey wares included ff. 268, 40, 38, 39, 274, 205, 276, 278, 277, 315 (fig. 5, A, 19, 20).

Thus we were left in doubt whether we were dealing with the rampart proper or with an accumulation of levels. The position of our trench, at the corner of a tower, might show the rampart to have been differently arranged at the towers than elsewhere. There may not have been a bank behind the towers.

In this connexion stands a surprising discovery at the bottom of the trench. The latter stopped on the surface of stiff loam already mentioned, and when the loam was cleared it revealed a very definite pattern of small post-holes (pl. IV, A). The 2-ft. rule in the picture shows their size; the centre of the largest is 26 ft. east of the SE. corner of the tower, measured from the offset level. The posts were square-pointed, indicating careful work, and of square or oblong section, the largest being 7 in. square. They had been driven, and the sizes of those on the left must be fairly accurately shown in the photograph. The two on the right were less perfect, and may have been enlarged upwards. No trace of the posts was observed in the layers above the loam.

It is tempting to see in these traces of a wooden stair for access to the tower and rampart-walk, for the position of these towers—apparently near the end of each street—would be the obvious site for such a pro-vision. However, the great depth at which they lie precluded further investigation, and one must not draw conclusions from evidence which may be only a small part of an extensive structure. The number of the posts and the variety in size call for caution in interpretation. Possibly some of them are later addi-tions to steady a structure originally too weak, or to repair it as it decayed. The model of the Balkerne Gate in the Museum incorporates a wooden stair at the end of the rampart, but this is pure conjecture.

3. SECTION I A

By MISS K. M. RICHARDSON, F.S.A.

In 1951 it was determined to cut a broad section through the rampart of the town wall, choosing some suitable place where, it was hoped, no comparatively recent disturbances might be encountered. The aim was to attempt to recover such evidence as might simplify, if not determine, the uncertainties of the narrow and less carefully supervised sections hitherto available. The work, organized by Sir Mortimer Wheeler in association with the Town Council, the County Council, and the Society of Antiquaries of London, was under the supervision of Miss K. M. Richardson, F.S.A., who reports as follows.

A trench 10 ft. wide by 37 ft. long was cut inside the wall and through the bank, about 213 yards north of the Balkerne Gate in the grounds of the Technical College, North Hill.[1] Along this length of the wall, as may be seen from its torn outer face, the courses are not laid horizontally, but parallel to the ground, following the steep gradient of Balkerne Hill. On the inner side the core of the wall projects barely 2 ft. or so above the present ground-level; the true face, however, lies immediately below the humus. When completely excavated the wall, with the buried face in mint condition, was found to be standing to a height of 13 ft. as from the Roman ground-level (pl. v).

The footings, which tended to narrow towards the base,[2] were 2 ft. deep and possibly about 11 ft. thick. They had been set in a relatively shallow trench dug in what is locally known as 'pug', in this case equating to all intents and purposes with the natural soil. Some clay packing was observed against the foundations, but the rest of the filling was loose sandy earth. The mortar spread sealing the wall-trench (mortar spread I) was covered with a scatter of septaria chips, the wastage from the trimming of the facing-stones. Coursing began as from just below the original ground-level. First came five rough courses of septaria capped by a tile course, which formed a first offset, 6 in. wide, more or less hidden under a second spread of mortar (mortar spread II). This capping was not a constant feature. Next came four stone courses and a 3-in. offset. From this point upwards the build was normal, four stone and four tile courses alternating. The only unusual feature was in an irregular line of mortar lumps adhering to the wall face at about 1 ft. above the 3-in. offset (see pl. v, B), the remains apparently of yet a third mortar spread (mortar spread III).

A small ditch (gully II) running parallel to the wall, and antedating it, had gone out of use before the bank was thrown up. An ashy layer sealing the infill oversailed the tail of the first level of the bank and was therefore contemporary with it. A second ditch (gully III), partially destroyed by a later gully, ran parallel to and equated in time with gully II. In both gullies II and III, the lowest infill consisted of water-laid sand and gravel.[3]

The make-up of the bank was composed largely of layers of loosely packed sand and

[1] Thanks are due to Alderman L. E. Dansie, J.P., F.S.A., for making all preliminary arrangements, to the Board of Governors of the Technical College for permission to work on the ground, and to Colchester Corporation for their ready co-operation. I am deeply indebted to Dr. F. Oswald, Mr. E. B. Birley, Miss J. Liversidge, Mr. B. W. Pearce, Mr. I. Cornwall, and Mr. M. E. Cosgrove for their respective reports.

[2] Compare Section VI (p. 47), where the foundation narrows very quickly.

[3] It is possible that these gullies are irregular cuttings made by storm water (p. 23). On this assumption they would be caused by stripping the vegetation from the line of the bank, leaving the soil free for erosion, and are incidental to the beginning of work on wall and bank.

gravel, with the exception of layers 4 and 6, two thin bands of hard, gravelly clay containing occupation material. The peculiarly rough and irregular build of the lower section of the wall up to the second mortar spread, and the unweathered appearance of the wall face proper, as seen in the sharply defined joint-marks in the pointing mortar, would suggest that the face was not exposed for any length of time. The third mortar spread adhering to the wall above ground-level implies that the wall and lower levels of the bank were built in alternate stages. Thus after the first five courses above the main offset had been built, the

COLCHESTER TOWN WALL, 1951

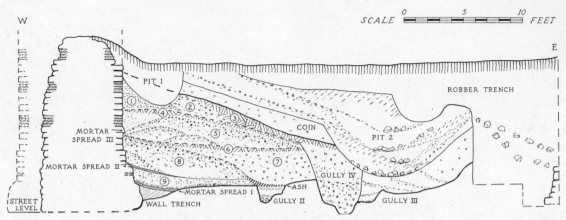

FIG. 6. Section IA, cut through rampart. [197], pp. 25 ff.

bank was thrown up as high as layer 6. Then the next 2 ft. or so of the wall were erected, and in laying the first course of this stage the third mortar spread was deposited, overlying the hard, gravelly, trampled surface of the last tip of the bank, layer 6, which served as building platform. A further 2 ft. were then added to the bank, the surface of which, at this stage, was defined by a second hard gravelly layer containing occupation material, layer 4.

When the bank was standing at this height, a deep trench (gully IV) was cut through the existing levels and through the underlying filling of the early ditch (gully III), down into the 'pug' (fig. 6). The reason for this feature is hard to explain. The almost vertical sides show no signs of timbering and could hardly have remained without revetting. In any event it was filled in immediately and buried under the upper levels of the bank. As the uppermost layers had been disturbed by later activities, it was impossible to say whether there had been a platform top to the bank in this section.

The tail of the bank had been entirely destroyed by a large rubbish-pit of the third century, but the 30-ft. width of the bank, established in other cuttings, agrees with the slope of the uppermost layers.

In conclusion, mention should be made of a coin recovered from the level over the bank, a variant of an *as* of Antoninus Pius (coin no. 3, p. 31), and of a piece of painted wall-plaster (see p. 31) showing traces of gold paint, a form of decoration hitherto unknown in this country.

The Date of Wall and Bank

The pottery from the silting of the two gullies underlying the bank (fig. 8, A) and the Samian base f. 27 from the wall-trench (fig. 7, 8) are Flavian. The rough pottery from the lower levels of the bank up to and including layer 5 (fig. 8, B) would not be inconsistent with a Flavian date, while that from the upper levels included, together with material still Flavian in character, the rims of several 'pie-dishes' dated hereabouts *c.* A.D. 70–170, as well as pieces of two plain dishes with tooled wavy lines, of a type the earliest of which are Hadrianic (fig. 8, C). These two distinct groups of pottery might lead one to question whether the upper levels of the bank might not represent a second-century addition to the bank, the wall and original bank having been built in late Flavian times. The Samian pottery, however, tells another story. The latest pieces have been examined both by Dr. F. Oswald and by Mr. E. B. Birley and both their reports have been appended. From these it will be seen that the lower levels of the bank (layers 5–9) produced a few sherds of *c.* A.D. 150, with one piece (fig. 7, 1) dated by Dr. Oswald perhaps to the second half of the second century. The latest fragment (fig. 7, 15) from the upper levels (layers 1–4) is dated by Mr. Birley to *c.* A.D. 140–70. This evidence would show the bank to be of one build. Further, as already noted, the whole of the present wall face was quite unweathered, which argues that it was protected by the bank from the start. The wall and whole bank may therefore, with some certainty, be ascribed to the Antonine period. Taking into consideration the fragmentary state of the Samian, which does not always allow for any exact determination, and since the level immediately over the bank yielded consistently Antonine material, including a pie-dish type later than the bank group (fig. 8, D), a dating nearer the beginning than the end of the Antonine phase would appear to accord with the evidence.[1]

THE SAMIAN POTTERY

Report by DR. FELIX OSWALD, F.S.A.

From Bank, Lower Levels

1. Form 31, cf. Niederbieber, *O.* and *P.*, pl. XLVII, 7. Second half of second century. From level 5.
4. Insufficient for exact dating, probably second century. From level 5.
5. Cf. f. 27, Wiesbaden Kastell, *O.* and *P.*, pl. XLIX, 16, Domitian–Trajan, and Newstead, ibid., pl. XLIX, 11, with inner groove, Flavian. ? Flavian. From level 5.
6. Fragment from side of a very large f. 33, a late variety, probably mid-second century. Lezoux. From level 6.
11. Cf. f. 42 from Guildhall Museum, *O.* and *P.*, pl. LIV, 6. ? Flavian, but too small for exact determination. From level 5.
12. Indeterminate. From level 5.

From Gully IV

2. Curle 11, rim thin and high, similar to *Margidunum*, pl. XXVIII, 7. Domitian–Trajan, A.D. 90–100.

From Bank Upper Levels

13. F. 18/31. Not possible to give exact date, but incised moulding seems to mark the Domitian–Trajan period; perhaps later. From level 3.

14. F. 37, Cupid with upraised arm perhaps similar to *O.* 440c, Lezoux. Possibly Hadrianic, *c.* A.D. 120–30. From level 3.
15. F. 37, probably lower part of a caryatid like *O.* 10201 by DRVSVS of Lezoux, *c.* A.D. 120–30. From level 2.

Report by E. B. BIRLEY, F.S.A.

From Gully II

3. F. 67, South Gaulish. Flavian.
7. F. 37, South Gaulish. Flavian.

From Wall Trench

8. Part of a f. 27 in South Gaulish ware, stamped and with an external groove on footring. The footring in profile corresponds closely to Knorr, *Aislingen*, Taf. XVI, 20. The stamp is broken in half lengthwise and is not readable. But the groove on the footring is a reliable indication of a date of manufacture not later than the time of Vespasian.
9. Base of f. 18, stamped OFMERC. Oswald, p. 202, lists similar stamps on f. 18 from Brecon, Chester, London, York, Vechten, and Mainz, to which may be added Corbridge. Mercato of La Graufesenque and Banassac made figured as well as plain Samian, using ff. 29 and 37. Unsigned figured Samian attributed to him or to BIRAGILLVS is widely distributed in Britain and on the Continent. His period of production was *c.* A.D. 70–90.

---

[1] But there is some reason to believe that in Colchester at least the more common Antonine types of pottery remained in use, almost unchanged, well into the third century.

From Bank Lower Levels

1. Rim of f. 31 in Central Gaulish ware, *c.* A.D. 150. From level 5.
4. Rim of f. 33, probably Central Gaulish ware, *c.* A.D. 100–50. From level 5.
5. F. 27, angular profile. Central Gaulish ware, *c.* A.D. 120–40. From level 5.

14. Small scrap of f. 37, ? Lezoux. ? Antonine. From level 3.
15. F. 37, Lezoux, attributable to DIVIXTVS, *c.* A.D. 140–70. From level 3.

From Level immediately over Bank

10. F. 33, small with good glaze, stamped SENNI. M. Cf. Oswald, *Index*, p. 293. Antonine.

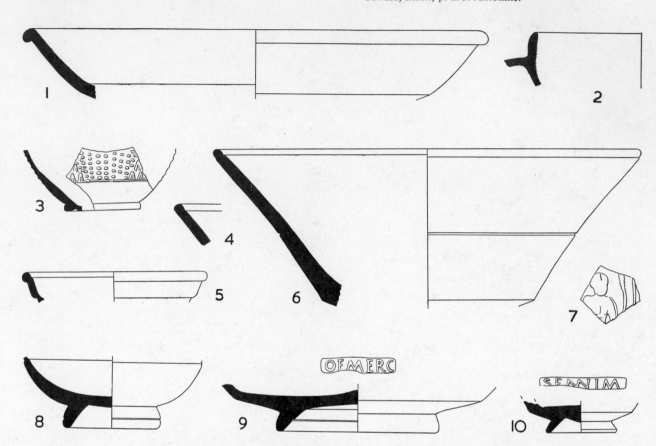

FIG. 7. Samian ware from Section IA. Scale ½ (stamps full size). p. 27.

6. Fragment of a large f. 33; height, thickness, and colour of glaze suggest it is Central Gaulish ware and that it may have been made *c.* A.D. 150 rather than earlier. From level 6.
11. Rim of bulbous jar, turned over and grooved, form uncertain. Central Gaulish. From level 5.
12. Rim of f. 18, probably Central Gaulish, *c.* A.D. 100–30. From level 5.

From Gully IV

2. F. 38, very small bowl with thin wall. Cf. *O. and P.*, pl. LXXII, 8. Poorly preserved orange glaze. Rheinzabern. Hardly earlier than *c.* A.D. 150.

From Bank Upper Levels

13. F. 31. Fragment showing part of rouletted internal pattern. Rheinzabern ware. Second half of second century A.D. at earliest. From level 3.

THE COARSE POTTERY

Fig. 8, A. *From Gullies II and III*

The majority of forms in this group are native derivatives, which continue into the Flavian period in harder romanizing ware. No. 1, a jug neck in soft sandy cream ware, is related to *Cam.* 146, but the neck is more cylindrical. Cf. also *Cam.* 140. For no. 4 cf. *Cam.* 232 and for no. 5 *Cam.* 218B, 217, and fig. 54.

Fig. 8, B. *From Bank Lower Levels*

This group does not appear to be much later in date than the above, and native derivative forms are still present. No. 15 is in relatively soft, dark brown native ware. No. 9 is a variant of *Cam.* 232 (15 others found). For no. 11 cf. *Cam.* 108 and 108D, 'which became almost universal in Flavian times and continues into the second century A.D.' Nos. 12 and 13, carinated bowls with everted rims, which begin in the Claudian period and are found at Sheepen from period II–IV, see *Cam.* 243. For no. 17 cf. May, *Colchester*, pl. XLVII, 198.

Fig. 8, C. From the Bank Upper Levels and Gully IV

Native forms have virtually disappeared from this group and

second-century forms are present. They cover the period roughly from A.D. 70–170 or 180. The present examples (14 all told) appear to be early in the series, and of these, nos. 24–26 are from gully IV. Nos. 28–30 are bowls with everted rims; no. 28, with heavy rim, is an early type; see above, nos. 12 and 13, and cf. *Cam.* 243. For no. 30 cf. *Cam.* 246A, which is rare at Sheepen

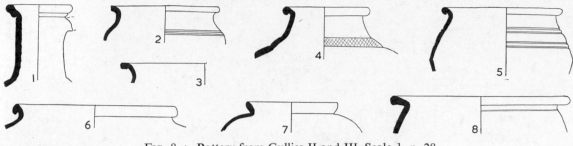

FIG. 8, A. Pottery from Gullies II and III. Scale ¼. p. 28.

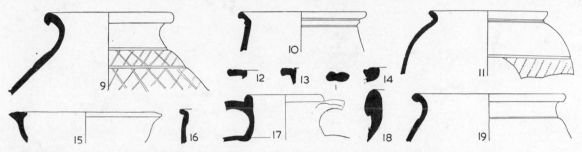

FIG. 8, B. Pottery from bank lower levels. Scale ¼. p. 28.

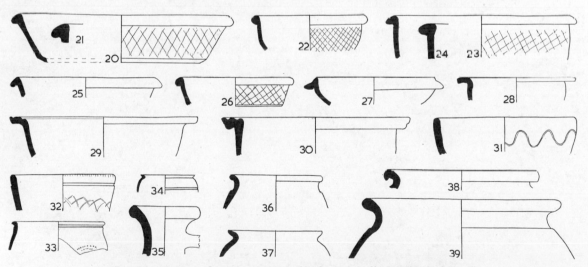

FIG. 8, C. Pottery from bank upper levels and Gully IV. Scale ¼. p. 29.

certain Roman forms appear for the first time; e.g. nos. 20–26, pie-dishes in fine, pale to dark grey ware with polished surface and faintly tooled trellis pattern. Mr. Hull notes that dishes of this type (f. 37) belong to the late occupation at Sheepen and none is found in stratified levels pre A.D. 64. They are common in grave-groups and provide the only link between groups containing forms found at Sheepen and those where definitely

but common in the early levels of the Colonia. Nos. 31 and 32 are bowls with tooled decoration. Of this type (f. 40) Mr. Hull remarks that the earliest is Hadrianic and probably post A.D. 120. No. 33 is a colour-coated beaker with soft core and bronze-red surface. These begin in the post-Conquest period. No. 34 is in hard metallic ware. No. 35, in hard dirty cream ware, is a second-century type.

Fig. 8, D. *From the Level over the Bank*

Nos. 40–42 are all three Antonine in date and associated with the Samian form 33 stamped SENNI. M and a coin dated A.D. 151–2.

Fig. 8, E. *From Pit 2*

This pit contained an assortment of material ranging from the second half of the second to the end of the third century A.D. The associated Samian is Antonine in date; the coins are chiefly worn barbarous radiates, with one identifiable coin of Victorinus (A.D. 265–7).

cisions made after casting points to the work of a provincial craftsman. From pit 2.

The casting was analysed by Dr. I. W. Cornwall, who reports as follows:

Two small samples were taken of the metal itself; A, from the casing, and B from the soft core. A qualitative analysis gave the following results:

'A. Mainly copper with some tin and traces of iron, i.e. probably rather impure bronze with about the usual 10 per cent. of tin.

'B. Lead with a considerable amount of tin, i.e. a soft solder, again with traces of iron.

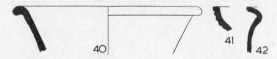

FIG. 8, D. Pottery from level over bank. Scale ¼. p. 30.

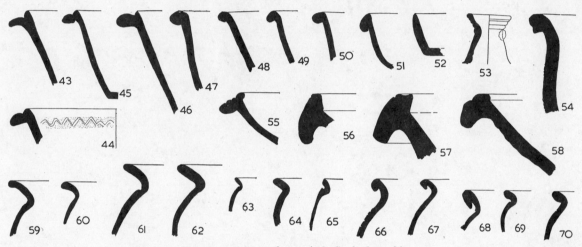

FIG. 8, E. Pottery from pit 2. Scale ¼. p. 30.

MORTAR STAMPS, ETC.
(FIG. 9)

Mr. Hull notes:

1. This stamp is of the Colchester potter whose name was, apparently, CVNOPECTVS, which we reach by collating several matrices (and this is a particularly good new one). He worked at the Sheepen kilns about A.D. 190, and made Samian ware and mortaria; we have his stamp on vessels of both groups. From pit 2, see fig. 8, E, no. 57.
2. Imperfect stamp in two lines, both framed in chevroned lines; the lower line reads CANCA. (retro.). Nothing is known like it. Mr. Birley regards it as Flavian. From bank level 5.
4. Fragment of wall-sided mortarium (f. 501B) bearing the graffito :: IMPTV.

SMALL FINDS

3. Part of a piece of furniture or a casket in the form of an animal's foot, a bronze casting with lead core. There is a rectangular opening in the top for a socket. No little technical skill was required to cast this, but the somewhat naïve rendering of the creature's fur by means of stitch-like in-

'The object therefore seems to be a hollow bronze casting filled with solder.'

The following objects were also recovered: From pit 2, a bronze scabbard attachment of a type illustrated by Collingwood (see *Roman Britain*, fig. 66, *b–g*), two bone pins, part of a bronze bangle, and a bronze stud. From gully II, a bronze pin and a bronze fitment. From gully III, a bronze ? toilet or surgical implement. From bank level 3, a bronze clip. From bank level 6, a melon bead. From bank level 1, a bronze implement similar to one found at Richborough (see I, pl. XIII, 4) and at Hofheim (see Taf. XVI, 51).

THE COINS

The coins were examined by Mr. B. W. Pearce, M.B.E., F.S.A., who reports as follows:

1. GALLIENUS. Anton. *R.I.C.* 164; *Rev.* APOLLINI CONS. AVG. A.D. 260–8. From robber trench.
2. MAGNENTIUS. Æ. cf. Cohen 68; *Rev.* VICTOR[IAE DD.
   NN AVG ET CAES] mm. TR̄ P. A.D. 350–3. From robber trench.

3. ANTONINUS PIUS. *As.* A new variety. *R.I.C.* 899 shows Bonus Eventus holding cornucopiae. Coins with BONO EVENTVI show corn-ears. The British Museum has neither coin (see *Num. Chron.* 6 s. xi (1951), 133, no. 1). *Obv.* ANTONINVS AVG. PIVS P.P. TR.P XV. Head right, laureate. *Rev.* BONVS EVENTVS COS. IIII S. C. Bonus Eventus standing left, sacrificing with patera over altar and holding corn-ears. A.D. 151–2. From level over bank.

Liversidge, to whom the piece was submitted, knows of no other example of the use of gold leaf in this context. She notes, however, that fragments of painted wall plaster from Nero's Golden House in Rome, now in the British Museum,[1] show traces of gold leaf. The paintings represent a frieze with confronted sphinxes perched on tendrils and a swan. Touches of gold or tiny squares or lozenges of gold have been used to decorate the sphinxes' headbands, the central finial, the left wing of the swan, and a tendril with rosettes.

FIG. 9. Small objects from Section IA, p. 30. (Scale $\frac{1}{1}$.)

4. VICTORINUS. Anton. *R.I.C.* 114. *Rev.* INVICTVS, Sol walking left. A.D. 265–7. From pit 2.

5–11. Three barbarous radiate and four indeterminate coins, all from pit 2.

STONE BUILDING MATERIAL

The following were identified by Mr. M. E. Cosgrove: 7 fragments of Vert de Mède (from pit 2, gully IV, and bank level 1); 6 fragments of Purbeck marble from pit 2, bank levels 1 and 3; and 1 fragment of Carrara marble from bank level 1.

WALL PLASTER

A small fragment of wall-plaster 3 by 4 in., with painted foliate decoration of green on a black ground, ornamented with a gold strip $\frac{1}{3}$ in. wide, and touches of gold (i.e. gold leaf) was recovered from disturbed levels over the bank. Miss J. E. A.

Unfortunately it is not possible to date the Colchester fragment accurately, but in all probability it was derived from the debris of a building of the Hadrian–Antonine period, equating in time with the hey-day of the Colonia.

From this point the wall continues in good preservation to the NW. angle. Most of the way down Balkerne Hill its foundations have been exposed, and at one point, where a doorway opens on to the hill, they are so elevated as to pass over the top of the doorway. Soon after, the roadway rapidly comes up to them and before the angle is reached conditions are normal, with the foundation well buried. The wall is largely obscured by a protecting apron of small stones, but there are frequent glimpses of the quadruple tile courses. The angle is much more rounded than the others, for

[1] Hinks, *Catalogue of the Greek, Etruscan and Roman Paintings in the British Museum*, 1933, nos. 55*a*, *b*, and *c*.

no apparent reason. There was probably an interior tower here, but no search has been made for it.

After rounding the corner the wall by the street is lofty but obscured by the apron mentioned. Farther east it ran behind some buildings which have been recently demolished. Here it is now exposed, without protection, showing only rough core, for the face is missing. Farther on it disappears behind the 'Coach and Horses', and so we reach the site of North Gate at the foot of North Hill.

4. THE NORTH GATE

Morant names North Gate without comment; Duncan knew of no remains of it. It is shown on Buck's prospect of the town, made in 1724, when it was clearly medieval in character. The late Mr. P. G. Laver held that there was no Roman gate here,[1] relying on the argument that 'If a line be pursued northwards from the gate (which is frequently mentioned in records from the 13th century onwards) it is found to pass over Roman burials on the site of North Bridge (p. 241) and immediately afterwards over the remains of a considerable Roman house or houses (p. 240). Thus no road lay here . . . .' But all this might be held as evidence for a road, which could run north across the river avoiding the remains just mentioned. Moreover, roads from the gate could have run west to the great brickfields at Sheepen, and east to the ford at Middle Mill; but all this is conjecture, for no remains of roads have come to light in this vicinity.

The question of the gate was settled in August 1944 when excavations were made to fix the fuse-box on the east side of the street.[2] The remains were excellently preserved and standing up to the level of the present pavement. The excavations were small and very restricted, so that observation was difficult, and only one photograph could be obtained (pl. VI, A).

The town wall, approaching from the east, exactly on the line shown on the O.S. 1:500 map (sheet XXVII, 12, 3), was curved in to the entrance in a similar manner to that at the NE. postern, but whereas there the corner only is rounded, with a radius of about 5 ft., here the curve covers the whole distance of the set-back of the gate, with a radius of about 8 ft., or perhaps a little more (i.e. the thickness of the wall), for the portion exposed was small and difficult to measure.

From the base of this curve to the reveal of the portal there is a straight portion of 2 or 3 ft., which carried the outer ring or arch of the gate. Its dimensions could not be more accurately observed. The reveal itself, which was only just visible in the bottom of the trench, was only $6\frac{1}{2}$ in. South of this the east wall of the passage-way was preserved for $7\frac{1}{2}$ ft., ending in a broken face where it had been cut away for a drain of recent date. This wall was preserved to pavement level, and consisted of tile and septaria in the same style of building as seen in the NE. postern. An opening cut through it, full of dark earth, was probably made a long time ago for a drain. The remains comprise part of an upper course of septaria; below this a quadruple course of tile and two courses of the next four of septaria. The tiles seem all to be imperfect, the longest side observed being only 14 in. The short side appears to have been 12 in., and the average thickness is $1\frac{3}{4}$ in. The excavation could not be carried lower than is shown in the elevation (fig. 10); in it the lowest courses were seen to have been well mortared and the joints marked out with the trowel, exactly as elsewhere.

At the exact point of the reveal or jamb of the gate the masonry had been robbed in ancient times, but north of this it rose again, and from the elevation it can be seen that here three courses of septaria remained, north of the tiling of the reveal, and beneath them a quadruple course of tiles, plastered and marked out as described. This was so well done that the sizes of the tiles could not be observed.

The septaria outside the gate are 5 in. high, the largest was 9 in. wide by 12 in. deep; inside the gate they were only 4 in. high. Owing to the restricted excavation it is not possible to state the relation of the interior coursing to that outside. They cannot have registered.

[1] *J.B.A.* xxvi, 30, 31.   [2] *Essex Rev.* liii, 133; *J.R.S.* xxxv, 83, fig. 11; *C.M.R.* 1947, 23.

The mortar of the outer facing was pink, of the inner core yellowish-white.

A sounding bar was tried, to feel for an offset which would indicate the Roman ground-level on the curved portion. At 2 ft. 1½ in. below the top of the quadruple tiles the bar struck solid tile, enabling us to show on

the house which stood on the west half of the street up to about 1845.

In the west half of the excavation, under the site of this house, the ground was softer, not apparently having been made up for a road. The west side of the old metalling was 14 ft. from the present west kerb;

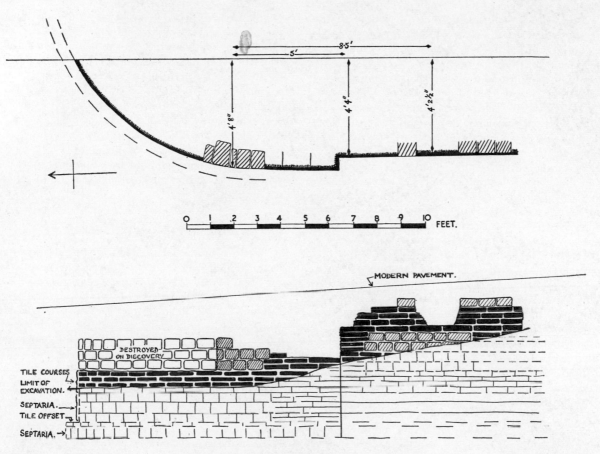

FIG. 10. Plan and elevation, North Gate, p. 32.

the elevation a conjectural offset at this level. Farther from the face the bar was firmly fixed in gravel at only 2 in. lower, which we take to indicate the Roman street-level.

The trench for the cables was taken westwards across the street at right angles from the south end of the elevation. The cutting was about 4 ft. deep to the middle of the street, rising to much less at the west pavement. The eastern half of the street, which was that in use in former times, overlay an old street of rammed gravel capped by large rounded flint cobbles, the whole very hard and very black, about 6 in. thick, with its surface about 3 ft. below the modern street. About the middle of the latter, and at about the same level as the black gravel, lay the brick foundation of

between 8 and 13 ft. from the kerb lay the cutting for a deep sewer, and the upper 3 ft. of the filling of this was almost entirely broken Roman masonry, which must have been broken from wall or gate when the sewer was made, probably in the third quarter of the last century. Otherwise the ground here was of soft made earth down to at least 4 ft., as the sounding bar assured us.

Thus we are left with no evidence for the lateral dimensions of the gate, and the pipe on the east side has deprived us of the position of the south face. The position of the last stones in the east wall of the portal suggests that the inner (S.) reveal (if there was one) must come within a foot of the broken end, and if we allow 2 ft. 3 in. for the inner arch (as at the NE.

postern), we have an over-all length of 10 ft. 6 in., which compares favourably with the NE. postern. There are, of course, other possibilities.

The position of the former street suggests that the Roman gate may have occupied only the east side of the present street. The width of the black cobbling, which lay right against the Roman masonry, appeared to be some 18 ft. The spaces at our disposal would fit a supposition that the gate consisted of one portal of 10 or 11 ft. in width, and this, with a counterfort of about 9 ft. width (as at the NE. postern), which may have been demolished to widen the street, would correspond to the width of the metalling. This would account for the absence of remains of the west counterfort in our trench, and the masonry in the sewer trench would come from the town wall just west of the counterfort.[1]

The larger curve at this gate might suggest that other dimensions were larger than at the NE. postern, but if this had been so we should have to have at least two portals, and this would put the west counterfort under the former house and in the line of the sewer. Now so massive a feature may well be removed by public work to widen a road, but is unlikely to have been removed so thoroughly in order to build a house. Had the sewer cut through its remains, at least a little of it should have been left on one side or the other; actually no trace remained, and it is certain that either no masonry (other than the normal town wall) stood west of the centre of the modern street, or it has been pulled down to lower than 4 ft. below the level of the bottom of our trench. P. G. Laver's observation practically proves the former correct.

The bottom, or under side, of the black gravel of the medieval road was found, on the curve of the wall, to be about half-way up the quadruple tile course; beneath it the filling was of dirty sandy silt with a water-washed appearance.

No pottery or other remains were found.

The masonry of the east counterfort runs continuously into the surviving and visible portion of the town wall, still standing, as the centre part of the core only, to a height of about 12 ft.; but whether this upper part is original or part of a rebuild is unknown.

From this point eastwards the course of the wall is concealed by buildings, and such of the masonry as remains is almost entirely buried. There is still an appreciable difference in level between the ground inside and outside. About 340 ft. from North Hill the line of the wall comes under the north pavement of Northgate Street, which gradually diverges, so that at the east end of the street it is under the fronts of the houses. Where it crosses the modern street, by the Mortuary (at II), it is quite invisible.

There is thus little hope of ascertaining the position of the tower which should lie about 310 ft. east of North Hill, or of determining whether a tower or a gate stood opposite Scheregate, another 370 ft. farther east.

Stukeley's map shows no break in the north wall of the town except North Gate, nor any river-crossing other than North Bridge. Morant's map and another a little later (Chapman and André) show a street passing through to Middle Mill and lying on the west part of the broad modern roadway by the Mortuary. On the 1805 map this is clearly marked as the Rye Gate. Most maps then show the wall without break as far as a gap just west of the NE. Gate, but Morant shows a gap north of the centre of the Castle, and the 1805 map one somewhat farther west. These both refer to the visible gap of some 23 ft. which we shall discuss in reference to the Rye Gate.

5. Section II and The Rye Gate

There is in the Museum an original drawing by Major J. Bale of a section of the Roman town wall at the end of St. Peter's Street, near the Rye Gate, 24 February 1908, prepared for Dr. H. Laver. The footpath of Northgate Street is shown on the right, which is the south end of the section, and the position of the south face of the wall is indicated, one wonders with how much certainty. To the north the wall has been robbed, but the piece of tile, topping a small offset, is easily recognizable as an old friend. It, with the stone below it, is the offset of the outer face. Below that Bale shows a foundation projection of 21 in., and we have little doubt that part of this has been robbed and that his dotted line completing it should have been set one course higher. Even so, we have only 21 in. depth of foundation, from which we may safely assume that the bottom was not reached.

The remains of the wall were just beneath the pavement, and probably are so still; the width between the upgoing faces, above the tile offset, is shown as 9 ft., and the section, on the whole, will compare very well with our others (figs. 5, 6, 16, 18, 22).

Immediately east of the last section (II) we have to begin to look for the Roman Rye Gate. As we have seen when discussing the town plan, the site of this gate is not so simply decided as it was held a few years ago. Reviewing the history of the question Morant[2] says, of the third of his three posterns: 'Rye-gate as it is vulgarly called; or rather Rhee or Rea-gate, that is the River Gate, as leading to the river. It was anciently

---

[1] As it seems it was observed to do by P. G. Laver, *J.B.A.* n.s. xxvi, 31 and plan (at J).   [2] p. 7.

named the North or King's Scherde. 'Twas taken down in the year 1659.' A footnote explains that it was probably very much damaged in the siege of 1648, and was sold by the town in the beginning of 1659. One John Woodroffe had 40 shillings allowed him out of the sale towards the expenses of pitching (paving) the Red Row (*Book of Assemblies*).

Duncan (p. 53) says: 'the wall is traced with great difficulty as far as the eastern side of the street leading to Middle Mill; this street led to the Rye or River Gate of which all vestiges are lost. It is tolerably evident that the Rye Gate was not of Roman origin, but that its formation was determined in Saxon or Norman times by the necessity of providing a fall of water for milling purposes above the ford which led through the river from the Roman gate towards the north. The Roman Gate is still to be made out, being situate at the base of the hill leading upwards to the Castle; a side wall exists, in a ruinous state, on the west side of the gate, and the wall is wanting for many feet. Standing close to the low-side wall, and looking riverwards, the position of the Roman way is seen, by the track of the lane, on the further side of the river, which even now comes down to the brink.'

'Three feet six inches of the side wall remains of length, and three feet of thickness, and there is no trace of the wall for 23 feet; this is space enough for a gate and to spare. The surface of the ground around the interior of the gate is a mass of broken tile; and some excavation may perhaps, reveal much that is interesting.' He goes on to mention the arch (no. **29** in insula 5) in the last house in Maidenburgh Street, which he suggests may be a drain.

R.C.H.M., p. 21, says: 'The Roman Rye Gate was still standing in the middle of the last century. It was a few feet east of the mediaeval Rye Gate and possibly gave access to the road from Stratford (St. Mary).'

The first part of this statement is an error, the second remains a conjecture.

Despite difficulties which will be now noticed, all writers follow Duncan. Even the late Mr. P. G. Laver wrote: 'the Roman Rye Gate (to distinguish it from its mediaeval namesake on the plan), was just below the present Norman Castle. . . . [It] has been so materially damaged that it is quite impossible to make out the plan . . . for there is a gap here in the wall for about 23 feet, in fact all that remains of it [the gate] is a small damaged piece of return wall, on the west side, which projects [inward] . . . for about 3 ft. 6 in., and is about 3 ft. thick. The piece of walling containing a culvert . . . [no. **29**, see above] may be part of it. This gate gave on to a ford across the river and a road

leading northwards. The gate was probably flush on the external face of the wall.'[1]

Now we can say at once that the inner face of the Roman wall is well preserved and visible on each side of this famous gap of 23 ft., that there is now no trace of any return-wall, nor any trace of any masonry ever having been attached to the inner face on either side. The gap is by no means enough and to spare for a gate, for even so small a gate as the NE. postern is 28 ft. over the counterforts.

So far as the position of the gap goes, a gate here will not fit in with the town-plan. A glance at the map (pl. XLI) will make this clear. Nor does it appear that there can be any doubt that this is the gap mentioned by Duncan and Laver, for westwards the inner face of the wall is well preserved and continuous until it disappears in a large mound upon which stands the north end of Ryegate Road and Maidenburgh Street (the name of the former is of no significance, being quite recent). Moreover, the arch (no. **29**) is not less than 145 ft. west of the gap and could not have been part of a gateway occupying the gap.

If the return-wall mentioned could be found one would feel there might be something in the story, but it cannot, and so, contrary to most of the views hitherto published, we hold that the plan must lead us to expect to find the Roman Rye Gate (if there was one) about the north end of Maidenburgh Street and Ryegate Road, and just at this point there is 'a few feet east of the mediaeval Rye Gate' a large mound under which the Roman wall is buried, and a very large gateway could easily lie hidden. Whether this is so, and whether the arch (no. **29**) is connected with it, can only be proved by excavation. The arch itself cannot be important, for it is weak, having only one ring of imperfect tiles, and the work does not look like that of a public building.

East of the Rye Gate the inner face of the wall is visible along the north side of the Park Folly. At the gap already mentioned the Folly passes to the outer side of the wall. All along insula 6, where it bounds the former 'Sheepshead Meadow' on the north, the inner face is exposed and well preserved. The outer side is much robbed and obscured by the protective apron.

37. On the east side of this portion there was a tower (no. 6) which was destroyed in 1853, the mark of which can still be seen (pl. X, A) on the face of the wall. The account of the damage done in 1853 is of interest, thus (Wire's Diary, 22/3/1853): 'The Town Wall at the bottom of Cheaping Field [= Sheepshead Field] is exposed to view by cutting a trench for a footpath, in doing which the remains of what appears to have been

[1] *J.B.A.* n.s. xxvi, 25.

a square tower was exposed to view.' Duncan (p. 53) has a longer account of the removal of the rampart behind the wall on this occasion: 'This rampart was not of earth thrown up by military foresight, but consisted of the ruins of buildings, of burnt and charred wood, tile and stone work, and of all kinds of Roman domestic utensils. The whole of the wall . . . to the end of the meadow on the east has had its inner face cleared . . . within the last three years [of 1858] . . . for no less than seven feet below the surface did the *supellex Romana* extend, and yet nothing was whole . . . the most interesting relics were large pieces of Purbeck marble, thin and polished on one surface, hundreds of pieces of Samian ware, and a long row of red tesserae [no. **37**, insula 6]. So continuous was the layer of red tesserae that it formed the base upon which all the ruins rested, and it gave the impression that the way by the side of the wall was formerly paved . . . a huge solid tower . . . was destroyed during the formation of the new path . . . solid as high as it could be traced—viz. twelve feet, and it extended thirteen feet into the town [sc. from the outer face], and was joined to 19 ft. 2 in. of the wall. It did not project without the wall, and the layers of tile did not pass through it, but faced the sides.'

The dimensions of this red pavement against the town wall are nowhere preserved. It is a remarkable phenomenon.

In *T.E.A.S.* ix, 124 it is recorded that the tower measured 19½ ft. by 6½ ft.; the latter is clearly the inward projection.

Not far east of the tower there is a breach in the wall, the history of which is not known. Beyond this we pass into the Hollytrees' Meadow, the north boundary of which is the town wall, in the same condition as the last portion, except that the rampart remains practically undamaged, and with the addition of a modern hedge-bank on the top. The inner face is invisible.

The outer face all along the Park Folly has been protected by a stone apron. Here and there the core or some tiles may be seen jutting through, and recently the Ministry of Works, when the apron breaks, has not replaced it, but preserved the original work to view.

During the excavations of 1927–9 a beginning was made of a section of this rampart, but it could not be completed. It was ascertained that it was composed here of a very dry and light-coloured loam, with nothing else in it to a depth of about 6 ft., at which work stopped. The only other fact worthy of mention is that a small opening was found in the wall, the size of one square block of septaria, apparently a putlog hole, but in the absence of others at all observed points, including the long length north of the Castle, this explanation will not serve.

In the NE. corner of the Hollytrees' Meadow lies the NE. Postern Gate, now to be described. Before we opened it up in 1927 it was closed by a modern wall and masked on the outside by the apron, so that it was quite invisible. A gap in the wall just west of it which is shown on several old maps has been similarly treated and is still invisible. But westwards from the gate, in our excavations, the town wall can be seen to be rapidly diminishing in height. Morant's map and others show a footpath leading from the NE. corner of the Castle Ramparts through this gap to Middle Mill, and Chapman and André show a path equivalent to the Park Folly coming to it from Land Lane, on the north side, and passing through it to run along the south side of the wall to Rye Gate.

6. THE NORTH-EAST GATE AND SECTION III

(PLS. VI, VII; FIGS. 11–15)

This was discovered in 1853 by Dr. P. M. Duncan, who published his work in *T.E.A.S.* o.s. i, 210–38 (1858), and there are several references to the work while in progress in Wm. Wire's Diary. In 1927–9 the Colchester Excavation Committee (1927) again uncovered and thoroughly explored these remains. After the upper part of the site had been cleared we were easily able to recognize the doctor's trenches, which we emptied first, leaving undisturbed deposits for examination.

The gate was small, and of very simple plan, with a single passageway of 10 ft. 8 in. wide, formed by returning the town wall inwards at a right angle at each side. Lateral piers or counterforts were thus provided to support the thrust of the arches of the gate and the weight of the tower above, while also, in part, retaining the ends of the rampart.

The foundations, and those of the wall on either side, are exceptional, for the subsoil here is hard gravel, and they are set on a layer of mortar laid directly upon it. The regular offset of 1 in. on the outer face of the wall is continued round the quadrant-shaped corners of the gate up to the outer rebate (pl. VI, B, C). The mortar foundation was at least 4 in. thick and projected 18 in. behind the piers, just as it does behind the inner face

The side walls of the entrance are recessed 8 in. between rebates for the valves of the gate. No trace of pivot-stones, hinges, or slots for the securing-bar could be found.

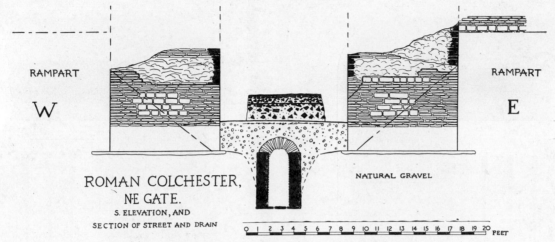

FIG. 11. Section through NE. Gate, p. 37.

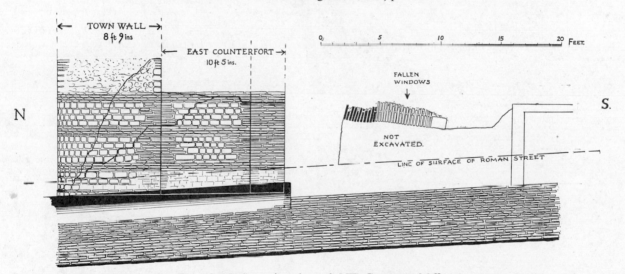

FIG. 12. N.–S. section through NE. Gate, pp. 36 ff.

of the wall. Through the passage-way and on the south side of the piers it was 6 in. wide. Wherever the face, which is continuous with that of the town wall, has been well protected by the rampart or road-metal, we found the joints had been plastered and marked out with the trowel.

The piers are 9 ft. wide and project inwards 10 ft. 5 in. and 10 ft. 7 in. respectively. They are quite solid, with the same interior construction of irregular coursing in mortar as the wall, the corners being carefully turned in tile, except the quadrant portions at the front, the radius of which is 5 ft.

The remains of the piers stand from 6 to 8 ft. high and the town wall, on the east, to 11 ft., but all slope away steeply to the north, where everything has been robbed down to the foundation offset. The robbers have left several traces. A large piece of masonry comprising several courses of tiles had been prised off the SW. angle and lay a few feet away. It has been restored to position, where it fitted exactly. A large part of the tower lies flat on the ground, opposite the centre of the gateway, on the inside. Duncan refers to this as the fallen arch of the gate, but it bears no resemblance to an arch. It is in several pieces, only the largest of which

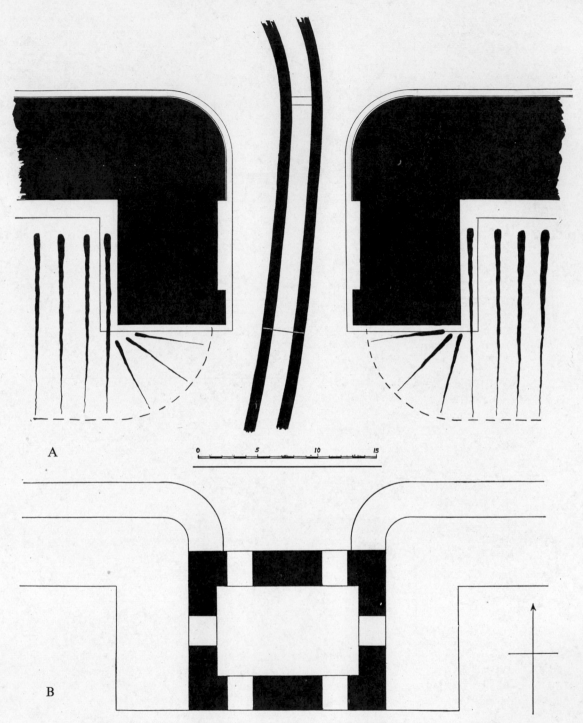

A

B

Fig. 13. Plan of NE. Gate: A, ground floor; B, 1st floor. (Scale of feet.) pp. 36 ff.

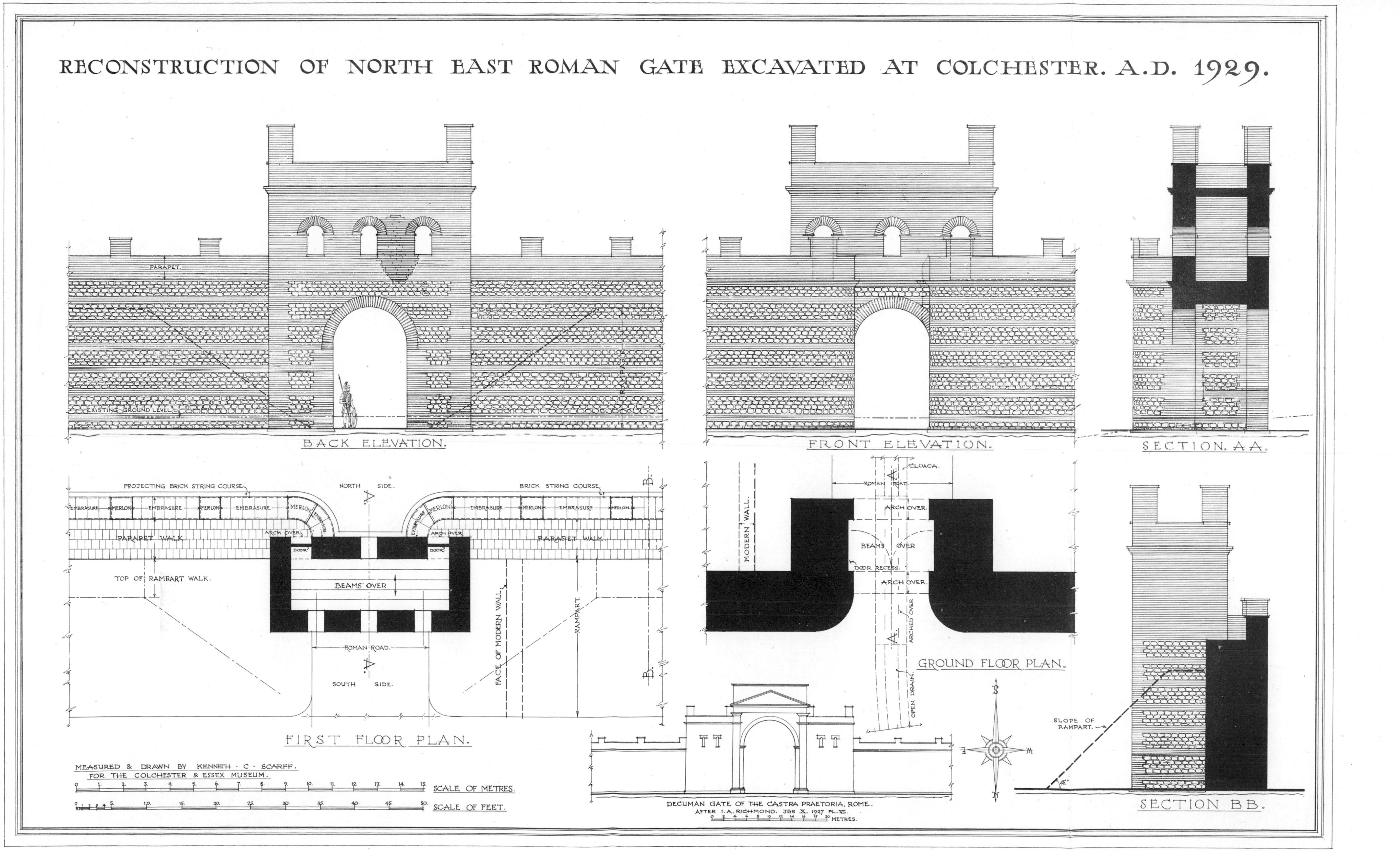

RECONSTRUCTION OF NORTH EAST ROMAN GATE EXCAVATED AT COLCHESTER. A.D. 1929.

BACK ELEVATION.

PARAPET

EXISTING GROUND LEVEL

FRONT ELEVATION.

SECTION. AA.

FIRST FLOOR PLAN.

PROJECTING BRICK STRING COURSE.

NORTH SIDE.

BRICK STRING COURSE.

EMBRASURE · MERLON · EMBRASURE · MERLON · EMBRASURE · MERLON

EMBRASURE · MERLON · EMBRASURE · MERLON · EMBRASURE · MERLON

PARAPET WALK.

ARCH OVER.

ARCH OVER.

PARAPET WALK.

TOP OF RAMPART WALK.

DOOR.

DOOR.

BEAMS OVER.

FACE OF MODERN WALL.

RAMPART.

ROMAN ROAD.

SOUTH SIDE.

MEASURED & DRAWN BY KENNETH · C · SCARFF.
FOR THE COLCHESTER & ESSEX MUSEUM.

SCALE OF METRES.

SCALE OF FEET.

GROUND FLOOR PLAN.

CLOACA.

ROMAN ROAD.

MODERN WALL.

ARCH OVER.

BEAMS OVER.

DOOR RECESS.

ARCH OVER.

ARCHED OVER.

OPEN DRAIN.

DECUMAN GATE OF THE CASTRA PRAETORIA, ROME.
AFTER I.A. RICHMOND. JBS X. 1927. PL. VI.
METRES.

SECTION BB.

SLOPE OF RAMPART.

FIG. 14

is of any significance, that on the east (pl. VII, A). It consists of the outer face of the south wall of the tower, above the main archway, and comprises over thirty courses of tiles, with indications that a few blocks of septaria were used in the spandrels of the windows. Parts of two windows are preserved, one side of each, with part of the arched head (pl. IV, B, C). The sides are 3 ft. high and 5 ft. 7 in. apart. Both windows had an offset of 1–1½ in. at the spring of the arch, following a regular Roman practice. The sides are square, not splayed, and consist of eleven courses of tiles. The curves of the arches as they lie suggest a diameter of 2 ft. for the eastern window and 4 ft. for the western, but all the joints are sprung by the fall, and this cannot be regarded as trustworthy.

We have here invaluable evidence of the design of the upper work of the tower. Much information has been gathered and published on the larger Roman gates which are so often well preserved on the Continent, and a few parallel cases can be quoted now in this country, but lesser gates have not received the same attention. Most readily available are those of Silchester and Caerwent,[1] but none are very similar to ours in plan, though the tower and first-floor plan may well have been so.

There is a notable parallel to our discovery in the contemporary print[2] of the remains of the west gate of Lincoln, found under the walls of the castle in 1836. This shows the top of one of the main archways still standing, and above it remains of a series of windows —apparently four or five in number—with a block of masonry closely resembling ours tilted a little from its original position. But this was a gateway of the larger pattern, and the information it gives is a repetition of the continental evidence.

The Restoration of the Gateway

The block of fallen masonry is probably the only remaining portion of the upper part of a Roman gateway in this country. Its composition has been described, and from it we gather that practically the whole of the upper works were of tiles. As to the plan of the first floor, there are two possibilities. The tower could cover the whole of the piers and passage-way, or the latter only.

Our first reconstruction (fig. 14) assumed the former was the case. The height of the town wall was taken as 21 ft. (after Duncan), but we now feel that this is far too much. It was also assumed that it was essentially practical to carry the parapet-walk over the gate without interruption. We do not know the thickness of the walls (the fallen masonry is outer face only), and the dimension here used is that of the depth of the ring of the main arch. The same dimension has been taken for the parapet wall, though this may have been somewhat thinner. In this way we get a tower 27 ft. 6 in. by 17 ft., entered from the parapet-walk on each side by a door at each front corner. We put one window in the north face and three in the south.

The defects of this plan are the exposed doorways, even when covered by merlons, the single fighting-window on the north, and the fact that a figure in it is silhouetted in the window behind him.

We then consulted Professor I. A. Richmond, whose restoration (fig. 15) is much more convincing. The tower covers the passage-way only, for which we have the authority of the Silchester gates. The doors are in the sides, and have steps in them to raise the parapet-walk over the main arch. The floor of the tower room is of wood. The most part of the top of the counterforts is left clear to receive, perhaps, steps giving access from the street. The reduced height of the wall makes the disposition of the rampart more understandable. The difficulty with this has always been that if we assume a width of 30 ft. (see section VII), or even 24 ft. (fig. 38), the natural slope of the bank would flow round the piers and cover the roadway if the rampart-walk (i.e. the top of the rampart) was brought up to the side faces of the piers at its normal level. In the model made in the museum we have assumed that the width of the bank was reduced at the gate, and the slope of it artificially retained steeper than elsewhere. This may have been so, but there are indications in some Roman forts that the bank did slope down to the gates and that the space in the corner was used variously, often as a latrine. There was, however, no trace of any such use here, and the preservation in the east corner was such that traces should have survived if there had been any.

The restored tower now measures only 12 ft. by 7 ft. 6 in. inside. This leaves but little room for access to a flat roof, so our model has a tiled roof. The evidence for flat and hipped roofs is about even; both were in equally common use.[3]

We have now only two windows in the north and south faces, and these are opposite, a weakness which we feel we cannot avoid.

Though the second of these two restorations is the more attractive, it should be remarked that the position in which the masonry lies indicates that if it fell directly below its original position (and it surely could

[1] *Arch.* lii, 750 ff. and pl. xxxi.

[2] I am indebted to Professor Sir Mortimer Wheeler for drawing my attention to this print, of which an example is in the Fisher Collections, Exeter City Library, F. 72733. Q. 942.

Another example is reproduced in colour in Professor I. A. Richmond's *Roman Britain* in the 'Britain in Pictures' series.

[3] Herbig, *Germania*, ix, 138, with refs.

deviate but little as it fell), that position would be shown in the first restoration rather than the second.

It is, of course, possible that the roof was flat, with parapet and merlons. In this case, with the merlons spaced as widely as they were in early Roman days, there would probably not be room for more than one on each corner, certainly in the second plan.

On the parapet of the wall we have shown the merlons with a wide spacing but closer than those on the Tiberian *castra praetoria*,[1] and not so close as the late Roman fashion, which approximates to medieval practice.

In our model we have shown steps simply revetted with wood, leading from the street up the rampart to the walk on top, and with a wooden stair to the parapet-walk in each corner, although, in any case, the rampart walk would be at a level such that access to the parapet walk would be easy at any point.

The Stratification in the Gateway, and the Drain

The E.–W. section (fig. 11) shows the street with the drain passing beneath. A careful examination (at which Professor Sir Mortimer Wheeler was present and gave invaluable aid) showed that the street, gate, and drain were contemporary (as Duncan had already observed).[2] The latter is completely enveloped in the gravel of the road, which is probably the same gravel that was excavated for the drain replaced. Nothing was found in this except a few lumps of pebbles cemented by iron, as if a few nails had been left in it.

The surface of this road showed little wear and bore only one thin repair, a layer of gravel 3 or 4 in. thick.

Duncan had removed the layers against the piers and also across the whole south face of the gate, but we were satisfied that the layers now to be described were restricted to the space between the piers. At any rate we could find no extension of them southwards.

The first (lowest) of these was 18 in. thick and consisted of fine dark soil full of broken septaria and mortar. Some of the septaria were large blocks and might have come from the wall. The whole was not at all compacted, but quite loose. That it was simply an accumulation of rubbish over a long period of neglect (and possibly of decay) was proved by the large numbers of empty shells of the common garden snail. The few sherds of pottery found included chips of colour-coated ware, some with decoration in white paint.

All this was sealed down by a compacted floor of chips of septaria and gravel. The large stones shown in the section were not a pitching for this. Actually in the under side of this layer, or on top of the layer below, lay a small bronze coin, unfortunately illegible, but apparently a diademed head, and undoubtedly of fourth-century date. The whole was covered by a continuous layer of charcoal 1 in. thick.

After this the floor was again made up in similar fashion with about 6 in. of rather larger pieces of stone with some loose mortar. The surface was of smaller chips, well rammed. Nothing was found in this. Upon it lay first a thin layer of greyish mud and then traces of an intense conflagration. The charcoal included large pieces of oak and lay from 2 to 4 in. thick. At the bottom remains of planks about 7 in. wide could be traced, lying north and south, and the bulk of the charcoal above them was of small, round brushwood. Had brushwood been piled against a gate or barricade and fired, and the whole mass fallen inwards, the result would be exactly what was found.

Approximately in the centre of the gateway there was a post-hole of about 8 in. diameter. It is probable that Duncan's trenches removed another on each side, and that we have here a trace of the barricade which must have closed this gate from a date not long after its erection (judging from the little use the road shows) until the troublous times of the fourth century. During this time the space of the gate would be full of weeds and fallen stones—a paradise for snails.

The two burnt floors (the heat of the last fire had turned the stones red) are only present in the gateway. They indicate that in the fourth century attention was once more turned to the gate, and the passage-way was floored; possibly the gate was re-opened for use, for a lead coffin has been found in the small cemetery outside, but also possibly the gate sheltered a guard. After the first destruction by fire the floor was replaced better than before, which suggests a public work, but this was followed by a most destructive fire for which we have good evidence that outside action was responsible. This may indeed be the best evidence we shall ever see of the end of Roman Colchester. It is unfortunate that all the ground above this level had been disturbed, either by Duncan or by the builders of the brick wall which closed the gateway. We cannot say whether more layers ever existed, or whether we actually had here the very last level of the Roman period.

---

[1] Richmond, *Papers of Brit. School at Rome*, x, pls. VII and VIII.

[2] But Duncan's references to differences in construction observed somewhere (west of ?) near the gate is developed by P. G. Laver into a statement that 'the mortar of the filling of this ruined gateway and a portion of the wall to the west of it is different to the rest of the wall'. This is much more than Duncan says, for he does not expressly include the gate. Anyhow, in our explorations we saw no differences (but we did not work westwards) save in the *foundations*, in which point we are at complete variance with Duncan.

The above account is of our findings. It is not so grim as Duncan's, who probably moved a great deal of evidence in digging round the fallen masonry, from which it seems clear that the traces of the last fire spread farther south than we could trace it. 'Mingled with them [the remains of the 'arch'] were human which is more attributable to Normans than to Saxons. The great litter of broken tiles and mortar extending many feet around the gate shows that the ruins were plundered for building material, and at no very remote period, for there is no occupation level above this spread.

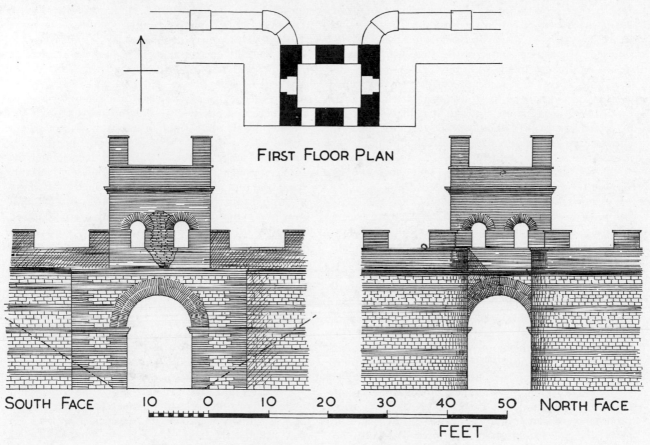

FIRST FLOOR PLAN

SOUTH FACE 10 0 10 20 30 40 50 NORTH FACE

FEET

FIG. 15. Second reconstruction of the NE. Gateway.

bones, horse bones, much charred wood . . . large pieces of burned fatty matter, in contact with charred wood, of disagreeable import; there were the remains of weapons, large human bones and lumps of semi-vitrified substance' (pp. 220, 222).

We saw nothing of this description, though we examined (in section only) the very black earth remaining under the fallen masonry. This had not been disturbed by Duncan, and could not be by us without ruining the masonry above it. It quite possibly is contemporary with the black layer at the south face of the 'forum' (p. 65 below) and if ever it is moved its contents should be of the highest interest. For it probably accumulated over the long period between the end of the Roman period and the demolition of the gate,

Section IV

(Just east of the NE. corner of Hollytrees' Meadow)

We cannot draw this, but can only give the remarks made about it in the middle of the last century, when a drain was taken through beneath the town wall. Duncan observed this in 1852 and says (p. 39): 'The foundation was very massive and broad. Composed of flints, septaria, and a dense mortar, harder even now than the stony part, it was laid upon a flat surface of sand, well rammed and beaten. First upon this sand some mortar was spread, then large flints and septaria, then more mortar was added and about two feet and a half of this irregular work was perfected.

'The first course of tiles was laid upon the foundation and every attention paid to its being perfectly level. The thickness of the wall is not equal to that of the foundation . . . [which] projects some 18 in. without and within the walls.' He 'walked beneath the wall, having its ragged base for my archway, the wall was eight feet thick, and its base eleven feet. There is no slope between the wall and its base; the first course of tiles is placed 18 in. within the boundary of the work below it, and then four rows of septaria are super-imposed. The lowest course of tile goes right through the whole breadth of the wall, but . . . the others are superficial. There are some exceptions to this rule.' Duncan here describes the foundation we have since found to be usual where the wall stood on sand, but his dimension of 8 ft. should be about 8 in. greater, which would reduce the offset of the foundation on the outside to more nearly the dimensions we have found elsewhere. We have never found the first course of tiles running through the wall.

It is remarkable that Wire, who saw the same exca-vation, says in his note (June 1852) that there was a projecting foundation 2 ft. wide on the garden side (S.), 'and it is *conjectured* [our italics] there is a similar set-off on the other side. There was no rubble dis-covered under it—because the builders found a solid mass of undisturbed gravel and set the wall upon it.' Now this statement flatly contradicts Duncan, but confirms our observations at the NE. Gate. Wire was a remarkably sound observer.

Eastwards from this point the wall is well preserved on the south face, and the rampart is preserved, to some extent, as far as the NE. angle (pl. VIII, B).

185. Excavations for 'fox-holes' during the invasion scare of 1940 exposed the corner of an interior tower standing approximately in the centre of the curve of the NE. angle.[1] It appears to have been of exactly the same nature as no. 1 (p. 22). It has not been exca-vated. We feel justified in supposing that there would be a similar tower at each angle.

Southwards from the angle to a point where the wall disappears among the houses on the north side of East Hill, the outer face has been almost entirely robbed and covered by modern retaining walls (pl. VIII, C). At one point where the latter collapsed the remains of the Roman work were found to be very thin, as indeed they are at the NE. angle—nearly the whole has been taken away.

It was on this length of wall that Wire made the fol-lowing note (Diary, 11/5/1848): 'A breach had been made in the original wall 60 ft. in length, which had been repaired in a singular way, for instead of the bonding tile as in the Roman part there had been, in imitation of them, a layer of plank covered with flat tiles similar to the modern house tile, and at different intervals billets of wood of various shapes, some round, had been inserted in the masonry, which in several instances had decayed and left a vacant space. The mortar is of a loose nature, similar to that I have observed in Saxon buildings although this is of a more recent date.'

Despite this clear statement it has been suggested by some that this may have been one of the points repaired by Edward the Elder (p. 15). But Wire is explicit. Some of the wood had not decayed, the tiles used were comparatively modern, and no doubt he was (as usual) quite right in saying it was of recent date.

Duncan, on the other hand, after mentioning the tower on the east wall in the grounds of Mr. J. Saville (who lived on East Hill) says: 'The rubble in the centre of this part of the wall presents numerous circular holes and cylindrical cavities, evidently once occupied by wooden beams. There is very little original struc-ture in this part of the wall and it looks very Norman.'

7. SECTION V—IN GARDEN OF No. 27 ROMAN ROAD

This very clear and useful section was cut about 1925 by Messrs. G. Farmer and the late E. J. Rudsdale, while still at school. The section (fig. 16) is reproduced, by permission, from their drawing. The subsoil here is grey clay, and their drawing shows the foundation of the wall projecting 18 in. on the inside; its depth was not ascertained. Its trench had been filled in with red clay, which contained, they say, 'a number of flint chips very like neolithic scrapers'. The foundation was of irregular septaria in white mortar, upon the top of which was 2 in. of grey clay [*sic*].[2] Upon this the wall was raised, beginning as usual with one course of squared septaria capped by one of tile, which makes an offset of 3 in. on the inside. The angle between this and the top of the foundation-offset was occupied by a mass of pink mortar, forming almost a half-round moulding, laid on top of the 2 in. of grey clay just mentioned. This pink mortar has not been noted else-where.

After an offset of 3 in. in the tile course, the wall face continued with three courses of septaria, then four of tile and four of septaria alternately, up to 5 ft. 9 in.

---

[1] *J.R.S.* xxxii, 111; *C.M.R.* 1944, 17, 21.

[2] This seems improbable, but in Mr. Rahtz's description of the foundation of the octagonal temple on Pagan's Hill, Somerset,

he refers to a layer of clay laid across the top of the foundation, in this case as a damp-proof course.

from the offset. Against this face lay the rampart, here of no great dimensions and consisting of four very distinct layers.

The lowest was the grey clay, which was not clean, as it contained patches of tile, and 6 ft. back from the wall, 2 in. below its surface, the T.S. sherd shown on fig. 20, A, which is late first century. It was shattered, as it lay, by the ramming of the bank above it. A little below it and farther from the wall lay fragments of a fine buff flagon.

Next comes a layer of clean sand, but with broken stone and tile in it near the wall. The thickness varies

pottery was found in this bank. It is only 14 ft. wide and 3 ft. 5 in. high, but had been made up, before any rubbish could collect upon it, to a more suitable size by the addition of a second bank of loose earth and stones, which increased the width to at least 23 ft. (the excavators say 'nearly 30 feet'). It may also have added to the height, but this we cannot know. On its slope was much broken tile and oyster-shells, &c., indicating an exposed surface. The whole was covered by garden soil, 2 ft. 9 in. thick against the wall and increasing to 6 ft. as the rampart sloped away.

Somewhere between Section V and East Gate lay an

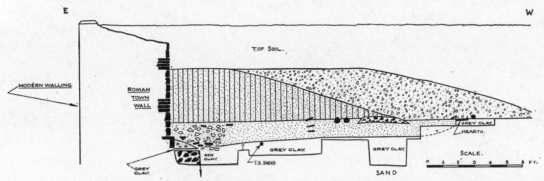

FIG. 16. Section V, in garden of no. 27 Roman Road, p. 42.

from 12 to 21 in., and farther back, on its surface, which seems to have been nearly level, lay odd blocks of septaria, and behind them a band of pieces of tile set in hard clay, 3 ft. wide and 5 in. thick, which so coincides with the tail of the next deposit that it would seem to have been laid down to secure it.

Upon this lies a bank of the peculiar very dry sandy loam used in local ramparts, containing no stones. Under it, on the sand, lay a Hod Hill-type brooch. No

interior tower, known to Duncan. Its position as shown by Wheeler and Laver is based on Cutts's plan but is anomalous. P. G. Laver says that it projected 6 ft. from the wall and was removed in making a path by the wall. The latter 'as at present uncovered shows no bonding of this tower'. We agree and think the tower has been wrongly sited. It probably lay a little farther south, especially since we are told that it stood on ground of Mr. Saville of East Hill.

8. THE EAST GATE

The town wall is very ruinous and inaccessible on the north side of East Hill. The site of the gate itself is under the modern street. Morant (p. 7), as usual, gives no description of it, merely saying 'East Gate fell down in 1651, and in the place where it stood were afterwards erected two brick pillars; and the like where Head Gate stood.' But in a footnote he adds: 'in Feb. 1651/2 it was ordered that the Chamberlain should be allowed, out of the town revenues, six pounds for the carrying away of the rubbish of the East Gate that was fallen down, and to make the way passable for carts and horses . . . and the Chamberlain to have such stones, lead, and iron as belonged to the gate for his own use. But it seems to have been repaired again. For 10 January 1675 the following order was made—"by reason East Gate is out of repair, and soe dangerous that it is believed that it will suddenly fall, whereby great mischief may be done, ordered, that Mr. Mayor and three of the Aldermen, together with the Chamberlain, taking with them such workmen as to them shall seem convenient, shall view and survey the said gate and pull down soe much thereof as they shall thinke in danger of falling, and the rubbish is to be disposed of as they shall think fit.'' Clearly the fall of 1651 involved only part of the gate.

Duncan (p. 33, note) says: 'I learn from one of the oldest inhabitants that the piers of the arches of the East Gate indicated a central carriage way and a footway on each side.' One has the impression from Morant that the gate had disappeared completely before 1748, but this is not correct.

The *R.C.H.M.* (p. 21) says: 'The East Gate, which fell down in 1651, was apparently the original Roman building and occupied the northern half of the present highway. It consisted, like the Newport Gate at Lincoln, of a central and two small side arches.' This relies upon Duncan.

Cromwell says that in 1825 there were no traces of the two brick pillars; but of the gate he says, 'indeed the structure does not seem to have been effectually removed until a still later date (than 1675)'.

We owe to the sharp eyes of the late E. J. Rudsdale the discovery among the several drawings of Colchester by John Constable, now preserved in the Victoria and Albert Museum, of a view of the south side of East Gate, made in 1813 (pl. IX). The east end of St. James's Church is unmistakable. The cottage (the old 'Clergy house', removed 1820) on the right has disappeared. The tall retaining wall of the churchyard has been rebuilt,[1] and did not then contain the modern door and flight of steps. The west end of the house (no. 1 East Hill) on the left ran right up to the face of the Town Wall, which is seen roughly squared-off, standing some 20 ft. high and projecting somewhat into the pavement. It bears a lamp. More important is the unmistakable fact that it extends considerably westwards as what must have been a wing-wall or counterfort of some sort. This is not as tall as the wall, for the upper part seems to be a wooden lean-to shed. By carefully comparing this view with the present one, and assuming the proportions of the drawing to be correct (as they certainly are for the church), the right-hand limit of the Roman masonry is some 21 ft. from the outer face of the wall. Allowing 8 ft. 8 in. for the latter, the wing-wall is at least 12 ft. long. Its face, which seems to have a lacing course indicated near the top and another lower down, with just a suspicion of stone quoins, is marked off from the wall core by an indistinct line which should show where the valve of the gate came, or the corner of a guardroom.

At the bottom of the wall, on the left, is an offset, and this suggests that the foundation is here exposed to a height of about 3 ft. This would be so if the gradient of the hill had been reduced.

The present street is so wide that the gate need only have occupied one-half of it. P. G. Laver noted foundations on the south side, under the pavement, which he took for part of the gate. He cut a mark, to indicate its position, on the brick wall, but this cannot now be discerned. This was, no doubt, the same piece of wall which was found in 1925, running N.–S. under the pavement, 21 ft. west of the outer face of the town wall (**111**). The line of the Roman street (if we have grasped it correctly) suggests that the main portal occupied the north part of the street,[2] and in view of this the wing-wall shown by Constable may well be

---

[1] In 1820, when the retaining wall was moved back, southwards.

[2] *J.R.S.* x, 89; why P. G. Laver (*J.B.A.* n.s. xxvi, 26) should site it north of the street is inexplicable.

the south wall of the south guardroom. If so, the gate is a large one. It seems that its plan could easily be recovered.

Only a few feet south of East Hill, in fact just south of Constable's wing-wall, the Roman wall is pierced by an opening with a double-ringed arch of tiles (pl. XI, A). It is 11 ft. above the present ground level (to inner crown of vault). The lower part is covered by a modern stone apron and has never been examined. The opening is 2 ft. wide. It is the outfall of a drain (see p. 59).[1]

From this point southwards the wall stands high, but is closely built up so as to be almost inaccessible except where houses have been cleared away. Here begins the series of rounded bastions which ornament the SE. parts of the wall.

Continuing southwards from the East Gate, and after passing St. James's churchyard, the town wall is behind the buildings of Priory Street, which turns the rounded SE. angle with it and runs on along the south side, continued by Vineyard Street and St. John's Street. The whole of the SE. angle was formerly occupied by the gardens of East Hill House, which have gradually been broken up, but a large part still remains open land, and that in the angle still belongs to the house. On its boundary stand bastions 1 and 2, the former being that nearest East Gate, from which it is distant about 240 ft. As far as bastion 3 the plan of the town wall, as shown on the O.S. maps, and as seen in fact, is remarkably irregular, a circumstance due to several causes. In the first place the ground here was probably not at all secure: there is water in quantity close outside. The wall may have had several repairs in Roman times. Certain it is that this part needed and received heavy repairs in the time of Richard II, when the bastions were added. Then, in 1648, this portion received the heaviest battering by the cannon of the besiegers, who actually claimed to have blown a breach in it, though this was denied by the defenders. Finally, as a result of its weakened condition it has here, more than anywhere else, been patched and repaired in a haphazard manner by any number of private individuals acting on no agreed plan or principle. It still, as by a miracle, acts as a retaining wall to the much higher ground behind it, and is still the town wall, but its date is of 'fifty-seven varieties', and it is crowned by a crumbling series of walls (Duncan's 'parapet wall') designed to bound the properties of those within the walls, but built just after the siege and now in a most dilapidated state.

In the garden of East Hill House, formerly known as the Berry or Bury Field, P. G. Laver carried out some excavations on the line of the wall. The gardener tells the writer that he (Laver) excavated bastions 1 and 2, going right to the base of them, and also sank a shaft midway between them, against the inner face of the wall, going to a great depth.

Unfortunately, all that Laver has left us is some slight information about his work on bastion 1.

9. BASTION 1

This bastion is rather dilapidated (pl. XI, D). The original work is the thick part; the more slender top is probably eighteenth-century ornamental garden-work. In 1923 (6 Feb.), Laver began to clear one side of the interior of it.[2] At first the whole seemed full of rubble and earth. Soon it was established that the projection of it, measured on the inside, was 11 ft. 2 in. Later Laver was able to make the diagram from which our drawing, fig. 17, is made, from which we can see the construction of the Roman town wall, with the subsoil below, and the manner in which the wall of the bastion butts up against it. We also have a photograph of the actual section as excavated (pl. XI, B).

The shaft was sunk to a depth of 7 ft. 3 in. below the foundations of the Roman wall. Of this the lowest 2 ft. was natural sand. Above this Laver shows 1 ft. 7 in. of sandy clay, then a 6-in. layer of sandy material followed by 3 ft. 3 in. of buff clay, which he regarded as a foundation for the wall. Upon this the foundation consisted of 3 ft. 5 in. of roughly coursed medium-sized rubble, capped by a single course of tile. Above this came the first four courses of septaria followed by four of tile and so on, in the normal manner. The photograph shows that this face was much damaged before the bastion was built, and it would appear (as one would expect) that the foundation projected beyond the face, but of this Laver has left no note.

The bastion seems from the photograph to have been of similar construction to bastion 5, the masonry of smallish blocks of septaria being so mortared over that the coursing is not clearly visible. It is shown as standing upon 4 ft. of clay, through which runs a thin band of lime. The bottom of the masonry was 1 ft. below the bottom of the Roman foundation, and the building seems to have run up, without any offset, to a height

[1] It became clear in March 1955 that this arch is so low down that it can only have been for a drain. The base of the wall-foundation is now 5 ft. above present ground-level.

[2] *J.R.S.* xii, 260; Diary, 6 and 9/2/23.

of 9 ft. 4½ in. above the tile course capping the Roman foundation, where Laver refers to an offset, but this is perhaps the upper limit of the original work, upon which stands a modern parapet wall.

Very little seems to have been found in the earth excavated, and the few pieces of glass and pottery are

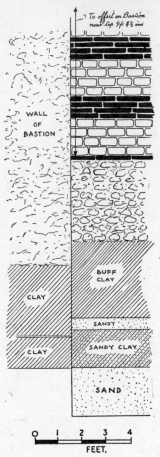

FIG. 17. Diagram, interior of
Bastion 1, p. 45.

all Roman. Coming from the filling of the bastion (we may make no other assumption), they are of no value as evidence. As at bastion 5, the filling seems to consist of soil taken from the surface near by, containing Roman remains in plenty, but nothing later.

The description of this work is taken from P. G. Laver's Diary, 6, 9, and 14 February 1923. The finds are in the Museum (C.M. 4417.23). There is also a statement that Mr. Duncan Clarke took measurements and made a sketch of the remains. A further note, on the 18th, records that Mr. Andrews also measured the bastion, and that it was apparently 5 ft. thick at the base. In the Museum is a water-colour drawing of the excavation, by K. C. Scarff.

The bastion seems a pretty good parallel to bastion 5, except that it is built where the wall was still standing, and so is closed at the back.

10. SECTION VI, IN GARDEN OF EAST HILL HOUSE
(FIG. 18)

In July 1948, by kind permission of the authorities of the Eastern Counties Institute, it was possible to cut a trench at right angles to the town wall at a point 70 ft. south of the centre line of bastion 1.

The point was selected with a view to avoiding the places where, according to the gardener, P. G. Laver had already dug, and also with an eye on the possible site of an internal tower.

The work was done by volunteer labour, but in the end it turned out to be almost the sole work of Lt.-Col. R. J. Appleby, M.B.E., F.S.A. The section was curtailed to the west by the presence of crops.

Immediately beneath the foundation of the modern (and ruinous) parapet wall the Roman wall was found standing 6 ft. 6 in. high above its foundations, but leaning outwards, the top 2 ft. out of plumb, and cracked horizontally in two places. The method employed was, having examined the foundation, to work back through the rampart material, throwing it forward towards the wall, in order to complete the section and to find any remains which might date the rampart.

The lowest point reached was 11 ft. 10 in. from the surface, which was the level of the yellow sand (A) under the foundation of the wall. Presumably this is natural, and into it the foundation trench was dug. The sand is very soft, and this trench would not long stand in any regular shape. It is assumed that the yellow sand and gravel (G) is also natural. We could see no clear line between it and (A), and nothing was found in either. The latter is subdivided by two black lines, about ½ in. thick, of which a sample was taken. It was like a coarse black sand, not staining the fingers. (Note the very similar case at tower no. 1, p. 22, where the black lines were described as 'peaty'.) The part of this sand next the wall was disturbed, containing odd pieces of septaria, and it will be noted that the lower black line curves down. Probably all this disturbance is due to the collapse of the side of the foundation trench.

The foundation (D) consists of an uncertain number of courses of rough stones in mortar, slanting back beneath, and 2 ft. in depth. What was finally left of the foundation trench was filled with grey clay (E). The internal offset (15 in.) of the foundation was capped with a very poor mortar, now dissolved to sand, and the grey clay was continued over it (compare section V, p. 42) and up the wall to cover two courses.

At some time the whole wall has slipped from its position some 6 ft. eastwards and outwards, tilting over at the same time. The gap left inside has been filled with earth, and into this has been dug a large pit, which had been revetted with wood. We are here without dating material, but it seems at least probable

wall was the object of special attack. The defenders lay in trenches behind the walls, and our pit (L) is probably one of these. The bottom was rounded, and a festoon of dirty gravel on the outer side may be the remains of a firing step. The pottery from (H and H') is Antonine.

After (L) had been filled in the trench (N) was cut in the bank behind and the upcast (O) was thrown on top

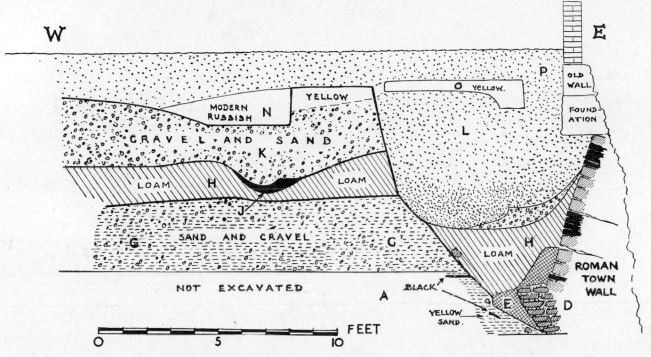

FIG. 18. Section VI; in grounds of East Hill House, p. 46.

that the pit is a redoubt or lager of the siege period. If it is, then the collapse of the wall is far anterior to the siege.

Back from the wall the layers of the rampart are clear. Upon the natural gravel lies (H), which is stiff loam, corresponding to the grey clay of section V. Above this lay the body of the rampart (K), which consists of yellow sand and gravel, but in dirty mixture, and is probably the main upcast from the ditch. It seals a dark line of ash and charcoal which marks the top of the loam, and reaches a maximum concentration in a shallow midden pit (J), which was full of shells of large oysters, mussels, cockles, and whelks, but no winkles. These lay in soot and charcoal, with a few animal bones and sherds of pottery.

The stiff loam (H), lying above the grey clay (E), cannot well be distinguished from (H) from which it must have slipped. Into it was cut the pit (L), which was full of very dark soil. During the siege this part of the

of (L). The space (N) thereafter filled up with recent building-rubbish. East of it the upper part of the (K) layer looks as if it might possibly have been deposited at the same time as (O), but the muddy line (shown broken) is more probably merely incidental to (K).

At a period when small bricks were in use, probably when East Hill House was built (c. 1710), (P) was cut as a foundation trench for the boundary or parapet wall, of which six courses remain. On top of this stands the thin modern wall, of small stones capped with brick, which is decaying.

The foundation of the Roman wall matches the construction at other points where it has been found to stand on soft sand. The clay packing is found again in section V, where also is a faint parallel to the decayed mortar. The wall begins with one course of septaria (here obscured by mortar) capped by a single course of tile with an offset of $1\frac{1}{2}$ in. Then follow three courses of septaria (with a crack between the second and third), then four of tile (with a crack above), four of septaria, four of tile, and one course of stone. The back of the upper stringcourse of tiles can be seen in the outside of the wall, which is therefore scarcely 1 ft. thick here. The outer side of the wall is very rough and overgrown, but it is possible that the next string-course below can also be seen.

The general build is normal. The stone blocks have faces about 5½ by 9 in.; they varied much in length. There is one particular difference. Here the pointing is left rough, elsewhere it was smoothed and the joints marked out with the point of the trowel. Also the

or 45 (2nd century), and a fragment of thin grey with dotted panels (fig. 19, 3, 7, 8, 14 Antonine). There were many food bones, and some iron nails, and one frag-ment of a 'lantern' in buff ware. A fragment of slate is probably intrusive.

From the black hollow (J) came 2 chips of buff flagon, 18 fragments of one jar f. 268, and 4 of one f. 108, 22 other grey fragments, with food bones, shells, &c. (fig. 19, 9, 10, late first century).

From the gravel and sand (K) came a sigillata beaker-base, a chip of a Castor ware beaker f. 391 or 392, buff fragments including 2 or 3 flagon necks,

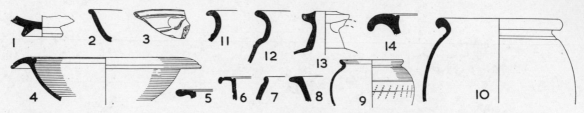

FIG. 19. Pottery from rampart in Section VI. Scale ¼.

1. T.S. base, f. 27 (?), level K.
2. T.S. rim, f. 18, level K.
3. T.S. rim, f. 36, level H.
4. Rim, f. 318, fine, polished grey, level K.
5. Rim, f. 246, dark grey, level K; cf. fig. 8, 12.
6. Another similar, thin hard grey, level K.
7. Rim, f. 124, coarse black, polished, level H.

8. Rim, f. 303, D. 7½ in., hard polished grey, level H.
9. Beaker, f. 108, fine grey, level J.
10. Jar, f. 268A, coarse grey, level J.
11. Rim, f. 221, grey-black, polished, level K.
12. Rim, f. 266, var. (?), coarse grey, horizontally rilled, level K.
13. Flagon-neck, f. 149, white-buff ware, level K.
14. Mortarium-rim, f. 195A, buff, with white grit, D. 9½ in. level H.

Nos. 3, 7, 8 from H are probably Antonine, 14 is probably Flavian; all those from
K could be first century, as should also nos. 9 and 10 from the charcoal at J.

untidy slope-back of the foundation has not been noted anywhere else.

These points may indicate a different working party or a Roman rebuild. If the latter was the case we have to note that care was taken to match the earlier work, and that there is second-century pottery in the rampart, as in section VII.

Owing to the fact that the section is incomplete on the west we lack the slope of the tail of the rampart, which would very much help the identification of the layers. As it is, it is difficult to be sure which layer matches which in other sections.

In a comparatively secluded corner of the general disturbance made by the slipping of the wall, in sand and gravel and against a brown mark like that of a horizontal timber beam, at X on the section, lay the fragment of decorated sigillata, f. 37, shown on fig. 20 B. Though it cannot be regarded as safely strati-fied, its general concordance with that found in Sec-tion V is of interest.

From the stiff loam (H) came Samian of forms 18 (large), 35, 36, 27; 6 fragments of buff ware, including a rim f. 46 (or possibly a mortarium), 24 fragments of grey ware, including a rim as Collingwood fig. 54, 44,

c. 40 fragments of grey ware, including ff. 246 and 278 (Collingwood 18–20 and 72); fragments of red and yellow roof-tiles, 35 fragments of painted wall-plaster, glass, charcoal, bones, and septaria. This can hardly be other than second century (fig. 19, 1, 2, 4, 5, 6, 11, 12, 13).

From the gravel 'step' in the pit (L) came Roman fragments plus one with brown glaze, which is recent. From the bottom of L came Roman wares plus 3 pipe-stems and 8 fragments of pottery ranging from white-painted gotch to brown glazed ware. Higher up was similar, still with much Roman, but with 5 more clay pipe-stems, and pieces of china and delft, Grenzhausen and Lambeth ware, these latter especially near the top. The remains in (N) were similar.

Very little of the pottery is worthy of illustration. Fourteen pieces are shown, fig. 19.

11. BASTION 2 (pl. X, B)

Measured centre to centre this bastion lies about 245 ft. from the first, and is likewise open (on the sur-face) to the garden of East Hill House. As has been said, we are informed that P. G. Laver excavated it,

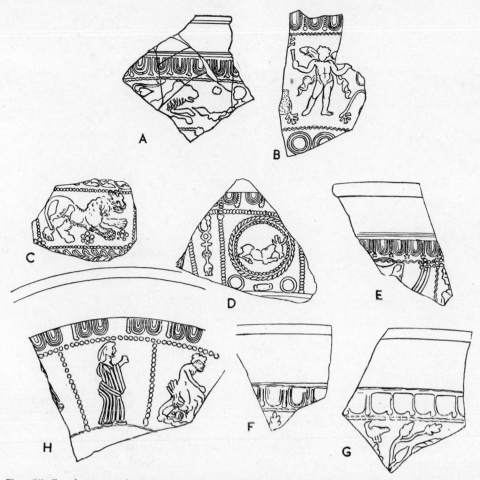

Fig. 20. Samian ware from rampart: A, from Section V; B, Section VI; C–G, Section VII; (H, not rampart). (pp. 43, 48, 54.) Scale ½.

A. Fine matt glaze. The decoration is well-known late-first-century style. Found under the rampart-bank, on grey clay in section **V.**

B. Good ware, light glaze. Cupid, Oswald 450, 'Trajan–Antonine', the wavy lines and band of circles below suggest a Trajan–Hadrian date for this. Found in rampart in section VI.

C. Good, bright glaze. The small bead-rows and seven-point rosette are Trajanic (*J.R.S.* xxv, pl. XVII, 1), and the horizontal wreaths agree well with such a date. Compare *Silch.* xxv, 17, 18, which are, perhaps, not so late as 'Antonine'. The lion is close to *Silch.* xxvi, 50. Found in upper, sandy rampart, section VII.

D. Good ware. The stag appears to be Oswald 1704A, broken, or Déchelette 847; compare *Silch.* xxvi, 46 and 48, stamped by *Doeccus.* The candelabrum is on *Silch.* xxix, 130, and of Brecon, fig. 71, 30 (smaller), attributed to Trajan. Our piece is perhaps a little later. Found in lower rampart, section VII.

E. Good, dark ware. The vase appears on Knorr, *Rottenburg*, p. 21, stamped by *Perpetuus*, compare *Silch.* xxix, 124; note the large wavy line and seven-point rosette; compare *Holt*, figs. 42, 43, 45, nos. 98–116; *Wrox. I*, fig. 13. Date *c.* A.D. 120. Found in grey clay under rampart, section VII.

F and G. Probably from one vessel, blurred in the mould, the tree-pattern with bird is well known; cf. Holt, fig. 37, 42 and fig. 40, 67; also *Richborough II*, pl. XXVII, 11, stamped MERCATO. *c.* A.D. 80–110. Found in lower rampart in section VII.

H. Unusual ware, with hard but unpleasant glaze. Crude work. The standing figure resembles Oswald 327, the ovolo is most distinctive, and the bead-rows are very large. Found in thick layer of old daub in insula 40, 87 ft. from town wall.

but if he did so he has left no word concerning it, nor about the shaft he is said to have sunk between the two.

12. BASTION 3

This is clearly shown on Morant's map of 1748, and on Chapman and André's of 1777, but it is now missing. Its interval from the last, again centre to centre, was probably 235 ft. The site has not been tested.

13. BASTION 4 (pl. XI, C)

147. The spacing of the bastions showed that there should be one on the site of some small slum cottages built against the wall in Dale's Court. In due course these were condemned and demolished, and in July 1934 we were able to excavate the site.[1]

After the removal of the cottages the wall presented a sorry sight. A deep recess in it had been bridged by a flat arch. On either side of this the wall, where visible through modern plaster and former interior decoration, was of a composite nature. High up on each side could be seen two of the quadruple lacing courses of tile, attesting the presence of the original Roman face. But elsewhere the face was a repair, of remarkably coarse and small masonry. It appeared that most of the Roman face had had to be thus replaced, and it may even prove that the lower part of the wall had been deliberately undermined at some time.[2] Inside the recess the masonry across the back presented rough core work only, of a nature rather different from the usual Roman core.

Excavation quickly revealed the foundations of the bastion, and also the lower part of the wall. The latter consisted of the sloping, or battered toe, neatly built of small squared septaria, the four lower courses of which were still partly standing, on a foundation of mortar-concrete 6 in. thick. Below this was clay, but whether natural or placed there is uncertain.

The approximately semicircular wall of the bastion had been bonded into this batter, the full ten courses of which were preserved at the west angle, but the bastion had pulled away, leaving a gap of several inches at the joint (pl. XI, C). It was surprising, as we uncovered the wall of the bastion, to find that it varied in thickness from 3 ft. (at top of batter) on the west side to 3 ft. 7 in. on the east side. All round, it was uniformly battered to match the town wall. Even more surprising was the difference in the foundations. On the west the foundation coincided with that of the town wall, as already described, but on the east the mortar layer was missing, and its place was taken by an extra course of the batter,

standing directly on the clay. P. G. Laver thought the clay on the west showed signs of burning. The eleven courses on the east gave a total height of 4 ft., and corresponded exactly with those of the town wall into which they had been bonded.

It will be seen from the photograph (pl. XI, C) that the lower part of the entire masonry, where it had been buried, is of a different nature from that above the present ground-level, and it is possible that the core in the recess belongs to the buried portion, which is certainly contemporary with the building of bastion 5, or approximately so. The quarrying into the wall had primarily occurred before this time, making the rebuild necessary, but it had occurred again, after the ground reached its present level, and had been repaired by the very poor work first mentioned (above). As this work stops at the angles of the tower, the latter must have been still standing when this was done. This puts us back to before the eighteenth century.

The bastion projected 11 or 12 ft. from the south face of the town wall exclusive of the batter, which is 18 in. The interior dimensions were N.–S. about 8–9 ft. and E.–W. 13 ft. 7 in.; over all E.–W. 22 ft. 9 in.

The site is exactly opposite that of the NE. postern, and in the interior of the bastion we found, below 19 in. of recent deposits, 10 in. of hard rammed gravel lying on firm clay. The remarkable thing is that the masonry of the bastion stops on this gravel, and must have sloped down from that level to the toe of the batter outside. There is little wonder that this projecting tower tilted to the south and pulled away from the wall behind, and this was probably the cause of its demolition.

There was no such gravel layer in bastions 1 and 5, and in any case it must antedate the masonry here. Its position opposite a gate in the north wall of the town suggests that it was a Roman street, the edges of which were destroyed when the bastion was built.

We therefore turn to the wall behind, looking for evidence for a small gate similar to the NE. postern, and immediately notice that the only Roman work surviving, i.e. the tile courses, stops short as if cut off, just short of the bastion. The shortest distance between the ends is 25 ft. 9 in. Here is just enough space for a gate of the type expected, and although the recess already mentioned goes deep into this space, it shows no masonry which need be Roman work. We conclude that the possibility that a gate stood here remains probable, but the ground-level inside the wall is so high, besides being mostly covered by a pavilion, that excavation has not been possible.

---

[1] *J.R.S.* xxv, 214–15; *C.M.R.* 1935, 6.
[2] There may have been several sieges of which we know nothing. The outward slip of the wall in section VI is most easily explained by undermining. Examination outside would be illuminating, but the wall there is in a dangerous state of equilibrium.

The history of the site thus appears to be: (1) a small Roman gate with road issuing from it; (2) Roman wall and gate deeply cut away beneath, perhaps in Saxon times; (3) when the walls were repaired under Richard II the opening in the gateway built up and the undermined wall restored to a uniform face with a batter at the foot, and bastion.

Fourthly the bastion leans outward to the south and is pulled down to ground-level, corresponding to modern level (nearly) and about the same time the face of the town wall is also seriously damaged. This could hardly occur before 1421, up to which date the walls were an object of much care. It probably happened in the seventeenth century, to which date the very coarse repair work belongs, or perhaps to the time of the erection of the cottages, which were of eighteenth-century date. The author finds he is at variance here with P. G. Laver's Diary, 21/7/34, where he states that the bastion wall was not bonded in, and that the wall to which it is butted-on is a broken-faced wall. This must remain a matter of opinion.

14. Bastion 5 and Section VII

In 1931 by the generosity of P. G. Laver, and by the kindness of the Eastern National Omnibus Company, it was possible to examine the town wall in insula 39 more thoroughly than has yet been possible at any other point. The prospects were not regarded as remarkably good, for no Roman work was visible, but in the event, it was found that a more informative point could hardly have been selected.[1]

Bastion 5 (pl. XII, A, fig. 21)

104. This picturesque feature stands in the middle of the south side of the space which was available. It is an external tower of D-plan, with open back, appearing as a round tower from the outside. Above the level to which the town wall is preserved the tower is continued by an eighteenth-century addition in the form of a summer-house, built of stone, brick, and tile, in pseudo-antique fashion, with a thatched roof.[2]

From the bastion to the garage on the west the level of the ground had been reduced about 4 ft. by the bus company, revealing that height of the inner face of the town wall (**110**), and also the existence of the opening in the back of the bastion. All this part of the wall is of one continuous build, of small pieces of septaria and without any tile lacing courses, and thus totally different from any known part of the original Roman wall. The only tile used was at the angle behind the bastion, and here only single tiles are employed to form the corners, whereas corners of Roman work are deeply tiled.

The first task was to explore this part of the wall. The corresponding corner was found to be exactly similar, and the opening, equalling the interior width of the bastion, proved to be exactly 10 English feet wide. The town wall itself was 4 ft. 6 in. thick, but there was probably originally a batter at the base on the outside, adding another foot or more (see bastion 4 above, p. 50). The wall of the bastion was only 3 ft. 9 in. thick, and this also probably had another foot of batter around the outside.

The upper 2 ft. of the inner face of the town wall are somewhat differently finished from the lower face, which lay below ground-level, and is obscured by the rough mortar which is left unfinished. The upper part, which probably was visible above ground at the time of building, is better finished, so that the small blocks of septaria can be distinguished.

The wall of the bastion was of one continuous build with this, and in exactly the same style, though the finished face extends lower than it does in the town wall. At a level about 7 ft. below the top of the wall there is a row of four (possibly five, for we only cleared rather less than half of the interior) rectangular openings like put-log holes, 6 in. square, corresponding to one block of septaria, which extended, originally, right through the wall. Some of these are now closed on the outside by subsequent patching and refacing. Three feet six inches below there was another similar row, one of which has a piece of tile above and below it. This hole still goes right through and was found to house a nest of wild bees, to the dismay of our workmen. There was also one hole of an upper row, at about the level of the ground inside the town wall, which may have consisted of two or three holes only. All are set directly above one another, so that they may indeed have been put-log holes, in which they would closely resemble the similar remarkable holes of which so many are to be seen in the walls of the Castle. There is also the possibility that they were constructional and housed timbers of a rectangular framework built into the masonry. Examination of those in the Castle shows that this was not the case, and the masonry is so thick that there was nothing to gain by doing it. The thinner wall of the bastion may have been judged to call for reinforcement of this nature.

It has also been suggested that these openings may have been for drainage purposes. We dismiss this as improbable. They were certainly not necessary, for the Roman town wall nowhere has any, and has not suffered from the lack of them.

The bastion and the town wall were clearly not of Roman date, and were found to have been built upon the ruined remains of the Roman town wall. Moreover, though conforming to the general line of the latter, the

[1] *J.R.S.* xxii, 212.   [2] Since this was written the thatched roof has been burnt.

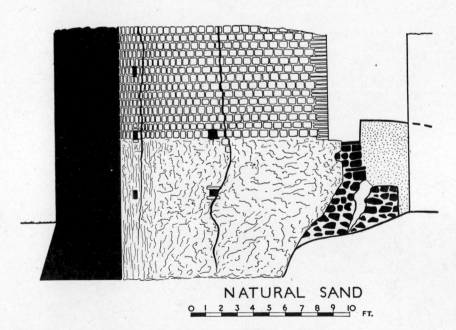

NATURAL SAND

FIG. 21. Plan and section, Bastion 5. [104], p. 51.

actual line of the rebuild is diverging slightly from the Roman line at the point where we were. The Roman wall is usually 8–9 ft. wide, so that the narrower rebuild leaves part of it uncovered. At the west corner of the bastion 2 ft. 7 in. of it can be seen; 20 ft. farther east this has increased to 2 ft. 11 in. (pl. XIII, B).

The foundations of the Roman wall are shown on pl. XIII, A and B. The subsoil is a very soft yellow sand, so a foundation of 2 ft. or more in depth of rough stones laid in mortar was laid down, projecting about 2 ft. on the inside. Above this there was a single course of septaria followed by one of tile. After an offset of 2 in. the inner face begins. The remains of the yellowish, sandy rampart could be seen overlying the projection of the foundation and ending on the face of the wall.

The depth to the bottom of these excavations was nearly 14 ft., and we were working with limited means and forced to use much timbering. Consequently it was only possible to reach the bottom at one point near the bastion. Corroborative evidence was, however, obtained in the next section.

The foundation of the Roman wall was found to have given way, possibly owing to the proximity of the ditch outside. The wall tilted outwards, and a large crack opened into the foundation, into which a man could thrust his arm. This is clearly seen in pl. XIII, A, and fig. 21. In the centre of the back of the bastion the fall of the wall had taken with it every trace of the foundation, and probing with a bar westwards of the bastion showed that over most of the length of the wall the case was similar, though here and there fragments of masonry remained.

It was probably not long after the fall that the wall was rebuilt, for the builders cleared the line of soil and rubble, and the Roman rampart must have been standing still to full height (which shows it was not thrust from it which ruined the wall), for the almost vertical face which it shows in the sections is that to which it was now cut back.

After removing all loose material from the ruins and clearing a building-line along them, slightly divergent, the builders erected their new wall partly on the remaining Roman work, and partly on the yellow sand, where they carried their work *2 ft. or more lower*[1] than the bottom of the Roman foundations. They did not, however, lay any special foundation differing from the main part of their wall. Their work still appears stable enough, but there are cracks in the bastion (fig. 21).

As has been said, the vertical line of the rampart was clear all along, and straight across the back of the bastion. The space between the bastion and the old rampart was filled chiefly with black topsoil which had been obtained from the surface within the rampart and also from the top of the rampart itself. This was proved by the identity of potsherds from both positions. The filling, however, was not even; a mortar layer near the bottom must have been laid down when building began, and there are irregular layers here and there which indicate that filling was added from time to time as the wall grew higher.

Everything from this filling was carefully collected in the hope that some clue might be found to date the rebuild. Except at one point nothing was found which was not Roman, and all the Roman material was jumbled up in the filling.

From 18 in. to 24 in. below the top of the (ancient) wall of the bastion[2] the filling was capped by a yellowish band. This also produced Roman sherds, but, in addition, the following: two fragments of orange-glazed ware, one with impressed patterns, date about 1650–1800; one dark green glazed sherd, seventeenth century (?); some Lambeth painted delft and enamelled earthenware of about 1650–70; lead glazed fragments of uncertain date; a piece of stone-ware later than 1670; a piece of thin glass from a diamond-pane; also a fragment with lead glaze with green traces of copper, and a white pattern, fifteenth century; and a fragment of a brown rim, probably fourteenth century.

It is clear that this represents the occupation level after the completion of the rebuild, and the earliest piece accords well with the obvious attribution of the rebuilding to the repairs of the town walls begun under Richard II and extending over some years (p. 15). The later wares might be imagined to lay some emphasis on the mid-seventeenth century, the time of the siege of Colchester (p. 16).

The full extent of the rebuilt portion of the wall is yet unknown, but it has been identified at a point 110 ft. east of Queen Street in the same form as at bastion 5. Eastwards of the latter it may well extend nearly to bastion 4, where, however, some Roman work again appears in position in the outer face. The new wall has here regained the outer line of the old one. Here and eastwards the rebuild is a patching of gaps in the Roman work (compare bastion 1). A survey is much to be desired, but the wall is not accessible in many places, and much of it is obscured by modern patching and refacing.[3]

---

[1] Compare other examples, e.g. bastions on London Wall, where the case is similar.

[2] i.e. below the floor of the eighteenth-century summer-house.

[3] The long-term town-plan provides for the clearance of the houses backing on the town wall in St. John Street, Vineyard Street, and Priory Street, widening those streets to a boulevard with space for car-parking against the town wall, which would be completely exposed. That would be the time for a survey. The appearance of the wall then may be gauged from pl. XII, B, which shows a portion with houses removed. It has been said that the spectacle of these old houses perched on the wall is more reminiscent of the old Roman towns of France than of England.

Section VII, in Priory Street (fig. 22)

About 20 ft. east of bastion 5 we secured a complete section of the rampart—the first under supervised excavation. On the right of fig. 22 is seen the rebuilt town wall, standing upon the Roman work, 10 ft. high on its inner face, and 13 ft. high above the modern ground-level outside. The offset half-way up is probably due to a later rebuild of the upper face. The Roman work corresponds exactly with what was found at the bastion.

The lowest part of the rampart here consists of a bank of grey clay, over 3 ft. thick, flat-topped over most of its width, and extending back 42 ft. from the face of the Roman wall, where it overlies the foundation. A few pieces of tile were found in it and part of a white imbrex (?). The pottery (fig. 23, A) consisted of three fragments of T.S. ff. 37 (fig. 20, E), 27, 18/31, and 81; a fragment of a platter f. 17, mica-gilt (cf. fig. 23, B, 9); a chip of a flagon with ringed and pinched mouth (prob. f. 366); grey forms 37,[1] 243, 246 (fig. 23, A, 5, 3, 12 and 14, 15, 18), 227, and a number of fragments of coarse grey cooking-pots, including thirty-five fragments of 4 or 5 f. 266 of Flavian (?) type (fig. 23, A, 8–11 and 16). There was also a coin of Cunobelin, Evans XII, 7, and a large fragment of a fine black, micaceous platter with a meaningless central stamp (fig. 23, A, 4); a Roman grey pedestal-base (ibid. 13), and a mortarium rim f. 195 (ibid. 6).

Though this bank was laid down when certain early pottery was still lying about, the forms 18/31 (T.S.), 81 (T.S.), and 37 show it was later than A.D. 65.

The recess cut into this bank and filled with gravel, not far from the wall, may or may not have been a continuous trench, perhaps an abortive foundation-trench. Six feet north of it there was a small hollow full of dark earth and gravel (compare section VI). Pottery ff. 14 (grey), 108, 246 (3), 266 (Neronian).

The clay lies directly upon the yellow sand.

Upon the clay lies a burnt layer, 7 in. thick, very definite in the centre, merging into the heavy black layer inwards and fading away towards the wall. It was of gravelly sand and earth, reddened by fire, and contained the following pottery: T.S., 2 chips f. 27; buff ware, 2 fragments f. 243, fragments of a very crude buff jug (will not draw), 2 fragments f. 187; grey ware, fragments f. 266, 8 fragments f. 246, also 2 fragments of ware stamped with concentric rings[2] and panels of small square impressions, and a piece of window glass.

There is nothing which could not be of Boudiccan date, except that we do not yet know the date of the West Stowe ware, but would expect it to be late first century. So this layer would appear to be Flavian, though the absence of later pieces may be accidental.

In any case the presence of a few blocks of septaria at the same level near the wall connects it with the building of the wall.

Above this level lies a composite bank of yellow sand intersected by black bands, which unite with the burnt layer and run back to the drain as a thick, dark layer. From this we have T.S. f. 27 and f. 18; coarse wares ff. 175 bis, 246 (5), 108, 266, and one rim f. 38 (fig. 23, B, 25). The latter (at least Antonine) spoils a first-century date.

From the sandy material of the main body of the rampart we have more pottery than from any point hitherto touched (fig. 23, B).

The most significant pieces of decorated Samian are shown in Fig. 20, C–G. E is from the grey clay bank, the others from the sandy rampart. They are all dated c. A.D. 100–150. Other Samian comprised ff. 29, 30, 18 (7), 27 (4), 31, 33 (3), 38, and we illustrate, Fig. 23, B, ff. Curle 11 a conical cup, 33, 46, 18, 31 and Curle 21.

Colour-coated ware included f. 391 (no. 8) in local ware, and eight fragments of Castor ware, including f. 308. In buff there were several mortarium rims (nos. 10–14, one stamped APRILIS) and forms 16 or 17, mica-gilt, 140 B, 156 (3), 195, 498.

Grey and black wares were plentiful, the best pieces are figured from among the following forms—17, 37 (14) 38 (3), 39, 40 (4), 108 (8), 120, 122 or 123 (2), 218, 221, 232, 246 (23), 266 (2), 268 A, 268 B (6), 278 (6), 320.

There were fragments of a globular, ribbed glass vessel, a roundel, and pieces of imbrices.

It is quite clear that we have to bring the date of this rampart down to the middle of the second century to accommodate Castor ware, the Samian forms, with coarse ware forms 156, 498, 278, and 40, agree with this. The date should not be very late, however, for f. 246 is still with us in numbers, and f. 38 is not at all numerous. A few pieces of f. 305 from the top of the rampart have been excluded as too late and not stratified.

It has been said that Castor ware does not appear before 170–180, but this is hardly proved as yet. Provisionally we suggest a date of about 150 for this deposit.

All this argues against a date later than A.D. 140.

The clay bank underlying the rampart is not explained. The decorated fragments of T.S. are not alone in showing that it cannot have been laid down before Flavian times. The complete lack of any kind of layer between it and the yellow sand indicates that the surface was probably cleared for it.

When the rampart was built it reversed the natural slope for drainage, and it became necessary to provide a drain at that point. To a lesser degree the clay bank had already spoilt the natural drainage, but no drain had been provided. The drain, carefully built of tiles

---

[1] This rim on drawing is definitely sloped inwards and may not be f. 37.

[2] As made at West Stowe Heath near Bury St. Edmunds, Proc. Suffolk Inst. Arch., vol. 26, pt. 1.

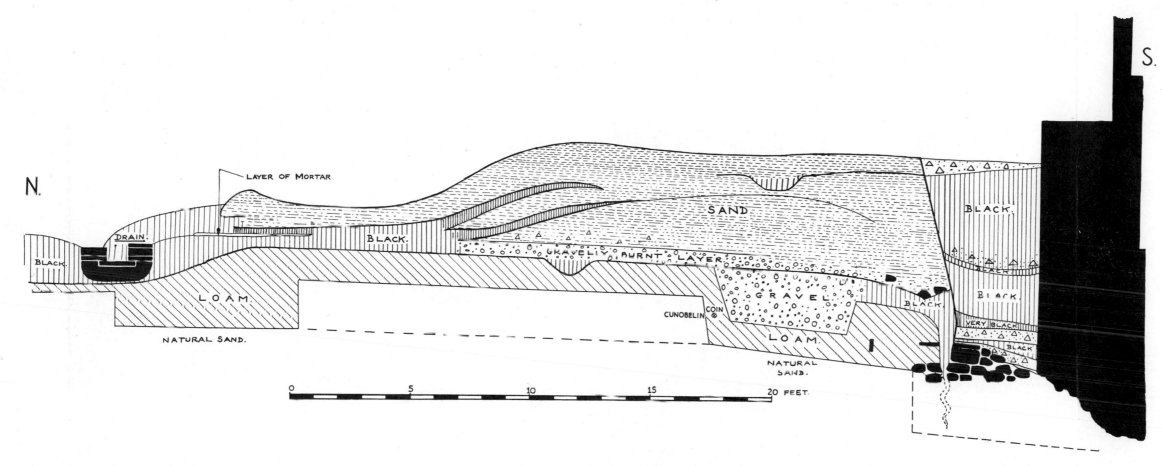

N.

S.

LAYER OF MORTAR.

DRAIN.

BLACK.

BLACK.

SAND

BLACK.

GRAVELLY BURNT LAYER

BLACK

BLACK

BLACK.

VERY BLACK

BLACK

LOAM.

GRAVEL

CUNOBELIN COIN

LOAM.

NATURAL SAND.

NATURAL SAND.

0   5   10   15   20 FEET.

FIG. 22. Section VII, p. 54.

and mortar and septaria, is 1 ft. wide and 9 in. high on the south side and 7 in. on the north. It was excavated into the thick black layer on the south side and into the loam of the ruined early buildings on the north side, with which the burnt layer is contemporary. Only 2 ft. away from it, on the south, the black layer is capped by a thin layer of hard mortar, which may have been a path of some sort, but did not seem strong enough for this, resembling more a floor where mortar had been mixed, perhaps for the drain itself. At any rate this would appear to have been the ground-level

It would appear that the yellow sand of the bank had not stood well (it would not) and has flowed down over the layers just described. At the same time the drain became blocked by a bank of yellowish loam, and the storm water seems to have flowed along the top of the north wall of the drain. This indicates a time when the administration nodded. There are no subsequent layers distinguishable, and we seem to have reached the end of the Roman period. On the other hand, it is remarkable that there are no late coins, and what late pottery there is is loose in the topsoil. We

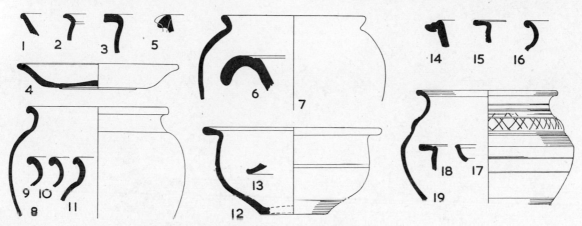

FIG. 23, A. Pottery from Section VII. Scale ¼.

1. T.S. rim of platter, f. 18/31. Hardly earlier than A.D. 100.
2. T.S. rim f. Walters 81, good glaze, cf. O. and P., pl. LXI, 8.
3. Rim of a red bowl f. 243, not polished. First century.
4. Part of a sub-Belgic platter in fine black ware, with meaningless stamp in centre. Date c. 60–70.
5. Rim f. 37, polished grey. Difficult to line-up for drawing and could take the extreme position shown by the outline.
6. Mortarium-rim f. 195B. Hard buff, with mixed grit; another similar is white, with white grit running over the rim. Late first century.
7. Rim of a jar in grey ware with black surface. Date uncertain.
8. Much of a cooking-pot f. 266 in sandy brown and black ware. First century.
9–11. Similar rims in grey and black ware.
12. Part of a bowl f. 246, hard grey, with fragments of several others quite similar. First century.
13. Rim of a small grey *pedestal* foot.
14. Rim of bowl f. 243, soft red ware, white-coated. D. c. 9 in. Another piece of this rim was found in the lower rampart.
15. Rim f. 246. Rough grey ware. D. 7½ in.
16. Rim f. 266, hooked. Grey-black ware. D. 6¾ in.
17. T.S. rim of f. Drag. 27, with fragment of another.
18. Grey rim f. 246.
19. Much of one bowl f. 218. Fine, thick grey ware, partly polished. The bulge on neck latticed.
    All nos. 14–19 came from the burnt layer over the grey loam and belong to the first century.

contemporary with the drain. It is also contemporary with the upper black seam in the rampart, which in turn runs out over the mortar layer as a 4-in. sandy layer, distinct from the sandbank overlying it. From beneath the mortar layer or path came certain sherds of ff. 38, 305, plus mortaria rims, the former postulating a third-century date. From under the drain, two sub-Belgic rims.

have to remember that much soil was removed from the surface to fill the space at the back of the rebuilt wall and this operation has probably destroyed or altered the upper layers. But even so, late coins were not found in the filling.

45.[1] H. Laver held that the Roman town wall was built over the remains of houses: '. . . In all parts of the wall on the west and south—I mention these sides

[1] We have retained this number, following Wheeler and Laver; it and **128** are the only cases of numbers in the Within-the-Walls List falling outside the walls.

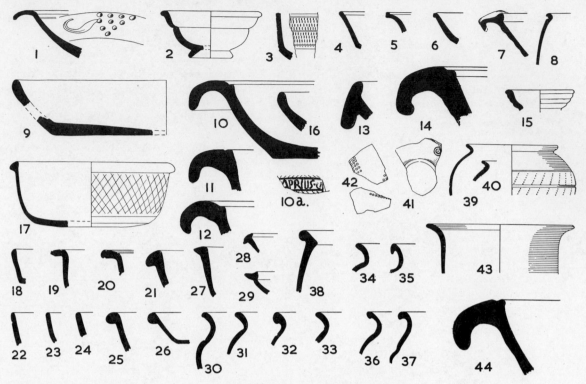

FIG. 23, B. Pottery from section VII. Scale ¼.

1. T.S. f. Drag. 36, deep, good red glaze, barbotine decoration. In lower rampart.
2. T.S. f. Drag. 27, poorish, thin glaze. In upper rampart, near top.
3. T.S. fragment of a conical, rouletted cup. Good ware and glaze. Ibid. Antonine.
   Could be Colchester ware, ref.: Oswald and Pryce, pl. LXXV, 13, and many fragments of this same form, in good ware, were found on the kiln site in 1933, but this piece could equally well come from Lezoux.
4. T.S. f. Drag. 33, one of three similar, all somewhat poor ware. Ibid.
5. T.S. f. Drag. 46, cf. O. and P., pl. LX, 9, 10, attributed to Trajan–Hadrian. Ibid.
6. T.S. f. Drag. 18/31, thin, rather poor glaze. Upper rampart. Antonine.
7. T.S. f. Curle 21, good glaze and ware. Upper rampart. Antonine.
8. Colour-coated beaker, f. 391, local ware. Ibid. Antonine.
9. Part of a large red dish f. 17, mica-gilt. D. 13 in. Upper rampart, near top. Mid-first century.
10. Part of a mortarium f. 195c, stamped APRILIS·OF (?). Hard yellow-buff, with sparse large white grit. Other stamps of this potter have been found in Colchester on this form. Upper rampart. Late first century.
11. Mortarium-rim, f. 195A. Buff. Upper rampart. Second half first century.
12. Mortarium-rim, f. 195B. Buff. Lower rampart. Trajanic (?).
13. Mortarium-rim, much battered and worn, f. 499. Light buff. Third century. Marked as 'lower rampart', but looks a stray.
14. Mortarium-rim, could be f. 195B, but is probably f. 497. Buff. Lower rampart. Probably Antonine.
15. Rim of a flagon, f. 156, in soft yellow-buff. Lower rampart. Antonine.
16. Rim of a fine grey platter, f. 17. Upper rampart. First century.
17. Bowl f. 37, typical of a number of rims and fragments. Fine grey-black ware polished inside and out, and latticed. Upper rampart, near top. Fragments also occurred in lower rampart. This form lasted from c. 70 to perhaps as late as 180.
18. Rim of a platter, f. 40 (not typical). Hard grey, not polished. Lower rampart. Date uncertain.
19. Rim of bowl f. 246. Rough grey. D. c. 7 in. Upper rampart, near top. Second half first century.
20. Rim of bowl (ditto). Upper rampart; there were several of these rims in the Lower rampart.
21. Large rim f. 37 (cf. no. 17). Lower rampart.
22–24. Three rims, f. 40, polished grey or black. No. 24 has a wavy line outside. 22 lower, 23–24 upper rampart. Antonine.
25. Very large rim f. 38. D. c. 12 in. Grey; another is black. Both upper rampart. Not earlier than Antonine.
26. A rim of the same form (38) from the tail of the lower rampart. Antonine.
27. Rim of a bowl f. 38 (?) in very hard, black cooking-pot ware, polished, uneven, as if hand made. D. c. 9 in. Lower rampart. Antonine.
28. Unusual rim, light grey, not polished. D. c. 7½ in. Lower rampart.
29. Rim of bowl or lid, f. 315. Grey-black, polished. D. 6 in. Upper rampart. Date uncertain.

[Continued at foot of opposite page

from having seen what I am about to describe—this earth (of the rampart) . . . is piled over remains of Roman houses, and in one place in Priory Street (**45**) I observed that the wall was built over and stood on the ruins of a house. Every one of these houses, without exception, showed that it was destroyed by fire, as did some outside the wall on the west, near St. Mary's Church.'[1] He was, naturally, of the opinion that these houses were pre-Boudiccan.

Laver was writing in 1907. The one spot he quotes which is closely marked is our **45**, and this is quite close to a point where we have since found that the town wall is a medieval rebuild under which the foundations of the Roman wall remain in fragmentary condition. Neither in section VII, nor in the section of the ditch about to be described, was anything like foundations of houses found under the wall, although we are only 30 ft. from **45**. In the years since 1907 we have seen no more from near St. Mary's, but we have seen sections I–VII, and in no case can we say that we have seen foundations of houses passing under the wall. We have seen remains of Roman occupation under the rampart, and the earliest levels could well include remains of wooden or clay houses, but we cannot say that this is positively the case. The burnt layer, or the lower occupation layers, under the rampart, may have continued outside the wall, but so far, except in the section now to be described, we have had no opportunity to observe them if they did. The critical point is that early buildings of flimsy nature *may* have extended beyond the walls, but we have no proof of it; as for buildings with masonry foundations doing so, we can say that we have never yet seen any evidence of such a thing. And if such were the case we should look also for metalled streets passing under the walls, but not even H. Laver has suggested this, for there is no slightest evidence for it (except, of course, on the lines of the gates).

15. THE TOWN DITCH
(FIG. 24)

In 1937 a trench was cut southwards from the face of the town wall at a point 45 ft. east of bastion 5 (just west of **45**). The aim was to obtain some information on the town ditch, which had never been seen. Here the outer face of the rebuilt wall should be about 10 ft. south of the inner face of the Roman wall. Exactly under the late face, and nearly a foot under the toe of the batter, a disturbance began, extending to 3 ft. 6 in. from the modern surface and 14 in. below the bottom of the later wall. The level soon rose again, and it would appear that the old surface, consisting of 3 to 5 in. of gravel, lying on sand, sloped gently down southwards from the wall. At a point 17 ft. from the face it ended in what must have been a gravel pit, but most of this 17 ft. of berm had been removed by a broad, upright-sided excavation 7 ft. 3 in. wide and 2 ft. 9 in. deep. It was full of black earth and yellow sand, and extended to form a new surface some 6 in. above the gravel level. This deposit would agree with the black deposit noted in the section of the south side of the 'forum' (p. 170) and may well be of the Dark Ages, though it contained nothing to date it.

The gravel pit cut through this latter very sharply and steeply, and had a flat bottom extending southwards. It has removed all traces of the Roman ditch, but it could not be examined farther than shown in the section, for the water entered so copiously that our timbering was shattered. The filling of this pit was mixed with mortar, which formed a layer on the east side of the trench at 7 to 8 ft. from the surface. This contained a cupped flagon neck (f. 156), two chips of T.S. ff. 18 and 33, another of a heavy bowl such as Curle 11; a fragment of a black bowl with scored branch pattern inside, a mortarium rim of f. 597, and

---

30. Coarse grey-black rim f. 221. D. *c.* 5¼ in. Upper rampart. Date uncertain.
31. Rim of jar f. 278. Normal grey-black, polished. D. *c.* 5¼ in. Upper rampart, near top. Date uncertain.
32. Rim of jar f. 268A. Rough dark grey. D. 6 in. Ibid. Date uncertain.
33. Rim of jar f. 278. Hard grey, not polished. D. 5 in. Ibid.
34. Ditto. Normal grey, polished. Ibid.
35. Rim of cooking-pot f. 266 (late and hooked). Ibid.
36. Ditto. Normal form. Ibid. Should be first century.
37. Rim of bowl resembling f. 217 or 218. Ibid. Should be first century.
38. Large rim, D. *c.* 11 in. very rough and hard grey. Ibid. Date uncertain.
39. Part of a beaker f. 108, fine polished black ware. Lower rampart, with grey fragments of others.
40. Similar rim, brown, black polished. Ibid.
41. Base of a bowl, probably f. 330, decorated with impressed concentric circles, grey-black, polished. Upper rampart. Perhaps West Stowe ware. Trajan–Hadrian (?).
42. Two fragments of beakers ff. 122 or 123, with panels of dots. Fine grey ware. Upper rampart.
43. Two fragments of an unusual rim of the finest light grey ware with high smoky-grey polish ('Upchurch Ware'). Upper rampart.
44. Rim of a mortarium in good yellow-buff ware. Large diameter, with small grit, mixed dark and white. Not impossibly f. 497 and Antonine, but more probably f. 195A. Found in the vaulted brick drain on the west side of the altar, south of the temple in insula 22 (see p. 176). Flavian (?).

[1] *Arch. J.* lxiv, 216.

some indeterminate fragments of pottery and bronze. The collection runs up to the second half of the second century.

The Roman ditch may have been extensively opened by street trenches observed by A. M. Jarmin in 1913,[1]

but his account is not at all clear, and no sections were taken or remains recovered. The large altar to the Matres Suleviae is said to have been found 'in the town ditch'[2] at the SW. angle of the Town Wall (41).

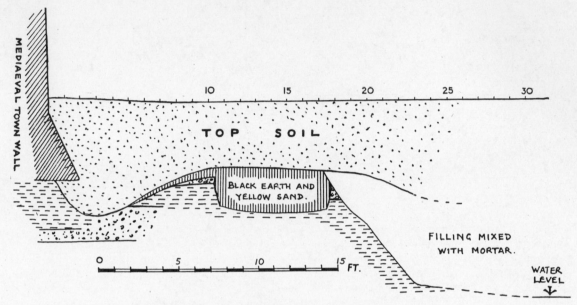

FIG. 24. Section outside town wall in Priory Street (p. 57).

16. THE SOUTH GATE

The gates on the south wall are little known because it has so long been closely built up. They provide ample scope for conjecture. Morant (p. 7) mentions 'St. Botolph's Gate, anciently called South Gate', but he is referring to the gate, hitherto supposed medieval, which stood at the south end of Queen Street, and which according to Cromwell (p. 173) 'was the last that remained to Colchester', for its traces did not disappear until 1817 or 1818.

R.C.H.M., p. 21, says that the road from Mersea (accepting Laver's line) should strike the town west of St. Botolph's Gate, and opposite Rye Gate, but that no record of such a gate is known. It would fall *about* the south end of Long Wire Street, but that street itself is full of Roman buildings; moreover the town wall can be inspected in the cellars of Messrs. Wilson's shop, where there is an opening through it. Both faces can be seen. Conditions are perfectly normal, and there is no trace of a gate. Of course, the area seen is small: a gate may lie to east or west, and it is noteworthy that Stukeley shows a gate in this position, besides St. Botolph's Gate. P. G. Laver also selects this position,[3] but on no very cogent grounds.

---

[1] *T.E.A.S.* xiii, 107, and see xii, 257.
[2] Existing now are remains of a very large ditch outside the north wall near the NE. corner (pl. VIII, A) and signs that something similar continued round the corner, possibly double along the east side. See p. 257 below.
[3] *J.B.A.* n.s. xxvi, 26. Laver did not favour the St. Botolph's

Gate site because, he says, Roman foundations extend across the site, there are remains of Roman houses just inside, and a Roman burial was found just outside. Unfortunately we have not the exact sites of these, without which we can make no judgement.

Thus the main south gate remains uncertain. It may yet prove to have lain at St. Botolph's (see p. 10 and note 5).

From Long Wire Street westwards the wall is well preserved, but obscured by modern buildings. Bastion 6 probably stood under the house on the north side of the Marlborough Head, while some remains of bastion 7 can be seen under the former Aberdein's Restaurant (which looks up Long Wire Street). There may well have been a bastion 8 250 ft. west of this at the back of the former Rose and Crown, but Morant shows only one west of Queen Street.

There was a small arch, with double ring of tiles, in the town wall just east of Scheregate. A good pencil drawing is in one of Wire's notebooks, and a reference to its discovery in the Diary, 31/3/1846. It cannot now be seen. Another, perhaps similar, is mentioned as in the base of the Roman (town) wall in the back yard of a Mr. Chaplin who lived 'half way down St. John's Street'.[1]

17. THE SCHEREGATE OR SOUTHSCHERD

97. Though often mentioned in medieval records, this gate is probably not Roman. It is passed over by former writers on the Roman gates. The ascent through it is so steep that it is stepped; moreover the town wall runs unbroken under the steps. It is supposed to have been made to provide a short cut between St. John's Abbey and the town. In 1926 a trench for a cable was cut through the steps (on the east side) and the masonry of the town wall was found to be at least 14 ft. thick, the outer face being imperfect.[2] It was assumed this was a gate-tower as at the NE. postern, but the subsequent discovery of other internal towers makes either tower or gate possible. If it is the latter, then the gate must lie east of the steps, for the wall continues under the buildings westwards. The inner face of the wall is 18 in. south of the south face of the top step.

18. THE HEAD GATE

Of this gate, regarded throughout the medieval period as the chief gate of the town, we know very little. The site lies under a broad and busy road-junction, and most trenches opened there are full of pipes and cables, so that all the ground has been disturbed. Morant says: 'Head Gate, called in records Heved or Haved Gate, and in Latin *Porta Capitalis*, is now [1766] taken down.' He adds that two brick pillars

were erected to mark the site, and that East Gate was similarly marked. On his town plan he shows a rough arch over the street at Head Gate, but this is probably a conventional sign.

The question of whether this was a Roman gate is fully discussed by Wheeler and Laver[3] with a bias in favour of a Roman date, and *R.C.H.M.* points out that the Domesday survey is based on this present London road. The discovery that North Gate was Roman has much strengthened the supposition. Wheeler and Laver remark: 'the presence of a Roman gate on the site [of Head Gate] . . . demands a brief explanation'. The latter is that the main Roman road was at some time in the late Roman period diverted from the Balkerne Gate to Head Gate, and Dr. Horace Round[4] is affirmed to have under-estimated the antiquity of the modern road which enters Head Gate from London.

Now the metalling to the Balkerne Gate has been seen several times (p. 3), but that of the road to Head Gate has never been seen, not even in the trenches made in 1913, to which Mr. Jarmin refers (p. 255), as I was informed by Mr. Rudsdale.

Dr. Horace Round (loc. cit. 199) was quite correct in pointing out that the road to the Balkerne Gate was obliterated when the Saxon open-field system was laid out in the area concerned. The date of this operation is not known, but it certainly would not follow directly upon the end of the Roman régime. In the interval the Roman road may have become much obscured. The main point is to decide when the Balkerne Gate ceased to function. Until this can be done we do not know when the London road was diverted to Head Gate, but in the absence of a Roman metalled road we prefer to regard this change as happening after, perhaps long after, the Roman period. Not before this could we place the extraordinary phenomenon which we encounter within the Balkerne Gate where the main street is built over on the west of the Head Street–North Hill line and that part of it lying west of the old Three Crowns was out of use as a street when our earliest records start (*c.* 1280).

No actual remains of Head Gate have been planned, and nothing very concrete is known regarding them. The following is the extent of our information.

166. A note in a manuscript book of Alderman H. Laver, dated 18/8/1893, reads: 'In excavating a trench in Head Street to replace a gas main the men came upon

---

[1] *T.E.A.S.* xii, 257.   [2] *C.M.R.* 1928, 6.
[3] *J.R.S.* ix, 151 f.
[4] *T.E.A.S.* xiv, 201 ff. Those holding the theory tended to

regard Head Gate as a late gate (*J.B.A.* n.s. xxvi, 26), but the discovery of a Roman North Gate gives it a companion and reduces this possibility.

some brickwork and also portions of a rubble stone wall at a depth of four feet, directly opposite the remains of the Roman wall in Sir Isaac's Walk.[1]

'As this was the site of the Head Gate, pulled down in 1753[2] they would appear to be portions of this gateway. The brickwork was of small bricks 2 by 4 by 8 ins.; part, possibly, of the mediaeval wall of the gate.

'Crossing the trench from E.–W. was a carefully built stone wall, and 15 ft. 6 in. further north lay a similar, parallel wall. The space between them at the bottom of the trench was filled with rubble similar to that of the Roman town wall. The brick wall ran from N.–S. between these two, as if it might be part of the side wall of the gate. The excavations did not reach the foundations of any of the walls.

'In front of these walls, to the south, was plainly to be seen the ancient level of the street outside Head Gate, as a pavement formed of cobbles and other stones was cut through at a depth of three feet from the street.[3] The tops of these stones show considerable wear, being quite smooth.[4]

'The later cobble paving of this town is mostly of water worn flints from the chalk. These earlier ones[5] are smaller and are of various materials, flints from the chalk, much water worn, lumps of quartz, bits of volcanic trap and other early rocks. They exactly correspond to the larger pebbles picked out of the local gravels.'

Some twenty years later Alderman Jarmin described similar remains[6] when a trench for a drain was carried 'practically through the old gateway . . . revealing the footings of the Roman structure a few feet north of the tablet . . . in the wall of the new Liberal Club. The footings consisted of the usual square Roman bricks or tiles with a course of septaria above.' There is nothing here which might not be town wall. He goes on to connect a cellar, probably Tudor, about 30 ft. farther north, with the gate-house. The latter we may disregard.

At this very spot or near it, portions of an arch of Roman tile were observed about 1933. They may have belonged to a Roman drain running N.–S. Such drains are known to have emerged through the wall near the East Gate and near Scheregate steps (pp. 45, 59).

In the absence of better facilities to observe these remains we have to keep in mind the brick columns mentioned by Morant. Certain Roman tiles built in an oblique line across the pavement (**128**) on the west side of Headgate Corner are to be taken with caution; they can hardly be of Roman date. Just to the north of them the foundation of the town wall remains in an imperfect state, under the pavement.

In point of fact, no definite remains of a Roman Head Gate have yet been proved, but it is probable that there was a gate, though not of any large size, on the eastern part of the present street. It would serve a road running out roughly on the line of the present Butt Road, which has large Roman cemeteries on both sides. (See also Jarmin's observations, loc. cit.)

Westwards from Head Gate the town wall stands high behind the houses all along the north side of Crouch Street, and is mostly very inaccessible. It has not been explored, but we can show photographs taken for P. G. Laver of a portion exposed behind Messrs. Bland's office in 1925 just west of Head Gate (pl. XIII, D). The face here is of the irregular work in small stones already noted as part of the patchings in Priory Street (p. 50). On the right there are traces of the tile courses of the Roman work. The lower part of the wall is of better build than the upper, but is not the normal Roman work. It is clear that the wall here is much repaired at more than one period.

The extreme SW. corner, which must have been very little rounded, is one of the few places where the wall has disappeared. Somewhere close to this gap was the 'Royal Battery' at the time of the siege, and the wall was destroyed by the orders of Fairfax (p. 16). Soon after passing the corner the wall is present again and in excellent preservation most of the way to the Balkerne Gate.

19. THE SOUTH-WEST POSTERN

Morant (p. 7) says there were three posterns, and of this one: 'The West Postern in St. Mary's Churchyard . . . sometimes called the postern near Colkyngs castell (Court Rolls, 15 Hen. VI and 35 Hen. VIII) . . . but when the church was rebuilt (after the Siege) that postern being low and inconvenient, part of the wall was taken down in order to enlarge the passage, and stone steps made instead of the sloping ascent there.'

---

[1] The remains of the town wall are not visible in Sir Isaac's Walk. They can be seen, by permission, in the cellar of the Liberal Club.

[2] Our only source for this date.

[3] Presumably, then, running over the masonry just described.

[4] Compare the cobbling at North Gate, p. 33.

[5] Laver implies he thinks the early road Roman; he does not say in what direction it might lead. We wonder whether it was a medieval surface he saw.

[6] *T.E.A.S.* xiii, 107 (1915).

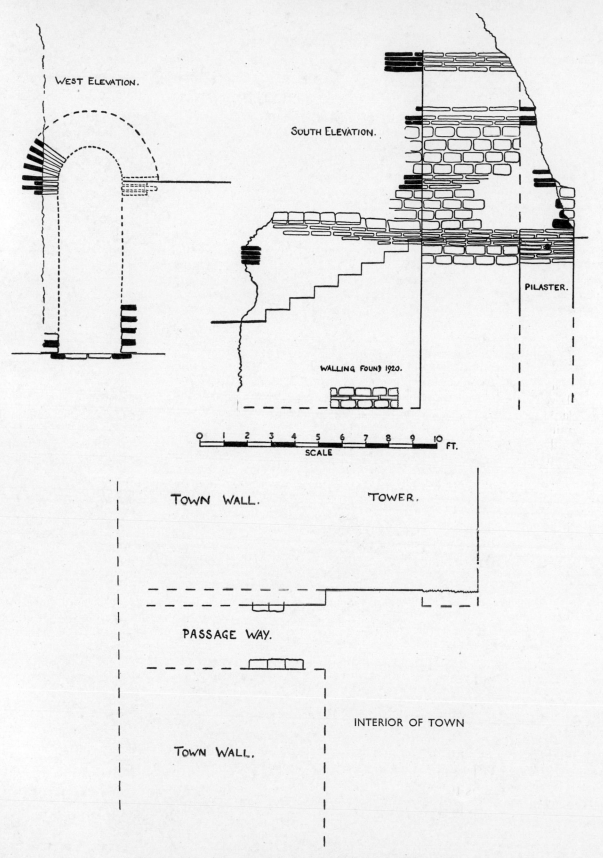

WEST ELEVATION.

SOUTH ELEVATION.

PILASTER.

WALLING FOUND 1920.

0 1 2 3 4 5 6 7 8 9 10

SCALE

FT.

TOWN WALL.

TOWER.

PASSAGE WAY.

INTERIOR OF TOWN

TOWN WALL.

FIG. 25. Elevations and plan, St. Mary's (SW.) Postern, p. 60.

Duncan, p. 57, says: 'there are evidences of an arch at St. Mary's Postern and of a tower'.

In June 1920 the steps were partly removed for an excavation, and, at the request of P. G. Laver, Mr. W. D. Clarke made drawings of what was revealed. The evidence was limited by the size of the excavation, but indicated that something unusual lay here.

In 1938 the steps were again disturbed and the writer was able to secure further information, with the aid of which the following account can be put together.

The tower, situated immediately north of the present opening through the town wall, projects 6 ft. 3 in. from the interior face of the wall and is 17 ft. 6 in. long. The construction is identical, and of one build, with the town wall, and, except in measurements, the tower is exactly like the other interior towers, save in one respect.

Part of the face of the south wall of the tower is preserved (below present ground-level) and at its east end it sets forward as a tiled pilaster 2 ft. 3 in. wide. Its tiles had been chipped away nearly flush with the wall-face. On the west side of this face the main wall itself had been similarly cut away when the breach in the wall was made in Morant's time.

The amount cut away is shown by Mr. Clarke's plan to have been 8 in. (see plan, fig. 25, C), which enables us to place the remains, which he not unnaturally took for a drain, on the plan. Using the level of the uppermost of the present steps as a datum, we can now arrive at the relative position of the remains of the arch still visible in the broken wall on the north side (fig. 25). The opening proves too tall for a drain and must have been a door.

The lower part was uncovered for a length of 3 ft. 6 in. in 1920. The passage was 2 ft. 7½ in. wide, floored with tile at the sides, and with stone slabs resembling Purbeck marble in the middle. They were worn as if by traffic. The walls were of alternate courses of septaria and tile, that on the south side with eight courses standing and a height of 2 ft., that on the north only 10 in. high, with three courses. From the face of the latter to the broken face of the town wall was 8 in. This is probably the distance of the opening from the face of the tower (see plan) and probably gives us the depth of the pilaster which stood at the SE. corner. The arrangement is very similar to the recesses in which

the gates folded back at the NE. postern. That the passage-way stopped at the inner face of the town wall is shown by the fact that the tiles of the vaulting cease at this line (see fig. 25). There are remains of four courses of them still in the wall, and (as can be seen in pl. XIII, D), assuming they were about 17 in. long they agree entirely in position with the reconstructed drawing, leaving little doubt of the main dimensions of the opening. The height, accordingly, from floor to spring of the vault was 7 ft. 1½ in., or 7½ Roman feet.

Nothing has been indicated to correspond, on the south side of this entrance, to the pilaster on the tower, but there is no proof that there was nothing there. The SE. corner of the opening is masked by brickwork which Mr. Clarke describes as medieval, and the ground opposite the pilaster has not been opened.

There can be no doubt, whatever the complete plan may prove to be, that the tower was solid to well above the level of the back of the vaulting, which must have been well below the level of the parapet-walk. One wonders how the pilaster was finished at the top.

The drawings are partly composite. The position of the steps and street level has been indicated. Much of the masonry shown in fig. 25, B is in different planes, as the damaged wall and tower slope away from the observer. Thus the pilaster probably had no septaria in it, those showing actually lying in the tower behind it. It is noticeable that one lacing course of tiles has only three courses for part of its length, and that the arch seems to have sprung from the lowest course of a normal band of four courses.

The outer face of the town wall here is not yet fixed. Existing tiles at one point suggest a position for it, but as this gives a total thickness of only 7 ft. 7½ in., instead of the usual 8 ft. 8 in., we do not propose to accept it at present.

20. The Date of the Town Wall, Summary[1]

Five recorded sections have been cut behind the interior face of the town walls, namely, sections I, V, VI, VII, and Miss Richardson's (IA) in 1951. Of these the most easily and completely observed was the last, which produced a clear stratification and a fair abundance of closely stratified pottery. It may be considered from two standpoints, (A) structural and (B) ceramic.

[1] This summary is by Sir Mortimer Wheeler, to whom we are most grateful for his careful consideration of the material.

(A) *Structural evidence.* For nearly the whole height of the inner face of the wall (10 ft.) the pointing was as fresh as on the day on which it was executed, and irregular ledges or lumps of projecting mortar remained at various points. The clear indication was that from the outset this face had been masked by a bank to a height of not less than 10 ft. at the wall. The bank in fact survived in section and could be subdivided broadly into two main parts, an upper and a lower, separated by a mixed layer which had to be considered as a potential occupation layer. A difficulty, however, in regarding the bank as of two periods was presented by the clean and sharp condition of the wall above the summit of the lower 'bank'. Furthermore, as a separate unit this lower 'bank' would have been of insignificant size.

(B) *Ceramic evidence.* The Samian sherds from *both* 'banks' extended down to the Antonine period, so that on the evidence available the two parts of the bank cannot be distinguished chronologically.

In this section, therefore, there is a clear balance of evidence in favour of a bank contemporary with the wall and not earlier than the Antonine period.

Comparable ceramic evidence was noted by Mr. Hull from section VII, where no clear earlier 'bank' could be detected and where the pottery led the excavator to date the bank as a whole to 'the reign of Hadrian'. This dating must be regarded as a *terminus post quem*.

Again, in section I the wall was cut through a layer ascribed to *circa* A.D. 100, and is therefore not earlier than that date. Whether or no the overlying material represents a bank was uncertain owing to the proximity of an internal tower: the material contained Antonine sherds.

In section V the bank again showed two separate heaps, but the upper was placed upon the lower 'before any rubbish could collect upon it' and the inference is that the work was all of one date.

Section VI was marred by a large intrusive pit or trench behind the wall, but the deposit of stiff loam, marked 'II' on the section, must on any showing have been part of the bank and produced 'rims of probably Antonine date'.

At the NE. Gate it was observed that the drain under the gate was contemporary with it and with the 'Mithraeum' in the Hollytrees Meadow. Unfortunately, however, it has not yet been possible to date the 'Mithraeum', so that synchronism carries us no further, though it may become significant at some future date.

In summary, there is a convergence of evidence upon the second century for the first construction of the Colchester defences, with an indication that the date was probably not earlier than the Antonine period. It may be remarked that this coincides closely with the most recent dating of the town wall of London, which was certainly not earlier than *circa* A.D. 180, whilst that of Verulamium is now shown to be of late second century date.

III

THE STREETS

1. THE MAIN AXIS FROM BALKERNE GATE TO EAST GATE

IN the Balkerne Gateway, under the blocking wall, there are 19 in. of gravel metalling lying on 9 in. of hard rammed loam, then sand.[1]

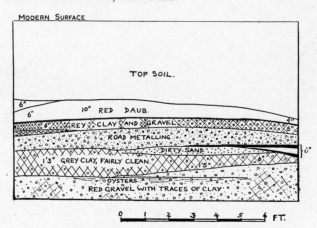

FIG. 26. Street section at Grosvenor Garage. [**121**], p. 64.

121. The metalling was partly revealed in a pit for a petrol pump in the Grosvenor Garage, at a point some 140 ft. west of the building line at the top of North Hill.[2]

At the bottom of the section (fig. 26), 7 ft. 6 in. from the surface, was a thick layer of red gravel, with traces of clay. A foot of this at least was seen, and it may represent the first roadway, though no really good surface was observed. The southern 9 ft. could have been a roadway, and a large stone on the north side may mark its limit. From this a layer of rubbish, including oyster-shells, spread southwards. There followed a make-up of fairly clean grey clay, to over a foot thick, with a lenticular patch of dirty sand above part of it, and overlapping this, on the south, occupation layers of charcoal, cinders, slag, and sand. Upon this lay a strong and undoubted road-metalling of gravel, cambered up to 10 in. thick and extending the whole 12 ft. of the section. Above this lay 5 in. of grey clay and gravel, with the appearance of a repair, as it follows the camber, but it can hardly have formed a good road-surface. P. G. Laver commented on the absence of any lime-concrete base such as he saw near East Lodge

[1] Laver, Diary, 6/12/1922.

(**112**, p. 146). Finally, we have an irregular heap of red daub, 10 in. thick at its maximum, representing the burnt walls of the surrounding buildings. Above this lay only the accumulated top-soil from the Roman period onwards. The burnt daub is very extensive; see the next section, and compare observations on insulae 9 and 17.

A parish boundary follows party-walls and fences right through from the south side of the south carriage-way of the gate to the modern building face on North Hill. This should approximately represent the south side of the Roman main street. Thereafter it lies under High Street, which is exceptionally wide for an ancient town. At the west end it is 57 ft., and about half-way along it is 72 ft. wide. Obviously the Roman street, which is nearly 40 ft. wide at the Balkerne Gate, and is unlikely to have kept so great a width throughout, would only occupy part of the modern street. The metalling has been seen at each end and south of the 'Forum'. Foundations of house walls have been found under the pavement of High Street on the north side, and under the roadway as far as 18 ft. from the building face on the south side, apparently running on. The latter find was, naturally, at the extreme south curve 350 ft. from Head Street (**82, 83**).

114. Outside the south wall of the 'Forum' the Norman ditch of the Castle has left in position part of the Roman street, of which several layers are preserved (pl. XIV, A, B; fig. 86). The first street was laid on the natural clayey loam and consists of a horizontal band of yellow gravel 7 in. thick. Between it and the building was a sloping footwalk of concrete, of the same thickness, divided from the street-metalling by a slot 6 in. wide. This had clearly held a stone or wood kerb. Against the foundation the concrete stops at the offset, leaving a slot, the width of the offset (8 in.), between it and the wall. This may have held a base for an ornamental marble sheathing. But it might also be argued that this is evidence that the masonry is cut through the concrete and is of a period later than it. The finished appearance of the edge of the concrete was against this view, and the slope up of the concrete to the building suggests that the building was there first. A slot such as this is not infrequently found, and actually recurs in the third period in this section. We therefore regard the building here as of the first period on the site, that is Claudian, and since it is so massive

[2] In 1935, *J.R.S.* xxvi, 254.

it must belong to some great public building, such as the temple.

At a later date the street was made up with yellow sand to nearly a foot higher, and upon this was laid a gravel metalling 9 in. thick. This made a new footway necessary, and this was again of white concrete, running right up against the wall, sloping to the street as before, and with a vertical end, where a kerb has been removed or has perished. Between this and the road-metal the ground was disturbed by the insertion of the drain in period III.

In period III 5 in. of sandy gravel were laid upon the second road surface, and then 7 in. of gravel, forming a third surface. Contemporary with this was the very fine tile drain set in the roadway. It was 3 ft. wide, with walls nearly 18 in. thick, the whole built of good building tiles (pl. XIV, A, C, fig. 86), four courses in the south wall and three in the north. From the drain to the wall the surface was level, made up with dirty gravel, and over the second footwalk a third had been laid, the stone kerbs of which remained in position. This was presumably the last Roman level, not only because of this, but because directly upon it comes the great accumulation of intensely black earth which has to be equated with all the years intervening between it and the under side of the gravel bank of the Norman rampart.

In the black soil filling the drain lay a coin of Antoninus Pius and nothing else.

East of this point the following exposures of the main street (E.–W.) have been made. We owe notes upon them all to the unflagging energy of P. G. Laver, in whose diary they are recorded.

112. In July 1921 drainage trenches cut in the middle of High Street, 400 ft. west of the site of East Gate, revealed a considerable length of the retaining wall (*sic*) of the Roman main street, with road-metal on its south side. The wall was 2 ft. wide, 18 in. high, and carefully levelled on top. The metalling was of gravel (including large stones) over successive layers of grouted stones and grey clay, to a total depth of about 2 ft. Objects found are in the Museum, and include part of the skull of a small child and a bronze brooch (4089.21), and the entry adds that the wall was of septaria and had an offset, and the operations caused the relaying of the pavement 'near the Gate House (East Lodge)'.[1]

21/11/1922: 'An excavation on the south side of High Street opposite Winsley's House and east of the gate of the Minories garden, exposed part of the cobbled surface of the Roman street. The trench cut was 19 ft. from the south building line. The cobbles were well-placed, close and very hard to get out. The bed on which they were set seemed lime, on top of old mortar and other filling, very hard rammed, containing a few large septaria stones and broken Roman tiles. Below this was hard rammed gravel and under this clayey loam, also well-rammed. Undisturbed sand was reached at 6 ft. . . . It is not usual, in fact I have not seen before, the paved surface of our Roman High Street, the side wall bounding the street was looked for . . . [but not, apparently, found] . . . that on the N. is 5 ft. 8 ins. from the houses . . . [thus] . . . the street must have been at least 31 ft. wide.'

On 27/11/22 Laver adds a further note: 'One trench was cut [i.e. in 1921] in the roadway against the N. kerb, opposite the W. jamb of the gate [of East Lodge]. Here the top 3 ft. 3 ins. comprised two feet of modern road metal and then about 15 ins. of very hard old road metal principally gravel. This lay on 9 ins. of lime and rubble of quite light colour, below which was one foot of grey clay, which rested on rammed sand. The distinction between the bands was very clear.'

'Another trench was cut N. of the kerb, across the gateway and as far as the next house east [Winsley's]. Here a piece of walling was exposed and followed to the east. It was 20 ins. below the pavement and the face was 5 ft. 8 ins. from the front wall of the house. It ran parallel to the line of the present houses, or very nearly so, perhaps having a slight trend NE., but as only 12 ft. were exposed too much must not be made of it. The wall . . . was identified as the boundary wall of the Roman road, for the metal, lime and clay layers, which showed a definite camber, came right up to the wall and no further. . . .'[2]

Another exposure was made in April 1937—'a water main laid outside Winsley's House showed road metalling beginning opposite the W. side of the W. window and extending to the centre of the E. window. The depth from the surface was about 18 ins. There was dark soil beneath it (This seemed too high up to be Roman, but remains uncertain). The metalling was 8 ins. thick, of large gravel, with some broken brick. A stone wall again appeared, coincident with the N. wall of the trench, opposite the E. side of the W. window of Hill Crest. It continued to the end of this house at least. The depth to the top was over 2 ft., height at least 18 ins.'

Now if a straight line be drawn from the north edge of the Roman street here to the north side of the main carriage-way of the Balkerne Gate it will also point to the East Gate, but it will put the main Roman street in a very strange position.

i. From here to East Stockwell Street it lies under modern buildings, and its north edge will be under the north pavement of High Street, exactly where walls

---

[1] Accessions Book, and *C.M.R.* 1922, 12.

[2] *J.R.S.* x, 89.

of Roman buildings have been found, but no street (**124**).

ii. From Head Street to West Stockwell Street it will run off the line of High Street and under the buildings on the north side, running exactly over the site of the Roman pottery shop (**127**).

iii. It will run under the George Hotel, exactly over the site of the red pavement (**157**).

iv. Hence it would pass under, and then behind, the houses on the north side of High Street, and opposite the Castle it would run through the Roman structure occupying the centre of the south side of the 'forum' (**114**), whereas these remains most definitely have an important street on their south side.

v. The parish boundary running east from the south side of the Balkerne Gate diverges from this line.

It is therefore necessary to conclude that the main E.–W. street was not straight, but, in some way, diverted southwards, so as to pass south of **114**, and if we suppose that it followed the parish boundary as far as the top of North Hill, or better, across the first two insulae, it could then run parallel to the rest of the grid as far as the crossroads east of **114**. Here it seems quite clear that it resumed its natural line.

This is curious treatment for a Cardo Maximus, but we cannot avoid it.[1] It may be compared with that at Trier, where the grid is much larger and more elaborate than ours, yet the Cardo Maximus is not straight. The forum is not yet well known, but the eastern part looks perilously near encroaching on the street (unless the latter passes through a forum covering three insulae). See the latest plan in *Studies presented to D. M. Robinson*, i, 494.

2. North Gate to Head Gate

Since we still do not know which was the main N.–S. street, we take next the first N.–S. street on the west, which runs from North Gate, by North Hill and Headgate Street, to Head Gate. It is the only Roman street whose whole course lies under modern streets. It seems to have had houses of the best class on both sides of it in Roman days, and to have come through the Dark Ages without losing its identity. (For the gates see pp. 32, 59.) The east side is pinned by the known east side of North Gate, which approximately coincides with the modern east kerb opposite Balkerne Lane. The gate may have been only some 11 ft. wide (we do not know), but the street would be at least 18 ft. wide.

15. The line is continued by a stone wall noted by Wire, who noted (Diary, 25/5/1842): 'While the workmen were digging on the E. side of North Hill to lay

down a drain of gutter bricks, when opposite the gates of St. Peter's Church they dug onto a wall of the same sort of materials as the town walls, which continued running up the hill about 10 feet, when it turned in towards the churchyard, and another wall of a similar description, reaching from the lower part of Mr. Hall's house down the hill to within about 10 ft. of the other, when it made a similar curve towards the churchyard. Between the two walls where they run towards the churchyard is a Roman road, which appears to have crossed the hill from the Waggon and Horses Inn yard, which is nearly opposite' (fig. 73).

The line thus obtained, projected, brings us to a point under the modern street at Head Gate, just over 10 ft. from the building line on the east side.

The 'Roman road' at St. Peter's Church is obviously the entrance to some premises in insula 18. The red pavement shown by Cutts (**177**) need not worry us, for Cutts's red overprint is inaccurate.

84. Here, in insula 25, Wire noted that he saw a concrete roadway, which he shows running N.–S., on the site of the old Dutch church, just west of Head Street, and rather farther west of the probable Roman street line. We know no more of this.

Trenches cut along the west side of Head Street from Head Gate to High Street were all clear of the street-metalling of Roman days, as indeed the plan shows they should be.

3. The First E.–W. Street North of High Street

This is a difficult subject. We may expect the insulae north of the High Street to be longer N.–S. than the average.[2] And on this line, if anywhere, we have evidence of change in street position, if not of grid.

This street has only been observed thrice, and in no case really satisfactorily.

125. In 1930 an extension was built on to the south side of St. Martin's House. A deep trench afforded a section of a Roman street running E.–W., but about 40 ft. south of the line expected. Three distinct road-surfaces could be seen, and several repairs. In the lowest road-metal a second brass coin of Nero was found.[3]

The section obtained (fig. 27) was 17 ft. long, but reduced to only 14 ft. lower down. From the modern concrete surface to the undisturbed sandy loam was 8 ft., the loam sloping down to the north. Immediately upon it was a patch of charcoal and above this, in the northern 8 ft., a 4-in. layer of gravel with 2–4 in. of

---

[1] The above was written and the plan drawn before **196** (which had been overlooked) was added to the plan. The confirmation is welcome (p. 150).

[2] Haverfield, *Ancient Town Planning*, 77 (and footnote), 88, 125.

[3] *C.M.R.* 1931, 8.

burnt clay upon it. These layers, which approximately levelled the site, may have belonged to early buildings. Or taken in conjunction with the shallow depression at its south edge, they might be the remains of an early street. In the absence of evidence for its continuity no more can be said.

Above this was a foot or more of sand, which had a burnt appearance. Upon this lay a hard metalling of 4 in. of gravel with an excellent even surface, only

however, have been quite the final phase, for we see part of what may have been a later roadway, consisting of 3–4 in. of gravel, lying upon it, to the right of the pink mortar. But it has been so damaged by a late-seventeenth-century pit that one cannot be certain.

Above this level the ground is all surface-deposit, with recent foundations here and there.

The workman who found the coin was very positive about its position, which is shown on the section.

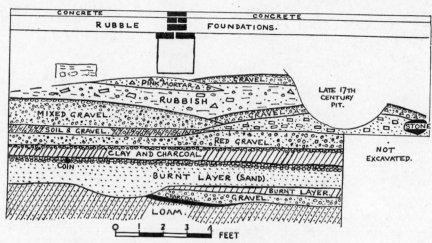

FIG. 27. Street section at St. Martin's House. [125], p. 66.

slightly tilted to the north. This is the first definite surface in the section, and contained the coin of Nero, which could not have got there before A.D. 64. Next above this lay 6 to 10 in. of burnt clay and charcoal, with another thin and even layer of gravel covering it, this time again practically level.

The next horizontal band is 9 in. thick, mostly of red gravel, but partly covered by a 4-in. layer of gravel and clay, upon which the street was made up anew, its main body being a foot of mixed gravel, with a strong camber. Nine feet, probably the northern half, of this show in the section. North of this we show a cambered bank of brick rubble, up to 6 in. thick, capped by a 4-in. layer of gravel and mortar, similarly cambered, with a definite surface. The large stone seen on the right may be part of the rubble, or part of a rough kerbing to support the north edge of what looks like a 9-ft. wide footwalk. The rammed gravel surface of the street projects into these two layers as if all three had been laid in one operation. Above it lies the great layer of destruction, represented by 6 to 15 in. of building rubbish covering everything, with a very prominent patch of pink mortar in the top of it. This may not,

156. Another point where this street has certainly been encountered was in the garden behind nos. 4 and 5 North Hill, when an air-raid shelter was made there in June 1940.[1] Owing to the great haste in which the work was executed no satisfactory observation could be kept. The following is the best that can be made of the matter. It will be observed that the line of the street is about 40 ft. north of that just described.

The site was excavated to a depth of 8 ft. and the shelter stood lengthwise (E.–W.) upon a Roman street. Scarcely anywhere did the excavation extend beyond the limits of the metalling, both sides of which, however, appeared to be uncovered, but their accurate plotting was rendered impossible by the many mutilations they had suffered.

The roadway was made up of a thick bed of yellow gravel, very tightly packed and very difficult to break through. The surface was found at a depth of about 5 ft. and the metalling was over a foot thick in the middle,[2] thinning towards the edges. The width, so far as could be ascertained, was about 17 ft.

Definitely from below the road-metal, in the NE. corner of the shelter, at a depth of 8 ft., but not

[1] *J.R.S.* xxxi, 137; *C.M.R.* 1944, 18.
[2] I do not understand Laver's note in his Diary, 5/6/40, which makes the road-metal 4 ft. 10 in. thick (!), with horizontal divisions or layers. He also supposes the centre of the road to

have lain near the south side of the excavation, interpreting the slope of the road to the north as due to camber. It may be so, but would make the road unduly wide, and to us it seemed otherwise.

definitely sealed, came a piece of T.S. f. 29, and several fragments of T.S. f. 37 in 'transitional' style. Other pottery found attested a mid-first-century occupation, including a stamp of *Licinus*.

The following coins were stated to have been actually found in the road-metal: an *as* of Claudius, Minerva type, a poor copy; three pre-Neronian second brass, one almost certainly Antonia, the others illegible; a denarius of M. Antony; three second brass of

roadway had largely been removed by later excavations. There was, however, a street on this line, at a low level, corresponding to the lowest levels of the N.–S. street found at the same time. Upon this lay a burnt layer, and an accumulation thicker than that on the N.–S. street. Above this the street had been made up again, corresponding to some of the later levels of the N.–S. street, but the uppermost of these had been dug away.

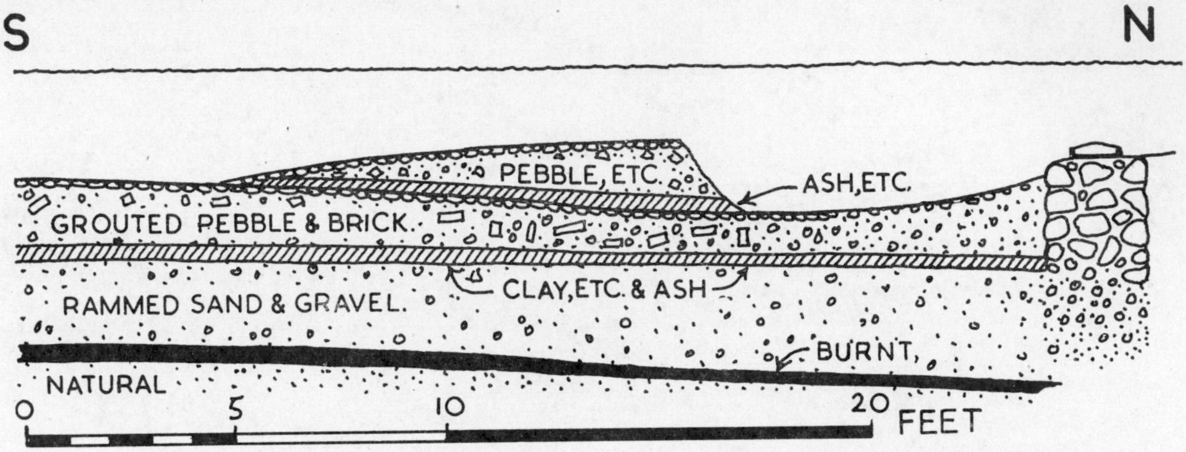

Fig. 28. Street section at Park Bandstand. [36], p. 68. (*After R. E. M. Wheeler.*)

Nero, one of Vespasian, and two illegible, but of first-century appearance.

Along the south side of the street lay a litter of building rubble and in it coins of Victorinus, Carausius, and Constantine I. The north wall of insula 18 had been robbed. It was probably, to some extent at least, a retaining wall.

In later Roman days a large pit had been cut so that its base passed right through the roadway (!), which clearly was, by then, out of use and buried from sight. The contents of this pit comprised pottery of all periods, and coins from Vespasian (?) and Hadrian to Constantine II, and a *Fel. Temp. Reparatio* type, probably also Constantinian.

Of the unstratified coins the latest is an illegible small brass of Honorius or Arcadius (or similar).

Of exceptional interest, however, is a single piece of pottery from the rim of a cooking-pot of thick black ware with brown surface like fig. 35, 5. It is hand-made and, to our view, undoubtedly Saxon. Although unstratified, there is no reason to regard it as a stray.

A large amount of pottery and other small finds came up in this excavation; they are all listed and preserved in the Museum.

Owing to the hasty nature of this work no more could be done than collect the finds. No section could be made. Over the garden wall, in the next premises to the east, a section was seen in 1950 (see p. 67), but the

For the rest of its course this street is uncertain. It was carefully sought at the south end of the insula 15 without success. The tower (**164**) at the Technical College must be close to its west end. The tower on the east wall is sited by Wheeler and Laver to the south, and by Cutts to the north, of this street. It should probably approximate to the east end of the street, the line of which also just passes the back of the temple, as happens, for example, at St. Bertrand de Comminges.

4. THE SECOND E.–W. STREET NORTH OF HIGH STREET

This is very poorly attested so far, except where it has been seen north and NE. of the Castle. The towers at each end have not been seen, but there is reason to believe that masonry visible in the grounds of the Technical College is part of tower no. 2.

The south wall of insula 6 was traced for 325 ft. It consisted of three to four courses of septaria on a footing of rammed sand and gravel, all grouted with yellowish-white mortar; the top was finished with a course of one, sometimes two, roof tiles with the flanges upwards and filled with mortar. The tiles were 14 in. wide, so that the septaria projected 6 in. on each side of them. Two sections of the street were made and showed widths of 23 ft. 7 in. and 24 ft. 6 in. of metalling respectively (fig. 28). The second cut showed natural loamy sand at 5 ft. 3 in. from the surface of the street. The metalling showed two periods, with incidental repairs. The stratum lying on the loam 'consisted of burnt material, principally wood, to an average depth of 3 ins.' (this layer was frequently observed at a low level in insula 6). Above this lay over 2 ft. of rammed sand and gravel, upon which lay 3–4 in. of clay, mixed with white mortar, oyster-shells, and much wood ash. Upon this lay the road surface of gravel and broken

Above the red gravel lay a bank of rubble and rubbish, from 4 to 11 in. thick, highest at the south of the road, and above this some 4 ft. of dark surface-soil. Two small patches of mortar lay on the dark layer which lay on the clay. They may have belonged to the floor of a room, or may be the mortar foundations alone surviving from late walls (visible above the shovel on right of picture).

The above account is from the writer's observations,

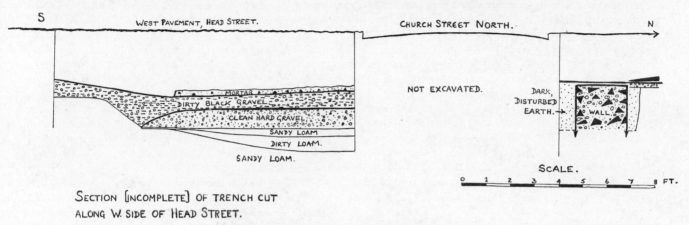

SECTION (INCOMPLETE) OF TRENCH CUT ALONG W. SIDE OF HEAD STREET.

FIG. 29. Section in Head Street. [135], p. 69.

brick compounded with mortar and iron hard, varying from 8 to 12 in. in thickness. The metalling was weaker along the north side, and sagged.

The road was made up in a narrower form by a bank of rammed sand and gravel, with some tile and much oyster-shell, canted to the south to counter the slope of the ground and running on to the older surface to the south, but leaving a gap of 5 to 8 ft. along the south of the retaining-wall. It lay on a layer of sand, clay, and ash, and had been patched at various periods. Pottery from the ash layer was not very determinate, but was considered not later than mid-second century, but may have been old when deposited. The second section, near the gate of the houses (see below, p. 84), was similar in the upper part, but showed the second road cambering down to the north, presumably to approach the entrance. The lower part was not excavated.

120. When the old Park Café was pulled down in 1930 a deep cutting was made in the west side of the bank of the Norman ditch for the basement of the new café. In it (pl. XIV, C) the street was clearly seen in the west face as a cambered bank of red gravel, 12 ft. wide and 8 in. thick. Beneath it was a layer of dark earth and stones about 2 in. thick. This lay on a black layer, about 1 in. thick, apparently of decayed wood. This capped a thick deposit of brown, cheesy clay, the upper foot of which was darker, the whole being 4 ft. thick at least and almost certainly natural.

largely assisted by a good account in Laver's Diary (24/2/30).

When the Hollytrees' Meadow was explored in 1927 9 this street was again found, 120 ft. farther east, where it was not at all strong, laid on clay, and of uncertain width, probably about 18 ft., with no camber. The metalling was only 4–5 in. of rather small and loose gravel and mortar. Farther east, the point where it should cross the tile-built drain was examined with interest, for the drain stands so high that it would be difficult to cross. Unfortunately, just here some 38 ft. of the west side of the drain had been robbed, and the ground thoroughly disturbed, so that no traces of a street could be seen, unless in the appearance of more gravel than usual in the confused top-soil. The east wall of the drain, however, was still standing and the street could hardly have passed over it.

5. THE E.–W. STREET SOUTH OF HIGH STREET

This safely started at the postern gate at St. Mary's steps (p. 60), but nothing has been seen on this line until we reach the Public Library.

169. In 1936 a trench for a water main was cut along the west kerb of Head Street, and the appearance of a street running E.–W. was noticed at the east end of Church Street North (fig. 29). The section shown begins 13 ft. south of the south kerb of the latter street. The main feature is a thick layer of dirty black gravel, reached generally at about 2 ft. 9 in. from the surface, but rising to only 2 ft. at the south end. It had been laid over a most pronounced, cambered bank of clean hard gravel, 9 in. thick, of which a width of 9 ft. was exposed. The cambered south side dipped to a small ditch caused by a definite rise in the sandy loam sub-soil. Beneath the clean gravel, which looked like a roadway, were two tapering layers of loam, the lower dirty, the upper sandy. The uppermost layer is seen as an irregular spread of mortar about 3 in. thick, partly overlying the black gravel.

The next 8 ft. 6 in. of the trench was tunnelled, and immediately after this came a deeply founded wall, in its foundation trench, its top only 2 ft. below the surface. It marks the north side of the street (if street it was) and the south boundary of insula 25. The maximum possible width of the street was, accordingly, 18 ft. This seems inadequate, and the position is 90 ft. north of the expected line. If a road at all it is possibly not a town street, but one of the several 18-ft. roads which have been found outside the walls, and which seem to have been laid down before the colonia was planned, possibly in connexion with an early military layout. Alternatively, its resemblance to a metalled road may be quite deceptive.

161–2. In 1938–9 the basements for the Public Library were excavated (pp. 209–10, fig. 103) and the work was watched for the Museum by E. J. Rudsdale. The NW. corner of the boundary-wall of insula 35 was found, thus fixing the position of two streets. Altogether some 40 ft. of the metalling of the E.–W. road were exposed, and it was 29 ft. wide between the walls of the insulae (27 and 35). It was pierced by a number of recent rubbish pits.

102. When the Wire Street Arcade was built in 1928 remains of a Roman street were exposed between insulae 30 and 38 at a point 70 ft. south of the expected line. The gravel metalling was much damaged and entirely destroyed at the west end. It was pierced by numerous pits and holes of later ages, so much so that it was difficult to find its exact line and width. 'It is about 20 ft. wide, made of rammed gravel, with a cobbled surface, a foot to 18 inches thick at the camber and tapering to the edges. At one part it was seen to run over the foundation of an earlier building, and coins, including one of Carausius, have been found under it.'[1] This is not surprising in view of its unexpected position. We may expect to find an earlier street lying more to the north.

6. THE SECOND N.–S. STREET

We have three exposures of this, and they do not line up. One is at the Public Library, where very little was seen of it; the next was at St. Martin's House, where a complete and measured section was obtained. The third, farther north, does not line up with these. We begin with it.

13. Laver, Diary, 'A trench cut in 1920 in Mr. Frost's garden 100 yards east of N. Hill, revealed a hard gravelled surface (probably road or passage). . . . Again, in 1922, extending a trench E. from the pavement (**14**) a road surface of fine road metal was found lying on black soil, below which was a heavier bed of metal, both showing camber, and in 1923 when three trees were dug out, 30 ft. from the N. wall of the garden, and opposite the W. end of the Three Cups stable a bed of hard rammed shingle was revealed on a bed of mortar, 10 in. thick. Below this was clay and shingle [sketch, 4 ft. of black topsoil]; gravel metalling 18 in. thick.'[2]

174. Naturally the above was taken as establishing the line of the street. But early in 1950, when an extension was added to the west end of the Telephone Exchange at St. Martin's House, it was sought, and found, again, somewhat farther west than was expected. Metalling was struck only a foot beneath the surface and turned out to be the surface of the N.–S. street. The section obtained (fig. 30) is the most impressive we have so far, despite the mutilation by later pits. From top to bottom (the natural sand) was nearly 6 ft., and the whole of this consisted of a sequence of road-surfaces separated by layers of mud.

The street ran between two stone walls, which are 25 ft. apart and not quite parallel. Neither, of course, belongs to the earliest period, they only came along when temporary buildings of wood or clay were replaced by stone. The earliest levels of the street, however, show that its line remained unaltered by the rebuilding.

The excavation (see p. 98) was carried out under difficulties and against time. The time spent on trying to plot accurately and individually each of the twenty-six layers of the road on the section proved useless; it was an impossible task. Though visible from a distance they could not be followed when close up.

The subsoil was soft yellow sand, the upper part of which was stained and dirty, presumably by worms, plant-roots, and possibly by cultivation and trampling. Upon this the first road was laid without any clay or loam bedding, and without stone or rubble foundation.

The first road was approximately central in the space

---

[1] *Essex County Standard*, 1/9/1928; *C.M.R.* 1929, 21, 22.
[2] Diary, under 19/11/23; *R.C.H.M.* 23, no. 13.

of the section, and had two cambered layers of gravel metalling, each about 5–6 in. thick, the lower of a greyish colour, the upper yellow. Mud appears on the surface of each, towards the sides, and upon this lay, on the east, a small bank of dirty gravel. A lenticular patch of gravel on the east side may represent a partial repair.

The presence of the great pit A has robbed the section of some of its significance, for the conditions are not the same on both sides of it. To the east all is street and road-metal, to the west the layers are much less

relationship to the roadways has gone. Above (F) is a layer of gravel and mud which looks like the last of the camber of a road. The last two levels under the concrete which crowns the section again indicate fire, the lower being almost entirely of burnt daub, the upper of mud, with burnt material scattered in it. Since neither appear in the roadway, perhaps the daub was used as hard core for a new pavement, but the burning belongs to the later burning of insula 10 (p. 98).

The pits are filled with black earth continuous with the top-soil and are of two kinds. (A) and (H) are large

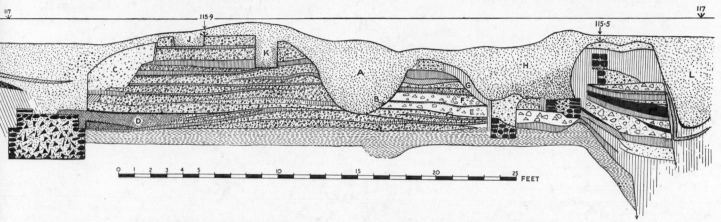

FIG. 30. Section of street and walls, St. Martin's House, 1950. [174], pp. 70 f., 98.

solid and do not tie in very well. They give the impression of having belonged to a footwalk of scarcely metalled nature. The first road would not appear to have had a footwalk, but the burnt layer which closes this period (D), while clearly covering the road on the east, is not clear under the lowest footwalk; on the contrary, there are heavy burnt layers higher up (E, F).

The subsequent road or roads were raised upon the burnt layer, in sequence, without further signs of fire, and seem to have been limited to the eastern part of the space. They consist alternately of layers of yellow gravel and mud. A curious fact was the way they were cut away on the east side, and the space filled by a light filling of sandy loam and fine gravel (C), as if there had been a ditch down this side. A similar feature occurs on the west (G), where the filling is similar, but in this case was possibly contemporary with the building of the wall.[1]

Taking the 'footway' next, the thick layer (E) was of muddy earth rather than gravel, with indications of fire. It had a defined upper surface upon which lay another thick layer (F) of muddy loam containing burnt daub, rubble, and tile. It is unfortunate that these layers are so interrupted (at B) that their correct

and rather formless, though it was later found that A went down deeply (on the south) as a well or shaft. (J) and (K) are rectangular and straight, and may represent the foundations of late buildings, though these would have been of wood, for no masonry or mortar was found in them. The remains in them included food bones and late Roman pottery, but no coins. The west side of the upper part of (C) seemed bounded by an upright dark line; compare the wooden structure in the road at Gurney Benham House (p. 6).

It is noticeable how high the street rides above the levels on each side of it. This is mostly due to excavations for stone-robbing, but it was noticed that the upper layers had actually been removed, and it is doubtful whether anything remained in position later than the second century, apart from the contents of the pits.

This road was perhaps the most valuable result of the excavation, which is described on p. 98. It was not possible to do much more with it. A large part of the metalling was removed by hand, in a search for coins, but none was found, nor indeed anything else, except the round, horizontal hole where, presumably, a hollow wooden drainpipe had been laid in the west side

---

[1] These conditions are closely paralleled by a street-section at Augst, Laur-Belart, p. 31.

of the metalling, following the direction of the street.[1] The north end, where a further section was most urgently required, was occupied by that modern cult-figure, the mechanical grab, which could on no account be moved. Around it the site was ruined. Only in the NW. corner was it possible to give a few hours to the study of appearances in the section.

In this corner there had been a street similar in nature, and at a similarly low level, to the lowest just described. This should be the first street north of the High Street. It also was covered by a heavy burnt layer, much thicker than our (D), giving the impression that much time had elapsed before the street was repaired. The restoration of the street lay at a high level. Possibly this may account for the coins of Vespasian found 'in the metalling' just west of this point. We were most anxious to see how these layers joined up with the N.–S. street, but the grab was in the way, and it was never possible to do so.

In the extreme SE. corner of the area, SE. of the new building, the slight reduction of the surface-level which first exposed the top of the N.–S. street, also revealed the appearance of a crown of a gravelled road running E.–W. It was not possible to dig to prove this, but its position would line up well with the section found in 1930 south of St. Martin's House (125). There is thus some evidence for two different street lines on this route.

The variation in depth to Roman levels within the town is remarkable. Several streets have been noted as scarcely a foot below the present surface. The impression here was that the street (N.–S.) had been retained for some time while an uncivilized populace dug and scrabbled among the remains on each side, and finally all had become overgrown, and the street too became subject to burrowing.

7. THE THIRD N.–S. STREET

99. This has only been seen at one point, but on two separate occasions. A trench for a cable, cut to no great depth, in the pavement on the south side of Culver Street, due north of the nave of Trinity Church, was cut through the strong gravel metalling of the Roman street. The surface was of large pebbles, such as some might term cobbles. The width observed was 18–20 ft., but a deeper excavation would probably have made it greater on account of the camber. Some

years later the opposite pavement was cut in a similar manner, and the gravel metalling was again observed, but not in such good condition. The general line of the street is well confirmed by the general town plan, and the presence of either a tower or a gate at Scheregate. It is curious that two of our oldest churches, Holy Trinity and St. Martin's, must stand partly upon the carriage-way of this road.

8. THE FOURTH N.–S. STREET

123. For this we have only one exposure. During excavations for a gas main in 1927 along the north pavement of High Street, a heavy gravel layer was noticed under the front entrance to no. 119. It had the appearance of a street running N.–S.; the width was 18 ft., with gravel metalling 12 in. thick and only 18 in. beneath the surface.[2] The position fits in excellently with the general plan.

9. THE FIFTH N.–S. STREET

This has only been seen once, when it received bare mention, lying by the side of a large red tessellated pavement which occupies the SW. angle of insula 6, but not quite opposite the possible position of the Roman Rye Gate and the ford of the river. Southwards, it fits in with the observed NW. angle of the 'forum' block, where it must have been dug away by the Norman ditch of the Castle, for a vaulted drain shows its broken end in the bank in the Park shrubbery, and such a drain must have run either under the road or by the side of it. Indeed, it has not been previously noticed that if our premises are correct some length of this drain projects westwards of the 'forum' wall, and all of this must have been under the road, which is a point for investigation.

On the south side of the High Street we have nothing. The continuation of the line should run down Long Wire Street, but this is quite impossible, for remains of buildings, and none of roadway, have been found all along this street. Nor did the excavations for the arcade expose any signs of a N.–S. street east of Wire Street. Possibly the street may have run by the heavy wall noted in insula 29 (61), but its course is beset with remains of pavements, unless it has side-stepped to the west.

---

[1] The use of wooden pipes in the streets is described by Laur-Belart, *Augst*, 134. It appears that they formed the water-supply and were found usually by the side of the street, but sometimes embodied in the metalling. The cavity was filled with sand and often contained a type of 'fur' from the water. The pipes were connected by iron rings. The diameter of the 'fur' was about 12 in. (think of the drill required to bore them out!). They would

have to be renewed from time to time, and in some sections as many as four pipes were found at various depths and belonging to different periods. There were lead pipes also here and there. Laver notes iron rings for wooden pipes in the exposure at **167**. See also Atkinson, *Wroxeter* (1942), 121, 219.

[2] E. J. Rudsdale in *T.E.A.S.* xix, 132.

10. THE SIXTH N.–S. STREET

The metalling of this street has not been seen north of the High Street. Its position is fixed by the SE. angle of insula 6, where its metalling had been destroyed, and by the NE. angle of insula 22. Its course points to the tower on the north wall.

129. South of the High Street one exposure has been recorded. In 1938 a long trench for a drain was cut eastwards from Queen Street on the south side of the back entrance to the Eastern National Omnibus Company's garage. The section then obtained forms our fig. 31, beginning a few feet east of the eastern manhole, and running west 44 ft. to the wall of insula 38. The work done included a complete re-levelling of the site, and the depths mentioned hereafter are measured from the former surface, while the surface shown on the section is that left after the workmen had finished, i.e. substantially what it is now.

The bottom of the trench here seemed to reach natural gravel, upon which lay two layers of diverse character, divided by a slot 9–12 in. wide, which was filled with black gravel and looks like a medieval palisade-slot. East of this lay 21 in. of yellow loam containing fragments of septaria, apparently continuous with the clay and loam layers already observed farther east. This layer sagged to the west and was there capped by 3–4 in. of mud. West of the slot the layer was of 10 to 18 in. of dark sandy soil in two layers, the upper the darker.

Upon this accumulation of earlier habitation the road-metal of yellow gravel had been laid, 9 in. thick at the east side, rising to 21 in. in the middle, where, however, it partly filled a hollow, and fading on the west as it approached insula 38. The total width of metalling was 25 ft. 6 in. The surface of the eastern half carried a very black layer 2 in. thick, and ended sharply at the slot.

The western half had a quite distinct surface, but lacked this black layer. Instead we find a heavy make-up of black gravel which seems quite continuous with that filling the slot, and its surface seemed also to be made up to continue the surface of the eastern half. It ended 36 ft. 6 in. from zero at 1 ft. 9 in. from the surface. Beyond this point the black gravel gave place to black soil.

As it approaches the wall on the west the road-metal fades into this black soil, and the dark, upper layer of the sand below here contained much burnt clay and other signs of fire. A block of septaria also lay in this.

The wall ran N.–S. at 44 ft. 6 in. from zero and was 2 ft. thick, built of septaria laid in yellow mortar, not faced, but the upper 5 in. were of white mortar. The depth was not ascertained.

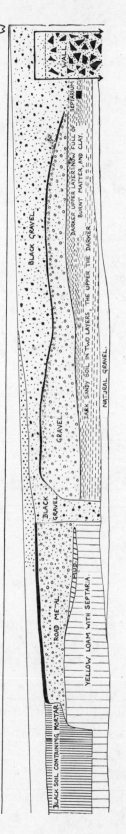

FIG. 31. Street section in Queen Street. [129], p. 73.

11. THE SEVENTH N.–S. STREET

The metalling of this street as it passes through the NE. Gate has been described (p. 40). In the excavations of 1927–9 three sections were cut across it, which leave no possible doubt of its strange course on the plan.

a. The first section (fig. 32, A) was cut 123 ft. south

A large pit (barren) had removed most of the centre of the road.

The road is thicker here than farther south; actually there is a slack in the ground, and there may have been some attempt to level this out. The natural drainage-slopes of the road met at this point and there was a large opening in the side of the drain to take the storm-water from the road.

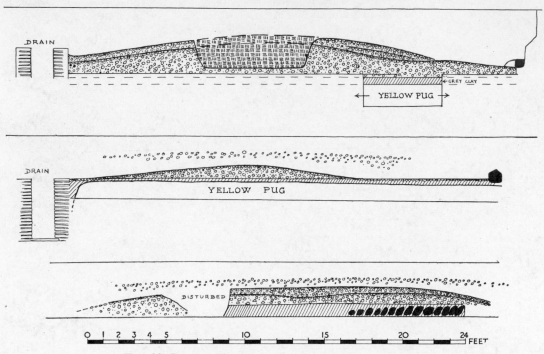

FIG. 32. Street sections in Hollytrees' Meadow. (p. 74.)

of the gate. The gravel metalling was 28 ft. wide and had been about 2 ft. 6 in. thick in the centre, steeply cambered to about 6 in. thick on each side. In it a dark line marked off two periods, and faint signs of minor repairs showed in these two major portions. The whole was laid upon 6 in. of grey, cheesy clay, which contained oyster-shells and pre-Flavian sherds (fig. 33), including a fragment of T.S. f. 29 and a base f. 27 stamped by *Murranus* (fig. 99, 25), a fragment of a T.S. bowl f. Ritt. 12 (1), the rim of a grey jar f. 266 (2), a large rim f. 273 (3), a chip of f. 120, and a piece of eggshell ware, probably f. 64. There was also part of a very corroded bronze disk, animal bones, and a piece of squared ashlar of oolite, all mixed with traces of burning. This layer may be dated to A.D. 61; and there was no street-metalling in its time.

The west side was bounded by the drain. On the east side lay a large block of septaria and a mass of pink mortar, remains of a building, or of the wall of the adjacent insula.

b. The second section was made where the drain turns westward, and was 485 ft. south of the gateway (fig. 32, B). Here the roadway is 26 ft. wide, but only the western 18 ft. are well metalled, and then only with 10 in. of gravel, cambering away to almost nothing at each side. This was laid upon a thin layer of grey clay. Below this was undisturbed (?) yellowish loam. The west side was bounded by the drain, against which was a packing of grey clay. To the east side lay two blocks of septaria, which may indicate the position of the boundary-wall of insula 16, with a gravel floor, like that of a yard, beyond it. There is quite an appreciable amount of gravel loose in the top-soil over the road, which may represent some post-Roman use of its course.

c. The third section (fig. 32, C) was made directly east of the SE. corner of the 'Mithraeum'. The bed here was of grey clay, with a pitching of lumps of septaria in the eastern half—an unusually prodigal use of this commodity. Upon this two successive banks of gravel metalling were clearly visible, with a total thickness of 2 ft. The width is 16 ft., but this is curtailed by a disturbance on the west beyond which a gravel bank, which completes the outline of the road, in section, does not continue any of the layers already noted, unless perhaps the lower gravel.

Over all again appears the spread of gravel, a little wider than in the previous section. (A similar appearance was observed in several sections of the road on the Camulodunum site.)[1]

The road may have crept westward. The disturbance in the section could have held a wall of small size; the gravel bank is a late addition.

167. This street may have been seen again on the High Street; if so, it has more or less recovered its line. In 1930 an excavation in the pathway at the entrance to Greyfriars revealed the surface of a Roman street running N.–S. Its east side coincides with the marks on the wall of East Hill House showing the boundary of All Saints' and St. James's parishes. The metalling was small gravel, exactly as in the former sections of this street, 2 ft. to 2½ ft. from the surface and 18 ft. wide.[2]

This is the sum of our knowledge of the streets.

[1] *Cam.* 97, sections 52–55.

There is some evidence for odd, as yet unconnected pieces, which may or may not prove to belong to a different grid, and there is some evidence that at a late date a larger insula was provided opposite the 'forum', if not at other places. We have suggested that a road may have entered by St. Botolph's Gate, dividing this

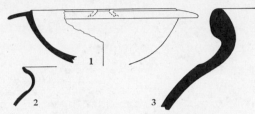

FIG. 33. Pottery from under street, Hollytrees' Meadow. Scale ¼. (p. 74.)

large insula N.–S., but apart from some slight evidence outside the walls (p. 10), this is still pure conjecture. Some of the apparent anomalies of the plan may simply be minor modifications of one general grid, but however this may turn out, the strange slant of the street in Hollytrees Meadow is original and shows no alterations.

[2] Laver, Diary, 3/9/1930.

IV

THE INSULAE

THE general plan of the town and the street grid have been described and discussed (pp. 64–75). There were forty insulae, of varying sizes, and we shall now go through these seriatim, beginning with no. 1 in the NW. corner. Much of the information was collected and published as a numbered schedule in the form of notes with references, with position indicated on the plan by numbered circles, in 1919,[1] and was used again, with additions, in the *R.C.H.M.* in 1923. Since then many more such notes have been made and most of these have been added to the map in the *Short Guide to Roman Colchester* published by the Museum. It is now time that these remains were published in more than note form.[2] The following is compiled from the large file kept in the Museum, in which the full details of every find are entered. The numbers used below are those of Wheeler and Laver's schedule, which has been extended. The notes in the Museum are very full, and we cannot attempt to reproduce them all, especially as regards quantities and types of pottery found and so on. The pottery has all been registered by a series of form-numbers, continuing upon those used in the *Camulodunum* report. This, done as a working convenience, now has to appear in public, although not prepared for that purpose (pp. 279–292 and figs. 118–23).

INSULA 1

No recent work has been done in this insula, which measures about 307 ft. E.–W. from the town wall to the centre-line of the Roman street, reckoning the width of the latter at 25 ft. The N.–S. dimension is much less certain. The area is at the foot of a steep slope and the general surface is level with the top of the wall. In the angle there should be an interior tower, and another at the SW. corner of the insula, but neither has yet been proved.

7. Wire, Diary, 18/3/1849. 'Mr. Man, bricklayer, informs me that he has discovered a red tessellated pavement of large size, but much broken, at the back of Mr. Stirling Maclean's, North Hill.' Identification of the house as now no. 45 North Hill is taken from Wheeler and Laver; the approximate position is also given on the plan in Wire's 'County Illustrations'.

8. The O.S. 1:500 map marks a tessellated pavement found under a shed, 290 ft. west of North Hill and 170 ft. south of the town wall, without date. Cutts[3] shows this or another one, indicating the same shed very clearly, but the position of the pavement is more to the west, 330 ft. from North Hill and 170 ft. south

of the town wall.[4] He states that this is the pavement found in the saw-pit in Bowler's Brewery (**10** below).

9. Wire, Diary, 22/5/1845. 'Portions of a Roman tessellated pavement has been discovered in a field behind the brewery[4] bottom of North Hill, under it was a quantity of charcoal.'

10. Wire, Album, p. 9, illustrates in colour three very small fragments of mosaic from a geometric pattern in black, red, yellow, and white, with a note that they were found in a field behind the brewery when digging for a saw-pit (see also *T.E.A.S.* o.s. v, 155; and *J.B.A.* i, 54).

11. Wire, Diary, 27/9/1844. 'Mr. Bowler . . . informs me that a tessellated pavement composed of different coloured cubes has recently been discovered at the rear of his premises.'

Nos. **10–11** clearly refer to the same pavement as shown by Cutts, who was unaware of any other, and all probably refer to no. **8**, which is probably the position of it according to H. Laver. Cutts's position (the left-hand cross) cannot be relied upon. No. **9** may be another pavement altogether. We have nevertheless shown nos. **8–11** as positioned by Wheeler and Laver, for the latter may have had unpublished knowledge.

---

[1] Wheeler and Laver, in *J.R.S.* ix.
[2] In some cases we are republishing previous reports which appeared in full. These must be included, but have been abridged.
[3] The red overprint on Cutts's plan is very often quite wrong.

[4] The two fields marked A and B on our plan were all one field in those days (O.S. map, 1876). They clearly form 'the field behind the Brewery'. Nos. **9, 11** and **163** cannot be closely placed.

The O.S. map has two marks, undated, showing where Roman coins have been found near the west side of the insula.

163. A sketch-plan in the Museum, dated 7/3/1914, shows some trenches cut by Mr. E. N. Mason. It is on a very large scale, and the site must have been behind the brewery. It shows a saw-pit by the side of a shed, but the saw-pit of 1844 had disappeared before 1876. The shed cannot be identified. His manuscript note identifies his saw-pit with that of Wire.

Five of his trenches proved negative, though carried 6–8 ft. deep. There is no record whether the subsoil was then reached or not. A trench at the west end of the shed revealed portions of walls of at least two periods, with no floors. There being no scale and no north point, we cannot enter this on the map.

In April 1921 a shaft was sunk close to the town wall for a water pipe connected with Mr. J. S. Askew's bungalow near Balkerne Hill. It would cut through the rampart. The pottery found is in the Museum and is from mid-first to early second century in date, with one piece of painted wall-plaster (CM. 4061.21).

In 1939, when making an air-raid shelter in the playground of the County High School, three coins were found, of Tetricus sen. (?), Urbs Roma, and Constantinopolis, and in 1933 an antoninianus of Tetricus was found in Cistern Yard.

INSULA 2

Lying east of insula 1, the dimensions of this are not certain, but should be about 340 ft. E.–W. by 310 ft. N.–S., the latter measured from the town wall. The area is below a steep slope and the surface is now level with the top of the wall, or higher. It is entirely covered by houses and gardens.

The street on the south is still uncertain, so that we do not know whether some of the remains lie in this insula or no. 10.

12. The earliest records are in Wire's Diary from November 1845 to March 1847. There is also a sketch-plan in the Album. Wire was informed that the mosaic pavement was found twenty years earlier but covered up again.[1] In 1847 it was again covered, to lie undisturbed until 1906, when part was again uncovered and removed to the Museum.[2]

In 1922, on the initiative of Mr. H. Lazell the owner, a trench was cut near the east end of the garden (sketch-plan in Laver's Diary). Here was 3 ft. 8 in. of black garden soil, then a 19-in. layer of Roman septaria,

mortar, and clay, beneath which were 2 ft. of old brown surface soil, and at 7 ft. 3 in., natural sand. The trench ran N.–S., the south end being 11 ft. 6 in. from the east wall and 33 ft. 6 in. from the south wall of the garden. There are references to the finding of two walls in this work, said to be shown on the plan, but they do not appear. Laver, Diary, 5–7 and 11/4/22.

Wire's notes would have been an excellent example of his work, but are too profuse to reproduce. Summarized they run: 28/11/1845, 'In Mr. Bryant's garden [fully defined and shown on sketch-plan] . . . a Roman tessellated pavement . . . tesserae one inch square. Several fragments of fresco house-wall . . .; 1/12/45, . . . pavement of greater extent than first supposed, it was covered with fragments of Roman roof tiles . . . most of the tiles were examined by me and none bore any letters . . .; 5/12/45, . . . made rough sketch of pavement . . . attempt made to take part of it up whole failed . . . its substructure is as follows . . . a bottom of clay and sand, the rubble consisting of septaria, then a concrete of pebbles and then another, after which a layer of mortar in which the tesserae were set. Mr. Bryant gave orders for it to be broken up . . .; 6/12/45, . . . more pavement discovered, buried again undisturbed . . .; 24/12/45, first brass of Postumus, said to come from this garden, shown by Mr. Bryant Junior . . ., 10/1/46, who says more pavement has been found, just like the rest . . ., 9/4/46, . . . Bryant jun. showed a white earth vase with neck and formerly a handle [thumbnail sketch of flagon] found in his garden . . . [the same one] . . . about eight feet below the surface . . .;[3] 7/5/46, . . . Mr. B. jun. showed a 3rd brass coin of Licinius found ibid. . .; 18/3/47, . . . another tessellated pavement was discovered this morning between nos. 18 and 17 running the whole length of the passage. . . . It is all red . . . probably connected with those found earlier . . . .'

Of this last discovery H. Laver wrote as follows: '. . . [it] appears to extend from the street into and under a large part of the gardens of the adjoining house (nos. 17 & 18) . . . the workmen carried their trench through it the whole length of the passage . . . further excavations in the garden exposed large areas at the back of no. 18 covered with red tesserae flooring . . . of a house or houses, it was impossible to say which, as from the erection of later buildings, and the destruction caused by the removal of the walls, which had been carried out almost completely, no plan . . . could be recovered. A short distance from the back door of the passage . . . the red pavement was found to

---

[1] *T.E.A.S.* o.s. v, 156.

[2] This is the smaller piece lying in the centre of the main hall, see ibid. x, 84 (fig.); *J.B.A.* xii, 289; *Minutes of Colchester Town Council (Museum)*, 23/11/06; *C.M.R.* 1907, 4, 10; *Antiquary*, xlii, 447; *Essex County Standard*, 24/11/06 (photograph);

O.S. 1:500.

[3] *J.B.A.* ii, 268, 'Mr. Sprague presented a drawing . . . of a Roman urn of elegant shape found in the garden of Mr. Bryant.'

be the border surrounding a very ornamental pavement . . . now mostly destroyed.' Laver thinks this portion was the one Wire says it was attempted to lift (but that was red). The complete design (pl. xv) is reconstructed from the fragment removed to the Museum in 1906, and from a mosaic of three vertical photographs, making a continuous whole, taken when more of the pavement was uncovered in the garden of no. 17, to the south.[1]

On this work, carried out in 1906, H. Laver con-

It is known that the continuation of these walls and floors southwards under no. 17 was also explored to some extent,[3] but there is no detailed record.

Goodyear's plan, it is to be presumed, gives us the position of the fragment of B, brought into the Museum. It is therefore the NW. corner of its pavement. The subsequent work done, as shown by our reconstructed drawing, must have been carried out south of this, and working from west to east, but in the garden of no. 17.

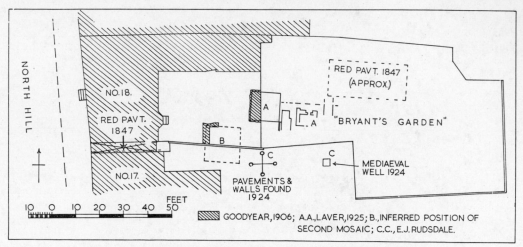

FIG. 34. Plan of nos. 17 and 18 North Hill. [12], p. 78.
A is the mosaic, pl. xvi; B is pl. xv.

tinues: '. . . Further excavations in the garden of no. 18 brought to light more of the pavements . . . and in the middle of the garden . . . another ornamental pavement, forming a square of 14 ft. . . . this was carefully covered up again' (pl. xvi).

We have a plan made by the Borough Engineer, Mr. H. Goodyear, to show the position of the pavements found in 1906, which are only two (A and B). Levels of the street and garden are given. The first piece of mosaic was presented to the Museum (B) by Mr. H. Lazell;[2] the rest of it should still be in the ground.

In 1925 the garden was again explored by P. G. Laver. The central pavement (A) was uncovered and trenches carried eastwards from it. Unfortunately, Mr. Laver published nothing, and the only material left, besides the small finds in the Museum, comprises two descriptions in draft form, some excellent photographs, and a plan by Captain H. E. Laver, which contains many valuable notes. No plan comprises all the finds of all periods, and our plan (fig. 34) pieces things together as best possible.

Pavement A was uncovered in August 1925 and removed to the Museum.[4] It measured 12 ft. N.–S. by 12 ft. 3 in. E.–W. The photograph (pl. xxiii, b) shows little red margin on three sides, but a good width (shown as 20 in. on the plan, with a note that it runs on to the south) on the south side, with part of the quarter-round moulding in position at the east end. Damage to the pavement was less than usual. One hole had been broken through it on the south side, and the NE. corner had sunk and lost its edges, having been laid over a pit or some earlier excavation which had subsided. The depth from the surface (at the higher level of the garden) was 4 ft. 5 in. Most interesting is the fact that a large patch of the pattern has been damaged and reset. It includes the whole of one of the corner flowers, which does not match the rest. Many other patches are present, but it is not now possible to say whether these were made by the firm who lifted the pavement or not (pl. xvi).

The bed consisted of 10 in. of red concrete, below which lay 3–4 in. of black soil, under which lay an earlier floor of red concrete, 6–8 in. thick, lying on fine

---

[1] So I understand; but there are difficulties.
[2] *T.E.A.S.* x, 84. The illustration shows that some of the

pattern was lost in removal. *Museum Minutes*, 23/11/06.
[3] *J.R.S.* xiv, 230 (1924). [4] *C.M.R.* 1926, 15; C.M. 5217.26.

yellow sand which contained fragments of Gallo-Belgic pottery.

The only trace of the walls was a gap of dark soil, 1 ft. 9 in. wide, all round, where the walls should have run; beyond this, on the east, H. E. Laver's plan shows a foundation (?) of red concrete 2 in. thick and 12 in. wide.

The plan (fig. 34) left by Captain H. E. Laver provides material for a very long description of complicated remains of floors, walls, &c. But since the work

are all classed by Wheeler and Laver as no. **12**. The references quoted are Wire, plan, and Diary; *T.E.A.S.* o.s. v, 156; n.s. x, 84 (fig.); *J.B.A.* xii (photograph), 289; *Antiquary*, xliii, 447; *Essex County Standard*, 24/11/1906 (photograph) and O.S. 10 ft. map. The latter is erroneous, for its mark lies some distance east of the true spot, in a larger garden south of no. 18. Cutts (p. 34) marks the site on his plan a few yards farther north than the O.S. map does, though still in the same garden, but with the description 'I, 9. In Mr. Bryant's garden'. The site of the 1925 pavement has been surveyed and added to the 1:500 map in the Museum by the Borough Engineer at the time.

The pottery and other remains from below the pave-

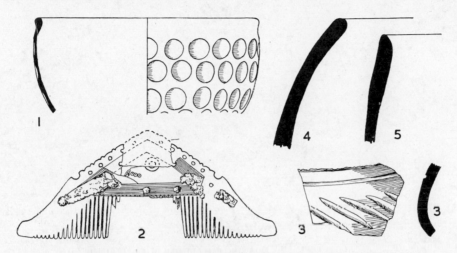

FIG. 35. Objects found at 18 North Hill. Scale ½. (p. 79.)

done was quite superficial, and no work was done on the strata (which, indeed, remain untouched for investigation), the only useful information is that remains of walls and floors are present, and that they belong to a series of periods. One piece of walling was exceptionally large for private building in Colchester. It stood 3 ft. high, with three courses of tiles at the bottom, followed by two of rough septaria and two of tile alternately. It was 7 ft. 4 in. long, broken at both ends, and with a large piece of the original plaster in position. It is shown as standing upon a red plaster floor 4 in. thick.

P. G. Laver collected and preserved a box of fragments of painted wall-plaster from the continuation of these remains under the garden of no. 17. These fragments chiefly show much white background with, apparently, leaves (and fruit?—lemons?) as the main pattern, many much faded, and others may have faded completely; there are also fragments showing panelling and two fragments are in blue.

There were also three fragments of marble veneer and five fragments of one, or possibly two, thin marble disks with a decoration of pointed ovals incised with a compass; and a roundel of marble.

Note. The finds in the garden of no. 18 (formerly Mr. Bryant's)

ment cannot be set out in full here. The list can be seen in the Museum files. It runs from Claudian forms, including millefiori glass, to colour-coated ware, which must be nearly mid-second century at earliest, and of eight fragments of T.S. form 37 two are second century. The pavement can hardly be earlier than Antonine.

Fig. 35 shows some of the unstratified finds from above the pavement. They are of interest. No. 1 is drawn from a fragment of Roman glass of opaque, milky-white colour and decorated with *cut* disks. No. 2 is half a bone comb which has been repaired with bronze rivets. Bone combs are rare in Colchester, and this form is never common. The remaining figures represent coarse, thick, brown-black pottery, made by hand. No. 3 has incised decoration; nos. 4 and 5 are from simple cooking-pots, of black to brown ware; no. 4 has small white grit. They seem to be Saxon; Mr. Dunning thinks them early seventh century. It is so unusual to find anything of Saxon date that the most must be made of such small finds.

Two large lumps of burnt clay, apparently from rectangular blocks 3¼ in. thick, are probably from clay building-blocks, from which some of the walls may have been made. The many food-bones included those of small animals, birds, oysters, whelks, mussels, and one cockle.

Coins included two, worn, of Vespasian; one, well preserved, of Domitian, all three *asses*; an antoninianus of Elagabalus.

INSULA 3

Very little is known of this insula. The town wall is buried under Northgate Street, and there should be towers on it at the north corners of the insula, perhaps even a gate opposite Scheregate. The width should be about 325 ft. and the depth N.–S. about the same. It has scarcely been touched by excavations in recent years and is covered by old properties. Even Wire has nothing of interest from it.

24. A red pavement in the yard of the public house formerly known as the 'Bishop Blaize'. There is difficulty about the siting of this. Wheeler and Laver place it on the crossroads of insulae 3, 4, 11, 12, slightly inside insulae 3 and 4. This is the NE. corner of the straight part of West Stockwell Street, where the Stockwell Arms stands. Now Laver, in *T.E.A.S.* x, 89, is explicit that it was at the NE. corner of Angel Lane or West Stockwell Street, and there is in fact another NE. corner to this street, at the end of the curved part, where the Locomotive Inn once stood.

Which of these houses was the 'Bishop Blaize'? P. G. Laver says the Stockwell Arms, reinforced by Pigot's Directory, which places it in Bear Lane (i.e. East Stockwell Street).

But the 1:500 O.S. map of 1875/6 shows the 'Locomotive' where we have said.

Now Wire, Diary, 10/9/1843, says that the 'Bishop Blaize', in Duck Lane (now Northgate Street), was later renamed the 'Locomotive'. Mr. G. O. Rickword, who is the authority on these matters, tells us that Thos. Rand renamed the 'Bishop Blaize' the 'Locomotive' in 1843. Later it was renamed the 'Victory', which was closed about 1919. There seems to be no doubt now that the 'Bishop Blaize' stood at the extreme NE. corner of West Stockwell Street and *Northgate Street*. We have accordingly moved this pavement to a position in insula 3, which we feel is right, and we cannot understand the error in Pigot's Directory.

149. Another red pavement is said to have been seen behind two houses just NW. of the Nelson's Head Inn and partly in the NW. corner of the inn yard. An ancient well was found under the eastern of these two houses, opposite the entrance to Garden Court. It was about 14 ft. deep and lined with stone,[1] with channels

of Roman tile running into it from the east and west. It may or may not be Roman. Wall-footings are also reported about 10 ft. south of the same house.

Speed's map of 1610 shows the houses in this insula forming an almost perfect quarter-circle, and the block in which they stand is continued in a more angular form in insula 4. In general there is sufficient similarity to the plan of the houses standing round the site of the theatre at Vieil Évreux[2] to cause us to suspect a theatre site here. The space thus demonstrated measures 350 ft. E.–W. and 250 ft. N.–S., measuring from the face of the town wall. This is room for a large theatre. A N.–S. street of the grid would strike it at the central point of the hemicycle.

INSULA 4

The position of the streets around this are approximate. The dimensions of the insula should be about 330 by 320 ft. Not much is known of it, and it has been partly discussed in insula 3.

186. A heavy foundation has been noted lying just west of Stockwell Street Infants School, between it and the next property. The position falls in with the suggested theatre site.

188. A red pavement is marked by Wire on the plan in his copy of Morant,[3] under a large building opposite the E.–W. portion of Stockwell Street.

INSULA 5

The southern limit may be taken fairly closely from insula 6, but the streets on the west and east are merely general deductions. The size of the insula should be about 340 by 320 ft. The town wall is invisible all along the north side, and very little is known of the insula.

29. Wire, Diary, 11/11/1849: 'In the cellar of the last house but one on the east side of Maidenburgh Street is an arch built with Roman bricks, each brick six inches square and cemented together with mortar in which is pounded brick and tile, presenting an anomaly, the bricks being the size considered Saxon [*sic*], but the mortar is undoubtedly Roman . . . above the arch the wall is built of Roman brick, but no pounded tile in the mortar. In the cellar of the next house is an arch of modern date . . . the arch could not be traced any further up the lane, as there are no cellars . . . till the Fencers Inn (now gone) is reached, where there are similar remains. Possibly the arch may be the remains of a Roman sewer.'

Wheeler and Laver (p. 161) recognize that the work

---

[1] It should be understood that stone walls or foundations in this part of the country imply a Roman date, or Roman material reused in later times.

[2] Bonnin, *Antiquités gallo-romaines des Éburoviques* (7860).

[3] With '4' against it. The numerals entered on this map must at one time have had a key to them, but it has disappeared.

is all Roman (the 6-in. bricks are imperfect tiles), and add 'the wall and arch are buried below the springing of the latter, but the wall is still visible to a height of six feet, and a similar breadth from E.–W. The work is good and probably not later than the second century.'

The arch, of one ring of imperfect tiles, is too wide for that of a sewer, and openings in the walls at East Gate and Schere Gate have double rings of tiles (see pl. XI, A) so that it hardly has dignity enough to belong to a possible Roman Rye Gate. Its distance back from the inner face of the town wall must be at least 30 ft.

28. A tessellated pavement and foundations are recorded by P. G. Laver in what was formerly Messrs. Truslove's yard, on the south side of Northgate Street, near the entrance to the yard, in 1920. No more than this is known of them.

INSULA 6

This is one of the few insulae which have been explored to any great extent. The town wall is well preserved along the north side, with a tower at the NE. corner. All three streets have been located, and the insula measures about 340 ft. N.–S. by 460 ft. E.–W. according to Wheeler and Laver's plan.

The finds in this insula are as follows (the field was part of the Castle lands, and was variously known as the 'Sheepshead' and 'Cheaping' Meadow). The removal of the rampart south of the town wall has already been described (p. 36, 37).

36. A red tessellated pavement was found in the field behind the Castle in 1892. It was about 18 ft. square.[1] Another note on this ascribes the discovery to when the Castle Park was being laid out, and states 'a portion where the lines of the tesserae were laid in a curve as if to suit some ornamental part, was covered by a glass roof and a much larger part was again buried.' The depth was about 3 ft.[2]

The following finds under this number all belong to one block of houses lying along the south side of the insula.

Wire, Diary, 22/3; 14/5; 21/5; 28/5/1853 notes that he secured from this field an iron spear-head, 3¾ in. long and ½ in. wide, a piece of decorated sigillata, a penny of Henry III, two bone pins, and a denarius of Caracalla. On 2/3/1855 he notes: 'Mr. Nason . . . informs me he has traced foundations for nearly 200 ft. on top of Cheaping Field (running E.–W.) . . . he only probed the ground by borer.'

In the summer of 1906 the outlines of at least two houses became visible near the bandstand and a plan was made by Major Bale. Excavations were carried out on a rectangular enclosure 100 by 50 yards in 1907. Wherever the lines in the grass had been seen it was found that masses of broken building material had been flung into the foundation trenches, evidently by Norman stone-robbers. Only in two places, each about 4 ft. long, was the original walling found. At least two Roman houses had existed. The foundations were covered up.[3]

In 1920 this site was opened up again by the Morant Club,[4] with Dr. R. E. M. Wheeler in charge. The work was limited by the necessity of avoiding park paths and fixtures (plan, fig. 36).

House I, so far as excavated, consisted of a range of at least seven rooms (plan, 2–8), most or all of which opened on a corridor on the west (1). The south room (2), which was doubtless subdivided into two, and part of the corridor lie under the present parade. At the south end, immediately adjoining and parallel with the retaining wall of the street, was a second corridor or open passage, the floor of which was of light gravel grouted with white mortar; it had been renewed at various periods, and at a depth of 2½ ft. below its final surface was a layer of burnt matter, with remains of an early cement floor which had been subjected to fire. The main corridor (1) was 6 ft. wide and paved with red tesserae, except at its south end, where the main entrance to the house may have been. Here, turned up on end, were blocks of a cement floor with black and white tesserae set in plain rectangular pattern; this probably formed a panel immediately inside the doorway.

The nature of the floor of the south room (2) was not clear from the small part laid bare. That of the room next north (19½ by 18½ ft.) consisted of a border of red tesserae enclosing a square frame 1 ft. broad of rather finer red tesserae. This was clearly intended to contain an ornamental mosaic. The present filling, however, is a rough patchwork of large yellow and red tesserae placed in careless disorder and partly breaking into the frame—evidently a later repair. North of this room were two small rooms (9½ ft. square, and 9½ by 8½ ft.) both paved with red tesserae. Room (4) was entered from the south by a doorway, . . . and opening from it into room (5), which is at a slightly lower level, is another doorway with a step. North of these is a large room (6) 19 ft. by 18½ ft., which, like room (3), has a border of red tesserae enclosing a central panel. A small fragment of this was preserved, in a poor state. It consisted of a well-laid strip about 18 in. long, of

[1] *T.E.A.S.* ix, 124.
[2] Ibid. x, 90, since damaged by frost and reburied.
[3] Ibid. x, 323.

[4] 'An Insula of Roman Colchester', by R. E. M. Wheeler, *T.E.A.S.* xvi, 7 ff.; *J.B.A.* n.s. xxvi, 214.

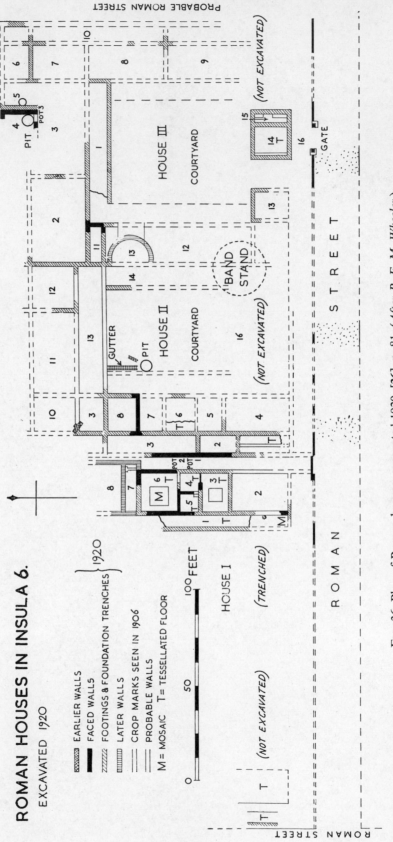

FIG. 36. Plan of Roman houses, excavated 1920. [36], p. 81. (*After R. E. M. Wheeler.*)

cable pattern within black and white linear borders. The colours were white, dark grey, red, and yellow. Two small gaps, each 1 ft. square, were purposely left against the south wall; unfortunately the floor was too badly damaged to show any corresponding gaps on the north side. Possibly they held wall-posts for pilasters to support the ceiling. On the east side some of the tesserae were scorched as if by a brazier. The debris on the floors of all the rooms included much coloured wall-plaster. No traces of earlier floors were found beneath those described.

The surviving walls are entirely of septaria. Rooms (7) and (8), at a somewhat lower level on the hill-side, show an intermixture of brick courses with the septaria; and as they are not bonded into room (6) they are evidently an addition to the plan, encroaching upon the passage to the east. Room (7) is narrow, with traces at the east end of a small compartment, which has no traces of burning, so is not a furnace, though no better suggestion can be made. Room (8) is of unknown extent; its north end is damaged and covered by a pathway.

No evidence for date of building was secured. The mosaic is well laid, and the paved rooms are possibly contemporary with the first-century buildings of house II.

House II and House III form a double building of the courtyard type. Each appears to have had ranges of rooms opening on to corridors surrounding an open court or garden. Their northern parts are denuded and the southern covered by the bandstand. There was some evidence, however, that house II had a corridor between it and the street. It certainly had an exterior corridor on the west, divided into three or more rooms of which (1) was paved with red tesserae, which ended abruptly half-way across the room with a border of yellow tesserae (here possibly was a staircase). The floor of room (2) was of smooth *opus signinum* (red cement), which also ended with an ill-defined edge about the middle of the room. The floor of room (3) had quite disappeared. The general level of house II is about 2 ft. above that of the open passage to the west of it, and it is possible that the limited extent of the floors is due to steps having existed here.

Nothing remained of the floors of the main western range save a small strip of red tessellated pavement in room (6). The south wall of room (8) retained a course of roughly faced septaria topped by a course of brick. Near this room, at a lower level, was an extensive layer of burnt wood, &c., similar to that found elsewhere on the site. Under the position of the north wall of room (9) was a short length of septaria walling showing the junction of another wall on its NE. side. This masonry lay below the footings of the west wall of rooms (9 and 10), and at an entirely different angle from the main

plan; it should probably be regarded in relation to another small piece of walling under the courtyard immediately east of the gutter.

Trial pits on the north part of the site showed that the floors and most of the walls had perished. South of corridor (13) were remains of a gutter floored with bricks about 11 in. square by 1½ in. thick, with sides of brick thickly covered with a yellow mortar. At the south end of the gutter was a rubbish-pit containing much oyster-shell, bone, and potsherds, chiefly of late-second- and third-century character (cf. Caerwent, house 3, *Arch.* lvii, pl. XL).

The eastern range was mostly inaccessible, but sufficient was uncovered to show that extensive alterations had been made at some time. Above the foundations of the original room (15) were the rubble footings of an apse, which had been anchored to the old east wall of the room by a rectangular projection at the apex. Large numbers of red tesserae found here suggested the apse had been paved with them, but the area could not be cleared.

The southern range of house III was trenched, but only a general outline could be recovered. This failed to confirm Major Bale's plan in detail, notably where the apparent outline of an apse was shown. At this point (room 4) was a short length of remarkably well-preserved wall of rubble, with five courses of roughly dressed septaria on the west face. The thickness was 4½ ft., but it was in two parts, the eastern of which was merely unfaced rubble with septaria footings. At the north end the western part returned west and ended in a square, brick-faced jamb. The position of the south wall or arcade was indicated by a rectangular patch of rubble footing, apparently for a pier or column, and by a marked change in the nature of the floor. At the SE. angle, below the first course of dressed septaria, stood the third foundation-pot (see below). The double wall owed its preservation to a cement floor, 6 in. thick, which had fallen against it and concealed it. Under and around this floor were numbers of flue tiles and several bricks, 8 in. square, of the type used in hypocaust pilae. The floor had been broken up to rob the tiles. In association with the floor were a rubbish-pit, much painted wall-plaster, and two or three quadrant-shaped bricks. Against the footings of the eastern half of the wall was a second smaller rubbish-pit containing unusually early pottery (see below). All further traces of this room had disappeared.

The northern range opened on to a tessellated corridor (1), which lay only 9 in. below the grass. The eastern range was mostly inaccessible, but enough was ascertained to show that it resembled the west range of house II. It had corridors certainly on the east, and probably on the west.

The south range was separated from the street by a corridor (16) with a floor of grouted gravel and sand, bearing some marks of tesserae. Opposite the gateway to the street was a square chamber (14) with a narrow room (15) on the east, both with good red tessellated floors. At some period the original walls had been removed and partly replaced by rough brick and septaria walls built actually on the tesserae of the floors. In the easternmost of these new walls was a doorway 4 ft. wide. The earlier partition was not rebuilt and the broad gap where it had been was allowed to remain. These new walls may have been of light timber framing above the footings. The purpose of such buildings is unexplained.

In room (14), opposite the gate, the tesserae are broken by two parallel ruts between 4 and 5 ft. apart. One of them has been roughly patched with brick. There can be little doubt that these are the wheel-marks of Saxon or Norman carts removing building material. The picture is complete even to a block of ashlar placed as a stop immediately behind the wheel-track.

The north end of room (13) had an *opus signinum* floor and west of it lay a mortar floor which could not be excavated.

Throughout the site painted wall-plaster was found in abundance. Most showed rectilinear borders, but one showed the spandrel of an arch, and others roughly daubed floral patterns. There were a few fragments of window glass.

Two trial pits were sunk west of house I. They revealed nothing other than the usual building rubbish. At the SW. angle of the insula lies the pavement uncovered in 1892, which was formerly partly preserved under glass. A trench was cut from the west of this to the park fence. It showed the extent of the pavement, also another narrow tessellated strip, like that of a corridor, west of it, and beyond this the street.

At a point south of the passage between houses I and II there was a break in the line of the wall by the street, which may at one time have been a gate. On the east side of this a small drain passed through the wall, coming from the south. The wall had been carried down, in layers of tile and brick, to form the top of it. The channel was 15 in. high and 8 in. wide; its sides and floor were of the hard rammed gravel which formed the edges of the road, and had also been plastered with clay. The upper part of it was still empty as far as could be probed, but on the floor was 3 in. of vegetable sediment surmounted by 3 in. of clay. It was not possible to trace this drain further.

The opening through the wall was almost closed by a length of similar walling, beginning from the opening of the drain and for some distance running against the north side of the retaining wall to the west.

Opposite room (2) of house III, 160 ft. east of the manhole to the drain, stand the two brick piers of the gateway. They were anchored on their outer sides by broadly spread brick footings, above which the piers, 2 ft. square, stood to a height of 15 in. They are of tiles measuring $11\frac{1}{2}$ by $7\frac{1}{2}$ by $1\frac{3}{4}$ in., and showed conclusively that the retaining wall had not been carried up in brick or stone. The opening was 11 ft. wide. Nothing remained to indicate the nature of the gates or their fittings.

The objects found in these excavations were mostly published in *T.E.A.S.* and included three foundation-offering pots from which Wheeler concluded that the walls where they were found were laid down 'not later than the last forty years of the first century A.D.'

The other pottery found was only partially published. The T.S. ran from Neronian times, with stamps of OF) CR(E)S(TI), f. 29; QVINT f. 27; and OF) NIGRI, f. 27, to a fragment of the so-called 'Marne ware', which is very rare in Colchester.

Objects of glass, bone, and metal were not important. The seventy-four coins were as follows: Claudius; Nero (2); Hadrian; Faustina I; Gallienus (6); Postumus (2); Victorinus; Claudius Gothicus (7); Tetricus (7); Helena (2); Constantine I (10); Crispus; Constantine II (4); Constans (4); Magnentius (4); Valentinian; local imitations of Constantine II; Constantinian (3); others (5); unidentifiable, one *c*. 250–80, and two probably Constans, and one *c*. 300–50, and two others.

Wheeler remarks that the coins are mostly later than 250 and do not agree with the pottery. The pottery published was from early pits only. As we have remarked elsewhere, the pottery commonly known as 'Antonine' is now known to have extended well into the third century, if not through it, and if there was not a great deal of this among the unstratified wares the site is exceptional in Colchester.

Two pieces of stone worthy of note were found, the first measured $13\frac{1}{2}$ by 11 in., material not stated. It has one face deeply inscribed with four concentric quadrants or semicircles, with part of a groove along one side. The other side of the same stone bears two concentric circles. The thickness was not stated. One edge was chamfered. This was found near the gate of house II. For conjectures as to possible purpose see Wheeler, p. 30.

A fragment of Purbeck marble from a slab 9 in. wide with ogee-moulded edges, found on the floor of the west corridor of house II, is possibly from the coping of a low wall carrying the columns of a portico (see photographs). There was also a fragment of a grooved stone, possibly from a window-jamb.

The bronze handle of a clasp knife in pierced work,

showing a dog chasing a hare, was found on this site in 1934 (C.M. 92.34).[1]

INSULA 7

The wall and gateway on the north of this insula have been described (pp. 36 f.) and the road on its east (p. 74). The road on the west was not, it seems, very substantial (p. 73), and that on the south not much better (p. 66). The insula measured 325 ft. N.–S. and about the same E.–W. The area has always belonged to the Castle and has never been built upon in the life of the Castle. In recent times it belonged to the grounds of Hollytrees House, hence it is known as Hollytrees' Meadow.

Early in 1927, by the gift of the then Viscount Cowdray, the Hollytrees and its grounds came into the hands of the Town Council, and this northern half of the meadow was designated for tennis courts. The Essex Archaeological Society secured permission to excavate and an Excavations Committee was formed. On 21 October work began under P. G. Laver, F.S.A., on the understanding that work was to cease on 29 February 1928.

No work of any magnitude could be undertaken. The programme was to uncover the gate again, and explore the drain which Duncan described (p. 87) and the northern part of the meadow. Later, however, permission was granted to explore the southern part of the field (insula 15), and by February 1928 we were able to demonstrate the importance of the remains of the gate, drain, and the building now described as a 'Mithraeum', and the matter became one of more than local importance. The Colchester Excavation Committee (1928) was then formed to raise funds and conduct the work, with the late Right Hon. Lord Lambourne, P.C., K.C.V.O., as President and Mr. C. F. D. Sperling, M.A., F.S.A. (President of the Essex Archaeological Society), as Chairman. The committee included representatives of the learned societies interested and of the Town Council.

Work was resumed in July 1928, under the same restriction that it must cease on 28 February 1929. Funds did not allow of more than three men being employed, nor would supervision for more have been available. The work was now under the supervision of the writer.

Most of the time and funds available were consumed by the work on the gateway, the drain (pp. 87–90), and the 'Mithraeum' (pp. 107–113). The work on the hypocaust was very slow (insula 15), so that but little opportunity occurred to explore the rest of the area available. Several weeks of iron-hard frost in February did not help. The clearing of the 'Mithraeum' alone involved the removal of over 1,500 cubic yards of earth, to a depth of 12 ft.

The thanks of the committee are due to Messrs. G. W. Farmer and the late E. J. Rudsdale for their continual assistance to Mr. Laver and the writer in the supervision. The former was present daily in the first season, and the latter collaborated throughout. We are also indebted to Mr. K. C. Scarff for making the survey and plan, for levels, and in many other ways, and especially to the then Borough Engineer, Mr. H. Collins, and his deputy, Mr. A. G. Andrews, for their readiness and courtesy in supplying men, material, and general assistance.

The excavations were visited while in progress by Sir Chas. Peers, Mr. J. P. Bushe-Fox, Sir Mortimer Wheeler, Professor I. A. Richmond, and others.

It is too late now to acknowledge the chief donations other than to recall with pride that the list was headed by the Town Council with £100.

The delay in publication has been due solely to the inability of the Essex Archaeological Society to raise the necessary funds. It is now some years since the Society of Antiquaries expressed willingness to act in this matter, but their own excavations on the site of Camulodunum had to take precedence.

Historical. The references to Dr. Duncan's earlier work in 1852 are *T.E.A.S.* o.s. v, 210; *J.R.S.* ix, 163, 169. The references to this field in Wire's Diary have never been published, so we give the useful parts now. They apply to both insulae 7 and 15.

2/3/1848. 'I am informed a tessellated pavement has been discovered in the meadow adjoining Sheepshead Field on the east.' (This cannot be identified.)

28/8/1852. 'Purchased portion of an enamelled fibula from the drain in Mr. Jas. Round's Field. Saw at Mr. Bottins Smith's a bronze fibula, a 1st brass of Hadrian, one of Carausius, one of Probus, a number of shells of small size, and fragments of bronze from the above drain.'

1/9/52. Describes his visit to Duncan's excavations with the local Archaeological Association. 'At some distance from it [the 'Mithraeum'] to the west is the remains of a pavement about one foot below the surface composed of red tesserae about 6 ft. long from E.–W. and about 4 ft. wide from N.–S. . . .' This would agree with the shallow pavements found on the west side of insula 15 (**118–19**).

4/9/52. 'Mr. B. Smith, Head St. has three second brass coins of Carausius, Pax type in good preservation, a first brass of Trajan and second brass of Hadrian in bad condition, beside some third brass of the lower empire in very bad condition, a (sketch of a narrow-mouthed flask) small urn of black earth, several fragments of Roman glass vessels and necks of earthen bottles, portion of a rather curious shaped earthen vase (sketch of a two-handled flask with rounded base), found in the remains in Mr. Round's field.'

6/9/52. 'Went with Dr. Duncan . . . to Mr. Round's field. . . . The drain is arched in several parts, but whether it was the whole

---

[1] *Essex Review*, xliii, 91.

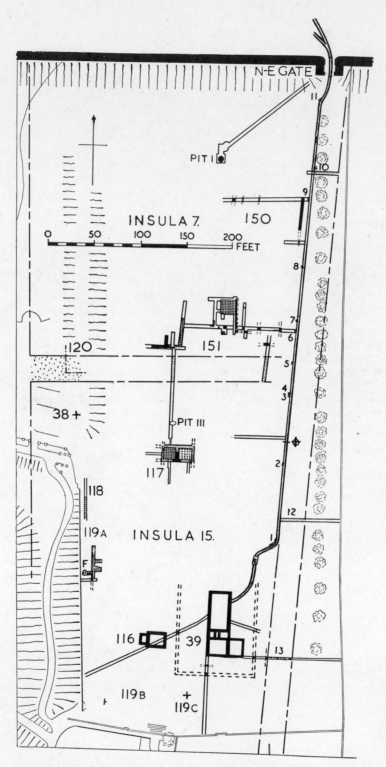

FIG. 37. Plan of excavations in Hollytrees' Meadow, 1927–9, pp. 85–91.

ength of it seems doubtful. My own opinion is that it was not. At that part of it nearest the town wall there are 16 tiles in the arch, two of them are cut wedge-shape to form a sort of key. . . . The chamber at the top of the drain has *in one instance* (our italics) a double wall, that is, one of Roman bricks with the other to strengthen it built of stone. . . .'

7/9/52. 'One of the labourers told me that three urns have been got out whole out of the chamber . . . and that two or three were broken.[1] He like[wise] brought some shells from the drain, of which there are quantities lying upon the top of one of the walls of the drain.'

9/9/52. 'Purchased a third brass of Carausius, rev. Pax type, a ae 3 of Tetricus and five other coins of the lower empire in poor condition, found in the excavations in Mr. Round's field. . . . Purchased a small black urn [sketch] . . . and a black . . . bottle [sketch] [spaces for the dimensions of these have not been filled in] from ibid. the bottle had the top broken off.'

10/9/52 and 9/10/52. Some small purchases.

20/12/52. 'Purchased a black . . . Roman urn [sketch], 5 ins. across mouth, 3½ ins. high, two bone and bronze pins, an old knife handle [sketch] 2 ins. long . . . a plain Samian base HELEN . . . MA another . . . ITA . . . SEE, a ae 2 of Carausius, a ae 3 same Emperor and same type, and several of the lower empire found in the old sewer, ibid.'

Duncan's account (loc. cit. 210 ff.) published in 1858 contains a number of errors in dimensions which must be ascribed to a faulty memory or misreading of his notes, or both. The 'bath' chamber was described as 30 ft. square, with double walls, clay being rammed between them.[2] The end of the drain is described as an arched opening 3 ft. above the floor and 2 ft. square! Compare pl. XVII, A. The statement that it was closed by a trap operated by a spiral spring when the water rose 5 ft. high is pure imagination. The most serious error was noticed in *J.R.S.* ix, 169, for while Buckler[3] places the building at its correct distance from the wall, Duncan followed by Cutts[4] plotted it 300 ft. too far north, and this despite the fact that portions of the drain near the 'Mithraeum' were left open to view (and still are so).

39 (part of). The impressive drain, to which reference has been made, is common to insulae 14 and 7. We propose to deal with the whole of it here. It begins at the NE. corner of the 'Mithraeum' and after a vaulted and serpentine length, extending to the limits of the 'Mithraeum' enclosure, it ran open along the west side of the street, nearly straight, to the NE. Gate. There it suddenly turns under the street and runs out through the gate, to curve sharply to the left and empty itself, apparently, into the town ditch. Its purpose was simple, to run off flood water, but its description will, unfortunately, have to be protracted.

At the south end, where it leaves the underground room, it has an opening 9 in. square at floor-level

(pl. XVII, A), and behind the demolished wall can be seen the beginning of the vaulted portion, which is out of all proportion to the volume of water which could ever pass through the square opening. It is 10 to 12 in. wide and 28 in. high, or, with the arch, 34 in. (section, fig. 38). The construction is entirely of tiles laid in white mortar, and the vaulting, though carelessly done because invisible, is very soundly built. Pl. XVII, B is a view inside the vault taken by flashlight from a point where it is broken looking south. While following a

FIG. 38. Section of vaulted drain north-east of 'Mithraeum', p. 87.

serpentine course for over 70 ft. to the NE. the width and height gradually increase, the vault ending with a flat, finished face 83 ft. from its beginning. Duncan left two brick-built openings covered by grills, as means of access, one of them at the breach and the other a little to the north where the vaulting ends (1 on plan). The breach was 18 ft. long and has removed evidence relating to the clay on the floor of the drain (see below).

The bottom is of flat tiles laid on a few pieces of lias limestone, and upon the tiles lie 3 in. of sandy silt. Above this lies a series of lumps of bluish clay up to 7 in. thick which are visible in pl. XVII, B. Neither clay nor silt produced any remains, which is not surprising under the vaulting. The clay seemed to run back, undulating in lumps as far as one could see. Ten feet south of the break we found the tile floor stopped, the silt, with the clay above it, resting directly upon the pieces of lias.

After the vaulting ends there is one more curve and then the drain sets a course following the side of the

---

[1] This agrees with our experience. We have never known so many pots to be found so nearly perfect as in the lowest deposit here, other than in a cemetery. Unfortunately, only one complete vessel can now be traced to Duncan's excavations (fig. 58, 7).

[2] Cf. Wire above, 6/9/52; the description applies to the two walls east of the stair-well and to no others.

[3] Buckler, plan facing p. 5.

[4] Cutts, op. cit. plan, gate, drain, and building are all wrong and too far west.

street to the gateway. The whole length of this was cleared. Though drawn straight on the plan, in fact the line was just slightly sinuous, and this to an extent which seemed definitely purposive and not accidental; pl. XVII, C will show this better than words. The tile floor was intact throughout the open portion, and where not disturbed by Duncan there was a considerable amount of sandy silt upon it, but nowhere outside the vaulting was anything observed corresponding to the lumps of clay. The width was not regular, varying from 17 in. to not quite 24 in., while the height of the walls varied from 28 in. where the vaulting ends to 4 ft. 6 in. at the gateway.

The walls were built in three sections. The whole length was first laid out with eight courses of large tiles measuring 17 to 17½ by 12 by 2 in., the uppermost course all of intact 'stretchers'. The total height is 21 in. The southern third was laid in white mortar, the northern two-thirds in pink. Perhaps two gangs were at work. The upper part, nearly all 'stretchers', but imperfect, was built upon this with a wide mortar joint between. At the level of this joint, in many places, openings about 4 in. square were left, generally exactly oppositely placed in the two walls. They are visible in several of our figures and are ringed with white in pl. XVIII, B. It cannot, however, be said that they are continuous and evenly spaced throughout. Their purpose is not understood. They are usually filled with mortar, with a small piece of tile.

The upper part is built of smaller tiles measuring 15 by 11 by 1½ in., in a varying number of courses according to the depth required. Ten courses make 24 in. height. At the south end, where the wall is lowest, the vaulting rests directly on the large tiles of the lower part (pl. XVII, B). The northern half of the upper wall is laid in pink mortar, the southern half in white. Near the middle of the course the wide joint showed the white lying on the pink very clearly. The difference in the size of the tiles can be seen in several of our figures.

It has been suggested, not very plausibly, that the sinuous line of the walls was to add to their strength. They average 4 ft. high, and being faced on one side only and built largely of halved tiles, which leaves the back unfinished, are not very strong, especially as, for the most part, they act as retaining walls.

Several small openings led into the drain from the west. The upper insula (15) only provided three. No. 1 lay on the last curve. It is 11 in. square and set in the upper part of the wall; no. 2 was 82 ft. farther north, and measured 18 in. wide by about 12 in. high, but had been damaged. It also was in the upper wall. At 23 ft. 6 in. north of this lay the zero point for our measurements, and here, a typical point, the width at the bottom was 21 in., at the top 26 in., the height was

36 in., with 15 courses in the east wall and 14 in the west. The width of the floor necessitated the use of two rows of tiles, one imperfect (pl. XVIII, A). In the walls the tiles are all 'stretchers', but in the upper portion many are imperfect.

Opening no. 3 lay 50 ft. north of zero and was 6 in. wide by 10 in. high, set in the lower wall, one course above the floor.

Opening no. 4 lay at 50 ft. 7 in., nearly over no. 3, and was 15 in. wide by 10 in. high (the top irregular), placed two courses above the top of the lower wall.

Passing into insula 7, opening no. 5 is in a broken part of the wall, and only the south side was preserved. It lay 85 ft. 6 in. from zero and was 10 in. high, in the upper wall.

No. 6 lay at 120 ft. 11 in. and was 10 in. long by 3 in. deep. It may well be only a damaged example of the small holes already mentioned.

No. 7 lay at 132 ft. 9 in. and was 10½ in. wide, placed three courses above the top of the lower wall.

No. 8 lay at 191 ft. 3 in., and was six courses deep from the top of the wall, and 18 in. wide.

No. 9 was a double opening (pl. XX, B). It lay 264 ft. from zero. The lower opening was 10 in. square, in the lower wall at floor-level; over it lay a somewhat smaller opening, a foot in height, in the upper wall.

No. 10 was a large opening nearly 2 ft. square in the top of the east wall just beyond trench II; the bottom was about 1 ft. above the floor. Placed at the lowest point of the N.–S. street, this opening drained the storm-water from its west side.

No. 11 is the last opening and occurs at the angle where the drain is deflected to run under the street by the gateway (pl. XVII, D). Its position shows that it was intended to convey the surface water, trapped by the rampart at the bottom of the slope, into the drain. It is 18 in. square, in the upper west wall, and there is, at the upper right-hand corner, an iron staple fixed in the wall, with the mark of a corresponding one at the other corner. These were for an iron grill. The position is 40 ft. from the inner face of the town wall.

It is remarkable that, with one exception, all these openings are fairly high up in the wall. The exception, no. 9, especially offered hope of tracing a drain back to a house, for a small brick culvert appeared in a parallel wall just west of it. But here, as in every other case, the made earth behind the opening preserved no trace of the direction or nature of the conduit employed. The openings as a whole seemed to have been planned in advance and built as part of the drain when it was first built.

The bottom of no. 10 is not understood. On the north side its straight wall descends nearly to the floor of the drain, but on the south it stops at the third course below the top of the lower wall. The masonry between is broken, so we do not know the shape of the bottom of the opening.

On reaching the gateway, at a point 40 ft. from the wall, the drain, now 4 ft. 6 in. deep, makes a pronounced turn (pl. XVII, D) to run under the roadway, but is not vaulted until it reaches the line of the south face of the counterforts. Here the vault begins and the side walls are continued a little above the spring of the arch. This was to enable the covering slabs, whatever they were, to ride high enough to close the opening of the arch.

Duncan (p. 223) says, 'often the great flat tiles forming the roof [of the drain] were in situ'. For this we must take his word, but we found none, nor any fragment to indicate a tile so large as to fulfil this purpose. The width of the drain at the top is such that a tile 3 ft. in length (which would be most exceptional) would scarcely have a 6-in. bearing at each end. Unfortunately, while implying that these tiles were in position from the gateway southwards—and his woodcut seems to show them—he does not state their extent.

Some such cover there must have been under the street, but if it extended over any large length of the drain it is very difficult to see how this became filled up to the top with earth full of pottery, bones, &c., especially in the silt and lower part of the earth. Although Duncan has recorded how he followed the drain along its full length, we felt certain that for considerable stretches he had not dug into it, especially south of the half-way mark. We found much of the filling quite undisturbed, including the silt in the bottom, and Duncan's description of the contents is quite sound except that we found no tiles of exceptional size.

He could not have found the covering tiles in position for very far. In a few places one or other of the walls had been badly robbed, the worst being about 100 ft. south of the gate, where the west wall was missing, affording a good view of the east wall and the tile flooring (pl. XVIII, A).

Where the filling appeared undisturbed, in the southern part of the drain, the sandy silt in the bottom varied in thickness; the uneven slope of the floor, or slight blockages, had caused deposits up to 15 in. thick in places; elsewhere there was sometimes only 1 in. It consisted of layers of washed sand and mud, and contained much pottery, some of it in large fragments, but rarely fitting together. A representative collection is shown in figs. 57–59, and the sigillata in figs. 50, 51. The bowl, fig. 51A, was found with only one piece missing, scattered over 18 ft. of the floor,

a strong argument that the drain was not covered at this point (just north of zero). The only coin found in the silt was an *as* of Hadrian. The accumulation dates from the end of the first century, slowly at first, more rapidly in the Antonine period, up to a time when the stiff yellow filling, similar to the last filling of the 'Mithraeum', was put in. This upper filling we found undisturbed from our zero point to the first curve southwards. In it lay two mortaria (fig. 58, 8 and 9). We found no coins, and Duncan's list running up to Valentinian may have included coins from the top-soil.[1] On the other hand, it may not be a coincidence that the latest coin in the 'Mithraeum' top level was a Valentinian. The top of the yellow filling was a foot below the top of the drain at zero, but as the walls became lower southwards, it rose and finally covered them. It practically corresponds to the level of the Roman surface outside, and from the point where it covered the walls there was mortar remaining on the upper side of the top courses. We do not know whether this signifies former covering slabs, or that the walls were at one time higher. But certainly it looks as if the drain had been filled in up to ground-level, and this perhaps at the same time as the hollow left by the demolished 'Mithraeum'.

Outside the gateway Duncan's plan and description is all we know, for this part was not reopened. He shows the drain curving to the west and forking, and he shows the right fork overriding the left, as if it were a later alteration. The width here was 21 in. The filling was thus described: 'the researches were directed first of all towards the river; but after clearing away the contents of the space between the walls for some little distance, they were found to terminate abruptly by a rude fracture and beyond, all trace was lost. The contents consisted, from the top downwards, of 1. earth mingled with pieces of Roman tile; 2. abundance of bones of ox and deer; 3. oyster shells in great quantity; 4. a most extraordinary collection of fractured pots and pans of the Roman period with fragments of Samian by the score; 5. some very fine silt. The silt was just above the flooring of tiles, and was very fine. It consisted of finely levigated sandy clay, such as is seen in the bottom of water courses subject to rapid flushing. There was no evidence of faecal matter.

'Several coins of the later empire were found, of these a few are in the possession of the Society, but the majority were stolen.[2]

'The ends of the walls were broken, towards the river, and by no mean violence. This fracture, and the portion of the walls anterior to it, proved that the

---

[1] The pottery is described on pp. 129–131 and the coins on pp. 115–117.

[2] Cf. Wire's references to Mr. Bottins [*sic*] Smith, p. 85,

but Duncan (p. 55) says 'Mr. Bolton Smith has preserved, for the benefit of the Museum, all the objects . . . .'

broad fosse . . . towards the N.E. was made later than the remains just discovered. . . . the walls of the cloaca (drain) could not be traced on the other side of the fosse towards the river.'

The curve of the drain outside the gate can hardly be for any purpose other than to direct it into the butt-end of the town ditch here. This ditch would be wet a little farther west, and most of the ground between wall and river would be marshy.[1] At some later date the ditch was widened and, probably, carried across in front of the gate, but this has not been tested (see p. 57).

Duncan, p. 223, mentions three coins of Carausius, one of Domitian, and several of Constantine as found in the silt of the drain just south of the gateway, and, generally, coins from Trajan to Valentinian, and, farther south, shells of freshwater molluscs, which show that the water was not unduly polluted. Farther south again he seems to state that two coins, of Tetricus and Claudius Gothicus, were found in the silt under the arched portion. This seems difficult to explain. It is possible that they came from the breach referred to above.

The peculiar fork to the left in the curved portion outside the gateway is dismissed by Duncan, p. 226, as probably a 'little mistake of the architect'. Is it possible the first was made before the ditch was cut, and had to be altered when the ditch was finished?— or that the first met a small ditch, and the second was made to meet a larger ditch?

As to the purpose of this drain, apart from its initial function of draining away the water from the 'Mithraeum', the several openings in its west wall and the large one at the bottom of the slope of the street on the east have been accepted as proof that it was a common drain or sewer. We are not, however, of the opinion that the detritus found in it gave any indication that it had been used for sewage, but rather for flood-water. The several connexions on the west can only have served private houses, but could nevertheless have been restricted to rain-water. In the face of this evidence of the drain serving private houses, whether as drain or sewer (or *cloaca*, as Duncan and many would have it), Mr. Laver quotes: 'In many hundreds of antique drains discovered in my time I have never seen a sign of communication with the houses lining the streets through which the drains passed. All side-channels belonged to streets or public buildings, none to private dwellings.'[2] Presumably cesspools were more popular, but only one had been found up to that time (these last words are Laver's).

As at Rome, so in the provinces, and so far we have not found a parallel case to our drain. At Augst the drains, where vaulted, had manholes as frequently as three in 80 metres. They were vertical shafts through the vault, closed at the top by a large stone slab. At street crossings the gutters of the lateral streets were led into them through sandstone blocks with oblique passages and with a stone block fixed in the wall opposite to receive the rush of water. There were no lateral openings between the street-crossings. One drain only was plastered inside.[3]

THE REST OF INSULA 7
(PLAN, FIG. 37)

Much of this was trenched in the excavations of 1927–8, but the circumstances were such that a thorough investigation was impossible. The aim was to ascertain the nature of the buildings present, if any, with the intention of concentrating upon the best. But the remains found were very fragmentary and had not belonged to houses of any great size or pretensions. In no case could sufficient time be given to the tracing of their plans, which, indeed, the evidence of our trenches showed to be a project at once difficult and without promise of useful results.

150. Having failed to find culverts leading to the houses from the openings in the drain, we turned our attention to the tiled arch behind opening 9 (pl. XX, B). But this wall proved to be in very bad preservation. It ran not quite parallel to the drain and was continued as a very ruinous rubble core, 3 ft. thick, for 33 ft. to the south. Ten feet farther south this was found to be a slight remnant of a stone wall only 14 in. wide, and not quite in the same line. The small arched culvert at the north end is at a level a little above the upper opening into the drain, with which it probably connected by a wooden conduit, for there is no trace left. The culvert is only 18 in. in diameter, and the tiles of the arch rested on made earth. Possibly there were here two large stones which have been robbed.

Searching for more information on this building, a trench was cut westwards for 90 ft. The top-soil was 2 ft. 6 in. deep with a foot of mixed clayey soil below it; beneath this was stony clay, which had been disturbed. At 42 ft. 6 in. and 65 ft. from the west face of the culvert we found traces of light walls of septaria. The remains were only about a foot thick and very fragmentary. At 72 ft. there was a patch of loose septaria and mortar 3 ft. wide. It is quite possible that this represented the west wall of the building. Nothing else was found in the trench save some battered and worn fragments of pottery.

---

[1] Stukeley shows it so, but a map of the Castle lands in 1622 shows it used as fields, with tenants' names.

[2] Lanciani, *Ruins and Excavations of Ancient Rome* (1897).
[3] Laur-Belart, *Augst*, 136.

151. On the south side of the area our trenches found the E.–W. street. North of it there was a gravelled area, probably a yard. No boundary walls appeared. About 30 ft. from the roadway remains of buildings were found and efforts to trace these resulted in a complex of trenches best followed on the plan. A foundation 2 ft. 3 in. wide, on which a few blocks of septaria still lay in position, was struck running E.–W. After running west for 12 ft. it returned north nearly at right angles. The return was followed for 13 ft., where it broke off without further trace. The angle of these two walls was built upon an earlier foundation of the same width at a lower level, which could be traced 14 ft. farther west and then no farther. A trench was carried 18 ft. north of the wall where first struck, but nothing was found.

Eastwards the line of the wall was indicated by the edge of a red tessellated pavement, 5 ft. wide W.–E. by 32 ft. N.–S. This was laid on an inch of red mortar on a bed of mixed clay and stones. The surrounding walls had been robbed so as to leave no trace. The beaker (fig. 59, 5) was found intact at the south end of this pavement, where it may have stood as a foundation offering at the foot of the wall. But it was not quite upright, and may have fallen, with black earth in which it lay, into the foundation trench after robbing.

After the pavement ceased there was a gravel area or yard of 15 ft. and then a dark depression like a pit, which proved barren.

So far our search for houses had been disappointing, so it was decided to dig one more trench across the intervening space to the drain, beginning near the north end of the tessellated pavement. After about 15 ft. width of clayey loam containing pottery of about A.D. 100 to 120 we came on a gravel path running N.–S., possibly of Roman date. Thirty feet from the red pavement lay the remains of an angle built of septaria and mortar. The return was followed north for 6 ft., and led to a very vague mortar layer, presumably a foundation, which we soon abandoned.

A little east of the angle just mentioned a number of broken Roman tiles lay high up and flat, as if laid for a garden path. This was probably of recent date. At four places beyond this fragmentary foundations were encountered. The first two were followed north, the first for 30 ft., as a very vague foundation. This led to another red pavement lying on its west side. The dimensions were 14 ft. N.–S. by 16 ft. E.–W., but the west side was incomplete. This pavement was ill laid in poor clay; no trace of mortar bedding could be seen. It lay only 18 in. below the surface, and on cutting through it in search of lower layers we found the remains of a brick floor 6 in. below. The bricks measured 5½ by 2½ by 1 in. and were of good red material. They were disturbed, but had probably been laid on edge in herring-bone fashion. The walls which surrounded this pavement could not be traced.

The second foundation struck a cross-wall to the south almost immediately and did not continue beyond. The cross-wall, running E.–W., was at a lower level. An attempt to follow it northwards also failed. The subsoil here is a yellow loamy clay, and in this trench at the point indicated on the plan there was a post-hole in this, with a block of septaria at the bottom.

A diagonal trench was cut SW. from the gateway. The first part, it was hoped, would find the intervallum road and a drain leading to the last opening in the drain. This NE. end of the trench was full of broken tiles, mortar, and gravel, the residue of the plundering of the gate for building material. At a depth of 3 ft. we were satisfied that neither road nor drain had existed here. The bottom of the trench was stiff loam and nothing was found.[1] A midden heap, almost entirely of oyster-shells, was found 118 ft. from the gate, and proved to be the overflow of a rubbish-pit (pit 1), which was circular, about 8 ft. deep and the same in diameter. The filling was almost entirely oyster-shells and pottery. No stratification was observable, and the filling had overflowed and formed three small mounds on top. Fragments of a number of decorated sigillata bowls of f. 37, of Flavian date, without the smallest sherd of f. 29, date it to the end of the first century. There was also a coin of Domitian and a fibula with rectangular enamelled plate. All these, with the pottery, are described below, pp. 118, 125–128. The pit is later than the yellow loam layer.

Before leaving this trench a hole was sunk into the stiff loam, which proved to be about 2 ft. thick. Beneath it lay a dark occupation layer about 8 in. thick, lying on the natural gravel. We were unable to return to this, so it awaits a future investigator. The total depth to gravel was 5 ft. 11 in.

The search for houses having produced nothing worth following, and the south part of the field being now available to us, it was decided to devote our limited time and means to the 'Mithraeum' site and that part of the field.

When the present Park Café was built in January–February 1930 a cutting was made westwards from the Norman ditch for a basement (pl. XIV, C). Part of the metalling of the E.–W. street was revealed (see p. 69).

Cutts on his plan of the town indicates two tessellated pavements in this insula, which cannot be traced to correspond with any records.

---

[1] These were early days. We have since learned that this stiff yellow loam which covers most of Roman Colchester is the daub from houses of the early period. The earliest level is beneath it, and it is itself full of Roman potsherds, &c.

INSULA 8

This occupies the NE. corner of the town, having the town wall on its north and east; in good condition on the inside, but robbed from the outside until only about 18 in. of thickness is left. On the north side the rampart can be seen still, on the east it is buried, and all is level. The width of this, being a marginal insula, is not less than 450 ft. The street on the south has not been found. With insula 16 this area was Castle land and not built over until about 1850, before which this part was a Botanic Garden, at least as early as 1805. Roman and Castle roads were begun in 1852, but not completed for many years. Wire has a goodly list of finds and observations, but since his time little has been observed in this area. The lack of records from the building up of the area is unfortunate and not a little surprising.

40. In May 1852 a tessellated pavement was found, 18 in. from the surface at a point marked on the O.S. 10-ft. map (with date '1852 and 1853') under Castle Road opposite Radnor Terrace. Of this Duncan (p. 36) says: 'I possess a glass unguentarium which was found with other antiquities, consisting of fragments of urns mortaria, Samian ware and tops of amphorae, upon a tessellated pavement in the Botanic Garden, which consisted of a bed of concrete and superimposed tesserae, under which was a coin of Diva Faustina and a classical head in terra cotta.'[1]

Wire has two notes on this: 13/5/1852. 'An ornament of metal gilt, moving on a joint, and has engraved on it some fabulous animal, it had originally been enamelled, some of it remaining. It was said to have been found under a tessellated pavement found there [Botanic Gardens] but one can hardly be brought to think it Roman but early Saxon from the fact of the foundation mortar being only two inches thick and set on the soil without any preparations . . . .' This is now lost.

14/5/52. 'Purchased several fragments of the above pavement which was made with the centre of black tesserae, the outer part of red . . . the dimensions as far as could be measured, as the whole was not uncovered, were 10 ft. from N.–S. and 30 ft. from E.–W., being the entire width of the road. It was only 23 ins. below the surface and about three yards south of the pond.[2] The foundation mortar is of unslaked lime and sand, the latter being in the greater proportion. Under it was found a 2b coin of M. Aurelius, rev. a temple and a part of a mortarium with potter's mark on it.

Duncan has a further note that between the town-wall and Grayfriars 'nearly midway, but towards the western end of the ground, a long tessellated pavement was cut across. It was about 18 ins. below the surface, it consisted of middle sized tesserae of brick, placed upon a foundation of concrete, into whose composition roughly powdered red tile materially entered. There was no pattern . . . in cutting through it a coin of Diva Faustina Pia, bronze, second size was found, well worn. It was below the concrete, close by the coin there was a terra cotta . . . head [f. 369] . . . on a level with the pavement were pieces of fictile ware and tops of earthenware bottles.'[3] (The woodcut shows ff. 369, 368, and T.S. f. 37.)

Cutts has three crosses (for pavements) and some other marks in this insula, but we cannot rely upon them.

41. Wire, Diary, 18/6/1852, says: 'Purchased a metal fibula plated with silver, a plain bronze ring, another fibula 3 ins. long made out of . . . [one] . . . piece of metal wire and a 2b coin of Vespasian, a metal box, a T.S. base stamped OF. PASSEN and several fragments of plain T.S. At the lower part of the Botanic Garden opposite Lot xi, a layer of wood ashes was discovered about 30 ins. below the surface, which continued ten feet, then an intermission of a few feet, then a commencement of it for four feet. Some short distance east of it was a floor of flagstones on which a fire had been made, this was about 6 ft. square, then more to the east, opposite lot vi, was at 3 ft. below the surface a floor of three Roman tiles of usual size continued by a path made with pieces of septaria and good sized pebbles; this extended the whole width of the trench dug for sewerage pipes—about 3 ft. wide—how far it extended underground each side could not be ascertained as no more ground was moved. . . .' (See also *T.E.A.S.* o.s. v, 159, where it is stated that these remains were a little north of no. **40**.)

185. The tower found in military works during 1940 has been mentioned on p. 42.

The following small finds have been made: an Antoninianus of Probus, found 6 ft. deep when digging a grave in the Friends Burial Ground (1908.09); handle of a vessel of pale yellow green glass found at the bottom of Castle Road on the west side, March 1930 (76. 41); a vessel of crude (native?) ware, variant of f. 266, found in a yard at the back of the Botanic Garden in Roman Road, purchased of Mrs. Cater (4011. 20).

Wire has further details not quoted above:

2/4/52. 'Purchased some fragments of Samian, decorated, two plain bottoms marked ELVTILLI and [sketch of rosette-stamp], a bronze stud inlaid with silver [sketch] . . . found on the Botanic Garden, which has been purchased by the Land Building Society and is now being made level and drained preparatory to selling it off in lots.'

---

[1] The mouth of a mask-mouthed flagon, f. 369.
[2] The position of the pond on our map is taken from Gilbert's map of *c.* 1845.
[3] *T.E.A.S.* o.s. i, 215.

22/4/52. 'Visited the Botanic Garden and purchased part of a decorated samian bowl, impressed on it a gladiatorial combat, and a plain samian bottom stamped MOXSIU. F found there.'

28/4/52. Ditto. 'purchased the front of a bronze bow shaped brooch probably Saxon.'

30/4/52. Ditto. 'purchased the following . . . found there . . . a red earth bottle [sketch], the top had been broken off just below the handle to admit the calcined bones of a child. A double wick lamp of very coarse earth, the eyes and nose of a man in very coarse earth, being part of some vessel, two samian bottoms, plain, stamped PAVLIM and [C]OMPRINNIM.'

1/5/52. Ditto. '. . . a small bronze stag one and a half inches high and two inches long, having the horns united at the top by a modius; a bronze stylus, two metal ornaments, a bone pin, and a 2b coin of Vespasian very much corroded, found in an artificial mound in the NW. corner of the garden.'

4/5/52. 'Purchased a bronze needle five inches long and a bronze chain seven inches long found in the NW. corner of the B. Garden.'

6/5/52. 'Purchased a red brick cut in the shape of a cinque-foil, part of a bronze chain, a globe, found in the B. Garden.'

8/5/52. Ditto. 'a bronze ornament [sketch] part of a bronze stylus, two bone pins and a bead of vitrified earth . . . the labourer says he has found an urn there.'

10/5/52. Ditto. 'a bronze hook [sketch] with ring attached, a small urn [sketch, a late beaker] of red earth [dimensions given], a T.S. base stamped VERVS and two fragments of decorated T.S., also a bronze Roman ring-key, a small metal ornament with a face engraved on it, part of another metal ornament.'

13 and 14/5. See above.

15/5/52. Ditto. 'a 2b coin of M. Aurelius, rev. Mars with trophy to right, and a 1b coin of Hadrian in very bad condition, found in the B. Garden.'

18/5/52. Ditto. 'a bronze Roman brooch, an iron spur, and some fragments of bronze.'

22/5/52. Ditto. 'part of a Roman fibula found when laying down the sewerage pipes from the B. Garden through the trench in the washing-place meadows.[1] . . . purchased a bronze Saxon fibula [sic] [sketch, Roman, Langton Down type, with curiously decorated bow] formerly gilt, 2 ins. long, two hasps of bronze, one plated with silver, a bronze ornament [sketch], a 2b coin of Faustina II, beautifully patinated, rev. a female seated left, . . . a 2b Trajan, rev. a seated figure, . . . and a piece of bronze, found in the B.G.'

24/5/52. Ditto, ditto. 'part of a bronze chain . . . .'

26/5/52. On the town wall section see p. 92 above. '. . . One of the fibulae noted under Sat. 22nd corresponds with Akerman's *Guide to Celtic, etc. Remains*, Pl. xii fig. 14.'

8/6/52. 'Purchased an iron key [sketch], the top of an earthen Roman lamp having impressed upon it a bust of Jupiter with an eagle displayed standing before it, two bronze studs and a fragment of an encaustic tile found at the B.G.'

14/6/52. Ditto. 'a bronze needle 12½ ins. long, B.G.'

28/6/52. Ditto. 'a bronze stylus [sketch] 4 ins. long, a 3b coin of Valens, another small brass coin of the lower empire and two pieces of bronze. B.G.'

3/7/52. Ditto. 'an iron arrow head 2¾ ins. long, square section with hollow socket, and an iron key 3 ins. long, top broken off. B.G.'

12/7/52. Ditto. 'a bow shaped bronze fibula, two buckles, an iron hammer-head, some fragments of decorated samian, a fragment or two of bronze, two plain samian bases stamped OF.PAR . . ., the other illegible. B.G.'

13/7/52. Ditto. 'a bronze nail-like ornament having a bust

engraved in outline upon it, from the B.G. . . . this appears to have been plated with silver or tin.' (figure).

15/7/52. Ditto. '. . . samian base OFCREST (retro), mortar rim SOLLUS F' (between rows of chevrons).

16/7/52. Ditto. 'an iron knife 5½ ins. long, blade 3 ins. long, 1¼ ins. wide at the broadest part. B.G. also an iron modelling tool 4½ ins. long, blade 3⅜ ins. wide, and a small bronze buckle. B.G.'

17/7/52. 'Purchased a three-square pointed needle in bronze, similar to the modern sack needles, found at the Botanic Garden.'

22/7/52. 'Purchased an iron knife 6 ins. long, the blade 3 ins. long and 1 in. wide near handle, handle 3 ins. long. The remains of wood on the blade lead to the inference that it was . . . in a wooden sheath. B.G. also an iron instrument [sketch, the spring part of a padlock] with a spring each side, length 4½ ins. It appears to have been in a handle or haft originally, also a well-burnt red-earth brick 5½ by 2¾ by 1½ ins., several bricks of these dimensions have been found in the same garden, but not in any brickwork, but at several parts of it. . . . It is rather singular no coins have been found there of late excepting Nuremburg counters.'

29/7/52. 'Purchased . . . tile, graffito PRIMV, fragment of plain samian with graffito RAECINVS (Graecinus) (part of the G visible), another, AIF; amphora handle marked Q . . . . F; rim of mortar with herring-bone mark; base silver coin of Severus Alexander.'

31/7/52. 'Purchased the bone handle of a knife with ring and dot pattern, saw a coin of Constantine the Great, found at the Botanic Garden.'

4/8/52. 'Purchased a silver Roman spoon, straight handle, circular bowl length 5½ ins., bowl 1 in. diam.; bronze bow shaped fibula; found in the B.G. Also a bronze buckle without tongue [sketch, medieval], a black earth Roman urn 5¼ ins. high, 5 ins. bulge, 3¾ ins. mouth [sketch].'

24/1/53. 'Purchased a 3b coin of Allectus, six oared galley type, found in the Botanic garden.'

1/1/53. 'An entrance has been made through the Town Wall into the footpath [Park Folly] at the NW. corner of the B.G.'

INSULA 9

Up to 1910 this insula, which lies against the west wall, was almost clear of buildings. The streets to north and south have not been accurately identified, but should not lie far off the lines of the very old boundaries between the Technical College grounds and its neighbours; marked on the north on the 25-in. map by a fence and scarp, on the south by the old stone wall between it and the former garden of the existing rectory of St. Peter's.[2] On these assumptions the insula was about 525 ft. E.–W. by 250 N.–S. The tower at the SW. angle (**164**) is described on p. 22; that at the NW. angle remains to be found, and is believed to be partly visible.

5. Here we have one of the very few Roman houses which have been excavated in Colchester. The first part of it was comparatively well done in February 1865, when a pavement was discovered 32 ft. from the

---

[1] i.e. the meadows on the south bank of the river, due north of the Castle.

[2] Not to be confused with the former rectory which stood where the Essex and Suffolk Fire Office now is.

town wall and 132 yards north of the Balkerne Gate. The excavations, with plans and drawings, were carried out by Mr. Josiah Parish.[1]

The walls had in many places been robbed even of the footings, some of which, however, remained to a depth of 2 ft. The rubble used in them was small and

Crossing the end of this row of tiles, and at an angle of about 80 degrees, was found a number of flanged tiles, with their flanges uppermost. These were left in position.

The concrete base for the pavements was of a yellowish sandy nature, on the average 4 in. thick, laid on rough stone rubble. This was spread with a

ROMAN HOUSE (5)
INSULA 9

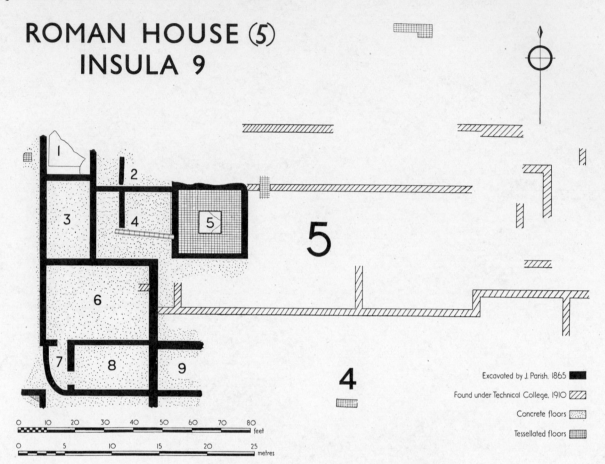

FIG. 39. Plan of house in Insula 9. [5 and 4], pp. 93–96.

looked like chippings from the dressed stones. Some of the latter, where left *in situ*, were as large as those in the town wall and of the same kind. A few pieces of Roman tile were also bonded into the walls in random rubble courses. One piece of wall, which had all the appearance of a foundation, was found standing on a concrete floor. Close to the corner of it lay a 'bronze box or vessel'. All masonry found was removed, at the owner's desire. There was an upright row of large tiles, standing at right angles to the foundation walls, eight in all, with about a foot of rubble concrete on each side of them and not a vestige of pavement.

very even surface, and then a concrete with a very large proportion of powdered tile was laid above it, about an inch and a half in thickness. On this was spread a thin coating of calcareous cement, in which the tesserae were bedded. The plain cement floors were of two kinds; the finest were red with crushed tile, the coarser yellowish.

The first pavement, in the NW. room, was a little over a quarter preserved. Only a lozenge-shaped centre can be missing. The border was of white tesserae and the pattern geometrical, not unlike that found in insula 15 (p. 115). A poor figure of it is given,[2] but there

[1] *T.E.A.S.* o.s. iv, 53, v, 161; *J.B.A.* xxxi, 69 note; O.S. map (Museum copy) 1/500, xxvii, 12, 3 and 25 in. xxvii; *J.R.S.* ix, 158.
[2] *T.E.A.S.* o.s. iv, pls. II and III.

is a large square of it in the Museum, composed of the main square surrounded by triangles taken from other parts. From these remains thus preserved the whole could be drawn out in detail. This floor sealed down masses of broken cement floors of an earlier house.

The second pavement was found in the NE. room, but only part of the guilloche border on the east side and part of a knot in one corner is preserved. The border is of red tesserae. The ornamental centre was 7 ft. 10 in. square.

The north wall of room 6 was very well preserved, sometimes still 3 ft. high. It was built of larger stones than the other walls, portions of fresco were adhering to both sides of it, and there was much more in the soil. The colour was mostly a brilliant vermilion. The depth from the surface was now 9 ft.

The east wall was 3 ft. thick, but much broken on the west side; its base did not go as low as the other wall by quite a foot. It stood on 4–5 in. of concrete. The south wall of room 6 was only 18 in. thick with fair faces, the bottom 7 ft. from the surface. After running west for 30 ft. it returned to the south, leaving a doorway 6 ft. wide between it and the short eastwards return, which was 2 ft. wide and 4 ft. long. The whole west wall was 2 ft. wide.

Room 8. The north wall is the south wall of room 6. It returns southwards, on the west, a distance which Parish says is 4 ft., but shows on his plan as nearly 9 ft.; then there is a doorway, shown 4 ft. 6 in. wide, followed by a short continuation of the wall to make this side of the room total 14 ft. 6 in. long. The south wall was 30 ft. long, but its structure is not described. This room was paved with concrete.

To the SW. of rooms 6 and 8 and in an angle between them lay room 7, formed by a curved wall of very inferior construction, composed of broken flue tiles, pieces of pottery of the larger kinds, and rubble stones. Parish thought it might simply have been a rough wall to retain a rubbish-heap, for a great number of bones, fragments of pottery and scraps of iron, and a heap of the best white lime concrete was found within it. At any rate the wall could never have supported much weight. (It is strange, however, to find the only two prominent doors opening into the rubbish-pit!) Shading on the plan seems to indicate that room 7 also had a concrete floor, which also is shown as extending beyond this building to the corner of the adjacent building, though not mentioned in the text.

Room 9. The north wall is shown on the plan as 3 ft. 6 in. thick, but Parish says it was very rough on both sides, and was at least so thick originally, but was so much broken that he could not decide how much thicker it had been. Here again there was a rise of about a foot in the ground and there was no trace of a floor (yet Parish shows and marks 'concrete floor' on both sides of this wall on his plan). Here there were no remains of wall-painting, and pottery was more abundant. In the wall were found four or five square tiles about 8 by 1 in., which were taken to the Museum. The eastern end of this wall could not be uncovered (nor has it since). The west wall, shown as continuous with the east wall of room 6, is described as only a trifle more than a foot in thickness, and was a little lower than the south wall of rooms 8 and 9. The interior measurement of room 9 N.–S. was 13 ft. This same N.–S. wall continued to the south, but could not be excavated (it runs into the former St. Peter's Rectory garden and could now be followed).

Room 1 is not so fully described as others. Apparently only the line of the foundations of the walls could be followed and these showed the room to be about 15 ft. wide: the north end of the room could not be excavated. The tessellated floor has been described.

Under this pavement, and quite 3½ ft. lower, a flue was found running westwards. It is not shown on the plan, but appears in two of the sections as a shallow trough with sloping sides. 'This flue inclined to the west about 1 in 20; its base was about 2 ft. 6 ins., but I cannot tell how much wider, as it had all been broken away, the sides only had the concrete rendering, for testing the bottom I found it was composed of half-burnt clay'; much vegetable charcoal was found in the bottom. The flue was traced as far as possible, and a large depression in the pavement had been caused by its collapse. Between the flue and the pavement the ground was made up of remains of an earlier building, including broken concrete and many fragments of wall-painting.

Room 2. Only the SW. corner was uncovered. The floor is indicated as of concrete, upon which at one place stood a portion of a wall with perfect faces. At one end of it the bronze box was found. The length of this room on the plan is shown as the same as room 4.

Room 3 lay to the south of room 1 and was of the same width. It had a red concrete floor and was 27 ft. 6 in. long. The centre was not excavated.

Room 5 contained the second pavement and was about 25 ft. square. The north wall is shown as very thick on the plan, but this part could not be excavated.

Room 4 may have been open to the air, for the corners of the rooms 5 and 6 do not connect. The north wall, very imperfect, was nearly 26 ft. long; the floor was of concrete. The space was divided by a wall 13 ft. 6 in. long running south from the north wall at 8 ft. from the west wall. The line of flanged tiles shown, with the flanges uppermost, must be that now referred to above, where reference is also made to a row of eight large tiles standing at right angles with the foundation walls, with a foot of rubble on each side of them and no trace of a floor. The row of flanged tiles crossed the end of this feature at an angle of about 80 degrees. Unfortunately, the plan does not show this clearly, which is curious, for the author regarded the feature as remarkable.

Close to the end of the dividing wall a complete urn was found, 'containing a small quantity of greenish earth. It was covered by a fragment of coarse ware about 1 in. thick.' Unfortunately, it is not stated whether this urn stood on the concrete floor or was buried under it. It was probably found under it and may be regarded as a foundation offering, but it is of little import now since the vessel cannot be identified.

Objects found included a stylus (figured), an iron spearhead 14½ in. long found with the building debris on the concrete floor, and three small silver rings. 'A Roman spur was dug up from under the concrete close to where the urn was exhumed' (this supports the view that the urn was found under the concrete). The complete skeleton of a horse was probably of post-Roman date; under it was found a piece of pottery 'with a blue vitrified pattern upon it' which the excavator did not think Roman. A few pieces of glass and a small fragment of a coin complete the list. A second list includes a piece of a colour-coated beaker with a large dolphin in relief from the rubbish-pit in the SW. corner, and there were bone pins and needles, mostly imperfect, also an iron knife and a knife handle of bone decorated with incised ring and dot pattern.

The corner of an adjacent building to the SW. was uncovered. The walls were similar to those of the SW. part of the first building and on the inside there were remains of a red tessellated floor. Parish's plan shows (by shading only) the space between the buildings as covered by a concrete floor. Whether this is accidental or not we cannot be sure. We are, however, so near to the line on which a street should lie that there is not room for a second building, and it would appear probable that the whole of the remains described belong to one house.

4. To this we would add the red tessellated pavement found under the summer-house in the garden once Mr. Halls's,[1] only about 20 yards east of Mr. Parish's discoveries, and no doubt part of a continuation of the rooms or passage the corner of which he exposed south of room 9.[2]

In 1910 the present Technical College was built on the site. Apparently no attention was paid to archaeological possibilities, for no record exists of what was found. A number of objects eventually made their way to the Museum, and were entered in the books in 1913 and 1914 as having been found '. . . during excavations for the new Technical College . . . .' The only other record of this important excavation is to be found in an entry on the O.S. 1/500 map in the Museum, presumably made by the then Borough Engineer (Mr. H. Goodyear). It comprises Parish's plan with the addition of a few fragmentary walls which show that the building was very extensive, measuring over 60 yards E.–W. by over 30 yards N.–S. (fig. 39).

A fragment of pavement, which must have extended at least 20 ft. in each direction, is mentioned by J. H. Pollexfen (1864), who goes on to record portions of other pavements 'of a more common description' nearby, and evidently belonging to the same building, at an average depth from the surface of about 2 ft. 6 in.

The position given clearly refers to Parish's excavation. It is the sole contribution by Pollexfen to the exploration of Roman Colchester.

The loss of the undoubtedly valuable information which could have been obtained from these works (at the college) is irreparable and much to be regretted. Mr. Wright said that he understood that the contractors did their best to avoid the work being visited by those interested in archaeology, the excuse being that this tended to interfere with the rapid progress of the work. Years later a workman told the writer that they uncovered great masses of masonry, some of them column bases 12 ft. in diameter [sic!], which were blown up with dynamite. He confirmed that archaeologists were excluded.

The only structural remains given to the Museum were three portions of a column or columns of Purbeck marble (or similar stone) 8¾ in. diam., one showing the moulding of base or capital (C.M. 2961.14),[3] a fragment of porphyry, measuring 1¼ by 1⅜ in. (C.M. 2971.14), and a number of fragments of painted wall-plaster (C.M. 2969.14).

The only coins from the site in the Museum are one of Constantine II, one of Gratian (435–436.39), and seven illegible of late empire. The writer has seen another Constantine II from the surface of the west half of the rectory garden.

Metal remains included a bronze 'dolphin' brooch (2972.14) and some small eyelets, &c.

The pottery (C.M. 2962–2968, 2970, 2980.14, and 3923–3924.20) includes no less than eight whole or nearly whole vessels. As there is no question of their being grave furniture at least some of them are most probably foundation-offering pots. They are of forms 266, 268 (2 exx.), 278, two globular beakers with bead-rims,

---

[1] Mr. Halls, fishmonger, NW. corner of High Street.
[2] *J.R.S.* ix, 158; marked on the O.S. 1/500 map, but without legend.

[3] Another piece of a shaft, 6 in. in diameter, was found in digging section IA.

and a rather tall fluted beaker, with brown colour-coating, f. 408. The last is not before about A.D. 190, and the 278 might go with it. The others may be earlier, the 266 certainly so; so that the vessels probably come from the foundations of more than one house, or from a series of rebuildings of the one house. The former is more likely, for Parish indicated the remains of two buildings superimposed under his room 1. One of the vessels is a T.S. cup form 33, quite intact, stamped MACERATI (Lezoux, Hadrian–Antonine); other stamps were MERCAI, f. Lud. Sb, and on coarse ware, ACIRG; CL PVDE; Q. M. CAL on f. 187, and APRILIS F on f. 195. The rest of the list is too long to give here.

6. A tessellated pavement was uncovered by Mr. Mason behind no. 44 North Hill in October 1923. It lay 5 ft. from the south wall of the property and 37 ft. from the back door of the house at a depth of 2 ft. 6 in. The material was large red tesserae with a few yellowish ones; painted plaster was also found, some plain white, and one fragment of red and yellow. This, says Laver, is the same pavement which was discovered in March 1849 at the back of Mr. Stirling Maclean's house, then, apparently, no. 47.[1] Wire says of this garden simply—'single tesserae are frequently dug up'.[2]

134. (Not shown on plan.) In April 1936 Mr. E. J. Rudsdale noted a red tessellated pavement only 15 in. below the surface in this same garden (i.e. no. 44 North Hill).

INSULA 10

This is of approximately normal size, though the exact dimensions are not known. They should be close upon 200 by 330 ft.

Much of the insula (and of insula 11) is a large open garden, in which excavations (never organized) have been made from time to time. Consequently there are finds which may have come from either, and none are well documented. The area is always in danger of being appropriated for a car-park or for building.

14. Wire, Diary, 3/5/1855: '. . . Mr. Smith, fruiterer, North Hill, informs me that he has discovered a tessellated pavement in the garden in his occupation behind the "Chaise and Pair", North Hill.' The reference is probably to this same garden, and Wheeler and Laver place the find approximately on the site of the 1922 pavement. We continue to assume the two are the same.[3]

In November 1922 Mr. A. W. Frost, then owning the garden, uncovered nearly half of a decorated mosaic pavement which must have been about 15 ft. square.[4] It lay at a depth of 4 ft. to 4 ft. 6 in. from the surface. Pottery and oyster-shells were found at the same level, and the pavement was covered by a burnt layer. Remains of walls and a deep cesspool were also found on the site. The pavement closely resembles that found in 1763 in insula 19 (**18**), and the floral pattern is the same as that found in insula 2 (**12**). The work is careful, little worn, and without ancient repairs (C.M. 4433.23).

165. A manuscript note by H. Laver dated 22/12/1909 states: 'Since I published my list of tessellated pavements . . . others have been discovered. One under the house at the entrance to Crispin Court, at the SW. angle of this court and North Hill. A fine one.' This should refer to no. 11 North Hill. Another note records that in 1909 a tessellated pavement was visible in the side of a small excavation 'just inside the entrance to Crispin Court, at the back of no. 11 North Hill,' but this could hardly merit the adjective 'fine'.

The large pavement (**14**) is now in the Museum. Of it P. G. Laver says there was nothing to show the date of its destruction. Just above it lay a T.S. base f. 18/31 stamped SVOBNI, which was covered, as was the whole pavement, by more than a foot of clay from the house-wall, with fragments of its decorated surface. This layer had never been disturbed after its fall. When the pavement was removed its foundations were found to be of septaria, many of large size, pieces of tile and pottery, all resting on a bed of light brown clay 3 ft. thick, which contained much pottery, including an amphora handle stamped T.ATII.ASIATICI and part of a T.S. bowl f. Drag. 30 of late-first-century date.[5]

Below this clay foundation was a black layer 1 in. thick, of ashes and charcoal, and beneath this, on what seemed the original ground surface, a second brass of Nero, Cos. III, the only metal object found.

The following can be gathered from the remains lodged in the Museum: Period I—on the subsoil, below the black ash and charcoal, the coin of Nero and a few sherds of no recognizable form, but of first-century character; an iron nail; no wall-plaster. Period II—from below the pavement, but above the black layer, coloured wall-plaster, first-century pottery, including spindle-amphorae, iron nails, a fused vessel of sea-green glass, oyster-shells.

There is some confusion in Mr. Laver's account of nos. 18 and 9 North Hill: the amphora stamp appears in both (but not in the Museum). The drawing of the pavement with section and site-plan was made by Mr. W. F. Hurry.

[1] But Wheeler and Laver are clear that (7) is in the garden of no. 45, and this is in that of 44. We regard the identity of (6) and (7) as doubtful and show them separately.
[2] Diary, 18/3/1849, and cf. *T.E.A.S.* o.s. v, 155.
[3] *T.E.A.S.* o.s. v, 159; *J.R.S.* ix, 159; xi, 221; *The Times*, 14/12/1922; *Essex County Standard*, 16/12/1922.
[4] *T.E.A.S.* xvi, 294, with coloured plate facing p. 251; *J.R.S.* xi, 221; *Essex Review*, xxxii, 41.
[5] Laver, Diary, 8/1/23 and 13/2/23 (with sketch of section).

There are two entries in the diary regarding this pavement: 31 October 1922: 'Patch of red tesserae found in Frost's garden . . . at depth of 3 ft. . . .', and in the same trench, on 15 November, a Roman drain, 25 ft. 4 in. from the west wall. This is followed by the same note about large tesserae, with reference to Palestine (16/11/22).

On the 23rd we read: 'handsome pavement found at A on plan of 2nd. Stamp of SVOBNI found'. It was still being uncovered on 8 December. On 1 January a new (red) piece of pavement was found, and a second trench was cut parallel to the first. There is no plan.

174. In 1950–1 an extension was built upon the west side of the Telephone Exchange behind St. Martin's House and a large basement was excavated 15 ft. deep, through all levels, to the sandy subsoil. The area measured 44 ft. 6 in. by 40 ft. A comparatively simple operation had been expected, for in the first place a road-junction should lie here, and secondly, remains of houses were alone expected otherwise. Previous experience led us to expect that the Roman layers would account for about 3 ft. of soil only. The facts proved very different, but the archaeological study of the area, despite the active co-operation of H.M. Ministry of Works, proved impossible in the presence of too large a gang of workmen and a huge mechanical excavator, which monster had to be fed incessantly.

In these circumstances not much could be made of a very curious site, which we will now try to describe.[1]

The only work which could be done at all carefully was a trial trench along the south side of the site. Another along the west side was attempted, but the exigencies of feeding the mechanical grab and the great depth prevented detailed investigations.

Roman remains, including stone foundations, were struck near the SW. corner as soon as the ground was broken, and even then, as it proved, the upper layers had been denuded. Fortunately, the most part of the site was occupied by the strong remains of the N.–S. street (see p. 70). The cross-roads which were expected remain somewhat uncertain; if there at all, they are very much staggered (plan, pl. XLI).

The subsoil is yellow sand, and the upper 15 in. or so of it is dark, perhaps stained from the layers above, in any case barren. In the SW. corner there had been a rectangular pit or cellar, with a deeper rectangular pit within it. Only part of the plan of these could be recovered. It was marked in a very strange way. The sides, being nearly vertical, must have been boarded, though no post-holes could be found. Where the boarding had been there was a very hard and dark brown lamina of sand 2–3 in. thick, which was like an iron 'pan' and very easy to follow. The pit was filled with darkish sandy earth containing early pottery, especially many fragments of amphorae of which one was whole and another could be restored (fig. 42, 1 and 2, and the flagon 3). The lowest occupation level tied up with this and could be traced all across the area as far as the road, where again there was an unusual amount of broken amphorae.

This lowest level (A) is Claudius–Nero (A.D. 50–61) and corresponds to the lower of two of three road-levels. (Cf. T.S., fig. 41, 3–7; mortarium 11; and rims 9 (*Cam.* f. 173) and 13.)

A deposit of dark muddy earth and charcoal lies on the east side of the road (B); on the west is burnt earth, daub, and charcoal (T.S. fig. 41, 1, and amphora stamp MIM. ibid. 12). The same is observed all across the site, dipping over the filling of the cellar or pit. This can be associated with the sack of A.D. 60 and partly overlies the earliest road.

Subsequent layers (fig. 30) only remained to a small extent, having been cut away by foundation trenches for walls and by later pits. They include very heavy burnt layers which contained slag, evidence of some industry on the site.[2] The pottery from them was very scanty, but the latest levels that remained, high though they were, were apparently not later than the second century. All later levels had been removed.

Whether any walls are second century cannot be proved, but some are definitely later. The whole section has much in common with the Verulamium sections, *Arch.* xc, 82, 83, figs. 1 and 2.

East of the road there was a stout wall of septaria and mortar, probably of fairly early date, but cut down through several layers. The length exposed was 37 ft. and the width was 2 ft. 6 in. widened below by two offsets to 3 ft. 6 in. No face remained, so that the whole was foundation and was 2 ft. 9 in. deep. From surface to top of the masonry was 6 ft. At the south end the foundation widened out on both sides forming a rectangular pier, all of one and the same construction, the length of which was not ascertained. The width was just over 5 ft., with the same offsets below.

This wall must have been nearly parallel to the street, and belonged to the westernmost building in insula 11. It had been completely robbed to the foundations, presumably in Roman times: the aspect of the stratification above suggests nothing else.

The walls west of the street were difficult. The great wall seen in pl. XXXII, A ran right across the site but was not quite parallel to the street. Its corners were not found, but it ran over the site of the E.–W. street, coming from the air-raid shelters behind no. 5 North Hill (156). At its south end subsequent work, after we had left the site, showed it made an approximate right

---

[1] *J.R.S.* xli, 133.   [2] No doubt connected with the crucible and bronze found at **156**.

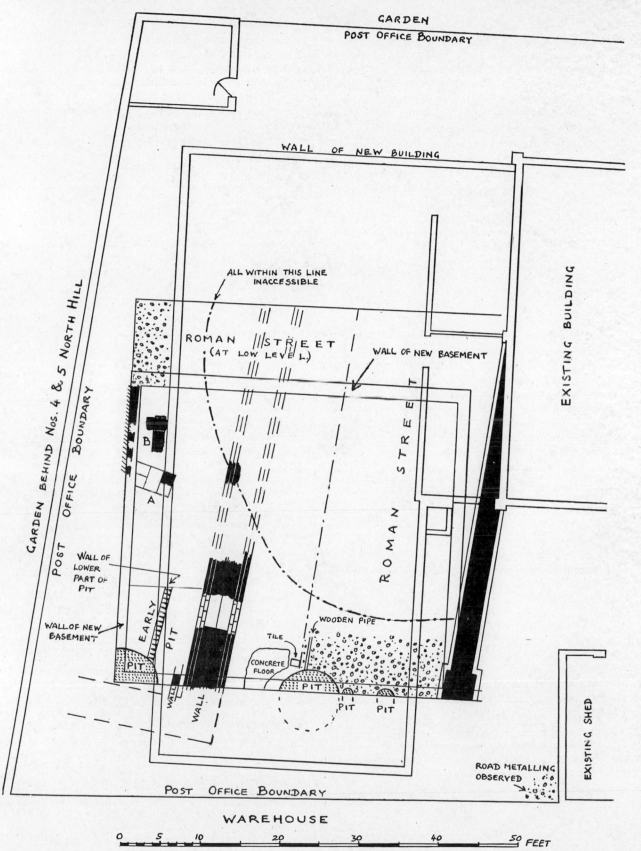

GARDEN
POST OFFICE BOUNDARY

WALL OF NEW BUILDING

GARDEN BEHIND Nos. 4 & 5 NORTH HILL

POST OFFICE BOUNDARY

ALL WITHIN THIS LINE INACCESSIBLE

ROMAN STREET
(AT LOW LEVEL L.)

WALL OF NEW BASEMENT

EXISTING BUILDING

B

A

WALL OF LOWER PART OF PIT

WALL OF NEW BASEMENT

EARLY PIT

WALL

WALL

PIT

ROMAN STREET

WOODEN PIPE

TILE

CONCRETE FLOOR

PIT

PIT PIT

ROAD METALLING OBSERVED

EXISTING SHED

POST OFFICE BOUNDARY

WAREHOUSE

0   5   10   20   30   40   50 FEET

FIG. 40. Plan of excavations at St. Martin's House, 1950 (N. at top). [174], p. 98.

angle to the west, which would bring it along the north side of the street coming from St. Martin's House (**125**). It was of late date because it cut through all levels and because of its poor construction. It had a massive foundation of rough septaria blocks, 5 ft. wide and 2 ft. 6 in. deep, laid in yellow mortar. This foundation appeared peculiar, but there was no possibility of uncovering and dissecting it. At places it seemed to be built in two parallel sections (cf. section, fig. 30). It was not impossibly of earlier date than the wall which stood upon it and may have been widened to receive it. Upon it stood the wall of a building of some size and importance. The only evidence for this was one brick pier (pl. XXXII, A) 3 ft. wide in the upgoing part, and at least 4 ft. 9 in. long, for the north end was broken. Its top was flat and mortared to receive two parallel stone slabs about 4 ft. long by 18 in. wide. The width of the wall increased downwards by several small offsets on each side, all fashioned in tile. The south end, however, was square, without offsets, down to the septaria foundation, which was rough on top. The whole presented a remarkably well-built and solid appearance. A slight trace of the tile-work of another pier remained in the south face of the section. Northwards we could not work because of the mechanical digger, which had to be kept working all the time, but the wall-foundation continued beyond the north boundary of the site, and we were able to get one measurement to the east side of the brickwork of it about halfway across, which checks its direction.

The solidity proved largely superficial, for it was chiefly due to mortar. The tiles used in the facing were all segmental ones,[1] mostly quite new. The concrete core was made up with a dry cement (with many lacunae) and small paving bricks, measuring some 5 by $2\frac{1}{2}$ by $1\frac{1}{2}$ in., others $4\frac{1}{2}$ by $2\frac{3}{4}$ by $\frac{3}{4}$ in.

Since the evidence, such as it is, is for a sequence of these piers, and since they would not carry a great weight, they possibly represent the *intervals* between the columns of a colonnade, the true column bases of which have been robbed, thus accounting for the flat south face of the pier. A column on a wall of this size would be of about 2 ft. diameter and about 18 ft. high.

No trace of a floor was found associated with this wall. On the contrary, west of it we encountered former excavations which presented complications insuperable under the circumstances. There had been a great excavation with vertical sides 12 ft. deep. It had been filled with rubble, in which no trace could be found of surrounding walls. This great pit or basement, which may have been multiple, had been recut in the rubble, again with vertical sides. No remains of retaining walls could be found. This later pit (or pits) was filled with

black soil resembling that of the late pits in the roadway and elsewhere, and all the pottery in it was of fourth-century date (fig. 41, 10, 14–18, and fig. 43). There was nothing whatever to indicate the function of these great pits, which were the size of large rooms.

Nevertheless part of a floor was found at the bottom. Here (A) lay several tiles bedded in mortar on sand, and one piece incorporated was cut to size from a worn-out mosaic pavement, turned face down. Upon them stood a small pier of tile and stone in mortar, 12 in. high and 18 in. square. Floor and pier were set at an awkward angle to everything else. Upon the floor, by the pier, stood a black, polished vase of the fourth century, intact (fig. 41, 10). North-west of all this, part of the base of a wall of septaria just showed in the face of the excavation (B). It stopped just short of the E.–W. street without a properly finished end. East of it, and distant 2 ft., stood a short length of similar walling. Both ran N.–S. and were not sunk below the level of the floor. But since the latter did not continue (or did not remain), their relationship is not clear. The east wall had another block of masonry loosely laid across it in an E.–W. direction. North of this lay a block of similar masonry, quite shapeless and obviously displaced. The stone-robbers had left a complete wreck which had no foundation trenches that we could find.

All this masonry is connected with the rubble fill rather than the later black fill, with which no masonry could be associated, unless it were the great wall with piers, against which the black filling impinged.

The masonry remains (A and B), though quite similar, need not be of the same period, for B was foundation work, while A, which lay lower, was a floor, perhaps part of a hypocaust, but carefully built, both in floor and pier. It seems that A is a scanty remnant of some building preceding the first basement, and B the scanty remains of that basement. A must be late enough for a mosaic floor to have worn almost completely away. B is fourth century. The second basement must have been of wood, and probably destroyed much of the ruins of A. It is fourth century or later and is possibly later than the great wall with piers.

To this late period also belonged a deep shaft or well cut in the SW. corner of the site, and the several pits full of very black soil, some large and formless, some neatly cut with vertical sides. Whether the upper Roman strata were removed before or after these pits were dug is uncertain, but the pits did not appear truncated at the top, so they should be later. Since some of them are cut into the Roman street (as at 5 North Hill (**156**) and Wire Street Arcade (**102**)) and they contained nothing which could make them medieval, it

---

[1] Subtending one-quarter of a circle of 2 ft. 6 in. diameter, and an angle of 100°.

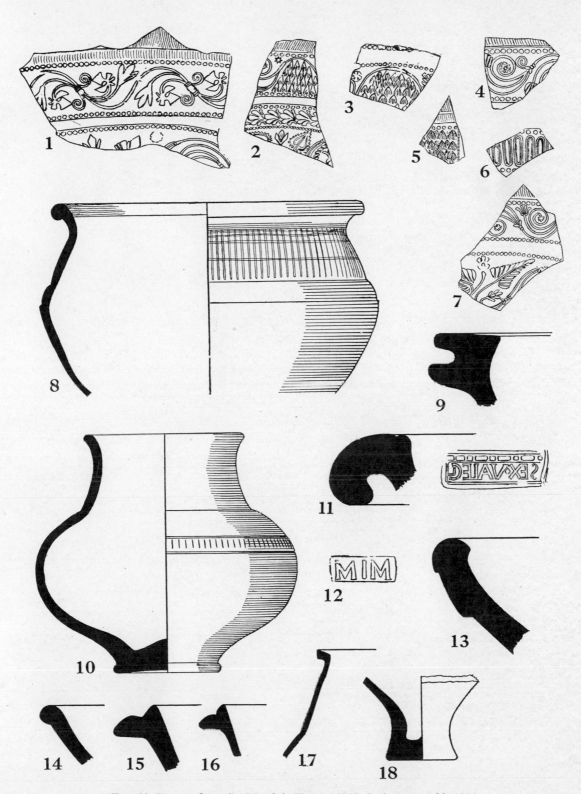

FIG. 41. Pottery from St. Martin's House, 1950. Scale ½. (pp. 98–100.)

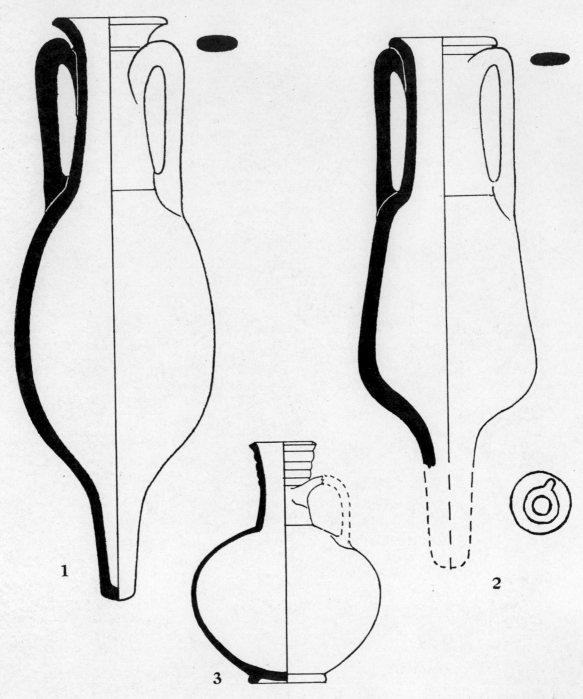

FIG. 42. Pottery from St. Martin's House, 1950. Nos. 1 and 2, $\frac{1}{6}$, no. 3, $\frac{1}{4}$ scale; the stamp beside no. 2 is full size. (p. 98.)

seems possible that they could belong to the Dark Ages and be witness of various digging activities going on then, off the line of the street and later, for other purposes, in the street itself, or perhaps after the lines of the streets had become indistinguishable. Nothing was found in them save scraps of late Roman pottery.

This excavation was in many respects a great disappointment. The situation regarding coins was quite

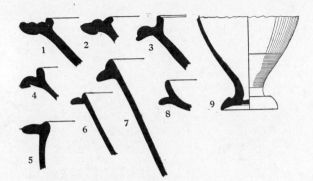

Fig. 43. Pottery from fourth-century pit at St. Martin's House, 1950. Scale ¼.

1. Mortarium, f. 500, white.
2. Mortarium, ditto.
3. Mortarium, f. 505.
4. Mortarium, ditto.
5. Rim of deep bowl, grey.
6–7. Grey rims, f. 305.
8. Rim f. 316A.
9. Lower half of pedestalled base in fine polished red ware, f. 296.

unsatisfactory. Many should have been found (compare what was found at **156** (p. 67) immediately west), but only two or three were handed in, none stratified.

INSULA 11

The street on the west has been well identified between insulae 10 and 11, especially in the excavations for the basement of the extension to the Telephone Exchange in St. Martin's House in January 1950. The other boundaries of the insula are uncertain, and its width N.–S. may have altered. The width E.–W. was about 300 ft. and N.–S. 325 ft. or 380 ft.

The insula is partly covered by houses and gardens of West Stockwell Street, and partly by the large garden already mentioned. There are several old records to begin with.

21 and **22.** In a letter of Dr. Guyon Griffith to Edward King[1] we learn there was found in the kitchen

garden of Dr. Piggot, physician, at a 'depth of a yard and a half . . . a Roman pavement, consisting of rude and coarse tesserae of brick, without any material difference of colour or any variety of figure. . . .' The labourer 'laid the ground open to the extent of five yards and a quarter in length, and two yards and a half in breadth, came to the extremity of the pavement on the west and south sides. It was every where entire, and lay in a direction parallel to the present surface of the garden, except at the SE. corner, where it rose in a kind of blister, about a foot square, . . . I went . . . to view the spot, and found a continued stratum of wheat running in part along the three sides of the lower space that had been dug (sc. down through the pavement). It was pure and unmixed with any earth or rubbish, and the whole of it appeared . . . as black as if it has been burnt. . . . The distance of the stratum from the bottom of the pavement was very unequal, being from 10 to 16 ins.; and its breadth was from 1 to 6 ins. The length of it on the north side was only 8 ins., on the west 4 ft. 4 ins., and on the south 2 ft. 4 ins.'[2]

Postscripts: 'The house, in the garden of which . . . it was discovered, is situated nearly opposite to St. Martin's Church, in Angel Lane . . . . Two years ago another pavement, still more rudely formed, with something of an arch under it was discovered in the further end of the same garden.'

20 and **23.** '. . . and some years before that, other fragments of the same kind were found, both under the house next above, inhabited by Dr. Daniel, and also under or near the house next below, inhabited by Mr. Wall, in the same lane.' Morant, p. 183, also refers to these finds, which are not indicated on the O.S. 1:500 map.

13. A trench cut in 1920 in Mr. Frost's garden 100 yards east of North Hill revealed a hard gravelled surface (the street, see p. 70), and 22 ft. farther east a tessellated pavement and foundations running N.–S. These were observed by P. G. Laver,[3] who also writes: 'account of the pavement found in the garden at the back of no. 9 North Hill—October 1920 Mr. A. W. Frost excavated in this garden and several walls and pavements were found, the latter being principally of red tesserae, in some instances mixed with buff, and some of opus signinum.' Since the above was written further information has come to hand[4] from Mr. C. A. Winkles, who excavated in this insula in 1939 and earlier. His plan suggests that Laver's '100 yards' is an approximation, for he shows a 'road' at a depth of 4 ft. from the surface exactly opposite the road found in 1950. True, he records it as 7 ft. wide, but had he

---

[1] *Arch.* ii, 287–90, dated 31/5/1771.

[2] There is a quantity of burnt wheat in the Joslin Collection. No source given.

[3] *R.C.H.M.*, no. 23; *J.R.S.* ix, 159. The site is not 100 yards

SE. of no. 11, but over 200 yards.

[4] Privately communicated to me by letters and plans, with photograph of the mosaic pavement. The plans, unfortunately, are not adequate for reproduction.

dug deeper it might have been wider. It is possible, therefore, that our **13** should be moved westwards, but Winkles also found a 'gravel path' east of this street at a depth of 5 ft., which corresponds with the general level of the floors of the house. This 'path' may be part of the same street, or of the house. If the former, then the street is not straight, and the house overlies part of it; if the latter, then Laver's 'street' may have been this path, and not the street at all.

The remains of the house just mentioned, consisting of tessellated floors at a depth of 5 ft. (the walls had vanished), extended some 18 ft. north of the garden wall north of **22** and may represent the same building. North of this again Mr. Winkles found remains of another house, with red tessellated pavements, and one of mosaic, at a depth of 4 ft. The mosaic he removed and reconstructed at Leicester; it is of chequered pattern, and of a type quite new to Colchester.

In the corner of the garden NE. of **13** and **22**, 27 ft. from the north wall and 32 ft. from the east, was found the concrete bed for a pavement, and the same again at several points in the corner SW. of **13**, at depths of 3 and 4 ft.

126. In 1926–7 the present Telephone Exchange was built in the garden of St. Martin's House. Unfortunately, arrangements made regarding the antiquities miscarried, and the only information surviving from this extensive disturbance of the Roman strata are a few objects which were collected by some enthusiasts and conveyed to the Museum.

The most noteworthy of these was a small hoard of twenty-seven coins found in a pot, which was, as usual, broken and lost. They were burnt, but nearly all could be identified. They are all *asses* or *dupondii* of M. Agrippa and Claudius. The hoard could well have been hidden on the approach of Boudicca in A.D. 60.[1]

Other finds included a crossbow fibula (5480.27), white metal spoons, a coin of Licinius, and four other illegible coins of the Lower Empire. Some finds from the insula are simply marked 'Frost's garden'. They include a small bronze figure, the feet missing, wearing 'mascles' or a kind of body-belt worn by charioteers, and a peaked cap (4677.24).[2] The list of pottery is not unusual, including stamps of OF. FEICIS, OF MACCAL, and CRESTIO (on Ritt. 8). The coins are Claudius (3); Nero (in road-metal); Vespasian (2); Trajan; Antoninus Pius; Faustina (?); Gallienus; Tetricus; Claudius Gothicus; Carausius (2); Licinius; Constantius II; a small bronze with SALVS reverse; and seven illegible.

125. In 1930 an extension was made to the south end

of St. Martin's House. The section of the street has been described on p. 70. A Roman foundation was found just south of the house, between it and the street. Farther east at the NE. corner of the new building a Roman footing was found 20 in. wide, of septaria, and running E.–W., but cut off on the west by a recent pit 5 ft. wide and $5\frac{1}{2}$ ft. deep.[3]

INSULA 12

This insula is almost completely built over and there is no great list of finds from it. The streets bounding it have not been seen, but to judge from the general plan the insula measured about 300 by 330 ft.

25. 'Indignation makes me write . . . having just seen a beautiful mosaic pavement in the yard of one Bragg, a baker, in Bear Lane, . . . which was discovered about two years ago and is going fast to ruin. . . . It is really much more beautiful than that engraved in Morant. . . . What remained of it is part of a circle (etc.) . . . the tesserae of the whole are very thin, not more than 1/8 inch thick, the colours are charming.'[4] The discovery was made in 1793. The pavement had a leaf border, and measured about 22 by 17 ft., extending beneath a stone wall into the adjoining garden where it could not be excavated.[5] There is an entry in the Museum register: 'Apr. 8, 1896, purchased of Thos. Foster of High Street a sketch of a Roman mosaic pavement found in the parish of St. Martins in 1794' (this sketch does not now seem to be extant).

The position was 36 rods NE. by N. of the pavement (**18**), and the design seems to have made a great impression: 'the vases are shaded . . . the colours softened into each other equal to any painting . . . the drawing . . . taken by Mr. Dunthorne is very accurate'. It was checked against omissions or elaborations.

26. This number covers two references in Wire's Diary—23/11/1855: 'The grave digger of Herrick's Chapel burial ground informs me . . . when digging a grave . . . he discovered a variegated tessellated pavement . . . and that under it were some chips of granite. Not far from this one . . . [was that one shown] in *Vetusta Monumenta*' (**25**).

14/2/1856: 'Purchased about twenty red bricks, $4 \times 2\frac{1}{2} \times 7/8$ inches . . . found in the burial ground attached to Stockwell Street Chapel (same Chapel as last). This constituted the ground work of a tessellated pavement of red tesserae in the following order; first a foundation of the bricks set edgeways, then about a foot thick of broken granite [*sic*], then the concrete on the top of which was set the . . . pavement. What was the extent

---

[1] C.M. 5355.26; *C.M.R.*, 1927, 24; *J.R.S.* xvi (1926), 229–30; *T.E.A.S.* xix, 57 (where I must apologize for my ignorance then that Nero struck no bronze before A.D. 64).

[2] *C.M.R.* 1924, 16. [3] Ibid. 1931, 8.

[4] Wire, in *Gent.'s Mag.* 1794, vol. xliv, 801; *Vet. Mon.* iii, pl. xxxix.

[5] *T.E.A.S.* o.s. v, 160; *J.R.S.* ix, 161 (not 200 yards but 260 ft. NE. by E. of no. 23).

of it the discoverer could not say . . . but he believes it runs under St. Helen's Lane.'

27. Wire also records the discovery of a pavement in the garden of the house three doors north of the Independent Chapel, some time before 1846. It is possibly the same as the small area 2 ft. square exposed on 29 January 1923 in the garden of no. 17, 70 ft. from the east face of the house. The tesserae were red, less than 1 in. square, and laid NE.–SW.[1]

Further notes from Wire:
28/10/1842. 'Mr. A. Frost, painter . . . removed a greenhouse near the old Chapel, St. Helen's Lane . . . [and] found a great quantity of Samian ware.'

like May 242 (nearly), which was in the possession of the Rev. D. H. Markham of Great Horkesley Rectory.

INSULA 13

The eastern limit is the 'forum' block, where the ditch of the Norman Castle has dug the street away, though some of it is said to be visible over the remains that drain against the west wall of the forum. The other streets are not known. The insula probably measured about 300 by 330 ft. On the south the limit should be, approximately, Sir William's Walk.

30. A short length of ancient walling, of septaria

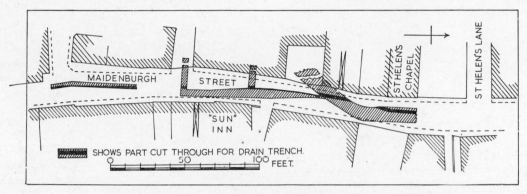

FIG. 44. Plan of foundations found in Maidenburgh Street. [152], p. 105.

24/1/43. 'Mr. Chas. Gunner, clerk of St. Martin's church, presented me with a few coins of the Lower Empire found in the burial ground . . . .'
10/4/43. 'Mr. Gunner brought . . . fragments of Roman pottery, found ibid.'
19/9/43. 'Mr. Gunner brought earth found 9 ft. below the surface, ibid. there was much charcoal mixed with it. Two pieces of Samian found at the same time.'
10/10/43. 'Mr. Gunner . . . digging a grave west side of the porch . . . dug on to a Roman urn, but . . . broke it.'
5/2/44. 'Digging a grave near SW. corner of St. Martin's Church half of a Samian patera was found.'
19/4/44. 'A black earth dish and several fragments of Samian and coarse black ware were found ibid. when digging Mrs. Fincham's grave.'
30/6/53: 'Purchased two bone Roman pins, each 4½ ins. long and the same pattern, a brass coin of Trajan, a silver one of Julia Domna, found in Stockwell Chapel burial ground.'
12/2/55. 'Purchased an iron instrument 8 ins. long having teeth on the face of it and the leg bone of an animal for a handle, 1 inch wide on the face, found in St. Martin's Churchyard' sketch, curious).
2/6/55. 'Purchased fragments of embossed Samian found in Stockwell Chapel burial ground.'

There are other small remains in the Museum. Chief of these is the small grey vessel of f. 282 (C.M. 3755.18), found in the churchyard and possibly fifth century. The material is very fine, hard polished grey ware.

Wire (Album, p. 43) figures a small cooking-pot,

surmounted by a triple course of Roman tile, is visible under the north wall of St. Helen's Chapel, of which it forms the foundation.[2] The Museum has mortar collected from 'the continuation of the wall' in 1924 (C.M. 6271.27).

In June 1940 part of a wall 3 ft. 2 in. wide running N.–S. near the NW. corner of the chapel, and 18 in. from it, on the west side, a small pier (of tiles) 18 in. square, were observed by Mr. Rudsdale, who also reported that many fragments of thin slabs of finely finished Purbeck marble (or similar stone) were found in the digging, all indicative that the site was of importance.

152. There is in the Museum a tinted plan (fig. 44), made in August 1891 by Mr. H. Goodyear, then Borough Engineer, showing remains of massive walls revealed when cutting trenches for drains in Maidenburgh Street. A section is also given, but there is scarcely any descriptive information. The portions of walls actually exposed are apparently shown in red, with conjectural restorations in paler tint. The reasons for the restorations are not given, and in fact we are not sure how much he saw and how much he conjectured.

We explain the plan as follows: the first piece of

---

[1] Laver, Diary, 29/1/1923.   [2] Presumably that meant by 30 in *J.R.S.* ix, 162, but 'adjoining' is hardly correct.

wall, in the centre of the street, opposite the Brewery Tap, is 59 ft. long (over which distance the trench cut away the eastern face) with a slight angle to the east near its southern end. The thickness is shown as 3 ft., but this seems conjectural. There is then a gap of 30 ft., but whether this space was trenched or not is not clear. Immediately north of this point the trench cut through an E.–W. wall which was 4 ft. thick, and, 41 ft. north from it, another similar. These walls are shown as continuing westwards as far as the building line of the street. The east side of the trench exposed about 13 ft. of the west face of a N.–S. wall running at more than a right angle south from the northern wall. The tinted outline of this N.–S. wall is incredibly irregular on the plan, especially in the thickness, and we do not know to what extent it is conjectural. The trench revealed its west face for 44 ft. north of the second E.–W. wall, with another slight angle in it. At the 44 ft. it joins a still more remarkable wall, which Goodyear has shown running in a curve. His evidence for this is the north and south faces which cross his trench obliquely and indicate a thickness of about 10 ft. for this wall. His plan and section end opposite the north corner of St. Helen's Chapel, but whether the wall was continuing northwards or not is not shown. The tinting indicates a wall 10 ft. wide running N.–S. down the centre of the street, curving away SW. just south of St. Helen's Chapel and broadening, but this may only be to indicate that the exact line of the continuation was uncertain.

The section shows the top of the wall as 2 ft. below the street over most of its course, but only 1 ft. in one place, while the N.–S. wall stands 4 ft. high, its base being 6 ft. below the street. The base of the masonry sinks lower after the joint with the curving wall, the maximum depth shown being 9 ft., after which the base runs horizontally.

We show the actual masonry uncovered in the drainage trench in black, and the shaded portions correspond to the paler shading on Goodyear's plan. It would seem probable that Goodyear actually uncovered these parts, but that he did not, in every case, clear the whole of the width of the walling, otherwise the variation in the thickness of the walls is inexplicable and incredible.

We have no word of description of the nature of this masonry nor of any finds made during the excavations. It is most remarkable that neither H. nor P. G. Laver has made any reference to the discovery, which was thus omitted from Wheeler's and Laver's list. The plan is so strange that it can hardly be an invention. Such massive remains could only belong to the Roman

or Norman periods, and the latter we feel is safely ruled out. If Roman, there is a general resemblance to one end of the stage and part of the auditorium of a theatre, but this is not plausible, because it is standing the wrong way to the hill-side (i.e. the stage is uphill, whereas it should be downhill); moreover, the dimensions are too great, though perhaps not impossibly so.

There remains the possibility that here we may have a hint of the presence of an amphitheatre, a thing which it is well known was most popular with the army, and therefore to be expected in a colony of veteran legionaries. Nor is it unusual for an amphitheatre to be within the walls of the town.[1]

INSULA 14

The large size of insula 22 encroaches upon this area so as to leave it very small. The north side is limited by the road found in insula 6, and the length E.–W. presumably corresponds with that insula and insula 22. On the south nothing was known until the excavations of 1950, when it was established that a street started westwards from the NE. angle of insula 22, but the width of this street could not be ascertained. Insula 14 was, accordingly, 440 ft. wide, but only about 150 ft. N.–S. Most of its area has been excavated away by the great Norman ditch, but when the foundations for the side walls of the steps to the rose gardens were cut in 1929, the Roman levels were reached and showed no trace of buildings, other than the usual layer of yellow loam and fragments of wall-plaster with very fine Pompeian red surface. Nor did a large bomb-crater near the NE. corner reveal any remains of masonry.

INSULA 15
(see plan, FIG. 37)

This insula is clearly demarcated except on the south, where we have failed to find the street. It was 310 ft. wide at the north but only 290 ft. at the south on the line where the street was expected. Its N.–S. dimension should have been about 330 ft.

There has been much interference with this area, especially in recent years. It is the southern half of the Hollytrees' Meadow, and was the object of excavations in 1927–9 (see p. 85). It had not been built upon since the foundation of the Norman Castle, and the Roman remains are not deeply buried. It contained a number of Roman houses of no great pretensions, the more elaborate building which we have called the 'Mithraeum', and a small shrine.

38. The O.S. 1:500 map marks 'Roman pavement

---

[1] e.g. Turin. Note also that if the lighter walls be ignored the building could well be a theatre, for the relationship to the hill-slope could then be correct.

and coins found, 1852 and 1853' under the site of the former shed where the Park Café now stands. For some reason Wheeler and Laver give the date as about 1848; other references are in *T.E.A.S.* o.s. i, 226; v, 157.

The remainder of the finds made in this area are chiefly the results of excavations by Dr. P. M. Duncan in 1853[1] and of the more extensive work undertaken in the winters of 1927/8 and 1928/9 on the initiative of the Essex Archaeological Society. In the first season the work was in charge of Mr. P. G. Laver, F.S.A., assisted by Mr. G. Farmer. Access to the area was only obtained very late, and all that could be done was to clear the hypocaust and cut exploratory trenches on the 'Mithraeum' site. In the following season it was possible, under the supervision of the writer, to uncover the whole of the 'Mithraeum', the whole of the drain (see insula 7), cut sections of the street, and explore a little farther for houses.

'THE MITHRAEUM'
(PLS. XVIII, C, D; XIX; FIGS. 45–46)

39. The building now to be described was first noted by Dr. Duncan in 1853,[1] and we found that he had cut one trench across room A opposite the end of the drain, and a trench along the north and east walls (inside) only. He quite reasonably mistook the building for part of a bath, owing to the concrete floor and the copious flow of water. We therefore began operations in the hope that we might have here the Public Baths of Roman Colchester, but very soon found that we were dealing with a comparatively small building.

In other respects, however, the building is so solidly constructed and so placed—at the corner of an insula, in its own walled temenos—that there can be no question of its having been a dwelling, shop, or works of any private owner. The plan itself suggests no such probability. It consists of a long parallelogram with the major axis nearly due north and south, and with an annexe on the east side. The over-all dimensions are 74 ft. by 42 ft. 6 in.

The ground falls away rather rapidly to the north, and the south rooms were built on the ground level; the northern large room D was sunk about 6 ft. lower at its south end (see section, fig. 46).

The large room A had a concrete floor 18 in. thick. It consisted of 6 in. of pounded tile in white mortar, laid on a 12-in. bed of rubble concrete, and measured 19 ft. 6 in. E.–W. by 18 ft. N.–S. It had been subdivided later by a partition wall, possibly of wood, the only trace of which was a rough trench cut in the floor, 11 ft. from the south wall. On the east side the trench was interrupted as if for a doorway.

The walls of this room, except that on the north side, were originally exterior walls and were 3 ft. thick and deeply founded. They penetrate 5 ft. below the Roman surface, and were built directly upon the natural gravel in the same way as the town wall at the NE. Gate (p. 42). On the south side the wall still stood to a height of 18 in., but elsewhere it had mostly been robbed to below floor-level. The rubble from its destruction lay directly upon the floor and upon the Roman surface outside. It contained many fragments of the semicircular tiles used for building columns, especially along the south side.

The north wall was only 2 ft. thick and the foundations only went down 4 ft. It had been robbed to below the floor, so that no traces of doorways remained.

The narrow space between rooms D and A was divided into three compartments. On the east was the entrance lobby (B) measuring 9 by 6 ft., including an extra foot obtained owing to the outer wall here being only 2 ft. thick. This is the only point where such a variation occurs: it should indicate the entrance, which would have been 6 ft. wide and must have had a double door.

The floor of this lobby was of stiff, yellowish clay. There may have been a boarded floor over it, for its level was about a foot below the concrete floor of room A.

The description of the two partition walls between B and C is complicated. Fig. 46, B shows them in section.[2] It will be seen that the eastern one was only carried down to the same level as that of the north wall of room A (both of these were built upon about 6 in. of dry stone chippings with scarcely any mortar), while the western one is carried right down to the level of the outer wall (so far as we could observe). At this point we must refer the reader to section C of the same figure to point out that the outer wall runs horizontally 5 ft. below the concrete floor as far as its north edge, where it descends the clay bank in room B to reach the lower level of the walls of room D. On the right of section B the east wall may be presumed to behave in a similar manner, but this point was not excavated.

The western of these two partition walls was built in one piece, in its lower part, with the south wall of room D, and still stands 6 ft. high. Its material is carefully coursed septaria and tiles, arranged as shown in the section, laid in white mortar. Its foundations were horizontal (i.e. they did not climb the clay bank, as did the outer wall, but entered into it), and when the clay was removed from them water gushed up in quantity.

An opening or doorway had existed in this wall at its south end. This had been 3 ft. wide, and its sill or

---

[1] *T.E.A.S.* o.s. i, 210 ff.   [2] Section taken on S. face of N. wall of rooms B–C.

threshold was 3 ft. below the level of room A, and just above the top of the clay bank. From its level, sloping down to the threshold of the door of room A, we

yet there is no reason for adding the east wall after the opening in the west wall had been built up. The clay produced no datable material, but the east wall must

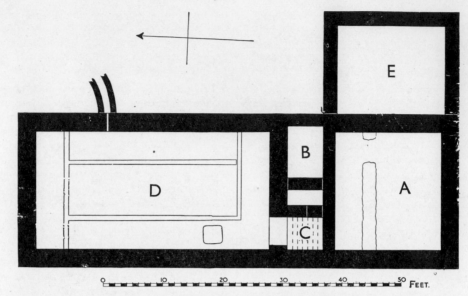

FIG. 45, a. Plan of 'Mithraeum' in Hollytrees' Meadow. [39], p. 107.

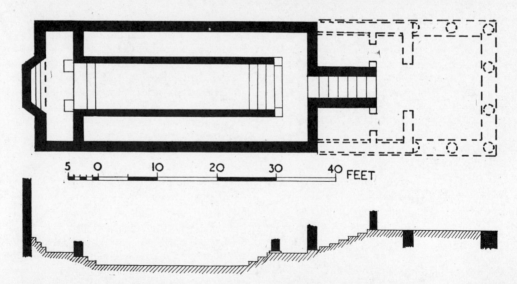

FIG. 45, b. Plan of 'Mithraeum' at Heddernheim. After Cumont, *Textes et monuments*.

thought we could see faint traces of the stringer of the wooden stairs still visible in the mortar of the wall. The corners of this doorway were carefully built of tiles. Later it was walled up with septaria and tiles.

These walls are difficult to understand. They are only 2 ft. 6 in. apart and the space between them was packed with clay. The opening in the western wall could not have been used with the east wall in position,

be later than the west, and it is butt-jointed at both ends.

The excavation of room C was complicated by the steep tilt of the strata, the depth of the excavation, and the presence of the blocking masonry seen in fig. 46, B and C and (partly removed) in pl. XVIII, C.

Uppermost in the section was the thick layer of mortar and rubble continuous with the broken wall-tops. It can be seen dropping down to become continuous with the rubble layer in room D. Under it the filling was exactly similar to that in room D, consisting of various tips of rubbish, including great quantities of pottery and roof tiles, with several intact imbrices inclined against the wall as if the roof had fallen in before the building was demolished.

The curious little bowl with rounded base (fig. 57, 11; p. 144) was found in the rubble on the top of the north wall of room A.

the lower courses of which had dropped several inches, without, however, affecting the wall above.

The doorway to room D was 4 ft. 4 in. wide and had had a very large wooden threshold 6 in. thick and the same width as the reveal (3 ft.). It had decayed away, leaving an open space under the flanking masonry.

Room D (pl. XIX) is the main room of the building and measures 39 ft. 3 in. long by 19 ft. 7 in. wide, obviously intended for 40 by 20 Roman feet. The walls are faced on the interior entirely with tiles laid in pink

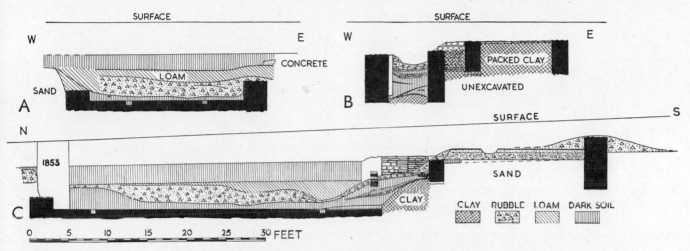

FIG. 46. Sections of 'Mithraeum', p. 107.

The masonry built across the entrance lay on top of the rubbish, and had not been cut through the mortar layer. It was therefore in position after the deposition of the rubbish and before the demolition. It consisted of four courses of square tiles set in thick mortar, but not bonded, for five tiles just over 10 in. square exactly fill the width of the doorway. Above them had been some septaria, of which little remained, indicated in fig. 46, C. The whole had sagged down as the rubbish beneath decayed, but very much more when the wooden threshold finally crumbled. This accounts for the deep sag and the gaps between the courses, filled with earth (pl. XVIII, C).

It has been suggested that this was the lintel of the doorway left as it fell, after the building was demolished. If so, it would have formed part of a tympanum over a wooden frame. But it lies *over* the rubble and is only the width of one 10-in. tile, so it is rather the remains of a makeshift effort to build up the entrance.

It is clear that room C must have housed a wooden stair. The space—6 ft. square—is not on the generous scale of the rest of the building. Perhaps this accounts for the alterations to the partition walls. The clay bank seems to have been put in to stop the flow of water from the spring. It gave way beneath the outer wall,

mortar, carefully pointed. Elsewhere the mortar is white; the two colours meet in the centre of the reveal of the doorway, which was plastered nearly completely over. (Frost has since peeled this plaster off.) The south wall is standing over 6 ft. high and the side walls drop rapidly at first and then run on about 2 ft. high. The north wall is 18 in. high. The floor is of rough concrete and still bears the marks of planks and vague footprints which were made upon it while not quite set. The channels in the floor, which Duncan found and planned on conjecture, were found to vary. They average 10 in. wide by 8 in. deep, but tapered with the roughly squared half-trees, which had been laid in them with the rounded side down. These are 4 ft. 10 in. from the walls and are symmetrical in plan, except opposite the door.

Directly in front of the door there is a sump-hole in the floor 3 ft. square with rounded corners. We did not break through the floor, but this hole is only well finished for 6 in. round the top; below this it is roughly hacked out of a solid mass of rough stones and mortar 18 in. deep, which may be assumed to be general under the floor and not limited to the vicinity of the sump-hole. So heavy a floor may have been demanded to withstand water pressure from beneath. The floor naturally floods from the clay bank at the entrance, but in the wettest weather, and with the drain blocked, the water does not (now) rise more than 18 in. above the general floor-level.

To prevent flooding, or to empty the room, a large and expensive drain was provided, with an aperture 9 in. square at floor-level, 8 ft. 8 in. from the NE. corner in the east wall.

The concrete floor was carefully examined for traces of its use or purpose. In some places transverse joists lying E.–W. had left clear impressions of the grain of the wood against the west wall. There was one certain impression of an end, and vague impressions of several others too uncertain to measure. During the building the workmen several times rested light battens vertically on the concrete, leaving the impressions of the ends (in no regular arrangement) measuring about 2 in. by $1\frac{1}{2}$ in. In the centre of the floor a similar impression was found measuring 4 by 7 in. and so exactly placed as to seem intentional. It was a chock-block, for the grain lay horizontally, not vertically. One other feature calls for mention: near the left centre of the north wall there was a clear-cut recess in the concrete floor in the form of an isosceles triangle, apex to the north, sides 12 in. long, base 18 in. wide, depth 4 in.

The sections show how the filling of this room was made up. The lowest layer varied from 6 to 8 in. at the centre to 3 ft. thick against the walls, where it sloped up rapidly, as it would naturally do if thrown in from the sides all round (*N.B.* this must presuppose the absence of a roof), and similarly running up the slope of the stairs in the entrance. This layer was extremely hard on the concrete and could be prised up in slabs about 2 in. thick. Between the south wall and the first beam in the floor it was soft and black; elsewhere it was mostly sandy loam cemented with calcium deposit from the layer above. Indeed there was so much lime in the rubble layer above that, in the course of centuries, it had been dissolved by water and deposited again, often as a thick incrustation on the walls and on the pottery not only in its own layer but in this layer below it.

As has been said, the lower part of this layer was very hard. It could well represent the slow deposit of a long period and contains no small finds. The softer, dark deposit above, sealed down by the mortar layer, was full of broken pottery, tiles, and other remains. The nature of the pottery fragments showed that this consisted of rubbish shot in as if in barrow-loads, for repeatedly the most part of a pot would be found within a very small area and then no more of it at all.

A few pots were intact. Many more were nearly so, but in no case was the missing part found, despite the most careful and exhaustive examination of all the fragments found.

The remains found in this layer cover a long period, but were probably deposited quite quickly. On the very bottom a coin of Constans was found, and the earliest contents, such as the worn sesterce of Trajan and chips of the rim of bowls f. 246 are so scarce that they only confirm the conjecture that the filling is rubbish thrown in from the surface of the surrounding area.

The sealing layer of mortar and rubble dates from the deliberate demolition of the building in Roman times, and this did not occur before the reign of Constans. There is no difference between the pottery of the two layers. Everywhere the mortar layer spread from the top of the broken walls. It is simply the useless rubble left after the building material had been taken away, and can only indicate that the building was deliberately taken down.

Above this there was another filling, which must have followed fairly quickly, for nothing intervenes which might be likened to a turf or other surface over the rubble. It was of stiff loam and contained much pottery and other remains, notably a coin of Valentinian. The only new element in the pottery is flanged bowls copying Dragendorff f. 38 in a fine red ware. They are of distinctive outline and have been found repeatedly in the town in late associations, but this is the best dated occurrence so far. This last filling more than covered the ruins to the north, but must have left some at least of the southern part of the building exposed.

The trenches around the building did not shed much light upon it unless possibly in one respect. The section of the trench to the south[1] shows two slots which may have held walls, one 8, the other 19 ft. south of the building. Trenches dug to the SW. and east showed a similar slot on each side, the interval being 30 ft. on the west side and 24 on the east. Another slot by the side of the street is also possible on this side. It may be the boundary wall of the insula. If it belonged to our building it would be asymmetrical, but it does not have to be parallel to the street. There are thus traces of two walls on south and east; could we have missed one on the west?[2] It is possible, for they were not of heavy construction and had been very thoroughly robbed. The inner one could have been a wall and the outer one a low wall or stylobate for a portico. There is not enough evidence for a decision. No trench was dug

---

[1] One has to draw the line somewhere, and we have not therefore figured these sections.

[2] Further work in autumn 1954 has confirmed the two parallel walls on E. and S. and shown a single wall on the N. The W. side was inaccessible.

northwards, but since there certainly was an enclosure, it is not unreasonable to suppose that its northern limit may have coincided with the point where the drain ceases its serpentine wanderings and its vault ends with a finished face.

The Purpose of the Site

To ascertain for what purpose the building was erected we have only its plan and construction and the objects found in it. Inasmuch as they are not self-explanatory (no one has advanced a theory which is at once and obviously correct), the solution demands every possible consideration.

The nature of the building, which is small in plan and area, must always be kept in mind. The walls are very thick, well built, and deeply founded. The position is isolated, and there are no signs of domestic offices; indeed there is no resemblance to a dwelling at all. All this points to the building having been of a public nature. Moreover, though we have not proved the continuity of them, there are certain traces of an enclosing wall, within which the ground was to some extent levelled, and the drain was vaulted. For some reason, too, its course was unnecessarily serpentine.

The connexion with the drain, which takes its inception from the large room, and which is soon after used as a public drain, and the plentiful supply of water, caused Duncan to think of the Public Baths, with good reason. But the limited plan now puts this quite out of the question.

The next natural suggestion is that it may have been a public water-supply. This is reasonable, for the position of the town precludes the possibility of supplying it from outside except by a long and expensive aqueduct, which certainly never existed. So far as we know the only supply within the walls was drawn from a number of wells, most of which would be private. The suggestion is attractive at first, but no similar water-supply is known, so our building must stand on its merits.

If, then, this was a water-supply, publicly owned, the rooms at ground-level are administrative—possibly a charge was made—and the large room was a tank, and the steps and door leading down to its floor-level would provide access to the water at whatever level it might stand. Thus several things are explained.

But far more are not explained, and one or two absurdities are caused. Unexplained are the elaborate floors, the evidence for columns at the south end,[1] the need for a surrounding wall, and the facing of tiles laid in pink mortar in the 'tank'. One cannot believe that so awkward a stair and entrance could have been devised for common use. But, far worse, the very drain which seemed to support the theory becomes its worst difficulty, for *this drain is not to keep the 'tank' full but to keep it empty*. Nor is this all: the 'tank', though every joint is carefully pointed (and, be it noted, with pink mortar), is not and never was plastered over. And such plaster was a normal *sine qua non* of Roman water-conduits and cisterns.[2] Moreover, while every provision was made to keep the chamber from flooding, there is no trace whatever of any means being provided for filling it. The water rises from a natural spring in the stair-well and its flow was limited by a bank of rammed clay. At present (with the drain not functioning) the water rises not more than 18 in. on the floor, and even allowing for a considerable fall in the water-table since Roman times (which is here improbable), the maximum depth obtainable could never have accounted for the height of 6 ft. to which the south wall still stands. There were also no means provided for closing the mouth of the drain if it was desired to retain the water.

And what of the slots in the floor?

Other suggestions advanced include that of a cesspool (there are no drains leading into it), which explains nothing. A fulling-works or tannery might account for the timbers in the floor, but no real parallel can be found. These timbers could have been the base of some contrivance used in some form of industry, but the building does not look industrial, and in any case we know of no industrial building, or of any plan at all, which contains similar slots for timber.

The next suggestion is perhaps feasible. It is that the building was the public *carcer*, or an *ergastulum* (a prison for slaves). This would account for one of our greatest difficulties, namely, why the chamber was sunk in the ground if it was not intended to contain water. It would account for administrative rooms at ground-level, and the beams in the floor would be for the attachment of shackles. The water-supply was found accidentally when the chamber was excavated, and the drain then provided to lead it away. Moreover the actual shackles (or some of them) were found in the building (pl. xxi, A), and one or two human bones and part of a skull.

But even if the building is of the best period (and we do not know it is), why line a prison with best tiles laid in pink mortar? The shackles were found in the rubbish of the first filling, which must have been thrown in after the building was out of use; but it is possible that they belonged to the building and were lying around upstairs.

---

[1] Since the discovery of a wall in insula 11 built mainly with quadrant tiles such tiles cease to be firm evidence for columns.
[2] Sir Charles Peers was the first to point this out to me.

There is another suggestion, which in the view of the present writer has the advantage of being based on the plan, and of satisfying nearly every requirement. There is a series of Mithraic temples which are orientated N.–S. (as is our building) to which the first two of the three found at Heddernheim belong (fig. 45, B). The resemblance between this plan and ours cannot fail to strike.[1] The long shape, with the well-sunken chamber occupying the most part of the plan to the north, the steps to the doorway in the south wall, and then the two rooms at ground-level, with door between, and finally, in both cases the indications of columns or half-columns around the southern room, all correspond closely.

There are also marked differences, but none is sufficient in itself to invalidate the suggestion. A reference to Cumont's great work[2] will show at once that the details of the plans of Mithraic temples were very elastic. The main chamber of the Heddernheim plan is typical, with its narrow banks all round, supported by low stone walls and with an alcove at the far end for the cult figure. But the sunken central aisle, while common, is far from invariable. To make our plan correspond with this interior subdivision we have only to suppose that wooden walls stood upon our timbers in the floor to provide the side banks. This theory is the only one so far to find a real use for these slots. The south room or rooms are so similar that no explanation is required. The lobby between, leading to the stairs, is present in both, but is different in ours because, as frequently seen in the pages of Cumont, the door is at one side instead of the centre. The several alterations already described show how inconvenient this was found.

There are further resemblances in our building to many in Cumont's work. Parallels can be quoted for our pit or sump-hole in the floor and for a drain leading out of the main room. There is evidence that the builders wished to be near running water—it is even stated that they wished to have water running through the building.

This theory accounts for more of the peculiar characteristics of our building than any yet advanced. It leaves unexplained the great thickness of the floors and of the outer walls. It must also be admitted that the wooden framework has a portion missing opposite the door which does not quite suit our explanation.

Had any relics of the Mithraic cult been found no one would have doubted the function of the build-

ing; as it is, there are none, and we are left to choose between the theories now propounded, or to find a better.

Because certain of the highest authorities have chosen to set their faces against the Mithraeum theory it is necessary to say a little more.

In 1929 Sir Mortimer Wheeler visited the excavations and, in company with the writer, decided that the drain and the town walls were contemporary (p. 40). We also decided that the 'Mithraeum' and drain were contemporary. It now appears that the town walls may be of Hadrian–Antonine Period (p. 62), so that the 'Mithraeum' may also be ascribed to a mid-second-century date.[3]

Now it is generally recognized that Mithraism reached its zenith in the third and fourth century, and to that time it has been mentally pigeon-holed, so that there are those who cannot imagine a Mithraeum at an earlier date. There is no doubt that by and large this has the support of the dating evidence from the many continental Mithraea, but there are some observations which must be made. First, although the dating has been disputed, the Mithraeum at Carnuntum on the Danube has been attributed to A.D. 79. Moreover, Mr. W. J. Williams has made out a case for some of the emblems on Roman soldiers' tombstones being of Mithraic significance,[4] which again takes us as far back as Flavian times.

The writer consulted Professor F. Drexel and M. Cumont himself (both of whom agreed at once with the Mithraeum theory), before committing himself to this view.[5] It is here offered as the one which seems to present fewest difficulties. On the other hand, it is only fair to add that contrary views have been expressed, for example, by the late Sir George Macdonald.[6]

The latest coin sealed in the lowest layer, near the floor of room D, was one of Constans as Augustus (337–50), in good condition. In the bottom also was one of Claudius Gothicus (269–70), and the rubble layer above contained numerous coins of the Tetrici, Constantines, and Valentinian (364–75).

So the rubbish of the bottom layer was still accumulating as late as 337–50, and the building must have gone out of use before then. At this time or later, but not earlier than Valentinian, the building was systematically demolished. The underground room may have gone first and there may have been some attempt to build up the door to it. But our impression was that the destruction had been thoroughly done in one

[1] The article in *Essex Review*, xxxviii, 109, was published entirely unbeknown to me.

[2] *Textes et monuments. Passim.*

[3] *J.R.S.* ix (1919), 143; xvii, 203; xviii, 202; xix, 198; *T.E.A.S.* xv (1921), 182.

[4] *Arch. J.* lxxxii (1925–8), 1–24, with excellent illustrations of

Colchester stones.

[5] *Illustr. London News*, 24 May 1930.

[6] In *Roman Britain 1914–1928*, British Academy Supplemental Papers no. VI (1929), p. 81; *B.R.G.K.* xix (1929), 56 ff., Abb. 41–43. *Archaeology in England and Wales*, 1914–31 (1933), 253–4.

operation. The masonry in the doorway probably belongs to the time of the deposition of the first layer.

In A.D. 311 Constantine adopted Christianity and by 325 was engaged in a general attack on paganism, razing temples and erecting churches. The impact of this was no doubt very uneven over the Empire. Apart from the comparative immunity of remote places, we now know that the effort was not generally successful anywhere (see p. 231) before the time of Gratian. Cumont quotes examples of savage suppression of pagan temples by the Christians, and in Colchester, where several temples have now been excavated, the destruction seems to have been most thorough. The buildings have had almost every stone removed, and in no case has a cult-object remained in association. Apart from statuettes, which could all come from private houses, the only cult-objects in the Museum are the altar to the Sulevian Mothers,[1] and the large bronze Mercury from Gosbecks. This is a poor showing from so many temples.[2]

It seems that the roof of room D became ruinous (tiles in the rubbish below) and was removed. Rubbish could then be dumped in from most sides. Possibly the place was 'desecrated' by throwing in filth and human remains. Then the building was taken down, leaving a large hollow over room D, covered with rubble. This may have been as late as 370. Finally, the hollow was filled up with a stiff loam (and perhaps the drain too was filled up now) containing a coin of Valentinian and late pottery. One or two patches of white mortar lay at high levels and might have belonged to later buildings on the site, but they are in the black top-soil and are of uncertain nature and date.

If this was a Mithraeum the owners had time to remove their treasures; there are no shattered remains of cult-objects. We think, nevertheless, that the possibility is there, and therefore wish to point out one feature, viz. the double door in the east side. Such a door was assumed to be in the south at Heddernheim because of the columns (which do not seem to have been very certainly indicated as regards detail): here it could not be in the south, because the south wall of room A still stood 18 in. high. Nor could a Mithraeum have a public and porticoed entrance, so we may assume some sort of use of part-engaged columns, probably on the outside, to give a religious appearance in the classical style. A reconstruction in the *Illustrated London News*, 24 May 1930, gives a general idea of what is suggested above, though the drawing is probably much too classical for a provincial town.

Only one definite Mithraic temple was known in Britain until quite recently, when to the almost vanished one at Housesteads was added the new and excellently preserved one at Carrawburgh, both on Hadrian's Wall in Northumberland. An underground chamber at Burham in Kent[3] has been rejected as a Mithraeum, but it is worth noting that its dimensions were exactly the same as those of our room D. At Carrawburgh, too, one dimension is the same; and in 1929 we conjectured the use of wooden walls for the side-benches, and suggested that they might have been so built at Burham. Now at Carrawburgh, in 1950, has come to light the first authentic and ineluctable example of such a practice.

We must finally mention the room E which was added, with straight joints, to the east side of room D. It is a lighter building and certainly an afterthought. The floor was of earth, with no distinctive remains, the walls of septaria, and the dimensions, inside, 18 ft. by 14 ft. 8 in.

THE REST OF THE INSULA

Exploratory trenches were cut outwards from the 'Mithraeum'. The first extended south from the SW. angle, in search of the E.–W. street. The rubble from the destruction of the building lay on the surface of the yellow loam at 4 ft. from the present surface, mingled with food-bones. Some 11 ft. from the wall the rubble faded at the edge of a slot which may have held a wall, or perhaps a palisade. This slot was 2 ft. wide at the bottom and less than 2 ft. deep, and full of clay and lumps of hard mortar (remains of a foundation?). South of it the yellow loam came up to only 2 ft. 6 in. from the surface. Its top from here on is uncertain, as if formerly cultivated. Eight feet farther on another trench crossed at right angles. It was nearly 3 ft. wide and 1 ft. deep and was filled with black soil and mortar. It could well have been the foundation trench of a low wall.

In the remainder of this trench there was nothing of much note of Roman date, and no trace of the expected street. The main feature was a large and smelly rubbish-pit of about 1650.

The second trench was cut eastwards from the SE. angle to the wall of the meadow. The Roman surface outside the east wall of room E was of dark tilth, at 4 ft. 3 in. from the surface, on sandy subsoil, covered by 3 or 4 in. of yellowish rubble, above which lay the white rubble from the destruction of the building. Pottery was of the same nature as that from the bottom of the 'Mithraeum'. Eleven feet east of the annexe a

---

[1] Found in the town-ditch near the SW. angle. A temple of the Matres should be somewhere near, possibly in Crouch Street. Even this altar has had its top destroyed.

[2] We have now to add the two plaques and bronze stag from temple IV, p. 239.

[3] *P.S.A.L.* xvi, 105, 248; xvii, 96.

foundation trench crossed at right angles, 2 ft. 10 in. wide and 4 ft. 5 in. deep. It was filled with black soil full of mortar and had a layer of yellowish mortar in the bottom. Beyond it at an interval of 9 ft. 6 in., lay another wall-slot with yellow mortar in the bottom, 2 ft. wide and 4 ft. 6 in. from the surface. Between the two walls lay a kind of raised floor of firm clayey, yellow loam, at 2 ft. 8 in. from the surface, with a scatter of pieces of very white mortar across it. There was much of this loose in the top-soil also. The second slot could be the wall of the insula, for it bounds the road, but it probably had a function also. Beyond the road, in insula 16, there was only a gravelled surface.

The third trench was cut diagonally SW. from a point on the west wall of room A. It revealed undisturbed soil at 5 ft. 6 in. with no signs of buildings or definite occupation-levels, and this space was bounded on the west by a much damaged wall-slot, a little over 2 ft. wide and 6 ft. deep, with mortar in the bottom. This wall had been to some extent a retaining wall, for the ground rises to the west (and rose outside the first slot in every trench), and just outside this wall lay the shrine which is described below. The rest of the trench was barren, save for a second- to third-century rubbish-pit. It was chiefly cut to test the strange statement made by Jenkins[1] that a vaulted drain (shown on his plan) left a round opening in the prison of the Castle, and ran across to the 'Mithraeum'. We now think we have disproved this at both ends.

The Shrine (116)

116. A small rectangular building lay 11 ft. 6 in. outside the last wall. Only the mortar layer of the foundations remained, 29–30 in. wide. It measured 21 ft. 6 in. long on the south, 17 ft. 4 in. on the east and west respectively, and 22 ft. on the north side.

A small porch was attached to the west side, 12 ft. 10 in. long and 7 ft. 8 in. wide. The foundations were 2 ft. 6 in. wide. A similar building was found in insula xxiii at Silchester.[2] We have styled it a shrine for want of a better name, although as shrine one would expect it to have the porch on the east.

Thirteen feet from the SW. angle of this shrine lay a rubbish-pit about 7 ft. square and 9 ft. deep. It contained dark earth with broken tile, flue-tiles, oyster-shells, bones, and very fragmentary pottery of the second century. Eleven feet beyond this there was a pitching of rough stones extending about 5 ft., and just beyond this a gravel floor. The foundations of the shrine lay 3 ft. below the surface, on the subsoil; the

stone pitching began at 2 ft. and went down to 3 ft. 9 in.; the gravel floor was 2 ft. 6 in. below the surface.

The trench was stopped just short of the boundary fence.

119B. Some months after the excavations were closed a small amount of levelling was done in this corner of the meadow, and remains of Roman walling were struck just below the surface. A fragment running approximately N.–S. was nearly 9 ft. long and 18 in. wide; three courses of septaria remained. On the east side of this another wall had abutted with a straight joint, but only about 18 in. of it remained. The thickness and materials were the same. These walls stood in gravelly soil, perhaps the subsoil.

119C. In 1939–40 Mr. E. J. Rudsdale noted a concrete foundation lying 45 ft. from the wall of Holly-trees lawn and 129 ft. 6 in. from the west end of the same wall. It was not explored.

117. Workmen planting a goalpost near the centre of the meadow came upon a red tessellated floor only 18 in. below the surface. It was found to measure 12 ft. 9 in. E.–W. and 13 ft. 9 in. N.–S. A quarter-round moulding of plaster had been run round the edges. There was a layer of pink mortar beneath it, dropping to the north to the edge of a hollow filled with mixed clayey soil containing pottery, broken hypocaust tiles, and the like. The pottery was very fragmentary, but could be attributed to the Antonine period (or later) with certainty; at least one vessel (the jar, fig. 59.3) is probably third century in date. Beneath this again was the ubiquitous layer of yellowish clayey loam, here about 6 in. thick, the pottery from which, wherever found, seems restricted to about A.D. 90–120. Below this was sandy subsoil.

Only to the east could any extension of the building be traced. Here lay a hypocaust (pl. xx, A), 12 ft. square, but the east and north sides were broken away completely and could not be traced. Remains of forty-four *pilae* stood in position, four of which were part-engaged in the west wall. Those on the south side of the room were much more closely set than those on the north. The tiles used were 8 in. square by 1½ in. thick. Only in the SW. corner was the preservation good. Here the wall was nearly 2 ft. high. It had four courses of septaria followed by four of tiles, the top of which probably indicates the floor-level. No traces of the suspensory tiles remained, for the floor had had a tessellated pavement upon it and the remains of this and its mortar bedding filled the whole space among the *pilae*. It had been completely broken into small fragments by robbers seeking the suspensory tiles.

The task of clearing all this and trying to salvage as

---

[1] *Colchester Castle* (1861), 33; (1869), 24.
[2] *Arch.* lvii, 235, several houses at Silchester have small square

buildings near them which might have been private shrines, but they have produced no proof of such identity.

much as possible of the mosaic and wall-plaster was slow and difficult. Most of the pieces of mosaic crumbled at the slightest touch, but enough was recovered to enable a conjectural reconstruction of the pattern. It is a geometric design in black and white, with a small floral panel in the centre and coloured guilloche panels and corner knots. The style is a common one here and elsewhere, e.g. the central panel of one found in 1793 near the Minster at Lincoln (according to a photostat from the B.M.).

The walls had been lined, at least to some extent, with hollow flue-tiles finished off with painted plaster, quantities of which lay among the ruined mosaic. These included fragments from the angles of the door and window-reveals, and curved fragments from a rounded recess. But all failed to yield any idea of the pattern of the decoration.

The *pilae* stood on a fairly level floor of pinkish mortar, the foundation of which was not examined.

The probable position of the walls of this room has been shown conjecturally on the plan. The building could not be traced farther, no sign of walls remaining.

From here we explored northwards looking for buildings. The Roman ground-level was roughly terraced, lying on the usual clayey loam, under which was the sand subsoil. The layer of broken flue-tiles and pink mortar rubble, 6 in. thick, from the demolition of the house, lay 18 in. down, in the top-soil, giving the impression that the Normans had done this. Beyond the midden there was an area paved with fine gravel, and beyond this lay the metalling, now becoming rather thin, of the E.–W. street, described on p. 69.

118 and **119A**. During the 1928–9 season the dry summer showed signs on the surface which led us to dig against the fence on the west side of the meadow. The remains of a wall were struck at once, at a depth of 2 ft. Later trenching exposed remains of several walls and plain red tessellated floors, all in a very fragmentary condition. The walls generally consisted of the foundation layer of mortar only, but here and there some blocks of septaria remained in position. The largest pavement was 19 ft. long by 6 ft. 9 in. wide, running N.–S. The west wall of the room had been robbed leaving a straight edge; the east edge was broken and a trench cut 3 ft. farther found the ground all disturbed. Nothing further could be found to north or south.

The wall first found proved to be part of an L-shaped fragment SW. of the pavement, and at the end of the western arm a pot (f. 268) for a foundation offering was found *in situ* (F). The wall is of septaria, about 2 ft. thick and roughly built, standing directly upon the gravelly subsoil.

When excavating for an air-raid shelter at the south end of the meadow (April 1940), a T.S. cup f. 33 stamped DIVICATIM was found almost intact; also the most part of a platter f. 18, with fine blood-red glaze stamped MATERNI. M (181 and 182.40). There were also found at the same time a fragment of T.S. f. 37, a fragment of a T.S. inkwell, and a fragment of a dark green glazed bowl decorated in moulded relief. Two other stamps on T.S. f. 33 were CELSIANI and BORILLI OF, and there was a second brass coin, possibly of Plotina.

In 1938 two emergency shelters were dug in the form of broad, traversed trenches, running N.–S. near the SW. corner, but east of the walls and pavements (no. **119**).[1] In this work the following coins were found: Nerva (?); Trajan (2); Hadrian (2); Alex. Severus; Postumus; Gallienus; Tetricus (2); Cl. Gothicus (2); Helena or Theodora; Constantine I (3); Constantine II (4); Constans; Constantius II (2, one a clipped silver siliqua); Urbs Roma (4); Constantinian; Valens or Valentinian (3); illegible third century (5); illegible fourth century (3), and various small finds, including another whole jar f. 268, probably a foundation-pot.[2]

When digging a large area west of the 'Mithraeum' for vegetables the following coins were found in the top-soil: Hadrian; Carausius; follis of Constantine I; Constantine II; Constans (3); Gratian; Decentius; Valentinian; Arcadius (2); two possibly Theodosian; three possibly Tetricus; another Constantinian; four illegible third century and an illegible silver denarius (2–19.41).

LIST OF SMALL FINDS FROM EXCAVATIONS IN INSULAE 7 AND 15, 1927–9[2]

COINS

The coins found were very few, especially in the first season's work, a fact which is to be attributed almost entirely to the fact that the work had to be done in the winter when the soil was sticky, for the ground in the park generally yields coins in good numbers continuously. Most of the coins were found during the first three months of the second season, while the fine weather lasted.

In the following list U means unstratified and C means condition when lost.

DOMITIAN A.D. 69–96.

1. *As*, M. & S. 723. Spes type. C, good; Rubbish-pit I, A.D. 77–78

2. *Sest.* Illegible, but head of Domitian. U, south trench; C, very worn.

TRAJAN, A.D. 98–117

3. *Sest.* Illegible, but head of Trajan. Bottom of room D; C, probably fair, but very corroded.

HADRIAN, A.D. 117–38

4. *Sest. Rev.* illegible. Lying against south wall of annex of 'Mithraeum' about half-way along. U; C, very worn.

5. *Sest. Rev.* illegible. U, south trench; C, worn.

6. *Sest.* Illegible (possibly Trajan). Bottom of room D; C, worn.

7. *Sest. Rev.* illegible. Ibid. 18 in. above floor, adhering to coin no. 3 above; C, good.

8. *Sest.* Illegible. Bottom of room D; C, probably fair.

9. *Sest. Rev.* illegible. Bottom of drain (?); C, fair.

10. Base *denarius*, possibly Hadrian; very mutilated. Bottom of room D; C, dubious.

C.M.R. 1944, 16.   [2] See also *C.M.R.* 1930, pp. 9–27 and 44–49 *passim*.

11. *As*? An empress, perhaps Sabina; illegible. South trench, in clay; C, very worn.

ANTONINUS PIUS, A.D. 138–61

12. *Sest.* Illegible. Bottom of room D; C, dubious.
13. *Sest.* Illegible. Found as no. 7 above; C, dubious.

FAUSTINA JUNIOR, died A.D. 175

14. *As*? M. & S. 1647. *Rev.* IVNO S. C. Bottom of room D; C, good.

SEPTIMIUS SEVERUS, A.D. 193–211

15. *Den.* M. & S. 265. *Rev.* FVNDATOR PACIS. (A.D. 198–201). Just under the late walling-up in doorway of room D; C, fine.

GETA, A.D. 197–212

16. *Den. Obv.* P.SEPT.GETA CAES.PONT. Laureate right.
    Rev. FVNDATOR PACIS, as last. Compare Cohen 63, M. & S., p. 317, note on Cohen 63. U; C, good.

CARACALLA, A.D. 196–217

17. Base *den.* Very broken and damaged, attribution uncertain. Bottom of room D; C, good.

JULIA DOMNA, A.D. 193–217

18. *Den.* M. & S. 559. *Rev.* IVNO. Bottom of room D; C, very good.

GALLIENUS, A.D. 260–8. All *antoniniani*

19. Partly illegible. *Rev.* Salus. In field P. U; C, poor.
20. M. & S. 207, IOVI CONS AVG. Stag. At SE. corner of annexe to 'Mithraeum'. C, good.
21. Possibly Gallienus. *Rev.* PAX AVG. Bottom of drain, at south end; C, fair.
22. Illegible, but head of Gallienus (?). *Rev.* stag standing left. U, south trench; C, fair.

SALONINA

23. *Ant. Rev.* illegible. U, over pit I; C, poor.

VICTORINUS, A.D. 265–7. All *antoniniani*

24. Cohen 92. *Rev.* PIETAS AVG. In rubble layer of room D, against south wall; C, good.
25. Cohen 131. *Rev.* VIRTVS AVG. In same rubble layer, with three others; C, good.
26. (Retains traces of silvering.) Illegible, Pax type. U, over annexe; C, fair.
27. *Rev.* illegible, prob. Pax. In rubble layer of room D; C, poor.

TETRICUS, T. A.D. 268–73. All *antoniniani*

28. Cohen 17. *Rev.* COMES AVG. U, over 'Mithraeum'; C, good.
29. Another, very corroded, in same position.
30. Similar. (COME?)S AVGG. Double struck and blurred. In uppermost layer over room D; C, fair.
31. Cohen 70. *Rev.* LAETITIA AVG. Same layer; C, good.
32. Cohen 17? Victory as on 28. Same layer; C, worn.
33. Cohen 70. U, over 'Mithraeum'; C, very good.
34. Orthodox obv. Barbarous *rev.* Uppermost filling over room A; C, dubious.
35. Pax type. U, over 'Mithraeum'; C, fair.
36. Cohen 95. *rev.* PAX AVG U, over 'Mithraeum'; C, worn.
37. Cohen 80. *Rev.* MARS VICTOR. Found near the bandstand in the Castle Park; C, good.
38. Pax type. On top of east wall of 'Mithraeum'; C, worn.

39. Vacat.
40. Illegible. U.
41. Illegible. In rubble layer of room A; C, worn.
42. Probably Tetricus. Illegible. Topsoil over room D, about 3 ft. down.
43. Illegible. U, over 'Mithraeum'. Broken.
44. Spes type. U; C, mint.
45. Another. C, fair.
46. Another. On top of the east wall of room D; C, fair.
47. Victory type. U, over room D; C, fair.
48. *Rev.* . . . MILL . . . Genius standing left with cornucopiae. In rubble layer of room D; C, fair.

TETRICUS II, A.D. 268–73

49. Cohen 6. COMES AVGG. U, over room D; C, good.
50. Another, ibid.; C, worn.
51. Another. U; C, fair.
52. Cohen 19. INVICTVS type. In rubble layer of room D; C, very worn.
53. *Rev.* PIETAS AVG. Found over red pavement against Castle ditch.
54. Another. Rubble layer in room D.
55. Another, in topsoil. Barbarous. C, fair.
56. Spes type. In rubble layer, room D; C, good.
57. PAX AVG. U, over 'Mithraeum'; C, good.
58. Barbarous *rev.* . . . PPIIL . . . Spes type. In filling of Duncan's trench in room D; U; C, worn.
59. Illegible. Just above rubble filling of room D; C, good.
60. Another. U, topsoil of south trench; C, worn.
61. *Rev.* . . . ITI VIC. Salus type. Pit in south trench; C, fine.

CLAUDIUS II, GOTHICUS, A.D. 268–70. All *antoniniani*

62. Cohen 109. GENIVS AVG. M. & S. 45? Top filling of drain in south part.
63. *Rev.* AEQVITAS AVG. In rubble layer in room D; C, worn.
64. CONSECRATIO, Altar. Filling of drain.
65. Another, same type. Top-soil over room D at 3 ft.; C, dubious.
66. *Rev.* VICTORIA AVG. Just above mortar layer in room A.
67. *Consecratio* type. Eagle. Same position.
68. Same type, large flan (25 mm.). Near culvert by drain; C, fair.
69. Same type. Just above thick layer on floor of room D at middle of south end; C, good.
70. Same type. Altar. In uppermost layer of room D.
71. *Rev.* uncertain. U, 'Mithraeum'.

AURELIAN, ? A.D. 270–5

72. Victory type. U, over 'Mithraeum'; C, fair.

CARAUSIUS, A.D. 287–93

73. *Rev.* Bull standing right, under it M (?); no other legend remaining. Chance find near 'Mithraeum'; C, rather worn.

ALLECTUS, A.D. 293–7

74. M. & S. 51. *Rev.* VIRTVS AVG, Hercules in temple. U, over floor of room D. C, good.

CONSTANTINE THE GREAT, A.D. 306–37

75. Gloria type, two standards, mm. TRS. U; C, good.

CONSTANTINIAN coins:

76. Constantine II, same type, mm. illeg. U, over south wall of 'Mithraeum'; C, fair.
77. Constantius II, Gloria type, one standard, mm TRS U, west trench; C, dubious.

78. Urbs Roma. mm. TRS. Module 14 mm. Uppermost layer over room D; C, good.

79. Constantinopolis. U, over south wall of 'Mithraeum'; C, poor.

80. Minim. No legends. Two soldiers and a labarum. mm. illeg. U.

81. Constans. VICTORIAE DD AVGG Q NN type, mm. $\frac{E}{TRP}$. Bottom foot of filling of room D, just inside entrance; C, very good.

82. Another, mm. $\frac{branch?}{TRP}$. In uppermost layer over room A; C, very good.

83. Another Constans, but *Fel. Temp. Rep.* type, Cohen 15. Top-soil over south part of 'Mithraeum'; C, worn.

VALENTINIAN I, A.D. 364–75

84. Cohen 37. SECVRITAS REIPVBLICAE mm. illegible. In uppermost layer over room D; C, good.

ARCADIUS. A.D. 383–408

85. VICTORIA AVGGG? Top-soil over room D, about 3 ft. down; C, fair.

Another forty coins are not accurately identifiable, they may be summarized thus:

A. *Stratified*

In the lowest layer of room D. 105, a minimus or small bronze extremely corroded, found 2 ft. above the floor, close to the entrance. In the rubble layer of room D, two radiate heads, nos. 95 and 116; in the layer above this four radiate heads, nos. 88 and 89, worn, and nos. 124 and 125, and a completely illegible, no. 123. In the rubble layer itself one small illegible (fourth century) no. 93.

In the third period in the gateway one small coin no. 111. As this coin is so important we describe it in full:

Obv. Diademed (?) head right.

Rev. . . . . . . VG. Device illegible. Module 11 mm. Found in the make-up of the second floor in the gateway. C, worn. Mr. Salisbury thinks this is a degraded *Fel. Temp. Reparatio.*

B. *Unstratified*

Radiate heads, nos. 91, 94, 101, 108, 109, 113 (very small and very barbarous, radiate draped bust right, *rev.* barbarous figure with attempts at legend), 115.

Barbarous radiate heads, nos. 86, 87, 97, 106 (*Fel. Temp.* type) 112, 113, 114, 122.

Diademed heads, no. 98, possibly *Securitas Reipublicae* type.

Illegible, second century, nos. 117 and 118, found over the gateway. Both ae ii.

Illegible, third century, nos. 99 and 100. Late, also 91.

Illegible, fourth century, nos. 90, 92.

Quite illegible, no. 96.

OBJECTS OF BRONZE AND IRON; AND OTHER SMALL FINDS

BRONZE OBJECTS (FIG. 47)

1. Bronze fibula, $1\frac{3}{4}$ in. long, tinned. Hinged pin, solid catch plate, the bow ribbed and moulded. It probably came from the west of England, cf. Caerleon, *Arch.* lxxviii, 162, 13 and one from Wroxeter in Shrewsbury Museum (B. 230). Many others could be quoted. This is probably second century. Unstratified.

2. Bronze fibula of light crossbow type, $2\frac{1}{8}$ in. long. Spring of at least 16 turns held in a half-cylinder on the head. Semicircular moulded bow with two lateral projections at middle and three

near the foot, which is faceted, long and straight, carrying a half-cylinder (now broken) beneath it to hold the pin. There is a slight moulding on the bow near the head.

No exact parallel has been found. It belongs to a large group which includes the brooches with a double or triple bow such as *Richborough II*, pl. xvii, nos. 12, 13. The characteristics of this group are the large cylinder containing the spring, the semicircular bow, the collars or mouldings on the bow near the foot,

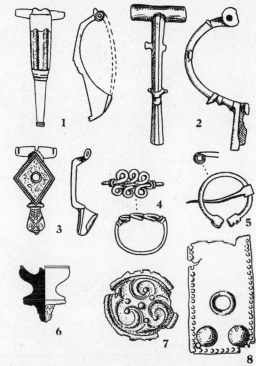

FIG. 47. Small objects (all bronze) from excavations in Hollytrees' Meadow. (Scale, full size.) p. 117.

and the long, box-like foot which takes the place of the catch-plate. Most of these features are characteristic of the later heavy crossbow type.

The nearest parallels are *Zugmantel*, Taf. ix, nos. 56–58, and see *Arch. Ael.* 3 s. vii, 185, figs. 20, 21, 23, 24 (Corbridge, 1910). The date is probably the first half of the third century. Found on the bottom of room D. Five others previously recorded from Colchester are similar, but lack the lateral knobs on the bow.

3. Small bronze fibula, $1\frac{3}{8}$ in. long, the pin was hinged. The lozenge-shaped plate has moulded and cross-hatched edges and has been enamelled. The foot is zoomorphic with two circular recesses like eyes, and a moulded snout. Above this there is some fine chasing. Found in pit I, Trajanic.

This is a very well known type, usually attributed to the Trajan–Hadrian period.

5. Small penannular brooch of bronze. Diameter $\frac{13}{16}$ in. The material is round bronze wire and the ends have been beaten out flat, coiled up, and the outer edges notched. Found on the bottom of room D.

The type was common at Camulodunum, *Cam. I*, 326, fig. 1–5, in the first half of the first century, and this is perhaps a rubbish survival, but many penannular types were long-lived.

4. Small finger-ring of bronze wire twisted into a knot as shown. Found on floor close to the preceding, in room D.

A ring almost identical, found in Colchester, is in the British Museum. The type is rare. Henkel, among the wire rings shown on his Taf. II, XVI, XXVIII, and XXIX shows only a few: nos. 323 (silver) and 707–9 (bronze). Of these 323 and 707 come from Nijmegen, the latter from the Augustan cemetery: it has two loops only on each side. No. 709 is from Niederbieber and closely resembles ours, but has five loops on each side. In a note on this ring Henkel observes that an almost identical ring in Königsberg Museum and was found with remains of the late Roman period, and that this fits in with a third-century date at Niederbieber.

7. Thin disk of bronze, diameter 1 in., with no sign of attachment on the back. Embossed with a repoussée design of distinctly Celtic character, it was probably cemented on the face of a disk brooch. Found in the rubbish-pit in the west trench.

8. Part of a thin bronze strap exactly 1 in. wide. The two corners are perforated. The sides are ornamented by a row of repoussée dots, and there is a large boss in each corner with a ring behind it, all pressed out from the back. Found in the filling of the drain.

6. Small knob of solid bronze, with remains of iron tang. A common type found in all sizes. Some seem to have belonged to lynch-pins (Ward Perkins, *Ant. Journ.* xx, 358 ff.), others were probably ornaments for furniture.

IRON OBJECTS (PL. XXI)

On pl. XXI, B we show six of a number of large and heavy split rings or washers, found on the bottom of room A. The ends overlap slightly and some are turned clockwise, some anti-clockwise. The cross-section is rectangular; the size varies from nearly 5 in. in diameter to nearly 3½ in. One only has a rounded, perforated end. Another has two perforated ends. Their purpose remains quite unknown, for Duncan's theory that they were the spring of a sluice-gate must be abandoned.

The same figure shows a neck-shackle found by Duncan and labelled 'from the gateway', with fragments of others. The complete example is rectangular in section, which is unusual. It is probable that the label is inaccurate and that these too were found in room A. The diameter of the top is 7 in.

Pl. XXI, A shows further shackles found by us in room A, all in the lowest layer. There are five large examples, diameter 6 to 7 in., two of them, left and right bottom, are a pair. The others are all arranged to clamp differently. The section, though very corroded, seems in all cases to have been round. There is also a pair of very well-preserved small shackles, diameter 2¾ in.

In all cases the links for fastening, both owing to their size and the looseness of the hinge, make very loose connexions when brought together. If these were manacles they are very crude indeed. They could better have been used to clamp round heavy beams for attaching a chain or rope. The smaller pair is perhaps neat enough to have been handcuffs, but none of these resembles known manacles such as those found at Echzell (*O.R.L.* 18, Taf. III, 5) or at Pfünz (*O.R.L.* 73, Taf. XVIII, 14).

THE POTTERY

DECORATED SIGILLATA

A. *From Pit I. Trajanic* (figs. 48 and 49)

1. Complete bowl, f. 37, but not stamped. The ovolo is between wavy lines and has rosette terminals of Flavian style. Upper zone also of Flavian character. Similar birds are used by *Virilio*, Knorr 81, 2; *Meddillus*, Knorr 54 and 13; *M. Crestio*, Knorr 28, 4, and by *Biracillus* and *Calvus*. The festoon is used by *L. Cosi*, Knorr, 25, 14, 15. The lizard appears in the B.M. catalogue, p. 105, M347, a larger one is ascribed to *Paullus* (A.D. 75–85), Knorr, 100, C. Oswald, *Figure Types*, 2149–51, quotes three lizards, all Flavian. Date, c. A.D. 70–90.

2. Part of a bowl, f. 37, with trifid ovolo with wavy line beneath. Decoration in two zones, the upper in large panels, the lower a straight wreath. The archer is used by *Valeri* (smaller), K. 18, 1; *Of Coeli*, K. 23, 1; *Meddillus*, K. 54, 2; *Justus*, K. 44; and *C.V.AIB*, K. 87, D.

The stag is that of *Coelus* K. 23, 5 and *Cens* K. 22, who also used an S-shaped motif.

The whole style is typically late first century; compare the bowl by *Vitalis*, K. 82, C.

3. Part of a bowl, f. 37. The ovolo has been removed in affixing the rim. Decoration in three zones, the lower as in nos. 1 and 3, the upper in panels, and the centre a continuous scroll.

The dog is an extremely common first-century type. The stag is that used by *Cens* and *Coelus*, K. 23, 5. For the general style compare *Passienus*, K. 64, F; *Pudens*, K. 68; *Mercato*, K. 57.

This bowl is signed with a stamp with sunk letters on a raised label (i.e. by the mould-maker) C. V. ALB (retro).

A fragment of a similar bowl with this same stamp was found at Richborough (ii, pl. XXVII, 7, and p. 67, where other examples are collected). Knorr dates a Nijmegen example (his Taf. 87, D), Vespasian–Domitian, and in view of the company in which we find ours, his judgement is vindicated, rather than the earlier date implied by the writer of the Richborough report. If the stamp C. VAL. ALBAN is really of the same potter as ours (which we do not doubt), it should be regarded as the earlier mark of this potter. Compare also *Silchester*, XXV, 5 and 6, stamped *Mercato*.

4. Part of a bowl, f. 37, repaired in Roman times by lead rivets. Trifid ovolo with wavy line beneath. Decoration in three zones. The upper and lower similar to no. 1. The middle zone is typically late first century in style. The figure on the left is part of a lion. The whole may be paralleled frequently on Agricolan sites.

Date, A.D. 80–90. Compare *Silchester*, pl. XVIII, A; *Wroxeter II*, pl. XII, 3, stamped OFIVCVN, in a deposit of 80–110; Pompeii (Atkinson, no. 57).

5. Two fragments of a bowl, f. 37, which had three zones of decoration. The ovolo is blurred. The upper zone has a festooning and birds in the same style as no. 1. The second zone is a straight wreath and the lower was probably similar to the middle zone in no. 3.

For the style compare *Wroxeter I*, pl. XIII, 3; ibid. II, pl. XIII, 4, stamped OF CRESTI, in a deposit of A.D. 80–110.

6. Three fragments of a bowl, f. 30, with a small ovolo and large scroll of polygonal leaves. The style is earlier than that of any other sigillata from this pit, and the glaze is worn. For the style compare Hofheim, Taf. XXVI and XXVII, 19. The rosette seems to be that used by *Maccarus*, Knorr 51, J and K. Compare also Knorr, *Rottweil*, 1907, Taf. VI, 4 (pre-Vespasian).

Fig. 50, 9. Two fragments of a bowl, f. 37, with trifid ovolo and decoration in panels; a slightly later style than that of the preceding pieces. Style Flavian. Cf. Knorr, *Rottweil*, 1912, Taf. XXII, 3 and 4.

Fig. 50, 10. A number of fragments, broken to splinters, of a bowl, f. 37 with poor decoration consisting of a large scroll, the lower hollows of which are filled with figure-subjects including a bird (Déch. 994). Compare O. and P., pl. XV, 2; *Brecon*, fig. 80, S 152, 'Late Flavian'.

B. *From under the N.–S. street*

Fig. 49, 7. The only fragment of f. 29 found stratified during the whole of the excavations. The separate details of the decoration

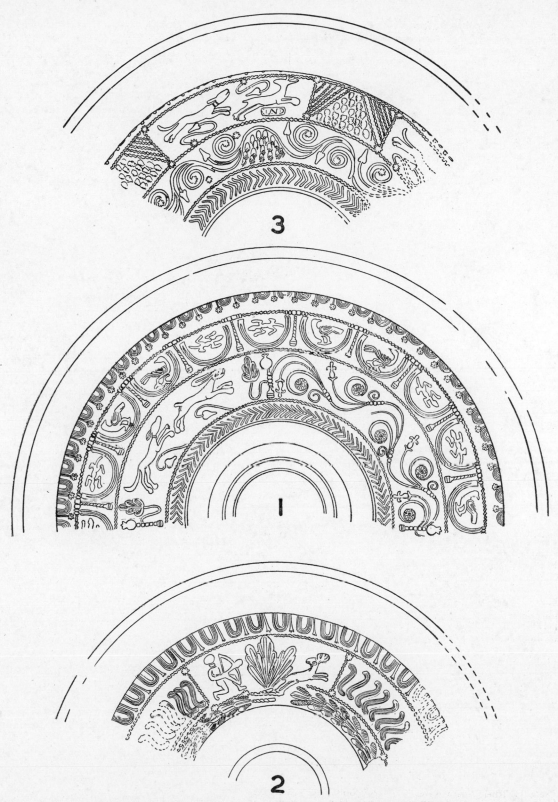

FIG. 48. Decorated Samian from Pit 1, *c.* A.D. 100. Scale ½. (p. 118.)

are too small for accurate identification, but the general style is pre-Flavian, as will be seen from the following examples of similar festooning in the lower zone with a zone of imbricated arrowheads or gadroons above: *Ardacus*, Knorr, 10; *Albus*, K. 5, A; *Carus*, K. 20, F; K. 93, C (Claudian); see also K. 94, B,

Ems, Taf. II, 20; *O.R.L.* 8, *Zugmantel*, Taf. xxv, 14, by COMITIALIS.

These two vessels were the only decorated sigillata found in this deposit. No. 11 is very worn. Both were probably in use in the Antonine period.

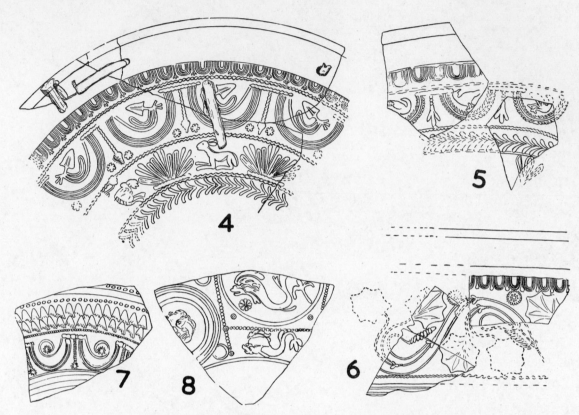

FIG. 49. Decorated Samian from Pit I, *c.* A.D. 100. Scale ½. (p. 118.)

which has a zone of SSS motif above the festooning and is attributed to Nero or early Vespasian, and Knorr, *Rottweil*, 1912, Taf. VIII, Claudian. Later examples have straight wreaths or chevron or SSS bands above. O. and P., p. 71, emphasize the Claudian date of pinnate leaves and Flavian of arrow-heads, but our arrow-heads are not used as filling for panels or scrolls, but occupy the position of pinnate leaves in the Claudian period. It is regrettable that so important a piece as this cannot be more closely dated than A.D. 60–75.

C. *From the lowest level in room D of site I* (fig. 50, nos. 11 and 12)

11. Half a bowl, f. 37. Decoration on panels with large medallions and figures. Stamped DOIICCI. The glaze is dark red. Further remarks are unnecessary save that Doeccus is a Hadrian–Antonine potter, who sometimes used a large D monogram, on which see O. and P. in the Brecon Report, 'Excursus. The Monogram D', pp. 193–201.

12. Complete bowl (restored), f. 37, with widely spaced ovolo and large medallions. Style of the East Gaulish potteries. The base of the tripod appears in Knorr, *Cannstadt*, Taf. XLII, 12 and 15, Rheinzabern ware. The very clumsy stag is Ludowici T. 121, the medallion B. 37, the boxer M. 42. See also *O.R.L.* 4,

D. *From the drain and elsewhere* (fig. 51 B)

Fig. 51B, 1. Major portion of a bowl, f. 37. The ovolo with rosette terminals has been cut away in affixing the rim. Style of animals free in field. The strange ornament in the field is the same as on the Maldon bowl (May, *Colchester*, pl. XIX, I), which is stamped CR (retro). The present example has part of the mould-maker's signature under the decoration, reading OF ATT (retro).

Compare this bowl with *Brecon* S205, and the Wilderspool bowl stamped OF ATT, in the same style. Ours may safely be attributed to Attius of Lezoux. Date, Trajan–Hadrian. Cf. also Benwell, *Arch. Ael.* 4 s. xxv, 59, no. 37.

2. Three fragments of a bowl, f. 37, found at the bottom of the drain. The large figure is Déch, 390 (*Butrio*). The figure on the left is D. 69 (*Maccius*). The caryatid standing on the mask may be D. 655a. Lezoux ware. Trajan–Hadrian.

3. Small fragment, f. 37, in incoherent scroll-work. Antonine.

4. Small fragment, f. 37, with ovolo and part of a sea-horse in a festoon. In upper filling of drain.

5. Small fragment, f. 37.

6. Very small fragment, f. 29, in upper part of drain, unstratified.

7. Fragment of f. 37. Free style like no. 1. Hadrian–Antonine.

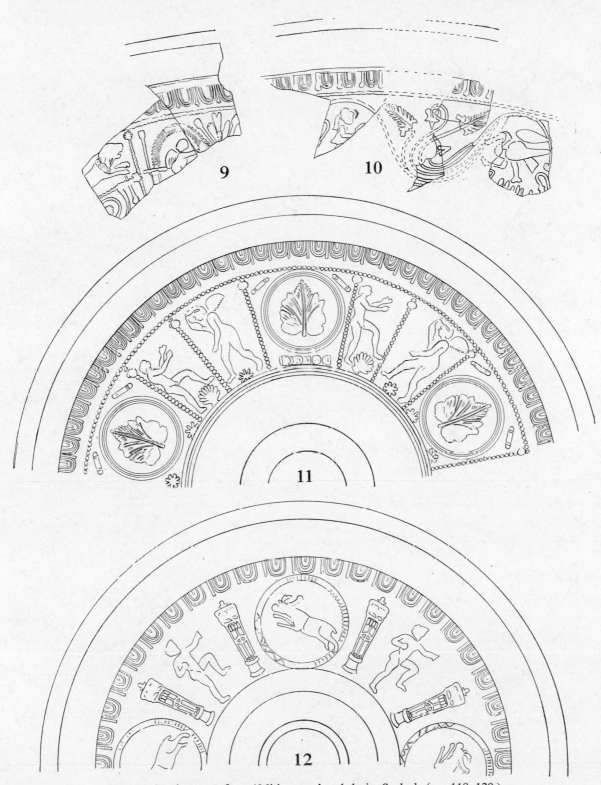

FIG. 50. Samian ware from 'Mithraeum' and drain. Scale ½. (pp. 118, 120.)

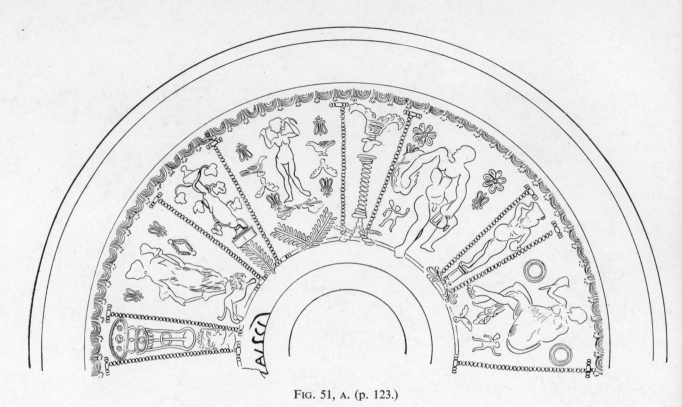

FIG. 51, A. (p. 123.)

FIG. 51, B. Samian ware from 'Mithraeum' and drain. Scale ½. (p. 120.)

8. Fragment of f. 37. Unknown figure in arcade. Diana with hound, not in Déchelette. Probably Trajanic.

9. Fragment of f. 30. Bottom of drain. Only ovolo and small lion preserved. Hadrian–Antonine.

Fig. 51, top. Bowl, f. 37, nearly complete. Bottom of drain, undisturbed. Fine ovolo with rosette terminals. Decoration in panels. Tripod like Déch. 1068 but smaller; Fortuna standing left with cornucopiae and rudder, below her a small lion; ornaments in field like *Cannstadt*, Taf. XVI, 1, but smaller; tree like Déch. 1092 but smaller; Venus braiding her hair, small orna-

the same arrangement and ligatures from Reillac (Creuse), and again, with addition of a point inside the first D, from Chantenay. His record from Poitiers seems the same as that from Reillac, as does the one in Clermont Museum. These four are the only continental records. Oswald adds York (f. 31) and Chesterford, *C.I.L.* VII, 1336, 1295.

The present case, and the forms quoted above, and the fact that the name seems to be that of the one potter throughout, casts a doubt on the 'Ritt. 8' at Poitiers; in any case we would now regard the potter as Antonine.

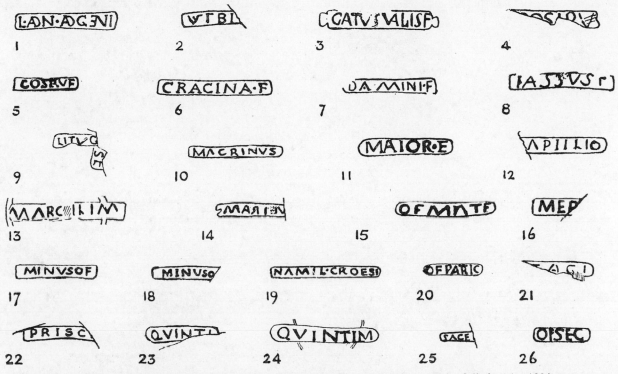

FIG. 52. Potters' stamps on Samian ware, from Hollytrees' Meadow. Scale, full size. (p. 123.)

ments include the leaf *Balmuildy*, pl. XXI, 9; pillar; Hercules drinking, as Déch. 449 but smaller; Silenus as Caryatid; unidentified figure with drinking-horn (??) similar to Déch. 94, but larger. Lezoux ware. Hadrian–Antonine.

Signed in the mould below the decoration . . . . AVSCA or . . . AVSSA.

This vessel is remarkably similar to one found at Birdoswald, *C. & W. Trans.* n.s. xxx, pl. VI, 2, where the style is the same, the same tree, tripod, and small leaf are used, with a rather different plumed leaf free in the field. Stated there not to be Lezoux ware, but no reason given. Compare also Benwell, *Arch. Ael.* 4 s. xxv, 58, no. 9.

POTTERS' STAMPS

a. On Samian ware (fig. 52)

1. L. ADN. ADGENI Base f. 33. Mithraeum I. Oswald, p. 5, makes this a double name only, and ascribes the potter to South Gaul, presumably on the strength of a Ritt. 8 at Poitiers, doubtfully 'Nero–Vespasian'.

Hübner, *C.I.L.* xiii, 10010, 41, shows the stamp with exactly

C. V. ALB (retro). Impressed on a raised label in the decoration of a bowl, f. 37, see p. 118 and fig. 69, 4.

2. ALBI . . . Base, f. 33, in upper filling of drain. There is not enough here to show whether we have an Albus or an Albinus.

OF. ATT (signature) large portion of bowl f. 37, from bottom of drain. See p. 120, and fig. 51B, 1.

. BELINICVS . F Base, f. 27. Pit I. This same form of the name does not occur in *C.I.L.* xiii. Oswald, p. 41, quotes it on f. 27 from Kettering and London. The potter is ascribed to Lezoux, Trajan–Antonine.

3. . CATVSVALIS F Large base, f. Lud. Sb. in rouletted wreath. Pit in west trench. Oswald, p. 131, gives Gatus and Valis as East Gaulish, of Antonine date. The continental records are chiefly from the Netherlands; in Britain there is one other from Wroxeter.

4. COSIRV Base, f. 18 (early), from the drain.

5. COS RVF Base, f. 27. Pit I. Cosius and Rufinus worked at La Graufesenque in the Flavian period.

6. CRACINA.F. Cup, f. 33. Mithraeum I. The only record of this same stamp is from the Pan Rock. Oswald, p. 93, under Cracuna.

7. DAMININF Base, f. 33. Top-soil over drain. The same form of stamp occurs on f. 33 at Langres. Daminus worked at Lezoux, Hadrian–Antonine.

DOIICI Complete bowl, f. 37. Mithraeum I. See p. 120, and fig. 50, 11.

8. IAS(S)VS F Base of large f. 31, in rouletted wreath. Bottom of drain. Probably Iassus of Rheinzabern and Westerndorf, Antonine.

sence of facsimiles this imperfect stamp cannot be identified. Perhaps MARINVS (ii) of Lezoux.

15. OF MATE Base, f. 31 or 18/31. Unstratified. Maternus of Lezoux, according to Oswald (p. 194, 'Domitian–Antonine'!).

16. MER... Base of large f. 18, with the two incised circles in rouletted wreath. Part found in the pit in trench III and part in trench IV. Probably Mercator of Lezoux.

17. MINVSOF Base, f. 33. Over top of drain.

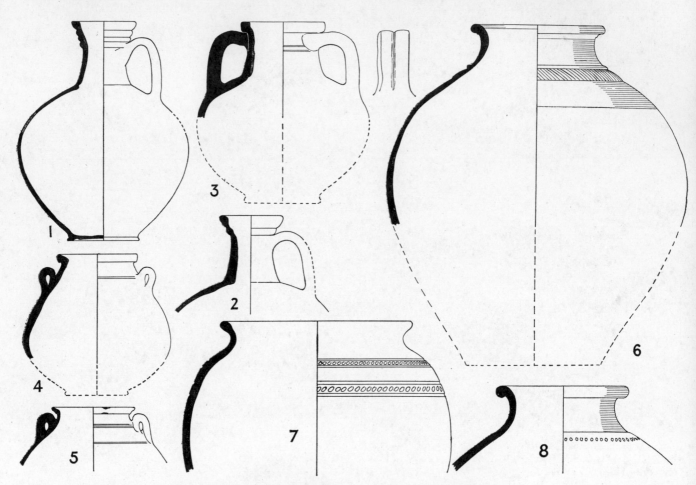

FIG. 53. Pottery from Pit 1, Insula 7, *c.* A.D. 100. Scale ¼.

9. LITVG(ENVS) F (two stamps crossed). This potter worked at Colchester in the late Antonine period. He may first have worked on the Continent, but where is uncertain, for his stamp only occurs about half a dozen times. See p. 249.

MCCIVS (?) Base, f. 18. Maccius, ascribed to Lezoux, but the ware looks South Gaulish. (Pit I.)

10. MACRINVS Base, f. 33. From upper filling of drain. Lezoux, Hadrian–Antonine.

11. MAIOR.F Base f. 31. Upper filling of drain. Graffito X beneath. Lezoux, Trajan–Antonine.

12. M)APILLIO (?) Base, f. 33. Top-soil over drain. Graffito X on outside. If Mapillus it is from Lezoux, Hadrian.

13. MARC(I)ILI M Base, f. 33. Unstratified. Probably the Rheinzabern pottery, although this exact stamp is not given by Ludovici (iii, p. 40).

14. MARIN... Base, f. 18/31. Top-soil of drain. In the ab-

18. MINVSO.. Base, f. 18/31. West trench. The Colchester potter.

19. NAMIL.CROESI Base f. 79. Bottom of drain. Lezoux potters ascribed by Oswald to Trajan–Hadrian, but f. 79 should be later than this, and indeed Namilianus occurs at the Pan Rock.

20. OF PATRIC Base, f. 18. Pit I. Trajanic. Patricius worked at La Graufesenque *c.* 69–90.

21. POT)TACI Base, f. 33. Upper filling of drain. Lezoux, Hadrian–Antonine.

22. PRISC(I... Base, f. 31 or Lud. Sb. Rouletted wreath. Top-soil over drain. There were potters of this name at Lezoux and at Blickweiler and Eschweilerhof. Both were Hadrian–Antonine.

23. QVINTI Base, f. 33. Drain. Unstratified. Graffito X under base.

24. QVINTI M Base,   33. Mithraeum I. Found under the door-sill. Probably Quintus (ii) of Lezoux, Hadrian–Antonine.
25. SAGE... Base, f. 33. Over the street in insula 14.

b. Stamps on mortaria and amphorae

1. MARTINVS F The well-known Colchester potter (see p. 249). The form is 497 as usual. Unstratified.

The Samian has been described (p. 118.)
The following coarse pieces are illustrated, figs. 53–56:
1. The most part of a flagon, f. 154, in fine, thin, red-buff ware, the foot roughly finished. A similar neck was in white clay.
2. Neck and shoulder of flagon, f. 146, in creamy-yellow ware.
3. Upper part of a two-handled jug in rough buff ware. Handles 2-ribbed. Apart from other circumstances one would have considered this vessel at least second half second century.

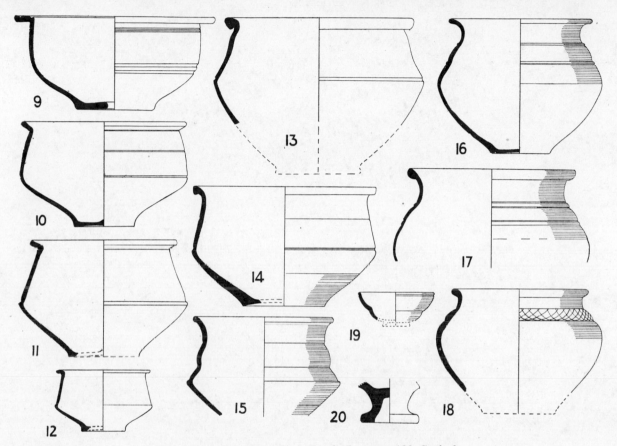

FIG. 54. Pottery from Pit 1, Insula 7, c. A.D. 100. Scale ¼.

2. BAL... On handle of an amphora, f. 187. Not elsewhere recorded.
3. CL PVD On longish handle of f. 187. Unstratified. *Richborough II*, same stamp and references there given. Not later than Ant. Pius.
4. PORLAI (?) On handle of f. 187. Top-soil over Mithraeum (C.M. 805.29). See *Richborough I*, 86, PO(R)AII and references there given, PORLAR, *C.I.L.* xiii, 10002, 27 and 25.
5. S. F. E. On handle of f. 187. From the drain. *Wroxeter II*, 44, fig. 17, no. 15; also at the Saalburg; *C.I.L.* xiii, 10002, 218; *Silchester*, 279; Corbridge; *Arentsburg*, pl. LXIV, 26.
6. ....SENTI...(?) On a mere splinter of a similar handle.

THE POTTERY FROM PIT I (FIGS. 53–56)

There was a very large amount of pottery in this pit, and it forms a very valuable deposit for Colchester, being fairly closely dated to about A.D. 100, a period for which evidence is otherwise scarce.

4. Upper part of a 'honey-pot' in white ware.
5. Rim and handles of another similar, buff ware. The form is 175 in miniature.
6. Upper part of a large flask, f. 232, in fine grey ware; the bulged band below the cordon decorated with oblique strokes.
7. Upper part of a heavy and irregularly made vessel of unclassified form; light grey clay, with drab grey surface; on the shoulder two bands of stabbed impressions between grooves.
8. Rim of flask, f. 285 (which was previously undated), with row of stabbing on shoulder. Hard, coarse, light-grey ware, with uneven surface.
9. Complete bowl, f. 246, with reeded rim; brown, with black surface.
10, 11, 12. Three biconical bowls with angular lip; gritty brown clay, thin and hard, with granular surface. The form is 241–2.
13. Similar bowl, in hard blue-grey ware with granular surface.
14. Another similar, grey-white paste with smoky blue-grey

surface. These are, presumably, the later version of ff. 241–2 in a ware more compatible with second century standards.

15. Upper part of a native bowl, f. 218 (simple form); paste red with tooled black surface.

16, 17. Two bowls, f. 218, one brown to black, the other rough brown. This form is very common at Colchester and was so in this pit. The second is very remarkable, because it is in the 'granular' brown ware and has never been smoothed.

dark grey fumed surface; with three cordons at top and broad band of rouletting.

29. Top of a curious bowl in brown clay charged with pounded shell, with black surface.

30. Platter, f. 17 with rim, smooth buff ware; unusual. Note survival of footring.

31. Part of bowl of curious buff ware; surface polished inside and out.

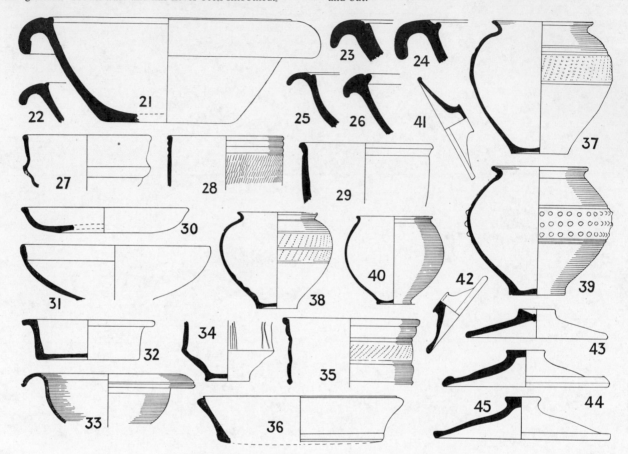

FIG. 55. Pottery from Pit 1, Insula 7, c. A.D. 100. Scale ¼.

18. Upper part of a bowl, simplified, f. 218, the bulge on shoulder latticed. Reddish clay with grey core; grey surface.

19. Fragment of cup, f. 333 (copy of f. Drag. 27). Red-buff ware, mica-gilt.

20. Pedestal-foot, of an incense-cup (?); white ware.

21. Mortarium, nearly complete, bar the spout; f. 195 C, dirty, grey-white clay, coarse and very much worn, so that no grit remains. White grit under rim.

22. Similar rim but smaller; white clay, with white and grey grit which runs over rim.

23. Similar rim, f. 195 B, buff ware, grit worn off.

24. Rim like no. 21, white-buff ware, with white grit; stamped A D I V . . . .

25. Slender rim like no. 23, white-buff ware, grit over rim.

26. Bunched-up rim, compare f. 194, but the offset inside the lip suggests the second century; buff, crumbly paste, grit over rim.

27. Part of a cup, f. 59; hard grey, well-finished.

28. Rim of a copy (perhaps) of f. Drag. 30; reddish-brown,

32. Upright sided bowl with smooth horizontal flange. Hard grey ware.

33. Parts of a fine bowl perhaps copying Drag. f. 35; thin, hard black ware with high polish.

34. Lower part of a cup in hard white ware; thick and coarse, with vertical incised lines on body. Cf. May, pl. LXVI, 313, our f. 331.

35. Small fragment from a bowl as shown; red with grey core, surface dark grey, decorated by oblique comb-stabbings. Possibly a Roman development from f. 85 (girth-beaker).

36. Rim of a platter like f. 33, but with a small upright lip on a thicker wall. Hard gritty, red-buff clay.

37. Beaker, f. 108, hard thin, slate-grey ware, with whitish interior; small cordon under rim, with broad band of oblique comb-stabbings between grooves.

38. Similar beaker, carelessly made; good dark grey ware.

39. Rusticated beaker of fine grey ware, polished on the smooth parts. The ware is brittle, shaling off in flakes. This type of decoration is very rare in Colchester.

40. Part of a fine beaker, f. 104, thin polished black ware; there was another in grey-black ware.

41. Lid, hard, slate-grey.

side and a vertical one, of round section, at the back. The remains of a large spout of unusual shape, with strainer, at the front are exactly reproduced by the spout in the form of a

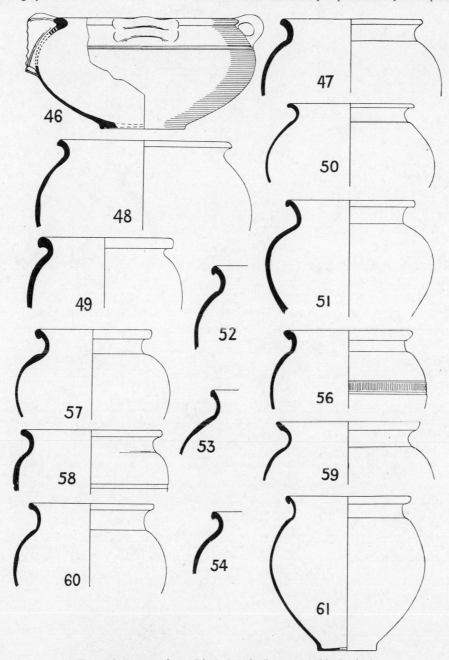

FIG. 56. Pottery from Pit 1, Insula 7, c. A.D. 100. Scale ¼.

42. Lid, grey ware.

43. Lid, dark blue-grey ware, hard and flaking. Knob hollowed on top.

44. Lid, coarse grey ware.

45. Lid coarse hard grey ware.

46. Nearly the whole body of a strainer-bowl in thin, fine, buff ware, mica-coated. There is a horizonatal handle on each

boar's head, in the same ware, illustrated *London in Roman Times*, 146, fig. 55, 2.

47. Black jar, f. 265, with fine, sandy white grit, rough black surface. Diam. 6 in.

48. Jar, f. 260 B, brownish ware, black-coated and smoothed. Diam. 7½ in.

49. Cooking-pot, heavily sooted, not a regular type; very

coarse brownish ware, surface dead black; some fine white particles in the paste.

50. Upper part of a thin f. 266, light drab or brownish clay, thin and hard.

51. Cooking-pot, f. 266; sooted outside, furred inside; brown clay with fine white grit, dark grey to black surface.

52. Similar rim, good grey ware.

53. Similar rim, brown paste with marks of chopped straw in it; and lumpy, dead black surface.

54. Similar rim, good grey ware.

This is a late form of *Cam.* 119, compare May, type 155. Although closely resembling the vessels in fig. 63, this vessel is in an entirely different technique.

2. (Fig. 59.) Small store jar, f. *Cam.* 270 or 272, of grey ware, irregularly formed, and the body full of small cavities where pieces of chopped straw seem to have burnt out. Height not quite certain. Neck and rim polished black, row of corded impressions on shoulder.

These two were found together in the slope of the rampart against the SE. corner of the east pier, at a depth of 4 ft.

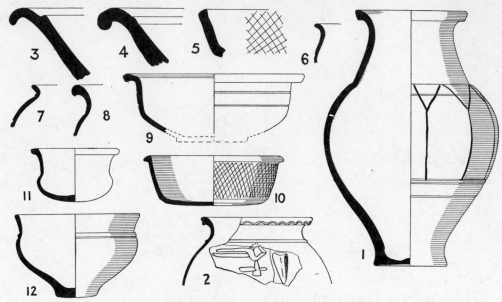

FIG. 57. Pottery from rampart and 'Mithraeum' (nos. 2, 11, 12). Scale ¼. (pp. 128, 144.)

55. (*Not used.*)

56. Grey jar, polished outside, very gritty inside; rouletted band of vertical incisions between girth-grooves. (Compare *Cam.* 108 Aa.)

57. Cooking-pot, f. 266, thin, hard brown ware, gritty, with darker, surface.

58. Rim, soft buff to black, unclassified.

59. Rim of f. 266 with slight lip, not undercut, typical of quite a series in this pit. Thin hard, grey ware, with dark grit and granular surface.

60. Similar rim, brownish clay, black coated, ill-levigated and flaking.

61. Jar of f. 266, brown ware, the rim sharply overhung and undercut. Hole in base.

The complete absence of ff. 268 and 278 is most remarkable.

THE POTTERY FOUND IN THE RAMPART (FIG. 57)

A large amount of very fragmentary pottery was found in cutting away the rampart around the piers of the gateway, but only in the pocket formed between the end of the rampart and the piers. The rampart itself was of clean sandy loam. The pottery was therefore not sealed down, but the main part of it obviously lay as it had accumulated, with the earliest pieces at the bottom. The best pieces are illustrated, figs. 57, 1 and 3–10; 59, 2.

1. Hard, fine buff ware, the smooth surface decorated with a pattern in red-brown paint. Height not quite certain. Diam. 4¼ in.

3. Rim of a mortarium, f. *Cam.* 496, buff ware with large mixed grit running over rim. Diam. 12½ in. Found against the back of the west pier.

4. Another rim of same type with mixed grit running over the rim. Diam. 14 in. These two rims should be Trajanic.

5. Rim of a bowl of unclassified form, in gritted cooking-pot ware, black polished and scored lattice pattern. Diam. *c.* 11 in.

6. Rim of a tall bowl or olla; the form is Newstead 46, our 299; light grey ware. Diam. uncertain. Antonine or later.

7. Rim and shoulder of a rounded beaker; the form is *Cam.* 108; fine grey ware, polished. Rim-diameter 4½ in. Probably Flavian.

8. Rim of a tall bowl or olla, good dark grey clay. Diam. *c.* 10 in. A wavy line is scored on the band below the slight cordon. Probably form *Cam.* 218 and Flavian or later.

9. Part of a bowl with reeded rim, form *Cam.* 246; coarse hard grey ware with unsmoothed surface. Diam. 7¾ in. There were two other such rims. They may be first or early second century.

10. Part of a bowl in thin hard grey ware with black polished surface decorated with a fine lattice pattern. Diam. 6 in. There is half of another and one or two fragments of others. These bowls are of long life, but do not seem to have outlasted the middle of the second century; not one fragment of them was found in the vast quantity of pottery found on the floor of room D in the 'Mithraeum'.

In addition to the pottery illustrated the following were found in this deposit: *Terra sigillata*, chips of forms 29, 27, 33, 18, and 30; coarse ware, part of a bowl as fig. 67, 101, and the rim of a very large dolium similar to fig. 119, 273; numerous lumps of iron and pieces of vitreous slag, an iron implement, animal bones, and many pieces of vermilion-painted wall plaster.

Pottery was found well down under the original roadway between the west pier and the side of the drain, but included no rims or any recognizable pieces.

4. Neck of flagon in hard sandy red ware, with grey core where thick. Has been mica-coated (same ware as fig. 62, 46). The elongated spout is semi-tubular. Handle plain, rectangular in section. Colchester ware, late second and early third century.

Handle of another, same ware, and spout of another. All from

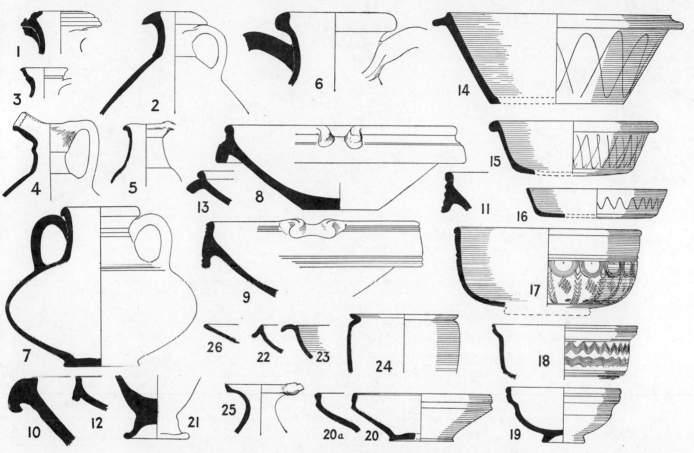

FIG. 58. Pottery from the drain in Hollytrees' Meadow. Scale ¼. (p. 129.)

POTTERY FOUND IN THE DRAIN (FIG. 58)

Jugs and flagons

Five necks of the 'screw' pattern were found loose in the filling; two are as fig. 60, 7; one as ibid. 8; two as ibid. 9; another, as 10, is from the bottom.

1. Conical mouth deeply grooved on top, had two three-ribbed handles. Buff ware, diam. 3½ in. Upper filling. Another similar, but smaller (diam. 1 in.), had only one handle. Compare *Arch.* lxxii, 235, fig. 5, 21. There are three others in Colchester Mus. undated, but the type was being made in the Colchester kilns about A.D. 190, our f. 370.

2. Conical mouth, one two-ribbed handle. White ware, diam. 2¾ in. Similar flagons, but smaller, are in second-century graves. May, pl. XCII, 11.

3. Small mouth not dissimilar to fig. 60, 11, but cupped inside. Red-buff ware. One two-ribbed handle, diam. 2 in. Top filling of drain. The complete outline is perhaps given by *Ospringe*, pl. XIX, 171.

top filling. Cf. *Zugmantel*, XVII, 34 and 50 and p. 168, date from Hadrian onwards, and *Heddernheim IV*, fig. 23, 2.

5. Neck of jug with slight pinched spout. Red ware with chocolate coating. Castor. Top filling, with part of another, larger. Should be fourth century.

Half the rim of a white ware jug of the type Hofheim 50 or 58 (*Cam.* 140 or 151) of the mid-first century is clearly a rubbish-survival.

6. Neck of a large amphora in coarse white ware, handles two-ribbed. The type is Niederbieber 76, our f. 355, which is second century. Diam. 5 in.

7. Complete jug, restored, buff ware, handles two-ribbed. Well made, with two shallow grooves on neck and two more on shoulder. Found in the drain by Duncan in 1853. Height 6¾ in., max. diam. 8 in. The type is May 199, our f. 167 C. Second century.

There were five rims of globular amphorae of standard type, and many fragments, with one stamped handle.

Honey-pots were represented by one unstratified rim, a three-ribbed handle, and a rectangular rim, reeded on top and on outside (a small vessel like fig. 53, 4 and 5). Not illustrated.

B 2567   K

Mortaria

8. Vessel in two complete halves. Drooping flange and tall rim. Small spout. No stamp. Upper filling, 1 to 2 ft. below top of drain, undisturbed. Mixed grit. Two similar, larger rims came from the bottom, but may have been in a disturbed area.

9. Vessel intact save for the bottom which is missing. The type is almost peculiar to Colchester, for the example at York (May, *York*, pl. XIX, 14) is stamped by MARTINVS of Colchester. Buff ware. These vessels have no grit on the interior. Diam. 9 in. Found with no. 8.

There are four other rims of this type, of which two were found near nos. 8 and 9 and two are from the upper filling elsewhere.

There were two large fragments of a rim of the type *Wroxeter I*, fig. 19, 46, in the upper filling.

10. Mortarium rim in white ware, stamped MARTINVS.F, Diam. 15 in. Found undisturbed 1 ft. below the top walls of the drain.

There are nine other rims of this type f. 497 (in which the groove outside the bead-lip is broadened to a wide, nearly flat fluting). All from the upper filling, save one from the bottom. Four have mixed grit, the others show none.

Of the bead-and-roll type as fig. 62, 70 there are four examples with the square finish beneath, of which two have 'herring-bone' stamps, and four with rounded finish, one of which has grit running over the rim. It is thus probably the earliest of this late collection, all of which are from the upper filling save one, which is from the bottom in an area which was probably disturbed.

Since the above was written the kilns of the local potters, including Martinus, have been found and excavated, and we recognize the above (except the early one) as products of our local kilns round about A.D. 190.

Of the type fig. 62, 71 there are four rims, all upper filling.

Of the type fig. 62, 72 there are three rims; two are very small worn fragments. The type is rare in Colchester. All upper filling.

11. A wall-sided rim of very unusual fabric, being of very soft buff ware charged with hard, sandy particles. The form is very rare in Colchester. Top filling. Diam. uncertain.

12. Another wall-sided rim, from the bottom. Hard buff, no grit showing. Diam. uncertain.

13. Rim of hard, dirty, grey-buff ware with black grit, diam. 9 in. Upper filling.

Bowls, cups, and platters

Of the reeded rims, similar to fig. 54, 9, there are five rims, two of heavy buff ware, all from high up. Bowls of f. 299, fig. 66, 74, 75, were very numerous; as fig. 67, 87 there is one rim in the usual very coarse grey-black ware, high up. Platters as fig. 67, 90, 91 were exceedingly many; 94 and 95 were not represented; 98 occurs, but not 99; 100–1 and 104 were numerous, but 102 and 103 rarely occur.

Bowls or lids as fig. 66, 79, two rims only.

14. Burnished black cooking-pot ware, scored intersecting arcs.

15. Grey ware, with smooth, black surface.

16. Good grey ware, black polished surface, faint scored wavy lines.

All three from the bottom of the drain, and obviously not much disturbed.

17. Large portion of a hemispherical bowl copied from the Samian f. 37. Decoration of incised concentric circles, upright fronds of impressed chevrons, lozenges of impressions of a toothed comb, and small impressed concentric circles. The ware is brick-red in the paste with a hard polished surface indistinguishable from some late sigillata. Found about half-way up the filling, undisturbed. Height 3 in., diam. 7¾ in. Cf. *Silchester*, LXXI, 164 and p. 171, where this type of decoration is assigned to the first century (!).

Compare a bowl from Chapel House Milecastle, *Arch. Ael.* 4 s. pl. I, iii, 29 (period I*b*), but there is a very much closer parallel from Colchester, perhaps from the same potter, in the fine bowl from the pit in Dr. Wirth's garden (see p. 247 and fig. 111, 4), which is in exactly the same ware, and has similar impressed decoration. In our view these two Colchester examples are third or fourth century.

18. Fragment of a copy of a bowl of f. 29 in rather coarse but thin blue-grey ware. The decoration in two wavy combed bands. Found high up. Compare *Arch.* lxxii, 228, fig. 1, 3 (Sandford).

19. Half a cup copied from f. 27, grey clay, fumed and polished. Found in the upper foot of the filling. Cf. *C.M.R.* 1927, pl. 5683.

20 and 20*a*. Two similar rims, of thick, sandy, brownish ware with drab surface and of crude fabric; these are finished on the outside only and are probably lids, and closely related to the similar vessels on fig. 66, 79. Upper filling.

21. Part of a pedestal base in good creamy ware, very much shattered. In filling.

22. Rim of a bowl, grey ware, slightly micaceous, diam. *c.* 7 in. In first foot of filling.

23. Rim of bowl, fair grey ware, with slate-blue fumed and polished surface. Not rouletted on top. Diam. 6¼ in. Upper filling. Cf. fig. 19, 4.

24. Complete upper half of a jar with remarkably upright sides, fine, hard grey ware, polished outside. Found in the silt on the bottom. Very probably f. 124.

25. Neck and several fragments of a buff ware jug, gilded with mica. Found in the silt on the bottom. These jugs were being made in the local kilns around A.D. 190, but how much earlier we do not yet know. Form 362.

26. Small fragment of the rim of a shallow bowl or platter with dark green glaze, very hard, like stoneware. Diam. *c.* 8½ in.

Other pottery from the silt was scarce compared with that from the upper filling. But there were long stretches of the drain which either never had any silt or had been disturbed by Duncan. The best preserved stretch was carefully cleared with the trowel by Messrs. Farmer and Laver. The pieces, with few exceptions, were very small, and, in fact, such as could be water-washed. They include nothing definitely early. The larger fragments are as follows:

A 'screw' neck of a flagon as fig. 60, 9 in the same ware as ibid. 4.

Two mortarium rims, like that by *Martinus* (fig. 58, 10), and one rim as ibid. 9.

A complete and intact bowl as ibid. 15, not decorated and of inferior manufacture. Small fragments of these and of nos. 14 and 16 were numerous.

There was one fragment of a Rhenish 'motto-beaker'.

The most part of a bowl in slaty grey ware, rough, as fig. 67, 87.

The complete bowl, f. 37, illustrated fig. 51A.

Half bowl or lid of the type fig. 66, 79.

Fragments of colour-coated beakers, rouletted and roughcast of second-century (and later) type.

Grey beaker, decorated as fig. 71, 148, but not fluted.

The grey jar top, no. 24 above, and fragments of two more similar.

The fragments of the mica-coated jug, no. 4 above.

It will be seen that the contents of the silt are not materially different in date from the majority of the pottery from the bottom of room D, and that earlier wares occur among the plentiful pottery in the upper filling. This filling was found undisturbed at least from our zero point to the vaulted portion on the south, and was of the yellowish loam which marks the Roman occupation level almost everywhere in the town. The conclusion is that at some date the drain had been neglected and silted up to a certain extent, and was filled in with earth taken from the surface round about. At the same time the building on site I was pulled down and the cavity left was filled first with some 3 ft. of rubbish and then with rubble and mortar and a thick layer of the yellow loam. The coins found in the drain are inadequate for argument, but those found in site I show that this or later filling was

POTTERY FROM PIT III AND BLACK LAYER IN TRENCH 3

This was less of a pit than a slack or hollow in the ground full of potsherds and food-bones, which continued for some distance as a black layer. The site was in insula 14, just north of the hypocaust.

Sigillata, forms 18, 27, 33, 36. *Coarse ware*, fragments of

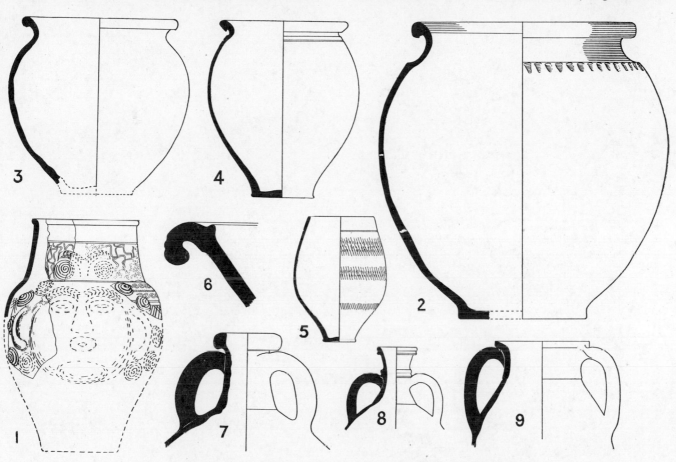

FIG. 59. Pottery from drain and rampart (no. 2). Scale ¼. (pp. 129, 145.)

not made before 330, at which time we must conclude that the local or the military authorities were engaged in levelling this area.

There remains for mention a number of small fragments of fine grey ware, with surface partly polished and decorated by scoring, which were found in the bottom of the drain, but near the gate, in that portion where the west wall had been robbed. They cannot be regarded as stratified. The fragments have belonged to a face-urn of peculiar pattern, and fit into a picture such as that shown on fig. 59, 1. The indication of horn(?) on a fragment of the neck is unmistakable, while a side fragment has part of cheek, ear, and eyebrow. The hair surrounding the face is done with whorls of clay in the manner of cake-icing outside which it is further indicated by straggling scored lines. Besides this decoration the vessel had horizontal continuous bands of decoration, partly of SSSS pattern and partly of latticing, visible on the right.

several jars as figs. 3 and 4. Half a brown bowl as fig. 54, 18, Trajanic. The following are illustrated (fig. 59):

6. Mortar-rim, f. 497, buff, with mixed grit, diam. 23¾ in. The very heavy, incurved ledge bears two horizontal flutings on the outside. c. A.D. 190.

7. Jug neck, two handles of D-section. Buff ware.

8. Jug neck, ringed, with two-ribbed handles. Fine buff ware. Compare *Heddernheim*, iv, fig. 23, 3, p. 136 and v, pl. ii, nos. 24, grave 90, p. 21; and 27, grave 49, p. 19; *O.R.L.* 18, Echzell, iii, 8, marbled ware. This looks, however, like *Cam.* f. 171, and might be first century.

9. Top of a curious two-handled vessel in white ware. Handles flat, two-ribbed. Compare Hofheim, type 63, rare, copied from bronze prototype. Cf. also Behrens, *Bingen Mus. Catalogue*, Taf. 17, m.

The date of this deposit appears to be about A.D. 100–20.

There was also a strainer-spout in polished grey ware.

The Pottery from the Lowest Layer in the 'Mithraeum' (Figs. 60–71)

Nearly a cartload of pottery was recovered from this layer and several of the vessels were whole. In all cases where it has been possible to restore a vessel from fragments the latter were found close together, an indication that they were shot in as rubbish and not thereafter disturbed.

*3. Nearly complete, in fragments. Very fine grey clay shading to red at surface, which is coated with a thick, highly polished white finish almost like ivory. Handle missing.

*4. Found high up in the bottom layer, lying on its side broken, and empty of earth. Similar to last but typologically of later proportions. Poor, sandy, tile-red ware with a thin white coating, not polished. Handle flat, three-ribbed.

Note the absence of foot-ring on these two.

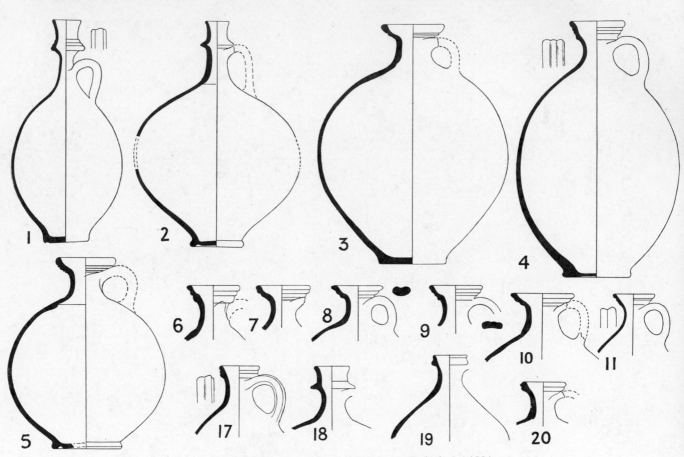

FIG. 60. Pottery from the 'Mithraeum'. Scale ¼. (p. 132.)

Vessels so nearly complete as to have been broken only shortly before being discarded are marked with an asterisk, as they are the most important for dating purposes.[1]

Flagons and jugs, nos. 1–47A

*1. Found at the door-sill. Very fine, thin buff ware with polished, mica-gilt surface. Handle flat, three-ribbed. A tall variant of the next type; note the poor groove under the foot. No very close parallel, and perhaps locally made. The height suggests fourth century.

2. Found with the last. Base and top, of thin, hard, white ware, polished. Height not certain, probably as restored. (Complete top and bottom, no other fragments.) On this very common type, which was well represented, see nos. 22, 24, 25, 30–35, 39–43.

*5. Top half and base found together in fragments. Buff ware, coated inside and out with a hard, dark coating of limy (?) deposit. Handle missing, but was wide and flat. The mouldings on the rim degenerated to incised lines.

6. Neck, unsmoothed, granular yellow-buff ware, hard.

7. Neck, unpolished, granular, white-buff ware, blackened as by fire.

8. Neck of smoothed white ware. Handle two-ribbed.

9. Neck of unsmoothed, granular white ware. Handle three-ribbed.

10. Neck of smoothed white ware. Handle missing.

11. Neck of buff ware, white coated, not polished. Handle two-ribbed. Thin and small.

12. (Not illustrated.) Neck very much as no. 9; unsmoothed granular white-buff ware. Handle missing.

---

[1] The following account, and especially the plates, were composed many years ago. They would have been presented somewhat differently but cannot be altered now.

13. Fragment like no. 6, but only two mouldings. Handle three-ribbed.

14 and 15. Chips like no. 9 (i.e. with four shallow mouldings). Buff ware.

16. The whole body of a flagon, probably of this type, but the rim is missing. Polished white ware. Found intact and half full of water.

There were, of course, many side fragments of these flagons. The type is well enough known in general (cf. *Cam. I*, ff. 154,

14, 15, which are Antonine, and those made in the Colchester kilns about A.D. 190. See also *Poltross Burn*, pl. IV, nos. 15, 17, 18, of uncertain date in the second century.

*21. Found nearly complete; good hard buff ware, smoothed. There is a slight groove under the base.

*22. Neck and several large fragments; fine buff ware, white coated, well finished, and decorated with three broad bands of brown-red paint. The stout handle has four lightly defined ribs. Base missing. Found low down near doorway.

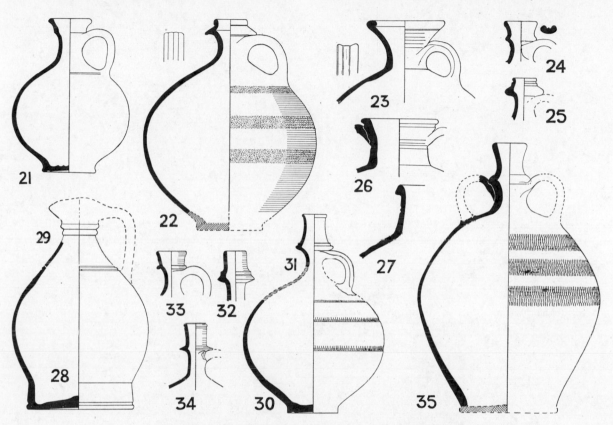

FIG. 61. Pottery from the 'Mithraeum'. Scale ¼. (p. 133.)

155). This series which we call f. 156, is one of the commonest vessels in Colchester, where the mouth is always (or nearly always) cupped as shown. So far it has not been possible to find a reliable chronological series of the variations in form of mouth, but it is fairly certain that tall examples are of late-third- to fourth-century date, and that a flat base, instead of the usual foot-ring with groove inside, is also a late sign. In the middle Empire, too, the material was always buff, while here we find a white coating applied to clay of other colours, even grey being used. Many close parallels to these Mithraeum flagons will be found in the pages of the Ospringe report.

17. Neck; same fabric as no. 4. Moulding of lip very slightly indicated. Handle two-ribbed.

18. Neck (like no. 40), rough, sandy buff ware, nearly white and unsmoothed. Handle missing. See under no. 34 below.

19. Part of neck and very sloping shoulder. Buff, carelessly finished and white coated. Handle two-ribbed.

20. Neck only; smoothed white ware, not polished. Handle of very small section.

Nos. 17, 19, 20 are similar to Curle, *Newstead*, fig. 33, nos.

The style of ware and painting is that of a tall flask found in grave 547, which was probably an inhumation. There are two others similarly painted in the Museum. The date is probably first half of fourth century.

23. Neck; buff ware, white coated, careless work. Handle three-ribbed.

24. Small neck; smooth white ware, not polished.

25. Small neck; red ware, white coated.

This dumpy neck, and no. 22 above, are presumably variants of the ledged necks 30 ff. below.

26. Neck of a two-handled jug, f. 167 c, with groove round the rim and two on the neck. Handles two-ribbed. Buff ware, white coated.

27. Rim only, of similar jug, nearer to the earlier form with conical neck (167B). Similar ware.

*28. Most part of the body (repaired), found low down inside the doorway. Fine creamy clay with dark chocolate coating (Castor). The drum-like base with groove corresponds to the pill-box base of late beakers of this ware. Two light grooves round shoulder. Neck and handle missing.

29. Part of the neck of a trefoil-mouthed flagon; same ware, but thick, light red coating. The two cordons are not pressed out. Drawn on top of the preceding, completing the type-figure (f. 375). Other small fragments contribute to this restoration, as do several complete necks in the Museum. See also May, *York*, pl. xiv, B, no. 1.

A fragment of a second such base almost certainly belonged to no. 29.

types than to those so well known from Ashley Rails (Sumner, pl. ix, 1, 2, 11–13); see Wheeler, *Segontium*, 167 and fig. 78, 49. A two-handled example in white clay was found at Sandford, *Arch*. lxxii, 235, fig. 5, 22. The body is generally globular (as no. 30) or oblately so (as no. 2). The neck is usually tall and slender with a very narrow throat (some will not allow of the passage of a lead pencil). The necks fall into two main types shown by no. 34 (two more not illustrated) and no. 31 (two more not illus-

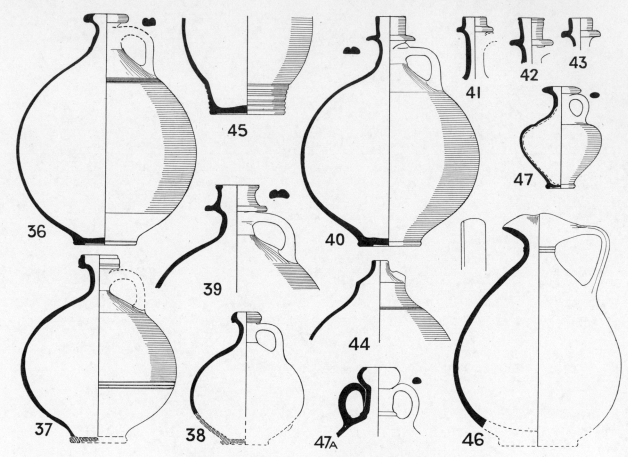

FIG. 62. Pottery from the 'Mithraeum'. Scale ¼. (p. 135.)

*30. Complete body; good white ware, with glossy, dark chocolate coating. Three rouletted girth-bands and a slight groove under base.

31. Neck and handle of fine creamy ware, with glossy chocolate to purple coating, showing light red where it is thin. Handle narrow, with deep central groove. Drawn over no. 30 to complete the type.

32. Mouth only. Same ware and coating as last, but not glossy. No trace of handle, which must have been attached much lower than usual.

33. Neck and handle of yellowish ware with light red coating. Handle with one deep central groove.

34. Neck only. Clay creamy with light red coating. Handle missing.

These flagons (f. 360) belong to an interesting and well-known type clearly connected with the ledged flagons which appear in Germany at the end of the second century and last to the end of the fourth. In outline of mouth they are nearer to the German

trated). The former are generally of much better finish than the latter. In both illustrations the lip is slightly moulded, but it is usually quite plain. In only two examples is the handle set low so as to leave the ledge free.

Fragments of at least 36 of these flagons were recovered in this layer, mostly as body-fragments. Of these 14 were red coated and 18 dark chocolate or black. Most have three lines of rouletting as no. 30, but 5 had been rouletted all over, generally in broad horizontal bands.

The bases are mostly similar to that of no. 2.

35. Neck and parts of the body of a two-handled jug of white ware with dull chocolate coating. The body with rouletted bands. Handles rather broad, flat, three-ribbed.

A parallel from Bottisham Fen, Cambs., 1847, is figured in *Cat. of the Antiquarian Collections of the Cambridge University Museum*, part i, pl. i, 28. Another is in the Bellheim find, Unverzagt, *Alzei*, Abb. 3, 15, and see his Abb. 12. Compare also *Richborough I*, pl. xxix, 119, fourth century, and another, somewhat similar to ours, from a skeleton grave at Colchester, *C.M.R.* 1944, pl. vi, 5.

The next few flagons are examples of a fabric which we have styled 'polished red ware'. It is of striking appearance; the vivid red colouring and high polish cause a most deceptive resemblance to Samian ware, especially when damp. Every vessel is most carefully finished, sometimes with elaborate small detail, and always with particular attention to the peculiar, broad and very low foot-ring. So far only two classes of vessel have been observed in this ware. One consists of small and large vases with frilled rims, sometimes bearing a face on the neck (*C.M.R.* 1928, pl. xvii, 6737. 27; ibid., pl. xvi, 7212.27). Of these no recognizable fragment was found in this layer. The second class consists of single-handled flagons, of which at least twelve to fifteen examples are represented by the fragments.

The characteristics of this ware are: the fine, sandy clay, which varies in colour internally from light red to greyish (remarkably similar to the 'terra rubra IV' of the *Cam. I* Report) which is always burnt to a more or less bright red on the exterior and very highly polished. The polish often begins only an inch or so above the base. The colour varies from a dark, blood-red to a light orange. The bases are neatly finished with a very low, wide foot-ring. The neck is tapered in both classes and on it the polish was applied by vertical motion, which produces faint upright striations, extending down to the root of the handle, which prevented the normal polishing on the wheel. At this level there are usually one or more scored lines. The space under the handle is left unpolished. Handles are D-shaped in section, with or without a bold central groove.

An exceptional vessel in this fabric is *C.M.R.* 1928, pl. xvi, 1635.27.

*36. Nearly the whole, in fragments, of a large flagon with flat, round mouth. Very high and brilliant light red polish.

37. Neck and half the body of a flagon, f. 365. Base and handle missing. Orange-red, the polish beginning 2 in. above the base.

38. Much of a smaller flagon like the last.

39. Neck and part of shoulder of a large flagon of the ledged-neck type (the commonest type in this ware), but this example is unusually modelled and finely treated. Cf. May, Sandford, *Arch.* lxxii, fig. 5, 22.

40. Flagon (restored), dull red surface, handle of D-section with central groove.

41–43. Three similar necks. An example like these in the B.M. is described as fourth century, probably because it has a graffito resembling the Christian monogram. There are five more rims of this type in the general collection at Colchester and one whole flagon in grave 149 (from the Abbey Field) which includes fragments of three others in the same fabric, two like our nos. 37 and 38 and the third of f. 361 (with semi-tubular spout) and there are examples in the Museum. Cf. *Richborough II*, nos. 164–5.

44. Two fragments only of a flagon of remarkable form. The mouth and handle have been cut or broken off and the edges filed smooth. Close to the stub of the handle a small air-hole was pierced before firing. The colour is brilliant red. Compare a complete example in York Museum (mouth as 41) from Dringhouses.

Two other fragments of the same outline were found. All have been filed down in the same way. Another fragment in the Museum is broken in the same way, but not filed.

45. One of three bases in red ware like the foregoing, but not so highly polished, corresponding in form to the drum-foot of no. 28: the upper part was also probably similar. They are polished all over, except under the base.

A base of this ware, like that of no. 40, had been cut down and the edge ground smooth to form a shallow bowl. Two other fragments show deep file-cuts, presumably due to abortive attempts with the same object.

46. Major portion of a trefoil-mouthed flagon in thick sandy red ware, with grey core and golden mica-coating. A similar example *O.R.L.*, *Zugmantel*, pl. xvii, 37, is dated to the time of M. Aurelius, but this need not apply closely to us.

There are a number of similarly mica-coated fragments which yielded no definite shape. Mica-coated ware begins at Colchester in pre-Roman days and continues right through.

47. Small flagon of rather coarse ware with a dull red glaze or polish which is flaking off. Found intact. The fabric is difficult to describe and might be a bad Samian ware. Cf. *Ospringe*, pls. xxx, 309 and xxxii, 341, described as Samian.

No single flagon found need be dated before A.D. 150, and all may be much later.

Tall, decorated beakers, late version of form 119

*48. Major portion and complete neck; sandy red-brown ware with grey core, with thick creamy coating which has largely worn off. It is decorated with three horizontal bands of red paint, one on the neck, one under the low cordon, and one at the constriction of the body. There is also a band within the lip and there are three triangles of six red disks, one of which is shown in the drawing. Foot missing. No parallel to this vessel has been traced.

*49. Numerous fragments of a single vessel; dark grey clay of good quality. Decoration of groups of three vertical scored lines only. There are several polished bands. Base missing.

One or two fragments were found of another similar, in thicker ware.

50. Similar vessel. Sandy red-brown clay with grey to brownish surface. Neck shoulder and base polished. No decoration.

51. A number of fragments of one beaker, hard dark grey ware, core nearly black, red surface black finished. The whole exterior polished except three matt zones with scored vertical lines. Three girth grooves and a low cordon on the neck. Rim missing.

52. A number of fragments, and the base, in fine grey ware. Three slight grooves at the neck and a bolder one below. Rim as nos. 48–49. Height approximately as shown.

53. Restored from fragments, dark grey clay, hard, with reddish core. Notched ridge under rim, low cordon on neck. Body polished save for two matt bands with combed decoration. On the shoulder a stabbed band between grooves.

*54. Finely made of thin slate-grey ware with lip hollowed for lid. Pressed-out cordon on shoulder, two rouletted bands, and two bold girth grooves. Nearly complete.

55. Large example of hard, very dark grey ware, gritty, but brought to a smooth, hard surface. The body rouletted with hatched rectangles (the German 'Schachbrett' decoration), traversed by three deep horizontal flutings.

Nos. 48–55 form a series with close affinities to the common late form of the butt beaker, *Camulodunum* f. 119. It is represented in May by his types 155–7, and there are seven more complete examples in the Museum. His very globular 157 is very like the urn in grave 15 (pl. lxxvii), which is with a f. 227 and a bowl f. 37 on tripod feet and should be late first or early second century. These strongly bulged vessels should provide the continuation of f. 119 in that period. One in grave 59 is still fairly rounded, but late enough to be accompanied by a T.S. beaker f. 67, a colour-coated beaker f. 391, and a ledged grey bowl f. 305. This group should be at least Antonine. A very broad example in grave 60 is with a f. 108 and should not be later than *c.* 120, but already shows incurve to the foot, which is small. Others occur in graves 61 and 62, both like ours, tallish with small base. Grave 61 includes a flask f. 286 which (see grave 104: May, pl. LXXXVIII) must be fourth century, and grave 62 has a large flagon of exactly the same shape as our no. 5. The above datings are uncertain to the extent that they rely on old discoveries: it is unfortunate that the type does not occur in any of the more recently found graves upon which full reliance can be placed. We may, however, say that there appears to be some

Large jars or vases

60. Fragment of a face-urn in thick, rather coarse grey ware, with frilled rim and four mouldings on the neck. Found low down in the doorway. There are many face-urns in the Museum, but nothing quite like this.

61. An isolated example in coarse soft, sandy *buff* ware. Base

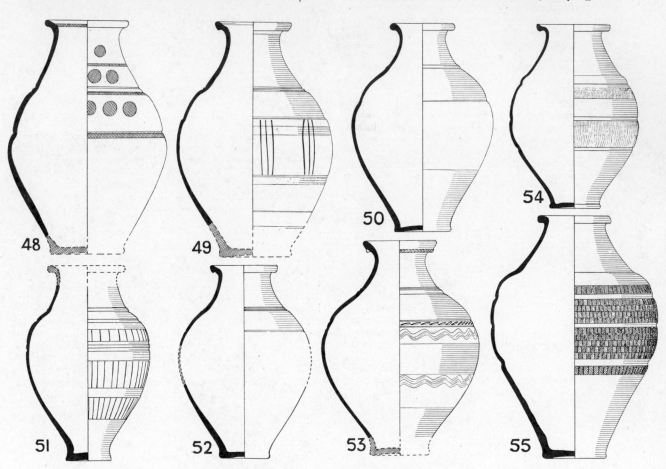

FIG. 63. Pottery from the 'Mithraeum'. Scale ¼. (p. 137.)

evidence that the form (119) runs right through, being most popular about the middle of the first century, and recovering popularity again in the early fourth.

56. Whole neck and several large fragments; size of the base uncertain. Fine grey clay. Hollowed rim, with slight cordon on shoulder. Body rouletted. One like this is in grave 252, covered by a local copy of f. 304 with bevelled foot (f. 304 is 102 below).

57. Curious flask-shaped vessel of grey ware, neck intact, base missing. Frilled rim, bold cordon on neck with line of stabbing. The whole polished, except the rouletted band.

58. Neck of a similar vessel, *found unstratified*, and only inserted for comparison. Fine grey ware, polished save the combed zone.

These two seem to be unparalleled.

59. A somewhat hypothetical reconstruction from fragments; finest slate-grey ware, highly burnished, with pressed-out cordon and decoration of scored vertical lines. There is a fragment of another such rim in the same fabric.

missing. Undercut rim, slight cordon on shoulder and double-girth groove.

62. Large urn, nearly complete; grey clay with bright red core, surface smoothed and darker; rim, shoulder, broad girth-band, and foot polished. Overhanging rim with cordon at neck. Round the shoulder a broad, unpolished band decorated with groups of three upright scored lines and three horizontal lines.

There were fragments of a number of other similar vessels. They are clearly in the same class as those found in the Signal Stations (Scarborough, pl. 1, 2) which, however, had counter-sunk handles, which do not occur at Colchester.

The type is our f. 280, which occurs at *Ospringe*, cf. II, 7, with another flask like nos. 108/9 below and a T.S. bowl f. 18/31; the same combination again on pl. XXIII, 202, 203, 205, and pl. XXVI, 394–6 (form Curle 15) and pl. XXXVIII (twice).

There are twenty-four or more complete examples in the Museum. The most globular of all is in grave 408 (Wire, MSS.) with a colour-coated lid of the usual form. Another in the definite grave 387 with a T.S. cup f. 33 stamped by *Asiaticus* (Hadrian–Antonine). This is more bulged than ours, as is one from the doubtful grave 162, with coin of Victorinus. The form apparently begins about A.D. 140.

63. Large urn of rather coarse grey ware, hard and heavy. Rim frilled, countersunk cordons at neck and shoulder. Upper part and base polished. Combed band on shoulder.

*64. Major portion of a wide-mouthed jar of hard grey ware.

67. Part of an elegant bowl of fine dark grey ware, very smooth, with three girth-grooves. Base missing.

This looks like a copy of a well-known type of Rhenish ware bowl.

68. Part of a bowl in red-buff ware, polished. Base missing. Compare the small red bowls made in the New Forest, of which this may be a copy.

69. Rim of a large bowl, fine grey ware with red-brown core.

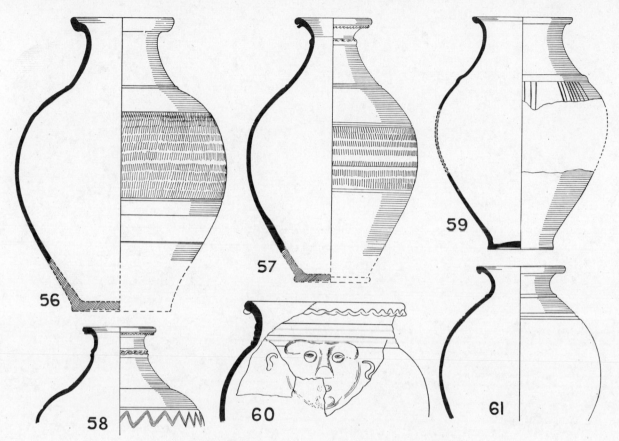

Fig. 64. Pottery from the 'Mithraeum'. Scale ¼. (p. 137.)

Surface polished. Decorated with four large scored spirals. Rim missing. Quite unusual.

65. Complete upper half of a bowl in dark grey ware. The hollow rim and shoulder polished, band lower down. Base missing. One or two other small fragments of this type were found.

This is our form 307, which is common at Colchester. A few fragments found at the Colchester kilns (1933) were perhaps not made there, but must have been in use about A.D. 190. But they were made in the somewhat later kilns excavated by Joslin, *T.E.A.S.* n.s. i, 192, and certainly lasted into the fourth century. Characteristic is the rim with hollow for lid, the steep shoulder and short side making an ungainly, wide base. The sides are often decorated with vertical or latticed scoring, always with horizontal polished bands.

66. Part of a wide-mouthed jar of fine grey ware showing some mica. There were several other similar rims. They are not easy to place, but may be late examples of f. 278 (see 115) with rim widened on the analogy of late f. 279 (e.g. no. 129 below), or perhaps are small examples of no. 78 below.

Surface black-polished down to the horizontal line. There were two more such rims, but the bases could not be identified. There is nothing like them in the Museum.

Mortaria

70. Half a mortarium, f. 497, of creamy clay, with mixed grit. Found just inside the entrance about 2 ft. above the floor.

This is the commonest form of mortar in the late second and third century in Colchester. It was made in vast quantities in several of the local kilns.

71. Rim of a white mortarium, f. 498, with mixed grit. This is the type favoured in the third and fourth centuries.

72. Rim of white ware, with biscuit-coloured coating. Form 503, which was never much in favour in Colchester. Probably third century.

73. More than half a small mortarium, f. 501B, buff ware, with a little mixed grit, much worn. Base missing. A common local type, produced in the kilns from *c.* 190 onwards. The best example is in grave 136 (May, pl. XCII, 14, with the 'Colchester

Vase', *c.* A.D. 190). One at York is stamped by the Colchester potter *Martinus*.

Bowls

74. Bowl, f. 299, grey-black micaceous clay, polished.

*75. Similar bowl, coarse whitish clay with grey core. Possibly a waster and the wrong colour.

and all sorts of wares. Indeed the rim-form is too common at all times on various forms of body to be of much use in classification.

Lids

Lids have never much appealed to the student of pottery, yet there are some which are worthy of notice.

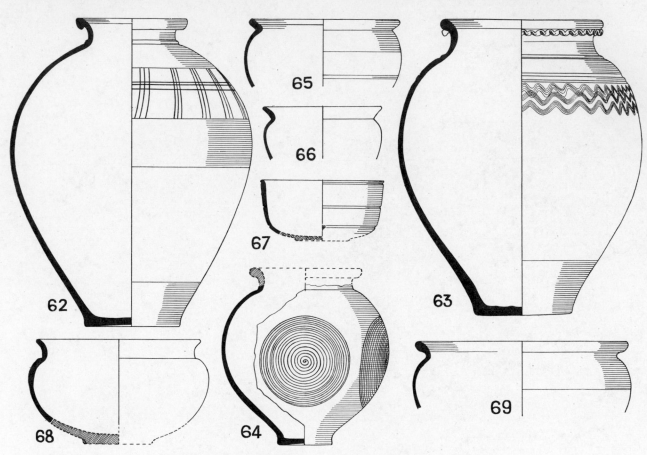

FIG. 65. Pottery from the 'Mithraeum'. Scale ¼. (p. 137.)

76. Bowl of similar type, with offset between neck and shoulder, very fine, thin grey ware. Fragments of two more.

*77. Much of one large and elaborate variant of f. 299 (?). Rim and shoulder polished, except for a narrow band bearing a wavy line. Foot burnished and, on the broad matt zone between foot and shoulder, which is the natural grey of the clay, five burnished lines. Two more such lines border the polished zone on the shoulder. All polished parts are black.

78. Large bowl of grey ware; rim, shoulder, and foot polished, and band round middle.

There are two types here. The first, with S-curve and no offset at the neck, always has the groove on the shoulder and is usually polished all over. It is our standard form 299, Curle's *Newstead* type 46. It seems to have been in universal use from Antonine times onwards, and shows little or no variation. Hundreds of fragments of it were found in the 'Mithraeum'.

The other rims with offset at neck are not so easily dealt with, for they occur with all sorts of variations (e.g. our 76–78 here)

79. Most part of a lid (?) of coarse hard grey ware, polished outside only. Knob or base imperfect.

80. Lid of common type of fine grey ware, not polished.

81. Lid of rough brown-red ware. There were two others similar. The type is not uncommon in Colchester and never appears with early remains. It is a standard, unvarying form.

Bowls (continued)

82. Incense cup of rough buff ware, with notched cordons on rim, angle of side, and base. The notched style is late: see Wheeler, *Gaer*, 225.

*83. A very fine bowl with skillet handle, of excellent red ware, almost as good as Samian, with glittering black glaze (similar to Greek glaze), and stamped on the interior of the base with a rosette stamp. The horizontal handle bears a moulded pattern in relief.

A fine red-glazed example of such a pan has been found at Richborough, and there is the handle of another in Colchester Museum.

*84. Wide bowl, exceedingly well made, of fine grey clay, with a horny, grey, polished coating, now chipping off. Probably originally black.

85. Fragment of an unusual bowl with sharp offset at shoulder and furrow in middle of body. Foot missing. Two zones of lattice pattern. Fine grey ware.

*86. Cup, copying T.S. f. 33, very earthy, drab-grey clay, polished. Found almost complete. Compare *Richborough I*, pl.

91. Similar bowl, but lacking the bevel at the foot. Clay light, soft, drab with darker grey surface, not polished, slightly micaceous. Three others similar.

92. Rim, same clay as last, unusual because bearing a wavy line between polished bands. Typically the form is not decorated.

93. Unusual rim. Slight bevel at foot. Grey ware. Lip slightly thickened only.

94. Unusual rim, grey ware, not smoothed, exterior latticed.

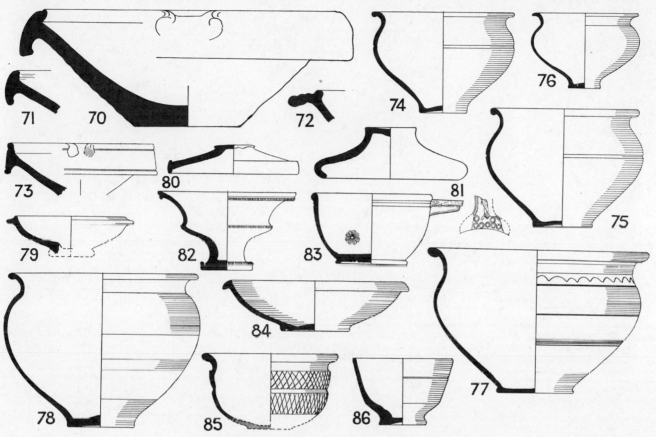

FIG. 66. Pottery from the 'Mithraeum'. Scale ¼. (p. 137.)

XXIX, 142, 'mid-fourth century'; and *Arch.* lxxii, 288, fig. 1, 2; *Silchester*, pl. LXXIII, 179; *Lowbury Hill*, fig. 17, 57–58.

87. Part of a bowl of very coarse ware, grey-black. Restored after a complete example in grave 495. A safe group, with forms 39 (101 below) and 391 and 392 (137 and 134 below). This form is common in Colchester, and seems to belong to the third and fourth centuries.

*88. Bowl, nearly complete, our f. 40, but without bevel at base and therefore almost certainly fourth century. Coarse grey ware, polished outside, merely smoothed inside. Another similar fragment lacks the groove (see no. 100 below).

89. Bowl with perforated base, forming a colander. Coarse hard clay with intense black interior and brownish mottled exterior.

90. Bowl of good, hard grey ware, polished, bears graffito BV on side. The form is our 38, and over 100 vessels of this type were counted among the fragments; some are very large, some very deep; a few are wide and shallow. This type begins in late Antonine times and runs right through.

95. Rim of light grey ware, polished and latticed. Another like it. These two, and possibly 94 as a variant, belong to our f. 37 and should not be later than mid-second century. They are to be regarded as rubbish-survivals.

Various

96. Small vessel in form of a crucible, but not so used, of coarse buff ware. Compare *Silchester*, pl. XLVII, 52, 53; *Baldock*, fig. 5, 4945.

97. Unguentarium of dirty drab-grey clay spirally grooved round the body; intact save for the top edge of the rim. This is our f. 287; such vessels were made in the Colchester kilns, but not necessarily this one.

98. Very large bowl of f. 40, black cooking-pot ware, polished. The lack of bevel at the foot indicates a fourth-century date.

99. Similar bowl, but of normal outline, with bevel. Fine, hard grey ware with fine black polish.

Of the fragments of this type found, only one lacked the bevel, and only one had the customary wavy line scored on the outside.

100. Similar bowl, but wide and shallow, as often, and lacking the groove under the rim, which is also quite usual. Black cooking-pot ware, polished.

Altogether there were over 40 examples with grooves and about 15 without. Numerous references could be quoted for this very common and universal type.

101. Fragment of a platter, f. 39, in black cooking-pot ware, polished and scored with intersecting arcs outside and with looped pattern under the base. A very standard type in this fabric. Four more similar. Three more are in good grey ware,

There was a pottery producing these bowls in great quantity at Sible Hedingham, 16 miles NW. of Colchester.

Large flasks

In general these vessels resemble f. 280, already described, in outline and detail, but have a narrower and taller neck. We have called them f. 281.

*105. Fine grey clay, polished neck and shoulder, and, in a poor manner, foot. Tall neck with undercut rim, cordon on

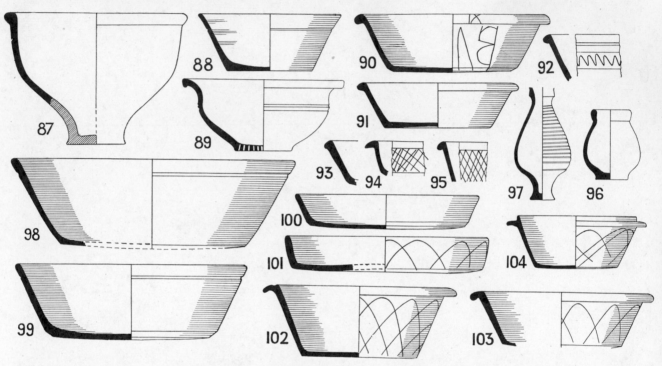

FIG. 67. Pottery from the 'Mithraeum'. Scale $\frac{1}{4}$. (p. 139.)

without decoration (as usual in the grey ones); one of them has a groove under the lip, a fourth-century feature. Cf. *Scarborough* (*Arch. J.* lxxxix, 220 ff.), fig. 4, 6.

*102. Bowl, nearly complete, of a standard third-century type resembling f. 305, but the inner lip never rising above the ledge. Black cooking-pot ware with (as, we believe, always) the usual intersecting arcs. There are at least 14 more examples and another 13 unstratified. This never had a bevel at the foot.

103. Several fragments of a bowl of the same fabric as the last. The type is very similar, with flat projecting rim. The base runs away at an angle and it is to be presumed that we are dealing with something like Collingwood's figs. 23 and 45. These hardly ever occur in Colchester. When they do they seem to be Antonine, but as Collingwood says of his no. 23, they probably lasted well into the third century.

104. Bowl in the same fabric. A well-known standard type. The earliest record of it is *Gellygaer*, pl. XXI, 11, but this must be regarded as in some way accidental, for it does not occur on Antonine sites, but later surpasses all bowls in number, especially in the late fourth century in the Signal Stations and on similar sites. There are seventeen more rims in this fabric and only nine in the grey ware which was so very common in the fourth century (e.g. at Scarborough, Crambeck, and Malton).

neck, and sharply rouletted band between grooves on the shoulder. Nearly complete.

*106. Small example in very fine grey ware. Better finished than 105, with scored wavy line below cordon and polished girth on body.

Another about the same size is very black and has a rouletted band on the shoulder, like 105.

*107. Hard slaty grey clay with black surface, polished top and bottom, with three polished girth bands.

*108. Very fine grey ware, darker surface, polished all over. Differs from the preceding in fabric, height of neck, and well-modelled foot-ring. The band on the shoulder is a sequence of finely cut chevrons made with a wheel. Nearly complete. Cf. *Ospringe*, pls. V, 35, IX, 70, &c.

*109. Fine grey ware. Shoulder, band below, and base polished. Half the vessel was found.

110. Upper half and some fragments of a flask in reddish buff ware. The reddish yellow surface is polished down to the bulge and decorated with three bands of reddish paint, so faded that they are not easy to see. No cordon.

There were a number of other fragments similarly painted. Small and more globular vessels like 108 occur in grave 8, which is otherwise definitely Claudius–Nero, but they look intrusive. Another like them in grave 20 looks more at home; it should be Hadrianic. Another is in grave 382 with T.S. f. 18 stamped I L L I X O and a green-glazed flask, probably about the same date. Not until graves 1 and 2, which should be third century, do we find flasks like our no. 107, and, in grave 12, two like our 106, with an urn like 62 and lid 81. In the distinctively late assemblage of grave 82 are two small flasks like our 113,

scored lines, and there is a curious angle in the side towards the base (see under 110 above).

114. Top of a narrow-necked vase in very similar clay to the last; on the shoulder a scored wavy line between grooves.

These flasks (105–14) are the most datable feature of the pottery from this layer. The fragments comprise nearly one-fifth of the mass and at least 80–90 different vessels are represented.

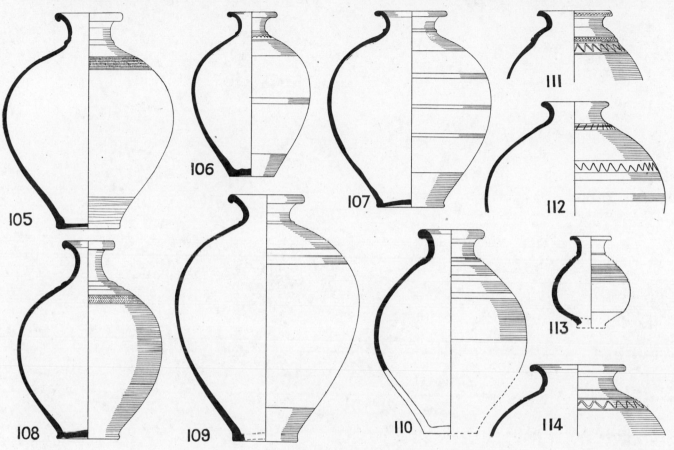

FIG. 68. Pottery from the 'Mithraeum'. Scale ¼. (p. 140.)

with red bands on white. Grave 318 has a flask like our 107 and 109 with a tall beaker (like *Silchester*, pl. XLII, 7), found with a skeleton.

These flasks of f. 281 may, then, have been in use in the first century, but this is doubtful. Small globular ones appear under Hadrian, but there is little evidence for this kind of thing until our present series appears in the third century, continuing into the fourth.

111. Top of a curious flask in very fine light grey ware. Rim frilled, cordon on neck enlarged as a bulge, bounded below by a band of stabbing between grooves, below this a scored wavy line and a groove.

112. Upper half of a flask in grey clay with reddish core. Simple lip, cordon evanescent and decorated with oblique and horizontal scored lines. Shoulder polished; below it a matt band with scored wavy line below which two more polished bands. Rougher material than that of the other flasks.

113. Small flask of nearly white clay, with smooth grey surface. Neck slightly offset; shoulder has two grooves and four

They vary considerably in form, as those illustrated will show. Possibly they were particularly popular about this period (for they are not numerous in graves up to 300, or about the time when inhumation begins). There is little possibility of confusing them with the Belgic examples of the first century (*Cam. I*, ff. 231–5 (but note that 232 runs through)), though May does so in his Colchester catalogue, p. 13, pl. II.

Jars

115. Fragments of a jar in reddish ware with dark grey core and brownish surface. Polished top and bottom, and bearing groups of upright scored lines.

The form is 278, and this was the commonest type of jar. There are twelve more rims of this size and a number of about 4½ in. diameter. They are usually of grey ware and usually latticed on the body. One of the commonest and most universal of Roman pottery forms. They begin perhaps in Flavian times and run through with so little variation that it is difficult to make any useful chronological observations. Note that no single example appeared in the Flavian rubbish-pit. Though, as May has pointed out, the proportions tend to change with time from short and broad to taller and narrower, and this can be seen on some large examples which may be attributed to the third century, on the whole such considerations are hardly reliable. In any case, as they require the complete outline they can rarely be used.

116. Nearly complete cooking-pot of hard grey clay; neck and shoulder and base polished. Latticed band narrow, lines very

122. Another similar rim, same description, but the stabbed line is on a matt zone.

123. Top and bottom of a cooking-pot in thin grey ware, with blackish surface. The form is 268.

124. Top of a similar vessel, with rather more erect rim.

These are fourth-century examples of the commonest type of cooking-pot found in Colchester. There were several more examples, and some like no. 126 below. The form runs right

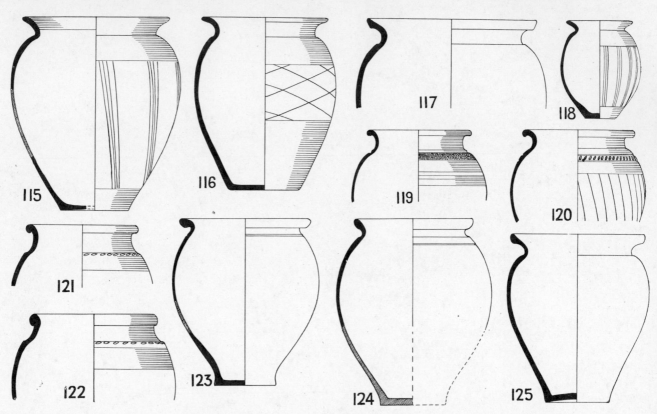

Fig. 69. Pottery from the 'Mithraeum'. Scale ¼. (p. 142.)

oblique. Form 279. The universal Roman cooking-pot the development of which from about A.D. 120 onwards is well known (Collingwood type 65 (where the lattice should cover the side), followed by his types 72 and 73).

117. Rim of a large jar, nearly white clay, with grey surface, not smoothed. This has quite the look of the Trajanic version of f. 266, and I prefer to look on it as a rubbish-survival.

*118. Small jar or beaker f. 278 (as 115), nearly complete. Fine grey ware.

*119. Top of a jar, very fine grey ware, rim and neck polished, small cordon and groove on neck, below which a band of fine rouletting; below this two polished bands with a scored line in the space between.

120. Top of a similar jar, same ware. Neck and shoulder polished, the latter bearing a band of impressed cordate buds between grooves. Oblique scored lines on body. The same decoration occurs on grey jars of the third and fourth century at Malton, Yorks.

121. Rim of a jar with undercut lip. Hard grey ware with reddish core. The upper part is polished as shown, with a line of stabbing at junction of neck; there is another similar rim.

through, from early graves like 126 (May, pl. XCI, 4), which must be Vespasianic, to the period of lead coffins. Wheeler (Ant. Journ. ix, 3) cuts the period of this type unduly short, and the coffin in question is probably much later than A.D. 150.

*125. Cooking-pot, nearly whole, of hard sandy grey clay with reddish core, surface mottled black, not smoothed. Interior heavily furred. The general outline, with the rim reaching the greatest diameter, is fourth century.

126. Cooking-pot in same ware as nos. 123 and 124. Base missing. The absence of the groove near the neck is unusual. The rim is more simply finished than the standard type 268.

*127. Cooking-pot of very coarse grey-black ware with rough surface and a certain amount of large black grit. Nearly complete. The form (277) is apparently fourth century. Examples in the Museum have a white grit of crushed shell, but are not common because the late layers of the town are destroyed, and few such vessels would get into late graves. One is shown C.M.R. 1932, pl. IX, 5.

128. The smallest example so far of f. 268. Foot missing. In these small examples the detail of the rim is often scamped, as too small to model.

*129. Most part of a cooking-pot of f. 279 of nearly the latest form, with narrow band of lattice and rim nearly exceeding the bulge. Gritted black cooking-pot ware, polished except on the lattice. Compare Collingwood type 73.

130. Cooking-pot of the same ware, with rather earlier rim and lattice. In the lattice is cut the owner's mark, a cross in a rectangle. Foot missing.

These two well illustrated a large number of fragments found in this layer. They are of local manufacture.

*136. Tall beaker f. 407B, but with beaded lip. Fine, hard, blue-grey ware with glossy coppery bronze coating, seven flutings, and three rouletted bands. Found in fragments at junction of the lowest layer and the rubble above. Possibly local ware.

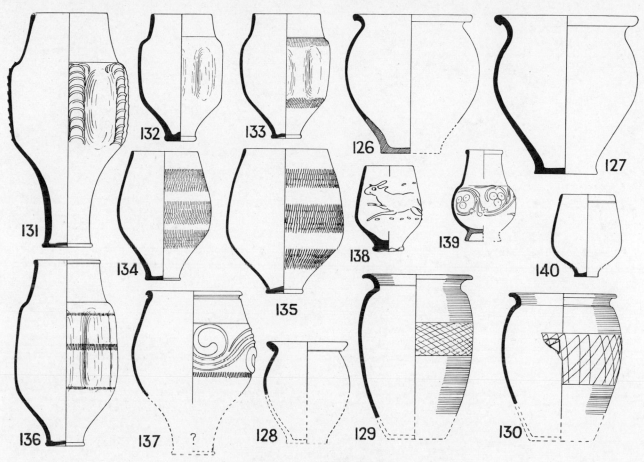

FIG. 70. Pottery from the 'Mithraeum'. Scale ¼. (p. 143.)

Castor ware and colour-coated and other beakers

*131. Tall beaker, f. 407. Fine, thin, hard red ware with grey core, coated a blue-grey metallic lustre. Seven flutings, the ridges bearing imbricated scales. These vessels were made in the kilns found by Joslin. One was found in grave 274 (stated to have been found all together at St. Mary's Hospital, Colchester) with two beakers of ff. 394 and 395 and a bronze lamp. A much shorter one is in grave 365, with a small f. 268.

*132. Fluted beaker of f. 407A. White ware with chocolate coating. Intact.

*133. Similar, hard red-buff ware with matt chocolate coating, rouletted above and below the fluting.

132 is from Castor or thereabouts. 133 is local.

*134. Beaker of f. 392 (with simple lip), thin hard red ware with grey core, surface red to chocolate. Three bands of rouletting.

*135. Similar, found by Duncan in 1852. Reddish ware with chocolate coating.

137. Large part of a beaker, f. 391. Whitish ware with dark purplish colour-coating. Castor ware, with barbotine scroll. The missing foot may have been tall, as shown, but this is uncertain.

138. Small and very crude hunt-cup, f. 391, in white ware, with purplish colour-coating. There were fragments of not more than half a dozen of these barbotined beakers, mostly of local ware. None quite so tall as May, York, pl. XI, 6, ascribed to the late fourth century.

139. Half the top of a beaker, f. 408. Creamy ware with chocolate slip, barbotine scroll, and berries in white paint. It is unnecessary to quote references for this well-known fourth-century type.

140. Beaker, f. 392. Thin reddish ware with grey core, matt chocolate coating.

There were perhaps a dozen of these, with or without the groove below the lip. All are in the same clay and several are nearly complete. They are of local manufacture.

141. Beaker, f. 408A (broad and rounded). Hard bright-red clay with grey core, polished. Groove under base. The type is exactly Niederbieber 33*a*, A.D. 190–260.

142. Beaker, f. 395, of very fine grey clay, highly polished. On the rim the graffito ||| , on body three crosses. The pill-box foot gives a fourth-century date.

143. Copy of a beaker, f. 391 or 392. Grey ware, darker surface, polished. Two bands of rouletting.

core, black surface, rather rough. The seven flutings covered by a broad band of deeply impressed rouletting.

*150. Beaker, f. 406, fine grey ware, rim and foot polished. Seven flutings.

151. Most part of an unusual little beaker of rough buff clay.

152. Top of a curious fluted vessel in soft reddish-brown ware with fine, grey polished surface. Deep groove under rim, cordon on neck and below this a scored wavy line. Flutings not polished.

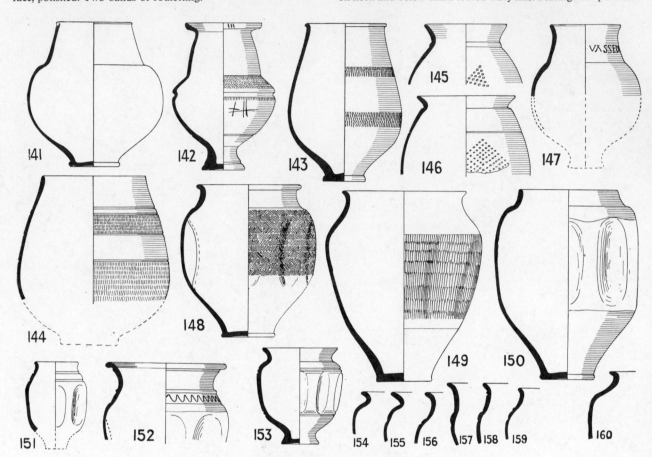

FIG. 71. Pottery from the 'Mithraeum'. Scale ¼. (p. 144.)

144. Part of another such copy, very fine grey ware decorated with rouletted bands and girth-grooves. Another fragment had no rouletting.

145. Top of a 'poppy-head' beaker, f. 401, in fine polished grey ware, panelled with dots. There were fragments of seven more.

146. Top of a beaker f. 400, clay and decoration as last, but slightly micaceous.

Eight examples of this fabric in this late deposit is surprising; perhaps this ware lasted longer than has hitherto been allowed it.

147. Upper part of a beaker, form not quite certain, of fine polished grey ware. The missing base may have been something like the drawing, one of which was found. On the neck the very neat graffito VASSEDO.

*148. Complete beaker (restored from fragments) of f. 406. Fine grey ware; six flutings covered by a broad band of striated triangular impressions applied with a wheel.

*149. Nearly complete beaker f. 410, reddish clay with grey

*153. Most part of a beaker, approximately f. 410. Fine grey ware with ten flutings, double groove above and below, rim and foot polished.

Nos. 154–59 are examples of rims of fluted beakers, which formed a large section of the fragments. Nos. 155–6 are curious, being simply jars of f. 278 in fluted grey ware.

Nos. 157–60 are representative of black and grey fluted beakers, of which there must have been about 100. Most are like nos. 148 and 150, but a number are like 160. The rest are unusual.

The following were overlooked and have been added to other plates (viz. fig. 57).

2. Several fragments of a 'Smith's Vase', which yield a drawing as shown. The clay is thin, hard, and brownish, with a dull white coating, on the outside. The rim is frilled, with a very small cordon on the neck. Two conjoining fragments preserve a pair of pincers, hammer, and anvil in high, applied relief.

11. Small bowl, nearly complete, found in the rubble on top of the south wall of the staircase well. Soft brown-black ware with

minute white grit (crushed shell), smoothed. The bottom is quite rounded. No parallel known.

12. Bowl of fine polished grey ware.

THE FOUNDATION OFFERINGS

Of these the first is certain, the others possible.

Fig. 59, 4. Olla of coarse grey ware with brown surface (f. 268). Height 7¾ in., diam. 5½ in. It is almost identical with that found by Wheeler, *Insula*, fig. 5, no. 3, and ascribed by him to the Flavian period, on the evidence of the grave groups in the Museum. Literally hundreds of these vessels were found in the bottom of room D with not a single fragment of first-century ware. The scarcity of the type in grave groups later than Hadrian can hardly be maintained, for the type lasted almost through the Roman period. The latest examples tend to have a taller neck, compare fig. 233, 32, and figs. 69 70, nos. 123, 124, 126, and 128. We prefer an Antonine to a Flavian date for these vessels. No other datable pottery was found in connexion with the building to which this pot belonged, but the foundations were on the subsoil and no earlier layers were present, so that a Flavian date is possible, though, we feel, unlikely. There was no lid, and the contents had left no trace.

Fig. 59, 5. Reddish ware with brownish-red slip. Found broken, against the end of the red pavement in trench 4 (insula 7) where the wall had been broken out. It may have stood in dark earth beneath a late wall, but more probably was dropped into position when the wall was pulled out. The type (f. 392) occurs in great numbers in the bottom of room A and in the filling of the drain (see fig. 70, 134). It is at least Antonine.

Fig. 59, 3. The most part of a cooking-pot of coarse gritted grey ware with brownish surface. The fragments were found all together under the layer of pink mortar under the red pavement of the hypocaust house. The foot was missing. Height *c.* 7½ in., diam. 6½ in. It is very similar to Wheeler's fig. 5, 2, contemporary with his no. 3 mentioned above. Compare the urns from Hatfield Peveril with a Flavian T.S. dish, *C.M.R.* 1931, pl. VII, 2, 3.

ANIMAL REMAINS

By DR. J. W. JACKSON, F.G.S.

The animal remains dealt with in this report consist of the shells of both marine and non-marine mollusca and of the bones and teeth of various domestic and wild animals. These are dealt with under their different headings.

MARINE MOLLUSCA

Common oyster (*Ostrea edulis*). Valves of this species are present from several different trial trenches, from the bottom of the drain, bottom of room D, and from the lowest road level.

Common whelk (*Buccinum undatum*). Three shells from different trial trenches.

Red whelk (*Neptunea antiqua*). One shell from bottom of drain.

Common mussel (*Mytilus edulis*). Two examples.

Common cockle (*Cardium edule*). One example.

NON-MARINE MOLLUSCA

Garden snail (*Helix aspersa*). One from a trial trench, many from yellow filling under lower burnt layer in the gateway.

DOMESTIC ANIMALS

Horse. There is a cannon bone or metatarsal measuring 248 mm. in length with a mid-shaft width of 29 mm., indicating

a small-sized animal of Exmoor pony type. Four upper molars are from upper filling of the drain.

Small ox. Bones of this animal occur in remains from various locations and on the whole indicate small animals. The hinder part of a skull with both horn-cores broken off resembles, in size and general appearance, the small Celtic Ox (*Bos longifrons*). Another imperfect skull is very similar; it is from the pit in trench 3. The horn-cores and frontals have been broken off as if to extract the brain.

Large ox. From the top of the drain comes a right horn core of a rough and robust type. It is deeply fluted along the inner curve and has the following dimensions: length along outer curve, 210 mm.; circumference at base, 186 mm.; diameter at base, 65 × 49 mm. From top of the stair-well (site I) comes a broad metacarpal measuring 210 mm. in length with a mid-shaft diameter of 44 mm. Both these specimens indicate a larger animal than *Bos longifrons* and resemble remains from the considerably earlier site of Woodhenge, Wilts.

Sheep. Bones of this animal are present from several locations. They indicate the small slender-limbed breed found so frequently on Roman and Romano-British sites in Great Britain. There are four half-skulls showing a hornless condition. These have been split down the middle as in the case of many from Glastonbury Lake Village (Pre-Roman).

Pig. This animal is represented by a few remains consisting of fragments of lower jaw and loose teeth.

Dog. The remains of this animal consist of several imperfect skulls and lower jaws with teeth from different locations on the site. They all seem to belong to a small type of dog.

WILD ANIMALS

Red Deer. This is represented by a fragment of antler from site I.

Roebuck. From the bottom of the drain there is a broken right ramus of the lower jaw with four teeth, and from the pit in trench 3 is another right ramus with full dentition; the length of the tooth row in this section is 61 mm.

Wild Boar? From trench 3 (on the E.–W. road) comes a brown-stained tibia minus the proximal epiphysis which may belong to the wild rather than the domestic pig.

Badger. From the top filling of the drain is a left femur and an innominate bone belonging to this animal.

Birds. A few remains of birds are present among the other bones. Some belong to goose or fowl, and one may be jackdaw.

REMARKS

The Celtic Shorthorn (*Bos longifrons*) has been previously recorded from Roman Colchester by John Brown (*Journ. Brit. Arch. Assn.* v (1849), 140–3, but this writer, following Professor Owen (*British Fossil Mammals* (1846), 510), was mistaken in regarding this ox as having lived also in Pleistocene times in association with elephant, rhinoceros, hippopotamus, hyena, &c. This matter has been discussed on several occasions by many authorities and the consensus of opinion is that *Bos longifrons* appeared in Britain in Neolithic times and lived down to and through the Roman period.

The Romans found large herds of small domesticated Celtic Shorthorn living in Britain and they improved the breed by crossing it with larger imported cattle.

The remains of *Bos longifrons* have been found in some abundance in Roman stations, such as Corstopitum, Newstead, &c.

The Kerry cattle are probably the most typical examples of the Celtic Shorthorn in the British Isles.

INSULA 16

The street on the west has been described; those to the north and south have not been seen. The east boundary is the town wall. Here, in the garden of no. 27 Roman Road, our section V of the rampart was cut.

Somewhere near the gap shown in the Roman wall on the O.S. 1:500 map (east of the NE. corner of Greyfriars) it should be possible to find the remains of an interior tower. It is indicated by Wheeler and Laver nearly 100 ft. farther north than we should expect to find it.

INSULA 17

The north boundary should be marked by the tower and by the old stone boundary wall of St. Peter's Rectory garden; the streets on the east and south are certain enough. The width N.–S. should be about 340 ft. and from E.–W. about 510 ft. The following remains have been found:

1. A tessellated pavement found at the SW. end of North Hill, under Simkin's furniture shop. Shown by Wire on his plan, p. 4 of his Album, see fig. 73, no. 14.

2. A tessellated pavement and flues behind the same shop, doubtless part of the same house as no. 1. Recorded by P. G. Laver.

In a lecture on St. Peter's Parish P. G. Laver said: 'on the site of Messrs. Simkin's furniture warehouse certain ovens etc. were found suggesting a glass blower's works'. No statement is made as to their date.[1]

3. Foundations, floors, painted plaster, &c., at a depth of 3 to 4 ft. found in the garden of St. Peter's Vicarage. See the passages from Wire below, 16/3/1843, 14/11/44, 24/3/45, and *T.E.A.S.* o.s. v, 155.

153. Wire has marked on the plan in his Morant a red pavement measuring about 90 by 65 ft. (clearly not to scale), immediately inside the town wall just north of the Balkerne Gate. The site is under the two western houses of Balkerne Gardens. It is numbered '1', but we find no text referring to it.

154. On the same map another red square indicates a pavement about 44 ft. square lying about 40 ft. west of North Hill under no. 60, opposite St. Peter's Churchyard. This is numbered '2'. On the map in his 'County Illustrations' Wire shows the same or another pavement at the west end of the garden of no. 60. He is careful to explain that positions are approximate.

154A. He also shows a long strip of pavement running E.–W. near the middle of Balkerne Gardens.

Wire's notes begin 6/3/1843 with the record of a '2b' coin of Nero found when the area was a field, and being converted to a garden. We only give the more useful entries. The others have several references to the discovery of iron cones, 4 in. long, which, it seems, are most probably pike-heads or butts of the siege period. If so, it is remarkable that they have only been found here, and at the Union House.

16/3/43. '. . . in [this] field, when in the possession of Mr. Sach some years ago a beautiful mosaic pavement was discovered and covered up again.'[2]

15/4/43. 'Obtained an iron spearhead found . . . [here].'

14/11/44. 'The Rev. S. Carr sent for me to go and look at a concrete found in the garden. . . . It is about two feet below the surface, and appears to be only a path . . . or the foundation of a tessellated pavement from which the tesserae have been removed . . . probably the latter opinion is right, as there is a very beautiful mosaic not far off in the same ground, which was discovered some years since, and covered up again at the time, as I understand, without any injury being done to it.' (We have a note 'A drawing of this is in Wire's MSS. somewhere'.)

24/3/45. 'The Rev. S. Carr sent . . . some fragments of Roman house-wall painted, found in the garden . . . . No part of it can be dug to the depth of 3–4 ft. but some Roman remains are found, principally foundations and concrete floors.'

There are the usual notes of finds of Samian ware and pottery, a coin of Tetricus, &c.

THE 'WAGGON AND HORSES' SITE

155. In 1935 the site of the restaurant, once Scott's and later Pallant's, which looked straight down the High Street, was cleared and a new building erected for the Prudential Insurance Society. Mr. Rudsdale noted 'a fairly uniform burnt layer over the whole site . . . much burnt daub'.

In the same year the old 'Waggon and Horses', close by on the north, was pulled down and a new building erected farther west. The former cellars were extended westwards and the earth to the south also exposed. A very clear section was obtained on the west side.[3] Our drawing of it is partly schematic, for the slope of the surface is judged, not measured (pl. xxxi, B).

The subsoil is yellow sand. Upon it lay, in the south half of the section, a sloping layer of brown loam, full of heavy layers of charcoal, especially at the bottom. Northwards, near the first wall-slot, this turned to a dirty sand and charcoal; beyond the wall its place was taken by a humped layer of sand divided in part by a dark sandy line resembling a 'pan'. The sand rested on the natural surface, which was uneven and carried no charcoal layer. To the north the bank of sand ceases steeply, giving place to a foot or more of dark, dirty loam.

In the southern part the top of the brown loam was marked by an even, whitish line of unknown nature.

---

[1] *Essex County Standard*, 11/3/1924. A photograph of a kiln on this site, undoubtedly part of the remains referred to above, has recently been given to the Museum. It shows a kiln of exactly the same type as those used to manufacture tiles in the thirteenth to fourteenth centuries, but very small.

[2] It seems certain now that this does not lie in the western part of this ground.

[3] *C.M.R.* 1944, 19.

At the extreme south the brown loam appeared also above this, but near the wall this had become a thick deposit of loamy sand, apparently contemporary with the upper heavily cambered banks of gravel (divided by several muddy lines, not all of which are shown) which filled the space between the two wall-slots and also extended northwards, the upper one extending over the dark loam.

The next layer in the southern half of the section was of yellow gravel, approximately levelling the site, and apparently contemporary with a layer of grey mud which lay upon the gravel to the north. Three feet from the south end of the section these lowest levels show a deep V-shaped slot, a foot wide at the top, running 1 ft. into the natural sand. Possibly a palisade stood here; but it will be noticed that the charcoal layers dip into it. (There is a possibility of a wooden drain.)

There now followed on the south a burnt layer 9–15 in. thick, containing charcoal, which stops abruptly against the first wall-slot. It was covered in part by a lenticular layer of stiff sand, perhaps mixed with mortar or clay.

The next occurrence on the site is most striking. There is a regular layer of about a foot of very red burnt clay or daub, capped by a thin layer of oyster-shells. Its edge is abrupt at the first wall, but the layer is found again, unmistakably, continuing for 2 ft. north of the wall at a level 15 in. lower. It ends abruptly in a heavy and deep burnt deposit full of loam, which continues to the north end of the section.

At the south end the remaining 2 ft. or more up to the modern concrete floor are of loam and burnt clay. The lower foot, of yellow loam and burnt clay has a thin layer of mortar and chips lying upon it; above this the loam is dark, still containing much burnt clay. From just south of the first wall this upper layer is missing, being replaced by modern top-soil, but north of this wall there is a layer of about a foot of pale, stiff loam, which may possibly be a continuation of that below the mortar layer to the south, though it does not contain burnt clay.

Two large recent pits mutilate the south part of the section. The first was full of dirty gravel, all in one filling; the second, deeper and splayed, was full of black earth. At 14 ft. from the south end of the section was a deep vertical slot, 2 ft. 6 in. wide at the bottom, which was 7 ft. from the surface. It was full of black earth. Seven feet 3 inches north of this lay another such slot, much similar and only 1 ft. 2 in. wide, with vertical sides, the bottom at least 6 ft. 8 in. from the surface, possibly a little more. It was full of dirty gravel, and the upper layers seemed to run across it

undisturbed except for festooning where they seem to have fallen into it. In the uppermost layer is a festoon of black earth, which appeared different from the top-soil.

At the north end there was a very large modern excavation full of black earth, the bottom of which was not reached. It cut an earlier excavation to the south, with very rectangular outline, which might be another wall-slot. The latter had been at least 1 ft. 9 in. wide; its bottom was 5 ft. 8 in. from the surface. If a wall-slot, it would appear to have been contemporary with the first wall and probably not with the second.

Farther north still lay another modern excavation filled with alternate layers of gravel and mud. Between these last two disturbances only a narrow tongue of the original layers remained.

Along the 17 ft. of the south side of the cellar only a partial section could be taken. Eight feet 6 inches east of the line of the section just described lay remains of a wall 2 ft. 6 in. wide (thus corresponding to the first wall above); the mortar layer for the foundation was 6 ft. 9 in. from the surface. West of it the section had been destroyed by modern excavation. East of it the original surface of the sand could be seen sloping down to the east, with disturbed sand above it, with uneven surface, and above this about 7 in. of dirty loam. There was then a narrow band of 1–4 in. of light sandy loam, corresponding in level with the yellow gravel of the first section. Above this was 9–10 in. of sooty loam containing oyster-shells. Upon this lay an even and continuous band of solid charcoal, and above this our deposit of burnt clay again, here 15 in. or more thick. Above this the ground was a recent make-up of dirty soil and clay.

Very little could be recovered from these excavations; we can only mention a shoulder fragment of an amphora f. 182 with the letters FAL LOLL in red paint in two lines,[1] two coins, of M. Agrippa and Gallienus, and a few fragments of pottery of first-century date.

Odd finds from the insula are mostly of little importance, but we mention the following. From Balkerne Gardens (formerly Provident Place, and before that Ivy Place), Wire 'purchased an ancient British copper coin ($\frac{1}{2}$ in. diam.), on the convex side S O S on the concave side a horse and circles . . .' (Diary, 3/3/1848). In 1933 a bronze Cunobelin (Evans, pl. XI, 7 or 8) was found there (387.33), and in 1936 a gold quarter stater of Tasciovanus (1113.36). A denarius of Augustus and second brass coins of Claudius and Antonia have also been found here.

A quantity of pottery was handed to the Museum as found when Messrs. Simkin's warehouse was built. But it included a vessel clearly marked as from another site (grave 316), so cannot be safely regarded as all from here. It includes an intact example of a large flagon f. 140, of peculiar appearance, the surface being almost vitreous. There are several potters' stamps on sigillata.

[1] *C.M.R.* 1944, 43.

173. In the late summer of 1945, by the good offices of Mr. W. Duncan Clark and the goodwill of the owner, Mr. E. Page, it was possible to make a small excavation in the garden of no. 60 North Hill.[1] The work was done by Messrs. G. H. Martin and I. M. Sparrow of the Royal Grammar School (fig. 72).

running N.–S. It was very clearly defined, but its west face was splayed outwards, as if it had fallen in that direction. In the immediately adjacent trench 5 an irregular mound of the same clay rising to only about 2 ft. from the surface may be attributed to the ruins of the same building.

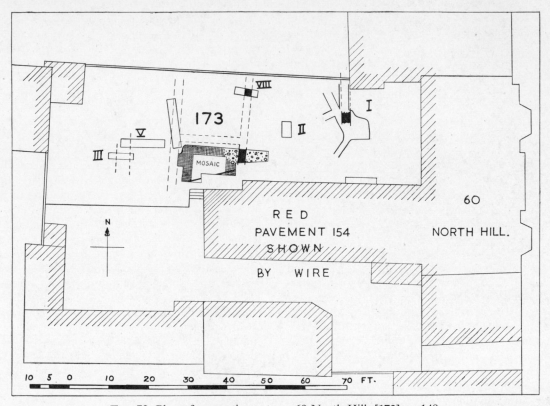

FIG. 72. Plan of excavations at no. 60 North Hill. [173], p. 148.

Wire has marked the red pavement, no. **154** above, under this very house.

The two parts of the garden are at different levels, the southern being 3 ft. 3 in. higher than the northern. It was in the latter that we worked, adjoining St. Peter's Vicarage garden on the north.

There was only 1 ft. of top-soil. Remains of a decorated mosaic floor were found at this depth, and it had been uncovered in the eighteenth century and then filled up again as a midden-heap.

The natural yellow sand was found at 4 ft. to 5 ft. 6 in. below the surface, sloping down to the east. Upon it lay yellow loam, thickening eastwards and tending to restore the level. The top of this merged into the earliest Roman level, which was about 3 ft. 6 in. from the surface but was nowhere very definite, unless in trench 3. Here was a layer of dirty soft sand, about a foot thick, into which had been set a clay wall 3 ft. 3 in. wide, and

At the east end of the garden, in trench 1, a small piece of wall 1 ft. 11 in. wide was found. The top was only 1 ft. 9 in. from the surface, the bottom 2 ft. 9 in., but the foundation (which had not shifted) was not level. It stood on a remarkable burnt layer which, just east of the wall, was at least 1 ft. 8 in. thick, consisting of mixed earth, yellow loam, fragmentary roofing tiles, and lumps of burnt clay, with patches of charcoal. The top of this lay 1 ft. 9 in. from the surface, but dipped abruptly to the wall and seemed still to dip beyond it. Close to the west side of the wall, and definitely below the foundation, lay a number of large pieces of burnt clay, including one fairly complete, which showed that these belonged to rectangular blocks measuring about 9 by 6 in. None of these showed any trace of marks of wattle.

The wall was of dressed septaria laid in yellowish sandy mortar. Only the lower part of the foundation

[1] *J.R.S.* xxxvi (1946), 141; *C.M.R.* 1947, 22.

was found, with remains of two courses of small blocks on the east face, and one large block, at a lower level, on the west. It appears to have been built on the sloping surface of the burnt layer.

Presumably this wall belonged to the other building remains which included the decorated pavement. A little over 23 ft. west of it another wall was found to run N.–S. Where it bounded the east side of the pavement it was well preserved, 1 ft. 11 in. wide, the top 1 ft. 3 in. from the surface; the bottom, which was not reached, entered the yellow sand at 4 ft. The materials were tiles (apparently all fragmentary) and yellow mortar. The east face, which we followed, was inclined outwards, which may account for a gap of 6 in. between its top and the edge of the pavement. Its northward continuation was found in trench 8, where nothing else was found, owing to gardening operations, which had reached down to 43 in. At this level lay a clay floor, 3 in. higher than the remains of the wall, and not running over them. In the disturbed soil lay an Antoninianus of Valerian senior.

The west wall of the pavement was not conclusively identified, but the trace of a wall in trench 4 can hardly have belonged to anything else. The bottom of the trench, at 3 ft. 6 in. from the surface, showed traces of a foundation of yellow mortar, occurring somewhat irregularly as shown on the plan. It should indicate a wall running N.–S. parallel to the last and 15 ft. 9 in. distant from it, and another E.–W., bounding the pavement on the north. Time did not permit of following this mortar down to check the depth.

The room which contained the pavement seems to have measured 15 ft. 9 in. E.–W. by about the same N.–S. On this basis the red border was about 2 ft. 9 in. wide all round, except on the west, where it ran to 5 ft. 2 in. of which 2 ft. 9 in. were preserved. This sounds suspicious, but we could not find another west wall.

The most part of the mosaic centre had been destroyed; all that remained recognizable of the pattern was parts of a rectangle bordered by a triple cable pattern, black, red, yellow, and white, between white bands, the outer 4½ in. wide, the inner 3½. The rectangle measured 8 ft. 6 in. E.–W. and apparently the same N.–S.

At some time the gap in the NE. corner of the pavement had been repaired with cobbling of large pebbles, which continued for over 8 ft. eastward from it. Below it lay four sherds of Flavian sigillata. Its surface had had much use, and was intensely black, as are most medieval cobbled surfaces in the town. Trench 2, which otherwise showed nothing but loam, had a layer of gravel at a corresponding level. The whole is at the horizon on which the eighteenth-century midden-heap was laid.

Reverting to trench 3, a pit had been cut into the remains of the clay wall; it had vertical sides, 2 ft. 3 in. apart and down to 3 ft. 3 in. from the surface. The bottom was filled by 7 in. of dirty black gravel, similar to that just described. Above this had been heaped a mound of mortar rubble which begins the modern deposits.

Above the remains of the clay wall lay 16 in. of sandy deposit, containing oyster-shells and charcoal, probably levelling work on the burnt layer. Sigillata chips of definitely first-century date came from the top of the loam, at only 18 in. from the surface. The only other find worthy of mention was an antoninianus of Victorinus, loose over the pavement.

The history of the site would appear to run as follows:

The initial occupation has left no clear mark, the earliest remains being trodden, or dug by cultivation, into the top of the loam. These included first-century sigillata with the bright glaze usually termed Vespasianic, but also found under Nero.

The earliest building on the site had clay walls about 3 ft. thick, and mounds of clay from these still lie about. Such evidence is in full accord with that from the earliest levels in other Roman towns, e.g. Wroxeter.

The early adobe buildings or a subsequent series built of clay blocks ended in a conflagration, the debris of which we met in the burnt layer of trench 1. The connexion (if any) between this and similar layers at the 'Waggon and Horses' (p. 147) and at the west end of the insula has yet to be shown. But it seems likely that ours here was connected with the disaster of A.D. 61.

The stone-built house followed probably in the second century, for it was not built until the burnt layer had consolidated. The subsequent history has vanished with the upper layers.

Much more might have been learned had time permitted.

INSULA 18

This is the insula in the angle between North Hill and High Street, and its dimensions are fairly closely known, except that we should very much like to know the exact position of the Roman 'High Street' here. The dimensions should be 300 ft. E.–W. and 310 ft. N.–S. Most of the area is covered by St. Peter's Church and churchyard.

The following discoveries have been recorded:

15. A sketch map on page 4 of Wire's Album (fig. 73) marks an old wall 3 ft. below the surface, forming the west boundary of the insula (p. 66), a concrete floor with powdered brick on the corner of High Street, and other remains mentioned elsewhere.

16. Wire, Diary, 12/12/1842: 'In digging a grave in St. Peter's churchyard adjoining Mr. Green sen. for his grand-daughter, about seven feet below the surface a concrete floor of Roman work was discovered, which probably was the foundation for a tessellated pavement.'

17. In 1849 (Dec.) a tessellated pavement was found during the rebuilding of the 'Peoples' Hall',[1] adjoining

156. The discovery of the Roman street behind 4 and 5 North Hill has been described (p. 67). A list of the many small finds begins with coins of Claudius and Nero and stamps of Licinus, and includes a small piece of tessellated pavement, all white, and coins up to Theodosian date. There were also thin slabs of sheathing of Purbeck marble, a fragment of a crucible, and fragments of waste bronze. A notable find was the

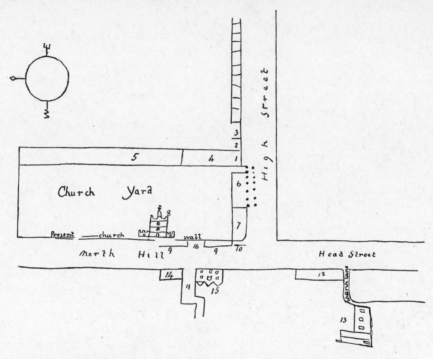

FIG. 73. Wm. Wire's plan of discoveries around the top of North Hill. (p. 66.)

the Corn Exchange. Wire tells us: 'It was discovered on the east side [of the site] . . . where the foundation is at the S eastern curve about eight feet below the surface. It was broken up, as only a portion of it was discovered, the remainder being under the building occupied by the Mechanics' Institution. The pattern was chequered.'[2]

An original drawing—the only one known—of this pavement, by Mr. A. Tibbenham of Ipswich (pl. XXIV, A), is in the Museum. The design is of 7-in. squares in black and white, surrounded by a red line and broad black and white bands. The number and size of the tesserae are only faintly suggested here and there. The margin is all buff.

Wire notes, 3/3/56: 'When digging on the N side of High Street near the Foundry Yard . . . fragments of Roman pottery were found at a depth of twelve feet . . . .'

rim of thick black ware with brown surface, hand made, which must be pagan Saxon.[3]

INSULA 19

The streets on east and west are only approximately known; those on north and south are, perhaps, fixed, but that on the north may have been moved. The insula apparently measured about 320 ft. E.–W. by 280 ft. N.–S.

196. A foundation of septaria in white mortar was found in High Street in April 1930 at a depth of 18 in. and 24 ft. from the front of the Cups Hotel. It coincides exactly with the conjectured line of the north side of the Roman street (*C.M.R.* 1931, 7).

18. Morant, p. 184, says: 'near half a very fine and elegant [pavement] was discovered, 12 May 1763, on the north side of High Street, in a garden belonging

[1] The site now of St. George's Hall.
[2] Wire, Diary, Dec. 1849; 'County Illustrations', plan no. 30;

T.E.A.S. o.s. v, 158; O.S. 1:500.
[3] *C.M.R.* 1944, 18.

to Mr. John Bernard, apothecary and chirurgeon, late part of a yard of the Falcon and Queen's Head Inn.[1] ... Mr. Bernard hath enclosed and covered it, in order to preserve it . . . an exact drawing of it was engraved and delivered with Lexden Hundred, when that part of the History of Essex was published'.

'Near this was found either part of the same or another, when a stable was pulled down, which was supposed to be an old Roman building.' Morant has the coloured drawing (p. 184) here reproduced (pl. XXIII, A). The original was drawn by Dunthorne, a local artist. There is another coloured print which differs only slightly. The pavement is stated to have been found in the garden of the Three Cups Inn about 3 ft. below the surface in 1763. The decorated portion must have been about 10 ft. square.[2]

It is no doubt of the same pavement that Cromwell remarks (p. 200): 'A fragment of . . . pavement was discovered in the market place, but which was then part of the garden of Mr. Wallis, a tradesman whose house fronted the High Street, and is now part of the Three Cups Inn, which is over the entrance to the market. It remains where it was found, at the depth of a few feet from the surface . . . being partly bricked over, and partly covered by a trapdoor . . . the largest pieces of the mosaic work are something more than an inch square . . . the whole . . . from neglect, and the admission of the rain is going rapidly to decay.'

Of the reputed Roman building we are told: 'And

at the Queen's Head Inn in the market place, the stable, as also the room above it, is of Roman building.'[3]

19. A mosaic pavement and foundations were found close to **18**: '23/5/1844. Mr. Bewick gave me a small piece of tessellated pavement being the remains of a beautiful one discovered in the gardeners' market some years since . . . .' Wheeler and Laver refer this to the western of the two marks on the O.S. map, presumably on the authority of Cutts (34, map, I, 7).[4] The second mark we have numbered **189**.

On 9/5/1856 Wire visited the Vegetable Market and got some small remains: 'A great quantity of septaria, mortar, fragments of Roman roof tiles, bricks and oyster shells have been come upon to the depth of nine feet, which appears to have been thrown in as rubbish to fill a hole for some purpose'; and on the next day 'a foundation of septaria and loose mortar was come up[on] about 5 ft. square, which was cut through . . . .' He collected a coin of Germanicus and three illegible small brass.

189. This number is allotted to the eastern of two marks on the O.S. 1:500 map of 1878 marked 'Supposed site of ROMAN VILLA'. Both were under the vegetable market, and are now under Victoria Chambers and the street south of them. We have no account of the discovery.

20. When Mr. Daniell's house was rebuilding, a pavement was found, 'together with an earthen urn, holding about a quart, and a metal one'.[5] Wheeler and

---

[1] *R.C.H.M.* 23; *Phil. Trans.* nos. 255 6; Gough's *Camden*, 1789, i, 58; Stukeley's *Letters and Diaries* (Surtees Soc.), ii, 162–3. There is an uncoloured print in Wire's 'County Illustrations'.

[2] The 'Falcon' is named in records from 1411 onwards, and was later known also as the 'Queen's (i.e. Elizabeth's) Head', then as the 'Royal Three Cups' and, after the failure of the 'White Hart', as the 'Three Cups and White Hart', now simply 'The Cups'. Of the three drawings mentioned that of Dunthorne is the best.

[3] Gibson's *Camden*, 1772, i, 358. The problem raised is of great interest and is beyond complete discussion here. Briefly, there are evidences for four 'Stone Houses' in Colchester. The first is planned on the 1:500 map of 1878, and was known as 'Hamo's Saxon Hall'. It was razed to the ground in 1886, despite opposition in the Town Council. It lay just west of 'The Cups' and measured 26 by 46 ft., with walls shown as 4 ft. thick. A water-colour drawing of the interior of its vaulted basement (by Lady Benham) exists, and a series of photographs showing it in various stages of demolition. The upper floor had large, round-headed windows. The second building lies under the middle of the Corn Exchange and all its northern part has been destroyed. The southern part is a mass of rubble, apparently some 40 ft. wide, with walls about 10 ft. thick. Most of the rubble looks modern, but the whole foundation must have an ancient core. Regarding this there is the following in a letter from Morant to Stukeley (dated 28/6/1762; Surtees Soc. lxxvi, 162): '. . . Some years ago the Queen's Head Inn in this town was looked upon as one of the most valuable remains of antiquity, there being in it a very antique building, which the old people still have a notion

of, under the name of temple. About fifty years ago it was all turned upside down, and new built in a slight manner. In digging for sand in the yard they have met with old foundations of Roman brick; and a few coins, viz. a brass one of Nero; obv. a winged Victory . . . one of Carausius, but not scarce, and a few of the Constantine family. And also fragments of large urns, and a whole one containing about 2 quarts, in which were the bones of a young person, and a little piece of wood.'

How reliable the record of the burial may be is uncertain. The piece of wood is suspicious in this dry soil, and if the person were young enough the burial might legitimately have been within the bounds of the town. In any case there is nothing to date it.

The third building appears on a plan of the area allocated for the new Town Hall built in 1845. In the NE. corner are shown parts of two adjacent buildings with very thick walls, obviously vaults, which were still then being used as prisons. These are 39 ft. back from the building line, which brings them exactly in line with 'Hamo's Hall'. We thus have three very old and massive stone buildings in a row along the south part of insula 19, and standing 65 ft. back from the estimated position of the north side of the Roman street. They are apparently at equal intervals, and present a parallel to the three buildings in the forum at Verulamium. But whether they are purely Norman or whether they had some Roman substructure is as yet quite unknown.

The fourth 'Stone House' lay opposite the Town Hall on the west side of Pelham's Lane. The plan is preserved and is purely medieval.

[4] Wright, *Essex*, i, 295; *J.B.A.* 1846, 366; *T.E.A.S.* o.s. v, 160.

[5] Morant, 183; *Arch.* ii, 287.

FIG. 74. Samian ware from the First Pottery Shop. Scale ½. (p. 154.)

Laver consider **19** and **20** as possibly two pavements; they state that Daniell's house was next south of no. **21**.

at a depth of 2–4 ft. lay a remarkable deposit of broken pottery, glass, and other wares, almost without admixture of earth, and so loose that fragments fell out

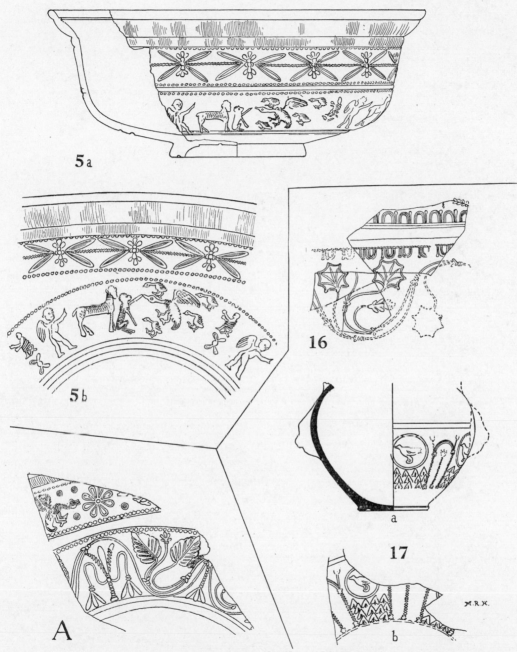

FIG. 75. Samian ware from the Pottery Shops. [**127**], p. 154. (Except A, see p. 206.) Scale ½.

127. In August 1927 workmen cutting trenches for Jacklin's new café brought into the Museum an astonishing collection of pottery.[1] On visiting the site the trenches were found completed. In a very small area,

in a tinkling shower when touched. No more could be collected, and that recovered is probably not one-hundredth part of what remains.

In October and November 1929 the adjacent site to

[1] *C.M.R.* 1928, 30 ff.

the west was cleared for the present building. Permission was obtained to sink two pits, and the work was done by Messrs. A. F. Hall, J. T. Jones, and M. J. Pakenham, to whom our cordial thanks are due.

The two holes were about 15 ft. apart; the top 3 ft. of soil was recent rubbish, while the lower 2½ ft. was a mass of brick rubble. This proved to be remains of daub which had been completely baked as red and as hard as brick. The marks of the wattle were clear—it was probably hazel, and the rods were nearly 1 in. thick.[1]

Below the daub was a thin stratum of burnt earth

have been of wood or thatch, for no tiles were found. When the ruins were cleared up the burnt clay walls were broken in pieces and the site levelled. No later layers remain, so its later history is unknown.

The homogeneity of the pottery and the number of vessels represented are sufficient evidence that here was a pottery store. After trying every piece to every other piece very few joins were found and so the numbers given below were arrived at. They give some idea of what still lies buried.[2]

Decorated Sigillata (fig. 74). Eleven fragments of bowls f. 29 (1–11); four of f. 30 (14–17); five small sherds of f. 29, and two

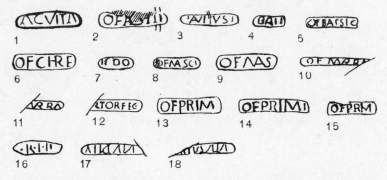

Fig. 76. Potters' stamps from the First Pottery Shop. Full size. (p. 154.)

or clay quite black in colour and lying on sand which showed signs of burning. Presumably this dark layer was the floor of the building.

The great bulk of the remains is red glazed sigillata ware, representing hundreds of vessels. The range of forms is small, so too the list of potters' names, several of which occur in numbers. Colour-coated or 'varnished' wares were also strongly represented.

Fine glass ware was remarkably plentiful. Most of it was, unfortunately, fused, but enough remains to show that a considerable number of elegant vessels were destroyed, many of them thin and delicately coloured.

The sigillata ware also is burnt, and examination shows that the various shapes were stacked bottom upwards in groups, and molten glass has dripped upon several of them. Heaps of broken glass have fused together, and, again, whole vessels are melted to shapeless lumps. In many cases these lumps have solidified upon the floor and show pebbles and earth on one side and the unmistakable rectangular impressions of charred wood on the other.

It is clear that the sigillata was piled on the floor or on a lower shelf, with the glass on a shelf above. The fire blackened some of the pottery before the piles collapsed. Then the glass dripped upon the sherds and finally the building collapsed upon all. The roof must

of f. 30. There was one small rim-fragment of f. 37, plain zone 1 in. wide. It is not burnt and may be intrusive.

There were also three fragments of one of the decorated jugs which are of rare occurrence (fig. 75, 16); another rarity is two fragments resembling f. 67 (fig. 75, 17 *a*, *b*), from which it differs in having a projection on the side which is not like a handle attachment, but rather resembles the junction between two vases of a triple vase. There is a further slight projection farther up for which no explanation can be offered. In the drawing the upper figure is a restoration. The shape and position of the projections have been shown on both sides, but only one is present on the small fragments preserved. These are burnt like the majority.

Plain Sigillata (the figure after the rule is the number of fragments): form Ritt. 9—6; f. 24/25—217; f. 16—1 rim; f. 15/17—261; f. Ritt. 1—5; f. 18—112; f. Ritt. 8—9; f. 27—84; f. Ritt. 9—2; f. Ritt. 12—2 (of one); there are also many fragments which might belong to either f. 15/17 or f. 18.

The potters' stamps on the above vessels are as follows:

1. ACVITA, twice on f. 27; once on f. 15/17. (Fig. 76.)
19. AQ)VITAN, once on f. 15/17 or 18. (Fig. 99.)
2. OF.ABITI, once on f. 24/25 (possibly ALBIN). (Fig. 76.)
3. AVITVS, once on f. 27. (Fig. 76.)
4. BAII, five times on f. 27 and 24/25. (Fig. 76.)
5. OF.BASSIC (Bassus and Coelus), once on f. 24/25. (Fig. 76.)
20. BIO, once on f. 27. (Fig. 99.)
6. OF CHRE (Chresimus), twice on f. 15/17 and 18. (Fig. 76.)
7. IIDO or ICDO (Edo?), thrice, quite clearly, on f. 27. (Fig. 76.)

---

[1] Compare St. Albans, *Arch.* XC, pl. XV, C, and XX, A.

[2] *T.E.A.S.* xix, 277; xx, 211; *Ant. Journ.* ix, 37.

21 and 22. OF.MAIO, twice on f. 15/17, or 18. (Fig. 99.)
(These appear identical except for the fifth letter.)
9. OF MAS, once on f. 24. (Fig. 76.)
8. OF MASCI, once on f. 24/25. (Fig. 76.)
23. OF MO... f. 18; and MO dubious, once on f. 24/25.
(Fig. 104.)

16. .R.I.II., four times on f. 24/25. (Fig. 76.)
17 and 18. VIRTVI (retro?), a dubious reading, the stamp
is very clear and occurs no less than eleven times, all on
f. 24/25. (Fig. 76.)
VITALI, on f. 27.
EGIDI (?), a dubious reading.

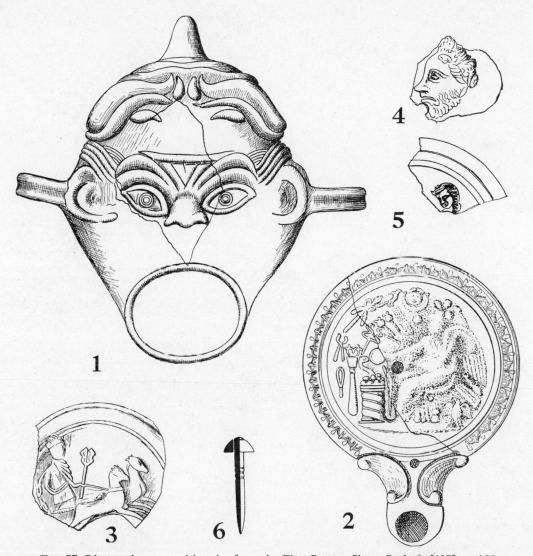

FIG. 77. Rhyton, lamps, and jet pin, from the First Pottery Shop. Scale ⅔. [127], p. 155.

10 and 11. OF.MVRRA, thrice, on ff. 15/17 and 18.
(Fig. 76.)
12. NESTOR FEC, once, on f. 15/17 or 18. (Fig. 76.)
NI)GR(?) on f. 15/17 or 18.
24. O PASSIEИ, (N reversed) on f. 15/17 or 18. (Fig. 99.)
14. OF PRIMI, twice on f. 27; six times on f. 15/17 or 18;
once on f. 15/17; six times on f. 24/25. (Fig. 76.)
13. OF PRIM, thrice on f. 24/25. (Fig. 76.)
15. OF PRM, twice on f. 27. (Fig. 76.)

Fragments of lamps (fig. 77). Twenty-six fragments were recovered, only four of which preserve any part of the decoration
of the disk. Two fragments have the angular, voluted nozzle of
Loeschcke's type I,[1] the rest are of his type IV. The best fragment preserves about one-third of the disk, and the design is
identifiable with the 'pantheistic deity' of Loeschcke's Taf. VI,
606, from which our drawing is completed.
Other 'varnished' ware. Of this the most interesting and important item is half a dozen fragments of a rhyton or drinking-cup

[1] S. Loeschcke, *Lampen aus Vindonissa*, Taf. I, A–C.

in the form of a human head (fig. 77, 1). The ware is thin and very hard, with a brownish, varnish-like coating. By the exercise of some ingenuity the accompanying illustration has been obtained from the fragments. These vessels are extremely rare, and it is possible that this is only the fourth recorded (for the Roman period). In the illustration the projection on the top of the head

The remainder of the fragments (fig. 78) consists of colour-coated bowls f. 62 (1, 2), and beakers f. 94A (3–4). Of the bowls there are at least five examples, of the beakers over fifty. Some of the latter are exceptional. One is rouletted outside, and there are four of unusual fabric decorated with panels of applied white dots, which appear yellowish through the coating (4).

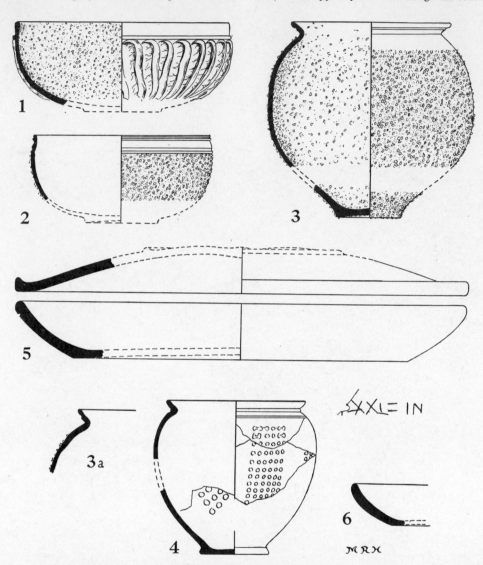

FIG. 78. Colour-coated ware from First Pottery Shop. Scale ½. [127], p. 155.

is entirely conjectural, but it is always present on the others, sometimes perforated.

The fragments have yielded one face very completely, but of the face on the reverse side only one ear is preserved. It should have been a bearded Silenus, as in the case of the other examples.[1]

A very similar vessel, in brownish-yellow ware, not coated, from the Trier kilns is illustrated in *Trierer Zeitschrift*, 1932, 42, Abb. 29. The second face is under the handle, the under side of the vessel bearing a palmette.

There are also a number of fragments of red coated platters f. 17B (6), and a few fragments of the lids used with them. The ware is creamy, very fine, and the coating (on the platters) is fine, but thin. The graffito illustrated is under the base of one of these.

There are a few chips of platters of Gallo-Belgic *terra rubra*. *Other coarse ware*. This is negligible, and may be intrusive. Six fragments of mortaria included two rims ff. 195A and 497; there was also the most part of a lid in white ware.

[1] Cf. S. Loeschcke, in *Haltern*, v, 195.

GLASS

By D. B. HARDEN, Ph.D., F.S.A.[1]

(FIG. 79)

A comparatively large quantity of glass in a very fragmentary state was found. It consisted mainly of the ordinary greenish or bluish-green glass as used in the first century A.D. for unguentaria, flasks, cylindrical and rectangular bottles, ollae, jugs, and open bowls and beakers. There was also, however, a number of fragments of dark blue or greenish pillar-moulded bowls, some

clear emerald green metal, cf. *Camulodunum*, no. 56, pl. 86. Glass of this turquoise-blue metal is sufficiently rare to make it worth while to record each specimen that occurs.

4. Fragment of rim and side of shallow bowl, opaque vermilion-red weathered to opaque cuprous green on both faces and on breaks, leaving only a core of red to indicate the original colour of metal. Mould pressed and rotary polished within and without. Sharp plain rim, convex side, flat base. Two wheel-cut lines on interior of base. Objects of this opaque vermilion-red glass are not rare in Egypt, but vessels made of it are infrequently met with. The transmutation of the red colour is due to

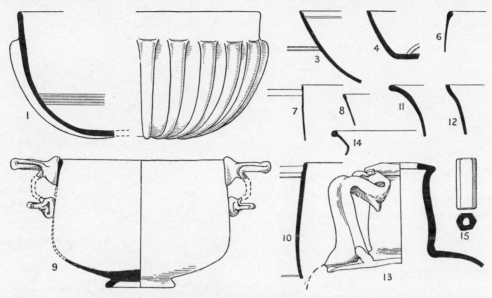

FIG. 79. Glass from the First Pottery Shop. Scale ⅓. [127], p. 157.

fragments of amber or dark blue jugs or flasks, a few fragments of bowls of yellow or colourless metal, and three pieces of opaque glass (one white—perhaps not ancient—one vermilion red and one turquoise blue).

Much of the glass was fused by heat into amorphous lumps and of the remainder much consisted of body fragments from vessels whose shape was not recognizable. It has therefore proved impossible to make anything approaching an inventory of the shapes that existed in this shop and we must be content with listing a few of the pieces that are interesting by reason of their shape or technique.

1. Seven fragments of rim and side, all perhaps from the same pillar-moulded bowl, bluish-green, mould pressed and rotary polished within, fire polished without. Heavy ribs spreading to under side of base, four wheel-cut lines on interior near bottom of side. Ht. 2⅝ in. Diam. 3¼ in.

On pillar-moulded bowls cf. *Camulodunum*, nos. 61 ff., pp. 301 f.

2. Nine fragments of rim and side, all perhaps from the same pillar-moulded bowl, dark blue. Shape and technique as no. 1, but only two wheel-cut lines on interior.

3. Two fragments of rim and side of shallow bowl, opaque turquoise blue with cream-coloured weathering flaking off, mould pressed and rotary polished within and without. Sharp plain rim, convex sides. Wheel-cut at rim on interior, two wheel-cuts on exterior of side. For the shape and technique, but in

red oxide of copper (A. Lucas, *Ancient Egyptian Materials and Industries*, 3rd ed., p. 218).

5. Fragment of side of bowl (?), opaque white. Free-blown. Shape of vessel uncertain. This may be modern and not Roman. It is more translucent than the other pieces of ancient opaque white that I have seen; yet it is weathered on both surfaces and on the edges. For Roman opaque white fragments cf. *Camulodunum*, pp. 298 and reff. ad loc.

6. Fragment of rim of bowl, colourless. Free-blown. Weathered to a frosted surface. Rim thickened in flame, sides slightly convex. This type of colourless bowl with thickened rim did not occur on the 'Camulodunum' site and is usually considered to be mainly of second- to third-century date. Its occurrence here is therefore instructive, as indicating that the type began earlier than has previously been thought.

7. Fragment of rim and fragment of side of bowl, colourless. Free-blown. Rim ground smooth, vertical sides. Broad wheel-cut on exterior at rim. Fine metal, very thinly blown. That colourless glass began to be made in quantity during the middle of the first century A.D. has recently been made clear by finds in London (Walbrook: finds in Guildhall Museum) and abroad (Locarno: C. Simonett, *Tessiner Gräberfelder*). This piece and the next are not, therefore, out of context.

8. Fragment of rim of bowl, colourless. Free-blown. Iridescent. Rim rounded in flame, sides taper slightly downwards. Fine metal, thinly blown.

[1] I am greatly indebted to Dr. Harden for giving his valuable time and knowledge to supply this section.

9. Four fragments of handle, rim, and base of handled bowl, yellow. Free-blown. Iridescent. Rim thickened in flame, sides vertical and slightly convex, flattened bottom with pad base-ring. Drawn handle with nipped thumb-piece at top. This shape is completely typical of the first century A.D., being found in metal, pottery, glass, and glazed ware. Glass examples are normally better made and of better glass-metal than this one, which is roughly made of common yellow glass.

10. Fragment of rim and side of carinated bowl, bluish-green. Free-blown. Dulled and iridescent. Rim ground smooth, sides convex. One broad and one narrow wheel-cut on exterior at rim, single wheel incision below carination. This type occurred at the 'Camulodunum' site, op. cit., p. 303, no. 68; see note ad loc. indicating that it is very typical of the mid-first century.

11. Rim fragment of bowl, bluish-green. Free-blown. Iridescent. Poor metal, bubbly and showing striations. Rim outsplayed and thickened in flame, sides taper downwards. Shape of complete vessel uncertain. The type did not occur at the 'Camulodunum' site and is not typical of the first century, so that the piece may be a later intrusion.

12. Rim fragment of bowl or beaker, bluish-green. Free-blown. Poor, very bubbly metal. Rim knocked off and ground smooth, sides taper downwards. The rim resembles that of Camulodunum no. 77 (op. cit., p. 303, pl. 88), but this piece has no trace of wheel incisions. The bubbly glass hints at a later date than first century and the piece may be intrusive.

13. Rim, neck, and handle of cylindrical bottle, bluish-green. Blown into a cylindrical body-mould. Iridescent. Rim folded inward, cylindrical neck with constriction at base, two-ribbed, drawn handle from rim to shoulder. The type, which occurred at the 'Camulodunum' site (op. cit., p. 306), is common and requires no discussion here.

14. Rim and neck of squat-necked jar, amber. Free-blown. Iridescent. Lip outsplayed, rim folded upwards and inwards. Amber glass is typical of the first century, though the colour occurs in later centuries also.

15. Bead, bluish-green, hexagonal, with cylindrical boring. The sides and ends ground smooth and the edges at the ends bevelled. A very finely made bead. Length 1 in. Diam. $\frac{3}{4}$ in.

It will be noted from the above list that though many of the types found here were paralleled at the 'Camulodunum' site this is by no means an invariable rule. Moreover it is noteworthy that there were only two or three pieces of early fine wares, and that none of the early polychrome wares so well represented at Camulodunum were found here. The stock-in-trade of this shop seems to have been predominantly, if not exclusively, the common blown glass—mainly bluish-green—of the period.

Jet. A fine jet pin, $1\frac{3}{4}$ in. long. The shaft runs through the hemispherical head and has three grooves about its middle (fig. 77, 6).

Stone. Four almost spherical objects of sandstone (pl. XXII, A). Each has one flattened side which looks as if it had been used as a rubber. They are perhaps pestles. Diam. about 3 in.

The pottery when examined in detail[1] gives the following results:

The decorated sigillata is pre-Flavian, more Neronian than Claudian. The plain ware, with the stamps, covers the period A.D. 45–65 approximately. Although it must be allowed that a shop may be burnt at any time, the natural idea that this one was burnt in Boudicca's sack of the town in A.D. 60/61 is supported by the fact that the site was not cleared up in the usual manner. Apparently the heaps of rubble were merely levelled for the next use of the site.

[1] *T.E.A.S.* xix, 277–87.

There remains for mention a number of shapeless pieces of lead and bronze, several of them fused, also lumps of a black vitreous substance, possibly pitch or bitumen (or, it has been suggested, commercial charcoal), and several small coins so burnt and corroded that even their century is dubious. There is a number of the short, perforated bone cylinders, which are held to have been used as hinges.

Of the later period of the site we know little. The remains were very few. They comprise a second brass coin of Hadrian with illegible reverse, and three mortarium-rims of late-second-century date. A later period still is represented by coins of Tetricus; Urbs Roma (2); Constantinopolis (2); a small Constantinian; one Gratian and an illegible bronze of the late fourth century. There was a little pottery to match the coins.

Wire's notes on this insula are few. The old Moot Hall was pulled down in 1843, and from the work for the new one Wire secured 'a lot of 2nd brass Roman coins . . .' (5/9/43), but he was forbidden access to the site by Alderman Vint and there was a clause in the contract claiming all antiquities found as the property of the Town Council.[2] The second Town Hall was pulled down and the present one built in 1901; a number of small objects then came into the Museum, but there is no record of any structural remains having been encountered, except for the plan mentioned on p. 151.

In 1856 drains for the Cups Hotel were cut through the Vegetable Market and were watched by Wire (7 to 14 May), who noted rubble and one piece of foundation. Coins collected then and subsequently comprise a sesterce of Germanicus, another of Trajan; three illegible third brass, and a few of the late empire. There was also a fine bone stylus. Add a coin of Antonia; a dupondius of Trajan, a coin of Constantine II, and one of Magnentius.

INSULA 20

The boundaries of this insula are merely inferred from the general conjectural grid. It should have measured about 330 by 330 ft. The N.–S. street on the east side has probably been seen under no. 119 High Street (p. 72).

31. Wire's Diary, 25/11/1842: 'A labourer . . . pulling down the Bear public house, corner of High Street and East Stockwell St., informs me that in digging for the new house on the spot a Roman pavement was discovered composed of different coloured tesserae, which shared the same fate as others found here . . . broken up and the tesserae were taken away by the proprietor, Mr. Catchpool.'

Ibid. 5/1/43: 'Mr. Jenkins, builder, who assisted in taking down the Bear Inn informed me that the tessellated pavement . . . was six feet below the surface, three feet long and six inches wide [sic!] and taken away by Mr. Catchpool. . . .'

Ibid. 29/3/43: 'When digging a cellar for the house where the Bear Inn stood, some Roman brass coins were found of the Constantine family, but in so bad a condition as to be worthless.'

Ibid. 13/1/45: 'Mr. Clark, bricklayer, informs me when digging to enlarge the cellar of the Bear Inn . . .

[2] Diary, 29/6/1843; 4/8/43 to 14/8/43.

he came upon a circular building between 20 and 30 ft. in diameter. In consequence of the almost impossibility of breaking it up the cellar was left at its original depth. The premises occupied by Mr. Dennis stand where the Inn did.'[1]

Obviously the whole circle was not seen and the building may have been an apse.

of the walls. The few coins were mostly illegible, but included a small Urbs Roma. The pottery was negligible.[2]

131. In October 1926 Mr. E. J. Rudsdale observed the remains of a wall running N.–S. by the east side of East Stockwell Street on the present site of Messrs. Cullingford's printing-works.

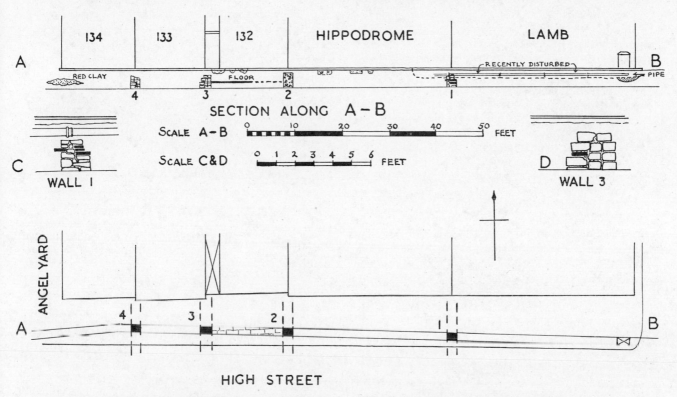

FIG. 80. Plan to show Roman walls crossing under the north pavement of High Street. **[124]**, p. 159.

124. A trench for a gas main, cut in 1927 along the north pavement of High Street, cut through a series of Roman walls (fig. 80). At the junction of the Lamb Hotel and the Hippodrome a brick and rubble wall, 2 ft. thick, was found 18 in. below the pavement. Similar walls were found opposite the boundary of no. 132 and the Hippodrome Café, between nos. 132 and 133, and between nos. 133 and 134. That between nos. 132 and 133 was 2 ft. 6 in. thick, built of brick and septaria slabs about 18 in. long, those on the outside squared off. Seven or eight tiles 'laid like a floor' were found between the café and no. 133. There was no wall at the entrance to the Angel yard, but a mass of brick and clay about 8 ft. wide was found.

No stratified finds were made, except for an antoninianus of Gallienus, said to have been found *under* one

168. In 1903–4 the site was cleared for the present Hippodrome, involving the destruction of the premises of Tabrum and Jones. The Museum has a hollow tile then found built into Roman foundations (600.04). Most of the pottery passed into the hands of Mr. List, antique dealer. The coins included Claudius (2); Vespasian (2); Hadrian (?); Cl. Gothicus; Carausius (?); Allectus; Constantine Gt. (2); Valens, and four illegible small bronze. In the next year a complete jar was found (961.05), which may have been a foundation-pot, part of a bronze finger-ring with intaglio, and six more coins, one being of Faustina (984.05). Among the pottery is an Arretine fragment, f. 15/17 (*Cam.*, p. 183, S6).

In October and November 1926 Messrs. Cullingford's printing-works were built. The Roman level was touched only in the deep stanchion-holes, at a depth

---

[1] Now Claridge's shop, no. 125 High Street.

[2] E. J. Rudsdale, in *T.E.A.S.* xix, 131.

of 9 ft. The only important objects found were some
illegible coins.

INSULA 21

The north boundary should approximate to St. Helen's
Lane or a little north of it. On the east lay the 'Forum'.
The dimensions should have been about 300 by 350 ft.

The following discoveries have been made.

32. A tessellated pavement was found and destroyed,
some time before 1907 in enlarging Messrs. Wicks's
wine-cellar, the next cellar west of the George Hotel.[1]

157. Another piece of red tessellated pavement was
found behind the south wall of the SE. cellar of the
George Hotel when alterations were made in 1936. A
section of it, with several layers visible below it, was
preserved behind glass for many years.

132. In 1927, when laying a gas main, a mass of pink
mortar about 4 ft. wide and 3–6 in. thick, tapering
towards the south, was found 2 ft. 6 in. below the surface in George Street just opposite the Oddfellows
Hall. (In the street, close to the kerb on the west, about
10 ft. from the corner.)

All that existed on the site of a supposed wall opposite 122 High Street was a large amount of fragments
of tile and rubble. A deposit of dark earth about 8 ft.
wide containing oyster-shells, pottery, bones, &c., was
cut through opposite 121A High Street.[2]

175. When the old premises of Messrs. Paull's (east
corner of George Street) were taken down a cellar was
made and three walls running parallel to High Street
were uncovered. The first, 2 ft. from the south boundary, was 2 ft. thick; it ran from George Street to half-
way across the property, where it broke off. North of
this lay the foundation of a tessellated pavement, extending for 18 ft. from George Street, and 19 ft. N.–S.,
from the first wall to the second. The second and third
walls formed a passage, parallel to High Street and
only 2 ft. 6 in. wide. The walls were only 1 ft. thick,[3]
and were seen in the middle part of the property only,
being broken at both ends. The foundation for the
pavement was over 1 ft. thick in front, but thinner at
the back; the middle portion seemed to have been
burnt, and was red: all was very rotten and covered
with a layer of clay (dirty and almost black), probably
representing the medieval floor.[4]

The small finds here included a block of stone with
moulded edge, measuring 11½ by 9½ by 6 in. (4638.23),
two fragments of marble slabs, and pottery.

INSULA 22

(PLAN, FIG. 81)

This exceptional insula is sufficiently outstanding, not
only in its area but also in the magnitude and importance of its buildings, to have been known for some
long time now as 'the forum', an identification advanced by Henry Laver,[5] though subsequent discoveries
both here and abroad have caused the question to be
reconsidered from time to time. It is still one of the
major problems of Roman Colchester, and the cele-
bration of the nineteenth centenary of the foundation
of the Colonia in 1950 was made the occasion for the
first controlled excavation on the site. The question
remains unsolved, though much more light has been
thrown upon it.

34. It can now be said that the conjecture of Wheeler
and Laver[6] that the great building under the Castle is
the substructure of the historic temple of Claudius has
been substantiated. The confirmatory evidence has
been obtained from time to time, but especially in the
excavations carried out in front of the Castle in 1932.
Accepting the identification of the building, we are
bound to consider whether the whole array of buildings
on the site did not belong to the temple and its appurtenances. If this is so then the forum, or trading centre,
is to be sought elsewhere. At present no alternative
site for a forum presents itself; nevertheless, it seems
most probable that for the period over which the Provincial Council met in Colchester, at least, the square
round the temple would be reserved for religious and
ceremonial purposes.

It is at present uncertain what the shape and size
of this insula was. It is, or was, circumscribed by the
great ditch of the Norman Castle, which may or may
not have cut away Roman streets only. The conjectural plan advanced by Wheeler and Laver[7] left a small
insula (14) to the north of it. The block itself was conjectured to have been some 350 ft. E.–W. by a little
more N.–S. The east boundary is probably fixed firstly
by the apparent position of the N.–S. street on the
east side of insula 6 (p. 72) and then by the position,
almost dead opposite this corner, of the apparent and
visible NE. corner of the buildings under the Castle
rampart. We assume this identifies the east side of the
block. The position of the west side is anomalous. The
corner of walling found in 1892 by H. Laver has a long
wall running south, and this is assumed to be the west
side of the block and agrees with the observed position

[1] T.E.A.S. x, 89.

[2] Ibid. xix, 131.

[3] Stone footings only 1 ft. thick are not infrequent; they can
only have supported timber-framed walls.

[4] Laver, Diary, 30/12/1923. With sketch-plan.

[5] Essex Review, ii, 3—an almost prophetic remark! 'it seems

possible that the castle itself will still be proved to have been
built, at any rate, on a Roman foundation and probably represents the old Forum and Temple of Claudius.'

[6] J.R.S. ix, 146–7; x, 87 ff.

[7] Ibid. 145, fig. 15.

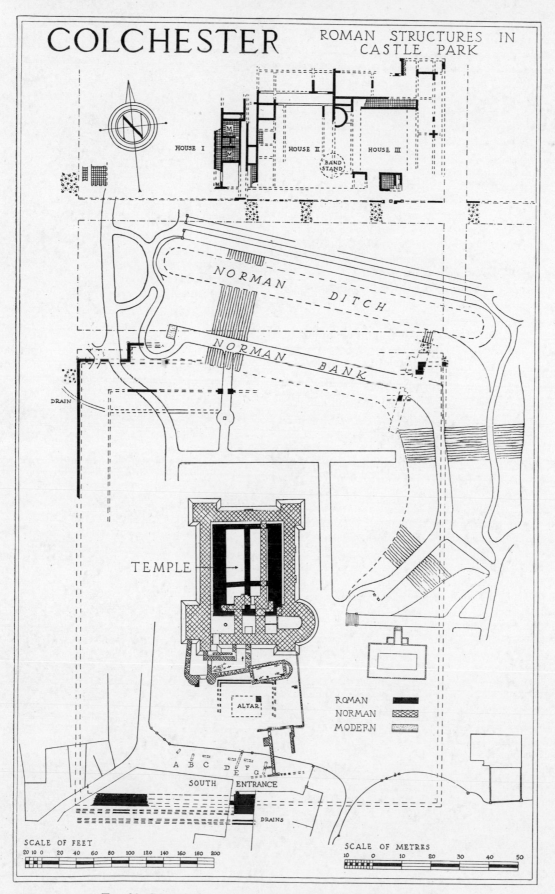

COLCHESTER

ROMAN STRUCTURES IN CASTLE PARK

HOUSE I   HOUSE II   HOUSE III

BAND STAND

NORMAN DITCH

NORMAN BANK

DRAIN

TEMPLE

ROMAN

NORMAN

MODERN

ALTAR

A B C D E F G

SOUTH ENTRANCE

DRAINS

SCALE OF FEET
20 10 0   20   40   60   80   100   120   140   160   180   200

SCALE OF METRES
10   0   10   20   30   40   50

FIG. 81. General plan of Insula 22 and part of Insula 6. pp. 160 ff.

of street metalling at the west side of insula 6 (p. 72). Outside this wall, in the Park shrubbery, is exposed the end of the vaulted drain reported by H. Laver in 1892. It was vaulted to run under the buildings, and also the street, remains of which have been observed to run over it. But a street on this line (which, it appears, we must accept) strikes the north wall of the town between the end of Ryegate Road and the gap in the wall in the Park, in which length the inner face of the wall is in perfect preservation, and where there has certainly never been a gate or tower. If this fixes the west wall of the insula the temple is sited about 18 ft. off centre towards the west. Another wall 18 ft. farther west would make the temple central, and would push the street over so that its continuation south of the High Street could miss the concentration of hypocausts and floors under Long Wire Street, but would not bring it far enough west to hit our conjectured position for the Roman Rye Gate. There is something yet to be explained here.

Assuming as facts the existence of road-metalling at the points stated, the width of this insula is not less than 426 ft. (from wall to wall, over all), which is quite exceptional, and seems to be shared by the blocks north of it.

The length N.–S. is now uncertain because, while a street has been found to come round the NE. corner, the NW. corner, formerly supposed to have been fixed by Laver, now proves to run a further 8 ft. north before turning east. We have, therefore, now no evidence as to the form of this side.

The south side was found in 1933, at a point where it was certainly encroaching some 15 ft., and perhaps even 28 ft., upon the line of the main E.–W. street. So the over-all dimension N.–S. cannot be less than 536 ft., which, in relation to the width, makes the whole rather too square to be classed with the great fora of Augst, Paris, and St. Bertrand de Comminges (see p. 189 below), but approximates to the proportions of the enceinte of the purely religious site on the Schönbühl at Augst.

The site is not, curiously, the highest point within the walls, and slopes gently down to the north. The northern half of it was made up nearly 5 ft. to obtain a level court round the temple.

THE TEMPLE OF CLAUDIUS

The *Colchester Chronicle* tells us that Eudo built the Castle of Colchester in 1076 on the foundations of the palace of Coel, 'formerly king'. Though the famous keep has been the study of many and learned antiquaries, who have produced many conflicting theories with regard to it,[1] it was not until 1920 that Wheeler and Laver remarked upon the fact that the vaults under the Castle belonged to an earlier and quite distinct building.[2] Morant[3] mentions them in his description of the demolition of the Castle by Weeley in 1683: 'These fine spacious vaults were full of sand, on which the arches were turned. The sand was taken out at considerable expense by John Weeley, who was endeavouring to pull the Castle down; and to carry off the sand he cut a cartway through the foundation wall near the NE. corner, where the wall is thirty feet thickness . . . .'[4] This passage-way (section, fig. 83) contains most important evidence which had been missed by all previous writers on the Castle, and which has been summed up as follows:[5]

'1. The vaulted substructure is independent of the Castle plan because:

a. A straight joint is visible between the two structures in Weeley's tunnel (fig. 82, A).

b. In this joint are traces of a pink cement facing which indicates that the north wall of the substructure originally had a free face (compare the cemented exterior of the Caerwent basilica).

c. The bricks visible in the tunnel . . . are apparently those of a formerly external lacing course.

d. Two enormous Norman walls (B, C) (one now reduced to its foundations) were thrown across the shoulders of these vaults at ground-level (see plan fig. 82 and fig. 83) in a manner which shows complete indifference to all laws of building construction, if we assume that, at the time, these vaults were standing free.[6]

It is not merely impossible that the Norman builders, generally overcautious, built these upper walls without first securing the disused vaults beneath them. The sand filling must surely date from this period.[7]

---

[1] The general consensus is that the Castle keep is Norman, built of Roman materials, between 1076 and 1086. There are two good accounts to be found of the building, the *History and Antiquities of Colchester Castle* (by J. H. Round), 1882, and the account by W. H. St. John Hope in *Arch. Journ.* lxiv (1907), 188 ff. See also F. M. Nichols in *T.E.A.S.* n.s. iii, 1 ff. and J. H. Round, ibid. 143 ff. Jenkins's amazing contention that the keep was the actual Temple of Claudius will be found in his '*Appendix to a Lecture on Colchester Castle with a reply to the animadversions of the Rev. E. L. Cutts*', 1853, and in *Colchester Castle a Roman Building* (a much more reasonable, though erroneous, publication) by G. Buckler, 1876. Another, who came close to the truth, was General Roy.

[2] *J.R.S.* x, 87.   [3] p. 7.

[4] This is an exaggeration, see fig. 82.

[5] R. E. M. Wheeler, in *J.R.S.* x, 88.

[6] The western wall (C) was completely taken down by Weeley. It had badly cracked the two vaults beneath it and partly settled. This would create sufficiently alarming rifts in the upper part of the keep to account for the decision to pull the Castle down. The amazing thing is that Weeley had his men cut away so much of the shoulders of the vaults. The podium only survives to its full height under the eastern partition wall. There is no doubt that Weeley did this demolition; the proof lies in the pieces of clay pipes found in the trenches cut by P. G. Laver.

[7] *J.R.S.* x, 88. We disagree profoundly. The Norman builders *did not know* the vaults were there. Nor can the vaults be called 'disused': they never were used at any time for any purpose.

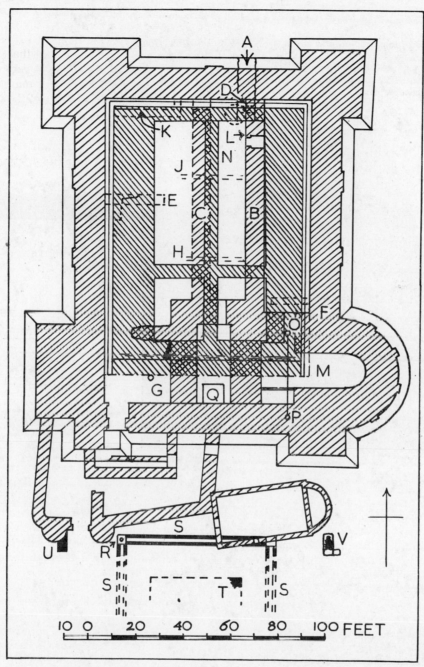

Fig. 82. Plan of Colchester Castle, with Roman vaults beneath, and Roman remains under chapel and forebuilding (shown black). [34 and 148], pp. 160–191.

e. The most cursory comparison of the building construction of the vaults with that of the remainder of the Castle makes it instantly clear that the two works are neither of the same date nor of the same epoch . . . .

'2. The substructure is, therefore, an independent work, and earlier than the Norman Castle . . . .

'3. Both the plan and the scale of the work put the Saxon period out] of court . . . the absence of any re-used material . . . constitutes strong independent evidence for a Roman and even an early Roman date.'

went about 4 ft. higher, and the uppermost foot was set back about 1 ft. from the main face. This is the only place where the recess for the upper moulding, corresponding to the plinth, has been seen.

Other cuts (E, F) made by Laver have proved that the inward projection of the Norman wall, which overrides the whole 3-ft. offset at the base of the Roman face, and is continued up to the level of the top of the

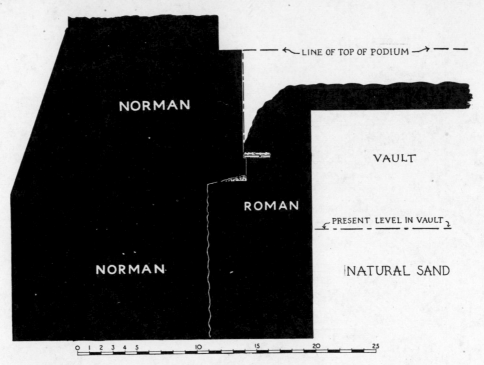

FIG. 83. Section through north wall of temple and of Castle. (Scale of feet.) [34], p. 162.

In fig. 83 the Roman ground-level is marked by a prominent offset 3 ft. wide, of which only part is probably foundation offset, for from this level there is a recess in the face 3–4 in. deep and rising 2 ft., which would very well accommodate a carved marble plinth running round the base of the podium. Below the offset, though the mortar of the two buildings is distinctly different, the junction of the Norman work with the unfaced Roman foundation is hard to follow.

Work done inside the keep (fig. 82) by P. G. Laver included a trench (D) a little west of our section, which showed that above the recess for the plinth the wall was 5 ft. 7 in. thick and had a facing of five courses of septaria, six of tile, and five of septaria, and the two lowest of the next band of tile. Unfortunately, the heights of the courses and the whole work are not given. Above this the face was not so well defined, but

podium, is to be found not only on the north but also on the east and west sides of the Castle, from which we *conjecture* that fig. 84 is a fair representation of the E.–W. section. On it the vaults, being accessible, are correct. The side walls have never been cut through, but the Norman offset has been seen here and there. In most places the Roman work has been broken out to a low level.[1] The width of the offset varies but little; it was shown to be 3 ft. 9 in. on the west in 1922 and the same on the east in 1932. The walls of the Norman keep are parallel, averaging 86 ft. 7 in. apart. The plan, fig. 82, after that in the *R.C.H.M.*, shows irregularity in the Roman foundations which could easily be rectified in the upgoing facings.

The south end of the podium lies under the Castle and is not well known. According to *R.C.H.M.* (p. 25) a small excavation made in the well-room (G)

[1] The only publication of this work by P. G. Laver, other than in Wheeler's and Laver's article, is in the somewhat superficial paper by A. M. Jarmin in *J.B.A.* n.s. xxviii, 203.

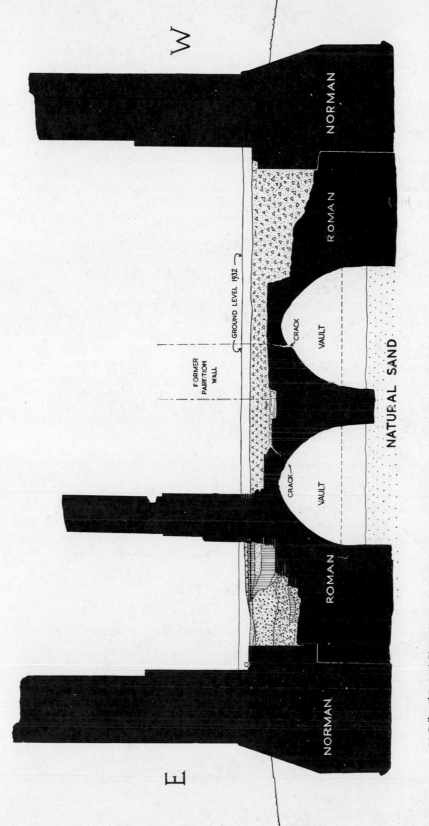

COLCHESTER·KEEP. MAY 1932. SECTION E~TO~W, ON ₵ 59FT FROM INTERNAL FACE N.WALL.

W

E

NORMAN

ROMAN

VAULT

CRACK

NATURAL SAND

GROUND LEVEL 1932

FORMER PARTITION WALL

VAULT

CRACK

ROMAN

NORMAN

0   10   20   30   40   50   60 FEET

Fɪɢ. 84. Colchester Castle, E.–W. section. [34], p. 164.

revealed the south exterior face: the small portion seen was wholly of tile. The thickness thus obtained for the south wall was 7 ft. 4 in. The stairs which now give entrance to the vaults (from the well-room) pass through a breach in the crown of the SW. vault and are partly cut into the south wall. The cut reveals the inner ends of the tiles of the facing, which must have run far back into the wall, as they did in one cut on the west side of the podium. They are continuous, not in bands.

The results of the trenches cut in 1922 by P. G. Laver are shown on plans left by him in the Museum, and these are partly incorporated in the *R.C.H.M.* plan. In 1933 he cut further trenches, one at right angles to the east wall of the keep (F) just south of the existing doorway. Here the Roman work had been robbed to a very low level. A drain-pipe lies upon the usual Norman offset, here 3 ft. 9 in. wide. Other trenches (H, J) cut up to the west face of the remaining Norman partition wall revealed the top of the podium, where protected by the base of the wall.[1] In 1925 the NW. angle was opened (K), and here the Norman offset was greater than usual, showing, it was thought, that the podium must have had a gap in it at that point. The face was again seen 36 ft. south at E. In each case the interval between the Roman face and the (upgoing) Norman face was about 3 ft. 6 in.

Knowing that there was a classical temple erected to the honour of Claudius here in Camulodunum in the year 50, and having before us a most unusual and massive Roman foundation, which certainly could be the podium of such a temple, and which clearly stood in a square with Roman buildings all round it, there is some reason to suppose that we have the actual structure mentioned by Tacitus and Seneca.[2] Further evidence for this will emerge later. In the meanwhile let us consider the monument as it has come down to us.

Such platforms were designed to raise the temple well above the general ground-level, and in districts where material was plentiful they were sometimes made solid. In Essex, however, the shortage of stone for building and for mortar has always been acute. There is nothing strange in the fact that the builders, here as often elsewhere, decided to save a large bulk of stone by making large vaults within the platform where there was no great weight to be superimposed.

The foundation trenches for the outside walls and the cross-wall were carried 13 ft. down into the soft yellow sand, with a maximum width under the side porticoes of 16 ft. These trenches were revetted or shuttered with timber supported by stout uprights measuring about 8 by 7 in. (pl. XXV, B). The trench was then filled with masonry, and the timber remained in position. After rotting it has left chases in the walls at intervals of about 5 ft. The foundation for the central wall, having little weight to carry, was taken down much less (pl. XXV, C and fig. 84) and did not have wooden uprights.

The sand from these great trenches was piled up and compacted on the inside and rounded off so that the vaults could be turned upon it. Boards were laid along the steep parts of the haunches, and the marks of them, about a foot wide, can still be seen in the vaults. But as soon as a point was reached where the sand would lie in position without boards their use was discontinued, and the masonry was laid directly upon the sand. The upper part of the vault shows in many places full proof of this in the way the masonry has sunk into the sand. In this way the need for timber centring was avoided. No opening need have been left in any vault, and none seems to have been left from one to another. The suggestion that they were filled with sand some time after completion is thus quite unnecessary.[3]

The vaults are four in number, two long ones underlying the cella and two short ones the *pronaos*. The former are 61 ft. long internally, the eastern 20 ft. 6 in. wide, the western 21 ft. 6 in., the latter are 27 ft. 6 in. long, and divided from the former by a cross-wall 5 ft. thick. The longitudinal dividing wall is 5 ft. 9 in. thick. The angles are not always exact right angles, as the *R.C.H.M.* plan shows, but are good enough for foundation work. The vaults are built of ragstone[4] rubble and their curve is that of a very irregular ellipse with flattened sides. The masonry of the cross-wall alone is somewhat crudely coursed in the upper part, with very large blocks of a rather different stone, perhaps sandy clunch from the Orwell. The thickness of this wall is considerably reduced upwards.

In our fig. 83 it can be seen how carefully the Normans built on the Roman masonry. The joint is so clean that it must have been washed down first. All limestone or marble would have been stripped off first to burn for lime. In the complete absence of any kind of entrance to the building they must have concluded that it was quite solid. That accounts for the structurally unsound position of the walls they built upon it, which ultimately cracked it.

From the end of the seventeenth century the keep

---

[1] There is a detailed description of the masonry in the Diary, 7/4/1932.

[2] Augst had two classical temples and some other large continental towns probably had; it is, however, audacious to suggest that Colchester could have more than one.

[3] *Pace* Wheeler in *J.R.S.* ix, 147; cf. Nichols, in *T.E.A.S.* n.s. iii, 6.

[4] The most part is of septaria stone, one at least of which has barnacles adhering, and very many are water-worn, obviously from a beach. There seems to be no Kentish Rag or Tufa.

stood almost entirely roofless and exposed to the weather. The only exit for all rain-water falling within the walls was through the vaults, and as time passed the mortar was deteriorated by the water, till under the exceptional rains of October 1931 the vaults, now cracked in many places, began to subside. With the advice of the Ministry of Works immediate steps were taken; concrete cross-walls had unfortunately to be added, and steel and concrete struts laid horizontally to brace the remaining Norman cross-wall against the west outer wall of the keep, thus relieving the turning movement on the central wall of the vaults. The cracks were grouted with liquid cement, of which they swallowed nearly 100 tons.[1] Since then the whole keep has been roofed over by the Town Council, after discussions which had lasted over a century, and the whole should be safe for the future.

We may now consider what this building looked like from the outside. The sections show that the flat top was almost exactly 11 ft. above the Roman ground-level, and that this coincides with the level of the Norman offset and the base of the existing Norman interior wall. The exact nature and height of the top of the podium cannot now be recovered. If it was of marble, as is probable, it would be robbed. The uppermost part left *in situ* is the bedding for the floor, consisting of small pieces of ragstone, septaria, and broken tile laid in a mortar rather whiter and of better quality than that lower down. This only exists in places where it has been protected in some way. The remains of the south end of the western Norman cross-wall stand upon an irregular surface of white mortar, from which a pavement may have been removed. In the section (fig. 84) the Norman footing of the remaining cross-wall can be seen standing upon the Roman work, which has been robbed to the limit. In one place there was a patch of rough foundation work, no doubt a Norman levelling-up of the top of the podium. The upper foot of the Roman work is of much finer quality than the rubble concrete below, and contains some tile.[2] The same can be seen in the break in the vault where the modern stairs descend in the well-room.

Pl. XXXI, A was taken at about L on the plan, looking east. Here matters are different. Four distinct courses of tile can be seen, the upper three forming a straight joint or step, and some less certain remains of tiles, above and to the right, seem to belong to the same construction, whatever it was. On the right is seen part of some more Norman levelling, and the five courses of the Norman footing can be seen reducing to four over the tiles. The masonry filling to the left of the

tiles does not look Norman in character, but neither does it match any of the Roman work.

It is little use to try to conjecture what the remains at this point represent. It is possible that they formed part of the masonry for the alcove for the cult-statue. It is perhaps more likely that they were connected with the interior architectural decoration; or it is even possible that they represent some alteration of the building carried on the podium, if and when its original purpose was abandoned.

The actual level of the finished floor of the podium must have been within a foot or so of the base of the east cross-wall, and this is very little below the Norman interior offset, with which it may have been level before it was robbed. On the other hand, the Normans, to some extent at least, laid a floor of Roman tiles, presumably throughout, but we have only seen it in trenches cut in the vaults of the sub-crypt (fig. 85, plan, M), where it was no less than 18 in. thick and most definitely post-Roman. A few tiles, with mortar backing, still lie in position at N on the plan.

The section O–P (fig. 85) was cut with great difficulty and by artificial light, in the small prison in 1931. Its direction is N.–S. It was made through a limited gap found in the Norman tile floor. At a depth of 20 ft. 6 in. we had to abandon the attempt to reach the bottom of the keep wall. The latter, on the left, was 12 ft. thick, with a small offset of some 3 in. Then came the usual interior offset, here at its maximum yet observed, 6 ft. Seven feet 8 inches lower there was a further offset of a foot, and nearly 8 ft. lower yet another, of a few inches of rough mortar. The wide offset coincides once more with the level of the Norman floor (eight courses of Roman tiles, seen on the right). We have assumed that this thickness, seen in both sides of our trench, and again in the adjoining prison to the east,[3] continued so over the podium, but this is, of course, not necessary.

Beneath the Norman floor the south front of the Roman work consisted of eleven courses of thick tiles with rather open joints, as if the mortar had weathered out. The eleventh course from the top projected a little, as if indicating a level. Below the tiles rough masonry, similar to that of the vaults, projected forward another 13 ft., sloping down to the south and ending in a nose only a foot high. We were unable to tunnel under this to find the outer (south) face of the wall of the podium, which remains unseen, unless it is visible in the well-room.

The evidence from the whole of the south face of the

[1] There were many cavities in the Roman work due to the concrete having been put in very dry, so that there was more to fill up than the cracks.

[2] Good photographs of all this were taken and can be seen in the Museum.

[3] Note that the prisons are not over the podium proper.

temple is very deficient. There is uncertainty about the total thickness of the south wall of the podium, which may have been ascertained in the well-room[1] (p. 164).

What they conceal we do not know, but it seems at least probable that a continuous flight of steps did not cover the whole front, and that this pit may occupy the

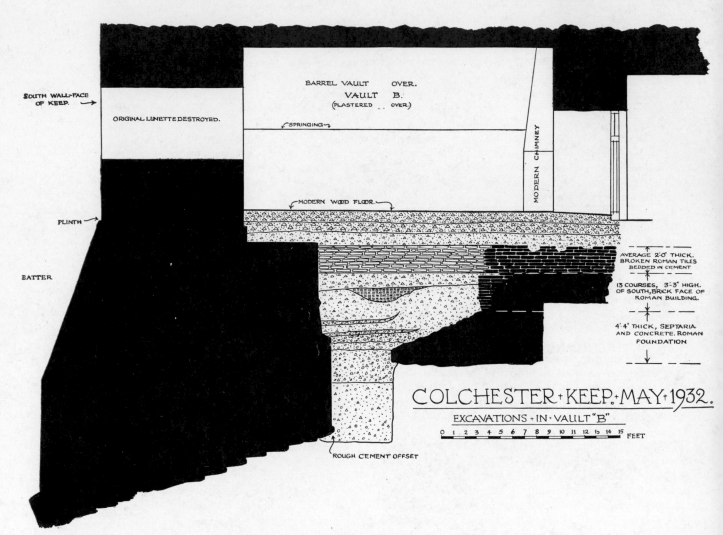

FIG. 85. Section in Small Prison on line O–P. [34], p. 167.

It is clear from the section just described that, in some parts at least, the Castle wall on this front is not built close against the podium as it is elsewhere. This is no set-back to the temple theory, but rather supports it. There were many ways in which the steps of a temple of this type might be arranged, and most of them would involve some breaking of the line of the front. In the central (Norman) vault of the south side of the Castle there is a large pit in the floor (Q on plan) 14 ft. 6 in. wide N.–S. Its walls are of large stones without mortar.

position of a large gap or recess in the plan of the steps.

What happened to the temple after its destruction in A.D. 61 we do not know. Presumably it was repaired or rebuilt on the same platform and of the same magnitude. The ruins could hardly be left as a perpetual monument to the success of Boudicca, even though there is some slight and inconclusive epigraphical evidence that the imperial cult was eventually transferred to London.

[1] The only record is in *R.C.H.M.* The original record has perished.

The Court and Buildings around the Temple

It is the northern part of the insula which has been the best and longest known, but it will be best for us to begin with the south side, so that we may suitably conclude with the excavations of 1950.

33. Little or nothing was known of the south side until 1931, when a flood of light was thrown upon it. We had already Wire's note of (19/6/1851): 'Visited the sewerage works in the street leading to the Castle [Museum St.] by Mr. Crosse's, broker. The foundations of the outer wall of the castle was discovered about 18 ins. below the surface and though built of the same materials as that structure it was a very difficult matter to break it up. I always thought the entrance to the Castle was here, but it could not be, as the remains testify. Upon an examination of an old map I find it was somewhere about Messrs. Joslin's workshop, Maidenburgh Street.'

We do not know what old map this was, and we do not know where the Norman entrances were. Morant (p. 8) says: 'The Bailey was formerly encompassed on the south and west sides by a strong wall, in which were two gates. That on the south was the chief. This wall was taken down by Robt. Northfolk Esq. who erected in the room of it a range of houses now standing in the High Street.[1] The west wall reached as far as the east side of St. Helen's Lane. On the north and east sides the castle was secured by a deep ditch and strong rampart of earth. . . . This rampart is thrown upon a wall that formerly encompassed either the Castle or Palace of Coel, on the site whereof the Castle is built; the buttresses and other parts of which wall have lately been discovered.'[2]

114. The demolition of some of Northfolk's houses in 1931 made a space accessible almost opposite the centre of the south face of the Castle. By the kind permission of the owner, the late Mr. Alfred Crowther (who also defrayed the expense),[3] we were able to secure invaluable information (plan fig. 81, and fig. 86). The site is on the line of the southern Norman rampart. Almost immediately under the surface we came on masses of pink mortar and masonry; and the section (fig. 86) makes it clear that this was the summit of remains which had proved too difficult to demolish completely, and that the Normans had piled the gravel of their rampart over them, exactly as elsewhere around the bailey.

As the work proceeded the massive nature of the masonry was only gradually revealed. The space for work was very limited, and it was impossible to obtain really good photographs. It is hoped the careful drawings will make up for this.

The upper part of the masonry ran N.–S., faced on the west side, broken away on the east, but still 5–6 ft. thick and 6 ft. high. On the north end there was also a face, to which was partly engaged a column, 2 ft. 6 in. in diameter, but with remains of a thick pink plaster in the angles, which would make it nearly 2 ft. 10 in. in diameter, that is 3 Roman feet. This plaster made it impossible to follow the bonding of the masonry in the angles between wall and column.

The west face of the masonry consisted mostly of small squared blocks of tufa, about 9 by 3 in. on the face. Eight feet from the north face a wall returned westwards. This was at least 5 ft. thick, the courses of its north face corresponding with those of the first wall. The south face was destroyed, which makes the exact thickness uncertain.[4]

South of this wall the west face of the first wall continued, but was now entirely of the small blocks of tufa, with a piece of tile here and there. The face north of the return wall is very different. Most noticeable in it is the bold course of large blocks of basalt (resembling Andernach lava), which are of a blue-grey colour, of varying length, and 8 in. thick. Above and below are courses of tufa and of tiles, in no very regular order. The tiles are 17 by 11½ by 3 in. (as used in the NE. angle of the insula), except in one course under the lava, where they are only the normal 1½ in. thick. The same mixture of materials is employed in the column, but the lava course is only 4 in. thick. The tile used here is broken pieces of the large segmental-shaped tiles frequently found in the town. Pieces of these also occurred in the concrete core of the masonry.

The mortar and plaster, except in the concrete core, is pale pink, full of crushed tile.

Though massive in itself this masonry is a mere shadow of what it has been. Determined efforts have been made to undermine or fell it from every direction and have wrought much damage. But a great deal remains below this level, where there is nearly another 5 ft. of solid masonry. The west face of this could not be examined, but the south (fig. 86; pl. xiv, A) was uncovered and showed six courses of squared septaria, very carefully built. The height was 2 ft. 6 in. There was an offset of 9 in. at the original ground-level, below which were three more rough courses and a foot of concrete foundation. Against this was the only useful

---

[1] Only one, no. 96, is now left.

[2] Morant omits mention of the ditch on the south and west sides. Northfolk had already filled it in. It is interesting to note that some of the Roman walls had been found before Morant wrote (1748). They are mentioned by Speed (1610), and Jenkins

says they are mentioned by Fosbroke, i, 79.

[3] Contributors to expenses of the later work are acknowledged in *Essex Review*, xli, 125.

[4] It was not possible to examine the foundations of this E.–W. wall.

small find, a T.S. cup base, f. 29 (?), stamped (P)ATRICI, but with no decoration preserved. The date is Nero–Domitian, which is not unexpected (fig. 99, 26).

On the north side the foundation had no finished face as on the south, but only consisted of rough rubble-concrete obviously intended to be underground.

whole plaque, which, with part of another, was found at the Union House about 100 years ago and drawn by Josiah Parish. The originals are lost.[1]

The demolition of the adjoining house to the east enabled us to follow the foundation in that direction. It proved to continue across the site and under the next

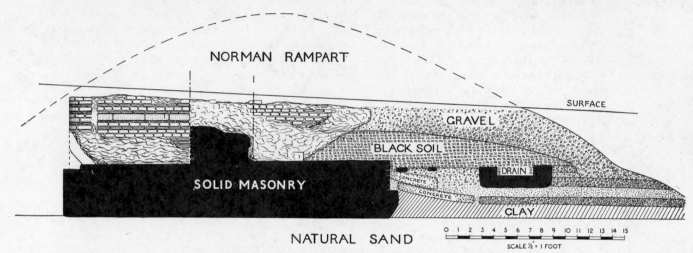

FIG. 86. Section, centre of south wing of Forum. [114], p. 169.

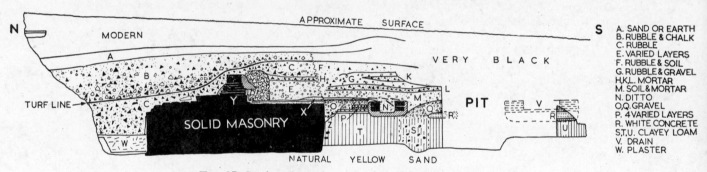

FIG. 87. Section through south wing of Forum, 1953. p. 171.

The ground-level on this side must have been about 2 ft. higher than the original street-level outside, but this difference would disappear after successive additions to the roadway.

Over all from north to south this foundation is no less than 28 ft. wide.

The core of the upstanding masonry was a rubble concrete, roughly coursed. Among it was found a fragment of a shaped and moulded plaque of terracotta (*Cam.*, fig. 66, 2). The left edge is rounded as if meant to fit some small architectural feature. Similar fragments have been found among the debris of A.D. 50–60 on the Camulodunum site. On pl. XXX, A we illustrate a

premises. It continued exactly as shown in fig. 86, where marked 'solid masonry', for an unknown distance eastwards: the total length uncovered by us was 26 ft.

The impression obtained was that this structure had been quite solid, with no chambers inside it, and that the first piece which we struck was the only portion which had defied the stone-robbers. This impression may prove wrong, but there was certainly no trace of internal spaces on the almost level surface of the platform which remains, and this is 2 ft. 6 in. above the original ground-level, where they should make some showing.

[1] The style is that of the 'Colchester Vase', which is of *c.* A.D. 200, but this need not date this plaque. We know of no parallel, but have not seen the continental plaques. Plaques of this nature

from an oppidum at Orgon (Provence) and another at Substantion (Hérault) are described in *Bull. Ant. France*, 1943/4, 380 ff.

33. The wall, mentioned by Wire, in Museum Street, has been seen several times by P. G. Laver, and also by the writer. It lies, probably, close to the SW. angle of the insula, but the remains seen are broken, so that they could belong to either the N.–S. or the E. W. wall. It seems almost certainly to have been part of a western continuation of our return-wall, and if so we are entirely without the Norman wall of which Morant speaks. We pass on to another piece of information. It is from a manuscript description by P. G. Laver of an abortive excavation by the Morant Club. A trench was cut northwards from the north kerb of High Street, on the site of the War Memorial 'opposite All Saints Church', so that it must have been at the west end of the site, a little west of **113**. 'The trench (largely interrupted by old cellars), was 15 ft. 10 ins. deep at the S. end, and 17 ft. at a point 21 ft. N. of this. Orders were then received that work must cease. The south end of the trench, next the pavement, showed [blank] ft. of made soil (containing nothing of interest), resting on a bed of yellow clay [blank] ft. thick. This clay was similar to that which we usually find here as a foundation layer under Roman buildings[1] and indeed, at one spot it was noted as being part of the foundation of the Roman predecessor of the modern High St. It is needless to add that such clay is normally foreign to the site.

'This clay rested on clean sand (it was on the sand under the clay that an early brooch was found in High St. in 1921).[2] At a point about 4 ft. from this S. end the sides of the cut began to show quite clearly such evidence as enabled a definite conclusion to be drawn. At a point about 4 ft. down a difference was noted in the material, that in the upper part being a filling composed of brick-rubbish mortar etc., below a brown earthy filling presenting evidence of gradual accumulation. This latter material had a sloping surface to the north, having a fall of 10 ft. in 16 ft., that is near the N. extremity of the cut, where, however, it was overlaid by a small bed of dark mud, somewhat greasy, and here the accumulated material had acquired a depth of about 6 ft. Below this was another bed of dark mud, wet, and 1 ft. 6 ins. thick, which rested directly on sand. The whole area beyond the first 20 ft. was of no interest till at a point 46 ft. from the pavement a mass of walling was discovered, but owing to its situation etc. its size could not be determined. This walling was obviously of early date — Norman.'[3]

There is no doubt at all that the above trench was cut across the Norman ditch of the Castle (the north

lip of which is seen in fig. 86) near its SE. corner; the walling, however, at 46 ft. from the pavement, falls into line with the Roman wall under discussion, while its position would appear to be rather too near the lip of the ditch to be Norman. There seems more than a possibility that it is Roman, in which case the alleged Norman wall on the south and west sides has never been found. One begins to wonder whether it ever existed.

Thus we have evidence for a wall about 5 ft. thick running along the south side of the insula. The exposure in Museum Street (**33**) may belong to its northward return at the west end.[4] The length is about 430 ft. In the middle is a massive foundation which can hardly be anything but a monumental entrance to the temple square. One has thought of a triumphal arch across the street, but the open drain and the part-engaged column (without die) are against this. The column could only have belonged to a colonnade, which could have run westward along the inside of the south wall or northwards towards the temple.

The street levels south of this central building have been described (p. 64). Between the latest recognizable Roman level and the under side of the Norman rampart lay a thick layer of intensely black soil, which must be attributed to the Dark Ages. It filled the gap left by the undercutting of the Roman masonry (see section, fig. 86). It was most remarkable that the undercutting was not connected with any layer of rubble. No trail of debris connected with this demolition work. The black soil was finely divided horizontally into many levels or layers, but, since nothing could be found in them, these counted for little.

The whole set-out here is remarkable. The building encroaches upon the line of the main street, pushing it southwards. The street is spoilt by the drain. One might conjecture that the building belonged, perhaps, not to insula 22 but to insula 30, but it appears to tie in with insula 22, and the section showing streets and pavements is not easy to transfer to the inner court of another insula, whether forum or baths.

THE KENT BLAXILL SITE

Part of the SW. corner of this insula suddenly became open to investigation owing to the destruction by fire of the western part of Messrs. Kent Blaxill's property in 1952. When the site had been cleared it was possible, with the cordial assistance of the owners, architect, and builders, to cut two trenches before work on building began and to watch all the builder's excavations

---

[1] It is the remains of daub buildings which preceded the more substantial later foundations.

[2] Unfortunately, we have no more exact information.

[3] Diary, 1/12/1921. Money was subscribed by the Museum

Committee.

[4] The exact point (**33**) is where the broken lines showing the W. limit of the Insula cut the N. kerb of Museum Street at the SW. corner of fig. 81.

attentively. The results are so important that they will require a separate report of some length, but a brief account must be included here (figs. 87, 88).

ditch of the Norman Castle, and the space between this ditch and the Roman foundation was largely riddled with cellars, pits, and wells, so that the other

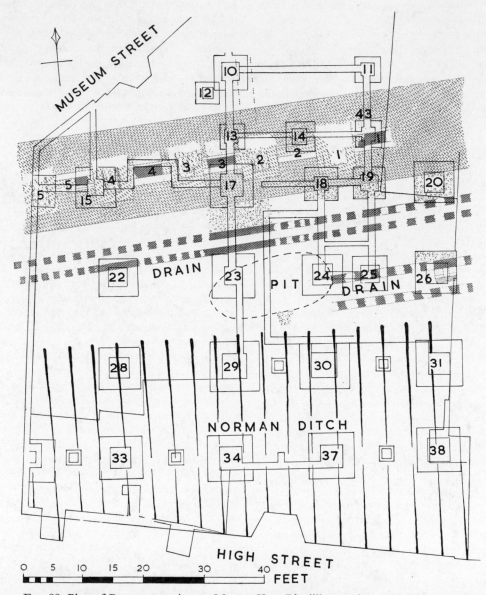

FIG. 88. Plan of Roman remains on Messrs. Kent Blaxill's premises. Colchester, 1953.
(*By courtesy of the Essex Archaeological Society.*)

The site lay astride the presumed line of the south front of the insula, and in fact the Roman work was found exactly where expected. It consisted chiefly of one continuous, massive foundation running east to west, 15 ft. wide and 4–5 ft. high. Its flat top served as a platform upon which an architectural screen in the form of an arcade had been built, facing south on to the main street. The latter had been removed by the

features to be mentioned were very much damaged, and were only partially uncovered.

Four feet 6 inches from the south edge of the platform there is a small open drain running parallel; it is 18 in. wide and 12 in. deep, the sides formed of two courses of stone, thinly plastered, the bottom of plaster only. At 16 ft. 6 in. from the platform runs a larger drain, also parallel. This is the same as that already described (p. 65), made of tiles and 3 ft. wide. Fragments only of this remained, but the identity of it was certain. We have assumed that its line was straight, and drawn our foundation to join the larger one farther east also at 16 ft. 6 in. from the drain. This orientation of the finds agrees perfectly with their incidence on the architects' plan of the new building.

The main foundation is of rounded cobbles of septaria laid in brownish mortar. Those in the face are roughly dressed to rectangular faces. Its flat top suggests the flat top noted farther east in 1933 was not accidental. The south face was well built and runs back in the lower part, as we have seen in fig. 86, but was not well finished or pointed and was not meant to be seen. It was covered by the deep layer of cheesy pug (T) which underlay the smaller drain, &c.

The remains of the building erected upon this platform show it as a series of separate units each about 6 ft. long, consisting of massive piers and short walls set alternately. The former had concrete cores which had been cased in fine ashlar of shelly limestone, at least around their lower part. In one case a block remained in position, and in most cases the mark of the blocks remained in the corework and in the very hard mortar on which they had been laid. The one stone left is a reused one.[1]

From pier to pier there had been arches formed of shaped voussoirs in tile, fragments of which arches were found, one fragment showing several courses of small septaria passing over the back (top) of the arch. At the back of each pier, presumably, there was a part-attached column built of coursed masonry, largely using the special segmental tiles. The most part of such a column lay shattered at full length behind one of the central piers. Everywhere there were remains of the material for columns, and it is possible that there had been a column in front of each pier.

The archways were closed by comparatively thin walls carefully built of tiles and septaria on a broader foundation with offsets. The walls we found appeared to be all different, but it is possible that one, which was removed so quickly that we got no details of it, would have proved to be similar to the one already noted. Yet in general scheme they were alike, for all had a steep and rather careless moulding of pink plaster along the north side, while the south side always shows two periods. In the first the offsets are covered by a skirting of fine white plaster, which itself has an offset in the middle. Later the floor was raised a foot and a new skirting was made consisting of a double moulding of red plaster. The differences lie in the thickness of the walls, which varies from 18 in. to 2 ft., and in the outline of the mouldings, especially the later one.

The floors north and south of the arcade have almost entirely perished. Parts of the northern one remain behind some of the piers, and I am told that its 3 or 4 in. of mortar are pink. This floor is very broken, and so is the outer margin of the platform, so that we have no idea what may have stood upon this part, if anything. The whole of this northern side of the building is roughly finished, compared with the south, and gives the impression that it was not meant to be admired. The ground-level is about 2 ft. lower than on the south, and the exposed face of the wall is faced with a rough plaster, the crude lower edge of which establishes the ground-level.

On the south side the top of the platform was levelled off with brown mortar which was finished with $\frac{1}{2}$ in. of fine pure white mortar. This seems to equate with the white plaster skirting, which certainly turned out at the bottom, as if to continue over the floor.

Presumably this floor became worn and it was decided to renew it; more brown mortar was laid over the white and by some means the floor was raised nearly a foot, up to the underside of the red plaster skirting. Fragments of a large block of Puzzolana about 6 in. thick have brown mortar on the under side and the upper side is smooth and glossy, as if it had carried a marble slab. But if this had belonged to the floor one would have expected to find more of it. On the other hand, this material is remarkably light, and it may have been used similarly, but in some upper part of the building.

However the floor was made, it seems probable that both it and the walls, or some part of them, were cased in marble, of which more hereafter. There were also very scanty remains in the rubble which call for note. Very occasionally there were found in the rubble core, or in paving, chips of bluish stone, probably lava, as found built into the masonry farther west. Two architectural fragments, one from a cornice and one from a string moulding, show badly weathered carving and a number of dowel-holes, as if they had had a replacement pinned over them. One stone bearing a recessed geometric pattern must have appeared on the façade. At least two pieces of Purbeck shale, shaped for building, were found, and some small building stones resemble granite. Very few pieces of marble were found in the rubble of the building; the vast majority of the pieces lay along the line of the smaller drain, mostly level with its top, but some were in the filling. The material is chiefly Purbeck, but there are red, yellow, white, and mottled marbles from Italy, Africa, and Greece. The pieces are mostly from sawn slabs, but a few are from carved panelling, and some in the form of leaves, tendrils, or geometric pieces are from inlaid

---

[1] The material has been identified as 'Forest Marble', but it is still under observation.

patterns. 'False Serpentine' is frequent among these. The slabs are thick or thin, presumably for floors and walls. The latter have small dowel-holes in the edges for the iron T-pieces by which they were secured to the walls. How or why these pieces lying along by this drain have been the only ones consistently missed by the stone-robbers is unexplained.

The following is a description of the section as shown in fig. 87 which is made up from the north end of one and the south end of another, about 10 ft. apart. The subsoil is soft yellow sand. At W there is a pit in this, which is full of hard white plaster, like that of the first skirting. This should be from a previous building, presumably the temple. On the south side the lowest layer is a thick make-up of soggy pug (T), which should be quite impervious, and would help to keep the drains watertight. At S this had been disturbed, and it was full of broken white mortar, probably from R. On top of this part lay a few sherds of mid-first-century flagon (f. 140). R is a fragment of a very good floor of white mortar, part of which was found 10 ft. farther west at the same level, but the most part of it had been destroyed by the large pit. Over this floor, here and farther west, lay remains of gravel road-metalling (Q), the first of which was certainly laid before the small drain N.

When the main foundation was built a few pieces of stone got into the pug (T) close to it, and at the top there was a space filled up with chips and mortar. The layers here (P and O) are very complicated. At P are four layers, each only about 2 in. thick; the lowest on the pug is of white mortar; the next is of clay mixed with chips of alabaster and septaria; the third is of chips of lava in red clay; the fourth of mortar. All are broken towards the wall. O is a gravel path with compacted surface partly worn away next the drain and with a layer of mud upon it.

But at other points the section is not so simple. Farther west it presented the appearance of a floor of white mortar running out from the platform to the drain, but dropping several inches, like a step, as it left the platform. Farther east it was noted that the hollow filled with rubble against the wall had been closed across the top with several inches of a mixture of mortar and wood shavings, which the builder's men recognized as a war-time expedient used in recent years. Here (the extreme east end of the site) a gravel surface seemed to continue to at least half-way across the platform, over the ruined pier; but this probably equates with E and N.

N is the layer filling the drain. It is of fine loam and fine mortar, with some rubble and gravel. In the drain it was soft, but on the whole it made a path of very uneven quality running into E. Now E flows round the cores of the piers, but in the trenches left by the robbers of the ashlar it consists of a fine comminuted mortar of a colour very distinct from that of the rubble cores. This helped much in recovering the limits of the ashlar. E also flows under the red plaster, filling the space beneath it very compactly; but it cannot be the original packing, for the under side of the plaster is quite smooth.

E could not have been deposited until the piers had been wrecked, but it is composite. It appeared that gravel had been laid down up to the level of the red plaster, replacing the upper floor, and upon this surface there was a deposit of fine black soil, which varied much in thickness from place to place. The same was noted lying on the concrete floor north of the arcade. This, then, was the state of affairs when the building was first demolished, an operation which left it as it now is and formed the rest of layer E, with a layer of rubble upon it, and the whole of layer C. All this is a confused series of tips and mounds of masonry and rubble lying on the disturbed black soil which had accumulated between the end of the Roman occupation and the demolition. In the black soil was a small amount of late-fourth-century pottery.

The whole bank of ruins is covered by a turf line separating C from B. Farther east it is indicated by the broken line at F, which covers more rubble-tips at G and K, belonging to the C group.

The second rubble-bank, B, is very distinct from the first. It is very loose, and there is a large proportion of lumps of chalk in it about the size of a man's fist. Towards the north side it is sometimes covered by a bank of yellow or red sand (A), and it appears that this bank must be connected with the digging of the Norman ditch and the completion of the Castle. It is difficult to see whence the rubble came, for it all lies above the turf line. The fact it is all Roman in character (except the chalk) means nothing on this site.

At the east end of the site the layer corresponding to O was a very carefully made path or road about a foot thick, of flint pebbles in pure white mortar, which did not extend over the edge of the platform; but here layer E was very gravelly, like a road, but with patches of mortar. But this did not extend north of the middle of the platform. Here, too, a patch of road against the north side of the large drain V was seen. It was strongly metalled with gravel, but nowhere in the whole length explored have we found any evidence of a way through the arcade.

The drain V could not be traced farther than a point opposite our easternmost pier, that is 115 ft. from where it was first found. Part of the north wall and floor remained. Only 10 ft. father west we reach our section (fig. 87) in which the pit has removed most of the evidence, but the small patch remaining at U shows that it has stopped or turned aside in this 10 ft. The position it would occupy if present is shown in broken line. This patch at U also shows the beginning of the excavation for the Norman ditch, with some alteration due to later pits and holes.

At U we have puddled pug, then a layer of 2–3 in. of grey clay, upon which lies a very good white concrete floor, 7 in. thick, with a smooth, flat surface, and upon this lies another 6 in. of gravel like road-metalling. The white concrete is, presumably, R again, which must have been quite extensive and flat.

Both the drains are additions to the first plan, whatever that was, and we have no evidence as to which drain comes first. The earliest work seems to have comprised the platform (in which no reused material was found), the pug T, the concrete R, and the composite layers at P. Whether all this was pre- or post-Boudiccan is not clear, for the plaster buried at W is still an isolated feature not yet noticed elsewhere and possibly accidental.

The arcade itself and the drain in front (N) contain reused material and may safely be regarded as post-Boudiccan. If the work had not gone farther than the laying down of the platform and T, R, and P, when the town was destroyed, we can imagine that when work was resumed the material from the ruined temple would have to be cleared away, and much of it could be used. Thus we find a reused ashlar in the casing of the piers, whole courses of damaged alabaster in the smaller drain, together with large pieces of white plaster moulding and a fragment of a carved wreath in sandstone. Broken marble from the temple would be burnt for lime, but the alabaster could not be so used.

Subsequent alterations are not many, but it is certain that the south floor was remade, with a red plaster moulding. The second drain may or may not belong to the same period. In any case there is a strong suggestion that the establishment was not abandoned after Boudicca, but actually only completed then, and remained in use long enough to require repairs and to receive them. It is to be noted, too, that this building was kept scrupulously clean: there is no deposit of rubbish of any kind until the fourth century, and all that was found could easily belong to a late period when the building had been abandoned. Only two coins were found, both quite unstratified; one was of Carausius, the other of Claudius.

THE ROMAN DRAIN AND ALTAR

148. Immediately before the south front of the temple and Castle, at 59 ft. from the latter and 92 ft. from the presumed face of the former, was uncovered a large,

well-dressed stone (fig. 82, R), measuring 2 ft. 5 in. long by 18 in. wide and $4\frac{1}{2}$ in. thick. In the centre was a round hole, $6\frac{1}{2}$ in. in diameter, with a $\frac{3}{4}$-in. rebate around it. The stone covered the corner of a vaulted drain SSS, in the manner of a manhole-cover, and the hole must have been provided for an iron grill or the end of a pipe (pl. XXVI, A).

The drain itself had been completely robbed from a point about 5 ft. south of the stone. The remains are well seen in the figure. The main construction was of small septaria and ragstones with some tile, mostly broken, with a tile vault, well executed; the interior walls were plastered. The general appearance was not in keeping with early Roman work, but the alignment with the main building is almost perfect, as will be seen below.

The position of the stone indicates, perhaps, a Roman surface-level, and the back of the vaulting, on the same level with it, is worn as by traffic. But we lack any evidence from any other spot for an old surface at this particular level (85 ft. above O.S. datum).

The walls of the drain completed a right angle, but the vaults were stopped off square where they met, leaving a square opening which was too large for the cover-stone.[1] The stone may be original, but when last placed in position it had been supported by odd stones carelessly placed without mortar, leaving spaces, which had been stopped by stones and tiles in a very insecure manner. Some of these easily fell away on the south side of the stone, as can be seen in the photo. On the left can be seen a large block of stone lying on the corner of the walls, which really formed the only secure prop for the cover. On the right is another large stone of irregular shape filling the space at the end of the eastern arm.

The drain is 18–20 in. wide and of about the same height plus the height of the vault. The floor is of tile, partly plastered over. This plastering has not been observed in other drains in Colchester, and, indeed, is more characteristic of water-conduits.

The eastern arm was traced on a course parallel to the south face of the temple, and was found to be 68 ft. in length (almost exactly 70 Roman feet). Where the wall of the Norman chapel crossed it the crown of the vault was broken and the wall of the chapel was taken down to the floor to secure a good foundation (pl. XXVI, B). This was close upon the eastern angle, where both vaults stopped as before, but concrete masonry remained in position, framing an opening and making a good bed for another stone cover, which, however, was missing. The drain continued away to the south and was not traced farther than shown on the plan.

[1] See p. 90.

Where the vault was preserved the drain was quite empty: it contained no silt, and no remains other than one fragment of a mortarium rim (fig. 23, B, 44) which is of late-first- or early-second-century date.[1]

The form of the drain, and general considerations, prompted a search for an altar, centrally placed. Time had become pressing, and only one hole could be dug. There was uncovered the NE. angle of a massive rectangular foundation of rough stones and mortar (T). It lay below Roman surface-level, and was clearly only a foundation. The northern edge had a well-defined rough face, the eastern looked as if a similar outer facing had been robbed. It lay 15 ft. 6 in. from the centre line of the drain on the north, and 14 ft. 6 in. from that of the drain on the east. If symmetrically placed it must have been about 33 ft. E.–W.; the other dimension remains unknown.

It is unfortunate that it was not possible to follow the drain farther south and so add to our knowledge of this interesting Roman plan, and that by this time the work on the Castle Hall had been filled in, for something may have lain under that.

THE ROMAN PEDESTAL

(Pl. XXVI, C)

The western tower of the entrance to the Norman forebuilding was found to stand partly upon a block of Roman masonry (U), finely built of tiles, with very little stone. It was not possible to reach the north end of this, but the width was 4 ft. 9 in. and the length not less than 9 ft. This block is 56 ft. west of the presumed centre line of the temple and altar, and would make a suitable base for an equestrian statue.[2]

Its discovery reminded us that we had observed what we took for a patch of concrete floor under the fragment of wall running E.–W. just SE. of the chapel (V). The distance of this from the centre line, as near as we can now judge, was 56 ft., as on the west, but the proof that the two things are a pair remains to be sought. One is reminded of the columns bearing Victories which flanked the Altar of Augustus at Lugdunum, and of the equestrian statues which also figured in that ensemble, and of the Victory which fell from its pedestal, perhaps on this very spot, in A.D. 61.[3]

That the foundations under Colchester Castle might prove to be those of the historic temple of Claudius was first suggested by Sir Mortimer Wheeler.[4] The earlier controversy over Jenkins's theory was absurd,

for Jenkins claimed the whole of the Norman building as the temple of Claudius, and there is no question of resuscitating this extravaganza. In any case it was settled in 1933 by the discovery of Norman pottery low down in the foundation trench of the keep.

Though the plan presented when the above discoveries have been plotted, despite the small extent to which each could be explored, corresponds well with known examples of a large temple of classical type with a large altar before it, and is therefore what we should expect to find on the site of the temple mentioned by Tacitus and others, it remains uncertain to what extent the several structures were contemporary. Only extensive further work could enlighten us, and in view of the difficulty of dating the much more carefully explored remains at the NE. angle of the courtyard it is necessary to reserve judgement on this very important point. Though the drain occupies the position of an ornamental screen for the altar, it is difficult to see what its function was, and it certainly seemed to us that no foundation lay close and parallel to it.[5]

It can scarcely be doubted, whatever future work may disclose, that we have before us the site of a centre of Emperor worship, and one which is in large part still accessible for excavation. Nowhere has such a site yet been excavated. The great prototype at Lyons–Lugdunum in Gaul has not been explored, indeed even its exact site is unknown. It is described by Strabo: 'In front of this town, at the place where the Saone joins the Rhone, is built the temple which all the Gauls in common have dedicated to Augustus. There is to be seen a magnificent altar on which are carved the names of 60 peoples, which are represented by statues. This altar is of considerable height. There is another altar to be seen, which is also very large.'[6]

The altar was famous for the delicacy of its carvings. It is said to have carried eight bronze tripods, the two in the centre bearing globes, signifying the power of Rome and Augustus. It appears, too, that there are portions of four columns built into the church of Ainay, which are supposed to have been those which, as we see on coins of Augustus, each supported a winged Victory, facing inwards to the altar. Besides the honours paid to the Emperor the celebrated fairs of Lyons were held near the forum, and the altar gained its greatest celebrity from these games, recitations of poetry and trials of eloquence, which were increased by Caligula, and became very fashionable. Juvenal and Suetonius speak of competitors thrown into the river after being defeated in these contests. The altar of

---

[1] Assuming it is of f. 195 and not 497. ·

[2] There is a finger from a bronze statue, over life-size, in the Joslin Collection (C.M.) and part of another, about life-size, in the Pollexfen Collection (B.M. 1870.4–2.97), both from Colchester. The fore-leg of a life-size bronze horse found at Lincoln

is at Burlington House, *Arch. J.* ciii (1947), 54; *Ant. Journ.* xxiv (1944), 5.

[3] Tacitus, *Annales*, lib. xiv. 32.   [4] *J.R.S.* ix, 147; x, 89.

[5] Presence or absence of it was not established.

[6] Lib. IV. iii, 2.

Augustus at Narbonne is said to have stood in the forum.

It will undoubtedly occur to the critical to exclaim at the fact that no smallest fragment of architectural or ornamental work has been found on the site. Apart from negligible scraps found during the work on the north and south wings of the forum, this is only too true. The explanation is that it is true of Colchester as a whole, and that it is due to the fact that all stone for carved work had to be imported. That the town had the usual rich decorations of the period, including imported marbles and porphyries, as well as great quantities of our own 'Purbeck marble', is attested by the many fragments found from time to time. The marble is found in great quantity at one spot in particular (p. 203) whence it has been conjectured that it was gathered together there from all the town, either by Normans or late Romans, to burn for lime. All limestone would be similarly treated. On the Continent lime-kilns have been found on the richer Roman sites: in some cases half-consumed column-capitals have been found in them. In the case of the temple we have the additional disadvantage that the ruins were completely stripped in order to build the Castle, and some clearing of the ancient layers seems to have been effected (see the remarks on the occupation levels found in the work of 1950 below, p. 182).

THE ROMAN REMAINS NORTH OF THE CASTLE

The area north of the Castle differs from that to the south. Here the Norman ramparts remain, wholly or in part. The ancient level has not been so deeply buried, e.g. the batter at the foot of the wall of the keep is largely exposed, and Roman masonry is visible here and there. The area, too, is not so large, and we have as yet no knowledge of any buildings lying in the court between the temple and the walls covered by the Norman ramparts.

35. The walls had been noticed in Morant's time (1748), and Jenkins published a sketch plan in 1861,[1] but the first excavation was undertaken by the Rev. J. T. Round, in whose garden they then lay, in 1845. Of this we have accounts by Wire and by C. Roach Smith. Wire's account is of interest (the dates are those in the Diary)

10/1/1845. 'Workmen are drawing a trench through the hill west side of the Bailey, others are opening the ground on the north side of the Castle immediately under the wall and excavat-

ing in the inner [east] quadrangle, also excavating on the south side of the pump [= well] inside the Castle where a drain was come upon leading in a southerly direction but, as it was found from the compactness of the material difficult to open it up, part of the brickwork of the well was taken down to obtain an entrance into it. [Strutt in his history of Colchester mentions this drain.] In the middle cutting in the garden terrace was discovered a thin layer of lime or chalk resting on the ground superimposed by one of concrete. Several bricks found in the drain had mortar adhering to them composed of pounded brick and lime, but set in a cement of a more modern character.'

15/1/45. 'Several fragments of pottery, apparently Saxon, have been discovered during the above excavations and the handle of an earthen vessel of Indian manufacture, but no coins that I am aware of.'

19/5/45. 'Purchased a 2b coin of Nero found in the Bailey.'

Roach Smith's account of Round's excavations for once puts Wire to shame. In *J.B.A.* i, 53 he says: 'Round dug to ascertain the nature of the wall under the rampart . . . his excavation was made . . . in the side nearer the Castle . . . .' The portion of wall exposed and seen by Roach Smith was 'six feet wide, twelve feet deep and two feet thick; the interior side had been broken down so that the original thickness could not be ascertained.[2] It was composed of cut stone, as in the town walls, with offsets about 4 ft. apart; the interior exhibits Roman tiles irregularly disposed and mostly in fragments; the mortar resembles that of the Castle, being soft (indeed!), without the lime and pounded tile. In excavating the approaches large quantities of . . . fragments of fresco painting . . . were discovered.'

In *J.B.A.* ii, 29 ff. Smith gives a longer account. He mentions 'masses of Roman masonry which were turned up in a partial excavation . . . on the south side [of the Castle]',[3] and then describes the later work by Round on the north side. '. . . In the side of the rampart, opposite the entrance on the north side of the Castle, at the depth of ten feet was discovered a pavement of well-cut broad slabs of blue lias (the remains of which are seen in the cut) laid upon a stratum of concrete five inches deep, of a reddish colour . . . which rests upon the native sandy soil. Three feet nine inches below were two well-built pieces of masonry, formed of stones and sandy mortar, similar to that used in the Castle. These foundations, which appeared to have been formed in caissons, were 5 ft. 10 ins. square, and descended to a considerable depth; the pavement extended as far as the inner line of the masonry, but not further, and it should be noted that the top of the squares is between five and six feet from the level of the garden . . . .'[4]

---

[1] *Colchester Castle, etc.*, 1861, facing p. 25.

[2] This description is now familiar; the height of 12 ft. we know; for 'wide' read 'long'; the interior side is that to the north (i.e. under the rampart); the offsets will be recognized in our sections.

[3] Probably the Norman forebuilding. It would be the work on this occasion which disturbed the skeletons found by us, and cut the wall.

[4] This seems to imply that the piers were level with the natural sand, and the pavement approximated to the level of the south

There follows a note that the previous piece of wall exposed was 23 paces away from this site. 'The wall which we have now met with in several places is most probably that referred to by Morant and *apparently subsequent to the other remains* [our italics]. The mortar in it is of that peculiar sandy kind which I have before mentioned as common to Saxon and Norman buildings.'[1]

A letter in the Museum from the famous geologist,

n.s. iii. 2) and Dr. H. Laver published an account of them, the first usefully conducted work on the site.[2] Two parallel walls were found, the outer of which seems to give us the NW. angle of the insula. At 45 ft. east of the angle this outer wall turns north for 19 ft. 6 in. and then east again. This emendation of 19 ft. 6 in. for the 15 ft. of Laver was established during Mrs. Cotton's excavations of 1950. The conjectural plan of the north side of this insula advanced by Wheeler and Laver[3] was

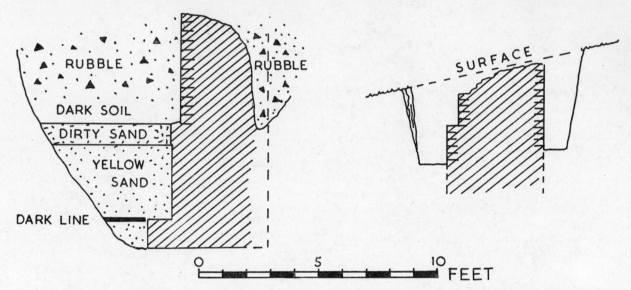

RUBBLE · DARK SOIL · DIRTY SAND · YELLOW SAND · DARK LINE · RUBBLE · SURFACE · 0 5 10 FEET

FIG. 89. On right, H. Laver's wall-section, on left, section obtained in 1929. [**122** and **35**], pp. 178, 179.

John Brown, dated 24/1/45, is a reply to Round, identifying samples of stone submitted to him from these excavations. They included two of calcareous tufa, one good; the other Brown thought must have been formed *in situ* 'by means of mineral water passing over fallen vegetables and entangling dead snail shells (fine specimens)'. He also lists mountain limestone from Derbyshire; Lias limestone, nearest source Uppingham; septaria, fossiliferous Chert; Upper Greensand or Firestone, from Surrey or Sussex; Oolitic limestone, full of shells, 'many possible sources', sandstone of fine white quartz sand, 'much like the old red sandstone of Shropshire', gypsum or alabaster, nearest source Derbyshire, conglomerate, and flint.

So the matter rested until attention was again drawn to these walls in 1892, when a path was made through them at the NW. corner (where an entrance may have existed previously in Norman times, see plan, *T.E.A.S.*

based upon H. Laver's plan and must be reconsidered in the light of Mrs. Cotton's work (p. 183).

The outer wall runs south from the NW. angle, under the west rampart of the Castle. It was described as 2 ft. 4 in. thick, with a 4-in. offset on the inner (?) side. The core was rubble, with a facing of squared septaria; the mortar, at least in parts, contained powdered brick.

The southern or inner wall was also 2 ft. thick and of a similar construction, except that no pink mortar was seen. It presumably formed a similar angle to the other (see plan) and they were 33 ft. apart. It is to be noticed that the outer wall, where now visible, is 4 ft. 6 in. thick, and that the Laver plan shows no variations in thickness (fig. 89).

On the west side, between the walls, Laver found two red concrete floors. On them were inhumation burials, described as almost certainly of early Saxon date.[4]

offset of our wall D. How did the piers come to be robbed so low and the (very useful) lias blocks left undisturbed? Were the piers remains of a building taken down in Roman times and the lias part of a later building? Also, what made up the level *between* the piers?

[1] The note in Wire's Diary (13/1/45), 'I am informed that a

tessellated pavement has been found in the Rev. J. T. Round's garden, near the terrace', is perhaps an error referring to the lias pavement.

[2] *T.E.A.S.* n.s. iv, 299; ix, 122.   [3] *J.R.S.* ix, 145.

[4] It should be appreciated that these lay under the Norman rampart, but whether sealed by it or not we do not know.

Of the skeletons Laver records they were five (in the notebook 'many'), laid side by side, the feet alternately east and west. The heads were protected by pieces of Roman tile laid on either side, with another laid across the top. There were no objects deposited with them. They showed no trace of violence.

Farther south the plan is conjectural, and it is still uncertain which of the two walls will line-in with the structures found under the west pavement of Museum Street, where a number of semicircular tiles, 19 in. in diameter, were found.

In 1919, using this data, Professor Wheeler and Mr. Philip Laver produced a plan for this area,[1] but they felt that the problem was still in its initial stages. They postulated tentatively a quadrangular area bounded on at least two sides by variously paved compartments between two parallel systems of Roman walls, of which the inner may have supported a colonnade.

122. In May 1929 a shaft was sunk on the line of the outer wall, 100 ft. east of the NW. angle. This established a middle wall, found to be standing 10 ft. high (fig. 89). It was entirely of septaria and was completely ruined on the north side. The upper part was still 3 ft. thick and had probably been 4 ft. Twelve courses stood 4 ft. 6 in. high and then there was a 6-in. offset. Below this it had been built in shuttering and had obviously served as a retaining wall, for the remaining 4 ft. were so finished that they were clearly not meant to be seen. At the base of this the foundation offset was 1 ft. wide,[2] and the foundations went down another 15 in. into the virgin sand. At the level of the foundation offset there was a dark line—the original ground-level. Above this was a make-up, to level the great court, of 3 ft. of clean yellow sand. Upon this lay 11 in. of dirty sand, the top of which was level with the upper offset, and must at one time have formed the ground-level of the court. There were about 9 in. of dark soil upon this, which continued up to the surface, but it was full of rubble from the demolition of the Roman walls. The little which could be done on the north side showed only the same loose rubble, which included parts of rounded tiles for columns, and small paving-bricks. The level of the upper offset is 9 ft. 3 in. below the floor of the summer-house on the terrace.[3]

Besides the two walls at the NW. corner, Laver reported in 1892[4] a vaulted drain, *c.* 20 in. wide and 2 ft. 5 in. high, built of tiles and septaria and lined throughout with Roman mortar. It runs under both walls, curving away to the north as if to cross under the Roman street and take up a line along the west side of it. It has been cut by the Norman ditch, and its remains can now be seen in the Park shrubbery. It has also been traced for some 120 ft. eastwards,[5] within the court, where it runs parallel to and south of the inner wall at an interval of 20 ft. The exposed portion shows that it is just over 2 ft. wide, with 2-ft. high walls of six courses of septaria. The floor and vault, which is remarkably flat, are of tiles. Those in the vault are of mixed sizes, a point not to be expected in an early structure.[6] This is the only feature so far found which

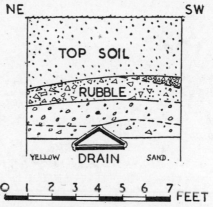

FIG. 90. Triangular drain, and stratification north of the Castle. [34], p. 179.

might correlate with the portico and drain round the temples of Augst, Paris, and St. Bertrand.

Many small bricks, $5\frac{1}{2}$ by $2\frac{1}{2}$ by $1\frac{1}{4}$ in. and 4–5 by 3 by $1\frac{1}{2}$ in., were found over the whole area of the Norman buildings south of the Castle, and also in the rubble of the Roman walls to the NW. They are from floors.

In 1940 the first of a stick of four bombs missed the Castle by inches and buried itself 33 ft. from the centre of the north wall without exploding. The bomb disposal squad removed it by digging a hole 6 ft. 6 in. square, when it was discovered that the bomb had turned and shot horizontally, cutting a peculiar Roman drain (fig. 90).

The top of the yellow sand is 5 ft. from the surface, with some 6 in. of mortary rubble lying upon it, but in one place there remained part of a floor of mortar, 3 in. thick, presumably corresponding to similar patches seen south of the Castle and presumably serving as a base for the paving of the Temple court.

The drain ran N.–S. and was of triangular section, formed of three building tiles mortared together as

---

[1] *J.R.S.* ix, 144–8 and fig. 15.

[2] The 'offsets 4 ft. apart' of Roach Smith (p. 177).

[3] We are indebted to Mr. W. D. Clark for assistance in recording this discovery.

[4] *T.E.A.S.* ix, 123. [5] *J.R.S.* xxxiv, 80 and fig. 7.

[6] Jenkins, *Appendix*, 19, is wrong in saying that this drain has a circular mouth, mistaken by King (*Arch.* iv, 409) for a well '. . . situate near the centre of the larger area' (i.e. inside the keep). He is also wrong in saying it runs beneath the west wall of the Castle, if by this he means the keep.

shown in the section (which is elongated because it is oblique) and partly sunk into the sand. It was partly filled with dark sandy silt.

Above the layers already mentioned came about 9 in. of gravelly soil and then a heavy rubble layer, with subdivisions, which may belong to the ruin of the Castle in 1683 or to the destruction of the Roman buildings. This drain must have started from about the middle of the north face of the temple.

THE EXCAVATIONS OF 1950

By M. AYLWIN COTTON, F.S.A.

190. The nineteenth centenary of the foundation of the Roman *Colonia* at Camulodunum, in A.D. 50, was celebrated at Colchester by holding a conference from 4 to 7 July 1950. An excavation in the Castle Park formed part of this programme. The celebrations were organized by a joint committee set up by the Mayor and Corporation of Colchester and the Society of Antiquaries of London, under the chairmanship of Sir Mortimer Wheeler, and the deputy-chairmanship of Professor C. F. C. Hawkes. Councillor L. E. Dansie acted as Chairman of the Executive Committee; Mr. M. R. Hull as Honorary Secretary, and Mr. K. R. Mabbitt as Treasurer.

Grants to cover the cost of the excavation were made by the Colchester Corporation, the Society of Antiquaries of London, the British Academy, the Haverfield Bequest Committee, and the Royal Archaeological Institute. Permission to excavate in the scheduled monument was granted by H.M. Ministry of Works.

At the request of the Committee, the excavations were undertaken by Miss K. M. Richardson, M.A., F.S.A., and myself, under the consultative advice of Sir Mortimer Wheeler, Professor Hawkes, and Mr. M. R. Hull. We wish to express our indebtedness to them for their invaluable advice and help. Our thanks are due also to Councillor Dansie and Mr. Mabbitt for their constant support; to Mr. Orchard, the Borough Engineer, and Mr. Richardson, the Assistant Borough Engineer, who lent us heavy equipment and a hut, and advised on engineering problems and helped with the restoration of the monument; and to Alderman W. C. Harper, Chairman of the Parks Committee, who facilitated our work.

Of our band of volunteer helpers, may we mention gratefully Colonel R. J. Appleby who led the local team; Mr. William Wedlake and his fellow members of the Camerton Excavation Club; and our colleagues from the Institute of Archaeology of London University, more especially Mr. R. Allchin and Miss J. Philips. For technical help we wish to thank Mr. Huntly S. Gordon who, assisted by Mr. Allchin and Mr. Stewart, did the surveying; Mr. M. B. Cookson and Mr. Evans for the photography; and Dr. K. M. Kenyon for advice on problems of stratigraphy.

Acknowledgements and thanks are due also to Miss Grace Simpson for the report on the Samian wares; Mrs. J. E. Morey

for the report on the marble veneers and building stones; Mr. B. W. Pearce for examining the Roman coins; and Miss M. Maitland Howard for the report on the molluscae.

THE ROMAN STRUCTURES

The point chosen for excavation was in the vicinity of the NE. corner of the Norman bank to the north of the Castle, where it is at its highest (pl. XXVII, A) and where a corner of Roman masonry was exposed about half-way down the bank. Two wide trenches were cut into the northern and southern sides of the earthwork. In addition the exposed masonry at the corner was cleared to its foundations. The Roman structures uncovered consisted of:

An earlier and later street separated by an intervening silt.

The walls and floors of part of a terraced masonry building.

A later demolished wall.

A sealing layer of earth which represented the occupation in the area from late Roman times until the arrival of the Normans.

The Early Street (pl. XXVIII, A and figs. 91, 92)

Underlying the tail of the bank on its northern side, street metalling was found lying directly on the old turf line. The northern part of this street had been destroyed when the Norman ditch was cut, so that its width was not determinable. Its southern edge lay 10 ft. north of wall A of the building found and it had no ditch on this side. It ran east and west and is parallel to the street on the south side of insula 6, which lies under the present bandstand and which was excavated in 1920.[1] It is separated from it by the space of a narrow insula of about half normal size. The metalling, of good quality and unrepaired, produced no finds, and the street cannot therefore be dated on this season's work. On plan, however, it appears to fit into the main street grid as originally postulated[2] and since confirmed in a number of places.[3] The existing evidence on the dating of the main street plan of the Colonia[4] suggests that it was not finished (that is, metalled) before the reign of Nero or even later.[5]

The Masonry Building (pls. XXVII, B, XXVIII, XXIX, A, B, figs. 81, 91–92)

The corner of this building, at the NE. corner of the Castle ramparts, has been known for many years.[6] Only a small part of it, all tile-turned, could be seen. Its continuation was exposed in the main trenches dug through the earthwork. Here the natural ground-level

[1] Wheeler, *T.E.A.S.* xvi (1921), 15–20.
[2] Wheeler and Laver, *J.R.S.* ix (1919), fig. 17.
[3] Hull, *Roman Colchester* (1947), map at end.
[4] Hull, *J.R.S.* xxxi (1941), 137.

[5] We are indebted to Mr. Hull for the information that the street grid of *Ara Ubiorum* (Cologne) was laid out many years before it was metalled when the dignity of Colonia was conferred.
[6] See above, pp. 160, 169.

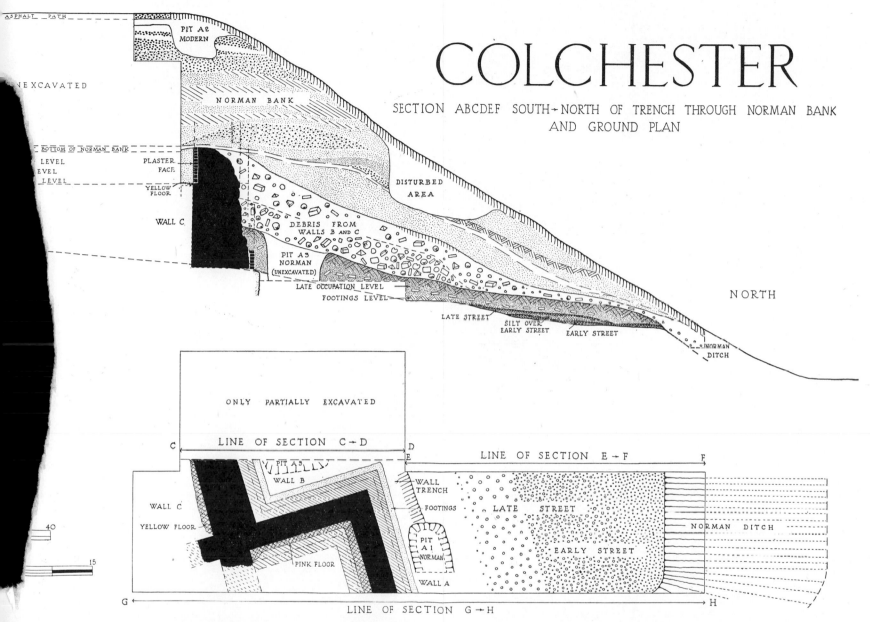

COLCHESTER

SECTION ABCDEF SOUTH→NORTH OF TRENCH THROUGH NORMAN BANK
AND GROUND PLAN

of the cuttings into the north-east corner of the Castle ramparts. [190] p. 180.

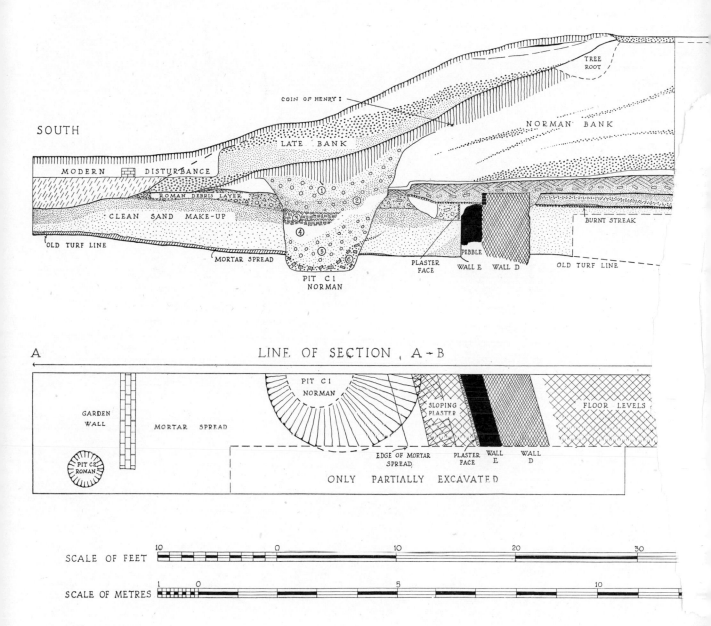

SOUTH

COIN OF HENRY I

NORMAN BANK

LATE BANK

TREE ROOT

MODERN DISTURBANCE

ROMAN DEBRIS LAYER

① ②

③

④

⑤

⑥

CLEAN SAND MAKE-UP

BURNT STREAK

OLD TURF LINE

MORTAR SPREAD

PIT C1 NORMAN

PLASTER FACE

WALL E WALL D

PEBBLE

OLD TURF LINE

A

LINE OF SECTION, A→B

GARDEN WALL

MORTAR SPREAD

PIT C1 NORMAN

SLOPING PLASTER

FLOOR LEVELS

PIT C2 ROMAN

EDGE OF MORTAR SPREAD

PLASTER FACE

WALL E

WALL D

ONLY PARTIALLY EXCAVATED

SCALE OF FEET   10   0   10   20   30

SCALE OF METRES   1   0   5   10

FIG. 91. Section ABCDEF and ground plan

slopes downwards to the north and falls away slightly to the east. The outer or northern wall of the building was sited just below the crest of the slope, and was built up against an artificially levelled area to form a terraced structure. The northern wall of the building had been robbed down to floor-level, but the lower

ruined wall was the corner of a yellow concrete floor. Its position showed that an internal offset, or offsets, equivalent to 1 ft. 3 in. must exist in these corner walls.

The corner was grooved and rubbed smooth at a height of 1 ft. 6 in. above the footings, presumably by the 'wear-and-tear' of traffic rounding the corner (pl.

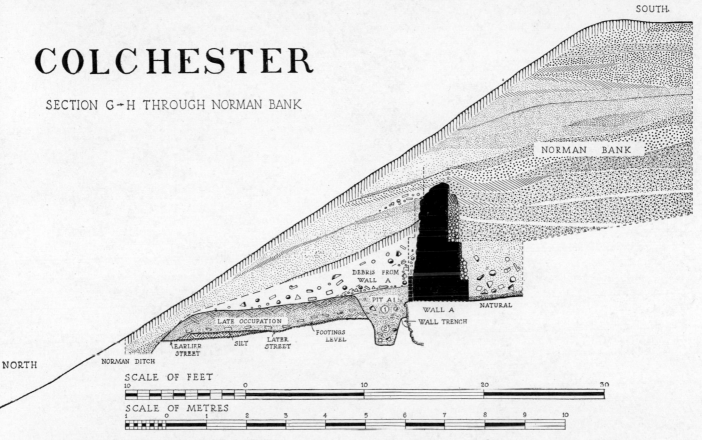

COLCHESTER

SECTION G→H THROUGH NORMAN BANK

SOUTH.

NORMAN BANK

DEBRIS FROM WALL A

PIT A1

WALL A
WALL TRENCH

NATURAL

LATE OCCUPATION

FOOTINGS LEVEL

EARLIER STREET

SILT

LATER STREET

NORTH

NORMAN DITCH

SCALE OF FEET

SCALE OF METRES

Fig. 92. Section GH of the east face of the cuttings into the north side of the Castle ramparts. [190], p. 180.

retaining section was preserved in the heart of the covering Norman bank. So much earth had therefore to be removed to expose this building that only a part of its plan and structure could be obtained. The findings were as follows.

The walls of the NE. corner of the building still stand 10 ft. above the footings level. They are faced with red bricks averaging 1 ft. 4 in. by 10 in. by 2 ft. 4 in. in size, laid alternately with their long and short sides outwards, but interspersed with an occasional narrower brick. The core of the wall was of rubble. The upper courses of the wall showed a few facing-stones of dressed septaria blocks. At the corner there were two external offsets, the lower, 5 ft. 4 in. above the footings, being 6 in. wide, and the upper, 3 ft. 3 in. higher, being 9 in. wide. At the top of the

XXIX, A). As this is low for wheeled traffic, it has been suggested that it was caused by wooden sledges rather than wheel hubs.

The north wall of the building was exposed in the main trench cut into the outer side of the bank. Here there was found a 5 ft. wide wall, wall A, which was in alignment with the north wall at the corner. Founded on a 4-ft. depth of grouted pebble footings, sunk into the natural, this wall, in its lowest seven courses, was faced with squared blocks of septaria. Above this, only the rubble core remained. Wall A stands just over 10 ft. high above the bottom of the lowest faced course, and the remaining core showed no evidence of brick bonding courses, but contained reused tiles and segmental quadrant bricks. External offsets, similar to those found at the corner, were found. The inside of this wall was explored down to the natural. At its foundation level it was shown to be 5 ft. wide and to have been built up over this width for a height of 1 ft. 9 in. It was then offset internally for 9 in., and on this offset was built a 1 ft. 6 in. high platform of roughly mortared flints. Except against the wall itself, this platform had been torn away, and some of the remaining flints were cracked by heat. Above this platform was a space 1 ft. deep in which the inside of the wall showed rough plastering. At this point the wall was again offset internally for a width of 1 ft., and on this second offset was another platform of flint-work standing 3 ft. 3 in. high, and supporting a pink concrete floor. As before, the floor and platform were torn away leaving only narrow remains adherent to the wall, and the resultant space was filled by the tips of the later enveloping bank.[1] The concrete floor was at the same level as the yellow floor at the corner, but was set more deeply into the wall so that wall A, at room level, was only 2 ft. thick.

At a point 32 ft. west of the corner the north wall of the building turned southwards for a length of 9 ft. 8 in. (wall B), and then turned westwards again (wall C) forming a re-entrant angle. Only a short length of wall C was exposed. Wall B formed the western boundary of the room with the pink concrete floor and had internal and external offsets and torn-away platforms similar to those of wall A. Wall C, however, had on its southern or inner face a yellow concrete floor set at a lower level with some remains of a plaster facing above it. It had external offsets like those of walls A and B, but, from the position of the floor, lacked the internal offsets, and the wall at floor-level was 3 ft. 9 in. thick.

Traces of partition walls were found bounding the east side of the yellow floor and the south side of the pink floor, but so deeply buried in the bank that they could not be traced properly. This evidence suggests a terraced building with three rooms.

In the southern trench a 6-ft. length of wall was found which, on its southern plastered face, had been built against timber shuttering.[2] This wall (wall E), built with a yellow mortar, had been destroyed and its lower courses partly incorporated in a wall of later build (wall D). Its width was not determined, but it projected to the south of wall D and was sealed by a thick layer of fallen plaster. The footings of wall E were cut directly into the old turf line and the natural soil.

To its south there was a spread of mortar lying on the old turf line. This had an uneven surface, showed no impressions of paving-stones, and stopped short of the wall. It was probably a builder's mortar dump associated with the building of the wall rather than a pavement level. Both to the north and to the south of wall E there was a deep make-up of clean sand which was contemporary with it. On the north it carried a yellow concrete floor which had been succeeded by a pink concrete floor. On the south the covering floor-level was wrecked. Whilst it was not possible to complete the trench through the bank in order to correlate these floors with those inside the north wall of the building, this fact was minimized owing to their having been destroyed. The two yellow concrete floors to the north of wall E are on the same level and appear to equate.

Wall D, which was sited on the northern part of wall E, was shown structurally to be of later date, as its wall-trench cut through both the yellow and pink concrete floors. Built with a pink mortar, it had been demolished down to the two courses above floor-level and was sealed by the late occupation level (pl. XXIX, B).

On the outside of the north wall of the building no levels were found which could be related to it. At the corner, the foundations of the building had been cut into the metalling of the earlier street, and it was therefore of a build subsequent to the street layout. This street was covered with silt and a later street metalling. Although the stratification on the outside of the north wall of the building was interrupted against it by later Norman pits, it could be seen that the level of the later street was well below the footings level of the wall (pl. XXVIII, A). It is suggested, therefore, that any levels contemporary with the build or use of this structure, lying as they were on a sloping surface, have been degraded down to the firm metalling of the earlier street. There is supporting evidence for such a theory from the excavation of insula 6 to the north. Here the parallel street was found to have on its northern side a retaining wall (fig. 81).[3] Should there have existed a street contemporary with the building, or occupation levels, they might also only have been kept in position by a similar retaining wall. If this had collapsed, these levels would have been washed down the hill.[4] The relevant evidence in this area has been removed in the cutting of the Norman ditch, but it may still exist farther west.

---

[1] Cf. Laver, *T.E.A.S.* ix (1906), 123 where he states that the inner side of the outer wall on the west was roughly plastered, and the stones were not pointed, showing clearly that it was intended for a facing to the mound of earth now overlying it. Portions were plastered in characteristic salmon-coloured cement.

[2] The wall found farther west (see p. 179) and the piers found by Round (see p. 177) had also been built against timber shuttering.

[3] Wheeler, *T.E.A.S.* xvi (1921), 19.

[4] We are indebted to Mr. Hull for the information that there appeared to be 'missing levels' also at the southern entrance to the temple precinct. Here he found a drain in the latest stratified Roman level, inexplicably open, which produced a coin of Antoninus Pius. The sealing level was of very late Roman or post-Roman date, and there was nothing in between.

Structurally this building is of later date than the earliest street found, and is presumably of earlier date than the silt over that street. The only level of contemporary date is the sand levelling to its south under the later floor-levels. The finds associated with this phase are, owing to the small area excavated, too scanty and indeterminate to permit of any secure dating of the building, and only preliminary indications of its period can be postulated. The upper date bracket depends on the date at which the early street was cut into. Should this street be proved to be part of a Neronic or later plan, a date posterior to that of Nero would then form the upper limit. The contemporary material found consists of a few sherds of coarse pottery from the sand make-up; the floors were sterile. These (fig. 94) are not sufficiently distinctive to serve as reliable dating evidence. The material from the silt over the earlier street contained a stamped Samian base of SENNIVS of Lezoux of Hadrian–Antonine date (fig. 93, 1) and a f. 18/31 Samian base dated as A.D. 150 (fig. 93, 2). The small quantity of coarse pottery did, however, produce a sherd of Castor ware which does not usually occur until c. A.D. 180, and the dating of this level depends on the finding of a fragment of a third-century radiate coin (no. 3, p. 188) which brings the date of the lower bracket down to c. A.D. 250 or later. It will be seen from this that further excavation is needed to reduce such a wide bracket and to date this building at all properly.

The Later Street (pl. XXVIII, A; figs. 91–92)

Over the silt was laid a later street-level of rough cobbling with many brick fragments. It was sited nearer to the north wall of the building than the earlier street. The pottery from this metalling (fig. 93, 3–6 and fig. 94, 5–6) is consistent with a late third century dating. No coins were found.

The Late Roman to Norman occupation level (pl. XXIX, B, C)

Sealing the later street outside, the demolished wall D inside, the remains of the floors to the north of wall E, and overlying the sand make-up level to the south, was a thick black layer which contained occupation material and many broken bricks and tiles. The surface of this layer was that on which the Norman bank was founded, and stratigraphically therefore it represents the gap between the fourth century A.D. and the arrival of the Normans in the eleventh century. The material contents were predominantly of late-fourth-century date. It was devoid of Samian wares. The coarse pottery (fig. 95, 1–26) found in the three subdivisions of this level (the late occupation level, the 'footings level', and the Roman debris level of figs. 91–92) included a number of sherds of pseudo-Samian wares which are most prevalent in the second half of the fourth century A.D. The coin series (nos. 2, 4, 7, and 9, p. 188) continues to at least the end of this century as it includes a coin of Theodosius I of c. A.D. 379–95. This suggests that wall D may have been demolished during the late phase of the Roman occupation. Its purpose was not determined, nor was it possible to say whether the floors and substructures of the building were destroyed at the same time.

The relationship of the building to other structures in the area (fig. 81)

In one season's work of limited extent it was not to be anticipated that the problems of the temple precinct area could be more than broached. The obvious starting-point was to add any information that could be obtained to the tentative plan of Wheeler and Laver of 1919.[1] It should be realized that this plan was based on the position of the NE. corner of the outer wall (which, being exposed, could be surveyed accurately) and Dr. Henry Laver's notes and sketch plans. That the latter were not susceptible to certain reproduction was made clear.[2] During the season several trial trenches were opened over the lines of the walls as shown in the NW. corner of this plan. These trenches were dug down only to the tops of these walls. Where examined, they were found in the position shown on the new plan (fig. 81), but some modifications of the original measurements were necessary.[3] Sufficient evidence was obtained to show that the buildings at the NW. and NE. corners lack the symmetry postulated, as the NW. corner has not the re-entrant angle in the same position as that found at the NE. end. On the other hand, the alignment and width of the outer wall of the two corners are comparable.[4] The inner wall of the Laver plan at the NW. end was not explored, and, as drawn at present, is not quite in alignment with either wall D or wall E, but, in the short length exposed of the latter, and having due regard to the other discrepancies found in the Laver plan, no great stress should be laid on this point.

[1] As illustrated in *J.R.S.* ix (1919), fig. 15.

[2] Op. cit., p. 144. This applies also to the discoveries made by Round in 1842; cf. Roach Smith, *J.B.A.A.* ii (1847), 36–38.

[3] Fig. 81 incorporates these. The modifications necessary to the account in *J.R.S.* ix (1919), p. 144 are: 'Under the north rampart are two walls running east and west, and parallel to each other, except that the outer or northern wall, at a point 58′ from the main north-west angle, turns at right angles towards the north for a distance of 19′ 6″ and then resumes its easterly course.'

[4] Mr. Hull has pointed out a second lack of symmetry. Assuming that the plan is correct, the temple is some 18 ft. west of the centre line of the insula.

In addition, there have been added to the general plan of the precinct area the positions of any other Roman structures discovered since 1919.[1] It will be seen that the general indication of a forum or temple precinct surrounding the podium of the temple beneath the keep still pertains. The findings all tend to suggest that the area as a whole was artificially levelled to form a platform which was perhaps paved, and which was bounded on at least the north and west by inner and outer walls with concrete floors between them, the upper having perhaps carried a pavement. The NE. corner of this enclosure certainly had rooms. The symmetry of the plan has been disproved, and the contemporaneity of the structures at the NW. and NE. corners is still unproved.

Conclusions

On the present evidence, it is suggested tentatively that:

1. Any pre-Boudiccan occupation of the area is still unproved.[2]

2. The initial Roman structure found on the site was the earlier of two streets which was laid on the original turf and was sterile and undatable. It appears, on plan, to form part of the main layout of the street plan of the Colonia.

3. At the NE. corner of an artificially levelled platform a terraced building was built, which contained at least three rooms. Its foundations were cut through the earlier street. This fact, and the reused material in the core of the walls, fail to support a Claudian date for its build, but lack of close dating evidence associated with its build or use, prevents its being dated at present within a wide bracket extending from the last half of the first century A.D. to the mid-third century A.D.

4. The inner wall of this building was destroyed and rebuilt on a more northerly line in Roman times. This later wall was of indeterminate use and was itself demolished during the Roman occupation of the area.

5. A later street-level was laid over the earlier during the late third to fourth centuries A.D.

6. Occupation of the area was attested to at least the end of the fourth century A.D., but no separate and distinctive occupation could be isolated which was attributable to the Pagan Saxon or Christian Saxon periods.

7. The question of whether the levelled and bounded area was the forum of the Colonia or the precinct of a temple is left open.

An account of the Norman earthwork, pits, and finds not of Roman date is to be published separately.

[1] These consist of houses and streets in insula 6 excavated by Professor Wheeler in 1920, cf. *T.E.A.S.* xvi (1921), 1–41; drains and the southern entrance, altar, &c., excavated by Mr. Hull.

[2] The old turf line cleared this season was sterile. No burnt

THE SMALL FINDS

The more noteworthy small finds of Roman date consisted of:

1. A bronze penannular brooch and pin with a faintly grooved ring and the terminals coiled frontally (cf. *Camulodunum*, p. 326, class A, for notes of the type). From an unstratified level.

2. A plain bronze ring made from a folded strip of metal. From the sand make-up level contemporary with walls A, B, C, and E.

3. A plaque of fine buff terra-cotta with part of a foliate scroll design like that of *Camulodunum*, fig. 66, 1–2; and three pieces of red-brown gritty clay antefixes with a tree design in moulded relief, cf. pl. XXX, B, top right.

4. A bone handle, bone pins and a needle, bone and pottery counters, and a whetstone were found also.

THE SAMIAN WARE

Report by MISS GRACE SIMPSON

FIG. 93

From the silt over the earlier street

1. Form 33. Base stamped SENNI M. SENNIVS of Lezoux was a Hadrian–Antonine potter. Cf. Oswald, p. 193. Cf. also May, *Colchester*, p. 288.

2. Form 18/31. Base from a large vessel. Central Gaulish ware. A.D. 150±.

In later street

3. Form 27, with an angular profile. Central Gaulish ware. c. A.D. 120–40.

4. Form 33. Central Gaulish ware with a rough finish. Antonine.

5. Form Curle 11. Cf. O. and P., pl. LXXI, 13 (or 12), which also have the internal thickening of the rim. South Gaulish ware. Flavian.

On later street

6. Form 18/31. Straight-sided. Cf. O. and P., pl. XLVI, 7, 10–12, &c. Central Gaulish ware. Antonine.

In Norman bank

7. Form 37. Fragment from a small bowl in the style of CINNAMVS of Lezoux, c. A.D. 140–70. The ovolo is characteristic of him, and usually appears on his small bowls. The decoration was arranged in panels and medallions.

8. Form 37, showing the tail of a dolphin to right. D. 1050 = O. 2382. The single-bordered ovolo is a rare one, and was used by the group of Lezoux potters associated with QVINTILIANVS. The small curved and serrated leaf was used by the potter LAXTVCISSA of Lezoux, who scattered it freely in his designs. It is also known on one Dr. 37 bearing the name-stamp of QVINTILIANVS, *Schaffhauser Beiträge*, 23 (1946), pl. 47, 1. The use of a wavy line and the double-ridged moulding below the decoration suggest a date of manufacture before A.D. 150.

Unstratified

9. From a small barrel-shaped beaker. The fragment comes from the lower part of the side, and shows a rouletted zone, closed below by two horizontal grooves; then a plain zone, as the vessel thickens slightly, and slopes in towards the base. The latter is indicated by four ridged mouldings. The sherd is well

level was found. The only objects found datable as anterior to A.D. 61 were the terra-cotta plaque and antefixes (p. 184) from post-Roman levels, and the Gallo-Belgic sherd (fig. 95, 28) from a Norman pit.

made and thin-walled; and the rouletting is regular and neat. The external glaze is good though slightly dull, and the interior has the same red colour, but is unglazed. Oelmann, *Niederbieber*, Abb. 20, 2, shows a vessel that may be of exactly similar form, though it is not in Samian ware. Mr. M. R. Hull has told me that six of these Samian beakers have been found previously

therefore, was found on which to date the building of these walls.

The silt over the earlier street, which is presumably of later date than the masonry building, produced sherds of coarse pottery which included one of Castor ware, but the broken third-century radiate coin (no. 3 of p. 188) indicated a date posterior

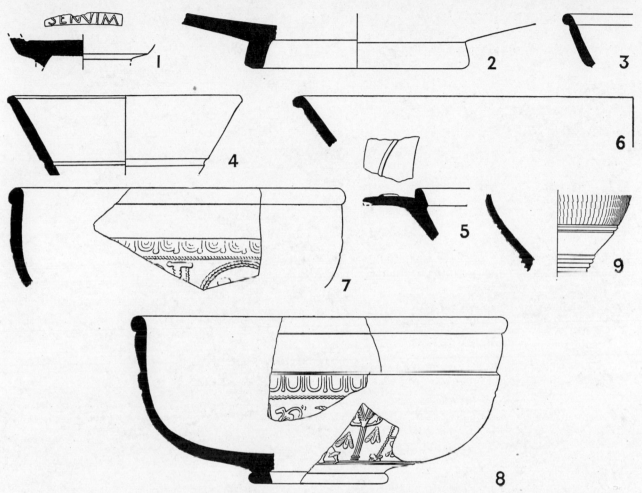

FIG. 93. Samian ware from 1950 excavations. Scale ½. (p. 184.)

at Colchester (May, p. 107, pl. XXXVIII, 108) but they are rare elsewhere in Britain. Stanfield, *Arch. J.* lxxxvi, 133–4, in describing nine examples known to him, wrote: 'These vessels were probably made in imitation of the barrel-shaped vessel, in coarse ware, which was produced throughout the Roman period, especially in eastern Gaul. They were manufactured during the second and third centuries.'

THE COARSE ROMAN POTTERY

The earlier street level, which structurally antedates the masonry building, produced no coarse pottery. In the clean sand make-up level, contemporary with the building of walls A, B, C, and E, only a few sherds of coarse pottery occurred (nos. 1–4 below). These were too fragmentary to be certain of their exact form or dating, except for no. 1, an unusual type for which no analogy has been traced. No contemporary pottery evidence,

to A.D. 250 for this level. The Samian pottery (fig. 93, 1–2) is of earlier date.

The coarse pottery from the later street (nos. 5–6) includes types of fourth-century date, and Samian wares (fig. 93, 3–6) mainly of Antonine date.

FIG. 94

From the sand make-up contemporary with walls A, B, C, and E

1. Cup or beaker of fine pale buff ware with traces of a green pigment below the rim outside, a 'blob' of green pigment inside, and a slight painted pattern on the body. The rim is flattened. No analogy to this form has been traced.
2. Necked jar or flask of hard, grey fumed ware. Cf. May, *Colchester*, pl. IV, 238–9 and p. 150, which shows that the form (Wheeler, type 2, cf. *T.E.A.S.* 2 s. xvi, fig. 5, 2) lasts from Claudian to Hadrianic times.

3. Necked jar or flask of greyish paste fired black and brown with a slightly pitted surface. Of the same form as no. 2 and probably of similar date.

4. Lid of yellow-grey paste with a polished grey-brown surface. Cf. *Camulodunum*, pl. LXXXV, 4, and p. 273 which shows that the tall conical and boldly domed forms tend to be early in date.

The sand make-up produced also a sherd of thin grey ware with a lattice-pattern decoration.

From the silt over the earlier street

The pottery sherds were too fragmentary to merit illustration, but included the base of a jug of pinkish ware with an external cream slip, two cavetto rims, which, according to *Jewry Wall, Leicester*, p. 99, are a form in use from *c.* A.D. 120 onwards, a sherd of an earlier rough-cast beaker, and a sherd of Castor

to the build of the Norman bank can therefore be assigned to a late-fourth-century date, but at present have yielded no stratified levels, in the small area uncovered, of Pagan Saxon or Christian Saxon date. Occupation of the site during this period is, however, suggested by the finding of odd sherds of contemporary pottery within the make-up of the Norman bank.

FIG. 95

'Footings level'

1. Lid of a Castor ware box or jar of white ware with a brown-black colour coating. The top is decorated with a band of rouletting. Cf. May, *Colchester*, pl. LIX, 290 which differs in that it fits outside the rim of the box and not inside as in this example. For notes on 'Castor boxes' cf. *Swanpool*, p. 67 and p. 77, which quote analogies, other Colchester examples, and show that this

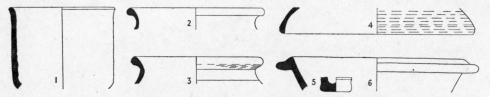

FIG. 94. Pottery from the sand make-up contemporary with walls A, B, C, and E, and from the street levels. Scale ¼. (pp. 185–6.)

ware from a red paste beaker with a grey-black metallic coating. Castor ware does not usually occur until after *c.* A.D. 170–80 (cf. *Jewry Wall, Leicester*, p. 119).

In the later street

5. Base of a Castor ware beaker of thick reddish-grey paste with a dull black slip. Cf. *Jewry Wall, Leicester*, p. 119, which states that this small high type of base was common at Verulamium in the late third century, appeared at Leicester *c.* A.D. 200–50, and was common there by *c.* A.D. 300–25.

6. Straight-sided flanged dish of thick grey polished ware. The flange is flat and triangular below a low bead. For notes on this type cf. *Swanpool*, p. 71, and *Jewry Wall, Leicester*, p. 84. At Colchester this form appears to begin early in the second century, cf. *Colchester Mus. Rep.*, 1928, p. 36 and pl. IX, 7189, but at most sites the coarser version, with a heavier flange as in this example, is typical of the late third and fourth centuries. Cf. also May, *Colchester*, pl. LVII, 258.

The later street contained also cavetto rims, pie-dishes, the base of a jug of buff ware with a yellow slip, rough-cast beaker, and lattice-patterned ware.

The coarse pottery derived from the levels posterior to the later street was predominantly of late-fourth-century date. In all levels anterior to the actual build of the Norman bank it was, however, of Roman types and fabrics.

The 'footings level', which overlay the base of the walls of the masonry building, produced a few sherds (nos. 1–3 below), the most distinctive being the Castor ware box lid. The late occupation level was the most prolific for pottery finds (nos. 4–21 below). They included Castor wares of forms prevalent in mid-fourth-century levels elsewhere (nos. 11–12), and imitation Samian wares which are dated to the second half of the fourth century (nos. 14–18). The coin evidence (nos. 2, 4, and 9, p. 188) supports a very late date for the accumulation of this level. The debris level over the sand make-up to the south of the building equated with this late occupation level and also contained a sherd of imitation Samian (no. 25), and a coin of A.D. 330–5 (no. 7, p. 188).

The occupation levels posterior to the later street and anterior

type appears to have been in use in the third century A.D., but notes that fuller discussion on the origin and development of these vessels awaits further investigation.

2. Straight-sided dish with a plain rim. Of heavy grey ware with a smoothed but unpolished surface. For notes on the type cf. *Jewry Wall, Leicester*, type B, pp. 85–86, which shows that in this heavy coarse version it is typically of fourth-century date.

3. Jar of dark grey gritty ware with a flat everted rim.

Other sherds in this level included the base of a jug of buff ware and fragmentary cavetto rims.

The late occupation level

4. Large storage-jar of heavy coarse grey ware fired red inside. The boldly rounded rim finished in a shoulder ledge decorated with a line of indentations. A graffito occurred on the top of the rim. Cf. May, *Colchester*, pl. LIV, 232 and analogies which are of late-first- to second-century date.

5. Large storage-jar of dark grey ware with a dull grey surface externally, a stabbed cordon on the base of the neck, and part of a wavy tooled pattern on the shoulder. This seems to be a more sophisticated version of the above type.

6. Large storage-jar of coarse heavy grey ware with a black coating on the lip and neck. Cf. no. 4 above.

7. Straight-sided bead-rim dish of coarse thick grey ware. It has no decoration. Cf. *Crambeck*, pl. III, 52–53 dated there from the end of the third century to A.D. 395, but cf. p. 30 which states that vessels of this form are so common that they are of little use for dating purposes. For general notes on the form, one especially prevalent in the second century, cf. *Jewry Wall, Leicester*, p. 86.

8. Straight-sided flanged dish of thick dark grey ware. Cf. notes on fig. 94, 6. This is a coarse example typical of a fourth-century date.

9. Jug or flagon of pinkish sandy ware.

10. Lid of hard brown-grey paste with a black fumed surface. The rim is squared off at the edge. Cf. May, *Colchester*, pl. LIX, 288 for form; cf. *Jewry Wall, Leicester*, p. 119, and *Swanpool*, fig. 5, G2, which both show that there appears to be no chronological significance in the form of lids.

11. Rim of a Castor ware beaker of grey paste with a dull black slip. The rim is vertical and is not thickened. This type of Castor ware rim was shown at Leicester to appear in period VIII, *c.* A.D. 250–300, and to be commonest in periods IX, X and disturbed levels *c.* A.D. 300–50; cf. *Jewry Wall, Leicester*, p. 119 and fig. 32, 21.

stamped with overlapping ellipses and the neck with rosettes. Cf. notes on no. 14 above.

17. Base of imitation Samian ware of dull red paste with few remains of the colour coating.

18. Base of imitation Samian ware of red-grey paste with an orange-red coating.

FIG. 95. Pottery from the latest Roman and unstratified levels of the 1950 excavations. Scale ¼ (except stamp). (pp. 186–8.)

12. Rim of a Castor ware beaker of white paste with a brown-black colour-coating. The rim is folded back. At Leicester it was only in period IX, *c.* A.D. 300–25, that the white ware was as prevalent as the earlier hard thin wares, and in period X, of mid-fourth-century date, it was predominant. Cf. *Jewry Wall, Leicester*, p. 119.

13. Base of a colour-coated beaker of red-grey paste with a dull brown-black coating.

14. Bowl of grey paste with a dull red colour coating. There is a faintly marked rouletted design on each side of a cordon on the neck. For discussion on these 'pseudo-Samian' wares, dated to the second half of the fourth century, cf. O. and P., p. 233; *Richborough I*, pp. 89–92; and *Jewry Wall, Leicester*, pp. 195 and 208–9. For an analogy fort his example cf. *Richborough I*, pl. XXIX, 126 and pl. XXX, 9.

15. Imitation Samian bowl of greyish paste with a dull red coating. Cf. notes on no. 14 above. Possibly a copy of a Samian f. 38.

16. Bowl of imitation Samian ware having a paste with a grey core and a dull brown-red coating. The cordon below the rim is

19. Cordoned bowl of grey ware with an external grey polish. Cf. *Camulodunum*, pl. LII, 209 for the Belgic prototype of this form.

20. Jug or flagon of coarse red ware.

21. Jar of hard, gritty, fumed grey ware. Cf. May, *Colchester*, pl. LV, 241.

This level contained also sherds of rouletted and white-painted Castor ware. The latter appeared at Leicester *c.* A.D. 300–25 but was not common there until the middle of the fourth century. Cf. *Jewry Wall, Leicester*, p. 119.

Roman debris level

22. Straight-sided plain rimmed dish of grey ware with a brown-grey polished surface decorated with a W-chevron pattern. This type occurs throughout the greater part of the Roman period and is not closely datable.

23. Bead-rim dish of grey ware with a polished brown-black surface. Cf. no. 9 above.

24. Storage-jar of grey ware with a brown-black pitted surface. Cf. May, *Colchester*, pl. LIV, 236 for an example dated to the first half of the second century A.D.

25. Jar or flagon of imitation Samian ware of red paste with a pinkish-red coating.

26. Jar of hard gritty fumed grey ware.

In the level there were found also part of a small amphora cover of white gritty ware, three sherds of black ware with a lattice pattern, two sherds of Castor ware of the earlier hard thin type and later white paste Castor wares with a white painted decoration.

The old turf line over the Norman robbing of the Roman walls

27. Mortarium of buff sandy ware with internal grits. It has a small square flange well below the bead. For notes on this fourth-century type cf. May, *Colchester*, pl. LVIII, 339 and pp. 172–3, and *Jewry Wall, Leicester*, type J, p. 80. Unstratified.

Filling of Norman pit C1, level 3

28. Sherd of thin hard Gallo-Belgic ware of a pink-brown paste

well smoothed externally. There is a graffito on the inside and on the outside a finely lettered stamp ROM. The potter may be ROMANVS(?). Cf. *Camulodunum*, pl. XLVI, 126 and p. 211. Unstratified.

IMPERIAL ROMAN COINS

Provenance of the coins

The broken third-century radiate coin, no. 3, was found in the silt over the early street and indicates that the layer could not have accumulated until after *c.* A.D. 250 at earliest. Nos. 2, 4, 7, and 9 were found in the late occupation level and the Roman debris level. No. 9, of Theodosius I, A.D. 379–95, is the latest in date and suggests that this level may well have continued to accumulate until well into the fifth century. No. 5 came from the filling of one of the Norman scaffolding pits, pit A1; nos. 1, 7, and 8 were unstratified.

Report by B. W. PEARCE, M.A., F.S.A.

No.	Emperor	Denomination	M. & S.[1]		Diam. in mm.
1	? Postumus (259–68)	Antoninianus	Indet.	Barbarous, but head suggests Postumus	..
2	Victorinus (268–70)	„	71	SALVS holds sceptre, not mentioned in *M. & S.* 71, but always present	18½
3	Radiate coin (250)	„	..	Broken. Figure holding patera	..
4	Barbarous radiate	„	..	Bead row in place of legend on rev.	13½
5	„	„	..	Clipped	..
6	„	„	..	Broken	17
			Cohen[2]		
7	House of Constantine (330–5)	Æ 3	17/19	VRBS ROMA. Mm. $\frac{|}{? \, \diamond \, e}$	15
8	Valens (364–78)	„	47	Mm. $\frac{|}{PCON}$	17
9	Theodosius I (379–95)	„	30	Mm. $\frac{P}{|}$	12½

[1] Mattingly and Sydenham's *Roman Imperial Coinage*.
[2] Cohen's *Médailles impériales*.

MARBLE VENEERS, WORKED STONES, AND GEOLOGICAL SPECIMENS

Report by MRS. J. E. MOREY (*Petrological Department, Geological Survey and Museum*)

(a) Marble veneers

1. A fragment of a white marble veneer 'veined' with parallel, silver-green and pale green bands; it is composed of fairly coarse grained calcite with a little dolomite; the bands are composed of green chlorite and phlogopite mica. This is undoubtedly Cipollino marble, from Greece. From the late occupation level.

2–3. Two fragments of a variety of Purbeck marble. It is a light grey limestone composed of somewhat larger specimens of *Viviparus* than in no. 8 below, with also fragments of other shells in a cream-coloured calcite matrix. The limestone is banded with alternate densely packed and less densely packed bands of shells. From the tumble of the Norman robbing of the Roman wall.

4. A white calcite marble or marble breccia heavily veined with micaceous minerals (including phlogopite), and stained with

limonite. Probably a variety of Carrara statuary marble. Cf. no. 6 below. Unstratified in the Norman bank.

5. A piece of a moulded marble veneer of a marble breccia of red, white, and cream-coloured fragments embedded in a grey matrix heavily veined with black material. It is composed of calcite and the coloration is due to staining. Cf. nos. 7 and 9 below. Unstratified in the Norman bank.

6. A white calcite marble, irregularly veined, and composed of coarse, interlocking calcite crystals. The veins are a silver and grey coloured mica. This specimen is most probably a variety of the white statuary marble of Carrara, cf. no. 4 above. Unstratified.

7. A fragment comparable to nos. 5 and 9.

8. A dark grey Purbeck marble or compact limestone composed of numerous whole and fragmentary shells of the small freshwater gastropod *Viviparus* (Paludina), which are cemented in a white to cream coloured calcite groundmass. The specimen is well matched with E. 9284 (in the Geological Museum) from Swanage. Unstratified.

9. A marble breccia composed of pink and white fragments and lenses set in a black coloured groundmass. The calcite of the

rock is stained by various concentrations of limonite and iron ores giving the coloration to the specimen. Unstratified.

(b) Paving-slabs

Several pieces of broken paving-slabs were found over the pink concrete floor, in a position which may equate with the 'blue lias' pavement of the earlier excavators, and also in the late street and unstratified levels. Some were badly weathered. These are of Purbeck marble. The calcite is stained pink, in a noticeable manner, by limonite, and a green coloration seen on a fresh surface is due to the presence of chamosite. Cubes and small grains of pyrites also occur in the matrix. The specimens may be matched with one that is exhibited in the Geological Museum (58043), a Purbeck marble from Peveril Point, Durlston Bay, Swanage, Dorset.

(c) Worked stones

1–2. Part of a 'pecked' stone and column with traces of paint, and a second worked fragment, were found in the Norman bank. They are a Jurassic, Purbeck limestone; a creamy-coloured limestone composed of a mass of comminuted shells, other organic remains, and very occasionally ooliths, cemented by fairly coarse white calcite. A very good match for this stone was E. 9509 (in the Geological Museum), a Purbeck building stone from Langton, Swanage, Dorset.

3. A small piece of a white moulded cornice is probably a brick made from a clay with a high percentage of gritty quartz grains.

(d) Geological specimens

1. In the Norman bank there were found specimens of a ferruginous sand composed of quartz and leucoxene grains, about 1·0 mm. in diameter on the average, but occasionally reaching 2·5 mm. The quartz is heavily coated and stained with limonite. Limonite is also present in small grains together with ilmenite and magnetite.

2. Slag was found in the sand make-up level.

Notes

The descriptions of the specimens have been confirmed by examination of a powder of the rocks, in oils, under the microscope. The search for matching specimens, for both the marbles and limestones, was very extensive. The only possible comparisons are those I have cited, so I think it rather more than a coincidence that the specimens of English rocks should come from the Swanage area.[1] Other well-known localities for the occurrence of *Viviparus* limestone are Charlwood in Sussex and the Isle of Wight.

Tiles and bricks

Some fifteen more or less complete Roman floor bricks were recovered from levels of different periods. These measured from 4–6 in. by 2 in. to $2\frac{3}{4}$ in. by 1–$1\frac{1}{2}$ in. Seven segmental quadrant bricks, which were sufficiently complete to measure, were 2–$2\frac{1}{2}$ in. thick, and had arc measurements varying from $7\frac{1}{2}$ in. up to 1 ft. 2 in. One whole large flat brick measured 1 ft. 2 in. by 1 ft. 1 in. by 3 in. Broken flanged tiles and tegulae occurred commonly. No die-patterned flue-tiles were found, but two tiles showed the imprints of fingers and a nailed boot.

HUMAN AND ANIMAL BONES

These have been examined and reported on by Dr. I. W. Cornwall. As the majority, and those of chief interest, were derived from Norman levels, his report will be published with the other Norman material. Those from the Roman levels consisted of ox (29), sheep (7), horse (3), and pig (9), and were undistinguished.

MOLLUSCA

Report by MISS M. MAITLAND HOWARD, F.Z.S.
(Member of the Conchological Society)

The shells submitted for examination are those which might be expected from Roman and Norman levels and present no special features. Other than oyster-shells, the species found consisted of:

15 *Helix aspersa.* (Late Roman debris level (1), late occupation level (7), and the make-up of the Norman bank (7).)

3 *Cepaea nemoralis.* (Late occupation level (1), the wall tumble from the Norman robbing of the Roman walls (2).)

5 *Cepaea hortensis.*
5 *Arianta arbustorum.*
2 *Oxychilus cellarius.*   (All from the wall tumble of the
1 *Vallonia pulchella.*   Norman robbing of the wall.)
1 *Caeciliodes acicula.*
1 *Retinella nitidula*

THE TEMPLE PRECINCT OR FORUM AS A WHOLE

(FIG. 81)

To the above excavation details and conclusions we add the following observations on the correlation of the Roman structures to the north and south of the Castle, together with notes on comparable sites.

The inferences so far to be derived all tend to the belief that the structure under the Castle is the podium of a classical temple, and if so almost certainly that of Claudius Caesar. The area round it was a public square, artificially levelled, at least where the ground sloped away to the north, with yellow sand. The latter demands some sort of surfacing, and remains of concrete bedding which may have formed this surface, or, more probably, carried stone slabs, have been found at various points north and south of the keep. Their correlation in time and level is a task for the future. The great square contained structures south of the temple compatible with those to be expected in front of a temple of great importance. It was surrounded by buildings which have proved to be asymmetric to some degree. On the north and west there were at least outer and inner walls with concrete floors between them, the upper perhaps having carried a pavement. The NE. corner was certainly provided with rooms. The south side has a monumental structure, of unexplained character, occupying a position which is certainly not central, and which has, so far as we know, only one wall on each side of it. There is some reason to suspect

---

[1] For an account of 'The Purbeck Marble Industry in the Roman Period' cf. Dunning, *Arch. News Letter* no. 11, March 1949, p. 15.

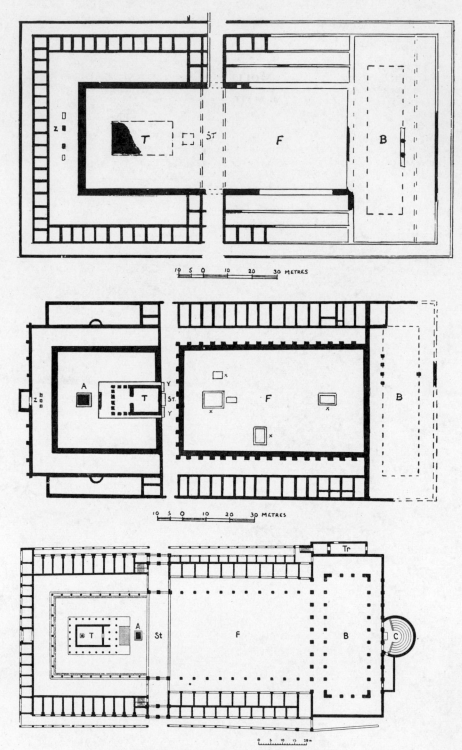

FIG. 96. Plans of Fora at Paris, St. Bertrand, and Augst.

By courtesy of 'Antiquity'

that the south side is different from the NW. and NE. quarters of the layout. There is no difficulty about this, but the main question as to whether the precinct was the Forum of the Colonia, or was devoted solely to the temple and its appurtenances and, possibly, some administrative buildings, remains unsolved.

As for size, the Colchester plan seems to measure 535 by 425 ft., or *c.* 177 by 107 metres, which is much larger than those at Augst, St. Bertrand, or Paris (fig. 96). It is also more nearly a square: two of the French sites are practically a double-square. Although exact symmetry is not found at either Augst or St. Bertrand, Colchester is markedly asymmetrical, not only in the temple being out of the centre, but in the plan of the two northern corners. If we assume that the street was brought through the court, as in the three French examples, the northern court is inconveniently abbreviated, although there was plenty of room, had it been desired, to run a double-square plan. There is another important difference in these plans. All four classical temples are surrounded by a masonry foundation, which served as a stylobate for a row of columns, with an open drain alongside. This at least is the case at Augst, and the same broad foundations at Paris and St. Bertrand seem to call for a similar interpretation. The portico thus supported surrounded the temple court on three sides and was for the temple alone, for the shops (if present) opened outwards. At St. Bertrand the broad stylobate is continued across the fourth side also.

These porticoes are of great width: from the back wall to the centre of the stylobate measures 14 metres at Paris, *c.* 9 metres at Augst (Schönbuhl), 7·5 metres at Augst Forum, and *c.* 8·5 metres at St. Bertrand. The Paris plan is very imperfect,[1] and some bases west of the temple, in the middle of the portico, may possibly represent a row of columns dividing it down the centre, making the span on each side 7·0 metres. A similarly heavy wall runs round the (forum) court opposite the temple at Paris and St. Bertrand. In all three examples the portico round this forum court is narrower than that round the temple.

But at Colchester we have no evidence, as yet, for any such portico. Its stylobate, elsewhere always over 2 metres thick, cannot as yet be matched here. Its absence on the south side, the only side at all extensively explored, is only to be expected. On the other three sides it is not known what structures may lie between the temple and the outer walls, but the drain at the NE. corner occupies a suggestive position within the court.

Another important difference between Colchester and these four temples is that they all face the east, whereas that of Colchester faces south. This is perhaps not a serious point, for many temples in Rome faced in southerly directions.

Thus, while it is quite possible to take a street through the court, as in the three examples quoted, this street is yet unproved, and the general impression and outline of the Colchester layout may possibly have a stronger connexion with that of the Schönbuhl at Augst.

The temple on the Schönbuhl[2] (fig. 97) is of similar type to ours, but colonnaded across the back. The length of the building over all, but omitting the steps, is 24·6 metres, and the width 16·5 metres. With the steps, which are in two flights, the length is 34 metres. The front is hexastyle. The surround consists only of a court bounded by a wall with porticoes inside and out. Six metres in front of the steps of the temple is the great altar. The architect was so determined upon his proportions that the porticoes have to project in places over the brow of the hill, and there they have to be supported on foundations going many feet down the slope, including spaces for rooms or shops at low level. There is in this some similarity to Mrs. Cotton's discoveries.

INSULA 23

Very little is known of this insula. The most part of it is covered by Hollytrees House and garden, and by the house and garden which were formerly adjacent on the east, now part of the Park. The north boundary has not been found (p. 113); the south boundary was found in July 1921, but only as a 12-ft. length of the wall bordering the street.[3] The west side is bounded by the forum; the position of the east side is obscure, owing to the peculiar line taken by the street from the NE. Gate where last seen, but according to P. G. Laver the street on the east lies where shown.

112. On the position of the main street see p. 65. The few objects found in those excavations are not worth recording here.

INSULA 24

This is the least known of all. Almost the whole of it is covered by the house and gardens of Greyfriars, which belongs to the County High School for Girls, and by the Post Office Engineer's Depot. Excavation work on the open ground here is much to be desired, for both the Roman and the later remains. The street

---

[1] F. de Pachtere, *Paris à l'époque gallo-romaine* (1916), plan iii.
[2] Laur-Belart, 99, Abb. 31–33.

[3] Laver, Diary, 27/11/1922 and 21/11/1922. Both entries are full and precise, and make it quite clear that for 400 ft. west of the East Gate (*J.R.S.* x, 89) we must read 584 ft.

on the north is unknown, and the town wall on the east is inaccessible. The streets on the west and on the south have been fixed (pp. 75, 65).

When extending Greyfriars in 1904 the following coins were found: a second brass of Vespasian; plated

(1707), with reservoir and tower, and the grounds of St. Mary's Rectory (1873), while the part bordering the east side has been built over.

84. A concrete road, apparently Roman, is mentioned by Wire (Album, p. 4) as seen west of Head

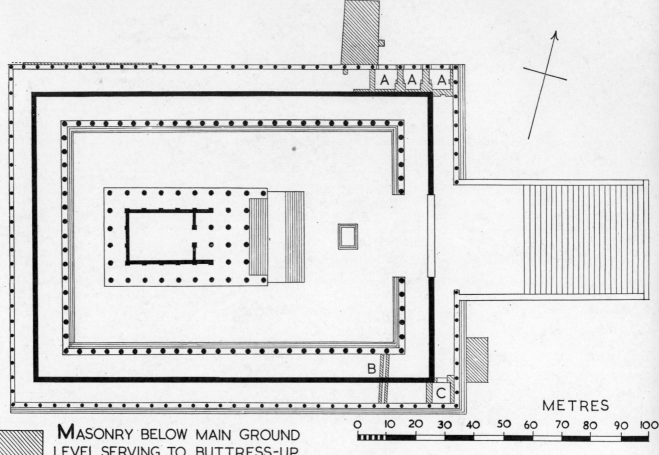

MASONRY BELOW MAIN GROUND LEVEL, SERVING TO BUTTRESS-UP THE CORNERS OF THE MAIN BUILDING WHERE THE HILL FALLS AWAY. A, SHOPS AT LOW LEVEL, B, STORM-DRAIN, C, LODGE(?), ABOVE GROUND(?).

FIG. 97. Plan of the Temple on the Schönbuhl at Augst, Switzerland. After two plans by Laur-Belart.

denarius of Saloninus; bronze Constantinian, and a very small late bronze coin (714.04).

INSULA 25

This lies immediately south of the Balkerne Gate. The town wall, in excellent preservation, bounds it on the west, and at the SW. angle lies a tower with the curious little postern doorway. The dimensions of the insula should be close on 534 ft. E.–W. by 350 ft. N.–S.

Recent finds in this area have been very few, for a large part of the insula is covered by the Waterworks

Street on the north side of the angle with Church Street. The account is not very convincing and has not been confirmed.

91. Morant, p. 183, says there is a tessellated pavement in the cherry garden belonging to the Rector of St. Mary's,[1] on the north side of the parsonage, not many yards from another in St. Mary's churchyard (no. **89**). The parsonage in Morant's time stood immediately north of the church; thus the site is marked on the lawn of the present rectory.

92. On the other hand, a tessellated pavement was

---

[1] Morant was Rector of St. Mary's.

found under the east wall of the SE. bay window of the modern rectory when it was built in 1781, together with foundations.[1]

In 1936 a trench for a water main was cut along the west side of Head Street, and a drawn section was made of part of it. One part has already given us a section of a possible street (p. 69); the portion north of this, falling in this insula, remains to be described. It is close upon the east margin of the area.

After the wall on the north side of the E.–W. street (if such it be) the yellowish loam which formed the bottom of the trench was capped by a thin layer of mortar, and above that was a continuous layer of hard gravel about 3 in. thick, presumably a yard. Above this the soil was all made and without stratification save for part of a tapering band of charcoal near the wall.

After another tunnel of 6 ft. we again find a wall, this time seen in the east side of the trench only, though a slot full of dark earth and charcoal may possibly indicate that it once continued westwards. The foundation was 2 ft. wide and 2 ft. deep, made of rubble concrete; the top was 3 ft. 3 in. from the surface. Beyond it the yellowish loam proved to be made, containing oyster-shells and pottery; upon it lay a thick burnt layer, varying in thickness from 5 in. at the north to 17 in. at the south, where it was flush against the line of the wall. Here the larger part of it consisted of crushed tile; the rest was particularly black on top and very hard, resembling a trodden surface. Upon this lay a thin band of greyish-brown clayey loam about 2 in. thick, and above this a double layer of mortar divided by a thin, dead black line. This layer would appear to correspond with the mortar layer noticed before. It contained loose mortar, gravel, and broken tile, and was 2 in. thick at the south and 5 in. thick at the north end. Above it was a 6-in. layer of hard blackish soil mixed with charcoal, which may have something to do with the charcoal in the previous section.

The length of the next tunnel and section was, unfortunately, not noted, but cannot have been much. The evidence from the section is only for a sloping and tapering band of gravel. After this there was another tunnel for 5 ft. and then the last section. In the first 2 ft. we see the ends of no less than five thin layers meeting at a point 2 ft. from the surface. The lowest is of grey loam, the next charcoal, the next red clay, followed by another of grey loam, and finally by one of mortar. Above this again we find the black layer, now reduced to about 7 in., and stopping suddenly near the end of our trench. In the centre of this last section another foundation of pebble-concrete, 2 ft. thick and

at least 2 ft. deep, was cut through. Its top was 2 ft. 4 in. from the surface. It was set in the disturbed yellow loam, without evident traces of foundation trench. There was some depth of made earth with charcoal lying to the north of it and extending over it.

The trench ended opposite Culver Street, down which it turned.

The pottery found in this insula cannot be listed here. But we must mention a mortarium rim found in 1936 bearing the graffito >IVSTI SVPIIRI.[2] Other finds include coins, mostly illegible, and a finger-ring of white metal with carnelian intaglio (234.38).

141. In September 1936 Mr. E. S. Rudsdale noted a red cement floor 'under the building east of Jumbo' (the great water tower). We do not know which building is meant.

177. Cutts shows a cross for a pavement in the middle of the junction of Head Street with High Street. His siting is often very wrong, but presumably this represents a pavement somewhere near here which is not otherwise recorded.

INSULA 26

The line of the streets around this insula is fairly well known, and the dimensions must have been close on 310 ft. N.–S. by 330 ft. The area was closely built over until Mumford's works were pulled down in 1938. A few trial trenches were dug at that time to see whether an excavation was desirable. It was found that the Roman level was 9 ft. below the surface, and because no notable remains were struck the project was abandoned. The area is now a car-park.

The following remains have been found:

81. Wire's Diary, 23/5/1856: 'A pavement made with red tesserae was discovered in laying a drain down Mr. Hitchcock's back way, Culver St. As the trench for the drain was very narrow there was no means of ascertaining the size of it. The master informed me that in one part it was considerably worn as if by a deal of traffic on it.' (Sketch-plan, showing the position as about opposite Bank Passage.)

This is probably the red border of that found 6 September 1886, partly under Culver Street and partly under adjacent buildings, at the gateway to Mumford's Iron Foundry, 60 yards east of Head Street. A large piece was raised and taken to the Museum. The depth was about 5 ft. The red border on the north side was at least 5 ft. wide. The pattern, chiefly black and white, strongly resembles that from N. Station Road (**82**, p. 240). Face downwards on the pavement lay the plaster from the walls, brightly coloured in patterns, but so decayed it could not be preserved.

---

[1] Cutts, plan, shows it well away to the east of the house; O.S. 1:500 map, 1875, xxvii. 12. 8.
[2] 'Of the century of Justius Super', *J.R.S.* xxxiv. 91.

The concrete under the pavement was unusually thin (about 3 in.) and lay on hard dry gravel. Parts of walls of septaria were found in the middle of the street.[1]

83. Foundations of Roman buildings found under modern buildings along the south side of High Street are marked on the 1:500 map at four places, 112, 154, 207, and 254 ft. from Head Street respectively, without any date, and we possess no description of these. They also appear on Cutts's plan, where they are five in number. The same map marks under the former Colchester and Essex Bank, now Messrs. Kent, Blaxill's shop (no. 3A), the site of the discovery of the bronze Cupid riding on a griffin.[2]

130. In August 1936 a water main was cut along Culver Street from Head Street, against the sets paving the south gutter. The first length, to past Bank Passage, was unproductive. The following notes were taken in the next section—the measurements are from the SW. corner of Bank Passage.

136 and **137.** Opposite this corner a red tessellated pavement was struck, which extended for 25 ft. eastwards. Just west of it stood a pottery vessel with shattered lid, and just east of it the sides of a doorway in tiles. Noted by Mr. E. J. Rudsdale, who also observed slight traces of a gravelled surface opposite the back gate of Barclays Bank, and, adjoining it on the east, another red tessellated pavement 10 ft. wide (**137**).

At 33 ft. 5 in. to 35 ft. 5 in. was the broken (?) end of a Roman wall of tiles, in the north side of the trench, at 3 ft. 8 in. from the surface. There was nothing to be seen on either side till 38 ft. 7 in., where the angle of a wall of tiles jutted into the trench, at an angle, from the south, at a depth of 3 ft. 6 in. Beyond this there were very broken remains of septaria walling, of which no face could be observed. It appeared to have been wider on the south side of the trench than on the north. P. G. Laver, who saw it, said it was the west wall of the room containing the black and white pavement, no. **81** above. We made it out to be 5 to 6 ft. wide on the south side, with a much smaller mass of septaria visible on the north, as if a corner had been cut through.

Farther on a wall of massive blocks of septaria was cut through exactly opposite the centre of Lay and Wheeler's building. Its thickness could not be ascertained. The mortar was of sandy colour.

Just beyond this there was a platform of several courses of tile laid flat, in good mortar. The depth was 3 ft. from the street. It began exactly opposite the SE. corner of Laver and Wheeler's and extended for 16 ft. to a point opposite the east side of the passage on the east of the same building, and may have continued another 3 ft.

The level of this platform, which included hypocaust tiles measuring 8 by 8½ in., coincided with a division line in the strata, above which the soil was black: below it was dirty yellowish and sticky.

Three feet from the passage-way another wall of septaria crossed the trench, and it is possible that this turned at once and ran along the north side of the trench, for large pieces of septaria, with mortar adhering, were pulled out all along this side.

Another wall, or remains of one, was found crossing the trench at right angles directly opposite the centre of the east valve of the doors of the Culver Heating Company. The width was 18 in. and depth from surface 27 in. The mortar was yellow, as before.

There followed an interval of about 6 ft., beyond which the bottom of the trench was on a copious layer of Roman rubble.

130. A Roman drain was found in this same trench opposite the door of Messrs. Benham's printing-works, but only the top of its arch was exposed, at a depth of 5 ft. 6 in., running N.–S. The position appears to place it by the west side of the N.–S. street. Observed by Mr. E. J. Rudsdale.

An entry at the head of a long list in the Accessions Book reads: 'Group of 4 Roman vessels coins and bronze objects found in High St.'; in the margin, 'Antiquities found in Colchester from Feb. 1888 to Feb. 1889 procured for the Essex Arch. Soc.' In the margin Mr. A. G. Wright has written after the words 'High St.' 'opposite the Corn Exchange in Feb. 1889'. This is presumably on verbal information from Alderman A. M. Jarmin, who collected all these objects for the Society. The alderman did not keep notes, and his observations are not always reliable. We cannot accept this alleged discovery of four vessels (by implication a grave) in the very course of the main Roman street.

Other excavations have produced pottery and coins. We cannot deal with the former here. In 1927 Barclays Bank was enlarged, and four bronze coins were found, one of Sabina (?). In 1874 alterations were made to Messrs. Benham and Harrison's printing-works, and in 1927 a tunnel was cut northwards under High Street from Barclays Bank; both of these works produced pottery only.

A foundation-pot, a grey jar f. 268, was found at Mumford's works in May 1896 (184.86).

INSULA 27

Except for the exact position of the Roman 'High Street', the streets bounding this insula are pretty well known. They give dimensions of about 350 ft. N.–S. by 368 ft. E.–W. No. **82** below is the best evidence we

[1] Accessions Book, Nov. 1886; *T.E.A.S.* n.s. iii, 207 (col. plate) and x, 88.   [2] *J.B.A.* i, 334.

have that the southern part of High Street, in this length of it, was built up in Roman days.

74. Very hard foundations are described as found at a depth of 5 ft., east of Trinity Street, opposite the house of Worts, surgeon (nos. 5 and 6). The O.S. 1:500 map marks the site under the fence in front of the doorway of the tower of Trinity Church. See also *T.E.A.S.* o.s. v, 158.

75. A tessellated pavement was found at a depth of 6 ft. at the back entrance (in Culver St.) to no. 1 Trinity Street, when excavating for a drain. No coloured tesserae were found, and the remains could not be traced because of surrounding buildings.[1]

76. Foundations were seen by P. G. Laver in 1880 in the garden of no. 1 Trinity Street. (The position indicated by Wheeler and Laver is important, for only Laver could fix it.)

82. Two walls of brick and septaria found under the modern High Street south of the former tram-lines, January 1920, are marked on the 1:500 map in the Museum. One extends to 17 ft. 6 in. north of the building line, the other to 6 ft. They were 354 ft. from the (then) SW. angle of High Street, lying apparently in an E.–W. direction, and were 2 ft. 6 in. thick and 3 ft. high; from the surface to their base was 7 ft. Observed by P. G. Laver.

93. In 1926–7 the present 'Oak Hall' behind Messrs. Wrights' Restaurant on Culver Street was built and the level of the ground reduced. In this work remains of walls of septaria were observed, two running N.–S. and one E.–W. They were very fragmentary and yielded no coherent plan. There were no floors. Much pottery was found, including a grey jar f. 278, standing on two tiles, almost certainly a foundation offering, and the following coins: Vespasian, Philip; Salonina; Tetricus; Cl. Gothicus; Carausius; Allectus; Constantinopolis; Constantius II (2); and twelve illegible third or fourth century.

98. A trench cut down Trinity Street, 5 ft. from the east kerb, lacked interest except that just south of Culver Street three parallel walls were cut through, the first lying 26 ft. south of the north building-line of Culver Street, the second 31 ft., and the third 40 ft. They were 2 ft. thick and of the usual character. The first was exposed again in another excavation against the west kerb. It was 2 ft. 9 in. thick, and 4 ft. from the surface. Its top two courses were of tile.[2] The small finds are listed in the Museum. There were no floors.

162. In 1938–9 the excavations for the Public Library exposed 23 ft. of the south boundary of this insula just east of the SW. corner. The wall was faced with small blocks of septaria: 24 ft. north of the street, under the north wall of the Library, near the NW. corner, lay a patch of red tessellated pavement 13 ft. long by 3 ft. wide, continuing southwards. Eighty feet east of the NW. corner of the Library, just south of the NE. corner, lay another small patch of red pavement, measuring 5 ft. by 3 ft. 6 in.

193. In October 1936 a Roman wall 2 ft. wide was cut through in Culver Street opposite the back entrance to the Essex Standard Offices. Noted by E. J. Rudsdale.

Other chance finds include: seventy-eight small paving bricks and fragments of others, from the site of the National Bank, 1925 (C.M. 5145.25).

Eight coins found on the site of Lloyds Bank during rebuilding comprised Claudius I; Claudius II (2); Victorinus; Constantinian (2); and two post-Roman (C.M. 5356.26).

Much pottery has come in from time to time from sites just west of Pelham's Lane. It includes some tenth-century ware, which is quite scarce in the town.

INSULA 28

The streets can be fairly closely planned except that on the east (which has not been seen south of High St.) and the dimensions should be about 325 ft. E.–W. by a little less (310 ft.) N.–S. This insula seems to have been pretty well covered with houses of good class.

66. Fragments of a Roman wall, consisting of ten courses of tiles on a rubble foundation, are standing in the cellar of no. 34 High Street on its east side. It seems to run E.–W. and its north face is 9½ ft. south of the south building line of High Street. The remaining brickwork is 2 ft. high and 2 ft. 1 in. wide. Its top is 22 in. below the level of the modern pavement.[3]

67. 'Another [decorated pavement] was found on the S. side of the Red Lion Inn, when part of it was converted into an iron warehouse. A great quantity of the pieces were preserved and set in an arbour in one of the gardens belonging to the Inn.'[4] This has long disappeared.

J.R.S. ix, 166 assumes that this is the same as the black and white pavement noted by Wire: '... a pavement composed of black and white tesserae in some design ... running E. to W. across the yard of the Red Lion ... as only about 18 ins. of this was uncovered it was impossible to see what subject was composed on it. Morant mentions a pavement of this sort being discovered on these premises ....'[5] The position is halfway between High Street and Culver Street, Wire, map in 'County Illustrations', no. 19 (1848).

68. In 1857 a very fine piece of pavement was found

---

[1] *T.E.A.S.* x, 88.   [2] Laver, Diary, 17/5/1928.
[3] *R.C.H.M.* 28; and notes in Laver MSS.

[4] Morant, p. 183.
[5] *J.B.A.* v (1849), 86; Wire, Diary, 3/1/1849.

in the Red Lion yard in making a drain, about 2 ft. underground. The ornamental part was about 25 ft. square. All attempts to persuade the proprietor to allow it to be taken up failed, and the drain was cut through it. A drawing in the Museum by J. Parish furnishes our pl. XXIV, B. It is made to the scale of 3 in. = 1 ft., and the tesserae were either exceptionally small, or he has drawn them too small. The pattern is exceptional in many ways, but there is no doubt that the artist is untrustworthy. He shows red and black only, with no yellow—or, more exactly, he has, we believe, coloured all white *and yellow* areas yellow uniformly. The portion shown is a hexagon only 3 ft. 6 in. across, with a red surround.[1]

68A. Just south of **68**, on 22/9/1882, part of a decorated mosaic pavement was found, apparently in the actual back entrance to the hotel yard from Culver Street. A drawing of it, with measured plan of its position, by F. Evelyn Morris is in the Museum (pl. XXIV, C). Within the red border are two white ones divided by a black one, within which is a cabled band of black, red, and yellow. Some of the buff tesserae have been replaced by white ones in part of the angle—probably an ancient repair. Within the cabled band is a narrow white band and then the main pattern begins, of which only a small portion of black and white triangles remains. The fragment is preserved in the lounge of the hotel.

There is no evidence that this is the same as any of those previously mentioned. That shown by Wire on his plan (fig. 100) and mentioned in his letter to Roach Smith is the one found in January 1849 (**67**).

180. Labourers laying a drain in the Red Lion yard found a pavement of small white tesserae.[2]

181. In February 1937 the east side of the Red Lion yard was converted into a large lounge. The trench for the new west wall revealed an ordinary red pavement at a depth of 3 ft., near the north end. It could be the margin of one of the preceding. Neither of these last two pavements can be marked on a plan of such small scale as ours.

69. In 1849 Wire reported: 'Lion Walk, at the north end a tessellated pavement of coarse red tesserae one inch square was exposed . . . and broken up' (no. 4 on his plan, fig. 98). Diary, 30/10/1848; see also *J.B.A.* x, 96.

73. In 1748 and subsequently a tessellated pavement has been uncovered in the garden of Trinity House, nearly 3 ft. below the surface (see insula 36).[3]

94. In February 1920 a Roman well was found 16 ft. east of the SE. corner of Pelham's Lane. It was 4 ft. 8 in.

in diameter and 33 ft. 6 in. deep. Recorded by the Borough Engineer on the 1:500 map.

95. In 1928 foundations were cut for a warehouse for Messrs. Woolworth on ground immediately east of the 'Red Lion' on Culver Street. The trench for the north wall 48 ft. from Culver Street exposed part of a wall running E.–W., consisting of 4–5 courses of septaria set in yellowish mortar. There was only 5 ft. of it, with broken ends, and no sign of any continuation. The top was about 4 ft. from the surface and the bottom about 7 ft. It stands on a layer of loose mortar rubble of whitish colour; below this there is about a foot of yellowish loam, then a very bold line of 2 in. of charcoal, below which is natural 'pug' over gravel. The trenches for the east and west walls went down to the same level, but in them the natural soil was only 5 ft. from the surface. The layers here were too confused to be of use, but a record was taken of them.

96. In January 1922 a pavement was found immediately inside the NE. corner of Lion Walk, when sinking a petrol tank. The plain red floor was tilted towards the middle, where it was spoilt by a pit of uncertain date. The end of a Roman wall 3 ft. thick just showed in the south face of the excavation. The pavement was 2 ft. 6 in. to 4 ft. 6 in. from the surface, and to the top of the wall was 5 ft.[4]

100. A rubble foundation 2 ft. wide was found 3 ft. below the surface of the east pavement of Pelham's Lane, near the north end and about 18 in. from the east building face. At the time the writer thought it part of a curved wall, but P. G. Laver saw it as straight, and we now incline to his view. It appeared to run N.–S. under the east pavement, and was seen at a point only a few feet south of High Street.

133. In 1936 Messrs. Sainsbury made alterations in the garden second west from the 'Red Lion'. A foundation trench cut along the east side of the extension revealed the foundations of three Roman walls. The first, about 3 ft. from the surface, was 2 ft. from the building line of Culver Street, and only 1 ft. wide. Nine feet north of it, 2 ft. 9 in. from the surface, lay another, 2 ft. thick. The third was 19 ft. north of the second, again about 3 ft. from the surface, but only 1 ft. thick. All ran E.–W., roughly parallel to Culver Street, and the spaces between them had been floored with clay, at 3 ft. 6 in. from the surface. The trench cut was only 4 ft. deep, so what lay below was unknown. The pit between the first two walls is recent. Observed by Mr. E. J. Rudsdale.

During alterations to the present premises of Messrs.

[1] *J.B.A.* x, 87.
[2] Wire, Diary, 3/1/1849; *T.E.A.S.* o.s. v, 158.
[3] Morant, iii, 21; Brayley and Britton, v, 293; Cutts, plan i, 12; O.S. map xxvii.
[4] Laver, Diary, 10/1/1922. The few measurements given do not suffice to enter these on the map.

Marks and Spencer remains of a decorated mosaic pavement were observed under the east boundary of the site (Feb. 1936). There was possibly another pavement running under Sainsbury's. The pottery found has been listed.

in Culver Street opposite Wolton and Attwood's, approximately central to the north face of the building, 3 ft. 6 in. from the surface and 24 ft. E.–W. Four days later there is another entry with a sketch showing part of Ager's house (next on west, now demolished); under

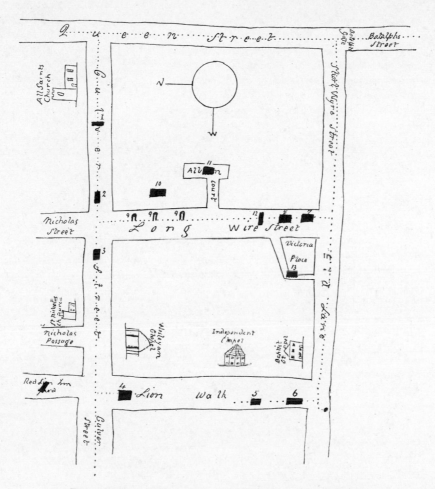

Fig. 98. Wm. Wire's plan of Insulae 28–30. (pp. 203–4.)

138. In September 1936 Mr. E. J. Rudsdale noticed gravel 2 ft. 6 in. thick overlying a stratum of burnt clay and daub in Culver Street east of the Roman street.

139. Gravel layers were also observed by him in Culver Street from Pelham's Lane to the corner of the public lavatories, and a wall running N.–S. opposite the NW. corner of the latter.

140. Pieces of marble have been found in Culver Street as far west as the 'Red Lion' Tap (see pp. 202–3). E. J. Rudsdale.

178. A pavement of red and buff tesserae was found

the east part is shown a Roman wall running N.–S., the top 3 ft. from the surface, the width not given. Under the west part, 3 ft. 6 in. from the surface, is a pavement of mixed red and buff tesserae, of considerable lateral extent.[1] The wall is probably the same as (**139**).

179. (Not shown on plan.) At the back of no. 17 High Street, close to the back door at the end of the passage from Culver Street, and under the wall of the adjacent no. 18, is a well about 60 to 70 ft. deep. The exact position is under an arch in the wall, close to the ground. It is about 6 ft. in diameter, made of Roman

[1] Ibid. 12/12/1922 and 16/12/1922. It should be made clear that wall and pavement lay under Culver Street.

materials and stuccoed from top to bottom. The plaster is very hard. There were several feet of water in it.[1] There are lists of pottery from the insula, also coins of Vespasian, Trajan; Hadrian; Antoninus Pius; Faustina; Tetricus (2); Victorinus; Constantine the Great; Constantius II; two illegible second brass; and one illegible third brass.

171. In 1927 a small extension was made to the west side of the cellar of Messrs. Currys' shop in High Street[2] (nos. 45–46), next east of the 'Red Lion'. At a certain point a heavy deposit of pottery was found, which, when collected, proved to be some 400 fragments of Terra Sigillata, a few fragments of yellow-green glazed ware, a sherd or two of grey ware, and one or two fragments of medieval ware, one of which was decorated with a broad scroll of white paint, presumably part of a fourteenth-century gotch.

There were over 350 fragments of plain T.S. The forms were all of early date, and not in great variety. Ritterling 1, 9, and 12

The stamps of the potters are as follows (fig. 99):

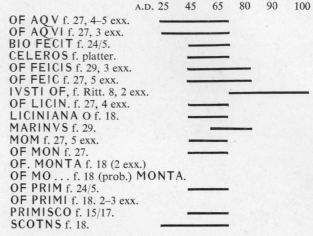

A.D. 25 45 65 80 90 100

OF AQV f. 27, 4–5 exx.
OF AQVI f. 27, 3 exx.
BIO FECIT f. 24/5.
CELEROS f. platter.
OF FEICIS f. 29, 3 exx.
OF FEIC f. 27, 5 exx.
IVSTI OF, f. Ritt. 8, 2 exx.
OF LICIN. f. 27, 4 exx.
LICINIANA O f. 18.
MARINVS f. 29.
MOM f. 27, 5 exx.
OF MON f. 27.
OF. MONTA f. 18 (2 exx.)
OF MO... f. 18 (prob.) MONTA.
OF PRIM f. 24/5.
OF PRIMI f. 18. 2–3 exx.
PRIMISCO f. 15/17.
SCOTNS f. 18.

Also IIVI., f. Ritt. 8; two illegible, same matrix, f. 24/5; two illegible, same matrix, f. 27.

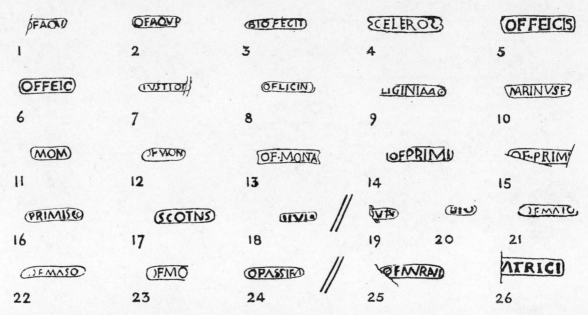

FIG. 99. Potters' stamps. 1–18, second shop (p. 198); 19–24, first shop (pp. 154–5); 25, see p. 74; 26, see p. 170.
Scale ¼.

are conspicuously absent. With the exception of one fragment each of forms 31 and 79 (with stamps ...VNIIM (?) and illegible) which are mid-second century or later, the whole collection is clearly from the stock of a pottery shop of the first century, which had been destroyed by fire, for many of the pieces are burnt brown.

The forms represented and the fragments found are as follows: f. 29 (c. 50); f. 15/17 (29); f. 18 (71); f. 24/5 (25); f. 27 (141); f. Ritt. 8 (18).

On these there are the following observations to make. The stamps AQV and AQVI are difficult to differentiate, and, indeed, may be one and the same. CELEROS has the S reversed; the only other British record is from London. Felix of Montans and La Graufesenque is dated by Knorr (for decorated ware) A.D. 60–70, by Oswald Claudius–Vespasian: see further on the decorated bowls below. On IVSTI OF see below. Neither of the two stamps of the Licinian firm occurred at Sheepen, where the name was very common. Whether MON is short for

---

[1] MS. note by H. Laver.　　　[2] *C.M.R.* 1948, 17; 1950, 18; *J.R.S.* xxxviii, 91.

MONIVS or MONTANVS we will not hazard. For SCOT-
NVS we prefer a date Tiberius–Nero, rather than Oswald's
Tiberius–Vespasian.

It is clear that Justus stands out from his fellows and has been

and Mommo in this case, and especially of Felix. The last appears most usefully more in the decorated ware, so that we can
add to our records almost complete drawings of three bowls
signed by him.

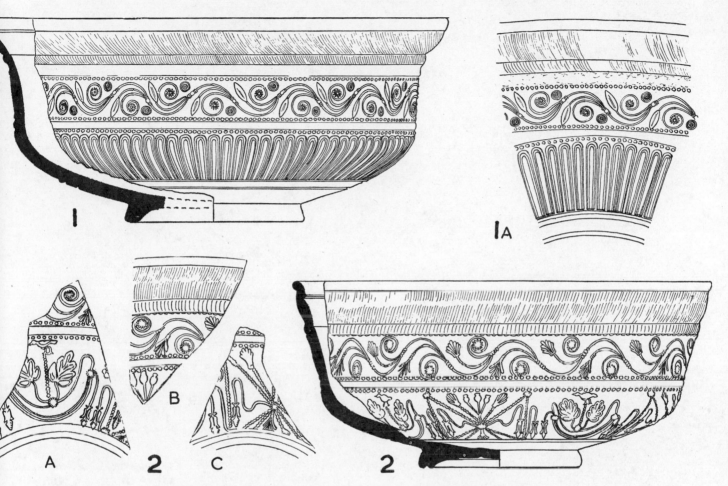

FIG. 100. Decorated Samian ware from the Second Pottery Shop. Scale ½.

misdated at A.D. 70–96 (Oswald). A line drawn vertically at the
year 61 falls within the main period of activity of our potters,
though admittedly near the end of that of Aquitanus and
Scottius. These pieces may have already been old at the time. As
for Justus, it is fortunate that the form of the cup Ritterling 8 is
well known to be at latest about A.D. 65, and since another
example of this form is known bearing his mark (Oswald, p. 155)
we can safely say that his period of activity must begin farther
back. Thus he becomes as firmly established in the picture as the
rest.

The decorated fragments number about seventy, and some are
very large. Some fit together, and we are provided with three
nearly complete bowls signed by Felix and a fourth not signed.
As with the plain wares, these decorated wares are all of a
character which would suit a similar date. It is noticeable how
the stock of the two shops tends to a repetition of certain names,
as if the cases of goods had come in largely bearing the stamp
of one potter. Compare the frequency of the stamps of Primus
and of Virthus (?) at the first shop, and of Aquitanus, Licinus,

THE DECORATED SIGILLATA

(FIGS. 100–2)

1. Large part of a bowl, f. 29, with very early decoration,
which might have come from the same mould as the bowl by
Licinus, *Cam.*, pl. XXXI, 1. The stamp is missing. (C.M. 177.47.)

2. Most part of a bowl, f. 29, parts of the lower band missing.
The upper frieze early and even simpler than the last. Compare
generally *Cam.*, pl. XXIX, 1 and 2, and in detail the fragment
pl. XXXIII, 7, where a similar leaf appears in the lower band. For
alternation of saltire and upright plant in panel compare *Cam.*,
pls. XXIX, 2, XXXV, 2, XXXVII, 1, and many other references
could be made. The motifs are all additional to those known to
Knorr (Taf. 52). The stamp is MARINVS, whose decorated
ware is rare, and who worked from about A.D. 50 to 80. (C.M.
178.47.)

3. Most part of a bowl, f. 29, with typically Neronic decoration. The opposite-leaved scroll of the upper band is uncommon,

cf. *Cam.*, pls. xxviii, 1, xxx, 21–23. The lower band, with its many leaved, but one-sided, scroll is not early, and the upright plant ornament, though early in use, is found with a late style upper band on *Cam.*, pl. xxxvi, 7. This bowl is stamped OFFEICIS. (C.M. 175.47.)

without any demarcations. The types are well known and belong to the style of LICINVS, but the bowl is signed OFFEICIS. These three bowls add materially to the motifs used by this potter as shown by Knorr, Taf. 32; see also Knorr, 1952, Taf. 23, 24. (C.M. 221.47.)

FIG. 101. Samian ware from the Second Pottery Shop. [**171**], pp. 199–200. Scale ½.

4. Most part of a bowl of f. 29, burnt brown. The beading of the rim is evanescent. The upper band is panelled in a latish style which hardly appeared at Camulodunum (pl. xxxvii, 4). The lower band is very badly double-struck so that much of it is obscured, but the style of the pattern is obvious. Several examples of the polygonal leaves and the winding wreath of leaflets will be found in the Camulodunum plates. This bowl also is stamped OFFEICIS. (C.M. 176.47.)

5. Fragment of early type with very upright rim. Decoration not so early, though the scrolls are double and not multiple-leaved. Both seem to be one-sided (part of a medallion is seen in the bottom right corner). The motifs include nos. 11, 21, and 22 of PRIMVS and the date is Claudius–Nero. Knorr, Taf. 65. (C.M. 180.47.)

5a. (Fig. 75.) Most part of a bowl, f. 29. The upper band, though a straight wreath, is not of early type. Other examples are *Cam.*, pl. xxxv, 10, 14–16. The lower band, though free figures are frequent in the Claudius–Nero period, is unusual because it is

6. Three fragments of a large bowl, f. 29. The upper scroll is double and simple, the lower also simple, but quadruple. Compare *Cam.*, pl. xxviii, 2, which also has the leaf of our no. 6 and is stamped OF CRESTIO, and for style, ibid., pl. xxx, 2, 3. The leaf is probably the same as that on *Cam.*, pl. xxxvi, 4, 5, and 17. Compare work of LIBERTVS, LICINVS, and MELAINI MA (Knorr, Taf. 44, 45, and 55). (C.M. 189.47.)

7. Much of a large thick bowl. The upper scroll is Nero–Vespasian; the lower, multiple, one-sided, with upright plant, is pre-Flavian: cf. *Cam.*, pl. xxxvi, 7. For general style compare DARIBITVS (Knorr, Taf. 31 E) AQVITANVS K. 1952, Taf. 4, 5. (C.M. 179.47.)

8. Fragment with similar upper scroll. Divided below into two bands: cf. *Cam.*, pl. xxxvi, 14, where the imbricated leaves may be the same; and ibid., pl. xxxv, 7, stamped SCOTNVS, with the same plume-like motif. (C.M. 187A.47.)

9. Similar fragment. Upper scroll one-sided, with medallions, the lower with free animals. The latter style is early enough: cf.

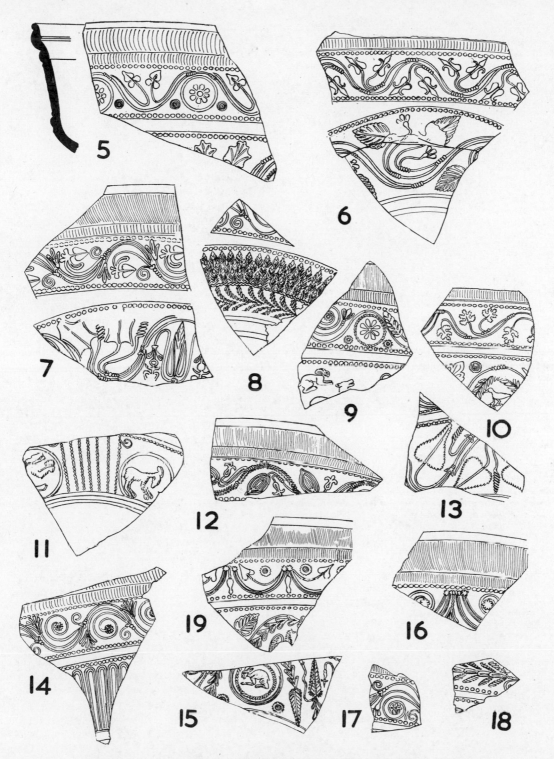

FIG. 102. Samian ware from the Second Pottery Shop, pp. 200–2. Scale ½.

Cam., pl. xxxvi, 3. Possible potters are LICINVS and PRIMVS. (C.M. 183.47.)

10. Another early piece with simple, double scroll in the upper band and the large scroll below incorporating the leafy wreath used by LICINVS. Compare *Cam.*, pls. xxv, 3, xxxii, 1, xxxiv, 1–6. The date is Claudian. (C.M. 194.47.)

11. Fragment of early ware panelled by wavy lines, with medallions of goats and bears. The former seems to be Oswald 1828 (Nero–Vespasian), the latter Hermet, pl. 26, 1. (C.M. 186.47.)

12. Fragment with upper band of early type with double and dissimilar leaves, scroll on a winding wreath. Exact parallels are *Cam.*, pl. xxv, 15–16. The date is Claudian. (C.M. 182.47.)

13. Fragment of large quadruple scroll, with a large leaf not in Knorr, but compare K. 1952, Taf. 35 A and 46 A (NAMVS). (C.M. 191.47.)

14. Fragment with simple scroll with spirals, gadroons below. Neronian. (C.M. 181.47.)

15. Fragment of lower band in rather free style. Several of the motifs are used by LICINVS. (C.M. 195.47.)

16. Fragment of upper frieze, with festoons or panelled scroll, cf. *Cam.*, pl. xxxv, 3–6. (C.M. 184.47.)

17. Small fragment of upper band, similar to that of no. 14 above. (C.M. 196.47.)

18. Small fragment of upper band with horizontal wreath in the later style, cf. *Cam.*, pl. xxxv, 7 (signed by SCOTNVS); 8 and 9 on the same plate are similar. The particular motif used does not appear in the Camulodunum plates, but cf. *Hofheim*, Taf. xxv, 11 and 13 and K. 1952, Taf. 34. (C.M. 190.47.)

19. Fragment similar to no. 16. In lower band the garland of LICINVS and an eagle. Compare *Cam.*, pl. xxxii, 1 and DARIBITVS (Knorr, Taf. 31 E). The leaf is smaller than that on no. 9, but both occur on *Cam.*, pl. xxxvi, 9, stamped by LICINVS. (C.M. 185.47.)

OTHER WARES

The deposit included seven fragments of brownish yellow glazed ware. The glaze is thick and bright, covering a decoration of white circles with central blob in a line round the bulge, which show through the glaze. The remains are of small globular beakers, of which no rim-fragment is preserved in this deposit, but there was one, with small beading, in the first pottery shop (pl. xxii, B). All are of the same type and series as certain beakers from the first shop, but there the glaze was very dark, thin, hard, and matt. Two quite different sources of supply are indicated, except for the rim just mentioned.

The potters' stamps are illustrated in fig. 99.

INSULA 29

This insula is very ill defined, especially on the east. It would be the same width N.–S. as the last, but its E.–W. dimension remains uncertain.

The following three records are on the O.S. 1:500 map, without date, and nothing further is known concerning them.

62. Tessellated pavement under the west side of the Sunday School of the Wesleyan Chapel, 104 ft. south of the centre of Culver Street and 176 ft. east of the centre of Lion Walk. O.S. 1:500 map.

63. Roman foundations in the centre of Culver Street, 210 ft. west of the centre line of Long Wire Street. O.S. 1:500 map.

64A. Roman foundations in the centre of Culver Street 130 ft. east of the centre of Lion Walk. O.S. 1:500 map.

60. Wire reported in 1849: 'opposite St. Nicholas Church . . . was a wall foundation of the usual adhesive character, and the operation of breaking it up was difficult. Further on, nearly opposite the Wesleyan Chapel a quantity of fragments of thin slabs of [Italian] marble, some white, others green, and some variegated; they no doubt formed a floor as all of them are faced[1] . . . it has been suggested that they were part of the tessellated floor [the Album says 'high altar'] of the adjacent church . . . [and some small objects].'[2]

Again he says: 'purchased a quantity of fragments of variegated thin marble. The handle of an amphora stamped by the Melissi . . . and three 2nd brass coins of Trajan in poor condition, found near the Wesleyan Chapel.'[3]

The position of no. **60** is shown by '3' on Wire's plan (fig. 98).

The following are classed under this same number: 'In Culver St., opposite no. 37 [corner of the Co-operative Stores] the sewer trench exposed a Roman wall running N.–S., the top was 5 ft. from the surface and the width was 3 ft. 6 ins. Though cut down by 4 ft. its base was not reached. The material was stone, with no tile. It showed on both sides of the trench. . . .'[4] This may be the same wall as **60** or another parallel to it.[5]

On the 25th Laver notes: 'Some more fragments of 4-inch Roman brick from Culver St. opposite W. end of Co-operative stores. The sand is reached at 9 ft. This appears to be the general depth all along the trench from Queen Street. For 18 ins. above this the soil appears to be old surface soil [so!] the rest being accumulation.'

As the trench reached St. Nicholas Passage fragments of marble began to appear, together with pieces of Purbeck stone. The marble was found up to a point just west of the Shaftesbury Hotel, amounting to a pailfull including some interesting pieces.[6]

61. 'The clerk of St. Nicholas [Mr. G. Mann] observed that in digging graves there it was no uncommon thing to meet with a foundation corresponding to the town wall and which appeared to run N.–S. He then named the circumstances that when digging the grave for Mr. Gentry it was originally intended to be nine feet deep, but in consequence of meeting with a

---

[1] One of Wire's few errors.
[2] *J.B.A.* o.s. v, 86.
[3] Diary, 10/10/1848.

[4] Laver, Diary, 22/11/1922.
[5] Ibid. 28/11/1922.
[6] *J.R.S.* xi, 221; Laver, Diary, 28/11/1922.

foundation it could not be of that depth . . . but . . . a lodgement was made in it for the coffin . . . it appears to be part of a Roman house.'

And on the same date: 'Mr. Mann . . . informs me that when digging a grave in that churchyard he came on what seemed to him a brick clamp for burning bricks, and on another occasion a quantity of wood ashes was found, apparently oak. To the question were they remains of coffins (he replied they were not) but ashes caused by a wood fire.'[1] Possibly there is a mistake here for All Saints.

'Visited the sewerage works, Culver St. A foundation of similar character to the town walls opposite the residence of Mr. Worts surgeon, has been found 5 ft. below the surface. So hard and compact is it etc. . . .' The site cannot now be identified.[2]

182. The end of a Roman wall showed in the trench, in the N. side, opposite the E. boundary of Beaumont's shop. It was . . . 18 ins. thick and 2 ft. high, the top 7 ft. below the surface.[3]

64. Another wall 4 ft. thick was cut through opposite the yard entrance to Potter's Dairy. The top was 7 ft. from the surface. This may be no. **64**, or another wall just west of it.[4]

65. Tessellated pavement found before 30 April 1842 on the premises of Mr. Salmon, linen-draper, of no. 50 High Street (now no. 48) and described as leading from there to the George Inn (!). Wire, Diary, 30/5/1842; *T.E.A.S.* o.s. v, 154.

115. When the new buildings for the Colchester Co-operative Society were erected in 1925 a foundation about 3 ft. thick was discovered running the whole length of the site from N.–S. and apparently lining up with the other heavy foundations recorded by Wire above (**60, 61**). At the same time a well was found, east of the wall, but it was pronounced post-Roman because its Roman materials were laid in Roman and later mortar. In the SE. corner of the site were large masses of burnt clay such as are found in the neighbourhood of pottery kilns. Some pieces were 'made into bricks' described as containing much straw and very soft; a fragment of one measuring $3\frac{1}{4}$ in. thick and 11 in. wide is in the Museum. These are clay blocks from a building destroyed by fire.

The following undated note on the marble was among the Laver MSS.: '. . . worked marbles of many kinds, of which several sacks full were obtained. Ranging from white through yellow and many other colours . . . they doubtless represent the ruined remains of more than one building. Generally they are badly broken, but some . . . remain whole, two leaves

of green porphyry being quite perfect. Many strips for inlay were found and in many materials—for there were other stones than marble . . . . Collectively they are . . . the largest find of ornamental stones found in England up to this date . . . some . . . showed evidence of being subjected to heat, and it is probable that they may owe their fragmentary condition to the destructive hands of the Normans.'

The Saxons also may have been responsible. It is easy to suppose that, as at Sanxay, the town was searched for marble and other limestone to burn for lime.

From time to time, whenever this area (under the street, just west of St. Nicholas' Church) is opened, further quantities of marble are found. Some have been submitted to the Geological Museum, which identified green porphyry from Italy, and red porphyry from Egypt has recently been identified. Fragments of marble veneers and inlay are found more generally than is realized in many towns and villas. We could not hope to quote the other cases here. It is a subject in itself.

Lists of small finds from the insula are in the Museum.

INSULA 30

This is a difficult insula. Lying directly opposite the great square containing the temple of the Emperor one would expect it to have contained important public buildings. Very limited evidence of any such has emerged, and we are in doubt as to whether the additional width given to the 'forum' insula and those north of it was carried on to the south of it. The main difficulty is that under Long Wire Street, where the street on the west should lie, there are continuous remains of buildings. There is, too, a feeling of doubt as to the position of the South Gate. Could this have been, not at the south end of Long Wire Street, but at St. Botolph's Gate, and could a street have divided this insula through the middle running N.–S.?

In 1849 Wire watched a sewer cut through several streets, and his notes and plan (fig. 98) furnish our earliest knowledge of this area.

49. 7 February 1849. 'Nothing was found in Culver St. . . . till the work proceeded nearly opposite the Grammar School,[5] where an old wall was found crossing the street nearly at right angles [about 5 ft. below the surface according to the Album], exhibiting the usual hardness and compactness. . . .'[6]

50. At the back of the Cross Keys Inn was part of a floor of Roman tiles, 18 in. long, 12 in. wide, 2 in.

---

[1] Wire, Diary, 23/12/1842.
[2] Ibid. 2/10/1848.
[3] Laver, Diary, 2/12/1922.

[4] Ibid. 4/12/1922.
[5] Now Messrs. Adams's Garage.
[6] *J.B.A.A.* o.s. v, 86.

thick, laid upon a bed of concrete of pounded brick (no. 2, fig. 98). Opposite St. Nicholas' Church, rather more to the east, was a wall foundation 'of the usual adhesive character . . .' (east is probably an error for west, or St. Nicholas for All Saints). Ibid., *T.E.A.S.* o.s. v, 158; and Diary, 4/10/1848; O.S. 1:500.

142. Remains of walling were exposed opposite the 'Cross Keys', in Culver Street, in 1922, but are difficult to follow from Laver's sketches. The most important was a portion extending for more than 12 ft. along the north side of the street, more than covering the opening into the 'Cross Keys' yard. In a first sketch, on 15 November, Laver shows this 12 ft. long with, it would seem, a return of no great thickness to the south at the west end. Another patch of walling (?) is indicated within the angle. But on the following day he makes a more detailed sketch, from which it appears that, after a small offset to the north, the wall continued to the east some 3 ft. farther, and there are no indications of return or patch at the west end.

This wall, the top of which lay 4 ft. below the surface, still stood 6 ft. high, and the bottom was not reached. The top two layers were of tile; below these were two of stone, two of tile, four of stone, two of tile, two of stone (possibly more); total height visible 6 ft. The thickness was apparently not ascertained, and the direction seems to have been uncertain, for on the 15th the wall is described as '12 ft. long or in section'; whereas on the 16th the sketch certainly implies a face to the south.

Besides this important wall the sketches show that in two places an oblique wall (or walls) was cut. The direction of these fragments was SE. to NW. One was opposite the doorway east of the 'Cross Keys' yard; the other was opposite the west jamb of the door of the saloon. They are shown as of no great width, 'walls indicated but not followed', and if joined in one straight line would cross over or under the first. No description of them is given.[1] Mr. E. J. Rudsdale records that walls and pavements were again seen here in September 1936.

51. We give Wire's own description: 'No. 9 [fig. 98] three hypocaust fire-places with round headed arches, formed with tiles 8 ins. square, near the middle one were two flue tiles 13 ins. long, of the usual shape, having lateral openings, and three tiles 18 ins. long, 10 ins. wide on the inside, with return sides 2½ ins. deep, having a vacancy in each return six inches wide, so that if two were placed together they would form a sort of box, the spaces in the reflex edges just holding

one of the above flues.[2] They, as well as the flues, were found standing on their ends . . . the tiles and pipes bear evident proof of having been used, as they are discoloured by smoke . . . with the fireplaces was found a quantity of charcoal and soot. They were covered up again unmutilated except the last which was partly destroyed by trying to get one of the tiles out for me.'[3]

The account in the Diary is interesting: 'Visited the sewerage works Long Wire St. Extensive remains of a Roman Villa has been discovered. Two hypocaust flues entire were found at a depth of six feet, but it appears that more remains are under the footpath and houses on the east side of the street. It was not possible to make a close examination as the excavations were carried out on a novel plan, places three feet wide, eight deep, were sunk at an interval of four feet, the intervening space being tunnelled through. Great quantities of Roman roof tiles, and bricks in fragments were thrown out, with septaria and mortar, composed of pounded brick and lime. The remains reached the passage leading to Smith's buildings, when some fragments of embossed Samian ware was found associated with charred wood. The flue tiles were discovered close to three hypocaust arched fire places and were covered on the inside with soot. The fire places were built with bricks 8 ins. square, and at my request were covered up whole, except one . . . [&c. as above].'[4]

52. In the same place in the Album Wire refers to no. 10 (fig. 98) on his plan, a pavement which he had not seen, but which he was told was 'a very pretty one', forming the floor of a soil pit a little east of **51** and said to extend farther in the same garden, at a depth of about 3 ft.[5]

53. A tessellated pavement is marked on the O.S. 1:500 map under Long Wire Street, opposite the entrance to Albion Court, with no date. There seems to be no further knowledge of this.

'Nearly opposite All Saints Court a wall of Roman construction was met with [sc. in Culver St.] running N.–S.'[6] This cannot be plotted.

113. In September 1930 a well-built Roman wall of tiles in white mortar was cut through under the north kerb of High Street directly opposite the die of the War Memorial and 40 ft. south of it. It ran N.–S. and was 4 ft. thick. The trench was shallow, so that only about a foot of it (in height) was seen. Its position, as can be seen on the plan, is anomalous, and shows how much we have to learn about the plan hereabouts. Recorded, with measured section by E. J. Rudsdale, and Laver, Diary, 10/9/1930.

---

[1] Laver, Diary, 15 and 16/11/1922.

[2] Quite irrelevant: a coloured drawing in the Museum shows the arrangement. There is no reason to suppose tiles were ever so used.

[3] Wire, Album, p. 151.

[4] Wire, Diary, 23/8/1848; *J.B.A.A.*, o.s. v, 87; *T.E.A.S.*, o.s. v, 157.   [5] *J.B.A.A.*, loc. cit., 86.

[6] Diary, 28/9/1848. All Saints Court was demolished in 1933. Its entrance was opposite the west boundary of All Saints Rectory.

There were four courses of tile on a slightly wider foundation of septaria, the base of which was not reached. With 1 ft. of wall and 15 in. of foundation the height exposed was 27 in.

192. (Possibly insula 31?) Wire says: 'Opposite the depository of the Society for the Promotion of Christian Knowledge and some distance up the street [Queen St.] the remains of a brick kiln were met with 3 ft. below the surface and was four feet thick [*sic*] of brick dust and fragments of brick. It appears to continue under the footpath; from the character of the rubbish one would hardly be led to estimate it at a higher period than medieval, probably Henry VI time when All Saints Church was built.'[1] Further: '. . . the upper part [of Queen St.] was found to have had the sand removed on some previous occasion and filled up with debris of a brick kiln, nothing else being thrown out scarcely but parts of bricks and dust of the same description. There was some considerable size[d] lumps of burnt clay with the rubbish which were considered by competent judges to have been the outer wall of a clamp when they were burnt, this particularly occurred near All Saints Church, not only in this street but some distance up Culver Street.[2] The most important discovery made here was part of a mill stone that had evidently been worked vertically as the edge showed similarly to the crushing stones of a modern oil mill. This as well as the fragment of a mill or quern stone . . . were made of lava.'[3]

Alderman H. Laver also noted the above. The following is from a MS. notebook: '. . . excavations for a new drain the whole length of the east side of All Saints Churchyard . . . found at about two feet from the surface a layer of white content (?), smooth on the top and about four inches thick, and beneath this a mass of red burnt earth, intermixed with fragments of Roman roof tiles and . . . numerous bricks about 4 ins. thick. These . . . were none of them whole and were formed of a clay which did not become hard in burning. . . . They had the appearance presented by a brick made of a very poor clay, which had been several times through the fire. Some of them were black inside, as if they had not been in sufficiently intense heat.

'Although no perfect bricks were found it was clear that they were portions of large flat bricks somewhat of the Roman shape and size and not at all like modern bricks' (Aug. 1903).

'In the following October the deposit was cut through again for a water pipe. There was a deposit of lime about a foot thick, extending 10–12 ft. along the trench. The whole deposit, more than five feet thick, in places came nearly up to the surface, and it had the appearance of having been made level and having been used to fill up a depression of some sort . . . may we have here the remains of a Norman brickyard or kiln? The thick, badly made bricks are certainly not Roman, but are exactly like bricks used in the lower part of the walls of the Castle . . . in the quadrangle. . . .' (Ibid.)

The deposit was again noticed by P. G. Laver when a sewer was cut along the middle of Culver Street in October 1922. It was struck at about 2 ft. from the surface and showed in both sides of the trench for about 30 ft. from Queen Street. Its thickness varied from 4 to 6 ft., and in it were many large pieces of brick-like material roughly 4 in. thick. A sketch-section, opposite the chancel of the church, shows a festooned bed of brown clay, 1 ft. thick, directly under the red earth, with a patch of charred matter on its surface.[4]

The writer has also seen some of this deposit opened east of All Saints Church, and it exactly resembles the blocks of burnt clay used to build the central supports of the potters' kilns (p. 249). One has also to bear in mind that buildings, even of importance, were sometimes built of blocks of unfired clay, e.g. at Caistor-by-Norwich. Such a building, if burnt, might leave a deposit similar to ours. There is also the possibility that the Normans may have burnt lime here. We would not agree that any tiles in the original structure of the Castle are other than of normal Roman fabric.

The small finds are unimportant, but it may be mentioned that the Museum has Roman pottery from this burnt layer. The only form recognizable is a rim of f. 265 (or similar) in coarse grey ware. It is a waster.

160. We find no reference in Wheeler and Laver to the marks on the O.S. 1:500 map showing Roman foundations found in two places, 94 ft. apart, in the middle of Culver Street, south of All Saints Church. There is no date against them, nor has any description survived.

The time has come to review the records from this insula. We have seen that masses of burnt clay are recorded from both the NW. and NE. angles. We think it very possible that these may be the remains of an important building facing the forum and constructed, in this part of it at least, of large blocks of clay, without wattle. There is the further consideration of the walls in Culver Street. There are now six of these marked, running N.–S., between Queen Street and Long Wire Street. The two easternmost have been mentioned; then comes the one Wire describes as

---

[1] Wire, Diary, 20/9/1848.
[2] The area is shown roughly on the plan in Wire's 'County Illustrations' as extending along Culver Street to opposite the middle of the church, and up Queen Street to opposite the south

face of the church.
[3] Wire, Album, p. 141, copy of a letter to C. Roach Smith, 1 Feb. 1849.
[4] Laver, Diary, 21/10/1922.

opposite the entrance to All Saints Court. Then a red line drawn N.–S. on the O.S. map in the Museum, which we take to be that noted by P. G. Laver between nos. 55 and 54 Culver Street (**183**) (both, unfortunately, long disappeared). Then comes the wall he noted opposite Adams's Garage (no. **49**), and finally a whole bunch of rather confused notes on remains seen from time to time opposite the 'Cross Keys', the oldest of which is the tessellated pavement marked on the 1:500 map (without date).

In Wire Street and in the Wire Street Arcade the impression given by the recorded remains is one of private houses of not very high class. At any rate, in the arcade, there was nothing to suggest a public building. In Wire Street the series of hypocaust flues makes one think of the town baths, but nothing has been found east of them to support this impression. The walls in question are a different matter, for they do seem to be of a fairly regular distribution, and between them there are not the usual red floors and small divisions of the usual private house. One floor has, indeed, been noted opposite the 'Cross Keys', but that is not enough to vitiate the argument.

183. Another wall was found in this same sewer trench; its position was about midway between the doors of nos. 55 and 53 Culver Street. The top was 6 ft. below the surface and the wall was 2 ft. 8 in. thick, standing 1 ft. high, crossing the trench N.–S. It stood on a layer of clay 18 in. thick and 12 ft. wide. There were 8 ft. of clay east of the wall and 4 ft. west of it.[1]

A piece of walling was revealed in the south side of the trench running E.–W. for 6 ft. 6 in., the face damaged. At its deepest it was 6 ft. below the street level and 1 ft. high. It stood on a layer of brown clay, 1 ft. thick, lying directly on the gravel. 'Direction and thickness not determined.' The position is opposite the party wall of nos. 67 and 66 Culver Street. Red mortar was plentiful in the work . . . 'This is probably the wall in Wire's plan (fig. 98, no. 1) but is farther to the E. than there shown.'[2]

Later another similar band of brown clay, 1 ft. thick, 6 ft. long, was found in the same position on the gravel. Its east end was exactly opposite the rainwater pipe between nos. 65 and 63. There was no trace of walling upon it. A large fragment of a T.S. bowl was found stamped OF MASCI, and (on the 28th) one of f. 27 stamped OF PRIMI.[3]

Another piece of wall was found opposite the entrance to Lissimore's yard (shown a little east of the centre), 6 ft. from the building-line and 2 ft. by 2 ft., the west face broken by a former branch sewer.[4]

176. On 24 February 1948 a shaft was sunk in Messrs. Adams's front showroom on the south side of Culver Street, and just south of the building-line. It was 5 ft. long by 3 ft. wide by nearly 9 ft. deep. The top 14 in. were of modern concrete. Under this was layer A, of black soil, containing modern slate, clearly marked off from:

B. The top 31 in. from the surface, consisting of yellow loam, containing a few pieces of tile and septaria. Two inches below the top it was traversed by a thin horizontal line of broken wall-plaster.

C. The top 40 to 45 in. from the surface, again marked by a thin layer of broken plaster. The yellow loam more stiff and compact. Layers A and B were cut through by a trench filled with the superposed black earth.

D. A very pronounced layer of broken wall-plaster (all round the shaft) lying on small and dirty gravel, 4 to 2 in. thick, and with a very pronounced line of soot, about ½ in. thick, beneath.

E. Was again stiff yellow loam, the top 58–56 in. from the surface, the bottom 70–63 in. down, and marked by another ½-in. band of soot which threw up a branch into the loam at the south end. Oyster-shells were scattered all along this line.

F. The lowest layer was 11 in. thick at the north end and 14 in. at the south, composed of stiff yellow loam, and only differentiated from the natural loam below (G) by a thin dark layer containing oyster-shells. On this lay part of a base which seemed to us to be of form Cam. 40.

The last 2 ft. of the shaft were natural loam or 'pug'.

A fragment of a fine early T.S. bowl, f. 29 (fig. 75, A), was found, the workmen said, in the lowest layer, with a chip of f. 15/17 and part of a glass unguentarium.

INSULA 31

Though much of the area lies under gardens, few discoveries have been made, and the streets are not too well known. The insula should measure about 350 ft. N.–S., but its width is as doubtful as that of insula 30.

The following records have been made:

A trench to connect a sewer in High Street, a little east of the party wall of nos. 72 and 73, was quite negative, sand being reached at 6 ft. 6 in.

158. In January 1924 a red tessellated pavement was found east of the arbour on the terrace of East Hill

---

[1] Laver, Diary, 2/11/1922; a later note of 15/11/1922 gives the average depth to the sand as 9 ft.

[2] Ibid. 25/10/1922.

[3] Ibid. 26 and 28/10/1922. We have elsewhere suggested that there may have been a large building on this site with walls built of clay blocks. Are these wide bands of brown clay the foundations for these walls?

[4] Ibid. 30/10/1922.

House, at a depth of 6 ft. 6 in. from the surface, extending for 7 ft. to the east and 'underlain by a floor foundation of an earlier building'.[1]

159. In October 1925 masses of white mortar and rubble were found under the pavement on the north side of the corner house of Queen Street–East Hill.

Fragments of flue-tiles, some with red mortar adhering, and a piece of painted wall-plaster in light blue, pink, and yellow, have been found in the Minories garden.

In September 1930 a new water main was laid up the High Street, a little north of the centre line. Opposite the west centre of Bedwell's shop there was an oak post 10 in. square, just under the concrete of the road. To the west of this there was a layer of red, burnt earth, extending 15 yards west of a point about opposite the centre of Adams's Garage. Mr. P. G. Laver says: 'at a depth of 2 ft. 9 ins., about, were remains probably of the road surface, but this is much damaged, and no definite layer could be made out, but much large road metal'.[2] The site referred to is due north of **49,** where one would not expect a Roman street.

191. A red tessellated pavement was found at a depth of nearly 5 ft. in the garden of East Hill House in 1951 and was covered up again undisturbed. The position shown on plan is exact.

INSULA 32

This lies immediately south of the East Gate. Its approximate dimensions are 350 ft. N.–S. and 460 ft. E.–W. Although it has not been built over to any great extent and most of it is still open ground, not many finds have been made in it.

42. A pavement is shown on the 1:500 map 40 ft. south of East Hill House (not 80 yards, as *J.R.S.* and *R.C.H.M.* have it), with no other information.[3]

43. Owing to the uncertainty of the position of the division between insulae 32 and 40, we place this pavement here, though it may lie in insula 40. It was of red tesserae intermixed with many white ones disposed in star-like form, and was found by George Wegg (owner of East Hill House) in time to be reported by Morant (op. cit. 183; *Arch.* xvi, 147).

J. H. Round's suggestion[4] that this is the same as a pavement discovered in 1907 is rejected by Wheeler and Laver. The identification of its site with the mark on the 1:500 map of 1876 ('Tessellated Pavement found') is presumably due to P. G. Laver. We regard it as uncertain.

111. A piece of walling, running N.–S., found 21 ft. from the present outer face of the town wall, under the

pavement on the south side of East Hill, seems likely to prove part of the East Gate. Noted by P. G. Laver and E. J. Rudsdale (see p. 44).

Coins are found from time to time in this garden (some of these will belong to insula 40); summarized, they are as follows: Claudius, Vespasian, Domitian, Trajan (2), Philip or Gordian, Postumus, Gallienus, Tetricus, Victorinus, Claudius Gothicus, Carausius, illegible radiate (2), Licinius, Helena, Constantine I, Constantinopolis, Urbs Roma, Constantine II, Constantius II (2), Constantinian, Valens, Theodosian, barbarous.

INSULA 33

This lies in the SW. angle of the town wall. The wall is in good condition except at the corner, where it is abruptly broken on the north, then continues as tumbled masses, after which it is missing for some distance. This would be part of the destruction of 1648 ordered by Fairfax after the capitulation. The insula is well defined, and must have measured about 520 ft. long E.–W. by nearly 300 ft. N.–S. The ground-level, as usual, is about 12 ft. above that of the terrain outside. At the SE. corner was Head Gate, at the NW. St. Mary's Postern.

85. Foundations and tessellated pavement at the back of the King's Head Inn,[5] found when making the strong room for Mr. Howard's office in Head Gate Court in 1893. Noted by P. G. Laver.

86. A tessellated pavement was found north of the last in Mr. Inglis's garden. No date given. P. G. Laver.

87. Foundations were found in the garden south of **85** in 1892. This was P. G. Laver's own garden and he excavated it subsequently, finding remains of a house or houses with several different periods. Few foundations remained, and only one small patch of red pavement. The maximum depth of the excavation would be about 5 ft. (Sketch-plan in Diary, 11/3/1931.)

88. A tessellated pavement was found about 1871 in the garden of St. Mary's Cottage. It was taken up and relaid in the veranda of the house. The site is marked on the 1:500 map and on Cutts's plan.[6]

In June 1922 some digging was done in this garden (St. Mary's Cottage) by Mr. May, of which P. G. Laver took notes and a sketch-plan. The NW. angle of a building was found, said to be 'some 30 ft. from the town wall'. But the sketch-plan shows this distance as about 60 ft. It lay due south of **88.** The wall was 12 in. thick, depth not ascertained, length of both arms about 3 ft. (so far as traced), depth from surface 3 ft. 6 in. The N.–S. arm is parallel to the town

---

[1] *T.E.A.S.* xvii, 119.   [2] Laver, Diary, 3/9/1930.
[3] *J.R.S.* ix, 164; *T.E.A.S.* xvii, 118; *R.C.H.M.* 27, no. 42.
[4] *T.E.A.S.* xvii, 38, the pavement is no. **44** in Insula 40.

[5] Not the small inn now on the Balkerne Gate, but a large hotel which stood on Headgate Court.
[6] *T.E.A.S.* o.s. v, 160; *J.R.S.* ix, 168.

wall and has a fair mortar surface; the other arm is level but the mortar surface has gone.

The sketch-plan shows two pavements; one is **88**, against the north wall of the garden. This Mr. May said was that recorded as being found in Mr. Unwin's garden and now in the Museum.[1] The other lies immediately west of the projection on the SW. face of the house, and is said to be similar to the other and still there.[2]

Another pavement is marked on the O.S. 25-in. map 70 ft. west of **88** with no information. The 1:500 map marks bronze coins only at this point. We think this is perhaps an error on the 25-in.

89. Pieces of tessellated pavement have been found at considerable distances apart during grave-digging in St. Mary's churchyard.[3] That here marked is shown on the O.S. 1:500 map, with the date 1871.

90. Foundations and tessellated pavement were found under the east end of St. Mary's Church in 1871. The only authority is the O.S. 1:500 map.

146. In 1934, by arrangement between the Ministry of Works and H.M. Postmaster-General, the site of the new G.P.O. was examined before the new building was begun. A broad band along the east side of the area, bordering Head Street, was useless because of a continuous series of cellars of the old buildings. Behind this there was a large area which had been yards and gardens, but the most part of this was inaccessible to us owing to the extensive dumps of building-materials.

A long trench was cut E.–W. across the centre of the site. The top 7 ft. of the ground was of varied composition, containing a jumble of remains of all periods from Roman to the present day, with frequent pits of recent date and of various sizes. The largest of these was the only one of interest; it produced an extensive series of vessels of the seventeenth century.[4] The unstratified finds in the top soil included a *firma* lamp, intact; an iron knife with ornamental bone handle, Roman or Saxon; pieces of bone possibly used in the manufacture of bone pins; and remains of a large cylindrical iron padlock. Below 7–8 ft., the limit of excavation, the pottery was entirely Roman, but there was no stratification worth noting. A notable find was a single fragment of a sharply gritted Iron Age rim exactly similar to ware found on the Camulodunum site. In general the pottery from this level appeared to be the earliest on the site (first century), and all the layers above had been destroyed.

At the west end of this trench things were a little different and here the only considerable discovery was made. Scanty remains of walls led us to a semicircular

bath, sunk to a lower level than the rest of the building (pl. XXXII, B). The interior diameter was 11 ft. and the walls were 1 ft. 9 in. thick. The floor was of small white tesserae laid on about 6 in. of fine mortar and carried about 6 in. up the walls. Above this the walls were evenly covered with a fine white plaster. The centre part of the apsidal wall and much of the floor had been robbed, also much of the NE. outer angle. The walls were of septaria in sandy mortar; only one was found leading away from the apse, near the centre of the chord on the north. It was 2 ft. thick, and broke off after only a few feet. It did not extend lower than the level of the floor of the bath, from which we conclude that it was a footing and that the apse floor lay below the level of the other floors of the house. Of the rest of the house no remains were left which we could follow; all around the soil was disturbed, as already described.

The floor of the apse lay 6 ft. 6 in. from the surface and the walls remained nearly 2 ft. 6 in. high. The filling contained a good deal of pottery, which seemed fairly consistent, except for two fragments of modern ware, which showed it was not undisturbed. The Roman pottery, so far as datable, seemed to belong to the end of the first century, but it cannot be regarded as safe evidence. There were also many fragments of tiles, chiefly imbrices and tegulae. None was large enough to give any dimensions. There was one piece of red-painted wall-plaster and another of purplish colour, two fragments of slabs of Purbeck marble, and a piece of window-glass.

A second trench was cut northwards and west of the cellars. Here conditions were the same as in the first trench, except that at 10–18 ft. from the latter we found a patch of the later Roman level undisturbed. It was simply a layer of light soil 4 ft. to 5 ft. 6 in. from the surface, containing pottery of first- to third-century date and some red and buff tesserae. Below this was a deposit of mortar at 7 ft. 6 in. from the surface.

A third trench was dug towards the NW. corner of the site. In the first 10 ft. of this from our second trench pottery was abundant, and below 3 ft. 6 in. it was all Roman, but there was no visible stratification. The pottery covered all the Roman period. The rest of the trench was disturbed, as elsewhere, but in the extreme NW. corner of the site we found a red tessellated pavement only 2 ft. below the surface and about 10 ft. square. The walls had been robbed and the edges were broken, so the exact size remains unknown. It appeared to have been repaired with two slabs of Purbeck marble, measuring 10 by 7 in., on the south side. On the east side lay some large stones, presumably from the wall. An antoninianus of Tetricus (?) lay on

[1] It is not known in the Museum.
[2] Laver, Diary, 27/6/1922.

[3] Morant, iii, 21; *J.R.S.*, loc. cit.
[4] *C.M.R.* 1935, 6; the Roman finds, *J.R.S.* xxv (1935), 214.

the floor.[1] The latter continued under the old Post Office northwards. In the edge of the south side there was a recess, as if for a pilaster, 1 ft. 9 in. wide and 7 in. deep, at 3 ft. 9 in. from the SE. corner.

128. In October 1931 a Roman wall 2 ft. thick and built of tiles was found running NW.–SE. under the modern pavement on the west side of Head Street, close to the corner of Crouch Street. (Recorded on hearsay evidence given to Mr. Rudsdale.)

135. In August 1936 traces of a Roman foundation were found in a sewer trench opposite the clock of the old G.P.O. in Head Street. This may be the north wall of the insula. Observed by E. J. Rudsdale.

The pottery from this insula runs from the mid-first century to the fourth century. There were two pieces of white marble sheathing. The only other coin to mention is a follis of Diocletian from Dr. Fell's garden. One of the very few tile antefixes found in the town, that with the Medusa-head (pl. xxx, B), was found on the site of the old G.P.O. (P.C. 1468.)

INSULA 34

This lies on the right as one enters Head Gate. Its NE. angle was fixed when the Public Library was built. The town wall is well preserved along the south side, though mostly invisible. The exact position or size of Head Gate is not known. Dimensions c. 310 by 320 ft.

The following discoveries have been made:

78. A Roman pavement, coins, and a lamp are shown as found under the former Friends' Meeting House in Sir Isaac's Walk in 1871–2. O.S. 1:500 map.

79. A tessellated pavement is shown under the house at the north corner of Sir Isaac's Walk and Head Street. The position is scarcely clear of the heel of the rampart.[2]

80. A fine pavement of geometric pattern with a large cantharus in the central octagonal panel was found early in May 1881 in what was then Mrs. Prosser's garden (which was later bought by Messrs. Mumford and built over) on the east side of Head Street (pl. xxxiii). H. Laver says: 'This pavement was about five feet deep in the soil, resting on it were evidently the remains of the walls of the house, the plaster lining the rooms being very brightly coloured, although unfortunately too much injured for preservation, the house having been probably destroyed by fire.

'The entire length of the pavement is about 18 ft., and the width about 15 ft. . . . the tesserae are of the usual colours, red, black and white etc., but of very small dimensions, some of those forming the vase being about one eighth of an inch square.' (This is very unusual, but recurs in the sea-horses on pl. xxxiv.)

'The coloured square is surrounded by a border 5½ ft. wide, of red tesserae. . . .'

A clue to the position of this pavement is given when it is stated that the pavement (no. **81**) was 100 yards north of it. This, though obviously a rough computation, gives an approximate position for it, just about under the Y.M.C.A. in the car park, where, in those days, lay several large gardens.[3] The pavement was not destroyed. We have positioned it according to Cutts's plan.

INSULA 35

The limits of this insula are now fairly well known. The NW. corner was found under the Public Library in 1938–9. The street on the east has been fixed and the south side is bounded by the town wall in good condition, though covered by buildings. There should be an internal tower at the south end of Sewell Road, and another, or a gate, at Scheregate (see p. 59). Dimensions about 375 by 380 ft.

The following records have been made:

77. A tessellated pavement was found west of Trinity Street 'in the garden of Francis the solicitor' and is shown on the O.S. 1:500 map and Cutts, plan i, 13; the former gives no date.

97. In 1927 the G.P.O. cut a trench for cables down Pelham's Lane, Culver Street, and Trinity Street, enabling a number of new observations to be made. The trench passed through the town wall at right angles on the east side of the steps at Scheregate, and here, although the cut was quite shallow, it was all in Roman masonry, which proved to be not less than 14 ft. thick (see p. 59).

101. In the same operation three shafts were sunk in the street just north of the steps; two against the south pavement were negative, being of no great depth; the third, on the rounded corner of Trinity Street and Sir Isaac's Walk, was deeper and revealed a red tessellated pavement at about 3 ft. from the surface. This is only 30 ft. back from the inside face of the town wall! See sketched section in Laver's Diary, 5/6/1928.

In 1934 the former site of Mumford's works was cleared for a car park, and with the co-operation of H.M. Ministry of Works the Museum was able to cut some exploratory trenches in the area. These were made in the eastern half of it and were almost without result, for it was found that the Roman surface lay nearly 9 ft. deep, and the only find of interest was a red tessellated pavement. Had important remains been encountered the work might have been continued, but under the circumstances it was considered too expensive. This part of the site was designated for the new

---

[1] The only other coin found was a second brass of Nero.
[2] Cutts, plan i, 3; O.S. 1:500 map.

[3] *T.E.A.S.* n.s. iii, 140 (illustr.); *P.S.A.L.* 2 s. viii, 543; *T.E.A.S.* x, 88.

Library. Air-raid shelters erected later on the north side of the Library did not go deep enough to touch the Roman levels.

161. In 1938–9 the basements for the new Public Library were excavated and the work was watched by

lated floor, of which two patches remained, extending at least 22 ft. southwards. Immediately east of the southern part of this two foundation trenches indicated the position of two Roman walls running N.–S., approximately parallel and only 4 ft. 6 in. apart. They

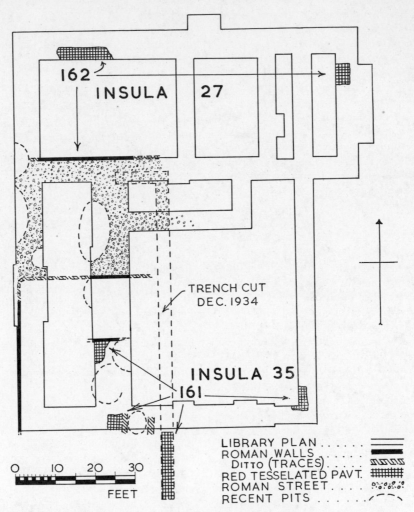

FIG. 103. Remains found under the new Public Library. [**161** and **162**], pp. 195, 210.

Mr. E. J. Rudsdale.[1] The NW. corner of the insula was found. Thirt-two feet of the west wall, bordering the street, were found, with a slightly rounded corner, and a similar return wall, which was traced nearly as far eastwards.

East of the corner, for 18 ft., the wall had been robbed, but thereafter 10 ft. of it remained in position, with a second similar wall parallel to it 15 ft. farther south. The latter had enclosed a room with a tessel-

may not have been contemporary. Between them lay a seventeenth- to eighteenth-century rubbish-pit. Farther east, under the SE. corner of the building, lay another patch of red tessellated pavement. Other recent rubbish-pits had disturbed such of the interior of the house as was uncovered, and a Roman rubbish-pit appeared to underlie the north boundary wall.

The tessellated pavement found in 1934 lies immediately against the middle of the south wall of the

[1] *C.M.R.* 1944, 17, with list of coins (Augustus to Constans) and other small finds.

Library. It was 9 ft. long from north to south, continuing in all directions except the north.

Small finds from the insula have been listed; they are not of importance. Coins found are: a denarius of Augustus; bronze of Claudius (?); Nero (said to have been found under the road-metalling); Vespasian (2); Domitian (2); illegible, probably Flavian (2); Trajan (2); Hadrian; Antoninus Pius (3); Faustina II; Severus Alexander; Constans; Constantinopolis; Constantinian; two illegible silver.

187. In May 1928 a pit for cables was sunk in Trinity Street opposite the north end of Potter's premises (next south of Marshall, solicitor). The end of a rubble wall projected into it from the west, about 2 ft. below the surface, and 18 in. thick, lying on made soil. The pit was carried down to 6 ft., where it was approaching original ground-level. All along the bottom, on the east side, ran remains of a Roman wall, its top about 6 ft. from the surface. (Laver, Diary, 14 and 16/5/1928.)

INSULA 36

The west boundary is fixed, and the south, which is the town wall, is clearly marked, though houses have long stood on top of the wall, and the outside, for many years similarly masked, is only now becoming visible again in places. On the north a line joining the E.–W. street at Wire Street Arcade with that at the Library passes through the site of the 1748 pavement (**73**), so that this line cannot be followed strictly. At present it is uncertain whether this pavement should be plotted in this insula or in 28. The street on the east is still quite uncertain. For the present we assume that it was just east of the wall between the Congregational Church and the Baptist Church, skirting the pavement (**72**) on its west.

The following records have been made:

70. Discoveries made in Lion Walk are shown on the plan in Wire's Album (fig. 98). On it, nos. 4 (insula 28), 5, and 6 are described in a letter to Roach Smith: 'Lion Walk . . . at the (south) end one composed of small and different coloured tesserae half an inch square was brought to view, but . . . the subject could not be discovered, as it appeared to have been . . . mutilated . . . no. 6, in digging a cesspool at the extreme SW. corner a great quantity of Roman roof tiles was thrown out. In Eld Lane nothing of importance was discovered.' (Here they were digging along the rampart.—M.R.H.).

71. Wire's Diary, 22/3/1844: 'Mr. Joseph Dennis, clerk of the Lion Walk Chapel informs me that when

he was digging a grave for the son of Mr. J. B. Harvey (about 30 ft. east of Lion Walk) in the chapel ground, he came upon a tessellated pavement, but could get none of it up whole.'

72. Pavement under the boundary between the Baptist Chapel and Lion Walk Church. The only record is the O.S. 1:500 map.

22/9/1848: 'Visited the sewerage works Lion Walk. A Roman pavement (**70**) has been discovered about twenty feet from Eld Lane composed with small tesserae.'

23/9/1848. 'ditto. a continuation of the pavement noticed before, but made with tesserae one inch square, has been met with and was probably the outer border. Under it was a pavement of flint stones similar to that discovered in Queen Street and very likely a foundation for the concrete. No coins of any description have been found here, but fragments of Roman roof tiles in abundance.'

26/9/1848: 'ditto. a foundation of Roman character has been discovered higher than the pavement noticed above which probably was the wall of the room [of the pavement].'

28/9/1848. 'ditto. Digging for a cesspool, corner of Trinity Poor Row[1] and Lion Walk, a vast quantity of fragments of Roman roof tiles were found, probably the covering of the house alluded to above.'

15/4/1856: 'Mr. Joseph Dennis, clerk at the Round meeting[2] discovered a pavement of red tesserae when digging the grave for Mr. Edward Brett near the wall opposite No. 5 Lion Walk, and he took a piece of it up, which I saw.'

73. 'In the beginning of the year 1748 [a tessellated pavement] was discovered in the garden of Peter Creffield, now of James Round Esq. in the parish of Holy Trinity east [not west, as *R.C.H.M.* has it] of Trinity Street, in the garden of Trinity House. . . . It was near three foot under the surface of the ground (as the rest generally are) and red, only a few whiter pieces were intermixed, but not in any regular order. The breadth of it was about three foot and the length fifteen, but it seemed to have been damaged at the sides. In the earth which was flung up there was the bottom and other fragments of a fine figured urn of red earth; upon . . . which was represented the head of Jupiter. There was also the bottom of another urn found, and a coin of Constantine Junior.'[3]

Coins recorded are of Antoninus Pius; Tetricus; Licinius; Helena; Constantinopolis; Constantius II; Constantinian (2). A piece of colour coated ware with a dog *stamped* on it in relief is worthy of note.

---

[1] i.e. Eld Lane.
[2] i.e. Lion Walk Chapel. The tombstones have recently been removed.

[3] Morant, iii, 21; Brayley and Britton, v, 293; Cutts, plan, i, 2; O.S. 1:500 map.

INSULA 37

The street on the west has been mentioned, as also that on the north, but this, where found under the Wire Street Arcade, is late and displaced to the south. The dimensions of the insula should have been about 300 ft. square.

In this insula Wheeler and Laver place their nos. 58 and 59, but the references they quote do not refer to these numbers, which occupy the positions of two marks on the O.S. 1:500 map, only one of which is a pavement. The following reshuffle has to be made.

51, 53. See insula 30.

58. The O.S. 1:500 map marks 'Roman Foundations found', without date, 70 ft. west of Long Wire Street and 145 ft. north of Short Wire Street. There is no mention of a pavement.

59. The O.S. 1:500 map marks 'Roman tessellated pavement found' under the east side of property in Victoria Place opposite the centre of the Baptist Church. No date is given, but Wire, in a letter to Roach Smith published in *J.B.A.* v (1850), 87 says: 'In Victoria Place, at the south west corner, a fine pavement was discovered some years since, but of what character does not now occur to me. I remember it was more firmly put together than most of them are, and with a little trouble might have been raised whole: it was about six or eight feet square, and two urns were standing upon it, one partly in the other.' The position is not at the SW. corner of Victoria Place but near its north end.

145. There is a red tessellated pavement under the front (east) wall of no. 19 Long Wire Street.

184. Wire's Diary, 28/10/1846: 'Mr. James Saxty of Long Wire Street, informs me that under his house is a mosaic tessellated Roman Pavement, and another in the yard, two doors north of Victoria Place, Long Wire Street.' These cannot be either of the preceding finds. It is not now possible to find out which was Saxty's house, but the implication is clear—that there are two pavements, one of them decorated, *north* of Victoria Place, and associated with Long Wire Street, which we can no longer plot accurately.

INSULA 38

A north boundary for this insula is given by the street found in the Wire Street Arcade in 1929, but this is almost certainly not the original line, which has not been seen (see p. 70). The south boundary is the town wall, which is closely built over, but which can be examined in the cellars of Messrs. Wilsons' shop. The street on the west is uncertain (see p. 72) and one found on the east seems rather far over that way (p. 73). See generally the remarks on insula 30.

The following records have been made; we take Wire first:

In 1848 extensive trenching was done in the streets for drains, and Wire watched these closely, keeping his diary, and reporting the finds to the British Archaeological Association in February of the next year and in a letter to Roach Smith, with coloured plan attached, which is preserved in his Album (fig. 98). Though he begins with St. Botolph Street we will begin with Long Wire Street, on the west side of the insula.

54. 'Visited the sewerage works Long Wire St., when continuing the drain down Albion Court a tessellated pavement was discovered opposite the third and fourth doors on the north side of the court' (Wire, Diary, 3/9/1848). Wheeler and Laver assume this to be the same as no. 11 on Wire's sketch plan in the Album fig. 98), but this is shown in the middle of the east end of the court. They may be one and the same, but we doubt it.

54A. (Possibly insula 38.) Referring to his sketchplan (fig. 98) no. 11 Wire says: 'Albion Court, at the bottom, is another pavement, but of what character I cannot say, not having seen it. . . .' The site is given so vaguely it cannot be plotted; about 100 yards east of **54** may be intended.

55. A wall crossing Long Wire Street at an angle (no. 12 on fig. 100). The exact position of this is not known.

56. Other remains south of the last. First (no. 8) a pavement of 'coarse red tesserae', indicated as approximately opposite the way through to Victoria Place. Then (no. 7) a floor of Roman tiles or bricks 'similar to no. 2' (which is part of the complex no. **50** opposite the 'Cross Keys', in insula 30).

Wire further notes, 14/8/1848: 'Purchased a T.S. patera and the lower portion of a red earth urn containing calcined bones, found in Eld Lane . . . Short Wire Street [corrected to the latter in *J.B.A.* v] . . . laying a common sewer.'

This find should be in insula 38, and would be of great interest could we appraise it. But the vessels are not now known, nor do we know whether they were sealed down by the rampart or inserted into it. Without this information the record is almost worthless.

57. In 1892 alterations to a house belonging to Mr. Locke (no. 18 Queen St.) involved the removal of a large brick chimney-breast, which was found to have been built upon an ornamental mosaic pavement of considerable size, for it extended over much of the house. Parts of it were taken into the Museum. A large piece shows eight-pointed stars and plain guilloche though the contemporary record says the design had a spiral border.[1]

We now return to Wire's account: 'To begin with

---

[1] *Antiquary*, xxvii, 24; *T.E.A.S.* x, 89; *J.R.S.* ix has wrong site indicated.

St. Botolph Street, nothing was found . . . when cutting through where St. Botolph's Gate stood part of the foundation was come upon. It exhibited the same appearance the town wall does excepting bonding tiles, which I believe were not used by the Roman architects in any part of a work hid from the eye.[1] No pounded or pieces of brick were discoverable in the mortar, neither is there any in the town wall but at the grand military entrance top of Balkon Hill.[2] Queen Street was nearly barren of interest, nothing being found but a bronze fibula of cruciform shape[3] . . . a 2b coin of Vespasian, consecration type, and a few of the Lower Empire, all in very poor condition. This relates to the lower part of Queen Street only, in the neighbourhood of the theatre. . . .'

46. P. G. Laver noted a pavement found in 1920 east of the former theatre (now in the National Omnibus Company's garage), near the SE. corner of Queen Street, and about 20 ft. from the town wall. The exact position is unknown, and it may lie in insula 38.

47, 47A, 48. Wheeler and Laver record a pavement or paved way west of Queen Street, opposite house no. 27, and refer to *T.E.A.S.* o.s. v and to O.S. 1:500 map. But these do not tally. The former is Wire's record of 9/9/1848, which reads: 'Visited the sewerage works, Queen Street and purchased some Samian ware bottoms—potter's marks MXIMI; OF.APRI; I.I.I.I.I, and a cruciform fibula. The workmen told me a paved way (**47**) had been come upon about three feet below the surface near no. 27 (this would be approximately in line with the late Roman street to the west) and that higher up a floor of Roman bricks (**48**) each eighteen in. wide 8 in. long [*sic*] and 1½ ins. thick, which was broken up.' The sewer trench was in the street, and these sites must be marked in the street, not west of it.

The mark on the O.S. map records a Roman tessellated pavement found behind a house west of Queen Street and just north of the Roman street found in the arcade. This is where Wheeler and Laver place their no. **48**, while **47**, representing the tile floor, is put farther north, but still west of the street. Both **47** and **48** are now resited, and to the O.S. pavement we give the number **47A**.

102. In 1929 many old buildings were demolished to make way for the Wire Street Arcade,[4] and in this and other demolitions about the same time Smith's Yard and Albion Court, well known from Wire's pages, disappeared for ever. Besides the trenches cut for foundations of the arcade there was an extensive lowering of the surface over much of the area. All this was watched

for the Museum by Mr. E. J. Rudsdale, but the nature of the work was not such as to provide scope for archaeological research.

The main discovery was the street, which has been described on p. 70. South of it lay remains of Roman houses at a depth of 4 ft., and two more red tessellated pavements were added to the map. One of these was 10 ft. 6 in. wide and stopped 5 ft. short of the street, from which point it ran at least 30 ft. southwards, and continued under the buildings. Its edges were clearly defined, though no walls were found. It seems to have been a corridor or portico serving rooms lying west of it, for nothing lay to the east.

Another such pavement, apparently the floor of a large room, but much destroyed by later pits and holes, lay 50 ft. east of the above. It was at least 34 ft. wide E.–W. and 24 ft. N.–S. The edges were not at all well defined, except that on the west it abutted on one of two parallel walls running N.–S. and 5 ft. apart. They perhaps formed a corridor along an inner court. North of the pavement lay a gravelled surface, which definitely abutted on the wall.

Between the two pavements lay a strip of red cement floor 9–11 ft. wide and 12 ft. long N. S., lying 12 ft. east of the first pavement. Its NE. corner abuts on a gravel surface with no intervening wall-slot.

A fragment of wall was found at the back of the second shop in the arcade against the party wall of Messrs. Boots, 40 ft. from Wire Street, but on the whole the west end of the arcade was disappointing in archaeological interest, for here the surface was scarcely lowered.

Mr. Rudsdale gave the following account to the press: 'The land rises slightly from Wire St. and then drops rather steeply to Queen St. so that near the centre it was necessary to remove 13½ feet of soil and debris of the last six or seven centuries. . . . Hundreds of pottery fragments have been found from which several vessels have been restored . . . [all of these were of post-conquest date] . . . Below all these a thin stratum of burnt matter can sometimes be seen. It is all that remains to represent the stormy period of the Saxon and Danish raids. Immediately below it lay the remains of Roman houses. When a main was connected under Wire St. remains of a hypocaust were found. Fifteen feet to the east was a wall footing of massive stones [not shown on his plan]. Even more interesting finds were made in Albion Court. Here were Roman tessellated pavements, the remains of walls and a Roman street. Some of the pavements

---

[1] They are used regularly in that part of the wall covered by the rampart.

[2] Note the difference in fabric between gate and wall, and compare conclusions at the Balkerne Gate (p. 17); Wire is well abreast of his time. He is among the first to recognize 'The Balkerne' as a gateway. His enlightenment may have come from Roach Smith.

[3] *J.B.A.* has 'circular'.

[4] *C.M.R.* 1929, 21, 22.

were laid over the remains of earlier buildings[1] consisting of layers of burnt clay or charcoal and fragments of walls, perhaps destroyed in the great Boudiccan revolt. A little below this was the natural subsoil. The nature of the pavements and the pottery found about them suggests they are the remains of poorer class houses, of the courtyard type. . . .'

It is impractical to list the small finds,[2] so we restrict our list to the coins, which were as follows: Vespasian (4); Domitian (5); an illegible Flavian; Nerva; Trajan (3); Hadrian; Antoninus Pius; Faustina I; Clodius Albinus (den.); Caracalla (found under the pavement in Albion Court); Postumus; Tetricus (4); Victorinus (2); Claudius Gothicus; Volusian; Carausius (4, one

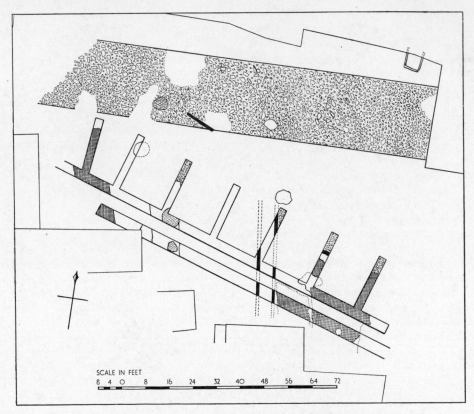

SCALE IN FEET
8 4 0   8   16   24   32   40   48   56   64   72

Fig. 104. Remains found under Wire Street Arcade, pp. 213–14.

In his report Mr. Rudsdale further mentions that under the east gutter of Wire Street two walls were found at right angles, bounding a concrete floor, one running N.–S., the other E.–W. The extent of the floor could not be followed. Against the N.–S. wall was a *pila* of eight tiles, 8 in. square. This was at a depth of 8 ft. and south of the recorded position of the three flues mentioned by Wire (**51**). At the same level, under the cellar of no. 18, a large storage vessel of f. 273 was found upright in the sand. The 'wall' 15 ft. from the street was a mass of loose blocks of septaria, 3 ft. thick, and below it, level with the hypocaust, was a stratum of burnt clay.

Under Smith's yard the Roman remains were encountered at a depth of 4–6 ft.

under the street); Allectus; Helena; Constantine I (5); Constaninopolis; Constans (4, 2 under the street); Constantius II (under street); Constantinian; Valens; Theodosian; illegible (3).

194. In December 1929 a shaft was sunk at each end of the front of the shop next but one south of the arcade, on the east side of Wire Street. At about 2 ft. 6 in. from the surface in the south shaft lay a red tessellated pavement, with a layer of charcoal less than an inch thick lying upon it; above this lay clay, presumably from the walls of the building. Upon the clay, reaching to within 8 in. of the modern pavement, was an old rubble wall, 1 ft. wide, on which the foundation of the present house was laid.

The bed of the Roman pavement was only 4 in.

[1] Beneath one pavement on the west side of the court was found a silver coin of Caracalla (455.28).   [2] See *C.M.R.* 1929, 33 ff.

thick and lay on a bed of clay, which was excavated to 10 in. deep, but its full depth is not known.

In the north shaft the pavement was missing, but the line of charcoal, now slightly thicker, continued at the same level. On these ashes, in the clay, was a second brass of Trajan in good condition (COS III). The rim of a large jar, f. 272, was found upright in the ground under the next house north.[1]

195. The excavations for building the new Police Station on the site of the former Soldiers' Home in Queen Street were carried out in 1939 with such speed that adequate observation of the finds was impossible. Remains of Roman walls were found, and red tessellated pavements, but they could not be planned. Two intact grey jars (ff. 268 and 278), complete with covers, were almost certainly foundation-offering pots[2] (C.M. 419–20.39). A rare denarius of Clodius Albinus was found (C.M. 155.40).

143A. In January 1936 a wall, judged by Mr. E. J. Rudsdale to be Roman, was cut through the east pavement of Queen Street opposite the corner of Short Wire Street and 9 ft. 6 in. south of the south corner of the National Bus Company's garage. It was 14 in. wide and 2 ft. 6 in. high. On its south side his sketch shows all the earth as modern rubble and made ground, on the other side 'mixed soil', presumably similar. There was sand over the top, and there is a note of a 'thin tile' apparently on top of the wall. The latter ran E.–W.

143B. In January 1935 part of a tile arch with pink mortar (part of a drain?) was found in the street opposite 45A (Wright's office). There was no sign of its wall. Noted by E. J. Rudsdale.

170. In February 1948 a shaft 8 ft. E.–W. by 6½ ft. N.–S. was dug in the NW. corner of the motor transport yard of the Police Station. The trench of a wall 2 ft. wide ran N.–S. very slightly oblique to the shaft. Its bottom was 7 ft. from the modern tarmac surface. On its west side a room had been paved with red tesserae on a poor base of yellowish mortar only 2 in. thick. The pavement was 50 in. from the surface and was irregularly broken. On the east of the wall had been a floor, of which 3 in. of very good white mortar remained. It probably supported a better pavement, possibly decorated, but no tesserae were found. It lay 4 ft. from the surface, i.e. 2 in. higher than the red floor. It was broken away at the north end.

The pavements had been broken by post-Roman excavations of varying depth, the pottery from which contained a few Roman sherds, but was otherwise fourteenth century (painted gotch) and Lambeth stoneware. Upon the pavements lay 15–18 in. of yellowish loam from the wattle and daub walls, and in the west

wall of the shaft this layer was full of broken tegulae and imbrices in large pieces. Beneath the pavements it was disappointing to find only yellow loam with no stratification and no artifacts, other than a small sherd of buff ware. Pebbles and an occasional oyster-shell showed it was disturbed down to 6 ft. 3 in. from the surface. Below that it appeared natural. There was thus no evidence that anything other than mud houses had preceded the house with the floors, and even that had probably only masonry foundations (which were completely robbed) with timber and wattle and daub walls.

INSULA 39

This insula is bounded on the south by the town wall, which it has been possible to examine more thoroughly here than anywhere else along the south side of the town. The west boundary is a street on the line of the east side of insula 22, but see **147** below. The north boundary is unknown. The east boundary would be a street continued south from the N.E. Gate which should strike the wall at bastion 4, but it has not been seen. The dimensions should be about 320 ft. N.–S. by 320 ft. E.–W.

Earlier discoveries are few.

109. (?) Roman foundations and part of a drain found east of **46** under the extension to the National Omnibus Company's garage.

144. In May 1935 Mr. E. J. Rudsdale noted a red tessellated floor at the back of the same garage, near the trench dug in 1931. Depth 4 ft. 6 in.

129. In March 1938 the back entrance to the same garage was made and a long trench for a drain was cut eastwards from Queen Street (this can still be traced by three manholes in the concrete). The section thus provided was measured and drawn, and most of it has been described as part of the Roman street (p. 73). The eastern 14 ft. or so were inside this insula, and of these the western 7 ft. comprised an excavation filled with black soil containing mortar. The bottom of the trench was 5 ft. from the surface, but the latter was later reduced in varying degree. The lowest 2 ft., exposed in the undisturbed strata, comprised two layers of yellow loam, the upper 4 in., the lower 6 in. thick. The top of the upper one was 4 ft. 3 in. from the surface. Below these was nearly a foot of clayey soil containing pebbles, earth, oyster-shells, and burnt material. The yellow loam layers were mixed with mortar and represent the remains of daub buildings. Above them lay about a foot of black soil, continuous (?) with the filling of the excavation to the west, and containing pieces of Roman mortar and tiles. The top of this came to within 2 ft. 6 in. of the surface.

---

[1] Laver, Diary, 19/12/1929.

[2] *J.R.S.* xxx, 173; *C.M.R.* 1944, 19.

This layer is late, but who shall say how late? It is level with the metalling of the street. The red gravel capping it is probably comparatively modern.

The Excavations of 1931

In 1931 a large garden, then belonging to the Soldiers' Home, was acquired by the Eastern National Omnibus Company and was made into the large concreted court now lying behind their garage. By the generosity of P. G. Laver, and with the willing co-operation of the owners, it was possible to do a considerable amount of work without the undue haste which is usual, and proper supervision was possible.

A single long trench was cut from a point a few feet east of bastion 5 northwards across the insula, to the north wall of the garden. This wall is still standing. The first 40 ft. of this section, covering the Roman rampart and a small drain, have been described (section VII) (p. 51). The masonry remains found are marked on the plan as nos. **105** to **108**.

105. Thirteen feet 6 inches north of the drain we cut through the remains of a wall 2 ft. thick, the top of it 5 ft. 6 in. from the surface. It was built of septaria, on a foundation of rubble concrete, the bottom of which was 7 ft. 4 in. from the surface. The section in the intervening 13½ ft. shows, lying on the natural yellow sand, first the tail of the clay bank which here formed the base of the rampart, the level of which continues as a layer of dirty sand. On top of this, which may be taken as the first-century layer, there is a deep deposit of yellowish, stiff loam over 30 in. thick, which varied in consistency. The southern 8½ ft. of this was well admixed with dark earth, the northern part much less so, and with a marked layer of dark earth about 5 in. thick underlying it. The yellow loam continued 6 ft. north of the wall, stopping at a slot, which, though only filled with top-soil, seems undoubtedly to have been for a wall. In this interval the lower, dark layer was absent.

The dark layer produced no datable material, but is later than the clay bank, and the foundation of the wall was cut into it. The yellow loam contained (1) a fragment of T.S. f. 37 (1577.31) and coins of Victorinus and Claudius Gothicus (all in the southern portion). This layer represents the materials of the walls of demolished buildings of wattle and daub, and, in the absence of any layer of masonry rubble from demolished stone walls, we may assume that the superstructure of the wall was of wattle and daub. The north wall of this building lay a little over 8 ft. north of the slot which we suppose to have held a wall and was represented by a slot 2 ft. 3 in. wide, full of loose mortar rubble, the top of which was 5 ft. 2 in. from

the surface, the bottom 7 ft. 6 in. The room between them had a red tessellated pavement on a mortar foundation little over 3 in. thick. It had settled badly, and the sagging surface was made up with dark earth, distinct from the top-soil.

The reason for the sag was a deep rectangular pit sunk in the yellow sand, in the earliest period, to a depth of 12 ft. from the present surface, but little over 3 ft. from the surface of the sand. The width was 5 ft. 6 in. (the plan was not recovered) and the filling dirty sand continuous with the lowest layer on each side. This also had sagged, and the space between it and the pavement was filled with yellow loam. This makes it clear that there was already a thick layer of yellow loam over the site before the foundations for the stone walls were cut. Between the pit and the north wall, in the dirty sand, there was a curious triangular deposit of clean sand which cannot be explained without further excavation.

106. Continuing northwards, there are traces of the earlier wattle and daub house consisting of the mortar foundations of two walls, the centres of which lie respectively 80 and 94 ft. north of the town wall, with traces of the trenches from which the material has been robbed. They are 2 ft. wide and 8 ft. from the surface, cut into the dirty sand layer, which is now rising to the north. The distance between these two walls is 15 ft. 6 in.; there was no trace of a floor. Above the dirty sand the thick layer of yellow loam continued, full of pottery, including several fragments of T. S. f. 37. At 83 ft. from the town wall there was a posthole 9 in. wide and 2 ft. 3 in. deep, filled with small stones. One thinks of a veranda connected with the wall south of it, but the levels seem to be against this. There is an indication of a later level visible in the top-soil over this wall, and it is possible that the posthole belonged to a building later than the second daub house.

107. Two more wall-slots, each 2 ft. wide and containing mortar rubble, corresponding to the first three described, except that the second is only 7 ft. 1 in. from the surface, lie at 102½ and 116 ft. from the town wall. They would appear to be those of the north wing of a courtyard house, to the south wing of which belonged the three walls first described. Against this interpretation is the fact that the yellow loam seems to run over the northernmost wall without a break and only stops at 132 ft. At 108 ft. there was some masonry of septaria and tile recessed into it, but not such as could definitely be described as a wall. This also may have had something to do with a later building. From 119 to 122 ft. there was a mass of broken tile pitched into the top of the loam, almost certainly the remains of roof-tiles slipped off in a heap.

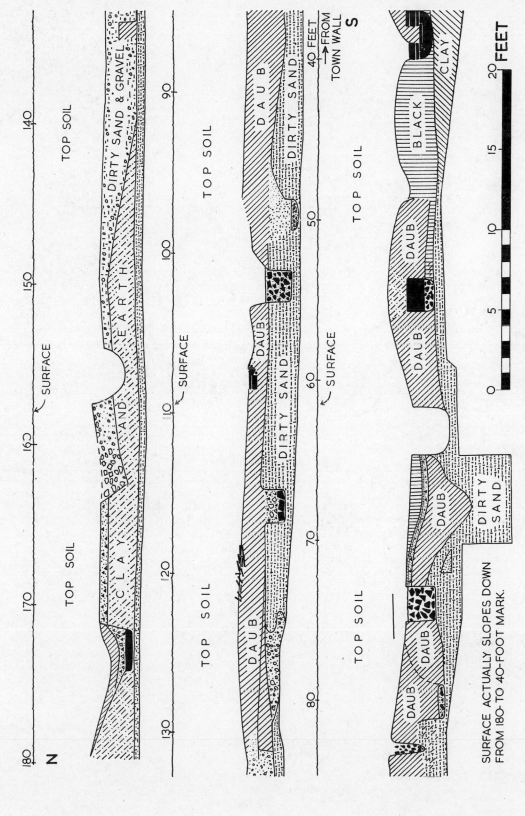

FIG. 105. Section N.–S. through Insula 39. [105–8], p. 216.

N

SURFACE

TOP SOIL

DIRTY SAND & GRAVEL

EARTH

CLAY SAND

TOP SOIL

CLAY

TOP SOIL

SURFACE

DAUB

DIRTY SAND

DAUB

DAUB

TOP SOIL

DIRTY SAND

DAUB

S

40 FEET
← FROM
TOWN WALL

SURFACE

TOP SOIL

DAUB

BLACK

CLAY

DAUB

DAUB

DIRTY SAND

DAUB

DAUB

TOP SOIL

SURFACE ACTUALLY SLOPES DOWN
FROM 180- TO 40-FOOT MARK.

FEET

108. At 125 ft. from the town wall occurs the only break in the layer of dirty sand. This consists of an irregular deposit of gravel over 5 ft. wide and partly underlying the sand. It would therefore appear to have been laid down at the same time. Above it there is a layer of stiff yellow loam (daub) into which, at 133 ft., a wall-slot is cut, 2 ft. 4 in. wide and 6 ft. from the surface. No rubble remained in it, and whether it can be connected with the last wall-slot mentioned or not is doubtful; more probably it is to be connected with the one before. Thus walls 4, 5, and 6 would belong to the first house and nos. 1, 2, 3, and 7 to the second, as is indicated by the stratification and levels. The yellow loam layer is not at all definite beyond the last wall, its place being taken by a mixture of dirty sand and gravel. This in turn runs up over a filling of a different nature coming down from the north and consisting of clay and earth, lying directly upon the dirty sand. The most outstanding feature in this northern part of the trench was a wall-slot, over 2 ft. 6 in. wide and 6 ft. 6 in. from the surface. The masonry foundation remained in the bottom, covered by loose rubble above which was a filling of yellow loam. Southwards from this wall a layer of mortar 6 in. thick extended for 8 ft., only ending where it had been cut away by an excavation filled with dirty sand and broken septaria. This was probably the foundation for a tessellated pavement, but no tesserae remained, nor any trace of a south wall, unless wall 7 could be regarded as such, which is hardly probable. North of wall 8, after six more feet of the clayey layer, the ground was all disturbed.

INSULA 40

This is the last insula, and of abnormal shape, owing to the form of the SE. angle of the town, which it occupies. The streets to the north and west have not been located. For a description of the town wall bordering it see pp. 45–56. The area formerly lay in the grounds of East Hill House, and was known as Bury or Berry Field.[1] It has probably not been built upon since Roman times, but in its use as paddock or garden it has become filled up with earth to the level of the top of the rampart and more. Very little has been done to explore it, and nothing systematic. It is in danger of modern development.

43. See insula 32.

44. While levelling the meadow in February 1907 for the bowling-green, a large piece of red tessellated pavement was found and, near by, a smaller piece of coloured mosaic of geometric design. They were to have been incorporated in the pavement of a pavilion,[2] but it appears that one piece only was built into the wall dividing East Hill House from the Minories. As this has no resemblance to a star pattern it can hardly be no. **43**.

172. On the map in Wire's copy of Morant he has marked in red a very large patch in the SE. corner of the insula as a tessellated pavement, but there seems to be no explanatory text (see *T.E.A.S.* xvii, 119).

103. On 14 March 1923, during the digging of a hole for rubbish, a large and nearly complete decorated pavement was found. It was 19 ft. square, including the red surround, and was 3 ft. 9 in. below the surface. The position (reported inaccurately as about 30 yards east of Queen St.) has been measured on the map by the Borough Engineer. The design is complete, except for one corner, which has sunk, owing to an earlier pit or well beneath it. Lying obliquely across the pavement at one corner (the extreme NW.) lay a skeleton believed to be that of a youngish woman. No further notes were made. The pavement (pl. XXXIV) was removed to the Museum (C.M. 4753.24).[3] Coins found in this garden include an *as* of Nerva, reverse NEP-TVNO CIRCENS CONSTITVT S. C., found about 1766. This reverse is not regarded as authentic by Mattingly and Sydenham (*C.R.I.* ii, 228). The coin is recorded in *Arch.* iii, 165, and is not in the Gray Collection in Colchester Museum. It is perhaps identical with the one in the British Museum.

LIST OF REMAINS FOUND WITHIN THE TOWN WALLS (Pl. XLI)

(The exact site is marked by a cross. If the site is not precisely known the cross is surrounded by a circle, the size of which reflects the extent of doubt regarding the position. When possible a wall is shown as a wall on the plan. Recognized street-metalling is hatched. No attempt has been made to differentiate between foundations, pavements, and other discoveries. Very occasionally a pavement can be shown in plan, e.g. 12 and 14.)

The first ninety-two numbers are those of *J.R.S.* ix, 157 ff. From 93 onwards the remains are subsequent discoveries or (and these are very few) omissions from the previous list. Since each item is fully described in the text, only the briefest description is given here, and only sufficient information to identify it.

1. Insula 17. Red tessellated pavement under Simkin's shop. Wire.
2. Insula 17. Behind the last. Another pavement and 'flues'. P. Laver.
3. Insula 17. Remains of buildings in garden area. Wire.

[1] Morant, iii, 21.
[2] *T.E.A.S.* x, 89; *Daily Telegraph*, 4/2/1907; *Essex Weekly News*, 1/2/1907.

[3] *T.E.A.S.* xvi, 295 (illustr.); xvii, 37 ff.; 119 (44 b); *J.R.S.* xii, 260; *E.R.* xxxii, 66, 90.

 4. Insula 9 (?). Tessellated pavement. O.S. 1:500; P. Laver.
 5. Insula 9. House, found 1865 and 1910, under Technical School, excavated partly by Parish. O.S. 1:500.
 6. Insula 9. Tessellated pavement behind no. 47 North Hill (old numbers).
 7. Insula 1. Back of McLean's House, 1849 (? same as 6). Wire.
 8. Insula 1. WSW. of Bowler's brewery. Tessellated pavement. O.S. 1:500.
 9. Insula 1. Tessellated pavement in field behind brewery, May 1845. Wire.
10. Insula 1. Tessellated pavement in sawpit, ibid., Dec. 1844. Mosaic. Wire.
11. Insula 1. Tessellated pavement at the brewery, Sept. 1844 (? new one). Wire.
12. Insula 2. Tessellated pavements, mosaic and plain, walls, &c., under nos. 17 and 18 North Hill.
13. Road found between insulae 10/11, in 1920. P. Laver.
14. Insula 10. Tessellated pavement in garden behind 'Chaise and Pair', 1855. Wire.
15. Insula 18. Boundary wall of insula on North Hill, and appearance of a Roman road or street running into the churchyard. Wire.
16. Insula 18. Concrete floor in churchyard, 1842. Wire.
17. Insula 18. Tessellated pavement (mosaic), under People's Hall, 1849. Wire.
18. Insula 19. Under Cups Hotel and Bernard's garden. Mosaic. Camden, &c.
19. Insula 19. Mosaic and foundations, west end of Vegetable Market. O.S. 1:500.
20. Insula 11. Pavements under Mr. Daniell's house, *ante* 1771. Morant.
21. Insula 11. Pavement opposite church, 1768; burnt wheat under it found in 1771. *Arch.* ii.
22. Insula 11. Pavement and arch, west of last, 1769. *Arch.* ii.
23. Insula 11. Pavement under or near house next north of no. 21 W. Stockwell Street, found *ante* 1771. *Arch.* ii.
24. Insula 3. In yard of the 'Bishop Blaize'. Tessellated pavement. Note that this is repositioned: the 'Bishop Blaize' was here. Wire.
25. Insula 12. In garden of Bragg, opposite St. Helen's Lane, 1793. *Vet. Mon.*
26. Insula 12. Mosaic, tile floor, concrete, in burial ground of the Independent Chapel (Herrick's), Nov. 1855. *Arch.* xvi.
27. Insula 12. Pavement in garden three doors north of the Independent Chapel, St. Helen's Lane.
28. Insula 5. Pavement and foundations in former Trusloves yard in Northgate Street.
29. Insula 5. Roman brickwork and arch in cellar of house.
30. Insula 13. Wall of septaria, with triple course of tile, under north wall of St. Helen's Chapel.
31. Insula 20. Mosaic pavement and 'circular building' at SE. corner of E. Stockwell Street.
32. Insula 21. Pavement under Wicks's shop.
33. Insula 22. Heavy wall under west pavement of Museum Street.
34. Insula 22. Vaulted podium under Norman Castle.
35. Insula 22. Walls and pavements under ramparts of Castle bailey on west, north, and east sides. Especially Round's excavation.
36. Insula 6. Foundations and pavements of houses around the bandstand in the Castle Park.
37. Insula 6. Pavement and debris south of the Town Wall.
38. Insula 15. Pavement east of Castle Park Café, *c.* 1848.
39. Insula 15. Building now known as the 'Mithraic Temple'.
40. Insula 8. Pavement under Castle Road.
41. Insula 8. Floors of flagstones and of Roman tiles, and traces of fire, &c. A little north of the last.
42. Insula 32. Pavement just south of East Hill House.
43. Insula 32. Mosaic pavement in garden of same house.
44. Insula 40. Mosaic and red pavements, site of bowling green, 1907, in the same grounds.
45. Just outside wall, insula 39. Alleged pavements and foundations under town wall.
46. Insula 38 (?). Pavement east of the old theatre, Queen Street.
47. Insula 38. Pavement or paved way.
47A. Insula 38. Tessellated pavement, west of Queen Street.
48. Insula 38. Roman brick floor, a little north of the last.
49. Insula 30. Stout wall running N.–S. under Culver Street opposite Adams's Garage.
50. Insula 30. Several walls and a floor of tiles, under Culver Street opposite the 'Cross Keys'.
51. Insula 30 (?). Hypocausts under Long Wire Street.
52. Insula 30 (?). Mosaic pavement.
53. Insula 38 (?). Pavement under Long Wire Street, opposite Albion Court.
54. Insula 38. Pavement in Albion Court. (In west side of circle.)
54A. Insula 30. Albion Court, pavement. (In east side of circle.)
55. Insula 38. Wall crossing Long Wire Street at an angle.
56. Insula 38. Pavement and floor of tiles under same street.
57. Insula 38. Mosaic pavement under Mr. Locke's house, Queen Street.

58. Insula 37. Pavement, in Victoria Place.
59. Insula 37. Foundations, east of last.
60. Insula 29. Wall running N.–S. under Culver Street.
61. Insula 29. Ditto (? the same wall) in St. Nicholas's churchyard.
62. Insula 29 (?). Pavement under west side of Sunday School of Wesleyan Chapel.
63. Insula 29. Foundations under Culver Street, 210 ft. from Wire Street.
64. Insula 29. Foundations under Culver Street 130 ft. east of Lion Walk.
65. Insula 29 (?). Pavement under No. 48 High Street.
66. Insula 28. Roman wall in cellar 50 yards west of 'Red Lion'.
67. Insula 28. Mosaic pavement under 'Red Lion', south side.
68. Insula 28. Mosaic pavement under 'Red Lion' yard, 1857.
69. Insula 28. Pavement under north end of Lion Walk.
70. Insula 36. Mosaic pavement under south end of Lion Walk.
71. Insula 36. Pavement in Lion Walk churchyard.
72. Insula 37 (?). Pavement near wall between Lion Walk and the Baptist churchyards.
73. Insula 36. Pavement in garden of Trinity House.
74. Insula 27. Foundations opposite west end of Trinity Church.
75. Insula 27. Pavement at back entrance of no. 1 Trinity Street, now under Culver Street.
76. Insula 27. Foundations in garden of same house.
77. Insula 35. Pavement in garden west of Trinity Street.
78. Insula 34. Pavement under former Friends' Meeting House in Sir Isaac's Walk.
79. Insula 34. Pavement under house at NW. corner of same street.
80. Insula 34. Mosaic pavement in garden once Mrs. Prosser's.
81. Insula 26. Mosaic pavement and foundations under Culver Street and running on south.
82. Insula 27. Two walls under High Street running E.–W.
83. Insula 26. Several walls running N.–S. under south side of High Street.
84. Insula 25. A concrete road west of Head Street, reported by Wire.
85. Insula 33. Pavement and foundations, under strong room of Mr. Howard's office.
86. Insula 33. Pavement in Mr. Inglis's garden.
87. Insula 33. Foundations in garden of P. G. Laver's house, now under the Gas Company's showrooms.
88. Insula 33. Pavement in garden of St. Mary's Cottage.
89. Insula 33. Pavements in St. Mary's churchyard.
90. Insula 33. Foundations and pavement under east end of St. Mary's Church.
91. Insula 25. Pavement in garden of St. Mary's Rectory.
92. Insula 25. Pavement under the same rectory, and foundations.
93. Insula 27. Foundations under Wright's ballroom, 1927.
94. Insula 28. Roman well under building on SE. corner of Pelham's Lane, 1920.
95. Insula 28. Wall running E.–W. under Woolworth's warehouse.
96. Insula 28. Pavement and pottery under NE. corner of Lion Walk.
97. Insula 35. Town wall cut through on east side of Scheregate steps and found 14 ft. thick.
98. Insula 27. Three Roman walls running E.–W. and parallel under north end of Trinity Street.
99. Insulae 27/28. Roman street cut through under south pavement of Culver Street.
100. Insula 28. Roman wall running N.–S. under east pavement of Pelham's Lane near north end.
101. Insula 35. Pavement encroaching upon rampart-space at SW. corner of Trinity Street.
102. Insula 38. Several pavements, foundations, and E.–W. street found under Wire Street Arcade.
103. Insula 40. Mosaic pavement, found in Lewis's gardens, 1923.
104. Insula 39. Roman town wall found under a later rebuild at bastion 5, June 1931.
105. Insula 39. Roman rampart, cement path (?), drain, and E.–W. foundations found ibid.
106. Insula 39. Pavement 70 ft. from town wall, ibid.
107. Insula 39. Foundations running E.–W. found as far as 180 ft. from wall.
108. Insula 39. Forms part of the last.
109. Insula 39. Roman foundations and part of a drain found when extending the omnibus garage west of the preceding, 1931.
110. Insula 38. Upper part of rebuilt town wall found under the south part of same garage.
111. Insula 32. Foundation running N.–S. under south pavement of East Hill, 28 ft. from town wall, Oct. 1925.
112. Insula 23. North kerb of Roman street, and metalling, July 1921.
113. Insula 30. Stout wall of tiles running N.–S. under street opposite the die of the War Memorial.
114. Insula 22. Massive masonry at centre of south side of insula, 1931.
115. Insula 29. Walling found under the Co-operative Society's premises on NW. side of Wire Street.
116. Insula 15. Small building (shrine?) west of 'Mithraeum'.

117. Insula 15. Hypocaust and foundations, with ruined mosaic.
118. Insula 15. Red pavement, 1929.
119. Insula 15. Red pavement and foundations, 1929.
120. Insula 7. Section of street at Park Café.
121. Insulae 17/25. Section of street at Grosvenor Garage.
122. Insula 22. Heavy wall 10 ft. high under north rampart of Castle.
123. Insulae 20/21. Appearance of a street running N.–S. under the entrance to no. 119 High Street.
124. Insula 20. Four foundations 2 ft. thick running N.–S. under the north pavement of High Street, Oct. 1927.
125. Insulae 11/19. Section of Roman street at SE. angle of St. Martin's House.
126. Insula 11. Numerous remains of Roman houses under the Telephone Exchange back of St. Martin's House.
127. Insula 19. Remains of burnt-out pottery shop under Willett's and Jacklin's premises.
128. At Head Gate. Roman wall of tiles, 2 ft. thick, running NW.–SE. under pavement on corner of Crouch Street, Oct. 1931.
129. Insulae 38/39. Section of Roman street at back entrance to National Omnibus Co.
130. Insula 26. Roman drain, vaulted, running N.–S., opposite door to Messrs. Benhams' works.
131. Insula 20. Wall running N.–S. by the east side of E. Stockwell Street at Messrs. Cullingfords' works, Oct. 1926.
132. Insula 21. Floor of pink mortar under George Street opposite the Oddfellows Hall, Aug. 1927.
133. Insula 28. Pavements and foundations on the east side of the back of Marks and Spencers, and another pavement (?) running under Messrs. Sainsburys', adjacent; also walls under Sainsburys'.
134. Insula 9. Pavement in garden of no. 44 North Hill, possibly same as no. 6 above.
135. Insula 33. Traces of foundations under Head Street opposite the clock of the old G.P.O.
136. Insula 26. Pavement under Culver Street extending 20 ft., and foundations.
137. Insula 26. Suspicion of a gravel road N.–S. opposite back gate of Barclays Bank, and a tessellated pavement adjoining the east.
138. Insula 28. Gravel 2 ft. 6 in. thick overlying burnt clay and daub, east of the Roman street in Culver Street.
139. Insula 28. Gravel layers in Culver Street from Pelham's Lane to corner of public lavatories, and wall running N.–S. opposite NW. corner of latter.
140. Insula 28. Pieces of marble found opposite the Red Lion Tap.
141. Insula 25. Red cement floor under building east of the great Water Tower.
142. Insula 30. Further walls and pavements found opposite the Cross Keys Inn, under Culver Street.
143A. Insula 38. Wall in Queen Street opposite Short Wire Street.
143B. Insula 38. Part of a tile arch with pink mortar, being part of a drain, found in St. Botolph's Street opposite Wright's office. No sign of wall.
144. Insula 39. Pavement found under back of the National Omnibus Company's garage near trench cut in 1931. (Close to no. 109.)
145. Insula 37. Pavement found under front wall of no. 19 Long Wire St.
146. Insula 33. Part of a building with apse floored with white tesserae, and remains of red tessellated floors found on site of new G.P.O.
147. Insula 39. Excavations at bastion 4, Sept. 1934.
148. Insula 22. Excavations in the Castle bailey, Roman drain, altar of temple, Roman bases, &c., Apr. 1932.
149. Insula 3. Well (? Roman) and red pavement.
150. Insula 7. Foundations and pavements of houses, 1927–9.
151. Insula 7. Ditto.
152. Insula 13. Curving wall 10 ft. thick found under Maidenburgh Street, Aug. 1891.
153. Insula 17. Red pavement shown by Wire on his plan.
154. Insula 17. Red pavement shown by Wire at back of house on west side of North Hill, opposite St. Peter's Church.
154A. Insula 17. Pavement in Balkerne Gardens.
155. Insula 17. Traces of walls, pits, and burnt layers at the 'Waggon and Horses', top of North Hill.
156. Insula 10/18. Roman street and other remains in garden behind no. 5 North Hill.
157. Insula 21. Pavement under south wall of George Hotel.
158. Insula 31. Pavement in front of arbour on terrace of garden of East Hill House.
159. Insula 31. Masses of white mortar and rubble under pavement north of shop on NE. corner of Queen Street.
160. Insula 30. Several walls running N.–S. under Culver Street south of All Saints Church.
161. Insula 35. Foundations and two or more red pavements under the Public Library.
162. Insula 27. Foundations and two pavements under the Public Library.
163. Insula 1. Foundations excavated and planned by E. N. Mason.
164. Insula 17. Tower on town wall west of Technical College, 1940.
165. Insula 10. Pavement at back of no. 11 North Hill just inside entrance to Crispin Court.

166. Walls on east side of Head Gate.
167. Roman street running N.–S. at entrance to Grey Friars.
168. Insula 20. Foundations under the Hippodrome, 1904.
169. Insula 25. Gravel like a street at east end of Church Street North, running E.–W.
170. Insula 38. Pavement found at petrol pump behind Police Station in Queen Street.
171. Insula 28. Burnt-out pottery shop under Curry's shop.
172. Insula 40. Red tessellated pavement recorded by Wire.
173. Insula 17. Adobe walls, foundations, mosaic floor, and burnt layer in garden of no. 60 North Hill.
174. Insula 18. Streets, foundations, and pits found when the Telephone Exchange was extended westwards in 1950.
175. Insula 21. Foundations under shop at SE. corner of George Street.
176. Insula 30. Shaft sunk at Adams's Garage.
177. Insula 25. Tessellated pavement marked by Cutts.
178. Insula 28. Tessellated pavement in Culver Street opposite Wolton and Attwood's.
179. Insula 27. Roman (?) well under back of 17 and 18 High Street.
180. Insula 28. Pavement of white tesserae in Red Lion yard (not marked on plan).
181. Insula 28. Red tessellated pavement, ibid., under east side at north end.
182. Insula 29. Roman wall running N.–S. opposite the east side of Beaumont's shop, Culver Street—probably the same as 63 and 64A. (Cannot be shown.)
183. Insula 30. Roman wall 'nearly opposite All Saints Court', 1848.
184. Insula 37. Tessellated pavement two doors north of Victoria Place.
185. Insula 8. Tower in NE. angle.
186. Insula 4. Heavy wall west of Stockwell Street School.
187. Insula 35. Roman walls in Trinity Street, May 1928.
188. Insula 4. Red tessellated pavement in E. Stockwell Street.
189. Insula 19. Pavement in the Vegetable Market.
190. Insula 22. Excavations by Mrs. Cotton.
191. Insula 31. Red tessellated pavement in garden of East Hill House, 1951.
192. Insula 30. Burnt layer east and south of All Saints Church.
193. Insula 27. Wall in Culver Street opposite Essex County Standard Office.
194. Insula 38. Red tessellated pavement and foundation in Wire Street, south of the Arcade.
195. Insula 38. Red tessellated pavement, foundations, and offering-pots found back of Police Station, 1939.
196. Insula 19. Wall of Septaria and white mortar running E.–W., 24 ft. south of the Cups Hotel.
197. Section IA. Cut in 1951 by Miss K. M. Richardson.

V

ROMAN COLCHESTER OUTSIDE
THE WALLS

THE ancient Borough of Colchester is of great extent (about 12,037 acres) and less than 200 years ago much of the ground was unenclosed. It was not until about 1820 that the town itself, which had remained almost unchanged in form and area for many centuries, began to spread and expand, especially westwards.

The oldest useful map is that of Chapman and André, published in 1778. It shows the heathlands, especially Lexden Heath, with many earthworks on it, and the tracks of the roads across them. Lexden Heath was enclosed about 1820, and in laying out and cultivating the new fields great damage was done to the earthworks. Thereafter a map made about 1845 by a local surveyor named Gilbert is very useful, because it preserves the field-boundaries of that time. It also professes to show certain earthworks, but with these we are not concerned here.

The complex of earthworks was by no means confined to Lexden Heath but spreads over much of the map and is complicated to the highest degree. Very little spade-work has been done, and without it it is not possible to conjecture how much of the whole is known to us, or the purpose and date of those parts of which we are sure. That much has been levelled and has disappeared since 1800 is certain, but much may have been destroyed before that, and some certainly in ancient times (e.g. Sheepen Dyke).

These works are still *sub judice*, and though they have for some years past been regarded as almost certainly of Iron Age date, there have been suggestions from time to time that they, or some of them, might belong to various other periods, including sub-Roman and Saxon.[1] Some have been more than once described as Roman roads.

The very large area outside the walls in which Roman remains are found has been divided, for many years past, into three areas known as North, South, and West. This was for convenience in keeping the records in the Museum. There is no East Area because of the proximity of the river on that side and because of the almost complete absence of remains east of the river.

The North Area consists of all the ground north of the river and south of it to the town wall and East Hill, between East Bridge and North Bridge. The West Area begins from North Bridge and covers all the area west and SW. of the town, as far as Maldon Road. The South Area extends from Maldon Road eastwards to the river. The outward boundary of all these areas is the same as that of the Borough of Colchester.

A separate series of numbers for the individual find-spots outside the walls has been employed. Within the walls we continued the numbers used by Wheeler and Laver and *R.C.H.M.*; outside the walls this has not been possible. To find any given number outside the walls it will be necessary to consult the list given on pp. 292 to 296.

[1] e.g. by P. G. Laver in MS. notes and by A. F. Hall (verbally).

(A) BUILDINGS

The Roman buildings outside the walls of Colchester have been reviewed in *R.C.H.M.*, pp. 29 ff. The remains are, in all cases, very fragmentary, and may be divided into the following categories:

    i. Temples, including the complex of buildings on Gosbecks Farm.

    ii. Houses.

    iii. Tombs, and buildings not yet sufficiently identified for classification.

1. Temples

95–97. *The Two Temples at St. Helena's School*

In the summer of 1935 the Colchester Excavation Committee faced the task of exploring the large field no. 613, adjoining the area excavated in 1930, and forming the largest part of our region 1. The area of this field was over 19 acres, and it was clear that only exploratory work could be undertaken unless something of outstanding importance was encountered.[1]

By this time we knew exactly what to expect in the way of remains of Cunobelin's city, and the area was trenched with the object of proving the extent over which the remains of huts, rubbish-pits, and all the copious litter of that intensive occupation was spread. There was, however, one other consideration. When the water-main was laid across the south side of the field in 1926 it was recorded that the trench cut through heavy Roman masonry, but the exact location of this was not known. Our trenches were accordingly planned with the aim of picking up this masonry.

It was not until late in the season that this came about. After, as it proved, missing again and again by inches only, we struck the precinct wall of the large temple about the middle of its south side. Thereafter it was not difficult to trace its course. In the meantime, quite early in the season, we had cut through the remains of the temple itself, which we took for a house. When the precinct was traced it became clear that we had to deal with a temple, by which time the season was far advanced. Not so much stripping could therefore be done as was desirable, but we were able thus to treat the entire cella and the east portico. Exploration of the interior of the temenos was, however, limited to two long trenches which were not at all adequate, for very large areas were not touched, and there may have been other temples, other buildings, and also a hall to

the east. However, two years later, when St. Helena's School was built the very extensive foundation trenches and basements revealed no new masonry remains at any point.

While the large temple was being traced we were also clearing up the last of the other exploratory trenches, and another building was found, even more thoroughly destroyed than the first, lying on a slight mound to the NW. This also proved to have been a Celtic temple, but of more normal size, much lighter construction, and of much later date. No precinct-wall or other boundary could be traced as belonging to it.

Further, just outside the SW. corner of the temenos of the large temple lay the very rough stone foundations of a building of late date which had been divided into two rooms. Both this and the second temple had not been built until the ground on which they stood had been covered by a dark occupation-level full of potsherds not earlier than the late second century, and probably actually third century. The concentration of such a deposit at these two points suggests that there had been occupation there, with wooden accommodation, over a long period. In the case of the third building wood was still the material in the end, for the stones were no more than a pitching for the frame of a timber building.

i. *The Large Temple* (*Colchester II*)

(Pls. xxxv–xxxvi, Figs. 106–108)

This was discovered accidentally by our exploratory trench (H. 11). The site showed as a slight mound, about 220 ft. in diameter and only 1 ft. 9 in. high. The field (O.S. 613) is fairly level, being part of the flood plain of the river Colne, which passes close by it on the north. The levels along the north hedge are from 26·6 to 28 ft. above Ordnance datum and the surface rises gently to about 30·5 ft. in the centre, the top of the mound being at 32 ft. Along the south side of the field the steep slope of the valley begins. The temple and its enclosing wall lie almost clear of this.

The top of the mound had been cleared very completely when the building was demolished, and had subsequently been worn down in cultivation, so that only 7 in. of top-soil overlay the undisturbed ancient levels.

Our section I is that of the first trench (H11) which crossed the site almost at right angles. Thereafter the lines of the foundation trenches were followed and their filling emptied in places in order to find evidence for the date of demolition, and to recover the plan. The interior of the cella and the east portico were completely stripped, but further stripping was not possible.

---

[1] Preliminary report in *T.E.A.S.* xxii, 45; *J.R.S.* xxvi, 252.

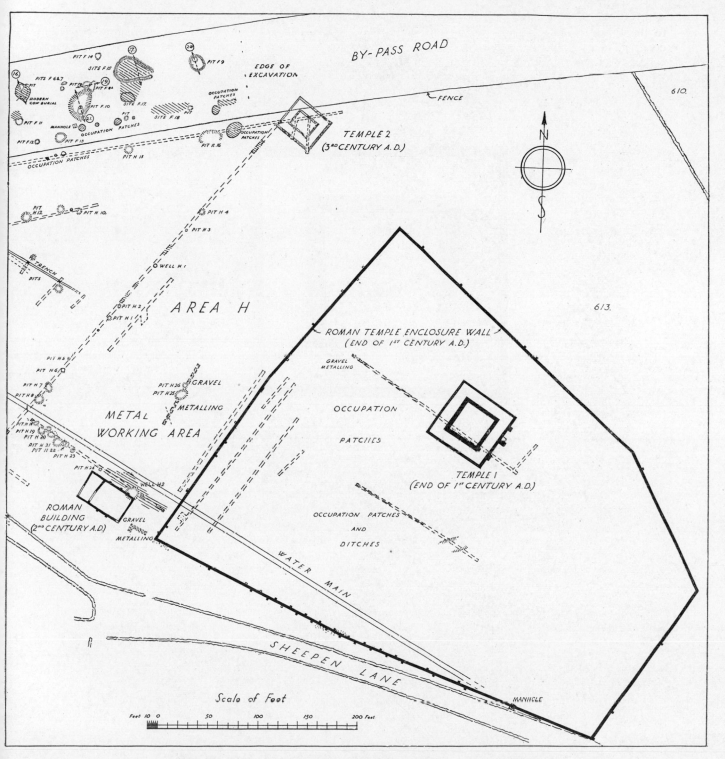

FIG. 106. Plan of Romano-British Temples on Sheepen Farm, 1935.

A broad diagonal trench was cut across the cella down to the subsoil, and a half diagonal to it in the SW. corner. The ground was extensively opened along the east side of the portico wall, but further work here, which was much to be desired, had also to be left. This proved to be the most interesting part of the building.

cella. In section A its place is partly taken by a burnt layer. The deposit was rapid and clean with little pottery and no coins.

The surface at the time of the building of the temple is shown by the top of the loam at the west face of the portico wall, and by the level of the base of the altar, the latter resting upon dark earth, on a level showing

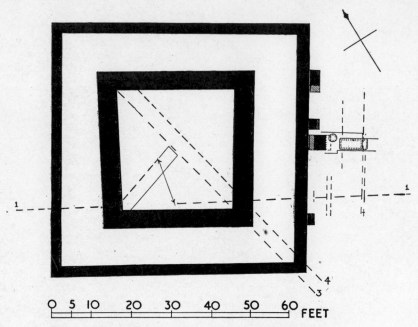

0 5 10   20   30   40   50   60 FEET

FIG. 107. Plan of Large Temple. [W 95], p. 224.

The sections (figs. 108, A, B, C) show the top of the natural gravel at a depth of 53 in. Upon this lies about 25 in. of stiff loam (the local 'pug'), the surface of which is rather irregular, the depth from the present surface varying from 2 ft. 2 in. to 3 ft. It is dirtied as if by trampling, cultivation, and the like, and corresponds in appearance and content with the level of the first occupation of the site, period I of Camulodunum, ending A.D. 43, but in parts (as largely here) remaining the exposed surface to a much later date. It produced the usual assemblage of potsherds of period I–III and coins of Cunobelin and Claudius, but no positive evidence of habitations.

Over most of the field we found periods III–IV (A.D. 43–50) represented by a sequence of layers of gravel, sometimes as many as four. Under the temple they are very few and simple. A lenticular patch 15 ft. wide and up to 7 in. thick is seen under the cella in section A, with a similar northward continuation. A corresponding layer is seen in section C in the SW. corner of the

stake-holes which we associated with leather tents of period VI (*Camulodunum*, p. 70). In section C the yellow make-up of the building-period lies directly upon the upcast of the trench for the portico wall, which is cut through the lowest gravel layer. No strata, therefore, intervene between the early period and the building of the temple.

The trench for the walls of the cella was 4 ft. 6 in. to 5 ft. wide and 4 ft. deep from the present surface. It had, of course, been partly damaged by the stone-robbers, so that accurate over-all dimensions could not be taken. Even so it was clear that the plan was not more than approximately square. The sides measured over all 39 ft. 6 in. on the north, 40 ft. 3 in. on the east, 37 ft. on the south, and 39 ft. on the west. The interior dimensions were, of course, about 9 ft. less. If we suppose a foundation 4 ft. 6 in. wide carrying a wall 3 ft. 6 in. wide, the actual cella must have been about 31 ft. square inside and 38 ft. outside. This is large, comparing favourably with Silchester,[1] Puy-de-

[1] 35 ft. square, *Arch.* lii, 745.

Dôme,[1] Avallon,[2] Autun,[3] Möhn, near Trier,[4] St. Paul, Austria.[5]

The stylobate of the portico (pl. XXXV, A) was similarly irregular in dimensions. The north side measured over all 64 ft. 9 in., the east 61 ft. 9 in., the south 64 ft. 3 in., and the west 63 ft. 6 in. The width varied from 2 ft. 3 in. to 3 ft., and the depth from the surface was about 3 ft. The foundation was thus not capable of supporting an exactly square wall, and we must accept the east side as having been definitely shorter than the other three, which could each have been about 63 ft. long. The case is similar with the cella, where, although a perfect square could be secured by juggling, the south side is 2 ft. shorter than the average. These differences appear intentional.

The foundation trenches were full of chips of septaria and mortar, most of the latter very pink and of fine quality. Much of this filling was removed, and though it produced sherds of Roman pottery of first- to fourth-century date, and black and white tesserae, nothing was found in it to suggest a post-Roman date for the destruction. The only stones (septaria) left by the robbers were a few at the bottom of the cella wall at the NE. corner and a length of the concrete foundation of the portico wall on the east side near the SE. corner (pl. XXXV, A). This latter was of small irregular stones and pebbles, similar in style to the foundations of the temenos wall, but without the admixture of broken tile, mortaria, and amphorae. The top of this concrete was only 16 in. below the top of the mound and only 15 in. below the grass.

The portico wall must have been very light; its maximum width may have been 2 ft.

Owing to the unequal length of the side walls the portico was of uneven width, but it averages about 10 ft. wide, with a maximum of 11 ft. on the east side. This, as is usual with temples of this type, was the main front and entrance.

The top-soil was removed over the whole interior of the cella. It was only 7 in. thick and lay directly upon the yellow make-up, the uppermost portion of which had undoubtedly been ploughed down or otherwise reduced long ago. Whatever floor had existed had been completely removed, but white and black tesserae, found loose hereabouts and in the rubble filling of the

foundation trenches, are evidence for a tessellated floor of a character superior to that of the portico.

Careful search was made for traces of any interior fittings or arrangements, the marks of which should have been very clear in the yellow loam. None were found, other than one doubtful hole nearly in the centre (section, fig. 108, A). The diameter was 25 in., but the hole was funnel-shaped, and, as a post-hole, unconvincing.

An irregular patch of mortar, 3 ft. 8 in. wide, against the west wall (section, fig. 108, A), was probably a place where mortar was mixed during construction. It contained eight fragments of pottery, all Claudian, a counter of opaque glass frit, and a fragment of thick native ware, thus agreeing with the upcast from the portico wall-trench already noted.

The yellow make-up, used to raise the level of the portico and cella to add dignity and a commanding position to the building, analogous to that secured by the Italian podium, was of a dry sandy loam. In it was found Claudian pottery in quantity, including T.S. forms 29, 27, Ritt. 12 (?), a fragment of a rim of yellow-green glass, a fragment of tile, a pig's jawbone, and two iron nails. There were also four British coins, two *asses* of Domitian, and a third illegible.

At one part the upper 6 in. were divided from the lower by a thin layer of white mortar. Here again the pottery was entirely Claudius–Nero, and there were also an iron nail, piece of sandstone, lumps of mortar, and a flint flake.

The top-soil contained the following: pottery fragments from the earliest period to the late fourth century, all in small pieces, worn by cultivation; white and black tesserae of about $\frac{1}{2}$-in. cube, and larger red and yellow ones of about an inch square. T.S. of forms 37 (Hadrianic) and 29; Rhenish and colour-coated ware; Antonine and later grey ware; window-glass, nails, iron buckle, coal or lignite, slag; the coins comprised one of Cunobelin, a small barbarous radiate head, one of Valentinian, and a late-fourth-century minim. There was also an iron brooch of *Cam.* type II, and a flat bowed brooch of type VIc (*Cam.* 312, sub no. 53), a fragment of a carved bone knife-handle, a small fragment of bronze (or possibly silver), a small iron buckle, and a flat, square-ended, tanged knife or chisel.

---

[1] 50 ft. square, dedicated to Mercurius Dumias, *Archiv. de la Comm. des Mon. historiques*, iv, pl. 2; J. Toutain, *Les cultes païens dans l'Empire romaine*, iii, 342.

[2] On Monte Marte between Girolles and Avallon, about 30½ ft. square, dedicated to Mercury, Domenico Romanelli, *Voyage à Pompei*, 1829.

[3] Fontenoy, *Autun*, 216, about 41 by 39½ ft., the best preserved of any of these temples, still standing 23·75 metres high.

[4] About 35½ by 40 ft., Hettner, *Drei Tempelbezirke*, apparently dedicated to a Celtic Mars.

[5] 31 ft. square, dedicated to Jupiter, *Anzeig. der Akad. der*

Wissenschaften in Wien, philos.-hist. Klasse, 1927, iii–iv. These references are taken from the summary by Wheeler in *Ant. Journ.* viii, 318 ff. (1928). To that list there are now several to be added both in this country and abroad; reference must be made in particular to S. Loeschcke, *Das Tempelbezirks bei Trier* (1928, two vols. so far); an additional note by H. Koethe at the end of his article in *Germania*, xvi (recording a temple with a menhir as cult object), and F. Oelmann on the classification of the many different types of these temples in *Germania*, xvii, 169 ff. (1933). An example with post-holes of an earlier building at Schleidweiler, *Germania*, xviii, 223 (1935).

The interior of the portico was too large for similarly complete treatment, but the whole of the eastern part was stripped. The level of the floor (or depth of top-soil) varied from place to place, but was fairly uniformly level with that of the cella. The latter would almost certainly have been higher originally. On the average it was about 15 in. below the grass, but in the SE. corner the top-soil was nearly 2 ft. deep (not seen on the section). Between the altar and the cella a thin layer of mortar capped the yellow loam floor and this may well have been part of the bedding for the tessellated floor. Large red and yellow tesserae (of tile) were frequently found in the rubble filling of the foundation trench for the portico wall. The finds made in the yellow loam make-up have been included in those mentioned under the cella.

Search was made for evidence of votive stones set along the eastern walls. Nothing positive was found against the wall of the cella, but outside the portico wall there was quite a series. The most important, which we have termed the 'altar', was set a little off centre, so that its south side rested on the centre line of the temple. Just north of it, against the wall, was a rectangular foundation of loose septaria chips, 18 in. deep and about 2 ft. 9 in. square. The top (as of the others, excluding the altar) was at 30·5 ft., which equates it with the penultimate period of the temple. Ten feet 6 inches north of the altar there was a similar but broader foundation of the same depth, measuring 3 ft. 9 in. N.–S. and 2 ft. 9 in. wide. On the south side it was extended another 21 in. by a rather slighter addition, which seemed to have been only 6 in. deep.

Sixteen feet south of the altar stood another such base, 2 ft. 6 in. N.–S. by 2 ft. wide. A slot in the early gravel layer, 2 ft. wide, 12 ft. south of the altar, may show where another stood, but, if so, it was earlier than the rest and was either made of wood or was a monolith.

The 'altar' itself (pl. XXXVI, C) was the largest and most central of these foundations, also the best preserved. On the other hand, it had no deep bed of stone chippings, from which we may assume that it carried no great weight. It was built directly upon dark, made soil, in which was found a coin of Nero. The lowest courses were laid as two offsets or steps, the facing-stones of which were carefully cut blocks of calcareous tufa. Apart from the face they were not well dressed, and varied much in size. The interior was filled with a concrete of mortar and fragments of stone, chiefly septaria, with an occasional flint. The facing-stones

remaining formed three courses (only one stone of the third remained), each nearly 4 in. high, the upper two each set back 3 in. The outer face had everywhere been plastered over to $\frac{1}{2}$ or $\frac{5}{8}$ in. thick, carefully smoothed and finally painted, but what colour could not be said. The appearance was a leaden grey. The eastern end had been robbed, leaving no trace, so that we lack the E.–W. dimension.

We have, very definitely, three sides of the second course preserved, forming a rectangle 3 ft. 8 in. N.–S. by at least 3 ft. 2 in. E.–W. Eccentrically placed near the centre was a block of Purbeck marble, or similar stone, resembling the broken stump of a nearly cylindrical column ($15\frac{1}{2}$ by $14\frac{1}{2}$ in.). If the third course of tufa blocks continued on all sides, reducing the area by 3 in. all around, the eccentric position of this stone, if used as a column, would be offensively prominent.

The first course, with its offset, is less complete. The only certain dimension is 4 ft. 2 in. N.–S. On the west it was clear that masonry of some sort had continued to the face of the portico wall, but most of it had been robbed. Enough remained, however, on the north side to show that the plaster of the face (but not on top) continued up to the portico wall across a span of about 1 ft. 8 in. Though in the coursing of the tufa blocks the outer rectangular foundation is treated as a separate entity, the plastering shows the fact to be otherwise. On the lowest course it is continuous, and on the second, where none was found on the west face, it may well have continued in the same manner.

The mortar remaining on the few stones in position between the main block and the portico was very flat, as though a large, flat slab had lain upon it. It was over an inch thick and rose up against the west face of the main block in places as if forming a thick mortar joint.

This leaves us in almost complete ignorance of what may have stood here, except that it was not of any great height or weight.[1] But we may assume that it was the most important ornament of the east face, and its plan suggests that it consisted of a rectangular, stepped base supporting a small altar. The small space behind it may have held a tall cult-figure (it is quite possible that a bed of stone chippings may underlie that particular portion) or it may have been utilized as a raised platform for the officiating priest.

One thing is quite certain: this stepped foundation was not steps in the sense of a stair to the portico, though steps are occasionally found in this position.[2] The altar was, naturally, usually in the cella, but frequently an

[1] The writer has collected all the plans of as many of these temples as possible. An outside altar is not unusual, but should be some distance from the portico. There is no parallel for a feature like this, which would obstruct an entrance in the normal, central position. The so-called altar of Hercules at Olympia, however, presents a plan remarkably like ours, but quite clear of any other building. The round block there incorporated is explained as a discarded column drawn from the Heraion. *Studies presented to D. M. Robinson*, 337, Abb. 1 and pl. 14, and ibid. 348.

[2] e.g. St. Ouen-de-Thouberville and Champigny-les-Langres.

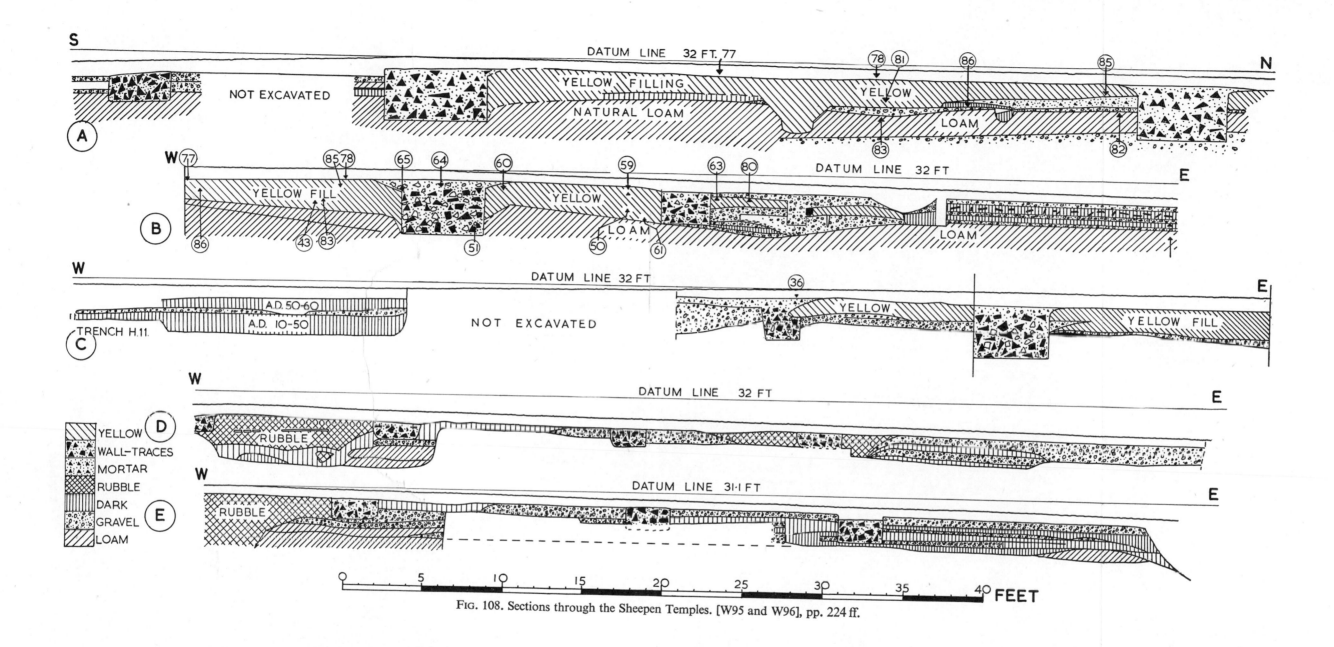

FIG. 108. Sections through the Sheepen Temples. [W95 and W96], pp. 224 ff.

outside one has been found, and others may have been missed in excavation. At Silchester the base of an altar was found at 24 ft. from the east side of one of the temples.

The ground east of this foundation was trenched in search of further information regarding it and the entrance to the temple generally. Only 3 ft. 3 in. from the broken east edge of the altar lay a long rectangular pit (plan, 107) measuring 7 ft. E.–W. by 3 ft. wide N.–S.; the depth was 27 in. below the layer of septaria The bottom was flat and the sides very steep. There was a shallower part at the east end, like a shelf, only 15 in. wide and deep. The filling contained nothing of interest, but over it lay so many pieces of septaria that at first we thought we had further masonry. All proved to be quite loose. Between this pit and the altar base, rather to the north, lay a small bowl-like depression 2 ft. in diameter, below the level of the lowest course, but whether made before the masonry or after could not be decided.

A section was taken along the side of this trench just north of the altar. The first terracing, seen in section B, does not appear, but the section was scarcely extensive enough at this point to be regarded as definite. There may well have been some diversion of the terracing before the latar. The yellow loam of the second terrace is well in evidence, the position of the outer revetment corresponding closely to that in section B, but the inner revetment is displaced farther east (at least 4 ft.) to give adequate clearance to the altar (which again demonstrates the importance of the latter).

Here the dirty loam of period I has no gravel laid over it until the close of the period of these two terraces. Thereafter the layer of septaria may be part of the final make-up of the terraces, or part of a period of decay, marked by broken tile in section i. The final make-up had mostly been disturbed, no doubt by stone-robbers or the like, but at one place remains were preserved of a final gravel floor with a black layer upon it. These two together must correspond to the final layer in section B. Directly upon the black lay the rubble of the destruction of the building.

No dating material was found here, other than the second brass of Nero found below the level of the altar.

We have seen the evidence from the interior of the temple is that the stone building followed directly upon the early levels with no recognizable stratum between the end of period VI and the deposit of the yellow loam, and that the walls and the loam belong to one period of construction. This is of the utmost importance in our approach to the east end of section B, that is, the portion outside the portico.

There is always the possibility, or hope, that some trace of an early building may be found under temples of this type, and in a few cases the hope has been realized. Section B has certain signs of slots for wooden sleeper-beams which might, were it not for the other evidence, be regarded as remains of earlier timber buildings. But we have concluded that there was no earlier building, and the true explanation of these remains is very different.

Further work around the outside of the temple was much to be desired, but could not be undertaken. We do not know as much as we would like, but the following appears to be the correct interpretation of the sequence here shown.

King-pins of the dating of this are the two coins of Domitian found in the yellow make-up of the east portico, and three coins found together, at a depth of 18 in., 28 ft. east of the portico, only 3 in. above the gravel layer capping period I; and these coins were of Tetricus, Constans, and another Constantinian. It follows that the two upper gravel layers here are Constantinian or later.

The evidence then, for the history of the temple, is as follows:

Period I. Occupation quite similar to that of the general area of pre-Roman Camulodunum, but without hut-sites or rubbish-pits, which is not quite usual. After aiming for the important site D1,[1] the road, which is presumed to follow a pre-Roman trackway, turns sharply in this direction, and it may be assumed that hereabouts, at this time, lay the holy of holies of Cunobelin's realm. This need not have been more than a sacred tree or group of trees.

Periods II–III. Little more than a single layer of gravel accumulates, though, in the midst of the intensive occupation of periods III and IV, the site cannot have been deserted. This means that it was in some way exempt from exploitation, as would be the case if it was regarded as sacred.

After Boudicca. No very great lapse of time can be allowed before the building of the stone temple, but we may confidently assume that so ambitious a work could not have been done while all the priorities (to use a modern term) were assigned to the rehabilitation of the colonia. When it was done the builders decided to build where they did, and on the scale they did, on one of two broad principles. Either, as we have supposed, the site was one of ancient sanctity and of a renown calling for an imposing foundation, or (we think much less probable) a wealthy body of citizens decided to found a temple which was to be so large that no room for it could be found within the walls of the colonia, and the site was chosen for reasons we can never know.

[1] *Camulodunum*, p. 97.

That such a work was promoted by romanized Britons rather than Romans can hardly be questioned. It would be costly because of its size alone, but the quality of the pink mortar and the tessellated pavements show that it was of expensive construction, though this did not run, it seems, to marble sheathing. We must therefore suppose it was put up at a time when things were easy, when business was prosperous, when public buildings in stone had become general, and when the glorification of the shrine of a native deity (even under a Roman name, as was very probably the case) would not be frowned upon by the authorities.

This must have taken place after the date of the coins of Domitian, so that a date in the late first century seems to be indicated.

When the temple was built, in common with most others of this type, it was so situated within its temenos wall that it left the central point unoccupied. This circumstance is so frequently repeated that it must have some significance. Normally the original sanctity of such places was not connected with a building but with a spring, tree, or glade, and there was no need for buildings until years of the Roman example, combined possibly with the demise of the already ancient trees, and a desire for higher standards, moved the devotees of the old gods to more modern and expensive establishments. But the site of the original sacred object remained central and revered. Nevertheless buildings were used on occasion in early times, and it is not impossible that, when a temple stands eccentrically in its temenos, an exploration of the central point might reveal the early building. For it would be reasonable to build a new temple alongside the old before pulling down the latter.

The altar was built on a low ground-level, without a sunk foundation, and the plaster demonstrates the ground-level of its period, which is presumably that of the first building and corresponds with the top of the black layer in section B, which is level with the top of the layer assigned generally in *Camulodunum* to period VI. It will also be noticed that the larger revetment slot is 4 ft. 9 in. from the portico wall, and so, approximately, falls in line with the east edge of the altar. Moreover, the recess against the portico wall shown in the same section is of the same width as the space between the altar and the same wall. This suggests that something of this width ran the full length of the east front of the portico—possibly a carved wooden screen.[1]

We must suppose that the altar, and therefore the stone building, was erected shortly after period VI. Evidence was found in region 4, south of the temple, that the area had been tidied up and levelled in Flavian times, probably under Domitian. It is reasonable to suppose that it was about the same time that the grounds of the temple were walled off and the new temple erected. The ground within the wall, however, was not levelled in the same way as that outside.

In course of time a step or terrace of 6 in. of gravel was made along the east face of the portico, burying the lower part of the altar and covering the former slot against the wall, which must by then have been obsolete. The outer revetment of this terrace has probably been destroyed by the subsequent one, for the next period saw the addition of further height to the existing terrace and the provision of a second one outside it. The material used is yellow loam similar to that used in the make-up of the cella. A foot of the altar was now buried. Of the revetments, only the slot of the inner remains. It was of wood 14 in. wide and 17 in. deep with a block of septaria, set in the floor of the outer terrace, marking the outer lip. This arrangement was contemporary with the 4-in. layer of dark occupation earth seen 18 in. below the surface on the right of the section, in the top of which were found the coins of Tetricus and Constantine, and probably with the gravel layer which comes next above.

A deep occupation layer then follows, in which the quantity of broken tiles (but not masonry) was most noticeable. This should correspond to a long period of neglect during which the roof, if not more, of the building decayed. But this was not final. There was another restoration in which the two terraces received a layer of gravel, which levelled them both into one, and which was revetted with wood, 7 in. wide and 21 in. deep. Outside this, another layer of gravel tidied up the surrounding ground.

The date of this is uncertain, but a coin of Valentinian, and another late-fourth-century coin, though found unstratified in the top-soil over the cella, may be regarded as evidence that the temple was in use, as is usual, even under the Christian emperors.

No evidence could be found for the date of the final destruction. This had been very complete. The trail of rubbish which it left was not very heavy, except in patches, and was found lying upon the surface of the last gravel layer and filling the slot of the wooden revetment. The evidence here is that the timber was drawn, rather than left to rot. The lack of tumbled rubble suggests that the building was taken down and not left to fall down. The site was swept clean of all remains, so that not a suspicion of a cult object has come to light. There is no clue to the dedication.

The greatest period of stone-robbing from the Roman remains here was in the late eleventh and early twelfth

---

[1] But continuity was not established, and this may simply have held early votive monuments.

centuries. So great was the supply available in the town that it is scarcely conceivable that the Normans, still less the Saxons, would have recourse to this building, and there is no sign that its materials were used in its immediate vicinity.

The evidence is that the building was taken down and the site cleared in late Roman times. The material must have been taken to the town, where, as was not the case in Saxon and Norman times, the existing buildings were still in use. The evidence is exactly similar in the case of the 'Mithraeum'. As to a more precise date, there does not seem to be any reason to suppose that circumstances were materially different here from those on the Continent, though it is not impossible that reasons for some divergence may yet come to light. Be that as it may, the latest evidence from the Tempelbezirk at Trier is that the complete triumph of Christianity over its pagan rivals did not become effective until the reign of Gratian (367–83).

The temenos wall which occupies such a large part of the field had been noted more than once at long intervals when trenches were cut through the field for mains or sewers. But it was simply recorded as a foundation, probably Roman. We first found it near the SW. corner, from which we will begin our description. Though much of the south wall was completely uncovered (pl. XXXVI, A), it was only possible to open up the other walls at frequent intervals, chiefly in order to recover the plan but also in the hope of finding the entrance. The latter hope did not materialize, but we recovered the general plan, though it was impossible to explore every buttress, so that our knowledge of these must remain incomplete.[1] At only one point was there any suggestion of any portion of the face of the wall remaining. This was about half-way along the south side; everywhere else there was only the concrete foundation (pl. XXXVI, A, B) made of white mortar and small stones, flints, fragments of tile and of large pottery such as mortaria and amphorae.[2] In many places even this had been robbed. Its width was usually 2 ft., but sometimes an inch or two more, and it was furnished with buttresses, alternately inside and out, set on an average 8 ft. 6 in. apart centre to centre. Each was 2 ft. square, but again occasionally exceeded this.[3] The depth of the concrete was not uniform. Usually it was 9 in. to a foot, but occasionally, as at the SE. corner, it exceeded this. The depth from the surface also varied, as will be seen from the following survey.

The South Wall. At the SW. angle (pl. XXXVI, B)

12 ft. of the foundation were uncovered, well preserved, with one exterior buttress. At 60 ft. east the foundation was 2 ft. wide, with 21 in. of top-soil, and no trace of gravel inside or outside. At 93 ft. it was similar, with a buttress 2 ft. wide, top-soil only 11 in., and no gravel. At 106 to 112 ft. there was a buttress on the south side, gravel at 18 in. depth on the north side, and top-soil 13 in. At 125 to 136 ft. the width was still 2 ft., the spoil-trench another 5 in., an exterior buttress at 125 ft., and an interior one at 134 ft., both 2 ft. square. At 154 ft. begins the exposure of a long section (pl. XXXVI, A) including an angle in the line at 192 ft. 6 in. Ten consecutive buttresses were uncovered, their spacing on one side of the wall averaging 17 ft. centre to centre, but with few inches variation. The spacing, if both sides be considered, halves this (i.e. 8 ft. 6 in.). As we are dealing with foundations, the slight variations or irregularities are unimportant.

At 215 ft. lies the zero point from which most of the field measurements were taken.

Just beyond 154 ft. the foundation reached its maximum width of 39 in., which is quite unusual; the adjacent buttress measured 2 ft. by 30 in. The top-soil here was 20 in., but only 10 ft. farther east it was only 12 in., and here was the only place where one course of the actual wall remained in position. The stones were small ill-dressed blocks of septaria. The width of the wall was 2 ft. Here too, outside the wall, lay a layer of gravel, 2 in. thick, at 22 in. from the surface, with a layer of oyster-shells upon it. Farther on, near where the foreman stands in the photograph (pl. XXXVI, A), is the slight angle in the wall, and here the gravel and oyster layers are on the inside, the oysters now 22 in. from the surface. At the end of this cut, at 282 ft., we left a gap and uncovered the wall from 293 ft. to 316 ft. Here the foundation was 27 in. wide and 17 in. below the surface. There was a layer of oyster-shells 4 in. thick lying level with the top of it inside and out, and immediately over all lay a 5-in. layer of gravel, 12 in. from the surface. This is the only point where any layer was observed to run over the remains of the wall. This cut revealed two more buttresses, one inside and one out, in their expected positions. The inner one was rather tapered in shape and built of small irregular pieces of septaria.[4]

The last cut was made to uncover the SE. angle. The total length of this southern wall was 483 ft.

At 230 ft. a trench was cut northwards into the enclosure to ascertain whether there were any traces of

---

[1] The curious polygonal plan is closely paralleled by that at Serrig, *Trier. Zeitschr.* (1931), 178, where the entrance seems to have been on the NE. side.

[2] But not of such a nature as to date the wall.

[3] The only similar case of the use of buttresses alternately so far known to the writer is the wall of the Byzantine reservoir

between Amari and Kaf, *Antiquity*, iii, 91, fig. 2. No connexion is suggested.

[4] Although one would expect the entrance to have been in the east wall, an entrance here would not be unreasonable, and might account for a gravel road over the footing and a rather better-built buttress on each side.

an interior portico connected with the buttresses. The section showed that there was no recognizable floor connecting with the apparent ground-level as indicated by the remaining few septaria blocks of the face of the wall. On the contrary a bank of oyster-shells nearly a foot thick had been left in position, and the foundation of the wall must have been laid in this layer. Beneath this the Cunobelinian occupation level lay at 3 ft., on top of the natural loam as usual. It had been followed by a layer of gravel crowned by a layer of trodden mud, and then the same two layers repeated. These represent Camulodunum periods II–V, and the oysters may well be of period VI. But the aim of the trench was to find traces of a portico. None was found; on the other hand, the evidence was that the ground had been left just as it was when the wall was built, and the unstratified accumulation of soil above was full, in its lower part, with chips of building stone, which was—remarkable to relate—chiefly Kentish rag. This debris may belong partly to the period of building and partly to the time of destruction; there was no means of determining which.

The oyster layer contained coin 73 (Claudius), and a layer of mud under it two *asses* of Claudius.

It is possible that the excavation which cuts through the early layers, or perhaps terminated the upper of them on the north, may represent a very oblique section of part of the road II and its ditch, last seen in the NE. corner of field 652 and then heading as if to traverse the north side of the temple enclosure.

The evidence here obtained that the ground was not levelled when the wall was built is supported by the stratigraphical evidence from trenches H11 and H12. It is nevertheless probable that, if not all, at least some of the area was made level with a spread of gravel.

The North Wall was in two sections, at an angle of 21 degrees to one another. The over-all length was 482 ft. The following description begins from the NW. angle. Nine cuts were made. The first 6 ft. of the NW. angle were exposed and then the wall foundation was exposed at 14, 28, 81, and 129 ft. At 28 ft. and 81 ft. there was an external buttress. Opposite the temple, where it was thought there might be some special feature, a long trench was opened. Two broken lengths of the wall foundation were exposed, the western 15 ft. long, the eastern 16 ft., with a formless gap of 3 ft. 6 in. between them. The ends were not so distinctly broken as to make a doorway impossible, but such a door is, we think, most unlikely (except perhaps as a postern), and the opening is not central between the two external buttresses, though it practically occupies the place of an internal one. At 209 ft. was a zero-point for our field measurements. A very straight line of wall all along this section could be followed by a brown line in the turf, so we were able to jump to 282 ft. and again to 301 ft., finding the usual foundation each time. At 354 ft. a long cut was made before the wall was found, for the angle in it at 326 ft. was unexpected, and the wall is in a very broken state here. Only one suggestion of a buttress was found, on the outside, at 348 ft. The remaining five cuts, including no. 14 at the NE. angle, exposed only wall foundations.

Along this side the foundation varied from 24 to 33 in. wide, and the top-soil over it from only 9–11 in., at the east end, to 22 in. Trial holes made both outside and inside the wall at about 376 ft. both showed a gravel floor 5 in. thick 1 ft. below the surface. At 336 ft. a short section was cut outside the wall to test the nature of the ground. This showed 6–12 in. of gravelly soil beneath the gravel floor, and below this an area of sand and another of black occupation earth. The bottom of the trench, at 31 in. depth, was yellow loam, possibly not undisturbed. We could observe no trace of an outside portico, unless the gravel floor had belonged to such. But this extended to beyond 19 ft. from the wall, quite even and unbroken, so that this is hardly likely. Length to the angle 326 ft., over all 479 ft.

The East Wall was well preserved at the NE. angle. From here frequent trenches were cut in order to follow the course, and careful watch was kept for traces of an entrance. In the end no such was found. The first 7 ft. of the foundation were uncovered and had no buttress; the foundation was uncovered at 23 ft. and at 40 ft., where it was low down, with spoil-trench visible above it. The same at 50 ft., where the width was about 29 in. and depth from surface about the same. A length was cleared from 62 to 80 ft., and this disclosed one buttress on the outside and traces of the next one west, inside. The wall was further located by short trenches at 87, 98, 117, 136 ft., and at 147 ft. 6 in. was an outside buttress. Here there was a big spoil-trench, and the depth to the wall was between 29 and 38 in., to the top of the buttress only 21 in. The width of wall foundation was 27 in. Finally the last 24 ft. to the SW. corner were uncovered, showing no buttress other than that on the corner. The total length of this side was 185 ft.

The West Wall. Beginning from the SW. angle, the first 29 ft. were uncovered, including two buttresses, the first outside at 7 ft., the next inside at 16½ ft. At 29 ft. the wall was completely robbed, but remains of it were found again at 60 ft., where were traces of an outside buttress also. The wall was proved at 71 and 86 ft. and at 100 to 105 ft., where there was a buttress inside, and another at 117 to 121 ft. Then a long cut was made at 138 to 194 ft., showing first 17 ft. of foundation with an outside buttress, then a gap of

28 ft., with jagged ends, and beyond this 13 ft. of foundation, but no buttress. At exactly 200 ft. is the angle in the wall. Beyond it numerous short trenches were cut to locate the wall. All along the depth is shallow, the top-soil being only 9–12 in. The width of the foundation varies from 2 ft. to 29 in. There were buttresses at 221, 266, 309, 328, and 341 ft., and possibly at 371 ft.; and the last 8 ft. to the NW. corner were uncovered, showing no buttress. The total length of this side was 396 ft.

The Area within the Temenos Wall

It was quite impossible to explore this area adequately. It was of more than three acres, and within it only two trenches, nos. H11 and H12, were taken down to the subsoil. Others made in search of masonry were not taken so deep, but they sufficed to show that in the western part of the area the same conditions applied as over the rest of the field explored, namely, that there was no definite occupation layer and no evidence of any concentration of buildings or population after the end of the early period, about A.D. 65.

The area enclosed by the temenos wall was, when enclosed, still as the previous occupation had left it, that is, rather uneven, with gravelled areas here and there interspersed with areas of dark earth, some of which are undoubtedly occupation levels and others perhaps areas which had been cultivated. In trench II11 and the east part of H12 this former level was only 12 in. below the surface; in their other parts it was somewhat deeper. There is no evidence anywhere that the area was ever systematically levelled either when the temple was built or afterwards. On the adjacent areas F and D a general levelling had taken place in the Flavian period, presumably for agricultural purposes. Moreover, in area D and possibly in area F there had been industrial sites working after A.D. 65 (e.g. metal-working and coins of Domitian round pit D4). There is no such evidence from within the temenos. On the contrary, the finds which are later than about A.D. 65 were lying upon the irregular surface which was left unaltered, apparently, until the end of the Roman period. There is no occupation level or layer which can be said to belong to the undoubtedly long occupation of the temple. This is not to say that such layer may not yet be found in connexion with other buildings not yet discovered, but it is pretty clear that the area enclosed was not used in such a way as to produce either an extensive occupation layer or a universal cultivation tilth. It was, however, used enough for most of its surface to become covered with a spread of pottery and coins, which extend to the end of the Roman period. If part of it was cultivated by the priests we have not found it. What we see suggests an untended space, possibly used as a camping-ground by visitors from a distance.

ii. The Smaller Temple (Colchester III)
(FIGS. 108, D, E; 109)

The remains of the second temple occupied the slight rise lying only 100 yards NW. of the first and now

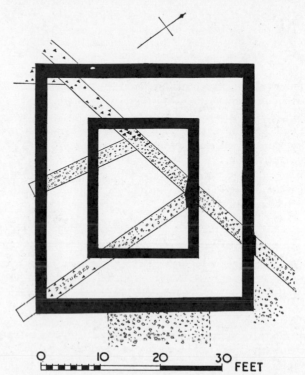

FIG. 109. Plan of Small Temple. [W 96], p. 233.

traversed by the south fence of the new by-pass road. They were even more scanty than those of the first, for while the walls were much smaller they had been no less thoroughly robbed and had been founded in made-up material which was very varied in nature.

The remains were so slight that the only useful result that could be looked for was the recovery of the plan, for which the evidence proved just sufficient. Owing to the inferior nature of the matrix in which they lay, the traces of the trenches which had held the foundations were more irregular in shape than those of the first temple, and the original thickness and exact course of the walls cannot be recovered with complete accuracy. The plan shown in fig. 109 embodies the data obtained.

The building apparently consisted of a rectangular cella 23 ft. E.–W. by 18 ft. 6 in. N.–S. The foundation trench was located in four places and varied in width, the minimum being only 18 in. The bottom of the foundation was only 1 ft. 10 in. from the surface. Such a wall, even if planted in solid subsoil, could not carry any great weight, and it seems possible that the super-structure may have been of wood.[1] Wattle and daub in timber framing is unlikely, for we found no layer of daub.

The outer wall for the portico was also located in four places, the SW. corner very exactly. It also varied much in the width of the foundation trench,[2] the mini-mum being 1 ft. 11 in. and the depth to the bottom 2 ft. The over-all dimensions seem to have been 41 ft. 6 in. E.–W. by 36 ft. N.–S. This allows of a portico an even 7 ft. wide on all sides.

There were no traces of any embellishments or luxury among the remains. Even the mortar was of a very common nature, and there was no trace of fine pink mortar from the superstructure. The floors were merely of native yellow gravel and were possibly in-tact, though their upper part may have been shaved off by cultivation, for they lay only 6 in. below the turf. In any case no remains of anything more elaborate lay scattered around, not even fragments of opus signinum or tesserae.

The site was not stripped, except a small area against the east portico wall on the outside, where it was neces-sary to seek for any remains corresponding to those found in that position in the larger temple. Only one notable feature was found. A gravel floor lay at the usual depth of 6 in. in the position shown on the plan. The sides appeared to have been straight, as shown, and the whole resembled a broad path leading to the entrance, set a little off centre, as was the case with the altar of the first temple.[3]

The slight elevation upon which this temple stood seems not to have been so homogeneously built up as the larger mound. The subsoil is the local 'pug' or loam, which at this low level near the river is perma-nently moist, and here has a greenish tinge. Its upper part, as usual, is dirty and contains potsherds trodden into it in the Cunobelin period. The later layers, our Camulodunum periods II–VI, are represented by a thick layer of fine greyish earth and a layer of gravel (see sections, under west side of cella, fig. 108, D, E) and a heavy occupation layer which is probably of period VI. The remainder of the mound is made up partly of a gravel floor and partly of a very mixed and dirty make-up full of broken septaria, tile, oyster-shells, small fragments of Antonine and earlier pottery, and food bones. As this deposit runs under the base of the wall (see section, at SW. corner) it must antedate it. This rubble make-up was observed outside and under the SW. corner and also inside the portico at both SW.

and SE. corners, with patches inside the cella on the west side and both inside and outside the portico wall on the north side. As will be seen from the section, the remains are so shallow that there is no possibility of the survival of any occupation level belonging to the period when the building was in use.

We can say that this temple was erected upon a mound which could not have been made before the Antonine period. Whether the rubbish composing it was brought from buildings near by, or whether it is a midden deposit in position, it is not easy to say. The section was too confused to give reliable indications whether any earlier building had existed on the site (other than in periods I–VI).

The pottery, loosely described as Antonine, could run far into the third century. There remains to men-tion a coin resembling those of Tetricus (no. 56) found in the rubble in the north portico and another illegible radiate head from the top-soil over the cella; and in 1930, when the large drain for the by-pass road was cut, it touched foundations, probably those of the NE. angle of this building, and near to these lay a coin of Gallienus and one of the Tetrici, and another, Con-stantinian (Mus. nos. 944–5. 30, 36. 31). A coin of Vespasian was found in the lowest gravel layer be-tween the SW. corner of the temenos and the building outside it.

COINS (*from the large Temple*)

Twenty-three British coins were found on the site; they com-prise one of Tasciovanus (*Camulodunum*, p. 136, no. 13), twenty-one of Cunobelin (nos. 22, 30, 41, 207, 71, 70, 77, 98, 104, and, found when building the School, 202–4 and 206–7 (Evans xii, 8 and xii, 9, four), 215, and 218–21), and one Evans xxii, 12; finally one illegible.

The Roman coins up to A.D. 65 have mostly been included in the Camulodunum Report, but we have a certain number to add. The list of post-Claudian coins is greatly swollen by those from the excavations for the School foundations, which lay mostly within the area of the temenos of the large temple, or immediately outside it.

REPUBLICAN (silver), L. PLAVTIVS PLANCVS. Worn. *B.M.C. Rep.* i, 576, *c.* 47 B.C. (F.R. 13).
    Q. ANTO. BALB. S.C. Date 82 B.C. School. C.M. 644.37. Quadriga right, no legend visible. School. C.M. 773.37.
    S.M.R. On *rev.* L. THORIVS BALBVS, lion leaping right, Q above. School. C.M. 895.37.
    ...CESTIANVS, helmeted head right. *Rev.* PLATORIVS M.F. AED.CVR..., eagle on thunderbolt. School. C.M. 1200.36 (cf. F.R., nos. 271–3).
AUGUSTUS, nos. 274–5. School. C.M. 772–4.37.
TIBERIUS, nos. 33 and 276.
AGRIPPA, nos. 44 and 277–84.
CALIGULA, nos. 47, 90, 112, 178, 287–8, 293–8, 300; no. 289 also comes into the picture.

---

[1] But 0·5 metre is quite a usual thickness for temple walls on the Continent.
[2] The reader is warned that the sections are oblique and show

a width greater than the fact.
[3] For gravel in the same position see Frilford, *Oxoniensia*, iv (1939), 1 ff., and several continental parallels could be quoted.

CLAUDIUS, nos. 138, 145, and no less than 29 from the School, 301–4, 307–12, 314–15, 317–20, 322–30, 332–3, 335–6; add nos. 305, 313, 331 from Sheepen Road.

Uncertain (all second brass), two or three; cf. nos. 186–221.

The following post-Claudian coins occurred:

NERO. *As*, with Victory, cf. M. & S. 329–31. Somewhat worn. Found just east of the altar of the large temple, below the foundation, in made soil.

Dup. Securitas type, M. & S. 287. Found with remains of a globular amphora, f. 187. School. C.M. 674.37.

Two corroded or worn *asses* found at the School may be of Nero. C.M. 177.37 and 818.37.

VESPASIAN. *As*. Cf. M. & S. 482. Fair to worn. Unstratified in the temenos.

As. M. & S. 497. Slightly worn. Found in the lowest gravel layer between temenos wall and 'Priest's House'.

Four *asses* of eagle-on-globe type. One is M. & S. 747, worn, C.M. 179.37. The others are more or less illegible, so as not to be precisely identified: C.M. 180.37, very worn; 307.37, good to fair; 683.37, very corroded; 684.37, corroded.

As. Spes type. COS III or VII. Worn and not more closely identifiable. C.M. 1201.36.

As. Temple of Jupiter type, but corroded and quite illegible. C.M. 178.37.

As. Like M. & S. 478. Fair to worn and illegible. C.M. 669.37.

As. Judaea capta type. C.M. 682.37.

As. For Domitian, probably M. & S. 724. Corroded, not worn. C.M. 673. 37.

DOMITIAN, *As*. M. & S. 422. Good to worn. Found in the yellow make-up of the large temple. Another similar, but dates illegible, was found at the School, slightly worn. C.M. 817.37.

As. Virtuti Augusti type, but corroded and slightly worn, dates illegible. School. C.M. 681.37.

As. Very worn and quite illegible. School. C.M. 1209.37.

As. Very worn, quite illegible, probably Domitian. School. C.M. 641.37.

As. Very worn and corroded, *rev.* uncertain. Within temenos at 2 ft.

As. M. & S. 422. Not worn. East of large temple at 1 ft.

NERVA. *As*. Corroded, not much worn, very uncertain, possibly Domitian. School. C.M. 368.37.

TRAJAN. *As*. M.&S. 392. Good, scarcely worn. School. C.M. 856.36.

Sest. Most probably Trajan, but quite illegible; corroded. From inner wall of large temple.

Dup. Cf. M. & S. 545. Unstratified in temenos. Fair to worn.

As. Cf. M. & S. 395. Ibid. at 18 in. Worn.

HADRIAN, *Sest*. M. & S. 970. Very worn and illegible. School. C.M. 672.37.

Dup. M. & S. 974. Worn but legible. From the adjacent slaughter-house. C.M. 348.40.

Dup. Probably of Hadrian, very worn and quite illegible. School. C.M. 897.37.

ANTONINUS PIUS. No. 243 of the First Report was found in this region.

Sest. M. & S. 977, obscured and worn. School. C.M. 863.37.

Dup. Probably M. & S. 953, but date illegible. Very worn. Sheepen Road. C.M. 1107.36.

As. Worn and illegible. *Rev.* sacrificial implements. From the slaughter-house. C.M. 350.40.

Dup. Corroded and illegible. School. C.M. 949.37.

As or Dup. Uncertain. School. C.M. 660.37.

M. AURELIUS. *Sest*. As M. & S. 1009, but date illegible. Worn. School. C.M. 1204.36.

Dup. M. & S. 1092. Corroded but not much worn. Slaughter-house. C.M. 349.40.

Sest. M. & S. 529. Somewhat worn. Within temenos at 2 ft.

COMMODUS *Sest*. Possibly M. & S. 312, but date illegible. School. C.M. 369.37.

Sest. Doubtfully M. & S. 580. Worn, dates illegible. Sheepen Road. C.M. 91.39.

Dup. M. & S. 292a or 296. Somewhat worn, dates illegible. School. C.M. 640.37.

Doubtful. Sest. Very worn, quite illegible. Might be of M. Aurelius or later. School. C.M. 770.37.

GORDIAN III. *Ant. Obv.* IMP GORDIANVS PIVS FEL AVG. Bust, radiate, draped, right. *Rev.* SECVRIT PERP. Securitas standing, legs crossed, leaning on column and holding sceptre. Slightly worn. School. C.M. 815.37.

Ant. Obv. as last. *Rev.* VICTOR AETER. Victory standing left. Scarcely worn. School. C.M. 816.37.

Ant. Exactly as no. 815.37, from the slaughter-house. Slightly worn. C.M. 351.40.

SALONINA. *Ant*. M. & S. 29. Worn. Sheepen Road. C.M. 332.38.

POSTUMUS. *Ant. Obv.* IMP C POSTVMVS P F AVG, radiate and cuirassed right. *Rev.* Uncertain. Slightly worn. School. C.M. 812.37.

Ant. Obv. as last. *Rev.* PROVIDENTIA AVG. Providence standing left holding globe and cornucopiae. Slightly worn. Sheepen Road. C.M. 857.36.

VICTORINUS. *Ant*. Cf. M. & S. 61. Hardly worn, but broken. Within temenos at 2 ft.

Ant. Obv. ...VICTORINVS P F AVG., radiate, draped (? cuirassed) right. *Rev.* PAX AVG, Peace standing left with transverse sceptre and branch. In field V and star. Not worn. School. C.M. 766.37.

Ant. Similar in all respects, but IMP C &c. Not worn. School. C.M. 954.37.

Ant. Obv. as preceding. *Rev.* PIETAS AVG, female figure standing left, before an altar. Worn. School. C.M. 953.37.

TETRICUS SENIOR, *Ant. Obv.* IMP C TETRICVS P F AVG, radiate, draped bust right. *Rev.* VIRTVS AVGG. Valour standing left with spear and shield. Little worn. School. C.M. 1202.36.

Ant. Obv. as last but cuirassed. *Rev.* PAX AVG, Peace standing left with branch and sceptre. Not worn. School. C.M. 243.40.

Ant. Illegible. Worn. School. C.M. 975.37.

Ant. Illegible, probably Tericus. Corroded. School. C.M. 651.37.

Ant. Small flan, only partly legible. *Rev.* of *Spes* type. School. Little worn. C.M. 245.40.

TETRICUS JUNIOR. *Ant. Obv.* C.PIV ES.... Radiate, draped right. *Rev.* illegible. *Spes* type, not worn. School. C.M. 182.37.

Ant. Three similar examples of the same type, almost illegible, C.M. 898.37 and 952.37, both School, worn, the latter barbarous. The third, CM. 867.37, also School, is very thin, much clipped. *Rev.* uncertain, not worn.

CLAUDIUS II. *Ant*. Oval. *Rev. Aequitas Aug.* type. School. C.M. 1205.36. Worn.

QUINTILLUS. *Ant*. Consecration coin of Claudius. Altar type. School. C.M. 893.37.

Illegible. Ant. Barbarous radiate. Worn. School. C.M. 308.37.

Ant. Three illegible radiate, C.M. 680.37 and 868–9.37, the latter two barbarous. All worn. School.

Ant. Barbarous radiate. Worn. Slaughter-house. C.M. 357.40.

PROBUS. *Ant. Rev.* of *Virtus* type. Very worn. School. C.M. 955.37.

ALLECTUS. *Ant*. M. & S. 55. Somewhat worn. School. C.M. 244.40.

Ant. Doubtfully Allectus. *Rev.* LAETITIA AVG. School. C.M. 762.37.

Licinius Senior. Æ. *Rev.* VIRTVS EXERCITVS, VOT XX. Mm. SF/TSA. Not worn. School. C.M. 945.37.

Æ. *Rev.* GENIO POP ROM. Mm. PLN, star in field. Slightly worn. School. C.M. 956.37.

Æ. *Rev.* Trophy between two captives. Somewhat worn. Sheepen Road. C.M. 333.38.

Constantine I. Besides the *Gloria Romanorum* coin found in Reg. 4 (F.R., no. 251) there are:

Æ. GLORIA EXERCITVS, two standards. Mm. illegible. Not worn. School. C.M. 944.37.

Æ. Similar. Mm. TR.S. Not worn. Sheepen Road. C.M. 311.37.

Æ. SOLI INVICTO type. Mm. SF/PLN. Not worn. Sheepen Road. C.M. 335.38.

Æ. VRBS ROMA. Mm. TRS. Very worn. School. 370.37.

Æ. CONSTANTINOPOLIS. Mm. uncertain. Slightly worn. School. C.M. 866.37.

Æ. Similar. Within temenos. Not worn. Mm. TRP.

Constantine II. Æ. Broken in half. *Gloria Exercitus* type, two standards. Not worn, almost mint condition. School. C.M. 255.40.

Constantinian. Æ. Small, *Gloria Exercitus* type, two standards. Mm. TRS. Slightly worn. School. 247.40.

Æ. Same type, one standard. Very worn. School. C.M. 365.37.

Æ. Similar, with chi-rho. Mm. CONS. School. C.M. 246.40.

Æ. Same type, two standards. Mm. TRS, slightly worn. School. C.M. 247.40.

Æ. *Victoriae dd nn* . . . type, mm. illegible. Slightly worn. School. C.M. 246.40.

Æ. Similar, much worn. School. C.M. 248.40.

Æ. *Rev.* uncertain. Worn. Within temenos east of temple.

Æ. Barbarous copy of *Fel. Temp. Reparatio* type. Found just west of the small temple at 2 ft. Not worn.

Æ. Similar coin, but orthodox. Very worn, with large hole for suspension. Found on the School site with another coin, also pierced. This second coin has on *rev.* an eagle as on the consecration coins of Claudius Gothicus, but the laureate head is of much earlier appearance. Corroded rather than worn. C.M. 958.37.

Æ. Illegible. Blundered in striking? Within temenos east of large temple.

Valentinian I. Æ. GLORIA ROMANORVM. Mm. OF/ III/CONST, slightly worn. Found on top of the cella of the large temple.

Valens. Æ. *Securitas* type. Found near the north wall of the large temple at 12 in. (Stolen while on exhibition during the excavations.) Not worn.

Æ. Another similar. Scarcely worn. Mm. OF III/CON... Sheepen Road. C.M. 312.37.

Illegible. Another coin, possibly as the last, but doubtful. Worn and corroded. School. C.M. 249.40.

Also three second brass coins of the first century. All very corroded. School. C.M. 371, 649, and 658.37.

118. *The Temple on the Grammar School Field*

(*Colchester IV*)

(Fig. 110 and Pl. xxxvii)

This lies some 1,200 yards SW. of the town, on the west side of the Maldon Road, in field 1266, and some 300 ft. west of the line of the Roman road coming in from Gosbecks. It was first observed in 1938 as a crop-

mark, which showed the line of the north and other walls. The mark recurs annually. The dry summer of 1947 caused more of the enclosure wall to be visible, and it was possible to plot three of the corners (NW., SW., and S.), besides affording much help to the work of exploration. This was carried out by members of the staff and boys of the School, led first by Mr. A. F. Hall and later by the Headmaster, Mr. J. F. Elam. Because the site is on a Rugby football ground the trenches were as small as possible and the work had to be done expeditiously. No great area could be uncovered. The depth to the natural gravel is 2½ to 3 ft., and this was usually reached; otherwise a depth of 2 ft. was found sufficient to prove a wall. Three long trenches were cut, two as diagonals to the enclosure and one along the main N.–S. axis. They were made in sections of 10 ft. in length. Many other smaller trenches have not been shown on the plan, except a few of particular importance.

The investigation was rendered most difficult by the very fugitive nature of the remains of the walls. Except in the SE. corner, where the overlay was deeper, the wall of the enclosure was founded on, but not in, the natural gravel. The foundations of the interior buildings were even more shallow. All that remains is chips of stone and mortar left by stone-robbers, and even the outline of the foundation trenches cannot be discerned clearly. In fact, since the litter of stone and tile was ubiquitous, it was the presence of mortar which became the final criterion in tracing the walls, and little confidence could have been put in the results were it not for the way in which the points plotted combine to make a quite coherent plan, with but one anomaly, the bulge in the west wall. The fact that the buildings are imperfect in plan means little, for they are commonly so on temple sites, even where the construction was of a much stouter nature than here.

It was observed that nodules of chalk occurred along the lines of the walls and nowhere else, and a few pieces of tile resembling red tesserae. The latter were so few that they may be accidentally cubical fragments. The former are puzzling.[1]

The maximum amount of tile was always near the enclosure wall, and indeed outside it, so that there may have been a tiled veranda outside.

The scarcity of mortar and stone suggests strongly that the buildings were of wattle and daub on stone foundations.

The Larger Building

This extends across the south end of the enclosure, facing the temple, as is so often the case. It is the

---

[1] Possibly this is agricultural chalk, which elsewhere is dissolved away by acids in the soil, but is preserved where there is already lime in the soil from the mortar of a wall.

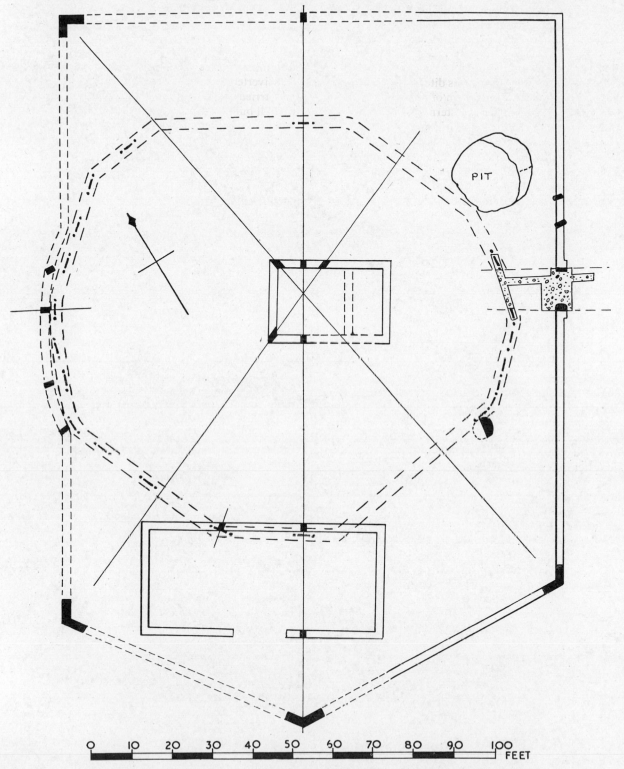

PIT

0 10 20 30 40 50 60 70 80 90 100
FEET

FIG. 110. Plan of Temple on Royal Grammar School Playing-field. [W 118], p. 236.

temple-hall, presumably a room for meetings and functions. Another notable example with one side open is that at Mare du Puits,[1] where, however, the hall was outside the enclosure and the open side was towards the temple. It is unique in having a hypocaust.

Our building is not centrally placed. From east to west it measures 61 ft. and from north to south 28 ft. 6 in. The existence of an opening 13 ft. 6 in. wide was proved in the south side. There were no traces of a floor. It is again to be emphasized that the traces of the walls were so sparse and uncertain that the plan is obtained by the general survey of them, and the dimensions of walls and buildings cannot be measured exactly.

The Temple

The central building was difficult to trace, for the reasons just stated. The excavators were satisfied they had what is shown. They were unable to trace part of the south wall and felt that they had not found the temple, because of the oblong shape and the lack of a portico. But if we suppose that a square (or nearly square) cella used the west wall, which is 21 ft. long, and that its east wall (which in any case might well have a gap in it for a door) has been too evanescent to find, we have a cella very nearly exactly central in the enclosure, with a porch 8 ft. deep on its east side. The whole building is 21 by 30 ft. over all. There is no reason to doubt that this is the temple. It was a common thing at first to dispense with a portico which could be, and often was, added later. If our portico was in wood it may have left little trace. The excavators mention that east of the building a conspicuous socket was found, but further search for others has not been made.

This building was floored with rammed soil. Though no trace of a portico-wall or stylobate was found, this floor extended outside the walls. In the middle of the building a large fragment of tile was found lying on it, with an inch-thick layer of mortar adhering to the under side, but it is dubious whether this could be part of a floor. The few and narrow trenches left most of the interior undisturbed.

The temenos wall enclosed a pentagonal space 126 ft. wide E.–W. The east wall is straight, with its NE. corner under the boundary of the property. It is 142 ft. long, with an entrance in the middle. The south end of the enclosure is closed by two walls at an angle, one 74 ft., the other 66 ft. long. The complete outline is closely paralleled by the much richer establishment at Faye-l'Abbesse.[2] The west wall is 151 ft. long, and all the evidence tended to show that it had a bulge in the middle 52 ft. long in which it made a maximum devia-

tion of 5 ft. from its line. Immediately within it, and so close to it that no significant width can be involved, an oval ditch was repeatedly found running on and even beyond the general line of the wall. There can be no doubt that it was to avoid a boundary represented by this ditch that the wall was thus diverted. If the western arm of the south wall had been carried on to match the eastern in length, and the west wall built on this line, it would have cleared the boundary, which may have been a stockade in the ditch, or a hedge by its side. Why this was not done we do not know.

In exploring the NE. part of the enclosure the bronze plaque (pl. XXXVII, A) dedicated to Silvanus by Cintusmus the Coppersmith was found lying on what was presumably the ancient ground-level. Near by there was a pit which will be described below. The plaque suggested a temple site, and the discovery of another plaque (pl. XXXVII, B) dedicated to Silvanus by one Hermes confirmed this.

The ends of the walls have been found on both sides of the gap 8 ft. wide for an entrance. Both ends seem, from the foundation trench, to have been wider than usual. This may have been to provide for a stone pillar or a wooden gatepost. The space between them is metalled with gravel, and this has been traced for 8 ft. outside the wall and 16 ft. towards the temple. The oval ditch comes up to it obliquely on each side and there stops, leaving a metalled passage-way 9 ft. wide.

Thus we may conjecture that our temple, first probably a simple square cella, probably of wood and surrounded by a polygonal stockade (or possibly a hedge and ditch?), was later rebuilt on stone foundations, with a porch, perhaps later a wooden veranda, and with a stone temenos wall which greatly increased the extent of the precinct, and was provided with an assembly hall 28 by 61 ft. At all times the main entrance remained at the same spot.

The Oval Ditch

This ditch, which the excavators have carefully plotted at very many points, indicated by line-and-dot on the plan, was first picked up under the north wall of the hall, and again under the same wall a little farther west. It is quite small, usually only 3 ft. deep from the Roman ground-level (reckoned as about 12 in. below the surface). It is described as irregular in outline, so that it has not been possible, when giving its centre line on the plan, to be very exact. This may account in some small part for the irregularity of its plan. Nothing is said as to its width, but the position of the west wall and of the pits shows that it must have been very narrow. Since it is clear that it was the first

---

[1] L. Deglatigny, *Documents et Notes Archéologiques*, ii, 7.
[2] *Mém. Soc. Deux-Sèvres*, xvi (1853), 65 ff.; *Bull. Mon.* xxi (1855), 52 f.; *B.R.G.K.* xxiii (1933), 45.

outer enclosure of the temple it is most likely to have been a slot for a palisade. Less probably it might have been a small ditch accompanying a hedge. In any case the plan seems to have been an irregular polygon as at Coblenz and Farley Heath.[1] Mr. Hall suggests that a secondary digging or cleaning might contribute to the irregularity, but this is assuming that it was an open ditch, which we much doubt. He advances proof: in places (e.g. east of the temple) there was a thin white primary silt below the normal dark filling, while at other places the fill sometimes reached the bottom, but with white material remaining at the sides. Here, apparently, the ditch had been dug to more than its original depth. We suggest that the second cutting was to replace a rotted stockade. Often the recutting left no white material at all.

The pottery found (all small worn fragments and second century) is from the darker fill, and does not date the origin of the ditch, but might date the second stockade. No earlier pottery was found in or around it. That the ditch is earlier than the enclosure wall and hall is obvious from the plan.

Pits

Two pits were found, both nearly circular, with vertical sides and flat bottoms, one being $8\frac{1}{2}$, the other 6 ft. deep. Both are sited so as to touch the outer edge of the oval ditch. A third possibly touched it also. The smaller pit has only been partly excavated, but the large one has been carefully cleared.

It was cut in gravel, presumably to win gravel, for the material from it was almost all taken away. The filling of dark soil has tile and building stone in it at all levels to the very bottom, but only sporadically, except for the layer over the top. Pottery and food-bones occurred as if thrown in. If the pit was dug for gravel it was subsequently used for rubbish, and a coin of Hadrian lay in the lowest layer. In layer 5 there was fine sand, perhaps from building-work, and in layer 6 crushed tile, and the HERMES plaque lay on the surface of layer 5. Then followed refuse, including mortar, which now first appears, and the level is now up to the surface. Finally, a lot of roofing-tile was scattered over the site.

The following small finds were made:

Bronze tablet with ansate ends, inscribed in punctured letters

DEO SILVANO
CALLIRIOD
CINTVSMVS
AERARIVS
V. S. L. M.

To the god Silvanus, called Calliriod(os?), Cintusmus the Coppersmith willingly and gladly fulfils his obligation. (Pl. XXXVII, A.)

C.M.R. 1947, 28, pl. VIII; J.R.S. xxxvii (1947), 178, fig. 8. We do not think it necessary to break up the second line, which is clearly the native name of the god, and will translate directly as 'King of the Woods', which seems a fair description of Silvanus.

This was found among stone and tile debris north of the large pit.

Bronze tablet with ansate ends, inscribed in letters made with strokes of a narrow chisel

DEO SILVA
NO
HERMES
VSLV

To the god Silvanus Hermes willingly and gladly fulfils his obligation. (Pl. XXXVI, B.)

C.M.R. 1948, 8, pl. II; J.R.S. xxxviii (1948), 100. Mr. Wright does not take the last V as a mistake for M, but reads V(ovit). He also remarks that most of the two dozen dedications to Silvanus in Britain are by soldiers, but those from Colchester are exceptions since one is by a coppersmith, and the other, to judge by his name, either a slave or a freedman, both civilians.

Bronze Stag (pl. XXXVI, C). A quite small and solid casting, *c.* 2 by 2 in., and it is difficult to see how it could stand or be fixed in position. The execution is broad and casual.

Votive bronze animals are scarce enough to be welcome finds. Another stag was found in Colchester by Wire (p. 93); its present whereabouts is unknown. A long list of votive animals found in Gaul could be given, and there is no doubt they are usually regarded in some way as attributes of the divinity, as in the present case.

This stag was found within the west edge of the pit, but so high that it could have been deposited after the pit had been filled. It is kept at the Grammar School.

In the same pit as the foregoing was found a very weatherworn fragment of white marble. It is from a slab about $\frac{3}{4}$ in. thick, which has been quite smooth on both sides. That which was probably the back is well preserved; the other, which bears a sharply and cleanly incised semicircle, is very worn. We have probably part of an O or C, and if so perhaps part of the dedication of the temple.[2]

In bone there were several pins, a die and some gaming counters, and an object like a duffle-button, and other objects.

In iron there was a large key, an object like a stiletto, and a stylus with the point missing.

The thirteen coins are listed below; only two have useful evidential value (nos. 3 and 8).

1. *As.* Julio–Claudian. Very worn, the reverse could be *Constantiae.* Unstratified.
2. *As.* Claudius, M. & S. 66; copy; unstratified. Pitted, not worn.
3. *As.* Domitian, M. & S. 325, A.D. 86 (*Fidei Publicae*); worn on one side only. 5 ft. deep, in pit.
4. *Sest.* Trajan, M. & S. 500 (*Fortuna*), A.D. 103–111; worn. Unstratified.
5. *Dup.* Trajan, M. & S. 502 (*Fortuna*), same date; little worn. Unstratified.
6. *Dup.* Trajan, M. & S. 563 (*Dacia*), same date; much worn. Unstratified.
7. *Dup.* Trajan, another as last; scarcely worn. Unstratified.
8. *As.* Hadrian, M. & S. 571 (*Fortuna Redux*); moderately worn. Found in the pit at 8 ft. 3 in.

---

[1] Coblenz in *Ant. Journ.* viii, 324, Farley Heath in *J.R.S.* xxxiv (1944), 84. [2] *C.M.R.* 1948, 8.

9. *Dup.* Hadrian, M. & S. 939 (*Restitutori Achaiae*). Unstratified.

10. *Dup.* Faustina Senior, M. & S. 1395 (*Felicitas*), A.D. 145–6; not worn. Unstratified.

11. *Sest.* Postumus, M. & S. 167 (*Victoria Aug*), A.D. 258–68; somewhat worn. Unstratified.

12. *Ae.* Constans (*Fel. Temp. Rep.*, Phoenix on globe); not worn. Unstratified.

13. A denarius, not sent to me, found at 18 in. depth, i.e. on the old surface at the entrance.

By estimating how much of the area has been examined Mr. Hall is able to compute that several hundred coins may still lie in the soil, so that the above short series may be misleading. There seems, however, to have been a Claudian occupation, perhaps distinct from the temple, and the temple was most frequented in the second century, the Trajanic representation suggesting that it was first established in his reign. After the Antonine period interest in this temple seems to have waned very much. The pottery too, which is chiefly second century, tells the same tale.

Other Possible Temples

The former St. John's Abbey lay south of the town, and its grounds still preserve their entity, but belong to the Garrison Officers' Club. Under these conditions they have not been touched for many years, and there is no recent information on the area. In December 1891 an ansate bronze tablet was found there with the following well-known inscription:

DEO. MARTI. MEDOOO. CAMP
ESIVM. ET VICTORIE ALEXAN
DRI. PII FELICIS. AVGVSTI. NOSI
DONVM. LOSSIO. VEDA. DE. SVO
POSVIT. NEPOS. VEPOOENI. CALEDO.

To the god Mars Medocius of the Campenses and to the victory of our Emperor Alexander, Pious and Fortunate, Lossio Veda, grandson of Vepogenus, a Caledonian, set up this gift at his own expense.

This inscription has many important points which we cannot discuss here; the reader is referred to the many previous writings about it.[1]

The Abbey of St. John was built on or near the site of a former wooden church of pre-Conquest date, which stood upon or near a mound. This mound, it is recorded, was removed by a later abbot.[2] It may well have been the mound of a Roman temple. There is still another mound standing in the same grounds at the south end. It has never been regarded as an object of great antiquity, but in fact nothing is known concerning it.

41. A large Roman altar of sandstone was found in excavations for a sewer in Balkerne Lane, just outside the SW. angle of the town wall and about 6 ft. below the surface. It is said that it was found in the town ditch.[3] The height is just over 4 ft., and it is about 2 ft. square. The whole of the top is broken, but the inscription, in a moulded panel, is intact and reads:

MATRIBVS
SVLEVIS
SIMILIS. ATTF
CI CANT
V.L.S.

To the Sulevian Mothers Similis, son of Attius, a citizen of the Cantii, gladly pays his vow.

An altar of these dimensions in such a place suggests the proximity of a temple of the Matres. The site is near to that of St. Mary's Church, which may be significant, but that is inside the walls and the altar was outside. The heavy masonry, however, noted near the Bull Hotel, could possibly have been a temple of the Matres.[4]

75. A foundation is noted in the Union grounds by P. G. Laver. We have no description, but his plan seems to show a square of about 18 ft. inside one of about 35 ft., and this resembles a temple more than a tomb.

2. HOUSES AND OTHER BUILDINGS

These are far more numerous than is generally understood. They were summed up in the *R.C.H.M. Report* in 1922 (iii, 29) under the nos. 3–15, which we shall now consider in more detail, and which we shall have to supplement. For despite the statement that 'on other sides the marshes made the ground unfit for habitation', there are dwellings on the low ground, and we have seen how low the most crowded part of ancient Camulodunum lay (*Cam.* 57). There is no doubt, too, that the houses with stone foundations and tessellated floors were not the only ones. Probably even more numerous were those built in the flimsy British fashion, which have left no structural remains, but whose presence, and that of a considerable extra-mural population, is witnessed by the extensive spread of broken pottery, food bones, &c., around the town.

i. *House at the Victoria Inn*

82–86. One house, or group of houses, lay north of the river. In 1880 when digging foundations for buildings at the back of the Victoria Inn, NW. of North

---

[1] Haverfield, in *Arch. J.* xlix, 188.
[2] Cotton MS., Nero D. viii, publ. in *T.E.A.S.* n.s. viii, 126 and 133.

[3] *T.E.A.S.* xii, 257; *J.B.A.* xxxvii, 227.
[4] On the altar see J. E. Price in *T.E.A.S.* n.s. ii, 266; *Arch. J.* xxxviii, 430; xxxix, 355; *Essex County Standard*, June 1881.

Bridge, a tessellated pavement was found at a depth of about 2½ ft. It appeared to be of considerable extent, but ran under the roadway and some buildings, so its full extent could not be ascertained. The part uncovered is illustrated in colour, and a restoration drawing shows the whole decorated portion as just over 16 ft. square.[1] Some of the tesserae were of Purbeck marble, which is unusual. The pattern is black and white, incorporating a large Greek key pattern or elaboration of the swastika, with mere strips of coloured guilloche pattern. The whole is remarkably similar to no. **81** in insula 26.

Red tessellated pavements have been noted running under the houses as far as the middle of the present North Station Road. Some of these were exposed when the pavement on the west side of the street was laid down (before 1909).[2]

More remains were found in 1927. A rubble and cement foundation lay about 12 ft. from the west building-line at a depth of about 3 ft. When a petrol tank was sunk in Messrs. Orfeurs' yard, 100 ft. from the street front, part of a pavement with a geometrical design in black and white was found 6 ft. below the surface. The mortar bed was red.[3] The tesserae were very small. The pavement was destroyed.

There are some valuable notes in P. G. Laver's Diary about this building. In May 1929 a water main was laid in North Station Road approximately along the middle of the street. Opposite no. 27, that is a little south of the junction of Albert Road, a Roman wall was cut through. It was 3 ft. 6 in. from the surface and 18 in. thick. It was only about 1 ft. high, and below it was gravel, full of water. It was 20 ft. from the building-line. There is a further note that some remains of walling exists from this point to a point opposite Albert Road. Very few fragments of pottery were found, and of these we can say nothing.

Nearer North Bridge nothing was found except what might be taken as part of the gravel road to the original ford of earlier Roman times—'here the gravel very dark, stained. Nothing found in it.'

Opposite the lane by the Victoria Inn the trench cut through another wall, very diagonally, so that it appeared to be 7 ft. wide.[4] Actually Laver estimated its real thickness at about 2 ft. 4 in. He recalls that Roman pavement has been found under the modern path and street opposite the Victoria Inn, and shows the area of this covering the end of the lane and extending about the width of the lane farther, both north and south of it.[5] The wall comes to within 2 ft. 6 in. of the surface and its base is at 3 ft. 6 in.; below this is a dark clayey layer about 6 in. thick, lying directly on the gravel. The wall is of good rubble with tiles.

On 4 October 1932 Laver notes a Roman wall running E.–W. under the west half of the street, 2 ft. from the surface, 2 ft. 6 in. high and about 2 ft. thick. His sketch shows the wall as just south of the Victoria Inn.

ii. *North Bridge*

81. Nothing was known of this until 1843 when **Wm.** Wire observed the building of a new bridge and made copious notes in his Diary. The northern abutment of the old bridge (a brick structure of three arches, built *c.* 1773)[6] was found to conceal a piece of massive masonry which roused much comment at the time, but the nature of which was never decided. Now that it has been proved (p. 32) that there was a Roman North Gate it can scarcely be doubted that it was the abutment of a bridge, the main body of which may have been either of stone or of wood, more probably the latter. We have to keep in mind the nature of the stream here, which was undoubtedly of the meandering type, and P. G. Laver observed an old channel, full of black mud and peaty silt, cut through in the street between North Gate and North Bridge. There may be more than one such channel, but, wherever the stream ran in Roman times, the evidence is that the present course at this point is over the site of Roman graves; and other Roman remains, including a similar south abutment, may have been destroyed by the stream.

The nature of this old work is not clear from the loose descriptions which we have. 'Upon removing the north abutment [of the recent bridge] it was found to be placed between the foundation of a wall of Roman character, which appeared to have been divided purposely for the reception of it. Under this foundation were discovered several earthen urns, apparently Roman, some of which fell to pieces . . . only two were got out whole . . . one red . . . the other black. The latter was inverted on a tile about 8 ins. square'[7] [grave 441].

On 31 May Wire wrote in his Diary: 'the old wall seems to have been built to prevent the north abutment shoving over to the north'.

This masonry must have been of considerable strength, for Wire records a series of attempts to destroy it with gunpowder extending over several days. On 7 June the blasting was still going on, and Wire writes: 'I have no doubt but it is the remains of a stone or brick bridge erected previous to the wood bridge mentioned by Morant or else the remains of an ancient fort built to guard the ford over the river there. It is rather singular that no such remains were found on the south side.'

On the same day he adds: 'Mr. Woolmer [Clerk of the Works] gave me an ancient brass spur and a piece of iron [sketched] found under[8] the concrete at the bridge works, several feet below

---

[1] *T.E.A.S.* n.s. ii, 189; iii, 129.
[2] Ibid. x, 87.   [3] Ibid. xix, 133.
[4] This was cut again and observed by the writer in January 1952.
[5] The pavement was also proved again in 1952.
[6] *R.C.H.M. Essex*, iii, 21, para. 5.
[7] *Gent.'s Magazine*, 1843, 189.   [8] i.e. at the foot of.

high water mark.'[1] (He previously says that the masonry was referred to as 'the concrete'.)

The evidence for graves 'under' the 'concrete' foundation is as follows: Wire, Diary, 31/5/1843, 'Mr. Woolmer informs me that a Roman urn containing a deposit by cremation was discovered under the concrete . . .' This was before the blasting was completed. The next day Wire inquired for the urn but could find nothing about it. Ibid., 10/6/1843: 'The men at work on the north side of the river dug on to a Roman pot which fell to pieces.' This was witnessed by Wire. Ibid., 12/6/1843: 'Purchased a Roman urn [sic] and a tile about 8 ins. square. The urn when found was inverted on the tile and contained charred bones. A hollow tile found under the old masonry the north side of the river. . . .' A drawing of the pot on the tile is found at the end of Wire's Morant, where it is definitely stated to have been found under the wall in question. It is added that the men stated that the pot had slipped to one side of the tile and exposed some fragments of bones. The pot is a black polished bowl of f. 305, which is late third or fourth century in date. The burial is grave 441 of the Museum list.

On the same day Wire records that the foreman 'showed me an urn of red earth and told me that a bronze vessel with two handles had been discovered there. . . . A few coins have been discovered at the bridge works, but of no value. . . .'

On 18/6/1843 Wire adds: 'The works at the bridge going on. The north pier of the old bridge was built upon what appears to be a part of the old wall found on the north side of the river and it is my opinion that the water did not originally run in this channel and in this I am borne out by the fact that a Roman pot covering calcined bones and inverted on a square tile was found by the labourers under the *north arch* of the old bridge.' For some days following the work in hand was the removal of this north pier. An entry in Wire's 'County Illustrations' clinches the matter; a plan is given showing where 'several Roman urns' were found '*south*' of the old foundation. 'Under' has been crossed out.

19/6/1843: 'Mr. Church junr. . . . purchased the red earth urn found at the bridge works. This he presented to the local museum.' (It cannot now be identified.)

22/6/1843: 'Mr. Woolmer informs me that a Roman urn was discovered when digging the foundations of the south pier. . . .'

28/6/1843. Wire visited the bridge works with Jenkins and both agreed that the river must have 'very much encroached upon the north side . . . founded on the fact of finding Roman fictile vessels in what is now the bed of the river at the bridge.'

Thus it seems that nothing was really found beneath the 'concrete', but rather in the river south of it. If undisturbed, as they seem to have been, these deposits should be older than the 'concrete', which, if Roman, should be fourth century in date. The whole, however, is much too vague to yield any definite conclusion.

71. On 3 October 1949 a Roman wall was found running N.–S. at the south corner of North Hill and St. Peter's Street. The top of it was 27 in., the bottom more than 76 in. below the surface of the street. The thickness of it was 2 ft. and the materials stone and tile. The ground to the east of it was well seen to be all made-up, chiefly of river mud and dark, wet earth. On its west side little could be observed, but what could be seen seemed similar to that on the east.

The function of this wall just here is puzzling, for the position is only 75 ft. north of the town wall and would scarcely be clear of berm and ditch. One thinks of the possibility of its having acted as a retaining wall for a causeway leading to a bridge, but the nature of the made earth on its west side did not seem to support any such theory.

No other buildings have been found on the north of the town.

iii. *House at the Waterworks*

73/74. Behind the Waterworks House at the bottom of Balkerne Hill are two reservoirs, one at least of which was in construction in 1808. Over both the O.S. 1:500 map writes 'Roman remains found', and Cutts marks pavements and foundations. The following is part of an article in the *Morning Chronicle*, 6/9/1808: 'Last week, while excavating the extensive reservoir for the Colchester Waterworks on Balcon Lane . . . the workmen fell in with the remains of some spacious Roman baths, and earthen pipes of a peculiar construction, for the letting in and out of the waters, with a quantity of Roman pottery. . . . What were taken up perfect are in the possession of Mr. Dodd the engineer . . .'; another report, 24/11/1808, relates how, later at the same place, 'the workmen fell in with a quantity of Roman pavement, and . . . beneath that some oak framing, almost perfectly sound . . .'; after a long description of a T.S. bowl '. . . most of the coins dug up are of Claudius . . . Trajan, Antoninus Pius, and several others hardly distinguishable from their state of corrosion; also gilt instruments [sic] used in their sacrifices. Few places lately dug have produced such a variety of Roman remains, but it must be remarked that the excavation and embankments have been very considerable, nearly the whole of an extensive field.'

If ever we should have to conclude that the public baths must have been outside the walls, this is a very possible spot. It could easily be well supplied with water.

Besides a coin of Cunobelin (Evans xii, 9) found 'near the Waterworks',[2] we have an interesting and early lot of pottery found at a depth of 8–10 ft. when sinking the 'new well' at the Waterworks at the foot of Balkerne Hill in 1891[3] (Mus. nos. 2033. 31 ff.). There were coins of Trajan, Vespasian, and Faustina jun. (one each); T.S. stamps of SCOTNS (graffito IAIINI...); OF MVRRA; ICCA...; CREST; PATRIC...; OF VIR... and fragments. Three fragments of early f. 30 and 13 fragments of f. 37, a large piece of a decorated Samian flagon,[4] a

---

[1] High-water mark means the level reached when the sluice gates of Middle Mill, lower down, were closed. There is no reference to the tide.

[2] Wire, Diary, 2/6/1842; illustr. Album, p. 49.
[3] *The Builder*, Feb. 1891.
[4] Stanfield, *J.R.S.* xxvii, 178, fig. 12.

bowl f. Curle 11 (restored), and many fragments of plain wares from the mid-first century onwards; the coarse wares correspond, and run up to the fourth century and to medieval gotches, including two stamps G. ANTONI QVIET and SEMPRON on amphorae.

In 1886 the Museum acquired a 'perfect small light earth amphora found some years since near Colchester Waterworks' from Mr. C. E. Bland (C.M. 16.86). In the next year Mrs. Bland gave 'three dark earth Roman urns found in Colchester', but whether from the same place or from her property on Lexden Road or elsewhere we shall never know (C.M. 27.86).

A brooch of Hod Hill type, found near the Waterworks, is recorded in *Arch.* xxxix, 509, no. 1.

iv. *Buildings on Lord's Land and at the Union*

The Union, now St. Mary's Hospital, was built in 1842 and occupies a large square of ground south of the Waterworks, and south of it again, separated from Balkerne Lane by the Chantry Lands (which belong to the Grammar School), lay another great square area known as Lord's Land. Both the latter are built over. The Roman road from the Balkerne Gate ran across them obliquely. The following remains of houses are known; other walls may have belonged to dwellings or tombs.

37. Roman coins, urns, and a tessellated pavement were found in 1803. The O.S. map 1:500 does not mark the exact spot, but indicates the centre of Lord's Land. *R.C.H.M.* omits this, but Cutts shows it.

38. A tessellated pavement is marked on the same sheet immediately at the rear of St. Mary's Villa, without date. It is actually just outside the gate. *R.C.H.M.* 7.

39. In January 1922 P. G. Laver noted the foundation of a pavement under the north pavement of Crouch Street, midway between the Excise Office and the 'Horse and Groom'. It consisted of reddish mortar laid on the gravel. It was not very wide N.–S., and E.–W. its limits were not found. A sketch-plan gives no measurements. There were no finer layers of mortar and no tesserae.[1] At the same spot, in 1925, were found remains of the pilae of a hypocaust, of square tiles, with pottery, tiles, tesserae, and other indications of a building.[2]

40. Not more than 40 ft. east of the last discovery (39) a red cement pavement was found in 1922, under the modern pavement, at the side entrance to the 'Horse and Groom'. Probably part of the same house.

110. Pavement shown by Cutts.

111. Cutts shows two rectangular marks which we have supposed to indicate foundations.

147. 'Another [pavement] nearly at the middle house in St. Mary's Road, on the south side, this has probably been recorded in my list.'[3] The list runs: 'Two examples . . . in St. Mary's Road. These are now built over.'[4]

In August 1876, at the famous meeting of the Royal Archaeological Institute, Dr. H. Laver showed excavations in progress described as follows: '. . . some of the party diverged . . . to the piece of ground between the Colchester Union and Blatch Square, where Mr. Laver on the commonly received belief that the old Roman way to Londinium from the Balkerne Gate . . . crossed to the London Road at the point where the Hospital now stands, conjectured that Roman remains might be found. A party of sappers and miners had excavated . . . the pavement of a Roman Villa . . . the party . . . found a large amount of pavement laid bare on the very spot selected for excavation. . . .' This pavement is not marked (or not dated) on the 1876 map, but may have been added later to revised editions. We are not even told whether the site was north or south of the Lexden Road; cf. *R.C.H.M.* 3; *Arch. J.* xxxiii, 420; *T.E.A.S.* x, 89.

(35). Several fragments of red tessellated pavement were found when cutting the foundations of the nurses' quarters at the Hospital (approximately covered by our 35). Some which lay in the line of the walls were removed and others were covered by the buildings.[5] We have no exact positions.

206. A small piece of red tessellated pavement found 3 ft. below the surface in Lord's Land in March 1895, in what is now Papillon Road. This could well be the same as no 37 above.[6]

207. 'A pavement of red tesserae has been discovered 30 ins. below the surface in the middle of the Chantry Lands. The foundation is of lime or chalk, about 1½ ins. thick, and one would be led to the conclusion that it was simply powdered lime or chalk, and had never been mortar when laid down. Fragments of wall-mortar, fresco painted, of Roman bricks and roof tiles and fictile vessels are found on the same land.'[7] This could be the same as 147.

208. A pavement of red tesserae was found on Lord's Land a few yards from the eastern entrance. Wire says: 'It was broken up before I saw it, but from the foundations, composed of septaria and fragments of Roman bricks and the mortar adhering to them being chiefly

---

[1] Laver, Diary, 23/1/1922.

[2] E. J. Rudsdale, and cf. *R.C.H.M.*, 29, 15a.

[3] MS. note by H. Laver, in Museum, dated 22/12/1909. It is preceded by a note of a fine mosaic pavement, but it is not clear whether this one is decorated or not.

[4] *T.E.A.S.* x, 89.

[5] *R.C.H.M.*, 29, 4; *T.E.A.S.* x, 89.

[6] *R.C.H.M.*, 29, 6; *Antiquary*, xxxi, 130.

[7] Wire, Diary, 1/1/1853; *T.E.A.S.* o.s. v, 159; *R.C.H.M.* 29, 8.

sand, with a small quantity of lime as a binding, I was led to the conclusion it was not very early. An urn, a glass vessel, and what was called a bone pillar, were found near the pavement. These I did not see, as they, with the loose tesserae, were taken to Mr. Wm. Bunting's residence in Sneak Lane.'

209. Foundations, tessellated pavements, and a roadway, near the NE. corner of the junction of Crowhurst and Papillon roads, are reported, but not described, by P. G. Laver, *R.C.H.M.* 15 c.

210. Foundations and walling south of the main building of the Hospital and east of the kitchen wing are also recorded by P. G. Laver, ibid. 15e. This should be just south of **183**.

A manuscript plan in the Museum by P. G. Laver shows a number of fragments of walls and pavements in the Union grounds or near them. Some may have belonged to tombs, others certainly did not. Though described as 'extensive' by P. G. Laver (*R.C.H.M.* sub 15), they are really disjointed, perhaps partly because so very fragmentary.

Wire says: 'visited the excavations for the foundations of the infirmary at the Union House, only a few fragments of pottery have been discovered, but a foundation at the NW. corner running west made with fragments of Roman roof tiles and bricks cemented together with a loose kind of mortar in which sand was the principal' (Diary, 5/5/1848). From time to time loose remains from buildings have been found in these grounds, e.g. two fragments of quarter-round moulding of red mortar, faced with fine plaster painted red; fragments of painted wall-plaster (red, and red-and-yellow) (C.M. 2889–90.14); more red-painted plaster; and parts of a red tessellated floor east of the infirmary (C.M. 708.29); fragments of slabs and veneering of Purbeck marble are quite frequently found. The levels to which these remains belong have not been observed, which is unfortunate, because the depth of soil here is apparently sometimes great. Objects are often recorded as found as deep as 12 ft., possibly in pits, but we do not know.

The O.S. 1:500 map shows 'Roman remains' found NE. of the Union and under the SW. corner of the fever ward, both in 1861, but does not state their nature.

v. *House at Stanway Green*

173. There is a note in the Museum Accessions Book against 5464.26 (miscellaneous pottery, mostly Roman of late-first- and second-century date, from a garden (not specified) at Stanway Green) that P. G. Laver says he has heard of a wall and mosaic pavement being found there many years ago. We have had no confirmation of this. (Off the map.) *C.M.R.* 1927, 20.

vi. *Buildings in Crouch Street*

50. 'Considerable masses of Roman masonry were met with opposite Dr. Renny's house (in Crouch Street) *in situ*, the footings evidently of a structure of some magnitude. The material was septaria and mortar [white].' A. M. Jarmin in *T.E.A.S.* xiii, 107; *R.C.H.M.* 9.

51. 'A mass of Roman masonry was found opposite the main entrance to the Bull Hotel, at a depth of about 8 ft. It had been broken up in places and cut through by the older sewer. More was now revealed, some *in situ*. One mass of square red tiles in courses, set in red mortar, and a few yards further on were masses of septaria set in ordinary white mortar.' Jarmin conjectured they formed part of a bridge over the ditch, although not opposite a gate! '. . . The bridge theory is supported by several fragments of stone which were evidently sections of columns.' (See further under inhumation burials.)

vii. *Buildings South and East of the Town*

63. We have discounted the alleged remains of a Roman house under the town wall east of bastion 5 (p. 55), but there was a house near. A tessellated pavement and an urn were found under the middle of Priory Street. Nothing further is known of them. O.S. 1:500 map (without date); Cutts, plan, i, 4.

171. 'Near the Bath Hotel [now gone], in the middle of Osborne Street, in excavating for the Electric Light Works, a red tessellated pavement was discovered about four feet from the surface. It was formed of rather large red tesserae, many of them being $1\frac{1}{2}$ ins. square.' *T.E.A.S.* x, 88; *R.C.H.M.* no. 11. The position on the map can only be shown approximately.

172. A Roman pavement was found at a depth of 11 ft. from the surface in Osborne Street during the making of a sewer in January 1903. It was opposite the corner shop (Greenwood's, Butcher) on St. Botolph's Street. Though possibly belonging to the same house, this is not the same pavement as the last, and is the one referred to in *R.C.H.M.* 12; *T.E.A.S.* x, 88; *Antiquary*, xxxix, 65; and *Daily Graphic*, 7 Feb. 1903. (C.M. 828.04.)

A decorated mosaic pavement was found in Osborne Street, and therefore somewhere near the preceding, in 1901. It is represented by a small fragment 'in white, yellow, light blue and grey tesserae of small

[1] Wire, Diary, 28/12/1852; *R.C.H.M.* 5; *T.E.A.S.* o.s. v, 159; x, 89; O.S. 1:500 map.

size' (C.M. 1351.07). It was given by Mr. J. J. Arnold of the Bath Hotel, and was found while deepening a well on the hotel premises, and is somewhere just west of **171**. *C.M.R.* 1908, 9.[1]

These pavements have led to conjectures that here, where water abounds, may have lain the public baths of the colonia, but it would be very strange to find the baths of a great town outside the walls. They do, however, witness to the presence of one, or more, luxurious houses.

The Building in the Garden of No. 22 Crouch Street

48. Of the main part of this building the only records are three. In *T.E.A.S.* xiii, 110, P. G. Laver says there are foundations and walling at the south end of Dr. Chichester's garden, near Burlington Road, and certain walls, indicating a rectangular building at least 100 ft. long, are entered in red on the Museum copy of the O.S. 1:500 map. There is a brief reference in *J.R.S.* xi, 221.

In February 1935 Dr. E. Wirth kindly allowed the Museum to investigate a piece of Roman walling in this same garden which it was intended to demolish for a rockery. Little work could be done, owing to lack of space, but the following results were obtained.[2]

The masonry proved to be the arc of an apse, which apparently formed part of the east end of the building. Our activity had to be limited to uncovering it. The masonry was broken away at both ends, and had there been so robbed that not even the foundation-trench could be followed. It is not now connected with the larger building to the west, and lies at an angle to it; nevertheless it is to be expected that it was connected in some way.

The garden dips into the small but marked valley where formerly ran the Chiswell Brook, though there is no watercourse now, and includes the lower part of the south slope. It is here, at no great distance from the stream, that the building stood, about a quarter of a mile south of the town wall. It would appear to have been some 110 ft. long, of unknown width, with an apse at the east end.

The apse was well built, of septaria blocks laid in yellowish mortar. The thickness of its wall was 2 ft., and the remaining height about the same. In the photograph (pl. XXXVIII, A) the height is increased by loose stones laid upon the wall while digging. In the far wall, facing the spectator, can be seen a double lacing course of tile, with only one regular course of septaria below it. This must, approximately, be the ancient ground-

level, for below this the masonry is rough and is set in the natural sand, which is here very soft and yellow. No traces of any sort of a laid floor were found, nor even of a definite occupation level, though there was a layer of rubble from the demolition of the wall.

Opposite the south end of the apse, and quite close to it, there was a small pit, cut 6–7 ft. deep. Remains of wood at the bottom showed that it had been shuttered to hold back the soft sand. It was most probably a well. At the time of its construction water could have stood in its bottom. On the other hand, there was no peaty sludge, such as is generally found at the bottom of a well. Nevertheless we are confident that we cleared it to the bottom and recovered all the contents.

The shaft appeared to be of about 3 ft. diameter, so that its wooden shuttering must have been quite narrow. In the mouth, and possibly used to close it, though not lying really level, was a large dressed block of sandstone. It was 30 in. square and 6 in. thick, with a string-moulding along one side. It apparently came from the entablature of a building. Such stones are very rarely found in Colchester. It is seen on edge in the photograph.

The contents of the pit were remarkable. Scattered throughout the filling, but with the earliest examples near bottom, were the following coins:

NERVA (or Trajan?). 1 dupondius.
TRAJAN. 1 sesterce. Both of these are very worn and cannot be more closely identified.
M. AURELIUS. 2 sesterces; one is M. & S. 948 (A.D. 166/7), the other is similar, but date is illegible. A third sesterce in poor condition, rather worn, no part of the legend legible, appears to be M. Aurelius, M. & S. 886 (A.D. 163/4) or 1397 (same date).
SEPT. SEVERUS. Sesterce, worn, Victory left, probably M. & S. 657 (A.D. 193).

The third century is better represented:
POSTUMUS. Antoninianus, M. & S. 75 (A.D. 259–68), in good condition.
VICTORINUS. Ant., M. & S. 57, 61, and 116, the latter marked V * (Cologne mint) (A.D. 268–70); all in good condition.
TETRICUS. 5 Ant., M. & S. 86–88 or 90; 109 (but Pietas seems to be holding an anchor); 270; all in good condition. The fourth and fifth are oval and worn, illegible.
CLAUDIUS GOTHICUS. 2 Ant., M. & S. 38; the other smaller, M. & S. 46, or possibly of Gallienus. No mintmarks.
ALLECTUS, Ant., M. & S. 128, mm. Q C (Colchester), in fine condition (A.D. 293–6).

The fourth century is very strongly represented:
THEODORA. 2 small Æ, Cohen 4, both Trier mint, c. A.D. 306.
CONSTANTINE THE GREAT. 11 Æ; viz. follis, *Principi iuventuti,* mm. P L N (London); slightly smaller, *Comiti Augg. NN.,* mm. – |* over P L N; three slightly smaller, *Soli invicto comiti,* mms T|F over P.TR, S|F over P L N, *|– over P L N (Trier and London); two, same size, *Sarmatia devicta,*

---

[1] The reference given to *Essex County Standard,* 29 June 1907, proves false and has not, so far, been traced. The fragment is not now recognizable in the Museum, but Mr. A. G. Wright's record must be accepted.

[2] *J.R.S.* xxv, 1935, 214; xxvi, 253; *C.M.R.* 1935, 7.

mms PTR ‿; PLO ‿ (Trier and London); one *Beata tranquillitas*, *Votis xx*, mm. STR (Trier), all of these in fine condition; the next three are poor, one *Gloria exercitus*, same size, mm. illegible; two smaller, one mm. .TRP., the other mm. illegible.

Constantinopolis. 11 Æ; mm. P.CONS; *PLG; SLG; ‿PLG (Lugdunum); TRS*; STRP; TRP; .TRP; .STRP (small) (Trier); all in good condition.

Urbs Roma. 11 Æ; mm. P.CONST; .PTR; TRP; TR.P; TR.S (Trier) and six more with mm. illegible; these are in rather poor condition.

CONSTANTINE II. A silver medallion, module 24 mm., nearly unique, but Mr. Mattingly says there is another in the London Museum. *Obv.* FL.CL.CONSTANTINVS P.F.AVG., diademed, draped bust right; *Rev.* CONSTANTINVS P.F.AVG. three standards, mm. TRS. The silver is poor and the impression not good, but the coin seems unworn, though the flan is cracked.

19 Æ; viz. (of the two smaller sizes) consecration coin of Constantine I, mm. TRS; one *Beata tranquillitas*, mm. PLON; another C|R over PLG; thirteen *Gloria exercitus*, mms RBS; RBS (?) (2 exx.); .PLG; .SLG; ⚹PLG; .TRP; TRP.; .TRS; SCONST; rest illegible, condition generally good.

CONSTANS. 13 Æ, all small size; one with Phoenix, mm. TRS.; ten *Victoriae dd augg q nn*, mms uncertain but three are of Trier, condition usually not so good; *Gloria exercitus* (labarum) two, one with mm. TRS; condition fair to good.

CONSTANTIUS II. 11 Æ, six of *Gloria exercitus* types, mms TRS; TR.S; RBT; SCONST; SLG, and one illegible; one of *Victoriae dd augg q.nn.* type, mm. illegible; and four of *Fel. Temp. Reparatio* type, one (orthodox), with mm. TSᴦ, one at least of the others a copy.

CONSTANTINIAN. 2 Æ, *Gloria exercitus*, mms illegible. A third, of dubious reverse, is also probably in this category.

MAGNENTIUS. 4 Æ, all *Victoriae dd* type (two Victories, *Vot. V Mult x*, modules 18 and 13 mm.), mintmark of one is RSLC, of the rest illegible.

JULIAN. AR siliqua; *rev.*, in poor condition, seems to be *Votis V, Multis X* in four lines in a wreath, mm. illegible.

JOVIAN. 1 Æ, *rev.* VOT V MVLT X in four lines in a wreath, mm. *LVG*.

VALENTINIAN I. 8 or 10 Æ, four (perhaps six) *Securitas reipublicae* type, mms SMAQ and SCON legible; four of *Gloria Romanorum* type (emperor dragging captive), mms SMAQP, and ASISCP legible.

VALENS. 13 Æ, eight of *Securitas* type, mms SISC P; SISTM(?), rest illegible; five *Gloria Romanorum* type, of which four have some form of the mm. CON, and the fifth SMAQP (?).

GRATIAN. 11 Æ, one follis *Reparatio Reipub*, mm. –|I over LVGS; and ten small Æ, two *Securitas* type, one mm. LVGP.; two *Gloria Romanorum* type, both mm. OF I | I over LVGS; six *Gloria novi saeculi* type, mms bad, but three are of CON.

Two other coins of *Securitas* type may belong to any of the last three reigns.

VALENTINIAN II. 1 Æ, *Salus reipublicae*, well preserved, but mm. illegible.

THEODOSIUS. 1 Æ, *Victoriae Auggg*, mm. illegible.

ARCADIUS. 2 Æ, *Victoria Auggg*, mm. SCON.

HONORIUS. 1 only, same reverse, mm. illegible.

THEODOSIAN. 1, same type, damaged.

This completes the list of what may be regarded as straightforward or orthodox issues. The very long run, and the frequent inclusion, from M. Aurelius onwards, of unworn or little worn

coins suggests that the collection is not a hoard of the usual type. When it is further noted that they were scattered through the pit, with the earlier coins at the lower levels, there is some reason to believe that they may have been cast into the pit as votive offerings.

The coins already listed we believe to have been correctly attributed and to be orthodox issues, or possibly, in a few cases, contemporary copies. Forty-one coins remain, and these call for very careful consideration. One thing they have in common is that they do not carry upon them the detail requisite to identify them with any orthodox issue. Three may be dismissed immediately as bearing insufficient legible marking to be of any use.

Twelve coins have a module of over 10 mm., actually, except one of 15 mm., varying between 12 and 13 mm. They coincide in general appearance with the small Theodosian bronze series. The obverse has a rather tall and narrow diademed head turned to the right, usually draped on the bust, perhaps always intended to be so. One in group III has a totally different and wider head. All reverses are of the type showing the legionary spearing a fallen horseman. The legends on both sides are imperfect or missing, what lettering there is varying from quite good to barbarous.

1. Could be orthodox, but *Obv.* ...TVS PI.... and *Rev.* ....PARATI, with mm. PLG. Lettering good, but device barbarous.
2. Could nearly be orthodox. *Obv.* ....VS PL AVG, *Rev.* ...TIO.
3. Barbarously cut both sides. *Obv.* ...VS FAV, *Rev.* ...REPAT....
4. Fairly well cut. *Obv.* ...S PF AVG (complete legend right of the head), *Rev.* ....EL.... visible on left margin.
5. Barbarous work. *Obv.* ....IIOII A(?), *Rev.* ....IIDOII, with L IC in exergue (imitating LVG); the whole reverse has been in a beaded circle.
6. Barbarous work. *Obv.* traces of letters only, *Rev.* ...ARTIO, with mm. PLG.
7. Bad cutting but good lettering, ...NS PCC.
8. Poor work. *Obv.* traces of letters, *Rev.* only PL(G?) in exergue.
9. Poor to barbarous. Traces of letters only on *obv.*; on *rev.* ....REPARTI.
10. Barbarous. *Obv.* wide head, no lettering, *Rev.* only T of TEMP visible.
11. Barbarous, oval and damaged. May have traces of letters on *obv.*
12. Barbarous, no lettering. Module 15 mm.

These coins may be contemporary (or even later) copies of coins of Constantius II, agreeing with his smallest module, or they may be of later date, for the style of the head is very Theodosian. But, if Theodosian, they are not copies, for this reverse was not then in use. The solution of this must await further evidence.

The next thirteen coins, with one exception, have the same reverse (where identifiable), and are of an average module of 11 mm., rarely reaching 12 mm. The heads are not so uniformly tall and narrow, but are not easy to assess, as many are too large for the flan. None, unless possibly the first, resembles an orthodox coin in quality.

1. *Obv.* Head has no diadem, no lettering; *Rev.* VOT V MVL(T) X in four lines in centre, on each side a blob, reminiscent of the two Victories?, over top possibly ....DD.... Copy of the well-known type.
2. Barbarous. *Obv.* CONHN...., *Rev.* ....IIPER.
3. Barbarous. *Obv.* TA....., *Rev.* no legend, CC in exergue (Colchester mint?).

4. *Obv.* fairly good work, CONS... (N reversed), *Rev.* barbarous, no lettering.

5. Barbarous. *Obv.* ..... TAV (?), *Rev.* no lettering.

6. Barbarous. *Obv.* traces of letters, *Rev.* TR in exergue only.

7. Barbarous. *Obv.* no letters visible, *Rev.* traces of letters on left edge.

8. Barbarous. *Obv.* no lettering, *Rev.* traces of letters in exergue.

9. Barbarous. Traces of letters on reverse.

10. Barbarous. Both sides show part of die only.

11. Barbarous. Both sides indefinite.

12. Most barbarous. *Obv.* a small barbarous head, well centred, with other traces behind it, and in front of it part of a beaded circle which could only fit a much larger coin, in which case the head would be far from central. *Rev.* confused device like that on some pre-Roman coins.

13. Barbarous. *Rev.* probably battle type (part of).

14. Very small and thick, with blob on each side, one of which is, no doubt, the head. Very barbarous.

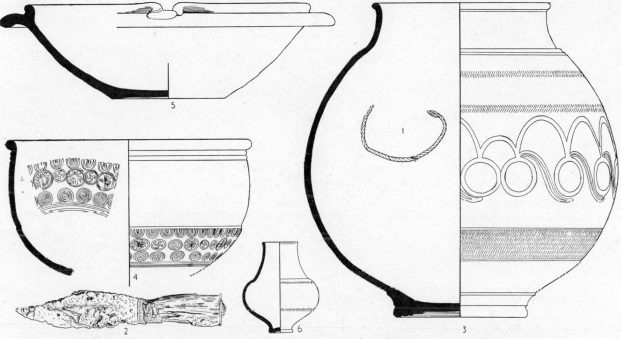

FIG. 111. Objects found in well or pit, behind no. 22 Crouch Street. Scale ¼. [S 48], p. 247.

10. Barbarous. No certain letters.

11 and 12. Barbarous. No letters. The latter nearly thrice the thickness of the rest.

13. Worn smooth on both sides.

Finally, there are fourteen coins of less than 10 mm. module, usually about 8 mm. There is great variety in thickness and weight. The dies are more barbarous than before, with occasional attempts at lettering, while often the device is only a fragment of the previous types, or even of crude and unrecognizable new (?) types.

1. CN visible on obv. *Rev.* part of man on horse.

2. *Obv.* has letters on right resembling DN AVG. *Rev.* Battle type, with CS in exergue.

3. *Obv.* DN VG ? in front of bust. *Rev.* battle type.

4. *Obv.* traces of letters in front of bust. *Rev.* part of the battle type with traces of letters in exergue.

5. No lettering but senseless marks in exergue. Little more than the exergue appears on reverse.

6. Very barbarous head. *Rev.* probably part of battle type.

7. Dubious traces of lettering on both sides. *Rev.* probably battle type. Thick flan.

8. Barbarous. Both sides obscure.

9. Small barbarous head of new type. *Rev.* fragment of battle type (?), thick flan.

Besides the coins the pit contained the following.

The most part of a human skull and a complete thigh-bone. These were found at the bottom, below everything else. There was also one indeterminate piece of burnt bone.

A silver armlet of twisted wire, tapering from the middle to the ends, which were secured by a hook and loop. It had been deliberately broken in the middle. The diameter must have been about 3 in. or less (fig. 111, 1).

A small silver ring, ⅝ in. diameter, of nearly square section.

An imperfect iron stylus, and an iron knife with remains of the wooden handle (fig. 111, 2). Part of an iron utensil, apparently a frying-pan, diameter 10 in., height of sloping side 1 in. The handle is a separate strip of iron 7½ in. long by 1 in. wide and ⅛ in. thick, thrust into a bent-up lug on the rim which is only 1¼ in. long, but which holds it tightly. There were also fragments of a rather large iron bowl, about 10 in. in diameter and fairly deep and rounded, with at least one flat, looped lug, ¾ in. wide at the top, riveted to the rim.

There were also found many iron nails, a quantity of painted wall-plaster, a piece of marble, and a great quantity of birds' bones.

Some of the pottery (fig. 111) was outstanding, namely: (3) fragments of a very large globular to pear-shaped vase resembling f. 408, of fine polished red ware, decorated with rouletted bands and a broad scroll pattern in white paint, the latter now very faint. Compare *Niederbieber*, type 32, but it is much shorter in the lower part. (4) Half a large hemispherical bowl in polished red ware, shaped and decorated in imitation of a T.S. f. 37, with impressed ovolo and medallions containing stylized floral motif and swastikas. (5) Half a mortarium, f. 503A. (6) A complete beaker, f. 408 (small), in Rhenish ware, and several fragments of three others, one with white painted decoration.

The remainder of the fragments run from a few fragments of T.S. (one small frag. f. 30, two of late f. 37, and ff. 18/31 or Lud. S*b*, 33, 43, or 45) to the end of the Roman occupation.

The whole is suggestive of a votive deposit dating from the late second century, but there is hardly sufficient evidence on which to class the building as a temple.

3. POTTERS' KILNS AND TILE-KILNS

These are to be the subject of a special Research Report, so that no more than a brief summary need be given here. The positions of them are shown on the three area plans (pls. XLII–IV). Some are very slightly known, and little or nothing is known of the wares they may have produced; others have been thoroughly excavated; some are dubious or conjectural. None of those we know is pre-Conquest, though great quantities of pottery, including some of the finest Gallo-Belgic variety, were certainly made here under Cunobelin. Belgic wasters were found amidst much soot and charcoal on site L2 in region 6 at Sheepen (*Cam.*, p. 122), but there was no trace of a kiln in the large area stripped. The earliest Roman kilns are just pre-Boudiccan; we refer to kiln XXIII in area L (**192**), which made forms 94B, 154, and 171, and the neighbouring pit L19, which was an unfinished kiln (*Cam.* 106, fig. 26, pottery fig. 58; and pl. XII). There was also a tile kiln XIV (**98**) lying just NE. of Sheepen Farmhouse, which has not been excavated.

The earliest discovery, kiln I, was found when building the Hospital in 1819.[1] It was found loaded, but the vessels were dispersed. Some are in the National Museum of Antiquities of Scotland. The exact site is not known. Two more, III, IV, were found in Dr. Maclean's garden, opposite the Hospital; the site must be at **185**.[2] Not far to the east, when a large new shop was built by Mr. Jarmin (**196**) in 1938, such quantities of pottery exactly similar to that from the 1933 kilns were found that we may assume a kiln or kilns lay near.[3]

Wire[4] heard that a kiln, II, had been found in the brickyard near North Station, which means somewhere near **184**.

In 1877 George Joslin excavated five kilns, VII–XI, in the SW. corner of field 497, just north of Kingswode Hoe (**186**). One was large and rectangular, the others oval, some double-ended. His report[5] mixes early and late pottery in illustrations much in advance of his day, but inadequate for our purpose. The early wares are from the Claudius–Nero occupation, and the late, which is third or even fourth century, includes wasters and belongs to the kilns.

Kiln XII was found in 1890 at Butt windmill, where others had been noted by Wire (V, VI).[6] This one made mortaria of late-second-century date (**187**). Fragments of it, and part of an unknown maker's stamp, are in the Museum.

Burnt earth and brick rubble found north of the town in what was Mr. Wallace's garden have been explained as a tile-clamp (**188**),[7] but we regard this evidence now as pointing more probably to the ruins of a building made of clay blocks and destroyed by fire. But however that may be, P. G. Laver always held that there was a potter's kiln near this point, and there is in the Museum a quantity of pottery from Serpentine Walk, at the corner of Margaret Road, which indicates that the firm to which *Martinus* belonged had worked there.[8]

Remains of pottery found in Mr. Duncan Clarke's garden[9] in Fitzwalter Road suggested a kiln, and fragments of vitrified kiln-wall and clay blocks establish the fact (XIIIB at **189**). Farther along the same road, in Alderman Piper's garden, exactly the same sort of remains were found (XIIIA, at **189A**). Part of a distorted tube resembles those from the Sigillata kiln, and there is a stamp of MICCIO and a new stamp, FIRMVS FE, both on Colchester ware. These kilns must therefore also be attributed to the same firm.

Pottery found in Queen's Road (**191**) consisting of grey jars and bowls (ff. 246 and 268) suggest that they were made on the spot.

In 1933 eight kilns were found where shown at **106** (kilns XV–XXII), four scattered to the west, and four in one enclosure on the east. The former are of the normal round or oval type. The enclosure was unusual in that besides two normal kilns (XIX, XXII) it contained a small kiln for colour-coated ware, an oven, apparently for baking bread or drying pots, and a large round kiln for firing terra sigillata.[10]

[1] *Coll. Ant.* ii, pl. XIII; iii, 37–38.
[2] Wire, Diary, 19/3/1855. The circle of **185** should stand where the **00** of **100** lies.
[3] *C.M.R.* 1944, 17.
[4] Diary, 28/3/1845.
[5] *T.E.A.S.* n.s. i, 192 ff.; *R.C.H.M.* 29; *J.B.A.* o.s. xxxiii, 230, 267; *Arch. J.* xxxiv, 302; xxxv, 70; *T.E.A.S.* n.s. v, 77; and W. F. Grimes in *Y Cymmrodor*, xli, 66; May, 160, 168, 173.

[6] See p. 257.
[7] H. Laver in *T.E.A.S.* x, 325; *C.M.R.* 1908, 10, 11; C.M. 1416–18 and 1429.08.
[8] *C.M.R.* 1944, 19.
[9] South-east of **162**.
[10] Full report is prepared and forthcoming; interim reports have appeared in the *Illustrated London News* and *Germania*, xviii, 27; *J.R.S.* xxiv (1934), 210; *T.E.A.S.* xxi, 300.

These kilns all seem to belong to one firm and period. The latest coin found was one of M. Aurelius, and the pottery is of a character suited to the last two decades of the second century. The sigillata types made are closely paralleled by the Pan Rock find, and the coarse wares and colour-coated wares made agree with this dating. The work may have lasted over into the third century, but there is no means of proving this. Every kind of product was made, including lamps. The enclosure, which had been surrounded by a stone wall of Kentish rag, was about 20 ft. square. The sigillata kiln ran into the hill-side to the north. In the NE. corner was kiln XX, for colour-coated ware, its entrance made of spoiled beakers. Between them was the oven. In the NW. corner was a small round kiln (XXII), which made unguentaria, and in the SW. angle lay remains of a large oblong kiln (XIX), which had been dismantled before kiln XXI went out of use.

The Sigillata kiln (XXI) was 13 ft. long; its oven was about 7 ft. 6 in. in diameter. It certainly belongs to the type described by Forrer and by Knorr and Sprater.[1] There were barrow-loads of the clay rings, tubes, lutings, and other apparatus, exactly as described by the continental excavators, and vast quantities of wasters of plain wares, accompanied by some of decorated ware. The latter was better represented by fragments of moulds for ff. 30 and 37, the fragments of which amount to well over 400. There are two distinct styles of decoration, being the work of two, perhaps three, different men. Though our potters had learned their trade on the Continent the motifs they use are almost entirely original. The paste is a flower-pot red rather than the pinkish-red of the imported ware.

The names of our potters on sigillata are as follows: ACCEPTVS.F (14 exx.); CVNOPECTVS (28 exx. in four varieties); GABRVS.FE (24 exx.); LIPVCA; LITVGENVS F (8 exx., from two matrices); MATVACVS (2 exx.); MICCIO.F (6 exx.); MINVSOF (28 exx., from three matrices); T.LITTERA F (4 exx.); REBVRRI OF; RECVI... (Regulus?) SENILIS FE (over 50 exx.); VIDVCVS FE; VIMPVS. Possibly also AMANDIN; ATTI..S.FE; CINTVGN. F; ELVILLI; and GRAN..NI.

The following stamps occurred on mortaria: ACCEPTVS F (who also stamped sigillata and colour-coated beakers with one and the same small stamp); BARO; DVBITATVS (variously spelt) (10 exx.);[2] MARTINVS F (nearly 50 exx. from eleven matrices); MESSOR (15 exx., from four matrices); RIIGALIS (retro) (5 exx., from three matrices); TITVS FE (12

exx.); VITALIS...; and a large variety of 'herring-bone' stamps.

Kiln XXIV was found when the foundations were cut on the Abbey Field for the N.A.A.F.I. Club.[3] Its remains lie under the middle of the west side of that building (**193**). It was of oval plan with a central support running out from the back wall, built of rectangular blocks of clay. The flues on each side of it had been vaulted with rings of clay voussoir blocks set about 2 in. apart. These gaps were filled with the same clay as was used for the floor, and through them passed the holes for the draught.

The pottery found was substantially similar to that from the 1933 kilns. It consisted chiefly of mortaria and colour-coated ware, the former bearing a stamp with meaningless imitation of letters. The date is a trifle later than that of the 1933 kilns, perhaps the first decade of the third century. The only coin found was a denarius of M. Aurelius (M. & S. no. 37).

Kiln XXV was found in 1952 in the playing-fields of Endsleigh School immediately west of Kingswode Hoe.[4] It was pear-shaped, with central support, made of clay blocks, attached to the back. The floor had vanished, but had in part been supported by long box flue-tiles perhaps laid horizontally, one of which lay almost intact on the floor of the flue. The pottery found in the filling of the flues was late, including wasters of colour-coated beakers of f. 395.

Across the stokehole was a tile-built block, and among the tiles were several fragments of tiles which must have been nearly 2 ft. square and ½ in. thick, with a nail-hole in each corner and combed decoration on one side.[5]

No coins were found, and a bronze brooch of type *Cam.* IV found in the filling of the stokehole is first century. Very little pottery was found outside the kiln, which probably produced mortaria (ff. 498 and 499) and other wares, but the only wasters were those mentioned.

It remains to mention that the chief brickfields of Roman Colchester, which supplied the vast quantities of tiles used in the town, have not been excavated. There seems but little doubt where they are. Westwards from where Sheepen Farmhouse stood, all along the south side of the By-pass Road the clay has been excavated. At the west end of the excavation the modern hedge stands on the edge of the steep face of the workings, and in the arable field beyond, in several places, the plough strikes buildings of tile (field 494 on pl. XLIII). As for the rest, it is in every way likely

---

[1] *Heiligenberg*, 29 ff.; *Blickweiler*, 112 ff.
[2] Occurs at Prittlewell, Southend; in Museum there.
[3] *J.R.S.* xxxvii (1947), 172; *C.M.R.* 1947, 26 and pl. VII.
[4] It was excavated by members of the staff and boys. Mark it

as **211**, ¾ in. west of the south end of Kingswode Hoe.
[5] Mr. Graham Webster tells me that large slabs like this were sometimes affixed to walls, leaving an interval, so as to form a large and uniform flue for heating purposes.

that earlier kilns have nearly all been destroyed as the brickyards expanded. The absence of very late kilns remains unexplained.

(B) THE CEMETERIES

The town is surrounded by cemeteries and scattered graves on all sides, though little is found on the east, where there is little space between it and the river. Apart from isolated references from the thirteenth century onwards, no one took much notice of discoveries until the nineteenth century, when about 1819 the Hospital was building, and soon after Wire began to keep notes, and the collectors appeared on the scene. Wire disposed of most of his material to Dr. Acton of Grundisburgh. The Acton collection was a very mixed lot, but comprised mostly material from Colchester, and was sadly dispersed in the end: while some returned to Colchester Museum, some went to Bury St. Edmunds, and some to the British Museum.[1] Probably some exists in other places. The objects at Colchester are not well labelled, and even in 1884, when Price catalogued the Museum, he could not attain complete clarity on the grouping of those vessels which were stated to have been found together. The collection is accordingly of less use to the student than it might have been. It includes 12 lamps, 17 vessels of sigillata, and 220 more or less complete vessels of pottery and glass.

149. In 1848 John Taylor began to build his house 'West Lodge' and found himself in the midst of the cemetery. His finds received much publicity, yet the accounts are not very clear. Thus we read: 'it was some time before he met with any [remains] in a perfect state; . . . about an acre of ground [was] dug from 16 ins. to 4 ft. deep; and without exception the vessels were found deposited on the surface of the subsoil of sand or gravel. He was aware of the danger of theorizing upon a subject of this kind, but it would be an interesting question to decide whether these vessels were originally placed on the surface with a slight covering of earth, or whether they were sunk down to the dry soil below.[2] There were still [1852] four or five acres which had not been disturbed. . . .'[3]

In 1849 the British Archaeological Association visited West Lodge and saw graves opened: '. . . although only a comparatively small portion of Mr.

Taylor's ground has been examined nearly two hundred vessels have been found; and he calculates that at least ten times that number remain unexhumed. . . .' The foundations from which came the inscribed stone found in 1850 and now in the Museum, which is from a tomb built of massive masonry cramped with metal,[4] were exposed at the same time, and from the words 'garden of Mr. Bunting adjoining West Lodge' we understand that Taylor's ground extended westwards, covering the area now occupied by the houses and gardens west of West Lodge Road and on both sides of The Avenue. In the same volume[5] we learn that up to this date (2 April 1849) Taylor had about 40 cinerary urns and about 100 vessels of pottery and glass, 1 acre had been dug and 7 acres remained. In all, the vessels presented by Taylor to the Museum amounted to some 170, with tiles from a tile tomb. Included are twenty-two burial groups which have been well kept, and of which we have coloured drawings by Josiah Parish, showing them as found.[6]

Taylor was followed by George Joslin, who collected in the second half of the nineteenth century. At his house in Beverley Road he assembled a large museum, almost exclusively Roman, and, we are assured, nearly all from within a quarter-mile of his house. Unfortunately he kept no plans or notes, and many of his 'groups' are suspect. An excellent catalogue of the collection was made in 1888 by Mr. J. E. Price, F.S.A., of which a special copy illustrated by photographs is in the Museum. Joslin bought the field south of his house in Beverley Road in order to excavate it, but left no account of his work. His museum is described when the Royal Archaeological Institute visited it in 1876.[7] In this account, alone, we learn that the main source of his material was 'Alexandra Road, Blatch Square [now Wellesley Road], and other places' and that grave 3 (with toy figurines) was found behind his house in 1866, and that with the many small objects belonging to a lady (grave 81) at West Lodge. From Price's catalogue we find, however, that Joslin received finds from the North Cemetery and from Lexden Cemetery. But the source is very seldom stated.

Joslin's large collection, the hobby of a lifetime, was purchased for the town in 1893[8] and formed the backbone of the Museum's collection. It comprises 126 groups from graves and a very large number of loose finds. In all there are 738 pottery vessels, 46 lamps, 44

---

[1] The Wire MSS. were purchased for the Museum by G. C. Round, Esq.

[2] This remark is interesting in view of the question raised by Mr. A. F. Hall as to whether urns were deposited with the mouth exposed. *Arch. J.* ci, 74, 75.

[3] *T.E.A.S.* o.s. i, 4.

[4] Omitted from *C.I.L.* vii; see *Arch. J.* xxxi, 346; xxxiv, 79; *J.B.A.* vi, 446. A reference to 'the foundations lately (20/4/1851)

discovered in the field at West Lodge' may refer to this (*T.E.A.S.* xviii, 279).

[5] *T.E.A.S.* o.s. i, 4; *J.B.A.* v, 9 and 133; ibid. iv, 400; *Gent.'s Mag.* 1848, 633; 1854, 70, 71; 1881, 311.

[6] May, pls. xci–xciii; 1–22, now numbered 123–44. *T.E.A.S.* o.s. iv, 257; v, 162.

[7] *Arch. J.* xxxiii, 421.

[8] For details see *Essex Review*, ii, 134.

glass vessels, 70 brooches, 63 armlets, and 1,024 coins. The most outstanding piece of all was, of course, the tombstone of the Centurion[1] (pl. II, A). A further quantity of remains was added later to this, but does not figure in the catalogue. All these later items bear the number 115.

Another large collection was formed about this same period by the Rev. J. H. Pollexfen, Rector of Lexden, but it went to the British Museum, except the British coins, which were bought for Colchester. Others were collecting on a lesser scale, and many still hold vessels dug up on their ground. The largest of these collections was that of Alderman A. M. Jarmin, which contained many vessels and some good groups.[2] Unfortunately it is quite without notes as to find-spots, and there is no catalogue of it. But we know that it came chiefly from the Barracks and Beaconsfield Avenue. It was purchased for the town in 1892.

The position of all these graves, thus disturbed by the collectors, is known in very few cases. The only attempt to map them, other than the isolated entries on comparatively recent O.S. maps, is found on the plan in Cutts, whose red overprint is often inaccurate. For what it is worth (and we have no other evidence in most cases) he shows grave 136/14 (May, pl. XCII) which contains the 'Colchester Vase' at **115**. Taylor's graves are shown as a block at West Lodge (**149**), and similar blocks of graves are shown west of the Hospital (**35**)[3] and east of the Grammar School (**112**). Who discovered these, or when, we do not know. We are left to wonder how many more such blocks remain unrecorded. It is believed that Bunting's garden (between **30** and **119**) and the grounds of St. Mary's Lodge (a square, now gone, lying west of **16**) were full of graves, of which indeed, an odd one is still found from time to time. The most outlying graves are at the south end of Cambridge Walk (**117**), one west of Altnacealgach (**21**), some scattered on the Sheepen area, and one in Errington Road (**121**).[4]

There is a discrepancy between Cutts's position for grave 3 and the O.S. map (**13** and **114**).

The general collection in the Museum, which has been accumulating at irregular rates since 1846, was not fully represented in May's *Catalogue*. It was cata-logued by J. E. Price (in MS.) in 1884, but had vastly increased by 1926. Since 1927, when excavations began, it has been very nearly doubled again.[5] Visible in the Museum are no less than 1,764 pottery vessels, 131 of glass, and 114 lamps; and hundreds of pottery vessels are in reserve. Other objects are in proportion, and a catalogue of the Roman brooches found in Essex, nearly all of which come from Colchester, exceeds 600 items.

No doubt a similar collection could be made from the soil of any Roman town of comparable size. If not, then Colchester must claim to have excelled in importance. But on the whole the *quality* of the remains found here is not remarkable; there is no suggestion of any exceptional wealth or luxury.

The earliest cemetery containing Roman pottery is that at Lexden, and it, originally, did not serve the colonia but Camulodunum. The earliest burials are purely Belgic (graves 166 (an omnibus number), 169, 172, 174 (omnibus number), 189, 195, 196);[6] these are followed by burials containing Gallo-Belgic ware, with some Arretine and some local Roman wares (graves 9, 294, 325),[7] and later we have purely Roman burials, perhaps after a gap, for some are certainly third century (graves 188, 212, 214, 503).[8]

The next earliest graves occur in the West Cemetery around the Grammar School and West Lodge, an area to which some early roads seem to have pointed. Though they are not numerous, there is no mistaking these graves. They are purely Roman and include the famous grave 3[9] which must be that of a child of a high official, for it dates to closely after A.D. 43. Here too were found the tombstones of Favonius and Longinus, which are pre-Boudiccan (pl. II, A and B).

From about A.D. 70 the occupation was again intensive (see the coin-list, p. 277) and no cemetery thereafter seems to have been limited in period, not even the North, where late evidence includes a jet necklace with a small carved bust as a pendant, a material otherwise scarce. Thus in most places where burials have been found in numbers they begin with Vespasian and run on to inhumations including coffins of stone or lead.[10] Later (to judge by Joslin's groups) incinerations are not infrequently inserted among earlier ones, and

---

[1] Discovery reported *T.E.A.S.* o.s. v, 87.

[2] May, pls. LXXXIX–XC.

[3] Since extended northwards by urns found when building new quarters for nurses in 1931. *C.M.R.* 1932, 3.

[4] But 'several others were found'.

[5] Most honourable mention must be made of the devoted work of Henry Laver and his sons H. E. and P. G. Laver. This family collected an immense amount of material and supported the Museum enthusiastically through difficult years lasting the most part of a century. Every effort has been made to give full credit to them in this work, but lack of space has precluded many references which might have been made.

[6] The Belgic pottery has been published from time to time in *C.M.R.* and some of it in *Swarling*.

[7] For Gallo-Belgic and Arretine ware see *C.M.R.* 1932, 26, 32, 35 (2056–58.31), pl. VIII, 1, 2; *T.E.A.S.* xviii, 270 and pls. (4932.24); May, pl. LXXVI (Joslin grave 9); *Ant. Journ.* xxii (1941), 59 ff., figs. 1–3; *J.R.S.* xxxi, 138, pls. XVI–XVII.

[8] The Roman graves are shown in *C.M.R.* 1927, pl. IV (5411–13.27 and 5400–1.27).

[9] May, pl. LXXV, 3a and b.

[10] There are nine lead coffins in the Museum, and others have been melted down.

inhumations are found not only on the edges of the cemeteries but also in the midst of the parts which had been long in use. Separate are some groups of skeletons, unaccompanied by other relics (e.g. outside Headgate, at the Park bowling-green, and in Cromwell Road); and these belong to the period between the abandonment of Roman grave-furniture and the institution of Christian churchyards. Some of them may be late Roman, but they are all probably more recent. For if we consider the best source of late burials (Butt Road cemetery) we shall find that we have a straight run of inhumations with Roman furniture, with iron tools or weapons (these are few), and with no furniture. There remains no clue whereby to date these at all closely.

Besides the large cemeteries there was a scatter of graves all around the town, with occasional concentrations which amount to small cemeteries in themselves (e.g. at the modern Cemetery (**197**), and in area C4 at **106**). Clearly there was no obligation to bury in any stipulated place. Moreover, there is a general litter of the *supellex Romana* among the burials (at least in the West Cemetery), which is, in the writer's experience, scarcely nearer the surface than the level of the bottom of the cremation-graves. It often is not found around a grave, and we hesitate to say that the two are confused, though they may so be in places. We have sometimes wondered whether this apparent occupation layer is simply a litter of fragments left by previous archaeologists or looters searching for graves, but on the whole the evidence is that outside the walls there were not only some houses with stone foundations and tessellated floors, but very many of wood, varying much in size and opulence, but mostly inhabited by native Britons. Not only were houses mixed with graves, but with potters' kilns also, and, no doubt, other industries.

The following comprises a very brief description of the cemeteries, from which all references to minor discoveries of pottery, coins, and other small finds have had to be omitted. These are fully recorded in the Museum files. The reader will realize that the vast majority of the finds were made in a period when interest lay solely in the objects found, and consequently in most cases no exact find-spot or details of discovery are preserved. The net result is that we have available a bulk of material relating to the life of a Romano-British town of first importance which is without parallel, but without documentation. It serves to show what may be expected from such a town, and how not to acquire it. May it serve to encourage other Roman towns to explore their vast untapped reservoirs by properly conducted investigations, and may the unfortunate exploitation of Colchester's cemeteries be an

'awful example' to other places, where the same might easily occur at any moment.

1. LEXDEN CEMETERY

We have said that the most westerly outlier of the great West Cemetery was the amphora burial, grave 163, just west of Altnacealgach (**21**). But another cemetery lay under Lexden Park, somewhat farther west.

Lexden Park was a large area lying astride the Lexden Dyke, but the eastern half has been split up into building-plots which are now almost all occupied right up to the dyke.

Some years previously to 1913 some adjacent fields were added to the park. Some odd finds had been reported as from Lexden, but without close location. Only one need be mentioned here. An amphora, f. 181, of the type usually found in pre-Roman tombs, is in the Museum labelled 'found in Park Field Lexden, 1823' (C.M., P.C. 700–2, 1871). These we may safely connect with the cemetery. Two other amphorae, broken, were also given, possibly from the same place, but the form is later (f. 186). They were given by Mr. G. H. Errington, owner of the park. Wherever these may have come from, the site of the first one is marked on the O.S. map just east of St. Clare Road (**3**). As for the others, we are told that the fields added to the park contained several tumuli, and they were examined before the levelling of the land. Pottery and other objects were found, and considered Roman.[1] The account stands strangely alone, for no one had ever noted or mentioned these tumuli, nor are any finds of significance recorded. Only two tumuli are now known in this area, one called the Mount, about 300 yards SW. of Lexden Church, the other, known as the Lexden Tumulus, 600 yards SE. of the church. Stukeley shows the former, marking it as 'Cunobeline's Tomb', and omits the second. Both are very large and prominent, but the Mount is much less worn down than the other, which, however, has been damaged, probably more than once. The O.S. map records that in it was found, in 1860, a Celtic amphora and pottery. From this it seems that it was possibly about 1860 that the depredations described above took place, although our map of *c.* 1845 shows the Lexden Tumulus already within the park.

The Mount was excavated by the Morant Club in August 1910. The flat top had a diameter of 50 ft., the sharpness of the angle with the side suggesting recent levelling. The excavation was disappointingly negative, but the consistent appearance of Roman tile throughout the mound makes a date later than about A.D. 50 necessary.[2]

---

[1] *T.E.A.S.* xii, 186.

[2] Full account in *T.E.A.S.* xii, 186 ff.

The second tumulus was excavated in July and August 1924 by the brothers P. G. and H. E. Laver, and a full report by the former appeared in the *Archaeologia*, vol. lxxvi (1926). To this we have little to add save one important fact which only came to light later. When piecing together the supposed iron tyres of the chariot-wheels for exhibition the writer found that they are not tyres. They are only broad flat bands for part of their circumference; in the other part they are of almost square section. The burial therefore proves not to have been a chariot burial. We are left to discuss to what manner of object these several iron hoops could have belonged. The general opinion now is that there was probably an elaborate funeral palanquin. A set of four pointed iron ferrules, as for spear-butts, but heavier, may have come from its legs. Our other comment is on the pottery. Firstly, of small pots only the most scanty remains were found, but these all belong to Belgic or Gallo-Belgic types, as found at Camulodunum; also we have to remember the mound was robbed of pottery in 1860. Secondly, attempts have now been made to piece together the many boxfulls of amphora-fragments. This has sufficed to show that there were several large amphorae of f. 181 and an incalculable number of f. 182. These latter are smaller, and of thinner material than the typical vessels so common at Camulodunum, and perhaps represent a special consignment.

In 1908 the water main was laid along the west side of St. Clare Road, and it was the trench for this, about the spot marked **151** (after the O.S.), which is 140 yards east of the Lexden Rampart and nearly 300 yards south of the London Road, that produced the first batch of funerary pottery and so identified the pre-Roman cemetery of Camulodunum. We have no plan or notes of how these vessels were arranged in the ground. It is certain they represent a number of different grave-groups and that they must have covered an area much larger than that marked on the map. The fact that more urns were found at the same place in 1913 shows that exhaustive search was not made in 1908.

Apart from this concentration of Belgic pottery here, which points to this as the oldest part of the cemetery, there are two other aspects to be considered. To the north a few scattered burials have been found, all of which, if not opulent, are certainly not of poor charac-

ter, and which contain pottery of the superior Gallo-Belgic technique almost unmixed with the pure Belgic, but mixed with pottery and brooches, showing Roman influence, some of it imported from Roman Gaul (**152**).[1] This is a later phase of the cemetery, possibly extending into the Roman period, for most of the material could very well be contemporary with periods III and IV at Sheepen (A.D. 43–61). The latter part of this time is less probable, and it may be that the use of the cemetery ended with the foundation of the colony in A.D. 50. Whether the expropriation of the lands of the natives had anything to do with this, or the establishment of Roman cemeteries to be used by all, is not yet clear.

Certain it is that burials in this cemetery begin again in the Flavian period, but in a small way, and finally they end in the third century.[2]

2. THE WEST CEMETERY

It is not easy to decide where this may be said to begin or end. It is convenient to regard the grounds of St. Mary's Hospital as a separate area, though there is no clear line of division. There seems to have been a gap between the West and Butt Road cemeteries, but even this may prove otherwise. At any rate burials have been found on each side of the Roman road on its course from the Balkerne Gate to the Hospital and Grammar School. Crossing the former 'Lord's Land' where now are Crowhurst, Rawstorn, Papillon, and Manor roads, it has tessellated pavements and foundations on each side (**37, 38, 110, 111, 146, 147**). At the Hospital and Grammar School occur blocks of graves already noticed (**35, 112**). In Manor Road the lower half of a civil tombstone was found (**36**) showing the lower part of a togate figure standing by an altar. There is no inscription.[3] Northwards, at **111**, lies a foundation noted by Cutts, and at **146** remains of a heavy foundation of septaria running parallel to the road, noted by the writer. At **35**, besides the urns, was found the Colchester Sphinx (**1**)[4] and another small bronze sphinx. Not far away lay part of a military tombstone.[5] There was much building material, with dressed Purbeck marble, and a large gilt letter V from some imposing inscription.

At the Grammar School the road runs into the maze

[1] *Ant. Journ.* xxii, 59 ff.
[2] *Cam.* 13, note 5; *C.M.R.* 1927, 17, pl. IV, 5411–13, 5400–1.
[3] Unpublished. The stone does not seem to have been finished; perhaps it was accidentally broken.
[4] Letter from Mr. Drummond Hay in *Quarterly Journal of Science*, 1821; *J.B.A.* ii, 38; *Gent.'s Mag.* 1821, i, 367; 1822, pt. i, 107–11; *J.R.S.* ii, 122, 148; Cromwell, pp. 369 ff.; *T.E.A.S.* o.s. i, 64; *Coll. Ant.* ii, 37.
[5] *C.I.L.* vii, 91; *Arch. J.* xxxiv, 78; Cromwell, ii, 374; Wright,

i, 295–6. The soldier commemorated apparently came from Nicaea, and two appointments mentioned were in Leg. III Aug. and Leg. XX Val. V. Another inscription found in 1713, exact site not known, omitted from *C.I.L.*, is described *Mus. Disneianum*, i, 99, pl. xlv, fig. 15; *Arch. J.* xxxi, 346; xxxiv, 76. We cannot omit mention of the remarkable inscription, *C.I.L.* vii, 92, which is imperfect and very difficult, but seems to refer to a tumulus.

of remains excavated by Mr. A. F. Hall (see pp. 6–8) and has burials on both sides, including the walled cemetery (**195**) which had in the middle of its south side the emplacement for a heavy monument.[1] On either side, too, lie places where burning has taken place. There are traces of other tombs. Remains of a monument at West Lodge have been mentioned. In 1909 alterations to the terracing on the west side of the Grammar School resulted in several finds, chief of which was a large female head, veiled and diademed, in sandstone.[2] It is on a square base and is clearly from a tomb. It was found where the balustrade now connects with the wall on the west (just north of the 3 in **113**). Part of an inscription was also found,[3] from a thinnish slab of Purbeck marble dedicated to a Roman knight, ending . . . *Val. Fron(t)ina. Coniunx et Flor. Cogitatus. et Flor. Fidelis. Fecerunt.*

Apart from a number of tile tombs which have been reported, some of which are in the Museum, there are some finds styled 'tomb' which may have been similar cists, or built structures, since nothing more is known of them. Such are those marked on the O.S. map in front of Highfield (**9**), behind Errington Lodge (without a cross) (**148**), one found in 1865 under Beverley Road (**12**), and another under the NE. corner of Wellesley Road in 1874 (**43**). Cutts shows an oblong building at the NE. corner of Beverley Road (**116**). But the so-called columbarium in the garden of No. 1 Queen's Road (close to **23**) is of recent work.[4] Our general ignorance of built tombs is probably due to the very complete stone-robbing such as had reduced the walled cemetery to 'ghost trenches' only.

In the grounds of Gurney Benham House, at about the spot marked **113**, remains of furnaces were found over the 'camp-ditch', and, north of the road, a pit full of burnt earth. A short description of these by Mr. A. F. Hall is appended and may be added to our scanty sources of information regarding Roman methods of cremation.

The road now begins to pass through the area of the earliest Roman graves. Crossing Beverley Road it passes the tombstones of the Centurion (**15**)[5] and of Longinus (**24**) (pl. II),[6] and not far away was the child's grave (Joslin grave 3) containing the toy figurines, and dated to shortly after A.D. 43.[7]

The cemetery extends about half a mile in length from east to west and is about a quarter of a mile wide.

Besides the blocks of graves already mentioned burials have been reported from all over this area in varying numbers. Burials by incineration are found in most of the area; how continuously or thickly they lay we cannot now know. Few of the hundreds in the Museum can be marked on the map. Those which can include our numbers **7, 8, 16, 20, 21, 23, 25, 26, 30, 31, 32, (34?)**,[8] **99, 104**,[9] **109**[10] (there were five here, one of which contained the glass cup with circus scene now in the British Museum), **114**,[10] **115, 117**,[11] **121, 157, 160**,[12] **174–7**,[13] **181, 189**. We know further that many graves have been found in the spaces between these marks, e.g. Alderman Vint excavated a number in his grounds (west of **16**)[10] and many have been found on Lord's Land and in the grounds of St. Mary's Hospital (over an area shaded on the plan), also in Queen's Road (just SE. of **119**). The shading could probably be well carried south to **43, 177, 19, 20** and north to **2, 31,** and **103**. The rest are outlying finds, with small cemeteries here and there (e.g. a close group of cremations and inhumations at **103–4**, another beside the pottery kilns at **106**,[14] and one of cremations only at **197** in the Town Cemetery).

Late burials can occur anywhere in the area, e.g. skeletons at **104, 150, 195,** and skeletons are still found around (e.g. **150**) Beverley Road. Lead coffins have been found at **19**,[15] **42**,[8] **100**,[16] **101–103** and as far afield as **106**[17] (and **105** on the south map). Stone coffins are less common; one made from large stones from the cornice of a public building was found in Burlington Road (**54**[18]), and one reused as a sink was found in High Street. Skeletons are also under Lexden Road and Crouch Street (**33**[19]). The account of the Butt Road Cemetery gives the impression that there were more inhumations there than usual elsewhere.

3. THE UNION CEMETERY

On the north of the Roman road as it leaves the Balkerne Gate lie the large grounds of St. Mary's Hospital. It will be seen that several fragmentary buildings are known here (**75, 77, 80**). The area is also the most productive, in every respect, of small objects. Up to nearly twenty years ago large pits were continually dug to dispose of rubbish and from this work a very large number of coins and other small finds were recovered for the Museum. Records of finds begin with

[1] *Arch. J.* ci, 68. [2] Apparently unpublished!
[3] *Essex Review*, xix, 164. [4] *R.C.H.M.* iii, 32 d.
[5] *T.E.A.S.* o.s. v, 87; *Arch. J.* xxxiv, 81; *J.R.S.* ii, 122, 124; *P.S.A.L.* iv, 271.
[6] *T.E.A.S.* xix, 117; *Germania*, xiii, 188; *Ant. Journ.* viii, 527; *C.M.R.* 1928, 8; *Essex Review*, xxxvii, 151; *J.R.S.* xviii, 212.
[7] May, group 3, pp. 251 f., and pl. LXXV, 3*a* and *b*.
[8] Marked by the O.S. at **13**, by Cutts at **114**.

[9] *T.E.A.S.* vi, 171. [10] Cutts's plan.
[11] *C.M.R.* 1929, 18, grave 222.
[12] Ibid., graves 229 and 230.
[13] Ibid., 18, grave 223.
[14] Cf. *C.M.R.* 1935, 18 ff., figs. 4–7.
[15] *Ant. Journ.* ix, 1 ff.
[16] Morant (2nd edn.) 183. [17] *C.M.R.* 1933, 10.
[18] *T.E.A.S.* o.s. v, 323. [19] *C.M.R.* 1931, 8; 33.

Wire, whose notes are too numerous to recount.[1] H. Laver also noted remains, especially interments in which the corpse was wrapped in a sheet of clay.[2] Interments have frequently been found, sometimes in numbers, but burials by incineration also occur. In no case has any deliberate excavation been undertaken, nor has any observation of the pits dug been possible. The depth of made soil is apparently great, being reported as sometimes 12 ft. The general impression is that much of the area was used as the general rubbish-tip for the town (resembling in this respect the *Schutthügel* at Vindonissa) since it contains a jumble of coins and brooches from the earliest times to the latest, the latter, of course, predominating. The pottery ranges from a Bronze Age sherd to late fourth century, if not later. It is quite impossible to state the relationship of the burials to the general deposit—they may be in it, under it, or separated from it. A controlled excavation would be valuable, if only one could know of an undisturbed spot.

Among the finds from here are fragments of inscriptions, including the corner of a Military Diploma[3] and part of a tombstone of Purbeck marble, found in 1889 (in Balkerne Lane), in which Professor Haverfield would see mention of the Coh. I. Vangionum, but this is highly conjectural.[4] Another fragment of Purbeck marble is recorded *J.R.S.* xxi, 249; *C.M.R.* 1931, 9.

4. THE ABBEY FIELD CEMETERY

So far as we know the graves of this cemetery are mostly concentrated in the NW. part of the large open area, formerly in the Abbey of St. John, later in the Lucas family, and acquired by the War Department about 1870. The extensive barracks which now surround it were begun about 1872, the first being the Artillery Barracks. Roman remains at once came to light. Foundations lying north of the main entrance of the Artillery Barracks on Butt Road are noted on the 1:500 map in 1875, and are indicated by Cutts, who shows a piece of wall running N.–S. with a short eastwards return at each end (58). This may have been a tomb. Urns were also found at two spots near the entrance gates in 1875 (44, 45). Cutts shows a row of red dots near the masonry, which probably represents a series of graves cut through by a drain. And, indeed, the numerous separate pots and grave groups in the Museum are almost without exception from the trenches

cut for foundations or drains, and workmen who saw these cut say that they cut through hundreds of pots 'like currants in a fruit cake'. The numbers extended eastwards across the 'circular road', for 'levelling the football field on the Abbey Field they came across an immense number of pots etc. They were arranged on the outside a large pot every few yards and between and inside many smaller. Many were Samian and many had figures on them and names on the platters. The area covered was at least 30 ft. There were many hundreds.'[5]

The positions of the finds also show that this cemetery must have been continuous with that to the west on Butt Road. To the north urns were found just south of Artillery Folley in 1863 (46) and just west of the Crown and Sceptre Inn in the Folley in 1874 (57). These are recorded on the O.S. map only. From here there is a scattered spread of graves right up to the town wall. The limit to east and west is not determined. A number of inhumations in Cedars Road (120) has been described by Mr. E. J. Rudsdale.[6]

Near the town wall Alderman A. M. Jarmin reported on a trench cut along St. John Street and Crouch Street in 1915,[7] and thought, because of the great depth of the overburden and the old name of the street ('Gutter Street'), that the trench was in the Roman town ditch. But observations made when the Playhouse Theatre and a warehouse were built in 1928 showed that 'to a depth of eight feet over most of the site the soil consisted entirely of Roman tip, containing pottery, animal bones, oyster shells and other remains'. Pottery was particularly abundant on the theatre site (at 125). There was Roman pottery in the top-soil and practically no medieval.[8]

This sounds like a second Roman tip, like that at the Union, but it is quite different in content. Samian is in great abundance, while fourth-century coins are scarce.

To the south the spread of graves becomes sparse. The most distant is a strip-lead coffin from Sobraon Barracks (105).[9] Burials from the Abbey Field itself can rarely be plotted. Messrs. E. J. Rudsdale and G. Farmer were able to excavate a number (mostly in very fragmentary condition) near the Garrison Sports Ground about 1925 (200)[10] and graves have been found opposite the Military Hospital (132, 133). All these were incinerations, but inhumations accompanied by colour-coated beakers and flagons were found at (130).[11] Remains of several incineration burials were found

[1] *Arch. J.* i, 156.　　　　[2] *T.E.A.S.* xi, 366.

[3] *C.M.R.* 1930, 9 ff. and pl. II; *T.E.A.S.* xx, 47; *J.R.S.* xix, 216.

[4] *Arch. J.* xlvii, 240; *Eph. Ep.* vii, 845; *Arch. Ael.* 2 ser. xiii, 358.

[5] Laver, Diary, 2/8/1922 (*verbatim*).

[6] *T.E.A.S.* xx, 289; *C.M.R.* 1932, 36 f., and 10, fig. 1; Laver, Diary, 29/9/1930.

[7] *T.E.A.S.* xiii. 107.

[8] *C.M.R.* 1929, 29; similar conditions prevailed at the Regal Cinema.

[9] *C.M.R.* 1932, 36.

[10] MS. in Museum.

[11] *C.M.R.* 1944, 40, graves 317, 318.

north of the married quarters when making an air-raid shelter (**131**).[1] But, on the other hand, many trenches have been cut in all parts of the field without turning up anything. In particular no trace of a road has been seen, although it must be admitted that in most cases there was no one present to look for any such thing. The number of vessels in the Museum[2] is very large. The earliest are of Iron Age C, but the exact sites of these are not accurately known. Of the later groups one, possibly two, are Claudius–Nero, after which there is a gap until the third quarter of the first century, after which the second and third centuries are well represented, with, of course, some falling off in incinerations in the fourth. As for inhumations, some are definitely fourth century, including those mentioned and also a lead coffin found under the Mersea Road (**107**).[3] We cannot go into the numerous records of urns and skeletons from this cemetery made by Wire, other than to mention that a number of inhumations were found when making the cellar of the New Inn (**134**) and several in Cedars Road (**120**).[4] Some of Wire's observations were published in *J.B.A.* iv, 82 ff. Drainage works in St. John's Street and Crouch Street were watched by A. M. Jarmin and he noted skeletons opposite Headgate (**52**) and in Crouch Street (**50, 51**). But this takes us westwards and we must turn to the Butt Road cemetery.

5. THE BUTT ROAD CEMETERY[5]

Probably the major portion of this cemetery was completely removed by gravel-working in the middle of the nineteenth century. It was, fortunately, watched by Wire, whose copious notes and drawings of objects cannot be fully used here. Afterwards still more material was collected by Joslin when Alexandra Road was built and by Jarmin when Beaconsfield Avenue was built. Unfortunately, only Wire has left records which are at all useful. They begin by relating how the top-soil was removed from the site on which Mill Place was built (in Butt Road) in 1839.[6] Since nothing but a summary can be presented here, let Wire make his own as he did to Roach Smith.

'There was the deposit of burnt bones simply laid upon a tile without any protection from the earth;—the deposit in urns of various shapes patterns and sizes, in some instances accompanied by other fictile vessels;—there was the deposit of the body entire, enclosed in a wooden box or coffin, as the large iron nails

testified, some of them accompanied by urns'; and in another letter: 'the number of skeletons was large, and with the majority of them were nails disposed . . . in such a way as to suggest that they had been used to fasten the coffins. These nails are very large, some of them twelve inches long (!); it is not improbable that the coffins were hollowed out of a solid trunk, and that the lid consisted of a very thick slab of wood, and was secured by these nails, which are usually four to six in number to each skeleton . . . most of them have wood adhering and . . . were embedded in black earth, evidently the remains of decomposed wood. Had this occurred only once or twice it might have passed unobserved, but with every skeleton exposed to view (and I daresay more than 200 were examined by me) there was a recurrence of these nails and black earth . . . with several skeletons I noticed the remains of iron, which clearly showed that some of the coffins or chests had iron handles. With others were iron keys, arrowheads, spearheads, bronze and glass vessels, bracelets, bone pins, metal brooches, bracelets in Kimmeridge shale and various other ornaments, such as are usually found in Roman burial grounds—still the nails in the same position.'

Roman coins of the lower Empire (chiefly) were also found with the skeletons. A tile tomb was noted with tiles propped against one another like the ridge of a house-roof, and there was a tomb 'constructed after the manner of the town walls'. Two lead coffins were found (**55**).[7]

In his manuscript book Wire says of the skeletons: 'they do not appear to have been buried in graves according to our custom, but in trenches with sloping sides, running the whole length of the ground, not east and west as now, but south-west and north-east'. Also (1842): '. . . Lowering the back part of the premises . . . for sand . . . more skeletons are discovered, but with no urns etc., but iron nails are still found with them in the same relative position; proving that the interments at the back . . . are of later date than those in front. These also are Roman, as is proved by the coins found, which are all of the lower Empire, chiefly of the family of Constantine.'

We have three plans, all very sketchy, two in Wire's 'County Illustrations', which supplement each other, and another in the Diary of 1/12/1848. From these and from early maps it appears that the part of the cemetery then removed consisted of a strip of land on the west of Butt Road, extending from the windmill on the

---

[1] *C.M.R.* 1944, 40, graves 562, 562A.

[2] All presented by H.M. Secretary of State for War, or deposited on loan by him from time to time.

[3] Colchester Museum, unpublished.

[4] *C.M.R.* 1931, 8, 31, 32; 1932, 10, fig. 1 (wrongly described as 'Abbey Field'). Observed by Mr. E. J. Rudsdale.

[5] The shaded area round 43A on the South Map.

[6] *T.E.A.S.* o.s. iv, 265; Letter to C. R. Smith in *Coll. Ant.* iii, 52, and pl. xiv, 3 and 4; and innumerable notes and drawings in the Wire MSS.

[7] Ibid., pl. xiv.

south to level with Burlington Road on the north, and to the properties on Maldon Road in the west. The area is now completely built over by Alexandra and Burlington Roads.

(55) Of the two lead coffins one was found west of Mill Place and one south. One at least had scallop-shell decoration. Both lay with head to west. In front of Mill Place, under the fence by the street, was 'a circular cist nearly full of urns, most of which were broken by the workmen'. Somewhat south of the middle of the west side is shown 'Roman grave of masonry', and in the middle of the south side 'kiln made of old materials full of fragments'. In the centre of the space is written: 'In this area was found great quantity of urns and other vessels, some with calcined bones, a glass vessel or two, a jet carved ornament,[1] rings and bracelets of bronze, fragments of bone brace-lets and a pair of *glass bracelets*, a bronze vessel, some *iron spearheads*, a knife blade, a few iron chisels, bronze keys, some few coins, principally of Constantine the Great's time and subsequent, one or two of M. Aure-lius, *no brooches*.' (The italics are ours.)

Graves were also found in the properties on Maldon Road, but not, so far as we know, west of that road, and in the garden west of the Windmill. Some graves have been recovered from the building of Beaconsfield Avenue along the south side of the cemetery. Two of these belong to the third quarter of the first century.

THE NORTHERN CEMETERIES

Two cemeteries lie in the northern area, one to the east and SE. of the North Railway Station, about a mile from the town, the other on the site of Everett's brickyard, near the NE. angle of the town.

6. THE NORTH CEMETERY

This was discovered by Wire, whose notes on it begin in 1842, and between that time and 1912, when it again came to the notice of the Museum, the most significant part of it must have been removed. Urns first came up when making the railway-cutting east of the station in 1843; an odd urn farther south was ac-companied by a coin of Trajan (grave 562); other scat-tered urns have been found between the King's Meadow[2] and the railway (87), but the main concentration was near the brickyard east of the station. The graves first found included two burials in globular amphorae (89, 90), one of which contained a coin of Faustina

junior. The second contained six vessels of glass which are illustrated in Wire's *Album*. In 1912 Mr. H. Money's collection of objects, including gold ear-rings, a silver spoon, and a jet necklace with pendant, came to the Museum, and in 1928 and 1929 the Mu-seum recovered thirty-two graves consisting of groups or single vessels. None of these were remarkably early, and the cemetery seems to have been used to a moder-ate extent fairly evenly from the end of the first century to the late third or beginning of the fourth.[3] The vessels include two fine glass urns.[4] There are no in-humations recorded but the necklace suggests there was one.

7. THE NORTH-EAST CEMETERY

This lies just outside the NE. Gate and its extent is not well known, for the vessels have been found from time to time as the brick-earth has been excavated and are mostly in the possession of Mr. J. Everett. Some he has given to the Museum, also a lead coffin (70)[5] which was found close to the surface not far from the gateway. Only this has been seen *in situ* and planned.

Even this site did not escape Wire, for in his 'County Illustrations' he marks on the map, in this area: 'No. 11. Two urns were discovered here in 1841, the one standing on the other, the lower one containing cal-cined bones.'

Eight graves are listed from this site in the Museum, the earliest being Flavian, another (grave 203) con-taining a coin of Hadrian. The cemetery seems to have been used at intervals from the late first century on-wards.

Westwards, on the Park side of the boundary, no vessels have been found. The area, on both sides, is traversed by the town ditch, which is very large and wide and has never been excavated. It has been sup-posed that it represents a medieval enlargement of the original ditch. In 1935 the outer lip of it was partly cut away in laying out the Park bowling-green.[6] Great quantities of pottery and other Roman objects were found, but the most striking discovery was that the upper 3 ft. of the earth (all that was moved) was full of disturbed human bones. It was as if the ditch had been enlarged after it had been used as part of a cemetery for a great number of inhumations. These skeletons presumably had no grave furniture, for even though they were disturbed, nothing of the nature to be ex-pected (late Roman vessels, or Saxon weapons) was found among the mass. The date of these skeletons

[1] The Cupids, illustr. Wire's *Album*, p. 111.

[2] Not 'King's Head Meadow', which has crept into common usage in the last few years. The meadow of the 'King's Head' was west of the Union, half a mile or more away.

[3] The 32 groups are published *C.M.R.* 1929, 21, nos. 232–5,

and 1930, 29 ff., nos. 239–65, no. 238 is omitted; noted in *J.R.S.* xix, 198.

[4] Ibid. 1939, pl. on p. 38; *J.R.S.* xxi, 236.

[5] *Essex Review*, xlvii, 103; *C.M.R.* 1944, 37.

[6] Ibid. 1944, 16.

could well fall in the darkest part of the Dark Ages, but of this there is no proof.

There are a few other records, of an indeterminate nature. Remains from near North Station include a bronze brooch; two bronze bracelets, a thimble, and ring found 'on the west side of North Station Road'. Remains of pottery, coins, &c., have been found in Serpentine Walk (in Strowlger's and Humm's

among the kilns themselves, these being interments of a much later period. Also in the sand-pit south of Sheepen Farm,[1] on the top of the hill farther south, and in the field to the east and on the site of the New Technical College.[2]

Wire has notes of remains both of occupation and of burials from west and south of North Station, including the site of Essex Hall, at the end of 1842 and

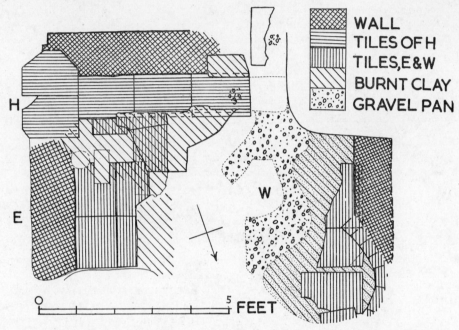

WALL
TILES OF H
TILES, E & W
BURNT CLAY
GRAVEL PAN

Fig. 112. Plan of remains of three furnaces found at Gurney Benham House. [113], p. 259.

ground), in Albert Street and Morton Road, and under the new Fire Station on the By-pass Road. The latter is all of the period A.D. 5–60. The records (in Wire) of finds in Nash's garden (between King's Meadow and the railway) are so numerous as to suggest that the whole area was a cemetery, or occupied, or both. But exploratory trenches cut at (88) in 1930 were negative.

8. Various Other Graves

A small cemetery in the modern cemetery has been mentioned on p. 252. The finds are published in *C.M.R.* 1947, 21, pl. v; 1948, 15 f., pl. iii; 1950, 22. Some cinerary urns found west of the great temple at Gosbecks are noticed on p. 259, graves at North Bridge on p. 241. Scattered graves have been found in Sheepen Lane and over the Sheepen site, especially on 'Site C4' (106) adjacent to the kilns found in 1933; and

the autumn of 1851 and spring of 1852. Of these we have no plan, and nothing has come from that area since (201, 202).

Inhumations have been found in Priory Street opposite St. Botolph's Priory, but their date is uncertain (137); others found east of the Priory are perhaps connected with it. There is evidence for one or two inhumations from the south side of East Hill, and a cinerary group (grave 154) from the East Yard Depot (139) and Rosebery Avenue (grave 313).

Four vessels at least have been found in the garden of St. Botolph's Vicarage (140). They are of first- and second-century date. Though ashes are not recorded from them, they were probably present.

Remains 'found at Old Heath 1913 or 14' include burnt human bones and remains of five vessels of second-century date (C.M. 2858.13). The exact site is not known.

---

[1] *T.E.A.S.* xix, 58; *C.M.R.* 1928, 60 (jewellery).
[2] Two urns, one in a tile cist, found at a point $\frac{3}{4}$ in. SE. of the figure 647 on pl. XLIII.

This scatter of graves around the town is roughly coextensive with the spread of other small finds, the list of which is great and quite beyond our present consideration.

9. FURNACES AT GURNEY BENHAM HOUSE (fig. 112)

The following is an abbreviated account of the report made by Mr. A. F. Hall on work done by him and others of the Royal Grammar School in 1937.

In trenching across the 'Camp Ditch' the remains of three flues or furnaces were found lying partly on the filling of the ditch. They had been built of tiles laid flat for floors, with walls of broken tile and shapeless pieces of black 'conglomerate'—natural gravel indurated by iron. The remains were fragmentary, and the materials had been laid in loam, which had been baked red by the heat. There was much of this about them. The burning blackened exposed parts of the tiles, but parts formerly covered by structure now gone are red. It is thus possible to plan the flues, even if much of the walls is missing.

The three flues overlap, in part; the earliest is W, laid on a bed of conglomerate, E followed, having no foundation, both lie partly over the ditch; finally H was built, partly over the others, but clear of the ditch. The last flue contained grey powder, containing phosphate and calcium,[1] pointing to bone.

These flues consist of a straight passage about a foot wide and up to 12 ft. long, ending in a nearly round chamber which seems not to have been specifically more concerned with heating than the rest, and may have been the base of a chimney. The structure is quite slight, and would not carry any weight. Similar flues have been found elsewhere connected with working iron, &c., and the ironstone conglomerate found in quantity here might be held to indicate this. But the ironstone is plentiful in the ditch-filling, which is earlier than the flues, and the ironstone found actually around the flues may have come from their structure. This black conglomerate is strange here, but we feel it was not imported for use in these kilns. It has been suggested that their purpose was for cremation, and the grey powder containing phosphates and calcium supports this view.

Our knowledge of the methods of cremation in Britain is at present slight, but there are many references to burnt spots in the vicinity of cemeteries, rarely, however, with an adequate description.

(C) THE GOSBECKS SITE

On Gosbecks Farm on Cheshunt field[2] there is a Celtic temple surrounded by a double portico, standing in its own temenos. Immediately adjacent, on the east, is another large enclosure, the length of the north side of the two together measuring 1,125 ft. Two hundred yards south of the temple is a theatre of simple construction, and west of temple and theatre lies a strange complex of quadrangular ditched enclosures, superimposed and overlapping. The fields all around, when deeply ploughed, show black patches here and there and are covered with Roman tile, pieces of stone, and Iron Age and Roman pottery. It is not yet possible to estimate the number of acres involved. (Plan, fig. 113.)

Deep ploughing in 1943 revealed remains, as described, in field 416,[3] pretty well covering the whole field. At C several burials were disturbed,[4] the plough slicing the urns in half as they stood in the ground. One or two of these reached the Museum, but in most cases the tops had gone long ago. The pottery is all Roman coarse ware. The evidence is scarcely sufficient to give more than a broad first- to second-century date. In 1948 members of the Roman Essex Society tried to get further evidence at this spot, but no burials were encountered. Instead a hearth was found over a small Iron Age pit (D), proving domestic occupation here in the time of Cunobelin; and a coin of Faustina was found near by to the east.

The ploughing showed patches of intense black soil; at other places it turned up yellow sand, presumably the upcast of excavations. The pottery found was of first- and second-century date, and there were also fragments of lava, millstones, and flue-tiles.

In the large field 1788, when ploughed, the line of the Roman road, known from the air-photograph, showed clearly as a band of yellow gravel in irregular lengths.

---

[1] Analysis by Mrs. Clarihew in the school laboratory.

[2] Or Chestnut, see P. H. Reaney, *Place Names of Essex*, p. 399, and cf. Chest Wood, near by, p. 318.

[3] This field has not been altered recently. East of it the present tenants of the farm have done away with several field-divisions. The field in which the temple stands was formerly several fields, now is no. 1788, of over 65 acres.

[4] *J.R.S.* xxxiv, 80.

Other traces of occupation were faint, chiefly small pieces of tile, but south of the mound, right up to the hedge south of the theatre, many patches of burnt

site in 1842, when unspecified 'agricultural operations' revealed the presence of extensive foundations. One would like to know whether these 'operations' were

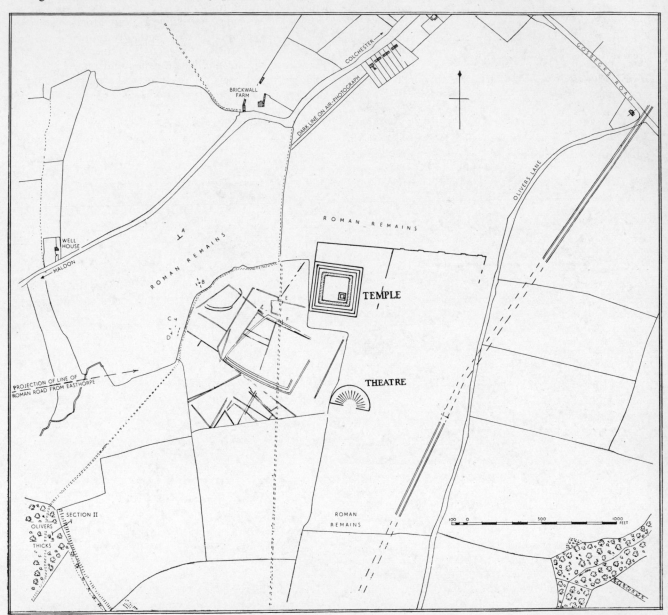

FIG. 113. General plan, Gosbecks site. pp. 259–271.

earth occurred, and in or near them dense patches of a peculiar, thin and heavy slag. The appearances suggest an extensive metal industry, and one piece of heavy sheet metal, of uncertain nature (? bronze), was found near the hedge.

The history of the site is short. It did not come to notice until the Rev. H. Jenkins excavated on the temple

actually the levelling of mounds in preparation for ploughing. Jenkins's results were published in *Coll. Ant.* ii, 53 ff., *J.B.A.* ii (1847), 45 f., *Gent.'s Mag.* 1842, pt. 2, 526, and *R.C.H.M. Essex*, iii (NE.), 207 and xxvii. He described the remains as those of a villa, but realized that it was of a strange plan. In 1932 the temple and its ditch and double portico and the ditched enclosures in field 415 were clearly visible on several exposures of an air-survey, made for us by the R.A.F. through the good offices of Mr. O. G. S. Crawford of the Ordnance Survey. So, too, the Roman road which passes the site on the east at a distance of about 840 ft. from the temple and about 160 ft. from the east side of the large enclosure. They have recently been seen again to even greater advantage, but obliquely, in pictures taken by Dr. St. Joseph (pl. XXXIX). Moreover the latter have shown that all around, for a great distance, and possibly even covering the most part of the 12 square miles of ancient Camulodunum, there are the traces of a former field system very much like our own, even to the green lanes serving the fields.

This is a new discovery of the utmost importance. The lines shown are those of small ditches, presumably hedgerow ditches. They have been observed in numbers, in section, in the sides of the long tank-trap ditches which were cut in 1940. They vary in size, but average about 3 ft. wide by 2 ft. deep, and are usually filled with a 'cheesy' clay. Sometimes the filling is of dark earth, but there is always the possibility that any such were comparatively modern.

Now these traces are so slight that they appear but rarely and very faintly on the R.A.F. photographs taken at 2,000 ft., but very clearly on Dr. St. Joseph's taken at 1,000 ft., *and they are the only traces of any field system at all antedating our own.* The first important observation is that they really do antedate our own, and are so entirely independent of ours that one must conclude that the whole area had reverted to the wild, and after a long while an entirely new system (the present one) was laid out. There are only these two systems, though both have gone through vicissitudes.[1]

There is thus no trace at all of either a rigidly reticulated Roman system or a recognizable Saxon strip-system.

Our own system remained almost unchanged from the time of the earliest maps[2] well into the nineteenth century, and, indeed, still is almost unchanged except in the towns. There is every reason to suppose that the old system now revealed to us was equally permanent. It may well have covered many more centuries than ours, and shows many more alterations than ours. The nature and date of these alterations must await a detailed study, for which many more photographs will be required.

Whatever the nature of the comparatively deep-ditched enclosures west of the temple and the remarkable enclosures near Lodge Farm, Lexden, the slight lines of the old field system can be seen running across both, but only to a limited degree. It would appear,

at least at Gosbecks, that the field system avoided field 415 until the enclosures were obsolete. That makes the system partly pre-Roman and partly Roman in date. These remarks are designed to draw attention to a new and remarkable field of study, and we must now leave the subject.

In 1936 a trench was cut diagonally across the temple enclosure from the NW. to the SE. angles of the double portico.

In 1948 the Roman Essex Society began to excavate in field 416 at the point A, where the air-photograph seemed to show traces of a building. Nothing was found save a few parallel grooves of varying length and intensity and irregular spacing in the subsoil. These were dismissed as due to ploughing. The site of the burials was then tried (C), and then site B (for which see p. 269). In 1949 the Roman Essex Society and the Colchester Museum turned to field 1788, with the excellent results set out below, and in 1950 the Museum, aided by members of the Society, explored the mound mentioned by Jenkins, which turns out to have been a theatre.

1. THE TEMPLE (COLCHESTER V)

The Gosbecks site is in flat and (now) very open country, only varied by a small valley which begins north of the NE. angle of the great eastern enclosure and passes along its north side, deepening to the west and passing so close to the NW. angle of the temple portico that the latter must have jutted out into it supported by a retaining wall. About 400 ft. west of this angle the old maps show a pond which was still there in Jenkins's time. From the pond the valley curves to the SW., and used to feed a small stream which is now piped. From the pond downwards the valley must have been very wet, and in one place (B) this has resulted in the fair preservation of a timber structure.

Since our work in 1936[3] was simply an exploratory trench its results are merely ancillary to what we can derive from Jenkins's account and from the air-photographs. The best account is that in *J.B.A.*, which runs as follows. The work was done after the corn was cut in 1842.

Workmen during the previous winter, while deepening the ditch of an adjoining hedge, had dug up a great quantity of broken Roman bricks and tiles, and fragments of coarse pottery, including part of a platter stamped MARTI. (The spot would be the SW. angle of the double portico.) When the autumn ploughing began 'the ploughmen . . . mentioned . . . their ploughs often struck on what appeared to them to be the foundations of a building: . . . a stone wall was discovered not more than six inches under the soil. This spot is at the NW. end of the villa, and the foundation was followed on the exterior wall on the

[1] No other system could have existed unless it depended on field divisions which left no mark in the soil. The two here

mentioned may possibly have coincided at some points.
[2] Often as early as Elizabeth.　　　[3] *J.R.S.* xxvii, 240.

northern side. Afterwards the foundations were traced on the other side; in some parts they were four or five feet under ground, and in some parts the stones had been altogether removed, but the space in which the foundation stood could still be plainly traced, . . . filled up to a certain height with rubble . . . and mortar. These foundation walls were three feet thick and consisted of septaria and Kentish rag. All the exterior walls were 288 ft. in length, except on the western side, where the wall was traced up to the hedge, and then it goes into an adjoining field, which was not touched; but no doubt the wall is of the same length on that side also.[1] There were four interior walls at the distance of fourteen feet throughout from the exterior wall; the whole building therefore formed a large square, having a spacious cloister around the whole interior, of fourteen feet in breadth. On the east and the west there were traces of rooms adjoining the walls, and in the centre of the square were discovered some very strong and thick foundations, four feet thick, built of septaria and Kentish rag; and adjoining these had been rooms of great depth, for the earth was opened to ten feet, and found filled with an admixture of earth, broken tiles, bricks, (some apparently from their rounded form, having been the pillars of a hypocaust[2]); there were also large quantities of stucco of various colours, chiefly red. At a short distance from these walls [? the 'strong and thick foundations'] were found a very large quantity of Roman tessellae of various colours . . . in single pieces. The building . . . probably centuries ago, appears to have been completely broken up, and the materials removed, to erect other buildings in the neighbourhood. The excavations therefore were discontinued, and the farmer . . . broke up the greater part of the foundations laid open and carried away about forty loads of stones.'

'At the south-western end, and along the southern exterior wall, to the extent of sixty feet, and at the distance of twelve feet, was discovered the foundation of a wall only 2 ft. in breadth, and composed of chippings of Kentish ragstone, laid in alternate layers with concrete or coarse grouted mortar.'

No account gives full reference to Gilbert's plan, which only appears in Roach Smith's account in 1852. It has numerals for reference, which no one uses, and has certain dimensions inserted which are useful. Perhaps the projections numbered 2 and 3 on the west wall are the 'traces of rooms'. The plan shows what the foundations of the temple itself looked like to Gilbert, and should, one thinks, have been more firmly indicated if they were really 'strong and thick'. The figure 122 at the SE. corner is quite without explanation.

It is noticeable that Jenkins somehow missed the outer wall on the north, east, and south, and the inner one on the west, but states the corridor was 14 ft. wide all round. On the west he should mean the outer one, with wall 3 ft. thick. But on the south he gives us the outer one (partially) as only 12 ft. wide and its wall 2 ft. thick. The inner angle of his walls at the SW. corner could be correct, but the same arrangement, shown at the NW. corner, is shown by all the air-photographs to be wrong. They also agree that Gilbert's outline of the 'central' 'strong foundations' is wrong, so that it is quite clear that Jenkins only got the general idea of the plan and not the details. We have not exhausted our sources. Wire says in his Diary, 2/8/1842, 'Received letter from the Rev. H. Jenkins containing a few particulars respecting a Roman Villa discovered by and being explored under his auspices at Gosbecks Farm, Stanway.[3] See C. R. Smith's *Collectanea* Vol. ii page [*sic*] and Vol. I of my Colchester Collection.'[4]

On 5/9/1842 Wire writes: 'went to see the foundations of a Roman Villa in Cheshunt or Chesnut Field Gosbecks[5] . . . which is being explored . . . the following measurements were obtained by me, 400 ft. wide from SSE. to NNW., and Mr. Jenkins sends me word that the crypto-porticus is 305 ft. long, this ran the whole length of the building.'

Now we can only get a length of 305 ft. by measuring, on Gilbert's plan, the inner of the two west walls shown, and this is short of an over-all measurement by one width of the outer corridor and the outer wall. If these were 14 ft. and 3 ft. the over-all of the building is 322 ft., barring buttresses such as that Gilbert shows at the NW. corner. Wire's 400 ft. is accounted for if we take it as the diagonal on the *middle* wall, that is the inner wall on Gilbert's plan.

Wire mentions no rooms, and we doubt the existence of any. The fact is that Jenkins found the ditch without realizing what it was, and thought he was in buried rooms; nowhere else could he have found a depth of 10 ft. Moreover, his description of the filling of the ditch tallies exactly with ours. Wire would realize there were no rooms, but mentions neither them nor a ditch, nor does he seem to have been impressed by the 'central' building even as much as Gilbert.

Since the air-photographs show nothing in the *centre* of the square we discount Jenkins's use of this word and suppose his 'strong walls' were those of the temple in the SE. corner, as, indeed, indicated on Gilbert's plan. Here we are to understand that Jenkins had

---

[1] We suspect he may not have found it so. Despite the curious form of the NW. angle on Gilbert's plan we believe the west wall continued to the north as the temenos wall, and it may have done so to the south as well, as it seems to have done on the north side at Champlieu (Grenier, *Man. d'archéol. romaine*, 181, fig. 10).

[2] Possibly; more probably for building columns.

[3] Most contemporary sources have 'Gosbacks', to which *R.C.H.M.* adheres, but Wire uses 'Gosbecks' and Gosbecks it

is universally today. It is also Gosbecks on early-nineteenth-century estate maps. See P. H. Reaney, *Place Names of Essex*, p. 399.

[4] The Diary, as we have it, was copied out from the original Journal; the *Coll. Ant.* volume is dated 1852. Of Wire's 'Colchester Collection' we know nothing.

[5] Chestnut appears on early estate maps, but we must remember the proximity of Chest Wood, the meaning of which is not clear.

actual masonry, yet Gilbert only shows the traces by broken lines! We are told the farmer removed the masonry uncovered, but we found no foundation-trenches in 1936, and we aimed to pass diagonally across the centre of the whole site, and must have been very near doing so.[1] We had, in their place, white patches where the subsoil was stained by lime. The air-photograph shows the walls very clearly; is it possible that the lime in the ground could, alone, give the effect, or did we make a mistake? Only further excavation can tell. It is possible that the temple stood on a mound, the removal of which has removed the foundations, save the lowest layer of mortar. If so, there is no mention of it in Jenkins, and the mound must have been levelled centuries ago. On the other hand, the photograph and Jenkins's account lead one to expect marked foundation-trenches, so clear that they can be measured, and even have suggestions of buttresses showing. The portico would be[2] about 48·5 ft. square and the cella about 33 ft. square. This is a temple of merely large-average size.

The actual centre of the enclosure had scarcely a foot of top-soil and no recognizable traces of buildings, though here and there were patches of mortar and chips of septaria. There was loam down to nearly 18 in. and then what appeared to be natural red sand. But a shaft was sunk to 4 ft. deep to test this and it showed six layers as follows: 1 (lowest), 7 in. of 'dirty oily sand'; 2·5 in. of clean yellow sand, which some thought contained mortar; 3·9 in. of red sand and gravel, divided from 4 by a thin layer of gravel; 4·6 in. of red sand and mortar; 5·8 in. sandy loam; 6·7 in. top-soil. It is clear that further exploration here is desirable, but the air-photographs show no building.

Our own description of the temple site in the SE. corner runs as follows. At 215 ft. (approx.) from the NW. corner came a small slot with vertical sides, filled with chips of septaria in reddish sand (cf. the slots east of the large temple at Sheepen (p. 229)). The width was about 16 in., the depth not ascertained. Beyond this the soil changed. The natural sand was at 14 in., capped by an even layer of 4 in. of clayey loam. At 227–8 ft. was another patch of septaria and mortar in the top of the sand, exactly as at 201 ft. At 237 ft. lay another slot 3 ft. 6 in. wide. Though opened up for 3 ft. on each side of the trench, this did not seem to be continued, appearing to be a rounded patch of septaria set in the middle of a square floor of fine gravel. The bottom of the trench was now only just over a foot below the surface, but the gravel floor went down to at least 15 in. (its top was 9 in. from the surface). Beyond this the loam continued, but at 251 ft. it changed to a whitish layer of fragments of septaria, mortar, and tile lying on fine gravel. The top of this was only 9 in. from the surface, and the sandy bottom of the trench was at 10 in. The edges of this white spread seemed to be quite clear and straight, crossing the trench at converging angles. Here were found numbers of white tesserae, peculiar, because not square, but measuring about 1 in. by ½ in. by ½ in. thick.

The trench continued, showing now a yellow gravel floor, to 279 ft., where lay another white patch extending to 284 ft. (i.e. 5 ft. wide), and after another 5 ft. was yet another white patch at 289–97 ft. Here the floor of the trench fell away somewhat, and it was 1 ft. 10 in. to the natural sand, upon which lay 13 in. of dirty gravel.

The remains of the temple are thus very ill preserved, and the exact position of the walls was not determined. It appears that the white patches must contain the evidence for the walls, as they certainly do of white tessellated floors and of the fine white mortar in which they were laid.

The Ditch of the Enclosure

This great ditch appears on all the air-photographs without any opening for an entrance, so far as one can see. Our trench cut it twice, each time, if our measurements were correct, in the exact angle. At the NW. angle the width was 47 ft. 6 in. from lip to lip, which means the actual width was 33 ft. 6 in. The outline was V-shaped and the depth 11 ft. 3 in. In the bottom lay 15 in. of fine dark silt. Above this there was a very substantial filling of dirty gravelly material, 3 ft. 6 in. thick, with, at one point, part of a layer of very black charcoal and ash. This filling, which is certainly ancient, made when the outer walls were added to the site, may represent the original upcast of the ditch thrown back; but the ditch is cut in sand, and this filling is quite gravelly. Above it the ditch had been finally levelled up with a uniform very dirty gravelly filling right up to the present plough-level.

Within the ditch our section continued with 9 in. of top-soil and natural red sand at 2 ft. The intervening space was filled with dirty sand or loose, red, gravelly material. Over some distance these could be differentiated into a vague upper and lower layer, and from 137 to 155 ft. there was a distinct spread of loose light gravel on the red sand.

At 302 ft. came the inner lip of the second section and the outer lip at 354 ft., giving a corrected width of 36 ft., but the SE. slope was at first very gradual, so that the exact position of the lip is not certain. The

[1] Can it be that, despite the fact that we knew where to look for them, and tried to find them, we missed these foundation-trenches?

[2] Reckoning the over all of the square at 322 ft.

depth was 11 ft., and in the bottom was nearly 2 ft. 6 in. of fine silt. Above this was all one yellow filling, full of gravel, tiles, and septaria, the latter with open spaces between, one containing a large 'cow' snail-shell. Below 5 ft. from the surface was found much pottery, including T.S. f. 79 stamped M..., the base of a cooking-pot, a heavy bronze pin with massive globular head, and many tiles and tesserae. Much mortar lay directly upon the silt, especially one patch which was 3 in. thick (many red tesserae were also found about 140 ft.).

In the silt was found a coin of Cunobelin, Evans pl. XIII, 2, in good preservation, and much of one native vessel of f. Cam. 231.

South-east of the ditch the top of the natural gravel was at 2 ft. 3 in., with 18 in. of yellow loam above it and 9 in. of top-soil.

The small finds made in all our excavations on the Gosbecks site have been very few. The site is very much denuded and the top-soil very thin. No real occupation layer has yet been encountered, even where a floor has been identified. There is no reason to attribute any of the following coins to any site other than that of the temple, except in the cases stated.

> A worn second brass of an empress, possibly Sabina or Faustina senior, was found in the temple ditch at a depth of 3 ft. 9 in. from the surface in the SE. angle (C.M. 1093.36).
>
> A second brass of Antoninus Pius was found unstratified near the site of the burials (A on plan), in 1949.
>
> A very worn and illegible first brass of M. Aurelius or Commodus was found on the surface of the field in 1929 (C.M. 501.29).

Besides the account already quoted Wire gives the following in his 'Museum' volume: '. . . a double wall of considerable thickness leaving a clear space of 14 ft. The measure of the exterior wall in length is 285 ft., and of the inner 265 ft. Numerous coins have been thrown up . . . amongst these a 2b of Titus, rev. Judeae Capta; 3b of Helena and Carausius in fine preservation . . . . the fragments thrown up are mostly of Roman antiquity . . . broken urns, bricks, tiles, boars' teeth, bones of animals, mortar etc. It appears from a hasty survey that this superstructure has been removed for purposes that may be hereafter explained. The ground we understand will be ploughed up . . . for cultivation.' (Cutting from the *Essex County Standard*, 9/9/1842.)

Wire further records a bronze coin of Claudius Gothicus found on the 'Villa' site, Diary, 22/2/1843; and ibid. 9/8/1843 we read that Mr. Root of Gosbecks gave Wire 'some Roman coins found in Cheshunt Field'.

Jenkins's account ends by recording that there were about thirty coins, in brass, found during his excavations; they were chiefly of Vespasian, Tetricus, Carausius, and the Constantine family; among them was a second brass of Titus (*Judaea Capta*), and a third brass of Carausius (*Pax Auggg*).

Judging by the present paucity of coins on the site Jenkins's excavations must have been very extensive.

2. THE ENCLOSURE WALLS

Jenkins found the temenos wall of the temple, but did not follow it very far, he says: 'In the same field and almost parallel with the eastern side of the villa, but at a distance of one hundred and seventy feet from it, was the foundation of a long wall, from two to three feet thick, with a return wall as indicated on the plan. In two spots near this wall, and in two other parts of the field, on the opposite side, where probably ran the return wall, large quantities of oyster shells, boars' tusks and broken pottery were found in pits or cesspools, which descended a considerable depth.'

Now Gilbert's plan shows this wall as 160 ft. distant from the middle wall of the portico at the SE. corner and 189 ft. at the NE. corner. It is therefore far from parallel. Moreover it had not a simple return, at the north end, for he shows it turning both east and west. The line of this wall does not show on the air-photographs.

In December 1947 Mr. A. F. Hall discovered that a ploughman named Beales employed on Gosbecks Farm had preserved in his garden shed for two years or more a fine bronze statuette of Mercury, 20 in. high, in excellent preservation. The figure (pl. XL) is quite nude, with two wings on the head, and no cap. The soles of the feet are pierced by triangular openings to receive securing studs in an uneven base (perhaps representing a rock) on which the figure had been fixed.[1]

Mr. Beales stated that he struck the figure with the plough, which partly broke the right leg. He had ploughed that field many times and never found anything, but had noticed the road which passes the temple on the east. This time, however, he was ploughing a few inches deeper than previously, and since then remains of stone walls have been noticed here and there. The missing arms of the figure may have been caught by previous ploughing and may still lie in the soil. Owing to the great size of the field it has not been possible to fix with any accuracy the exact find-spot, which according to the finder was in the bottom of the valley about 100 yards NE. of the NE. corner of the temple portico.

Nevertheless, in 1948 the Roman Essex Society made an attempt to explore the site, using a mine-detector.[2] Much agricultural iron was found, but no ancient remains. We also have reason to believe we were not really on the right spot. But trenching in the vicinity exposed Jenkins's N.–S. temenos wall, and it was decided to try to follow this east and west farther than

---

[1] The size is exceptional; the nearest parallel is one from under the temple of Mercury in the Trier Tempelbezirk, *Germania*, xii, 104 ff. and Trier Tempelbezirk Report, Heft i, Taf. 18; *J.R.S.* xxxviii, 91; *Essex Review*, lvii, 86; *T.E.A.S.* xxiv, 43; *C.M.R.* 1948, 8.

[2] *C.M.R.* 1950, 16.

he had done. We had found the N.–S. wall and a coin of Antoninus Pius among the rubble of it. It was followed north. Practically nothing was left but the foundation trench, full of broken mortar and fragments of tile and stone. Here and there a few large stones were

least 38 in. wide and the depth to its bottom was 46 in., but this is exceptional owing to the rise of the ground to the south. Five trenches were cut between this point and the corner of the temenos. At half-way the bottom of the foundation trench was 38 in. from

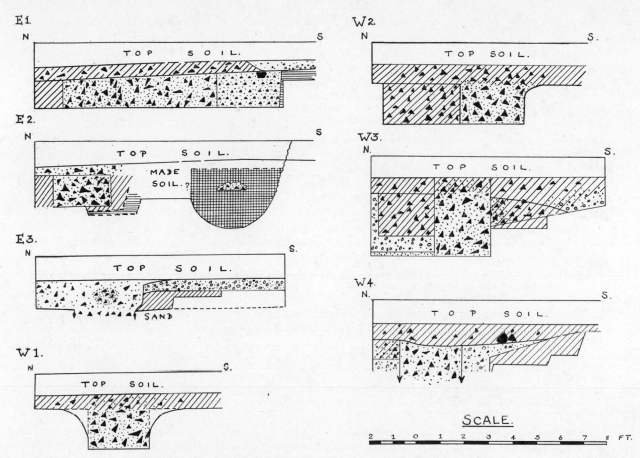

FIG. 114. Sections through north enclosure wall, Gosbecks, pp. 264–7.

found which had been missed by the robbers. On the whole this foundation trench had been but little damaged and was easy to follow. It was usually sunk about 12 in. into the brown subsoil and was 26–30 in. wide, occasionally as much as 35 in.

The total length of walling subsequently traced was no less than 1,125 ft. E.–W. In this length are comprised the north walls of two distinct enclosures (see fig. 113). That on the west contains the temple. Its north wall is 508 ft. long. The NW. corner was found opposite that of the double portico of the temple, which it probably struck exactly at the angle, but we did not uncover the angle itself. In effect the line of the outer west wall of the portico is continued for 120 ft. in a straight line. In the slope of the hill against the corner of the portico the foundation trench was at

the surface. The depth to the top of the rubble filling of the trench varied from 20 to 25 in., and over it there was a layer of yellow loam 7–10 in. thick. This was observed in nearly every trench of these excavations, and shows that most of the robbing must have been done so long ago that this layer has accumulated since. Nothing was ever found in it to date it.

At the NW. angle itself there was a buttress on the west face 4 ft. 5 in. long and projecting 1 ft. Some septaria lying against the position of the north face suggested there was a shorter buttress on that side also, approximately 3 ft. long. Depth to bottom of foundation, 32 in.

A number of trenches were cut to trace this wall eastwards, and all went well until 140 ft. from the corner. Here the centre line of the wall was found to be 3 ft. north of the prevailing line (section W1, fig. 114). But in the next cut, at 166 ft. it was back on the original line.[1]

All along, the depth was 32 in. to the bottom, except at 140 ft., where it was 38 in.

At 186 ft. (W2) the depth was 41½ in., with the natural loam at 21 in., so that the extra depth is not due to increased over-burden. At 235 ft. there were 7 in. of rubble, with large lumps of stone and tile, lying outside the wall on the natural subsoil. The wall itself was 31 in. wide, and the loam on each side of it was full of white streaks, like boulder clay, which it cannot be. This is a strange feature of the site, to which we shall refer again.

At 270 ft. again there was rubble outside the wall. At 360 ft. the top-soil was 12 in., then over the wall 2 in. of loose rubble, followed by firm rubble at 14 in. To the bottom was 33 in. On the south side of the wall was a layer 2 in. thick, about 1 ft. from the surface, of pale loam containing some pebbles; below it was the natural dark reddish loam. On the north side the 2-in. layer is full of blobs of mortar or chalk; even in the bottom of the trench this appears (at 31 in.). The limits of this feature (cf. the cut at 235 ft.) were not ascertained. Compare also the cut at 186 ft., where this streaky material filled an extension of the foundation trench, again to the north; but the soil is yellower here at 360 ft., and there are about 3 in. of streaky trench-filling on the south side also.

At 384 ft. the wall was found with its centre line 18 in. south of the centre line followed so far. There are 12 in. of top-soil over the loose rubble, which spreads out on both sides, and firm rubble is at 15 in., level with the clean brown loam. The next three cuts take us right up to the NE. angle and give us one straight line all the way. Something therefore happens to the wall between 360 and 384 ft. which is yet unexplained. It may have something to do with the unusual conditions at 153 ft., and both may be connected with the supposed series of bays in the wall about to be described.

At 371 ft. there is again some trace of an extension of the foundation trench (or an earlier work) to the north, here 2 ft. 5 in. wide. It would fit in exactly with a continuation of the original straight course from the NW. corner. The evidence is quite clear (see fig. 114, W3), for the wall-trench is cut through the mortar rubble filling of an earlier foundation slot. This earlier one is 3 ft. 4 in. deep, the later is 4 ft. 2 in. The subsoil is hard yellowish loam. The rubble of the earlier trench is mixed with this loam, that of the later is homogeneous throughout, with no

loam. On the south side of the later wall the natural ground-level was not found within the limits of the trench (i.e. to 5 ft. south of the wall) until 25 in. down, and it sloped down to 36 in. against the wall. The wall-rubble lay over it to a great extent, but at the south end of the section, under the loose rubble, there was soil and pebbles, the latter very hard at the bottom. The subsoil here is hard yellow loam with *white flecks in it*.[2] On the north side of the wall the subsoil is fine gravel and sand, becoming red lower down.

At 450 ft. the subsoil is a very bright red sand. The wall-trench is clear, cut through an earlier trench of which nearly 5 ft. width is seen in the section (fig. 114, W4), again with a sloping surface to the natural yellow loam on the south. This earlier trench would approximately line up with the more southern of the lines of the wall of the *east* enclosure. At 475 ft., the last cut, the wall-trench was normal, with yellow loam at 12 in. and some spread of mortar from the wall on the south side.

At the corner itself a trench was cut, but work here was not of sufficient extent to be useful.

The return wall southwards was followed for only 67 ft. Jenkins had traced it for over 440 ft. and made the angle 84 degrees; we made it 82. For 8 ft. from the NE. angle its course was marked only by a dark and rather shapeless trench which may or may not have been made by Jenkins. Beyond this it was normal.

Up to the time of writing no more can be said about the temple temenos. We do not know how far south the east wall runs, nor have we any clue to the course of the south and SW. parts of the wall. There may also be buildings within it, so far unsuspected.

The Wall of the Great Eastern Enclosure

This wall presented some difficulty at first until we realized that we had two different and almost straight lines, parallel and about 4 ft. 6 in. apart centre to centre. The clue was found exactly 48 ft. from the NE. angle of the temenos, where there was a pronounced angle which joined the two lines, and therefore promised a sequence of rectangular bays. But the true significance of this was not proved until the plan was drawn out after the work was completed; otherwise we would have uncovered all the NW. angle of the temenos to find how the wall from the east joined on. As it is we must take Gilbert's plan, which shows the two returns (east and west) quite straight.

In section E1 (fig. 114)[3] the wall is shown returning southwards, while E2 shows it just before it does so. The bottom is 32 in. from the surface. In E2 was noted

---

[1] Possibly there were bays in this wall, as in the next.
[2] It is hard to believe this is not artificial.

[3] E1 is the E. wall of our trench, E2 the west wall of the same trench.

the appearance of an earlier trench under the wall with a filling of two colours, a curious white deposit (which may, however, be natural) below and a darker, brown soil above. This feature needs further examination. The return wall in E1 is, at its south end, clearly cut into an earlier foundation trench which is now full of comminuted rubble, with a septaria block near the top. The soil south of this is again white, but probably natural. A band of yellow loam, rubble, and gravel runs over all, but turns to gravel and earth near the south end of the section.

Corresponding to the position of the extended or earlier foundation trench in E1 a distinct mark crossed our trench obliquely (this was of the white earth already mentioned and may not be of serious significance) and led us to a curious feature on the west side of the bottom of the trench (see section E2). A hollow in the subsoil had been filled with a very stiff and hard red-brown clay mixed with small pieces of mortar. The position where we struck it may have been an angle, for the rounded hollow ran on westwards and appeared in the next trench, cut to look for it. But the same feature also ran southwards. This needs further exploration.

At 117 ft. the wall was on its southern line, at 206 ft. on its northern, presumably in a bay. Between 300 ft. and 360 ft. six trenches were cut, establishing a bay not less than 20 ft. long. But on our final plan, if the bays were accurately laid out symmetrically, this bay would be 30 ft. long. Moreover, at two spots 6–10 ft. south of the wall the plough was reported to have struck masonry, and these fall *exactly* 10 ft. east and west respectively of the ends of a 30-ft. bay. There would seem here to be some building running southwards from the wall and it would be 50 ft. wide.

At 490 ft. the wall was normal, on its southern line, and so it remained to a point 34 ft. from the NE. angle. Here it early presented such trouble that at last it was uncovered for two long lengths, which gave us the double return of each end of a bay. Thus the first bay came to light, which gave the clue to the others. It is 23 ft. 6 in. long over all, and the first return is 11 ft. from the NE. angle.

The total length of the north wall of the great enclosure is thus determined, at 615 ft. If we make the first bay on the west the same size as the last on the east they measure, centre to centre, 525 ft., and the halfway of this definitely falls in the middle bay, suggesting it was really central. To make it so, however, we have to suppose it was 30 ft. long instead of 23·5 ft., which is no difficulty, for it certainly was longer than the rest.

All the way along this wall the depth to the bottom of the foundation trench was normally 32 in., the width was usually 27 in., and the depth about a foot. At several points there were remains of a gravel floor on the inner side (e.g. in E3). The east wall was traced for some 10 ft., and its last 2 ft. consisted of large blocks of septaria without lime. The trench then stopped abruptly and we were unable to explore farther. The angle here is 81 degrees, so it is obviously meant to be parallel to Jenkins's N.–S. wall.

Very much more work is required on this wall, and the east and south sides are yet to be traced, though the farmer is able to indicate the line of the southern side by its contact with the plough. As to what the enclosure may contain, the air-photographs tell us nothing, but this perhaps means little, for it seems that it is only where walls were disturbed by *recent* stone-robbers (e.g. after Jenkins's work) that they show up clearly on the photographs, and where they were robbed in antiquity they seem largely to escape the camera.

3. THE THEATRE

In his account of the temple[1] Jenkins says: 'At the SW. extremity of the field [fig. 113] is a very large artificial mound not more than six feet high, but the top has evidently been lowered. The bottom on the west side was full of loose stones and Roman bricks; but in the centre of the mound nothing but earth was found, to the depth of the original soil. The earth of which the mound is formed differs from that of the soil of the field.' The O.S. map marks 'Roman pottery found 1842', presumably in Jenkins's exploration.

In 1948, after the discovery of the size of the temple enceinte, and the existence of the great eastern enclosure, the resemblance to the layout of Champlieu and other Gaulish sites led the writer to look for a theatre. The removal of the hedge had made the mound much more visible, and it proved to be almost exactly semicircular, and to extend about 300 ft. E.–W. by 200 ft. N.–S. These dimensions are approximate, for the ascent from the level field begins almost insensibly, so much has the mound been ploughed down. Only on the west side, where a hedge still exists, clearly preserving the old line of the wall of the theatre, if only for some 40 ft., is the edge of the mound still quite steep at the line of the wall. A preliminary survey showed that the highest point on each radius from the apparent centre lay on a semicircle. It only remained to find a masonry building and ascertain its plan.

A trench sunk at the highest point (A, fig. 115) proved Jenkins correct. The mound is artificial, of very light earth with no pebbles in it, and the height from the old turf line is 6 ft. Set into the old surface at the west end of the trench was a sleeper beam of large dimensions,

---

[1] *J.B.A.* ii (1847), 47.

crossing the trench obliquely. So we have to think of a wooden building as occupying the site first. A wholly similar, but smaller, trace was found cut away by the inner lip of the foundation trench of the perimeter wall at the NE. of the building.

The material of the mound is very distinctive. When first cut and damp it is compact, stiff, and 'cheesy', and distinctly whitish. After exposure the upcast be-

of the mound over it. The deepest point on this line was 5 ft. 5 in. at 37 ft. west of C, where there was some suggestion that a wall might run off both north and south. The east end of this wall was found 30 ft. east of C, where the last 3 ft. 6 in. of it was 6 in. narrower on the north side than elsewhere,[2] and the end of the trench was rounded, possibly not intentionally. If not, the wall must be shortened by a little.

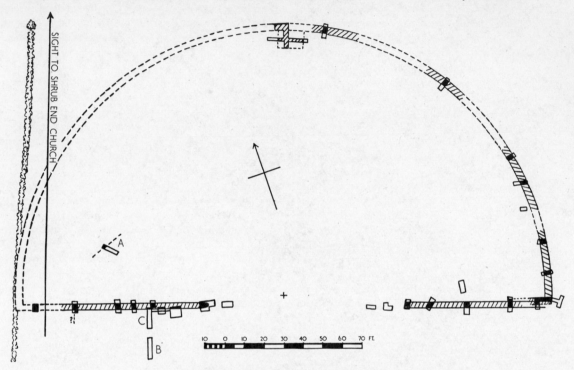

FIG. 115. Plan of theatre, Gosbecks, pp. 267–9.

comes perfectly soft and floury. It can only be the top few inches of turf and humus removed from the ground for some distance around.

The work of 1948 can be very briefly dismissed. There is much more mound than wall, and we looked for walls at too high a level, but at the end we had, we thought, two walls at point C, one E.–W. and one N.–S. They were simply foundation trenches, at a very low level, filled with chips of Kentish rag and mortar.

In the summer of 1949,[1] with the aid of some members of the Roman Essex Society, and other volunteers, work was resumed with the intention of following the plan of the walls, beginning from point C. There turned out to be only one wall, running E.–W., and its trench was 3 ft. wide. The depth varied according to the height

Some 70 ft. of this wall was thus traced, and it stopped at the right place for the orchestra, judging by the contours of the mound. The projection of its line enabled us to pick it up on the eastern arm of the mound. Trenches were cut, assuming the two walls to be on the same line. This is perhaps not so, for some difficulty was encountered, which has not yet been solved. The western two trenches have not found the wall, and although they are disturbed by tree-roots, they should show more traces of it than they do, if it was present. East of them 32 ft. of the wall were traced, apparently on the right line, but the last trenches at the SE. corner provide the conflicting evidence shown on the plan, which makes this wall apparently not straight. More work must be done here.

---

[1] *J.R.S.* xl, 107, xli, 134. We have to express, in the highest terms, our gratitude to the brothers Barber, tenants of Gosbecks Farm, for their cordial support at all times and their continued willingness in the promotion of our excavations and their inter-

est in them. Never has permission to dig been more willingly or lavishly granted.

[2] As at Aizani.

It was possible, however, to fix the inner SE. angle of the building, and this enabled us to begin tracing the perimeter wall. It proved exactly similar to that which we had been following—3 ft. wide and of the same depth. After the first two or three trenches the correct diameter was found, and thereafter, in each cut, the inner edge of the wall-trench was found exactly where expected. The trenches were cut deliberately to avoid an entrance, until we were nearly half-way round and the semicircular form of the wall could be regarded as proved. Then our last cut was made to see whether there was a central entrance at the north. There was. Removal of the top-soil showed that here was a rectangle, projecting inwards, but continuous with the perimeter wall, 13 ft. wide and extending 9 ft. inwards. It was not excavated.

The whole building, so far, is little more than a semi-circle, the centre being about 6 ft. inside the south face. The inner radius is 132 ft., the outer 135 ft. The over-all diameter is 270 ft., equivalent to 81·5 metres.[1] All the walls so far found served as retaining walls for the earth mound upon which the seats, stepped gangways, and concentric passage-ways were constructed of wood. The stone-robbers had worked from the outside, and in no place had they left any masonry in position. The wall-trenches were full of loose mortar, including very large lumps, chips of stone, and fragments of tile. The stone was almost entirely Kentish rag, with very little septaria. The rubble was very uneven. In places the trenches may be almost empty of it and difficult to trace; in other places they may be full to a considerable height, and often, in this case, the rubble contains many large stones. Some of these are irregular lumps from the foundations, others are roughly dressed facing-stones, their faces varying from 3 by 3½ in. to 3 by 5½ in. They are about 8 in. long and wedge-shaped. Tile is frequent, and one complete building tile was found lying flat in the body of the mound against the inner face of the wall. The SW. corner is, apparently, exactly under the hedge.

The site of the entrance on the north is 2 or 3 ft. east of the apparent centre-line. At this point the crest of the mound is perceptibly lower than elsewhere, and this suggests that the entrance was vaulted, passing into the interior at ground-level, and under the outer diazoma, which may have been 9 ft. wide.

A shallow trench was dug very quickly across the eastern arm of the mound from the perimeter wall towards the centre, taking advantage of the very white appearance of the mound material at about a foot depth. No traces of any concentric walls within the cavea were found, but this is, perhaps, not conclusive. A similar search was made with the idea that a pair of walls would continue the line of the north entrance towards the orchestra. This also was fruitless, but a better start will be gained by the excavation of the entrance.

The orchestra is still a problem. At the end of the wall and just east of it there was an old floor of pebbles at 3 ft. 6 in. depth. Efforts to find a wall for the orchestra have so far failed. When the material of the mound is disturbed (i.e. thrown down or ploughed), it becomes yellowish to brown, and that has happened around the orchestra. More work is needed here. No floor could be found, surprisingly, south of the south face, where there should have been entrances, for the mound material is solid to the north of the wall.

No determined effort has yet been made to find the stage-buildings, but tentative probing leads us to suspect that they were all of wood.

All our efforts so far have been directed solely to trying to recover the main outline of the plan. We are now satisfied that the building was a theatre. But since all the work was devoted to tracing wall-trenches, occupation levels and finds were not to be expected—except where we missed the walls. Mostly this occurred in mound material, which is barren. But even outside it we never found a recognizable occupation level with pottery, &c. No coin was found, and only a poor handful of pottery was found in brown disturbed earth some distance above the ancient ground-level, and therefore unstratified. It is of Antonine date. In a similar position on the west side a small fragment of Iron Age C pottery was recovered.

Though the field is strewn with tile and stone from Roman masonry the mound is on the whole neither more nor less so, but just beneath plough-level the old surface is sometimes found to be littered with masonry, presumably as left by the stone robbers. Among this litter was an iron spear-head with hollow socket. Nothing was found to date the destruction.

It is too early to discuss the form of this theatre in detail.

4. Site B

It remains to say something about B (fig. 113), which lies near the hedge and would be near the side of the former streamlet. A trial trench here was made in three sections.

The made ground is deep and is composed of washed material, deposited by water. The site must have been marshy. Most of the overburden is dark grey, formerly mud, the lighter deposit above having formed since draining. In Roman times the marsh-level was lower, and there had been here a kiln of some sort, built of

---

[1] A good average size, approximating to Drevant, Sanxay, and Vieux.

large pieces of building tiles, which included large seg-mental tiles for columns. All are much more orange-red than those found in Colchester, so presumably tiles for use in the buildings at Gosbecks were made on the spot. The kiln was so ruined that, in the space of one short trench its plan, and therefore its nature, was not recovered. The one fact gathered was that it had had a flue at least 2 ft. wide, which was marked by the usual glazing produced by the action of heat and wood ash on the clay walls. The floor of the flue was covered by about an inch of fine white substance, and then by an inch or more of charcoal and ashes. The few scraps of pottery found were all Roman, probably second century.

A trench cut parallel and to the west failed to find any continuation of the kiln. Instead it came upon well-preserved remains of a wooden structure, consis-ting of a horizontal member held by two vertical posts, the whole perfectly solid and immovable. Whether this is a building or is something connected with manipu-lating clay and water must be left to future investiga-tions.

The white material from the kiln we judge to be lime, and it is not improbable that this was a lime-kiln. It was not a potter's kiln.

5. THE FIELD WEST OF THE TEMPLE

This field (415) has long been known to show, when ploughed, parti-coloured patches, on which Roman pottery and tiles can be picked up. Since air-photo-graphs were taken (pl. XXXIX) about 1932 it has been known to contain a complicated system of ditches, which have been somewhat loosely termed 'Celtic Fields'. Since then other photographs have shown us much more of what is almost certainly the Romano-British field system, and only part of it can apply to this area. In any case an examination of the marks shows that they are not, so far as the major works are concerned, a field *system*. The only work done so far has been the cutting of a section across two of the ditches. The position of these two sections is seen by the two white spots on pl. XXXIX.

The main feature is a trapezoidal enclosure, appar-ently without entrance, but the east corner is invisible on any photograph. Its NW. and SW. sides are gently bulged outwards, and the SW. and SE. sides have a double ditch. It should be noted how the ditches vary in width and that the outer one wobbles considerably at the south angle. After these ditches we come to much narrower marks, some strong, some slight, and it has to be remembered that, comparing them with the temple site, some may be walls.

Next most noticeable is a large enclosure, including that already noticed and partly coinciding with its

SW. side. This large enclosure is different; its boun-daries (probably ditches) are straight, but the west corner is rounded. The north corner is angular and seems to have an entrance. Not far along the NE. side the trace seems to turn south and join an irregular and indefinite complex best seen on fig. 113. This is not a parallelogram, as one might gather from the plate, and the nature of its west side, as seen on fig. 113, is not borne out by the plate. On the latter, on the right, is a very strong trace, quite straight, which could be the SW. wall of our large enclosure.

A few strong traces confuse the issue. They run NW. from the north angle of the first enclosure, seeming on fig. 113 to form another angle outside it. To what extent they are part of the next complex to be men-tioned is uncertain.

We next come to the slightest marks, which are so light that they may indeed belong to the field system. They cover the rest of the field, but only invade the west part of the first enclosure. The oblique views of these ditches tend often to give an impression that they are rectangular in plan. In fact scarcely a rectangle can be found amongst them. They include traces of farm-roads serving fields. Similar marks are to be sus-pected in all the fields around and are actually visible in the field north of the Maldon Road.

As already suggested (*Camulodunum*, pp. 10 f.) it was thought possible that somewhere in or about field 415 might lie a pre-Cunobelin Iron Age settlement. Such a site would have a holy place which might well be developed into the large temple which we see. Un-fortunately this has produced nothing earlier than Cunobelin, though it has certainly hardly been ex-amined.

In June 1949 Lt.-Col. R. J. Appleby, assisted by Mr. E. C. Lamb and supervised by the author, made test sections across two of the ditches (E and F on fig. 113). The first was made just east of the footpath and parallel to it, cutting the NE. side of the first enclosure. At subsoil level the ditch was 18 ft. wide and 6 ft. deep, the depth from the modern surface being 8 ft.

The rapid silt was marked off from the upper filling by a spill of yellow sand on the north side. The filling was all uniform darkish earth, and it ran imperceptibly into the brown earth which occurs everywhere just under the plough level. The southern lip was 2 ft. from the surface, the northern nearly 18 in., the bottom 8 ft. The subsoil is red sand and gravel.

Nothing, unfortunately, was found in the rapid silt; the rest of the filling contained mostly Iron Age C pottery, but near the bottom were two pieces of thin buff flagon, presumably Roman, and two or three of the fragments of ollae were doubtfully Roman. Above these occurred fragments of blackish clay daub from a building (or clay hearth?), charcoal, and a fine Langton Down brooch of the straight pattern like *Cam.*, pl. xCIV, no. 89. There was also one fragment of sharply gritted 'Hallstatt' ware, which we attribute to Iron Age A. Nearer the top (at 4 ft.) Gallo-Belgic ware is represented by two fragments of f. Cam. 64 (black eggshell ware) and f. 120, by Roman grey chips, and two small chips of south Gaulish T.S., but the native ware was still in the majority. Recognizable native

(D) EARTHWORKS

1. THE ALTNACEALGACH SITE
(FIGS. 116, 117; PL. XLIII)

In 1939, in view of certain plans put forward for a new school, and of the suggestion that the Sheepen Dyke might have continued southwards across the Lexden Road, the writer was asked by H.M. Ministry of Works to make an archaeological reconnaissance of

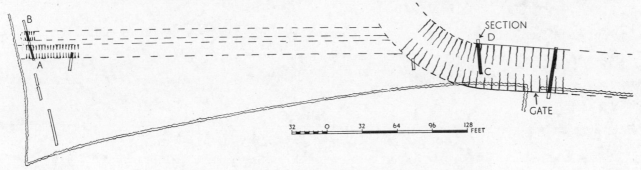

FIG. 116. Plan of ditches, Altnacealgach site. [W 17], pp. 271–3.

forms were Cam. ff. 64, 120, 212A(2), 229A(var.), 253?, and chip of lid, 271.

The trench was continued northwards for 16 ft. and south for 4 ft., but was barren.

The northern cut was across one of the smaller ditches, which appear secondary on the plan. From lip to lip at subsoil level (1 ft. below the surface) was 12 ft., and the depth was 3 ft. 6 in., or 4 ft. 6 in. from the surface. There was no noticeable rapid silt, and the major portion of the filling consisted of dark sandy loam, running imperceptibly into the brown earth. This filling formed a festoon, being 2 ft. 6 in. thick in the centre and thinning to about 9 in. at the lips. It was marked from the rest of the filling above by a clear old-surface line. This upper filling is of light sandy loam. The ditch must have lain a long time, visible to the eye, before being levelled for agricultural purposes.

The Roman content here is greater than in the first cut. The lower filling produced native fragments but also the following Roman: rim f. 16, chip of white bead-and-roll mortarium, fragments of flagon and amphora (f. 187), and two good fragments of red tile.

From the upper filling came a mixed lot of Roman and native fragments but also modern tile and pottery and clay-pipes, with some flattened buckshot. In filling-in a fragment of a T.N. cup f. 56 was found.

The evidence thus is that these ditches are pre-Roman in origin, but remained open late enough for Roman wares to get into them. The large ditch was the earlier and was, it seems, filled in before the smaller.

the school site. This occupied field 1222 on the 25-in. O.S. map, Essex, N. xxxvii, 2. The school has not been built, and the site is still vacant.

A series of short trenches was cut from the north end of the spinney on the west of the field to the east hedge, the line almost coinciding with that of a hedge or fence shown on the 1923 map, but of which no trace remained in 1939. This was done in such a manner that no ditch or other feature of any size could pass this line without detection.

The result was negative. The natural subsoil was found at a depth of about 2 ft.

A similar series was then cut parallel to the south side of Park Road, from the NE. corner of the garden of Altnacealgach to a point NW. of the buildings where we actually overlapped the line of the first series. Again nothing was found, although P. G. Laver told us that burial urns had been found in Park Road, approximately opposite the buildings, and the workmen said they had heard that skeletons had been found in the NW. corner of the garden. The subsoil here was about 2 ft. from the surface, but at frequent intervals it dipped as if we were crossing small ditches at oblique angles, but in no case was anything found to suggest that these were artificial.

21. One or two trenches were then cut in the centre of field 1222 near the spot where the O.S. map marks *Roman Amphora found* A.D. *1907* (grave 163 in the Museum). Here the subsoil was about the same depth, but we were digging in a cheesy brown loam which made it difficult to decide between made and undisturbed ground. In it at one spot were stains of charcoal and a few sherds of pottery. They were very fragmentary; what could be recognized was of second-century date.

17. Before abandoning the area it was decided to test the west side of the field, where the long spinney

A series of trenches was next cut along the north side of the second field to the south (1273), by the kind permission of Mr. Charlsley. The result was negative. Attention was turned again to the west side of the spinney, but our ditch was not found again till we were back to within 50 ft. of our first trench. Here it was found to be turning sharply westwards. Underesti-

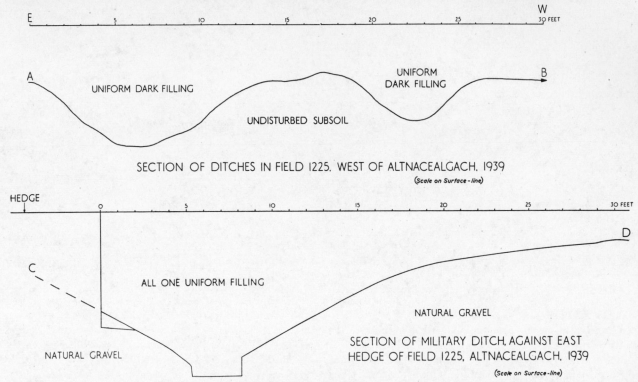

SECTION OF DITCHES IN FIELD 1225, WEST OF ALTNACEALGACH, 1939

(Scale on Surface-line)

SECTION OF MILITARY DITCH, AGAINST EAST HEDGE OF FIELD 1225, ALTNACEALGACH, 1939

(Scale on Surface-line)

FIG. 117. At top, ditches at (**W 17B**), p. 272; below, ditch at (**W 17A**), p. 272.

looked like an old boundary. Permission was readily granted by the Post Office to trench in the next field west (1225). The first trench was cut immediately west of the north end of the spinney and at right angles to it. It at once revealed a large ditch running N.–S., which we naturally thought to be a continuation of the Sheepen Dyke. The whole width could not be cleared because of the hedge which covered the eastern side.

The section (fig. 117) was, however, not that of a dyke. The ditch proved to be of V-shape, with a rectangular trench about 1 ft. deep and 2 ft. wide along the bottom. The maximum depth was 9 ft. 7 in. and the filling was an even mass of dirty sand, gravel, and loam. In the bottom were two or three small sherds of pottery, two of soft Roman buff ware (flagon) and one of rough, romanizing, grey-black cooking-pot ware, as found commonly on the Sheepen site and dated Claudius–Nero. The total width of the ditch must have been at least 32 ft.

mating this turn we again sought it along the south hedge, and there found two small ditches (**17B**). These also run N.–S., and are of rounded outline. The eastern was 14 ft. wide by 4 ft deep from the old level, and the western, following after an interval of only 4 ft., was 8 ft. wide by about 3 ft. deep but was wider in the north side of the trench, as if coming to a butt-end. There was nothing distinctive about the filling of dirty sandy gravel and loam. Another small trench cut farther north checked the eastern ditch, which seemed to be running on a straight course; but the two need not be parallel.

The next move was to examine the point at which the two small ditches should join the large one, towards the centre of the field. But permission could not be obtained. The final cut therefore was made 25 ft. north of the spinney to confirm the course of the large ditch. In doing this we were able to cut through the hedge and so obtain the full width, which proved to be 40 ft. The trench was not carried to the bottom.

It now seems possible, even probable, that this is the ditch of a semi-permanent camp or fort, one angle of which we have found. The NE. angle may well lie under the two cottages on Park Road, for the angular parcel numbered 1224 on the O.S. map is all below the normal ground-level and may represent the partly filled ditch. If it gives us the position of the NW. angle, it indicates a camp of almost rhomboid shape. The sides would be about 450 by 320 ft. long (inside the ditches) and the area about 2·84 acres.[1]

As for the two ditches to the south, there was some suspicion in our trench that the western one was just coming to a butt-end. In any case we obtained no check on its direction. The other runs on as if to join the larger ditch, and it, possibly the other as well, might be the ditch of an annex lying south of the main camp.[2]

2. THE 'CAMP DITCH' AT GURNEY BENHAM HOUSE

The plan (fig. 1) shows how Mr. Hall's researches have traced the road from the Balkerne Gate to this house, but not beyond, and his discoveries of other roads converging in a remarkable manner upon the same point. This most naturally suggested that hereabouts lay the entrance to an important site antedating the colonia and therefore probably military. The diagram as now drawn out may possibly not be so readily explained in this way, but if we have indeed so many roads running in so many different places and directions as our survey of them shows, it seems very probable that some of them not only lead to military sites but may be interior streets of such sites. The problem is to find the defences of these military works.

Now the south ditch of the three-track road (p. 6) is large, and different from the north ditch. Moreover, it is not quite parallel with the road, but converges upon it towards the east, and is accompanied by a small slot or gully in the southern track of the road, which is quite parallel to it. Their line is parallel with the south face of Gurney Benham House, but the line of the road is 3½ degrees different. Mr. Hall thinks that it possibly is deflected a little by the ditch, which would thus prove to be the earlier of the two.

In *Camulodunum* (p. 20) we suggested that this ditch had a character at least not incompatible with that of a military camp. The point has now to be reviewed critically, for it was not possible to go into details then. The outline of the ditch is rounded, and not V-shaped. The impression gained from it is that it is in some respects irregular, so that one wonders whether it is an unfinished military ditch, or a spoil-trench for gravel for the road, or of some other character.[3] Mr. Hall has pursued it into the next garden to the west of Gurney Benham House, where, in a very small space, and with the remarkable kindness and forbearance of the late Mrs. P. Green, J.P., he was able to sink some trial pits, which had to go to depths of 10 or 11 ft.

The results are not at all convincing.

At CD/7 two points were found where the north lip of the ditch could be identified, and just clear of the lip, that is to the north, of one of them there seemed to be a post-hole.

At CD/8 there was an interruption of the ditch, like a crossing, where most of the ditch had not been excavated, and the slightly lower level on the line of the ditch may have been due to wearing-down. The crossing was only examined in the southern half of the ditch-line. East of CD/8 the ground was disturbed down to 9 ft., but here we ran into foundations of old buildings and nothing further could be obtained in this direction (e.g. at CD/4).

Where examined, says Mr. Hall, the crossing at CD/8 had a vertical face to the east, while the west edge was taken down in wide steps. It was not wide enough to have been intended for a road, but it may have been used as a path across the ditch. Upon it, in a brown layer which capped it, were found two coins of Domitian.

---

[1] In 1955 a sewer trench has been cut southwards from Leeden Road across the E. half of the 'camp'. There was no ditch on either the N. or S. side of our conjectured 'camp'; instead, a smaller ditch, possibly the eastern of the pair just mentioned, was found running E.–W. in the SE. corner of field 1225, so that we now do not know what to conjecture of this layout.

[2] But since this was written, Mr. A. F. Hall has pointed out that the eastern of these two ditches can be seen as a crop mark running on southwards a considerable distance, and not quite straight, across field 1265.

[3] Mr. Hall has since found an apparently analogous ditch on the north of the NW. road near C3, which he thinks supports the spoil-trench theory.

At CD/10 the most complete section was secured, and even this has had to be completed by the addition of three lines from other trenches. It shows a rounded ditch of about 16 ft. wide and 5 ft. deep (from the old surface). It is buried 5 ft. deep under made earth. The filling showed a sandy silt falling in from the north and earthy silt from the south. Above this there were two marked festoons of dense rubbish. Lumps of gravel conglomerated by iron ('pudding-stone'), but unusually black, were found in the lower festoon. The pottery has been dated by Professor Hawkes as from mid-first century A.D. to early second century at the level of oysters and broken tile which runs over the ancient deposits.

At CD/1 undisturbed subsoil was found in the line of the ditch, with a small post-hole in it, at a depth of just over 4 ft. A trench cut eastwards from this soon found the edge of the gravel, which proved to be a vertical face running SW.–NE. The depth to the gravel lip was 5 ft., and to the bottom 10 ft. The filling was presumably of Roman date, but barren.

Two trenches were cut at CD/3 and one seemed to produce a north lip for the ditch at 11 ft. north of the house (no. 17 Beverley Road). Another trench was opened, but the excavators came upon a skeleton and the trench was filled in. But the evidence at CD/1 suggested that the ditch was turning to the south, and a further trench at CD/2 was dug[1] to a depth of 10 ft. in made soil. To a depth of 6 ft. this seemed disturbed, but below it seemed old filling, and in it, at 7½ ft., lay a complete bowl, f. 246, inverted; near the bottom lay fragments of a bead-rimmed porringer with bevelled foot and latticed sides, which is of late-first- to mid-second-century date (f. 37).

Thus since the ditch seemed to turn south, Mr. Hall tried to find it at CD/11, south of Gilberd House. The result was negative. The lip which appeared at CD/3 was not examined very thoroughly, but if it was truly a lip it could well belong to a smaller ditch belonging to the road. An attempt to pursue this line at CD/9 in Mr. Curry's garden again brought the excavators down upon a skeleton at 5 ft. depth, and the trench was abandoned.

The great amount of work which Mr. Hall has put in on this search was justified by the hope of finding a military enclosure. In the end, when we review the results, we are bound to come to the conclusion that this end has not been achieved. The vertical faces at CD/8 and CD/1, the narrow crossing, the rounded outline of the ditch, all combine against a military origin. The varied finish, rounded, stepped, vertical faces, and small 'crossing' all speak for an unfinished work, or a trench simply cut to obtain gravel for the road. The trench then seems to have been filled up fairly quickly, to the level where the festoons appear. The sandy silt from the north would wash from the road-works, the earthy silt from the south from the top-soil of the excavation, thrown out on that side.

Since it is of the highest interest to know whether there was a military enclosure in the neighbourhood of the Grammar School, it seems to be to the point to publish the following observations on a trench traversing the area, and also to remark that many short trenches have been watched from time to time in the whole area of the west cemetery, but never have any remains of military equipment turned up. The old surface may have been destroyed, but there is certainly no perceptible military occupation.

The trench began in Wellesley Road and was 2 ft. deep. Opposite no. 24[2] there was a skeleton just under the surface. Nothing further was found until Creffield Road was reached, when a few sherds of Samian turned up. The trench then followed the south side of Creffield Road. Up to half-way along, the soil was 3 ft. deep black mould, then became sandy, ending as clean sand immediately under the surface at the top of the hill. Opposite the back entrance of St. Alban's House two Roman rubbish-pits were cut through. The first was about 6 ft. wide and 3 ft. deep, containing a few coarse sherds and oyster-shells. The second was 12 ft. wide and over 3 ft. deep; the bottom was not reached. It contained quantities of pottery, bones, and oyster-shells, a bow-shaped fibula and a needle. The brooch and pottery are mid-first century (ff. 108, 119, 154), but this dating is vitiated by the presence of a scaled colour-coated beaker f. 396 and a T.S. base f. 18/31 stamped OFRONTI . . .

Nothing further was found until the corner of Beverley Road was reached, when grave 230 was found near the back door of no. 11 (**160**) Beverley Road, and, on the corner, grave 229, which is second century, containing a T.S. dish f. 18/31 stamped NASSOF.

The trench continued along the north side of Queen's Road, and along the Folley to Park Road. Another rubbish-pit was cut behind St. Mary's Lodge (at **119**). It contained many sherds of coarse Roman wares, including a jar f. 266,[3] which is first century, but the majority were Antonine or later. From Queen's Road onwards a smaller trench, less than 2 ft. deep, was cut. 'This undoubtedly explains why nothing was found in the grounds of Altnacealgach and at the back of Lexden Park' (*C.M.R.* 1929, 24).

This trench is a fair example of the nature of the terrain and what is likely to be found.

---

[1] By Mr. Reginald A. Smith.   [2] About midway between **43** and **177**.   [3] *C.M.R.* 1929, pl. VIII, 475.28.

3. VARIOUS WORKS ON FIELDS 1266 AND 1266A

The fact that the Laver Line crossed these fields led Mr. Hall to dig in an attempt to prove or disprove that line. As we have said, his trenches, cut in the SW. angle of 1266a, proved quite negative. He found reason, however, to do further work, and apart from the temple, which is described in a separate section, we have now to relate his other findings.

At the north end of the same field there is undoubtedly a large excavation extending to 5 ft. deep and containing Roman and sixteenth- to seventeenth-century pottery. It has not been explored sufficiently to give its outline and it cannot be said whether it may be a military work of the siege of 1648, or an ancient ditch, or even simply a gravel pit of comparatively recent date. Here was found the bronze statuette of Jupiter in 1844. There must be both recent and ancient disturbance here, for the Jupiter cannot have been disturbed, nor the cinerary urn of first-century date which was found at the spot marked (20). Thus Mr. Hall reports a small ditch (marked on plan) 'curiously constructed'. In this was much Roman pottery at one point, including a fluted beaker of f. 407 (third or fourth century) in fragments.

Midway along the west hedge there was another small ditch. 'Not far east is spectacular gravelling on natural gravel top', but this is not, it seems, to be associated with the Laver Line.[1]

Along the south side of field 1266 Mr. Hall has long struggled with features, especially a ditch or ditches, which appear and disappear. This area is not yet understood. In the SW. corner of the field, however, is a feature which is regular enough. It is part of a long oval hollow (now filled, and level with the surface) exactly 100 ft. wide and, so far, at least 250 ft. long. It continues under the next field. The floor in the middle is quite flat, at 6 ft. below the surface, and is formed of a layer of pebbles set in clay, which becomes incredibly hard in dry weather. The sides have a slight slope, steepest at the margin. What this feature may be is so far unknown.

South of the temple traces have been found of a small ditch or trench nearly parallel to the south hedge of field 1266. So far it is the only place outside the temple enclosure which yields building material. There is a straight line of tile and stone debris, about 2 ft. wide with very little lying off the line. It would therefore be evidence for a wall were it not for the fact that there is not a trace of mortar anywhere in it.

(E) COINS

Roman coins have been found in such quantities in Colchester that we find Wire, in the middle of the nineteenth century, casually recording that he sold to a customer 'about a peck' of them. The several collectors also collected coins, and Charles Gray had two cabinets of them and a manuscript catalogue. Some, if not all, of these coins reached the Museum, but not the catalogue. The others had collections in proportion. We are told that Taylor's were chiefly of the early Empire, as if this were unusual. Normally the series should run from consulars to Honorius, as did Duncan's. Speaking of the coins from the western cemetery generally, Duncan says that those of Carausius abound, but those of the Constantines are 'in excess'. The Grammar School site produced comparatively few.

As will be seen from the general list here appended, his remark on Carausius is not borne out by the facts, and, indeed, the coins of Carausius found at Colchester are not more numerous than on comparable sites, nor do they exhibit a larger proportion of the mint-marks C, CC, or CL, which have been attributed to Colchester.

The question of the mints of Carausius and Allectus has been exhaustively studied by Mr. P. H. Webb.[2] The three chief and certain ones are indicated by the letters L, C, and R, of which the first and last stand for Londinium and Rotomagus (Rouen). The C mint

---

[1] Subsequently Mr. Hall tells me that he is not at all convinced even yet that there is nothing at all on the Laver Line, but that he suspects certain traces here in field 1266a and at the entrance through Gryme's Dyke, not, however, suggestive of a main road.

[2] In *The Reign and Coinage of Carausius; The Coinage of Allectus;* and in vol. v of *The Roman Imperial Coinage.*

remains a matter of debate, though generally accepted as Camulodunum (or Colonia), as it provisionally is by Webb. Claims have been put forward for Corinium (Cirencester) and Clausentum (Bitterne, near Southampton). But we occasionally find the mark CC, which fits for Colonia Claudia or Colonia Camulodunensis better than Corinium. CL, which occurs on coins of Allectus, and a CLA, doubtfully recorded by Stukeley, have been used in attempts to place the C mint at Clausentum. It is regarded as certain that C and CL were used at the same mint, for the style of all the C coins is uniform and distinct. This being so, Clausentum can hardly be regarded as having held the status compatible with an important mint-city, even if it was, for the time, the headquarters of the British fleet. Mr. Webb further points out that about the time CL appears Lugdunum (Lyon) in Gaul was using C as a mint-mark, and the L may have been added to the British mark to distinguish it.

The QC of the Colchester mint is explained as including a mark of value (Q = quinarius), for, with one exception, the coins are of smaller size than the others.

Generally speaking the lettering of the Colchester mint is better than that of London, the strokes of A and V joining accurately in a point, for example, and the styles are distinguishable even without the mint-marks.[1] Of the Colchester mint Mr. Webb says: 'The coins of Colchester are generally neater in execution, but there is perhaps greater virility in the London portraiture. It is probable that the mint at Colchester was not established until some time after that of London, and therefore produced few, if any, coins of the roughest style. Some of its later pieces are the work of a very competent engraver, well designed and well centred, but perhaps a little conventional. The improvement in the work of both mints may be due in part to the influence of imported engravers, though the distinctive British style was never lost.'[2]

After the death of Allectus in A.D. 296 the Romans did not maintain a mint at Colchester, and we have no record of coins struck here until the Saxon King Æthelred II began to mint his Danegeld here.

Up to the time when the writer took charge of the Museum nearly all the coins, however secured, had been selected as Museum specimens, and in consequence the aggregate list was not representative and was particularly weak in those reigns in which the coinage is normally bad but common. Since 1926 all coins have been accepted (provided they were of local provenance), and the reigns of the Gallic usurpers and of the late fourth century, and the 'barbarous' issues in general, have rapidly swollen in numbers. The list therefore is more representative than it was, but is still unbalanced, and the many years of excavation on the Sheepen site have resulted in an overloading of coins up to about A.D. 60, which is not balanced by any large excavation in the colonia itself, for the work of 1927–9 was not extensive.

Nevertheless the increase in numbers under Vespasian shows that vigorous economic development did not have to wait for Agricola. The figures thereafter are not abnormal in comparison with other towns. There is the usual gap in the early third century, on which (and on the whole subject) see O'Neil in *Arch. Journ.* xcii, 64 ff. There is no evidence in our series to support any idea that the Roman way of life continued in Colchester to a later date than in any other Romano-British town.

Not included in the list are several hoards of coins which have been found in or about the town. The most notable of these was the large hoard of denarii and antoniniani which was reported in full in *Num. Chron.* 1891, 413 ff. (and see *J.R.S.* xxii, 92). Of the 3,169 coins, the last of which is dated to about A.D. 233, 351 are in Colchester Museum, the rest in the Evans Collection in the Ashmolean Museum.[3]

---

[1] Though not, of course, invariably.
[2] *Roman Imperial Coinage*, v (2), 433.
[3] Letter from Sir John Evans in Museum letter-book. The hoard was found in a bronze jug (*C.M.R.* 1907, 4) in the vicinity

(it is said) of an old barn on the Maldon Road. The law of treasure trove which prevailed at the time caused it to be concealed, with the result that nothing more is known concerning it. The jug is in the Museum.

A hoard of antoniniani came into the hands of Alderman A. M. Jarmin. Of this also nothing whatever is known, except that it was found in Colchester.[1] The coins are in very poor condition and consist of Victorinus (11), the Tetrici (22), and one of Claudius Gothicus.

Much more interesting is another third-century hoard reported by Mr. A. H. Baldwin.[2] It came to light in 1927, with the statement that it was found whilst rebuilding an old wall a few miles from Colchester—a most doubtful story. The coins were in a pot which was broken and lost. They came into the hands of a local man, who told no one in Colchester, and it is not known now where the hoard is. It consists of 298 coins ranging from Gallienus to Maximian, but of these no less than 102 are of Carausius and 167 of Allectus.[3] Of the former, 51 were of the London mint and 24 of Colchester; of the latter, 114 London and 53 Colchester. One Maximian was struck at Colchester.

Whether to be considered as the same as one of the preceding, or quite different, we read that 'Early in August [1906?] a considerable find of Roman coins was made in Colchester and about 50 of them have been secured by Dr. Laver and deposited in the Museum together with fragments of the vessel in which they were found . . .'; all were of the reigns of Gallienus, Victorinus, and Tetricus. The remains of the vessel cannot be identified, nor the coins.

A hoard of forty barbarous coins held by the Rev. J. H. Pollexfen passed from him to Mr. Golding of Sudbury and thence to Mr. W. C. Wells, who bought them in 1901 and allowed Mr. H. Mattingly to publish them.[4] It seems that they were probably found in Colchester between 1870 and 1880. There are thirty-one imitations of the radiate coins of A.D. 265–73, one of Constantinopolis, and seven of FEL.TEMP. REPARATIO type. The wear of all coins is about the same, so all are approximately contemporary. It follows that the barbarous radiates were being made at the same time (or nearly) as the barbarous Constantinian.

A small pottery unguent pot found at Colchester full of coins of Constans was in Museum Disneianum. *Arch. Journ.* vi. 85 (1849).

A small hoard of fourth-century coins, forty-nine in number, all very small, are of Constans, Gratian, Gratian? (7); Valentinian II, Theodosius; Arcadius (16), Arcadius? (4), Honorius, and 14 unidentified. It was found in West Lodge Road. There is no record of the circumstances. *C.M.R.* 1927, 23 (C.M. 5291.26).

The small hoard of Claudian coins found in insula 11 has been mentioned on p. 104.

On 3/4/1845 Wire wrote: 'A lad said that not long since two small lead boxes containing gold and silver coins were found there [the Union House]. . . .'

On 19/3/1849 he wrote: 'On Friday last [16/3/49] a hoard of 800 brass coins was found at the Union House in a heap, and had probably been buried together in a wooden box, as fragments of wood were discovered with them. I purchased 263 of them, they are very small and *many among them were blanks* [our italics]. From what few of them could be read they are Constantine the Great, and probably were intended to pass current during the Saxon period, as no coins have as yet been appropriated to the East Saxon kingdom, and no doubt were buried in some emergency.'

LIST OF ROMAN COINS KNOWN TO HAVE BEEN FOUND IN COLCHESTER

This list will also serve as a list of the Roman Emperors, with their dates.

Republican (up to 27 B.C.) . . . . . 48 }	
Marcus Antonius (died 30 B.C.) . . . . 16 } 66	
Julius Caesar (died 44 B.C.) . . . . . 2 }	
Augustus, 27 B.C.–A.D. 14 30	
Tiberius, A.D. 14–37 21	
M. Agrippa, Claudian 42	
Germanicus 10	
Caligula 37–41 68	
Claudius I, A.D. 41–54 . . . . . 239[5]	
Antonia, wife of Claudius 21	
Agrippina, mother of Nero 2	
Nero, A.D. 54–68 128	
Galba, A.D. 68–69 7	
Otho, A.D. 69 2	
Vitellius, A.D. 69 6	
Vespasian, A.D. 69–79 299	
Titus, A.D. 79–81 19	
Domitian, A.D. 81–96 169	
Nerva, A.D. 96–98 30	
Trajan, A.D. 98–117 201	
Plotina, wife of Trajan 2	
Illegible first century 42	
Hadrian, A.D. 117–38 238	
Sabina, wife of Hadrian 17	
Aelius Caesar, A.D. 135/6–138 7	
Antoninus Pius, A.D. 138–61 208	
Faustina senior, wife of Pius 67	
Marcus Aurelius, A.D. 161–80 136	
Faustina junior, wife of Aurelius 68	
Lucius Verus, died A.D. 169 16	

[1] C.M. 1119.06, definitely acquired and presented by Jarmin.
[2] *Num. Chron.* 1930, 174.
[3] The Jarmin hoard could be part of this.
[4] *Num. Chron.* 1934, 255.

[5] No attempt has been made to distinguish between orthodox issues and the copies used as occupation money, on which see C. H. V. Sutherland in *Camulodunum*, 142 ff.

Lucilla, wife of Verus	27
Commodus, A.D. 180–92	57
Crispina, wife of Commodus	12
Pertinax, A.D. 192	2
Clodius Albinus, A.D. 193–7	6
Illegible second century	35
Illegible first or second century	55
Septimius Severus, A.D. 193–211	104
Julia Domna, wife of Severus	51
Caracalla, A.D. 198–217	66
Plautina, wife of Caracalla	5
Geta, A.D. 209–12	38
Macrinus, A.D. 217–18	2
Elagabalus, A.D. 218–22	42
Julia Paula, wife of Elagabalus	2
Julia Severa, second wife of Elagabalus	2
Julia Soaemias, mother of Elagabalus	10
Julia Maesa, grandmother of Elagabalus	17
Severus Alexander, A.D. 222–35	78
Julia Mammaea, wife of Alexander	25
Orbiana, second wife of Alexander	1
Maximian, A.D.	8
Maximinus, A.D. 235–8	12
Maximus, A.D. 235–8	2
Balbinus, A.D. 238	1
Pupienus, A.D. 238	1
Gordian III, A.D. 238–44	53
Philip I, A.D. 244–9	37
Philip junior, A.D. 244–9	5
Otacilia, wife of Philip senior	7
Hostilian, A.D. 249–51	1
Trajan Decius, A.D. 249–51	6
Etruscilla, wife of Decius	2
Herennius, A.D. 249–51	3
Trebonianus Gallus, A.D. 251–3	8
Volusian, A.D. 251–4	3
Valerian I, A.D. 253–9	30
Valerian II, A.D. 253–5	5
Saloninus, A.D. 253–9	7
Gallienus, A.D. 253–68	194
Salonina, wife of Gallienus	42
Postumus, A.D. 259–68	88
Victorinus, A.D. 268–70	145
Tetricus I and II, A.D. 270–3	628
Marius, A.D. 267	2
Claudius Gothicus, A.D. 268–70	212
Quintillus, A.D. 270	124
Claudius or Quintillus	2
Aurelian, A.D. 270–5	11
Severina, wife of Aurelian	1
Tacitus, A.D. 275–6	9
Florian, A.D. 276	2
Probus, A.D. 276–82	25
Carus, A.D. 282–3	2
Carinus, A.D. 282–5	3
Illegible radiate heads (many probably barbarous)	557
Barbarous radiate heads	38
Diocletian, A.D. 284–313	24[1]
Maximianus Herculeus, A.D. 286–308	15

Carausius, A.D. 287–93	143
Allectus, A.D. 293–6	72
Constantius I, A.D. 293–306	9
Helena, wife of Constantius	60
Theodora, second wife of Constantius	51
Galerius Maximian, A.D. 293–311	4
Severus II, A.D. 305–7	1
Maximin Daza, A.D. 305–13	4
Maxentius, A.D. 306–12	2
Licinius I, A.D. 303–24	33
Licinius II, A.D. 317–24	8
Constantine the Great, A.D. 306–37	354[2]
Fausta, wife of Constantine	2
Crispus, A.D. 317–26	38
Delmatius, A.D. 335–7	1
Constantine II, A.D. 317–40	182
Constans, A.D. 333–50	243
Constantius II, A.D. 324–61	157
Constantinian	450
Magnentius, A.D. 350–3	54
Decentius, A.D. 351–3	10
Fel. Temp. Reparatio	72
Julian, A.D. 355–63	6
Valentinian I, A.D. 364–75	95
Valens, A.D. 364–78	124
Securitas Reipublicae	14
Gratian, A.D. 367–83	56
Valentinian II, A.D. 375–92	17
House of Valentinian	10
Theodosius I, A.D. 379–95	24
Magnus Maximus, A.D. 383–8	4
Eugenius, A.D. 392–4	2
Arcadius, A.D. 395–408	38
Honorius, A.D. 395–408	15
Theodosian	102
Gloria Romanorum	10
Gloria Novi Saeculi	1
Salus Reipublicae	13
Victoria Auggg.	4
Illegible	888
Justinian I, A.D. 527–65	1
Leo, A.D. 457–74	1[3]

Finally, mention should be made of the presumably fictitious coin published in Bishop and Norton's Camden (1607), pp. 67 and 73, purporting to be issued by the Colonia on its foundation. The obverse reads TI.CLAVD.CAES.AVG.GER.P.M.TR. P.XII.IMP.XIIX (a legend totally different from any other known, and the latest date known is TR.P.XI = A.D. 52), and the reverse, showing a veiled figure with two oxen yoked to a plough (illustrating the foundation ceremony) reads COL. CAMALODON.AVG.

The misspelling of Camulodunum gives it away, and the fact that no such coin has ever been seen. Later editions of Camden illustrate it as a middle brass with the legend given above, but every text omits the P.M. It was reproduced by Rouse in his *Views of Hastings Castle*, but was rejected at last by Gough, Camden (1789) in note D on p. lxx.

[1] The paucity of coins of Diocletian and his colleagues, who reigned comparatively long, is remarkable when compared with those of the short reigns of Carausius and Allectus.

[2] Including impersonal coins such as Constantinopolis, Urbs Roma, and Populus Romanus, many of which were probably issued by succeeding emperors.

[3] These last two coins are said to have been found in Colchester, but the circumstances are unknown.

(F) APPENDIX ON POTTERY

For the right understanding of much that has been printed in this book it is necessary to add a conspectus of the Roman pottery of Colchester. It is impossible to convey, to those who have not had first-hand knowledge of it, the size and scope of the collection in the Museum—not to mention the collections from Colchester in other museums.

It is not the purpose of this book to publish the Roman pottery of Colchester,[1] but reference to the pottery of individual finds has been necessary throughout.[2] The practice of using form-numbers to describe the type of vessel meant has proved the only way to avoid long and repeated descriptions and reiteration of paltry drawings of rims. For the early period the form-numbers used in *Camulodunum* have proved almost completely adequate, for the later period the normal work of the Museum demanded they should be extended. This was done, but it became clear that the Camulodunum forms should have been numbered in groups (i.e. platters, bowls, flagons, &c., should each have formed a group numbered from one onwards so that new forms could be added to the group). Failing this it has not been possible to keep to groups, as was done there. In the following list, already so rooted in the Museum records that no alteration to it can be contemplated, some numbers have been placed in the gaps left for the purpose in the Camulodunum series, but most extend beyond it.

Properly any such conspectus as this should conclude a careful treatment of the contents of the hundreds of graves from the cemeteries, of the many potters' kilns, and of the fragments from the Roman occupation levels. Each form should have a description and statement of the evidence for dating. All this has been quite impossible for this volume, and all we can hope to do is to present the forms, with a chronological table to show our present ideas of their dating.

The value of the present report is that it publishes the pottery from a rubbish-pit dating from about A.D. 100, and the great quantity found in the lowest layer of the 'Mithraeum', with a coin of Constans. The pottery from the Colchester kilns will, it is hoped, follow immediately in another report. There is no present hope of publication of the cemeteries.

The following list is merely explanatory in function and remains unpublished in detail. The proper place and time for that is with the Roman cemeteries of Colchester. We give here the briefest possible summary of what we can say, or what we feel we dare say, about the forms and their dating.

At the moment of writing, it must be admitted that for various reasons it is seldom possible to do more than Koenen did so many years ago when he divided the forms of vessels between Early, Middle, and Late Empire.[3] Lack of systematic excavation is chiefly responsible for this, especially lack of material known to be Hadrianic, and lack of dates in the third and fourth centuries. It is unfortunate that we have to print this list before making a final revision

---

[1] May's *Catalogue of the Roman Pottery in the Colchester and Essex Museum*, published in 1930, covered little more than half the collection at the time, and the collection must have at least doubled since. The report on *Camulodunum*, published in 1947, contains a very full account of the pottery of the site up to about A.D. 65. In it the coarse pottery is catalogued by *forms* (i.e. by shape rather than by material or colour).

[2] And lack of space has compelled this to be reduced to a minimum.

[3] *Gefässkunde*, 1895.

of the dates of the graves. When this is done it is almost inevitable that many alterations will have to be made. We hope, however, that they will not be of a major character.

A time-chart like that in Camulodunum had to be abandoned for lack of space. The information given is cut to a minimum and the full account must be given elsewhere. Attention is chiefly given to form and dating, but fabric and incidence receive what attention is possible.

TABLE OF FORMS OF POTTERY VESSELS

Nos. 1–275 have been published in *Camulodunum*, with some gaps left for insertions. The latter are marked by an asterisk. Of the later numbers nearly all are standard forms; very few rare forms have been included. The dating is from local sources, which we consider most desirable in Roman coarse wares. Numbers marked with a dagger are not illustrated here, those lower than 275 will be found in the *Camulodunum* plates.

1. Terra nigra platter. Scarce. Tiberian.
2. Terra nigra platter. Highly polished. Common. A.D. 25–50.
3. Terra rubra and terra nigra platters. Common. A.D. 25–50.
4. Variants of last, terra nigra. Rare. A.D. 25–50.
5. Terra rubra and terra nigra platters. Common. A.D. 25–50.
6. Terra rubra platters. Scarce. Tiberian.
7. Terra rubra and terra nigra platters. Common. A.D. 25–50.
8. Terra rubra and terra nigra platters. Common. A.D. 25–50.
9. Fine terra nigra platters. Rare. Claudian.
10. Fine terra nigra platters. Rare. Claudian.
11. Terra rubra platters. Rare. A.D. 25–50.
12. Terra nigra platters. Very common. A.D. 25–50.
13. Terra nigra platters. Not so common. Claudian.
14. Poor terra nigra, or (mostly) grey. Common. Claudian and later.
15. Fine terra nigra. Fairly frequent. Claudian.
16. Terra nigra and fine grey. Common. Claudius–Flavian.
17. Pompeian red, becoming very debased, finally Roman grey. Claudius–Flavian.

But this type occurs in various wares and forms throughout the Roman period.

21–33 are 'sub-belgic', that is native imitations of Gallo-Belgic platters, in soapy brown-black ware. Claudius–Nero.
*37. Fine black or grey, highly polished and latticed. Rim triangular in section. Very common. *c.* A.D. 70–150.
*38. Black or grey, polished, with half-round rim. Not latticed. Omission of bevel at foot is fourth century. *c.* A.D. 120–400.
*39. Black cooking-pot ware, or fine grey. The former with scored pattern. Really continues f. 17. Fine grey runs throughout; the black not earlier than Hadrian–Antonine. *c.* A.D. 120–300.
*40. Fine grey or black, with or without groove and scoring. Very common. *c.* A.D. 100 (?)–400.
41. Porringer, native and Roman grey. Rare. Claudius–Nero.
42. Porringer, light, rough grey. Rare. Claudian.
43A. Flanged bowl. Rare. Neronian.
43B. The same, very large. Brown to grey. Rare. Claudian.
44A. Unusual bowl. Native and various. Rare. Claudian.
44B. Similar to 43 and 44, very large. Rare. Claudian. (But see 243 and 247–8.)
45A. Similar bowl on three feet. Native. Rare. Claudian.
45B. Tripod-bowl in fine pale grey. Rare. Claudius–Nero.
46. Roman bowl, resembling mortarium. Scarce. Claudius–Nero.
47A and B. Carinated bowls, native. Rare. Claudian.
48. Bowl, beaded rim, ware various. Rare. Claudian.

49. Deep bowl, high kick and footring. Terra nigra, grey copies. Rare. Claudian (?).
50. Later copy of the same. Terra nigra abroad, buff here. *Claudius*–Nero.
51. Bobbin-shaped bowl with high kick. Gallo-belgic, various wares. Tibero–Claudian.
52A. Carinated bowl with everted rim. Grey. Solo. Claudian.
52B. Porringer with footring. Fine pale grey. Rare. Claudian (?).
52C. Hemispherical with moulded rim. Grey. Rare. Claudian.
53. Copy of Arretine cup. Various G–B wares. Rare. Tiberio–Claudian.
54. Similar, bell-shaped. Terra-rubra. Rare. Tiberio–Claudian.
55. Imitation of Arretine cup. Red. Solo. Claudian.
56. Copy of Arretine cup. Terra rubra and terra nigra. Both common. Tiberio–Claudian.
57. Copies of same, native or Roman. Rare. Claudian.
58. Copies of Drag. 24/25. Terra rubra and terra nigra. Common. Claudian.
59. Native and Roman copies of 56–58 or their prototypes. Claudius–Nero.
60. Carinated cup (or lid?). Fine native. Rare. Claudius–Nero.
61A. Hemispherical cup, deep. Various wares. Solo. Augustus–Tiberius.
61B. Similar. Red wares. Rare. Tiberio–Claudian.
62. Similar. Standard type. Soft buff, colour-coated. Common. Claudius–Nero.
62B. Copies of last. Reddish wares. Rare. Claudius–Nero.
63. Similar bowls on three feet. Buff, colour-coated. Rare. Claudius–Nero.
64. Similar bowls in black egg-shell ware. Fairly common. Claudius–*Nero*.
65. Bowl in white egg-shell ware. Solo. Claudian.
66. Fragment, polished grey. Solo. Nero.
67. Native cup. Soapy black. Solo. Nero (?).
68. Copy of Drag. 29. Fine grey. Rare. Claudian–Flavian.
69A. (Hofheim 28B.) Terra rubra. Solo. Claudian (?).
69B. Copy of Drag. 30. Fine red-brown. Rare. Claudian–Flavian.
70. Handled bowl. Dark grey, white coated. Solo. Claudius–Nero?
71. (Not Colchester.) Copy of Arretine crater. Terra rubra. Augustus–Tiberius.
72. Pedestalled copies of Drag. 29. Terra rubra (not yet found at Colchester). Tiberio–Claudian.
73. Bell-shaped beakers. Terra rubra. Rare. Claudius.
74. Similar, carinated. Terra rubra. Scarce. Tiberio–Claudian.
75. Various similar, with cupped mouth. Terra rubra. Rare. Claudian (?).
76. Ditto. Terra rubra. The commonest rim. Tiberio–Claudian.
77. Similar, almost cylindrical. Terra rubra. Rare. Claudian (??).
78. Similar, conical and carinated. Terra rubra. Occurs (?). Claudian (?).

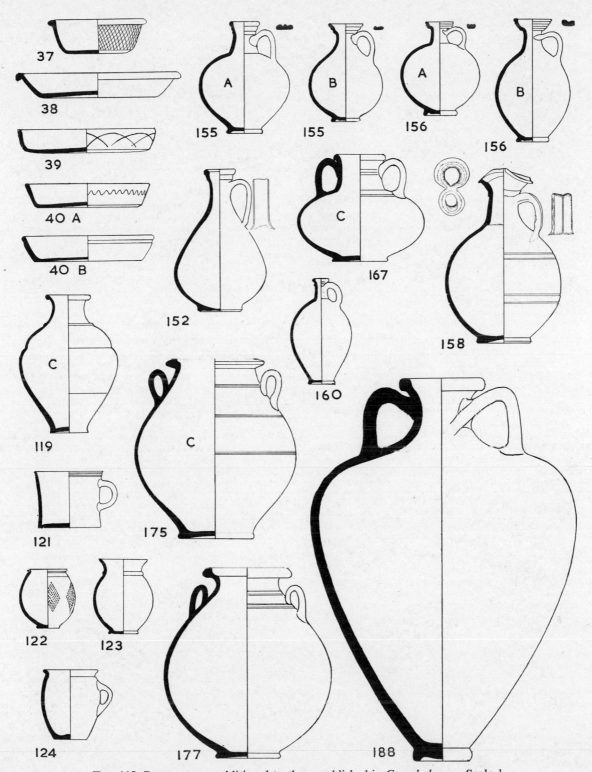

FIG. 118. Pottery types additional to those published in *Camulodunum*. Scale ⅙.

79A. Similar. Terra rubra. Scarce. Tiberio–Claudian.

79B. Native copy, polished black. Solo. Nero.

81. Barrel-like beaker, cordoned. Terra rubra. Occurs (?). Claudian (??).

82. Carinated girth-beaker. Terra rubra. Rare. Tiberio–Claudian.

83. Copy of same. Native brown. Solo. Claudian.

84. Similar, not carinated. Terra rubra. Common. Tiberio–Claudian.

85. Copies of same, native and Roman copies. Rare. Claudian.

86. Funnel-shaped girth-beaker. Terra rubra. Occurs (?). Claudian (??).

87. Copies of same. Native and Roman. May occur. Claudian (?).

88. Roman girth beaker? Thin fine grey. Solo. Nero.

91A and B. Globular beaker on pedestal-foot. Terra rubra. Fairly common. Tiberio–Claudian.

91C. Native copy, red-brown ware. Rare. Claudian (?).

91D. As 91A, but rim everted. Terra rubra. Rare. Claudian (?).

92. Native copy of 91A, black-polished. Fairly common. Claudius–Nero.

93. Small beaker, very thin, horn-coloured. Rare. Tiberio–Claudian.

94. Ovoid to globular, colour-coated and rough-cast. A. Full-bodied, fine ware. Continental. Common. *Claudius*–Nero. B. Taller, poor ware and coating. Local. Common. Claudius–*Nero*.

95. Bossed beakers, mica gilt. Rare. Claudius–Nero.

96. Beaker with pointed studs. Roman grey. Rare. Claudius–Nero.

97. Beaker with blunt studs. Thin hard black. Rare. Claudian.

98, 99. Rusticated beakers. Grey ware. Both rare. Claudius–*Nero*.

100. As 94A, but decorated in barbotine (Hofheim 118). Here only in grey. Rare. Claudius–Nero.

101. Folded beakers. Thin hard black (as 97). Rare. Claudius–Nero.

102. Ovoid beaker, upright rim grooved. Mica gilt. Fairly common. Tiberio–Claudian.

103. Unusual cordoned beaker. Grey, black-polished. Solo. Claudian.

104. Ovoid beakers with short rim. Black, almost egg-shell ware. Sometimes stamped. Rare. Nero–Domitian.

105. Small globular beakers on pedestal, buff, red-coated (Nero); another, not coated. Rare. Uncertain.

106–7. Vacant.

108. Ovoid beakers, taking the place of the rusticated type, the surface roughened instead by lines prodded with a comb. Very common. (Fig. 55, 37, 38.) Claudius–Hadrian.

108B. Similar vessels, but much larger, and usually with two bands of prodding. Despite strong resemblance, this series seems distinctly later. All the evidence agrees in dating it from about 160 to 250.

109–12. Absent.

113. Butt-beaker in white pipeclay, and copies. Scarce. Not after Nero.

114. White beakers with gilt rim. Scarce, in graves of Claudius–Nero.

115–18. Absent (?).

119. Butt-beakers with distinct neck. These run through, almost without change (except in decoration), from the earliest times to the fourth century, when they are exceptionally numerous in the 'Mithraeum' (with coin of Constans). Fig. 63, 48–55; fig. 64, 56, 59. Polished grey and black.

120. Sharply carinated beakers. The finest black (Gallo-Belgic) ones are absent. Inferior copies (some quite good) occur in graves up to Hadrian (i.e. *c.* 120). Claudius–Hadrian.

*121. Handled mug with curved and outsplayed wall. Mid-first century (grave 9).

122. Beaker, fine polished ware, decorated with panels of raised dots. The evidence is poor, but these seem to run from *c.* 150 to 350.

*123. Taller beaker of 'poppy-head' shape, similar ware and decoration. Seems to occur in graves from about 100 to 200, but is still with us in the 'Mithraeum' (fig. 71, 145). But the two fragments of ff. 122 and 123 found there may be rubbish-survivals.

*124. Tall ovoid beaker, with or without handle. Rim very small. Not rare. Of over a dozen in the Museum few are datable. One at the Gaer was dated early second century; our series seems to run evenly and continuously from *c.* 100 onwards. The evidence is from graves, and ends with two in a grave of about 350 and one with an inhumation.

125–38. Vacant or absent.

139, 140. These possibly occur in the colonia. Buff. Mid-first century.

141. Occurs in the west cemetery. Brown-buff. Scarce. Mid to late first century?

142. Vacant.

143 and 144 rare in Colonia. Buff. Mid-first century.

145. Vacant.

146. Buff flagon. A neck in pit I (fig. 53, 2) extends the life of this form to about 100.

147. Black flagon. Absent. Mid-first century.

148. Flat- or conical-mouthed flagon. One in a grave of Flavian date. Not common.

149. Similar, with short neck. Not uncommon. Claudius–Nero, and possibly later, but proof lacking, except that there are later derived forms.

150. Similar with tall, straight neck. This form certainly occurs in graves of Trajanic date. Period Claudius–Trajan. There is a doubtful reappearance of the type in the mid-fourth century.

*152. Tall, pear-shaped flagon with long neck. Buff. This is an early type on the Continent. Here it appears in graves of about A.D. 80 and 120.

153. Ring-mouthed flagon. Early form. Absent. Tiberian.

154. Ring-mouthed flagon, Claudian form. The rings are many and are never boldly stepped outwards; the ringed portion, too, is usually but little outbent. There is a distinct foot-ring. The typical form is common, but during the Flavian period modifications began to creep in. Nevertheless f. 154 is still frequent in pit I, *c.* 100, and the form continues popular in graves of Trajan–Hadrian date.

*155. This is an omnibus number for the variants which fall between 154 and 156. It includes vessels like 154, but with markedly trumpet-shaped mouths, or without offset between neck and shoulder. It also includes vessels in which the rings are few and thick, as shown in the Camulodunum plates. The chief incidence of this type is from about 70 to 130, judging by the graves. One example of apparently about 175 is probably a stray.

*156. This is another ring-mouthed flagon, like the last, but the mouth is markedly cupped inside. The footring is marked off by a deep groove from the centre of the base. The form is one of the most typical and local to Colchester. It is very common in the Trajan–Hadrian period, and hardly less so in the Antonine. It was still being made in quantities in our kilns about 190, and continues to be found in graves, and elsewhere, at least up to 350 ('Mithraeum', fig. 60, 3, 4, 5). In the latter part of its life a tall form appears alongside the familiar globular form, and the footring tends to disappear.

157–9. Three forms of spouted flagons. Incidence in colonia not yet known.

*160. Tall flagon with narrow cylindrical neck. White ware. These are scarce. One in a grave seems to date to about 140.

161–6 do not occur in the colonia, though the commoner varieties occur in graves up to about A.D. 60.

167A. Augustan (as at Haltern); B, Claudian (as at Camulodunum). C is the late form, in which the outline is blurred and softened. The way in which this is done can be seen in figs. 53, 3, and 61, 26, 27. The former is c. 100, the latter c. 350. The type is very common, but not in graves. A complete example is shown fig. 58, 7.

168–74. Absent from colonia.

175. The typical early form has been described in *Camulodunum*. With modifications it lasted on to about 140 (pit I, fig. 53, 4, 5, and graves).

176 and 177. Absent (but see 413).

178–81. Vacant.

182–4. Spindle-shaped amphorae, common in the colonia in the pre-Boudiccan level.

185. Sausage-shaped amphora; probably occurs as last, but not easily recognizable.

186. Radish-shaped amphora. A, with slender neck; B, similar, neck wider; C, neck very wide, rim now very short. All occur in Claudius–Nero level, but C is latest to appear and possibly lasts into Flavian times. Common.

187. Globular amphora, the commonest of the Roman period. Fragments are everywhere in the early and middle Empire. One has the impression that in the fourth century the vessels passed out of use, but there is no direct evidence. They are often used to contain burials and these are not later than about 200 (in Colchester).

*188. Amphora with high shoulder and small footstand. This occurs not infrequently, but never in graves. It is post-Boudiccan, but otherwise not yet dated.

189. Small, carrot-shaped amphora, horizontally fluted. Typically Claudius–Nero. Occurs in the colonia, doubtfully as late as Vespasian, certainly not later.

190. Vacant.

191. Wall-sided mortarium. Early (Augustan) type. Very common on the Camulodunum site under Claudius and Nero. Less so in the colonia. Not post-Boudiccan.

192. Heavily flanged mortarium. Neronian. Hard to identify among fragments from the colonia. Same date as last.

193. Small mortaria with stubby rims. Absent (?). Pre-Boudiccan.

194. Mortarium with 'bunched-up' rim. Absent (?). Pre-Boudiccan.

195A. Mortarium with broad, flat flange (favourite form of Q.VAL. VERANIVS). Frequent in colonia, and apparently Vespasianic.

195B. Flange short, thick, curved, with grit over it. Frequent. Flavian.

195C. Flange broad, very much curved, arched above rim. Frequent, date Flavian–Trajanic.

196 and 197. Unguentaria of thin fine red ware. Rare. Date uncertain, but perhaps all first century.

198. Incense cups. These have not been closely examined and there are many different forms.

*199. Cheese press. The base has concentric furrows and ridges inside, with perforations in furrows and in wall. Not uncommon. Period uncertain. One is Neronian, others first century.

200. Vacant.

201–5. Pedestalled vases, absent.

206. Various Roman pedestal-bases. Little can be said of these, for many of them probably belong to incense cups. One from pit I is shown fig. 54, 20.

*207. Large, buff, pedestalled vases. These were very common in the kilns of about 190. The only example which can be drawn complete is rather lighter in build than these, and is painted, which none is from the kilns. It may therefore be somewhat later.

208. Vacant.

209. Squat, carinated bowl with generous mouldings. Native, and rare, but lasted on through the Flavian period to reach pit I (fig. 54, 15), c. 100.

210–17. Native bowls. Absent.

218A. The native form, or the Roman copy of it, remained in use up to about 100 (pit I, fig. 54, 16–18). It is frequent in the colonia.

218B. The copies soon began to be latticed on the neck. The hard grey ware shows these to be developed Roman copies, and they appear in graves which may be dated up to 140. This latticing first appears (locally) about 70.

219 and 220. Absent.

221 and 222. Wide bowls with small cordon (or not) at base of neck. No dating can be given for this very simple and characterless type, which occurs everywhere at all times.

223–*226. The first three are native and absent, the last is purely Roman, but cannot be dated at present.

227. Bowl with incurved neck. The Roman series are true copies of the native original and are frequent in graves of the Flavian–Trajan period. Its continuation beyond 100 is dubious.

228. Somewhat similar bowl, also derived from a native prototype. Possibly same dating.

229, 230. Absent.

231. Absent.

232. Large, tall vase with narrow mouth. Bulge at base of neck, between cordons, scored oblique strokes or latticed. Runs continuously from Claudius up to pit I (c. 100), fig. 53, 6, and thereafter appears in graves up to about 180.

233–5. Absent.

236. Small flask with oblate body and strong cordon or bulge at neck. Rare type; occurs in a grave about 100.

237–40. Vacant.

241. Cancelled, now vacant.

242 (includes former 241). Biconical bowls with everted, flat rim. Numbers of these appear in pit I (fig. 54, 10–14) in Roman ware, thus continuing the popularity of this common Claudian type. But how long it remained in use after 100 we do not know.

243–5. Absent or very rare.

246. Grey bowl with flat, reeded rim. Common in the earlier levels, latest appearance in pit I (fig. 54, 9). Very rare in graves, and the evidence as to its use after about 100 is inadequate. One would not be surprised if it was current until about 120.

247 and 248. Vacant.

249–63 do not occur in the colonia.

264. Native cooking-pot. One of these occurs in a grave (141) which is probably Flavian.

265 and 266. The most common cooking-pot of the mid-first century, with offset neck and beaded lip, often undercut. Begins in native ware and romanizes to hard grey. Peculiarity is that the base is polished. The greater the polished area the later the date. Very common in graves from Claudius to Trajan. Not so common in pit I (fig. 56, 47–53 and 58–60) as might be expected. Late and tall examples (B) seem to be early second century, but so far positive evidence is lacking for the demise of the type.

267A is absent; B, with flat rim, occasionally occurs in graves of the first century, up to about 90. The type is never common in Colchester.

*268. Ovoid cooking-pot, smoothed, but never polished anywhere. Underside of foot always bears mark of the wire which cut it from the wheel. Rim nearly always undercut; neck short, with groove on shoulder.

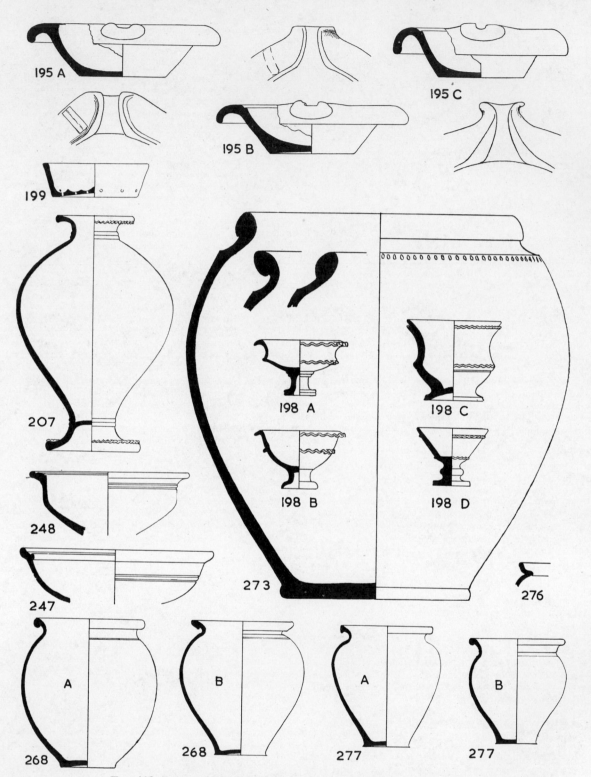

FIG. 119. Pottery types additional to those in *Camulodunum*. Scale ⅙.

*268A. Rim fat, and roundly curved outwards. Material often rather coarse and gritty. Body usually squat. One of the most common Roman vessels. Most numerous in graves which we judge to be Hadrianic, but probably begins about 100 (not seen in pit I). An example in grave 126, which is not later than Flavian, is abnormal and may be intrusive; at any rate we hesitate to begin the type so early. It continues to appear in graves up to 250, and is still present in the 'Mithraeum' with a coin of Constans.

*268B. Rim thinner, flat on the inside, the ware usually thinner and finer, the body often markedly incurved to the foot. Doubtfully represented in graves round about 100; well attested thus and in general use from about 120 to 200; not proved, but no doubt present from 200 to 250, when it again appears in a grave, and in the 'Mithraeum' about 350, and with inhumation burials.

These are beyond question the commonest vessels in Roman Colchester.

*269. Jars or cooking-pots with hooked rim-section. This type is not yet substantiated.

270–1. Large storage-jars of native ware. Absent except in the Claudius–Nero levels.

272. Large storage-jars of f. 266 but with polished rim and band of finger-tipping on shoulder. They begin full and round (*Camulodunum*, pl. LXXXIV) and gradually become taller. The type is one of the most common and was much favoured for burials up to about 140. Thereafter its continuity is in doubt. There is a possible burial about 220, and in the 'Mithraeum' (c. 350) the type is only represented by two miniature vessels (fig. 69, 121–2), which can hardly be accounted of the same class.

*273. Very large storage-jars about 2 ft. high and nearly as much in diameter. Roman development of the native 270–2. Rim fat, oval section, may be upright or sloped inward or outward. Begins round about 60 and runs on. A complete example in the Museum contains a grave of about 150 or soon after. Its later history is quite unknown.

274. Vacant.

275. Large storage-vessels with broad, flat, inturned rim. The few examples in the colonia are all probably Claudius–Nero.

276. Jar with tallish rim deeply hollowed inside. These are usually of a very coarse ware and seem to be of late date, but good evidence is lacking.

277. Jar or cooking-pot similar to 266 but rather tall, with rim cut off vertically. Does not appear in datable graves, and may belong to the period of inhumations.

278. The common grey (or black) latticed jar, ubiquitous on Roman sites. Always popular, its maximum frequency here is from c. 100 to 140, and is scarcely diminished up to 200. It still appears in graves throughout the third century and is still with us in the 'Mithraeum' c. 350. How soon it started is uncertain—probably in Flavian times, for it does not appear before about 65. The form changes scarcely at all. Taller examples may be third century.

279. The common black cooking-pot with latticed side.

279A. Fairly broad, with tall lattice and short almost upright rim, often with a wavy line scored round the outside. Hadrianic on Hadrian's Wall, the type is so scarce in Colchester that we have no dating evidence for it.

279B. Still as broad, but the rim now almost as broad as the greatest diameter. The latticing tends to become wider spaced and not so upright. Sometimes it is reduced in height. The form is universal, but in Colchester local products held the market, and it is not common in graves. One can be dated to about 200. Another was found in the 'Mithraeum' with coin of Constans, and another with an inhumation burial. The dating is therefore about 200 to 350.

279C. The latest form is smallish, and tall, with the rim now

very wide and often exceeding the width of the body. The lattice occupies a narrow band, and its angle is 45° or less. The evidence is 'Mithraeum', a grave of about same date, and an inhumation. Date, fourth century, c. 325 to 400.

280. Large narrow-necked storage-jars. These resemble the handled jars of the Yorkshire Signal Stations, but have a long life. They possibly begin under Hadrian, appear in graves of c. 150, are most numerous in graves of 200 to 250, but run on to 400. Early examples are full and round, later ones are taller and ovoid. Very common.

281. Flasks with narrow necks. There are many of these, and it is not easy to decide how many types to make (cf. f. 282). The present form is nearly globular at first, nearly always with a small cordon at neck. Two in grave 8 are very doubtfully Neronian; then they appear now and then in graves from about 100 right through, being especially numerous in the 'Mithraeum' (c. 350) and occurring in inhumations.

282. Flask with narrow neck, shoulder sloping up to neck. Commonly white coated, with painted bands. In graves from c. 250 to 350.

283. Tall flask, buff, with painted bands. First appears, apparently, about 200, but more usual about 300 to 330, and occurs with inhumations. Chiefly fourth century.

284. Vacant.

285. Large, tall, narrow-necked jars. Usually with finger-tipping round neck. Though frequent, the evidence for date is small. Latter half of first century (pit I, fig. 53, 8).

286. Ovoid flask with tall cylindrical neck. Copied from a glass form, rare. Three occurrences in graves seem to date to 160, 260, and 380 (approximately). Further evidence is needed, but the form seems late.

287. Large grey face-urn, no frill or handles. Undated. Rare.

288. Frilled face-urn with (usually) three handles. Buff ware. Many whole vessels in Museum, fragments are not rare. Datable graves seem Hadrianic, but one is about 200. Date c. 120 to 200.

289. Large buff face-urn. One only, not dated.

290. Face urns of polished red ware. These are small and quite distinctive. There is no evidence for dating save the activity of the potteries which made them. Possibly fourth century.

292. Face-urn of white ware. Features painted. Rare, no dating.

291 and 3 5. Vacant.

296. Tall ovoid flask on pedestal-foot, very finely made of polished red ware. Late fourth century. A standard type.

297. Vase of f. 119, but with frilled rim and prodded cordon on neck. Rare. Two in 'Mithraeum' c. 350; one in grave 320 may be of about 290.

298. Carinated bowl with broadly outcurved top. The base often pierced as a strainer. Date uncertain, but occurs in 'Mithraeum' c. 350.

299. Bowl of S-shaped outline. Usually of fine, pearly grey ware and slightly micaceous. Groove on shoulder. The form is Newstead 46. In Colchester it was certainly common by 150, and in use through the third century, and is still frequent in the 'Mithraeum', c. 350.

300. Buff bowl, with wall-side, like late mortaria, small. Rare. Was made in a Colchester kiln of c. 200.

301. Bowl resembling 298, but rim more upright. Rare. Seems Flavian in grave 45 and Antonine in grave 90.

302. Bowl shaped like a small cauldron, bulged below and straight above, with or without handles containing rings which may be loose or fixed. Not common, but several examples. Only date so far grave 408, c. 275.

303. Platter of polished black cooking-pot ware with flat rim. A well-known type which begins under Hadrian or Pius and is typically Antonine or later. One fragment in the 'Mithraeum' may be an intrusion.

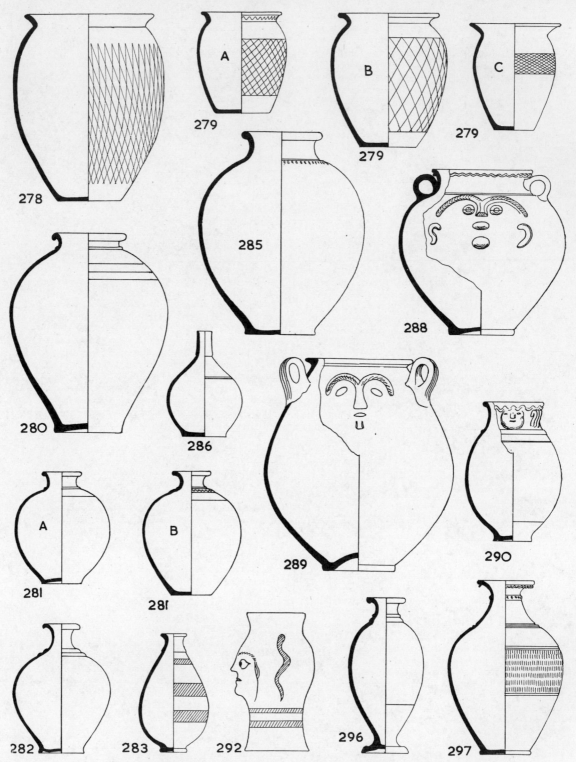

FIG. 120. Pottery types additional to those in *Camulodunum*. Scale ⅙.

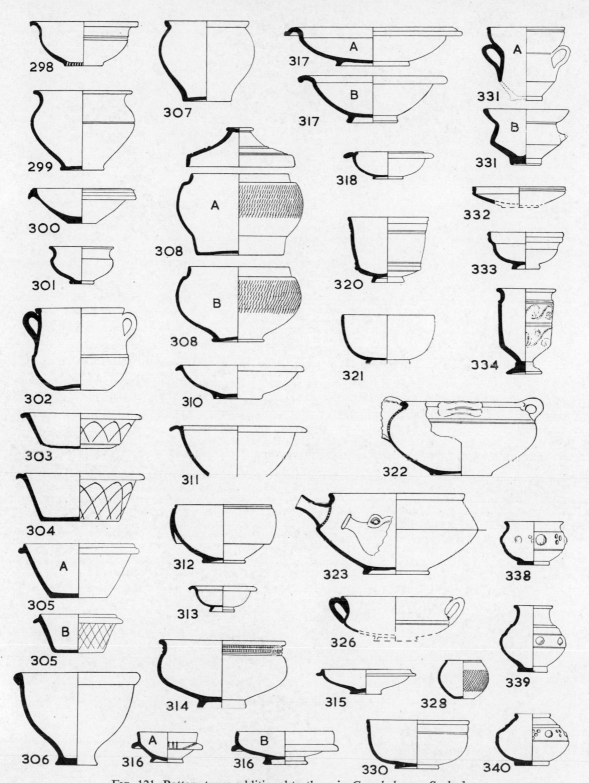

FIG. 121. Pottery types additional to those in *Camulodunum*. Scale ⅙.

304. Similar bowl, deeper, same ware. On the flat rim is a groove. Side scored as on f. 39 and f. 305A. Common, but dating uncertain. Not in graves. Probably Antonine onwards, certainly in 'Mithraeum' (15 exx.) about 350.

305. Bowls with ledged rim. Straight side, no bevel.

305A. Black polished cooking-pot ware. Exterior scored as ff. 39 and 304. A very common late Roman type, probably in use from about 250 to 400. Earlier evidence still lacking.[1]

305B. Polished grey ware. A wavy line on the inside wall does not occur in Colchester. One of the commonest of late Roman vessels. Occurs in grave with coin of Postumus, and in another which may be fourth century. Rarely used in graves.

306. Bell-shaped bowls of coarse grey ware. Dating uncertain; one in a grave seems late Antonine. Fragments occur in the 'Mithraeum'. The dating seems approximately 175 to 350 or later.

307. Wide bowls, with broad base, grey ware, with barrel-markings. The rim often hollowed for lid. These begin about 200, occur in graves in the first half of the third century, and are still with us in the 'Mithraeum', c. 350. Fairly common.

308. Colour-coated bowl, with lid. Sometimes angularly built (Corbridge, *Arch. Ael.* 3s, viii, pl. XII, 63); here they are always rounded. The ware may be Castor or local. The ugly base of *Ant. Journ.* xx, 506 occurs here in Castor ware in flagons and in polished red ware, e.g. figs. 61, 28 and 62, 45. Large examples are not uncommon, but are fragile and fragmentary. An unusually small one is in a grave of c. 190; none in 'Mithraeum'. Date c. 180–200, perhaps to 300.

309. Bowl with incurved lip like f. 251. Rare. Late Antonine.

310. Wide bowls with beaded rim, copies of T.S. f. Lud. Sb. These occur from time to time in various wares. A fine grey one is in a Hadrianic grave. Fine polished grey one in 'Mithraeum' (fig. 66, 84) and one in Castor ware in grave 394, of about same date (c. 350).

311. Small bowl, beaded and flanged (copy of T.S. f. Ritt. 12), the bead evanescent. Flange often rouletted. Fine hard polished grey. Type seems early. Neronian. Not common.

312. Bowl with wide vertical collar. Not dated. Rare.

313. Bowl with curved rim. A good example in pit I, c. 100 (fig. 55, 33). Not dated at present.

314. Carinated bowl with necked and beaded rim. Nearly always in red coated ware, generally ascribed to the New Forest. Often decorated in white paint. Occurs in inhumation graves only. Fourth century, and perhaps second half only.

315. Shallow, rounded bowl with ledged rim, and footring. There are possibly subdivisions, for one is in a grave of Trajan-Hadrian date and another was in the 'Mithraeum' (c. 350). Little known as yet.

316. Bowl copying T.S. f. 38. The form varies somewhat. The New Forest examples are very true to the original. A series which occurs fairly regularly in very late deposits in Colchester is wider and shallower, with a heavy, squarish footring. The ware is a red-buff, partly polished. All seem to be second half of fourth century.

317. Bowl with flatly curved rim. Copied from sigillata forms, especially by New Forest potteries. Usually red ware, red-coated, sometimes decorated with white paint. Fourth century.

318. Hemispherical bowl with curved flange and bead-rim. Little known as yet. There are two examples in a Neronian grave.

319. Vacant.

320. Conical beaker on footring, copy of T.S. f. 30. These are made in red or black polished ware, variously decorated with impressed patterns. Some were made in kilns at West Stowe near

Bury St. Edmunds. See P. Corder, in *Ant. Journ.* xxi, 296. Date uncertain, perhaps late first and second century.

321. Hemispherical bowl with simple lip. One in pit I (fig. 55, 31), c. 100. Others, quite small, are in New Forest ware (red-coated) and are fourth century.

322. Wide bowl with strainer-spout in form of a boar's head. Fine thin buff, mica-coated. Occurs in pit I (fig. 56, 46), c. 100. Not common.

323. Similar bowls, carinated, the spout usually quite simple, but sometimes showing eyes and tusks of the boar. Polished grey ware. Fairly frequent. No dating as yet.

324. Vacant.

325. Vacant.

326. Wide, carinated bowls with two handles. Buff ware. Fairly frequent. No dating as yet.

327. Vacant.

328. Grey jars resembling f. 278, except that the rim is a small beading. Dating perhaps much the same. One in a grave of Trajanic date.

†329. Wide bowls, copies of T.S. f. 29. Fine polished brown, grey, or black ware. Decorated with groups of incised lines, often in festoons. Made at West Stowe (see f. 320). Not rare.

330. Hemispherical bowls, copies of T.S. f. 37, in same ware and decoration as last (see f. 320). Not rare.

331. Carinated bowls with tall, cupped rim and two handles. Usually white ware, poorly finished, sometimes with scored groups of lines on wall. Not rare. Dating uncertain save one in pit I (fig. 55, 34), c. 100.

332. Wide bowl with vertical, reeded rim. White ware. Rare. No date.

333. Copies of T.S. f. 27. These are in grey or buff ware, sometimes mica-coated. They vary much and are infrequent. One in pit I (fig. 54, 19) is c. 100.

334. Tall cylindrical beaker on pedestal foot. Rare. Red, red-coated New Forest ware, decorated with white paint. Presumed late fourth century.

335. Vacant.

†336. Cup or bowl with curved, drooping rim. Rare. No date.

†337. Small vessel with thick, beaded rim. Coarse whitish ware. These were sometimes used as crucibles. *Newstead*, Type 20.

338. Small bowl, polished grey ware with round impressions and bosses. Late fourth century.

339. Small flask with large bulge round shoulder. Fine polished light red, decorated with bosses. With inhumation burial. Fourth century.

340. Similar vessel, without bulge. Fine polished grey ware, decorated with bosses and hollows. Rare. Presumably fourth century.

342. Oblate, rounded beaker, with tall curved rim and simple lip. Rare. No date.

343. The same, later form, taller, and the neck now little curved. Typical are the small, fine, black glazed Rhenish beakers, which first appear about 210 (?). Others are still with us in the fourth century, e.g. fig. 71, 141, and 41, 10 (St. Martin's House), the former red, the latter black. The very tall neck appears alongside the short.

†344. Hemispherical bowl, copy of T.S. f. 37, in red ware, with some slight incurve at top. Flavian. Rare in Colchester, more common on military sites. *Newstead*, Type 44.

345–54. Vacant.

355. Large two-handled jug, white ware, not yet dated.

356. Tall flagon with incurved lip, offset shoulder and cordons on neck. Castor ware. Late fourth century.

357. Two-handled jug. Castor ware. Late fourth century.

358. Flagon in buff ware. Not dated.

---

[1] We regard *Gellygaer*, pl. XII, 11, as a stray.

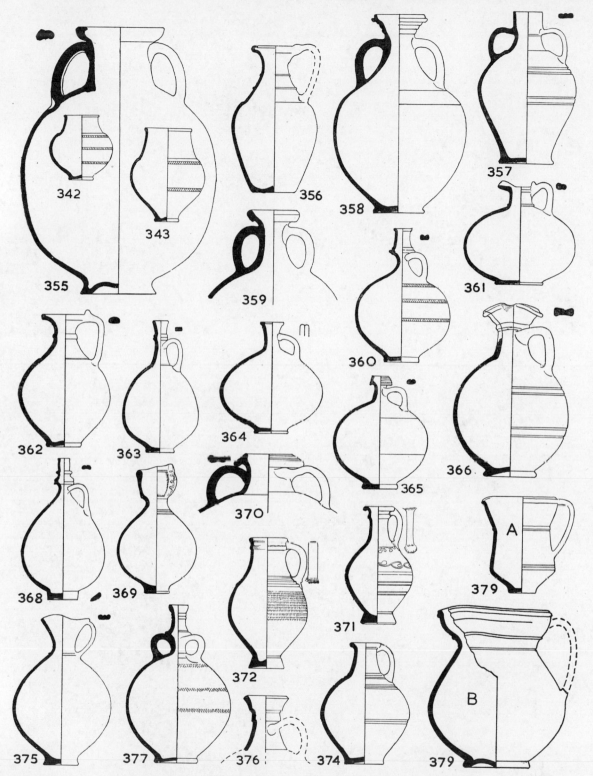

FIG. 122. Pottery types additional to those in *Camulodunum*. Scale ⅙.

359. Two-handled jug with cupped mouth. Little known. No date.

360. Flagons with ledged rim. In various wares, with various modifications of form. In Castor ware with coins of Tetricus. Common at Niederbieber (190–260). Wheeler dates them *c.* 220 to 350. Common in Colchester, perhaps from *c.* 200 on.

361. Flagons with beaked spout. Usually red ware, mica-coated. Made here *c.* 190. Terminal dates unknown. Bronze original also made here, one containing a hoard of about A.D. 230. Not common.

362. Flagon imitating a well-known bronze form. Usually red ware, mica gilt. Made here about 190. Not uncommon.

363. Flagon, no dating, probably *c.* 190–210.

364. Flagon with very narrow neck, tall and curved, with simple lip. Mostly in fine polished red ware. Not dated, but probably third to fourth century.

365. Flagon with conical, reeded mouth. Usually in the same polished red ware. Occurs in graves from about 240, and in 'Mithraeum', *c.* 350.

366. Flagon with pinched spout, the sides lapped over. Handle below mouth. No dating at present, possibly *c.* 190–210.

†367. Flagon, late second century.

368. Flagon with elaborately moulded mouth, neck very narrow. Fine polished red ware (see ff. 364–5). Probably fourth century.

369. Flagon with human mask on mouth. These are in many different wares, some white, with features coloured brown-red. Occur frequently with inhumations, presumably *c.* 350–400. Common.

370. Two-handled jug with conical-reeded mouth. Buff. Rare. No date.

371. Tall, colour-coated flagon. The ware seems Castor. Decorated with white paint. Rare. Should be fourth century, but this uncertain.

372. Tall flagon copying a bronze form, with or without pinched spout. Castor ware here. At Silchester with coins to Arcadius, and seems equally late here.

†373. Two-handled jug with cupped mouth. Buff. Rare. No date.

374. Flagon with conical neck and beaded rim. A late type, but no dating as yet.

375. Flagon with pinched spout, handle on rim. Castor ware. Not common. Possibly fourth century.

376. Flagon, buff, unusual shape. No data.

377. Two-handled flagon with narrow neck and ledge. Castor ware. One in 'Mithraeum' (fig. 61, 35), another with an inhumation. Rare.

†378. Pear-shaped flagon with cylindrical neck and upright collar-rim. One with an inhumation. Rare.

379. Flagon with wide mouth, shaped to spout. One in grave possibly *c.* 100.

380. Flagon with conical mouth and very narrow neck. Fine polished red ware. Occurs with an inhumation. Not rare.

381. Flagon on pedestal foot. Colour-coated ware, decorated in barbotine (check). Occurs with inhumation.

382. Tall, pear-shaped flagon, white ware, or buff, mica-coated. Occurs in a grave of *c.* 200.

383–5. Vacant.

386. Vacant.

387. Colander, with upright, collared rim. Grey ware. No dating.

389A and B are forms of unguent-pots which seem to be numerous throughout the period, though commonest, perhaps, in the second century. They were made in kiln XXII.

390. Large jars with several small cups on the shoulder, against the rim. No dating material as yet.

391. Cup or beaker with corniced rim. The greatest diameter low down (in contrast to f. 94). A short; B tall. Base beaded and grooved, or quite plain. Not before A.D. 120 (?) and then runs into the fourth century. Very common.

392. Vessels of the same outline except that the lip is quite simple. Appears later, perhaps not before 150. Both forms are typically colour-coated ware. There are grey copies of both. Very common. A short; B tall; C tall with almost a carination.

393. Similar beaker, tall, with rounded base and footring. Third to fourth century? Colour-coated ware.

394. Colour-coated beakers with cylindrical foot. Fourth century. Fairly frequent.

395. Colour-coated beaker with a rouletted bulge at base of tall neck; globular body with small foot. There are grey copies. Fourth century.

396. Globular beakers with upright, outcurved rim. Colour-coated ware; plain or folded. Late second and early third century. Not common.

397. Similar beakers, but the body variously constricted. Rare. Late second century.

398. Similar beakers, the body horizontally fluted, the top tapering to simple lip. Rare. Third century (?).

399. Small vase of colour-coated ware, very scarce. Fourth century.

400. Vacant.

401. Fluted beaker of conical outline. Grey ware. Fourth century.

402. Tall colour-coated beaker with cupped mouth and cylindrical foot. Sides with four foldings. Fourth century.

403. Similar beaker, but globular body, with four flutings. Fourth century.

404. Ovoid beaker, colour-coated, with several cordons at lip. Rare. Late second century.

†405. Ovoid beaker with everted lip, fluted on body. Grey ware. Uncertain.

406. Similar beaker with marked shoulder, insloping neck, with sharply beaded rim. Grey ware, fluted. Late second and early third centuries.

407. Tall ovoid beaker with tall neck, conical or curved, the lip simple. Fluted. Colour-coated and grey ware. Third and fourth centuries.

408. Oblately ovoid to globular beakers or bowls with insloping neck and rim as 406. Beaded base. Various wares, copying the fine metallic Rhenish ff. 342, 343. Sometimes fluted. Third and fourth centuries.

409. Similar beakers with tall, almost straight neck, rim beaded. Foot usually very small. Colour-coated. Sometimes fluted. Fourth century.

410. Ovoid beaker reducing below to very small foot, sometimes pedestalled like 394. Fluted. Grey or black ware. Fourth century.

411. Upright beaker, the sides nearly parallel, marked shoulder with medium tall, straight, insloping neck with simple rim. Common in colour-coated ware and copies in various wares. Late second and third centuries.

Honey-pots

These vessels are most striking to the eye, but are difficult to classify, and we have little upon which to date them. Some early ones are already dealt with under 175–7. Possibly the following could be telescoped to fill the three numbers 178–80. They are too many and varied to be illustrated here.

412. Honey-pot. Fat rim, two small handles close up. Greatest diameter low down. Buff. Mid- to late second century.

413. Honey-pot. Fat rim, always hollowed inside. Very similar to last. White or buff. Frequent. *c.* A.D. 120–50.

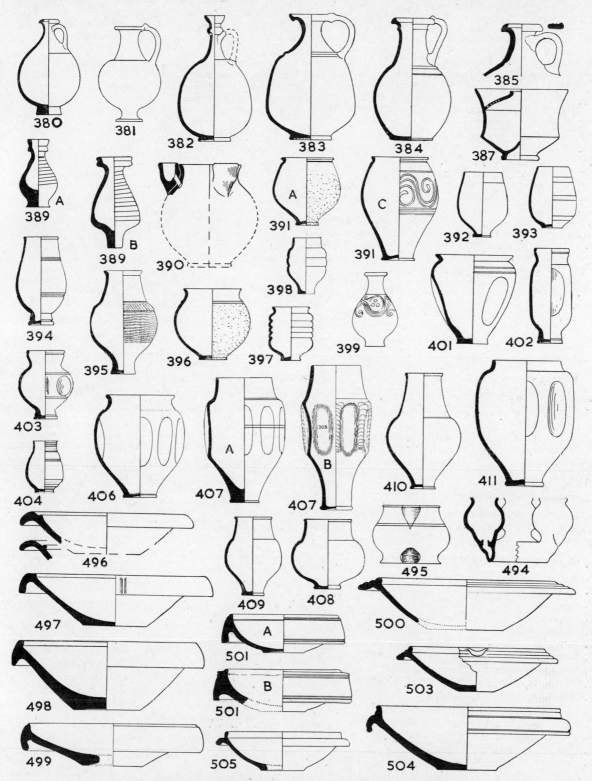

FIG. 123. Pottery types additional to those in *Camulodunum*. Scale ⅙.

414. Honey-pot. Tall and ovoid, greatest diameter very low down. Handles fairly low. Nero–Flavian.

415. Honey-pot. Body very evenly rounded, greatest diameter in middle, handles high up. Foot heavily beaded. Buff. Rounded rim has a groove inside. Mid-second century (?).

416. Honey-pot. Similar to the last, but more full-bodied. Buff. Rare. Third century.

417. Honey-pot. Rim broad, grooved on edge, no neck; handles close up, three-ribbed. Solo. Unknown.

418. Honey-pot. Fat rim with groove inside. Body ovoid on a tallish foot. Handles high up. Buff. Unknown.

419. Honey-pot. Like 414 and 418, but taller, no groove on rim, and upper part nearly conical. Third or fourth century (?).

420–93. Vacant.

494. Triple vase, three cups, without offset shoulder, standing on a hollow ring. Buff, not polished. Rare. Uncertain.

495. Triple vase, the three cups almost globular, on small feet, with tall, offset necks. Usually red, white, or buff coated, once buff ware; one painted as fig. 63, 48. Rare. Fourth century.

496 (follows on Cam. f. 195). Mortarium with rolled rim rising above the beading. Buff. Uncommon in Colchester. Trajan–Hadrian.

497. Mortarium with rolled rim of approximately quadrant-section. The beading level with it, or rising above—great variety in outline. Very common. Buff. Late Hadrian–Antonine.

498. Mortarium, similar, but rim at a very steep angle. Common. Buff. Late second and third century.

499. Mortarium. Similar, but lacking beading. Buff. Frequent. Third century.

500. Mortarium. Large beading, ledge more or less horizontal and fluted. Buff, often biscuit-colour. Rare. Third century.

501A. Mortarium. 'Wall-sided' type, wall sloping outwards, buff or white. Common. Second half of second century.

501B. The same, but the wall nearly vertical. Late second century.

†502. Mortarium with upright beading; the broad ledge smooth, but beaded beneath. White, buff or biscuit. Common. Late second century onwards. Resembles 505.

503. Mortarium. Similar, but the ledge fluted. Not common. Buff to biscuit. Late third to fourth century (?).

504. Mortarium with prominent beading of squarish section, the ledge rolled down as a quadrant in section. White. Frequent. Late second to third century.

505. Mortarium, similar, but the beading is usually grooved on top, and the narrow ledge is always beaded beneath. Buff or red ware, white-coated, grit a coralline pink. Common. Fourth century.

†506. Mortarium. 'Hammer-head' type. Very rare here. White or buff. Fourth century.

†507. Mortarium. Rim bunched up. Rare. Uncertain.

(G) LIST OF REMAINS FOUND OUTSIDE THE WALLS

The following numbered list is a key to the finds marked on the three plans. Of these plan II shows remains north of the town, plan III remains west of the town, and plan IV remains south of the town. Such remains as lie east of the town are included on plans II and IV. A few numbers are not to be found on these plans, being too far out from the town.

When the shape of an object can be shown it is so, otherwise a site is marked by a cross when known sufficiently exactly. When the position is approximate the cross is ringed, and the size of the ring indicates the measure of approximation. The letter N, W, or S is added to each item to show in which area it lies.

1. The Sphinx. At NW. corner of Hospital, 1820/1. W.
2. Remains found when building 'The Turrets', Lexden Road. W.
3. Amphora found east of St. Clare Road, 1823. W.
4. Remains found under Lexden Road opposite 'Deoban'. W. (Just off map.)
5. Glass vessels found in front of the 'Oaks', Crouch Street, in 1837. W.
6. Bronze statuette of Jupiter found west of Queen's Road, 1844. W.
7. Urn and bottle found, north end of Avenue, 1853. W.
8. Vase and unguentarium found west of Avenue, 1860. W.
9. 'Tomb' found in front of 'Highfield', Lexden Road, 1860. W.
10. Amphora, urn, and two bottles found in Beverley Road, 1865. W.
11. Amphora and pottery found in Lexden Tumulus, 1860. W.
12. 'Tomb' in the middle of Beverley Road, 1865. W.
13. Figurines found at corner of Creffield and Cambridge roads, 1866. W.
14. Other remains found ibid., 1866. W.
15. Centurion's tombstone found 1868. W.
16. Urn, found west side of Bunting's ground, 1874. W.
17A. Ditch of Roman fort, found 1939, west of Altnacealgach. W.
17B. Smaller ditches connected with same. Ibid. W.
18. Remains found south of Queen's Road, 1875. W.

19. Lead coffin found in Creffield Road, 1887. W.
20. Roman urns found at north end of field 1266A, near no. 6. W.
21. Amphora burial found west of Altnacealgach, 1907. W.
22. Remains under house south of West Lodge. W.
22A. Remains under house west of West Lodge Road. W.
23. Remains in garden of Ingleglade, south of West Lodge. W.
24. Tombstone of Longinus found west of Beverley Road. W.
25. Remains found east of no. 23 in same garden. W. Two urns (grave 190) east side of this garden; also grave 192.
26. Burial under east side of Beverley Road. W.
27. Pottery found 1923 in SW. corner of Grammar School playground. W.
28. Pottery found when making Grammar School swimming-bath. W.
29. Remains found at west end of Creffield Road. W.
30. Glass vessel found at NE. corner of Bunting's ground. W.
31. Roman vase and bottles found in field behind the 'Oaks', north side of Crouch Street. W.
32. Beaker found in front of the 'Oaks' stables, in Crouch Street, 1925. W.
33. Skeleton with jet bracelet found under Lexden Road, 1930. W.
34. Burial urns found NE. of the Grammar School. W.
35. Part of a military tombstone found just west of the Hospital. W.
36. Part of a civil tombstone found in Manor Road, north of the Hospital. W.
37. Remains found in Mr. Brown's garden, Crowhurst Road. W.
38. Pavement found at back of St. Mary's Villa. W.
39. Hypocaust under north pavement of Crouch Street opposite Maldon Road. W.
40. Red cement floor east of same. 1922. W.
41. Altar to the Suleviae found at corner of Balkerne Lane. W.
42. Lead coffin found (no date) west of Wellesley Road. W.
43A. 'Tomb' found 1874 east of the same road. W.
43. Roman coins found north of Alexandra Road, 1874. S.
44 (two marks). Burial urns found at entrance to Artillery Barracks in Butt Road, 1875. S.
45. Urn found south of same, 1875. S.
46. Burial urns found south of Artillery Folley, 1863. S.
47. Sigillata found under St. John's Terrace. S.
48. Building in garden of no. 22, Crouch Street. S.
49. Human remains found, 1874, south of the preceding. S.
50. Foundations under street opposite no. 22 Crouch Street. S.
51. Foundations under the street opposite the Bull Hotel, east of the preceding. S.
52. Skeletons found under street opposite Headgate. S.
53. Skeletons found under street opposite the Bull Hotel. S.
54. Lead coffins found 1873 at corner of Burlington Road. S.
55. Lead coffins found 1838 (and 1845?) at back of Mill Place (on Butt Road). S.
56. Human remains found 1871, SE. of Mill Place. S.
57. Burial urns found west of inn on Artillery Folley, 1874. S.
58. Roman foundations found just east of Butt Road, in the Artillery Barracks, 1875. S.
59. Burial found 8 ft. south of fence of Napier Road, south of the mound in the Abbey grounds, 1947. S.
60. Roman bronze coins found under Hollington's factory, 1875. S.
61. Roman (?) road metalling found under west pavement of St. Botolph's Street, 1933. S.
62. Ditto. ditto, opposite the 'Marlborough Head', 1934. S.
63. Tessellated pavement and urn under Priory Street. S.
64. Nine skeletons found east of St. Botolph's Priory, 1939. S.
65. Roman burial found under the Britannia Works (grave 160). S.
66. Roman foundations found east of St. James's Church. S.
67. Human skull found in river at East Bridge. (Off map.)
68. Traces of rubble foundations at north end of Brook Street. (Off map.)
69. Roman rubbish-pits in Everett's Brickyard, 1926. N.
70. Lead coffin in Everett's Brickyard, 1938. N.
71. Roman wall, running N.–S., found outside North Gate, 1949. N.
72. Roman amphora found under cottages on Sheepen Road, 1889. W.
73. Roman foundations found under reservoir at Waterworks. W.
74. Roman remains found south of same. W.
75. Roman building (temple?) found in Union grounds. W.
76. Remains found in Union grounds, 1861. W.

77. Corner of Roman building. Ibid. W.
78. Remains found in Union grounds, 1861. W.
79. Ditto, 1929. W.
80. Roman walling found ibid. W.
81. Roman walling found under north abutment of North Bridge. N.
82. Mosaic pavement found west of Victoria Inn, north of last. N.
83. Red pavement found at end of same lane, 1929. N.
84. Roman walling under east pavement of North Station Road. N.
85. Ditto, running E.–W. under west pavement of same street. N.
86. Ditto, running N.–S. (continues 84) under east pavement, 1932. N.
87. Grey urn found on south side of Serpentine Walk, 1926/7. N.
88. Ground trenched in 1930. No burials found. N.
89. Amphora burial, planned by Wire. On line, east of station. N.
90. Second ditto. Ditto. N.
91. Approximate position as marked by Wire, of discovery of bronze busts (definitely in a side-dike north of the railway embankment and some distance west of the Dilbridge cutting). N.
92. Position of same busts as given on the O.S. 25-in. map, in the Dilbridge cutting. N.
93. Roman pottery found in a gravel pit just outside the ramparts SW. of Moat Farm. (Off map.)
94. Complex of ditches, apparently a moated Roman farmstead, revealed by air-photograph, in field 500, SE. of Moat Farm. W. (Cancelled, Medieval.)
95. Large temple and temenos at Sheepen. W.
96. Small temple at Sheepen. W.
97. Small building SW. of large temple. W.
98. Tile kiln east of Sheepen Farm. W.
99. Urn found in field 1085, north of St. Mary's Terrace. W.
100. Lead coffin found in Windmill field opposite the Hospital. W.
101. Lead coffin found about 60 yards north of the Lexden Road, 1880. W.
102. Lead coffin found at the back of the Salvation Army Barracks, 1887, with other inhumation and cremation burials. S.
103. Lead coffin found under the lawn just NW. of the house 'Silver Birches' (now destroyed), Lexden Road. W.
104. Two cremation and seven inhumation burials at front of the same house. W.
105. Strip lead coffin and urn found in the Sobraon Barracks, 1931. S.
106. Lead coffin found in Lockhart's field, 1933. W.
107. Lead coffin found in the Mersea Road, opposite the Officers' Mess of Hyderabad Barracks, 1937. S.
108. Roman and Saxon burials, arms, and urns found, according to Cutts, in Cromwell Road east of the Mersea Road. S.
109. A quincunx of burials shown by Cutts at the NW. corner of Wellesley Road. W. (One contained the circus glass cup.)
110. Pavement marked by Cutts on Lord's Land. W.
111. Foundations shown by Cutts in SW. part of Lord's Land. W.
112. Number of burials shown by Cutts east of the Grammar School. W.
113. Position of Centurion's tombstone as shown by Cutts (probably quite wrongly). W.
114. Position of grave 3 (with figurines) according to Cutts, in Creffield Road. W.
115. Position of grave 136 (Colchester vase) according to Cutts, west of West Lodge. W.
116. Rectangle shown by Cutts (for a building) north of the house at the NE. corner of Beverley Road. W.
117. Position of grave 222 at south end of Cambridge Road. W.
118. Temple on the Royal Grammar School playing-field. W.
119. Roman rubbish-pit found in footpath west from Queen's Road. W. Grave 300 found in Queen's Road south of this; also graves 304 and 301.
120. Inhumation burials in Cedars Road, west of St. John's Green. S.
121. Grave 463, in Errington Road, position vague. W.
122. Remains found under Wellington Street. S.
123. Small Castor ware painted pot, opposite Headgate Chapel. S.
124. Skeleton north of same. S.
125. Sigillata found under house on NW. corner of Chapel Street. S.
126. Urn and patera found in St. John Street. S.
127. Two or three urns found under west end of St. John's Terrace. S.
128. Cremations found at Osborne House (now the Electricity Offices). S.
129. Grave 501, SE. of Camp Post Office, Abbey field. S.
130. Graves 317 and 318. North of last. S. In spinney behind R.E. drawing-office.

131. Graves found in 1939 north of the A.T.S. quarters. S.
132. Remains of graves found when building huts north of the Military Hospital. S.
133. Ditto, farther west. S.
134. Skeletons found under the New Inn, Chapel Street. S.
135. Roman road found under boiler house of Hospital. W.
136. Marks showing foundations in the Pinnacle garden, west part of Abbey grounds, according to Cutts (probably part of the Abbey). S.
137. Burials in Priory Street. S.
138. Skeleton found east of Eastleigh House, East Hill (? site). S.
139. Grave 134 in Borough Engineer's East Bay dump. S. (Off map.)
140. Graves in garden of St. Botolph's Vicarage (SE. of town). S.
141. Pottery found near Roman Catholic Church, Priory Street. S.
142. Coin of Postumus and bronze key, garden of Winnock's Almshouses. S.
143. Timber structure and Roman pot north of the Woolpack Inn. S.
144. Well found at bottom of East Hill. (Off map.)
145. Trench observed at Scheregate Steps. S.
146. Foundation at corner of Manor Road.
146A. Two cremation burials in the bank, west side of Mersea Road. S.
147. Pavement in St. Mary's Road (mosaic). Manuscript note by Henry Laver. W.
148. Tomb behind Errington Lodge. W. (NE. corner of West Lodge Road.)
149. Site of West Lodge, John Taylor's house. W.
150. Skeleton found in front of Gilberd House. W.
151. Celtic vessels found behind St. Clare Road. W.
152. Site of grave 188. Ibid. W.
153. Graves found. Ibid. W.
154. Site of grave 325. (Just off map to west of 152.)
155. Grave on Chantry Land on Balkerne Hill. W.
156. Early Roman pit under Mrs. Coats Hutton's house, Lexden Road. W.
157. Grave 220, found SE. of last. (Antonine?) *C.M.R.* 1928, 56, pl. xx. W.
158. Roman road-metalling seen in cutting in St. Clare Road. P. G. Laver. W.
159. Traces of Roman road crossing river north of NE. Gate. N.
160. Graves 229 (Hadrianic) and 230 (Ant. –200). Corner of Creffield and Beverley Roads. W.
161. Grave 194 (Antonine). Married quarters. S.
162. Section of Roman road crossing Fitzwalter Road. W.
163. Section of Roman road crossing Lexden Straight Road, exact position unknown. (Off map.)
164. Section of Roman road seen in field ditch SW. from Iron Latch Lane. W. (In Lucy Miles Lane.) (Off map.)
165. Ditch of Roman road (?) observed opposite Lexden Union. (Off map.)
166. Roman road observed crossing Fitzwalter Road north of the Lexden Tumulus. W. Laver, *Diary*.
167. Roman road observed in garden of P. G. Laver's house 'Ethelstowe', in St. Clare Drive. W.
168. Section of Roman road cut in Iron Latch Lane. (Off map.)
169. Section of Roman road cut on Rayner's Farm. S. (Off map.)
170. Site of excavations on Lexden Straight Road. W. (Off map.)
171. Red pavement under Osborne Street. S.
172. Pavement found at NE. corner of Osborne Street. S.
173. Alleged wall and mosaic pavement at Stanway Green. S. (Off map.)
174. Site of grave 324 at Gurney Benham House. W.
175. Site of grave 171, on site of 'The Oaks', 1852. W.
176. Site of grave 223 at corner of Maldon and Constantine roads, outside house called 'Northwood'. S.
177. Site of grave 312 in garden of no. 23 Wellesley Road. W.
178. So-called 'Circus' on Grammar School playing-field. W.
179. Ditch on same field. W.
180. Roman coins, &c., found in sand pit on By-pass Road. W.[1]
181. Burial (?) shown by Cutts in the Artillery Barracks. S.
182. Grave 509 (3rd–4th century). S. On Abbey Field (not marked).
183. Kiln I, on site of the Hospital, 1819. W. Cannot be shown.
184. Kiln II, at brickyard near North Station. N.
185. Kilns III and IV, on Lexden Road opposite the Hospital, before 1855. W.
186. Kilns VII–XI, excavated by Joslin, 1877. W.

[1] These included Claudius II, Constantine I and II, a barbarous radiate, and an iron arrow-head.

187. Kiln X found at Butt Windmill, 1890. S.
188. Kiln in Wallace's garden. N.
189. Kilns XIIA and B, in gardens in Fitzwalter Road, 1918–29. W. (See Addenda.)
190. Burials in Sheepen sand-pit (fourth century). W.
191. Pottery found in Queen's Road. W. (See Addenda.)
192. Kiln XXIII, found in area L near Sheepen Farm, 1938. W.
193. Kiln XXIV, found on Abbey field, 1946. S.
194. (Marks south end of Bluebottle Grove.) W. pp. 3–4 and *passim*.
195. Walled cemetery at Gurney Benham House. W.
196. Pottery found on Jarmin's premises. W.
197. Burials found in west extension of Colchester Cemetery. S. .
198. Road section opposite Crowther's Factory, E. Hill. N.
199. Burials on Garrison football-ground. S.
200. Burials on Garrison sports field. S.
201. Remains found at the North Railway Station. N.
202. Remains found at Essex Hall. N.
203. Skeletons found at Park Bowling Green. N.
204. Remains of a burial. (Red cup, &c.) N.
205. Corner of Margaret's Road. N.

ADDENDA

Insert on the maps, pls. XLI–XLIII:

191, on curve at EE in Queen's Road.
206. Red tessellated pavement, Lord's Land, 1895. W.
207. Ditto in middle of Chantry lands, 1853. (Between 147 and 38.) W.
208. Ditto. Lord's land, exact site not known.
209. Foundations, tessellated pavements, and roadway. (Place red figure 209 against roadway shown between 110 and 147 on pl. XLII.)
210. Remains south of the Hospital. (Place red cross and figure 210 immediately south of 183 on same plate.)
    Mark 189A in a circle in the garden SE. of 162 on same plate.
    Mark 189B in a circle in the garden north of i in Fitzwalter. Mark 191 about $\frac{1}{2}$ in. south of 119, same plate.
211. Kiln XXV at Kingswode Hoe, mark 1 inch S of 6 in 186, same plate.

INDEX

PLATES

PLATE I

A. Tombstone of M. Favonius Facilis, centurion of the Twentieth Legion. Scale *c.* $\frac{1}{13}$. [15], p. 3.

B. Tombstone of Longinus, *duplicarius* of *ala I Thracum*. Scale *c.* $\frac{1}{17}$. [24], p. 6.

PLATE II

A. Roman town wall and north tower of Balkerne Gate.

B. Balkerne Gate, south footway, looking east.

C. Balkerne Gate, doorway of south guardroom, looking east.

PLATE III

A. Interior tower on town wall at the Technical College. [164], p. 22.

B. The same tower seen from the north. [164], p. 22.

PLATE IV

A. Post-holes found adjacent to the interior tower at the Technical College. [164], p. 24.

B. Fallen window-head at the NE. Gate. p. 39.

C. Fallen window-head at the NE. Gate. p. 39.

PLATE V

B. Section IA. Close-up view of inner face of town wall. [197], p. 25.

A. Section IA. View of wall from the east.

B. NE. Postern, outer west angle. p. 37.

c. NE. Postern, outer east angle and town wall in Park Folly. p. 37.

A. East side of North Gate, looking south. p. 32.

PLATE VII

A. General view of NE. Gate. pp. 36 ff.

B. East side of NE. Gate after conservation. pp. 36 ff.

Photo. by L. C. Cosser

PLATE VIII

A. Broad ditch outside NE. angle of town wall (visible in background). p. 257.

B. NE. angle of town wall, looking NW. p. 42.

C. East wall of town, looking south from NE. corner. p. 42.

PLATE IX

A drawing by John Constable, R.A., showing the south
side of East Gate. p. 44.

Reproduced by permission of the V. & A. Museum

PLATE X

A. Inner face of town wall in Castle Park, showing face repaired where tower was removed. p. 35.

B. Bastion 2 from the NE. p. 48.

PLATE XI

A. Arch in Roman town wall just south of East Gate. p. 45.

B. Interior of Bastion 1. Roman town wall at back. p. 45.

C. Excavation of foundations of Bastion 4. [147], p. 50.

D. Bastion 1 from south. p. 45.

PLATE XII

A. Bastion 5 and (rebuilt) town wall from the SE. p. 51.

B. The town wall in Vineyard Street. p. 53.

PLATE XIII

A. Broken foundations of Roman town wall. [104], p. 53.

B. Foundation of Roman town wall at Bastion 5. [104], p. 53.

C. Roman town wall at St. Mary's Steps, showing remains of arch. p. 60.

D. Town wall (rebuilt) behind Messrs. Bland's offices, west of Head Gate. p. 60.

PLATE XIV

A. South wing of 'Forum', showing successive pavements, brick drain on right. [114], p. 169.

B. South wing of 'Forum', the wide brick drain. [114], p. 169.

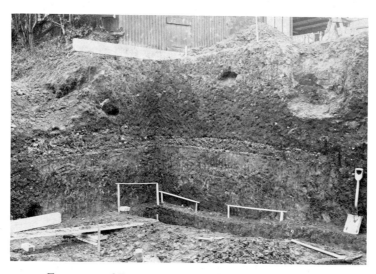

C. Exposure of Roman street at Park Café. [120], p. 69.

PLATE XV

N

W

E

O 1 2 3 4 5 6 FEET S

Pavement B, Insula 2. [12], p. 78

PLATE XVI

N

W

E

S

Pavement A, Insula 2. [12], p. 78

PLATE XVII

A. End of vaulted drain, and opening into it on floor of 'Mithracum'. [39], p. 87.

B. View inside the vaulted drain. [39], p. 87.

C. The same drain, looking north. [39], p. 88.

D. The same, just inside NE. Gate, looking south. [39], p. 88.

PLATE XVIII

B. Drain, showing difference between upper and lower parts, and line of holes filled with mortar. [39], p. 88.

D. Entrance to underground room, east wall of stair-well. [39], p. 109.

A. Drain, near NE. Gate, showing construction. [39], pp. 88, 89.

C. Entrance to underground room of 'Mithraeum', showing blocking masonry. [39], p. 108.

PLATE XIX

A. The 'Mithraeum' main chamber, looking south. [39], p. 109.

B. The same, looking north. [39], p. 109.

PLATE XX

A. Hypocaust in Insula 15. [117], p. 114.

B. Openings in west wall of drain and arch in house-wall
opposite near the NE. gate. [150], p. 88.

PLATE XXI

A. Shackles found in the 'Mithraeum'. p. 111.

B. Remains of shackles, and large split rings or spring washers. p. 118.

PLATE XXII

A. Examples of pottery pestles or rubbers from the pottery shop. [127], p. 158.

B. Yellow-brown glazed ware from the pottery shops. On the left from the first shop [127], on the right from the second [171]. The first are matt, the second glossy, but the chip of the rim, bottom left, is from a glossy beaker identical with those on the right. pp. 156, 202.

PLATE XXIII

A. Roman pavement found at the Three Cups
Inn, after an old print. [18], p. 151.

B. Pavement A, Insula 2, *in situ*. [12], p. 78.

PLATE XXIV

A. Mosaic pavement found under the 'People's Hall' in 1850.
[17], p. 150.

B. Roman pavement at the Red Lion
Hotel. [68], p. 196.

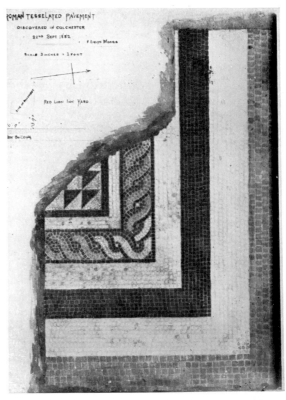

C. Roman pavement found at, and preserved in,
the Red Lion Hotel. p. 196.

PLATE XXV

A. The large NE. vault under Colchester Castle. [34], p. 166.

B. Slot for post in vaults under the Castle.
[34], p. 166.

C. Foundation of central dividing wall
between vaults. [34], p. 166.

PLATE XXVI

A. Roman drain and man-hole cover, south of Castle. [148], p. 175.

B. Roman drain under Norman Chapel. [148], p. 175.

C. Entrance to Norman forebuilding, showing part of Roman brick pedestal beneath (in background). [148], p. 176.

PLATE XXVII

A. View of north side of the Norman bank. [35], p. 180.

B. View of the cutting into the northern side of the Norman bank. [35], pp. 180 ff.

PLATE XXVIII

A. The east face of the cutting into the north side of the Norman bank, showing wall A of the Roman building, and the upper and lower street levels. pp. 182–3.

B. The re-entrant angle of walls A, B, and C from above, showing the torn-away floor levels and flint platforms. [35], p. 182.

C. The re-entrant angle of walls A, B, and C, from the north. [35], p. 182.

D. The brick-faced NE. corner of the Roman building and street level. [35], p. 181.

PLATE XXIX

A. Close-up of the NE. corner, grooved by the wear and tear of traffic. [35], p. 181.

B. Walls D and E in the cutting into the south side of the Norman bank and the late occupation level sealing them. [35], p. 183.

C. The west face of the cutting into the north side of the Norman bank, showing half of the unexcavated late occupation level over the streets. [35], p. 183.

PLATE XXX

A. Terra-cotta plaque, found at St. Mary's Hospital. (From a drawing by Josiah Parish.) Scale unknown. p. 170.

B. Roman ante-fixes in red clay, found in Colchester. pp. 184, 209.

PLATE XXXI

A. West face of cross-wall in Keep, showing tiling in the Roman work beneath. [34], p. 167.

B. Section of Roman levels on the site of the 'Waggon and Horses', North Hill. [155], p. 146.

PLATE XXXII

A. Pier of brickwork on stone foundation, found at
St. Martin's House, 1950. [174], p. 98.

B. Apsidal bath lined with white tesserae. G.P.O. site. [146], p. 208.

PLATE XXXIII

Mosaic pavement found in Insula 34. [80], p. 209.

PLATE XXXIV

Mosaic pavement from the Bury Field, Insula 40. [103], p. 218.

PLATE XXXV

A. Remaining masonry of portico wall; large temple. [95], p. 227.

B. Site of the large temple from the SW. [95], pp. 224 ff.

PLATE XXXVI

B. Base of 'altar' seen from NW. [95], p. 228.

C. South angle of temenos wall looking NW. [95], p. 231.

A. Temenos wall. South side, looking NW. [95], p. 231.

PLATE XXXVII

A. Bronze plaque.

B. Bronze plaque.

C. Bronze stag.

From Temple IV. [118], p. 239. *Scale: full-size*

PLATE XXXVIII

A. Apsidal building in garden of no. 22 Crouch Street, looking east. (*Photograph, T. C. Gall*, Feb. 1936). [48], p. 245.

B. The Colchester Sphinx. [1], p. 253. ($\frac{1}{7}$).

PLATE XXXIX

View of Gostecks temple and field SW. of it, looking NE. pp. 259 ff.

PLATE XL

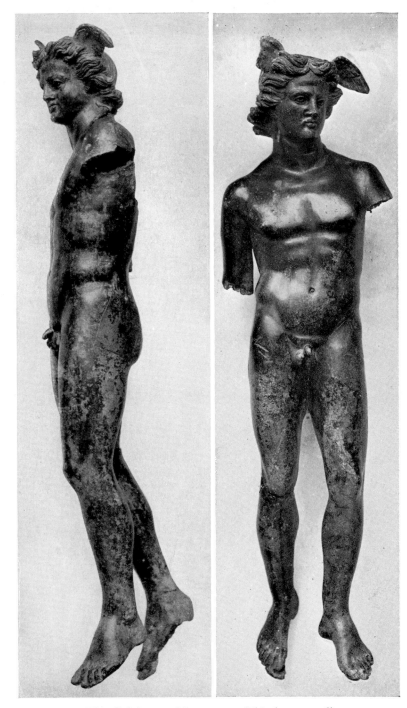

The Colchester Mercury. p. 264 (approx. $\frac{1}{3}$).

PLATE XLI

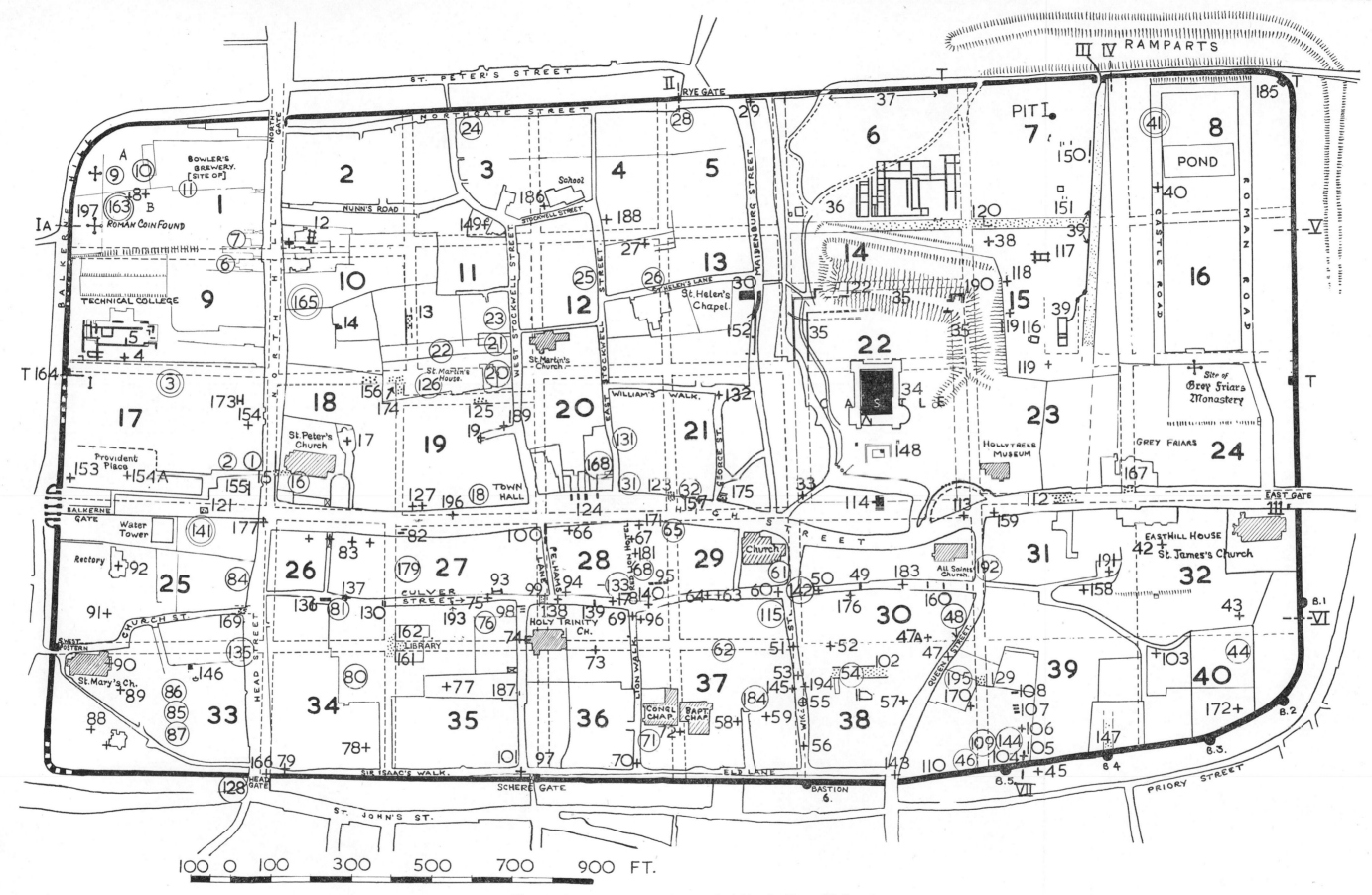

Plan to show remains found on and within the Town Walls.

PLATE XLIV

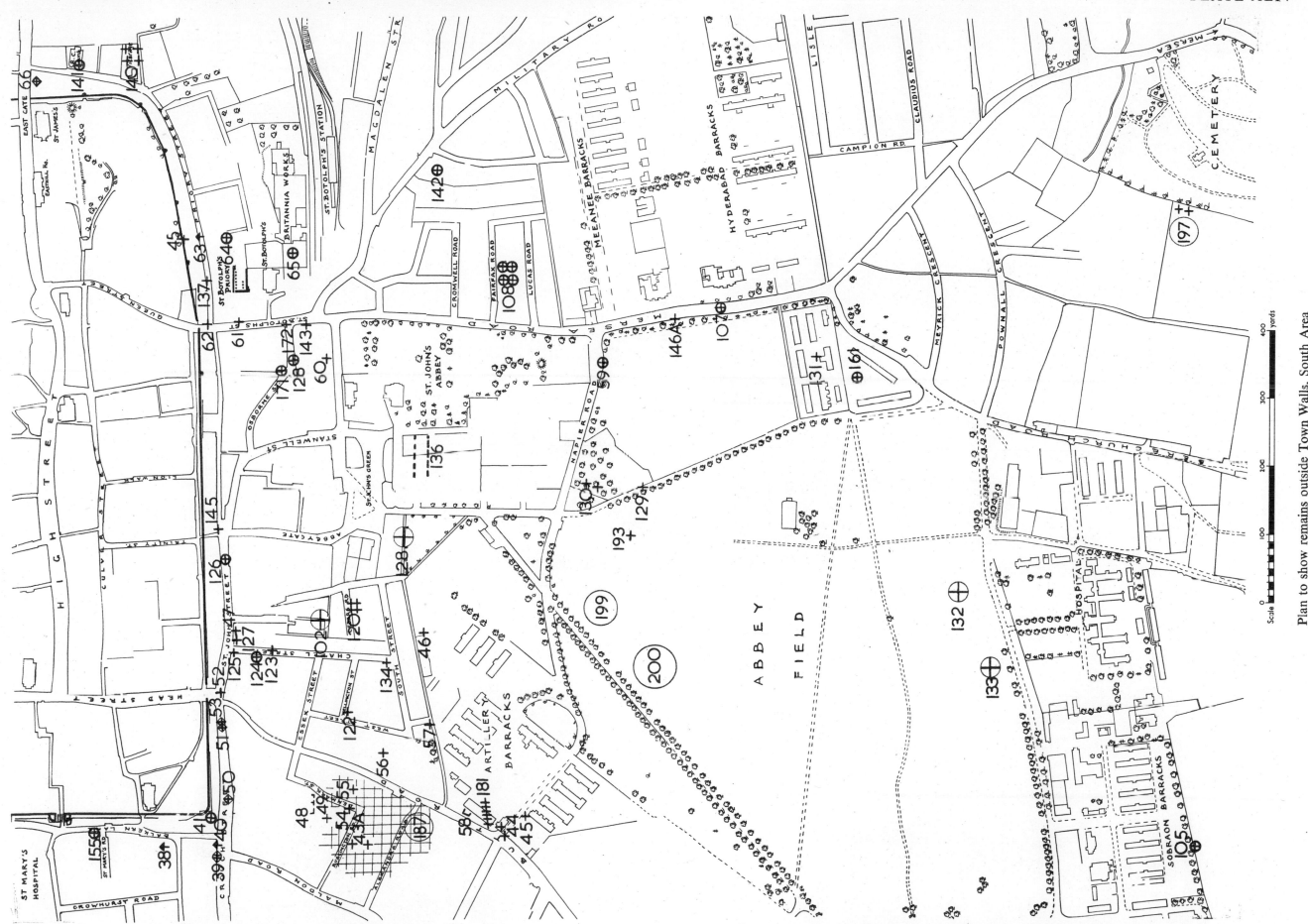

Plan to show remains outside Town Walls, South Area